BETWEEN EARTH
AND SKY

By the Same Authors

Hollywood Films of the Seventies:
Sex, Drugs, Violence, Rock 'n' Roll and Politics

We Are Not Afraid:
The Story of Goodman, Schwerner, and Chaney
and the Civil Rights Campaign for Mississippi

SETH CAGIN & PHILIP DRAY

BETWEEN EARTH AND SKY

How CFCs Changed Our World and Endangered the Ozone Layer

PANTHEON BOOKS
NEW YORK

Copyright © 1993 by Seth Cagin and Philip Dray

All rights reserved under International and Pan-American Copyright
Conventions. Published in the United States by Pantheon Books, a
division of Random House, Inc., New York, and simultaneously in
Canada by Random House of Canada Limited, Toronto.

Library of Congress Cataloging-in-Publication Data
Cagin, Seth. Between earth and sky: how CFCs changed our world
and endangered the ozone layer / Seth Cagin, Philip Dray.
   p.   cm.
   Includes bibliographical references and index.
   ISBN 0-679-42052-5
   1. Chlorofluorocarbons—Environmental aspects.   2. Ozone layer
depletion. I. Dray, Philip. II. Title.
   TD887.C47C34   1992
   363.73'84—dc20   92-1239

Map of Antarctica, page 264, © 1993 Heather Drake

PHOTOGRAPHIC CREDITS
AP/Wide World: page 3 below, page 5 below, page 6 below
Culver Pictures, Inc.: page 4 above & below
GMI Alumni Foundation/Collection of Industrial History: page 2,
   page 3 above
NASA: page 8 above
NCR Corportion, Dayton, Ohio: page 1 below
William Shurcliff: page 6 above
Susan Solomon: page 8 below
University of California, Irvine: page 7
UPI/Bettmann Archive: page 1 above, page 5 above

DESIGN BY GLEN M. EDELSTEIN

Manufactured in the United States of America

First Edition

CONTENTS

INTRODUCTION

THERE ARE MANY CAUTIONARY tales in environmental history of the unintended consequences that result when mankind oversteps nature's bounds. Pesticides that poisoned food and industrial chemical spills that rendered communities uninhabitable are but two examples. With ozone depletion and the closely related problem of global warming, however, the world is experiencing the first wholesale disruption of a global natural system caused by humans.

Beginning in 1974, for more than a decade scientists, politicians, environmentalists, and the world's leading chemical corporations argued bitterly about whether it was possible that a family of widely used industrial chemicals—chlorofluorocarbons—could deplete the layer of stratospheric ozone that shields the earth from harmful ultraviolet radiation. That debate is now over. Actual ozone depletion has been monitored, not only above Antarctica, where a dramatic springtime ozone hole was discovered in 1985, but over the earth's mid-latitudes as well. Moreover, this depletion has been linked irrefutably with CFCs. Although today questions remain regarding how best to replace these useful chemicals, and whether the phaseout schedule now mandated by international agreement will take effect in time to forestall further serious damage, the nations of the world have established an important precedent by negotiating to end the manufacture of CFCs.

We began work on *Between Earth and Sky* in 1988, a year after the first treaty to control CFCs was signed, drawn to the subject by other questions this unprecedented global crisis had raised. How did mankind reach the brink of environmental catastrophe? Why was it so difficult for governments, and even for science, to recognize that the sacred ideal of technological progress can carry a tremendous hidden cost? Does our brilliant capacity for invention—as epitomized by CFCs, but by no means limited to them—now exceed the tolerance of the earth's natural systems to accommodate it? Can we invent new legal, political, and diplomatic institutions able to manage and control modern industrial technology?

The CFC story begins in Dayton, Ohio, a mecca of early-twentieth-century technological endeavor, the Silicon Valley of its day, where in 1928 researchers responded to an urgent demand for a safe refrigerant. The refrigerants then in use were either toxic or flammable or both, ensuring that the iceman would remain a familiar figure in millions of American homes. A new and improved refrigerant, some of the nation's most farsighted entrepreneurs recognized, could improve the quality of life and be the cornerstone of a vast new industry.

The solution was chlorofluorocarbons, first synthesized by General Motors researcher Thomas Midgley, Jr., and his close friend Charles Kettering, the head of GM's Research Corporation. Midgley and Kettering were already two of America's most highly regarded industrial pioneers. Kettering was renowned for his invention of the electric automobile starter. Midgley was responsible, in the mid-1920s, for discovering that when lead was added to gasoline, it took the "knock" out of car engines. His invention, known as ethyl, provided greater acceleration and allowed the manufacture of bigger and more powerful cars. With Kettering's help, Midgley had successfully defended ethyl against attacks waged by America's first occupational-health specialists, who claimed that the manufacture of the substance was dangerous to workers and that its distribution might harm the general public.

For Midgley and Kettering, it was unthinkable that a technological innovation with such obvious and useful applications as ethyl gas could be held up by such fears. Certainly, there were problems to overcome with the introduction of any great invention, but as Kettering liked to remind people, "The price of progress is trouble, and frankly I don't believe the price is too high."

These two optimistic scientists personified America's faith in technology and progress, a faith that had withstood numerous challenges—not only from "health cranks" but from nineteenth-century romantics such as

Henry David Thoreau and John Muir, who had expressed a spiritual attachment to nature and sought to protect it from the advance of civilization. The realization that technology could have profound unforeseen and harmful effects on the environment gained widespread credence only in 1962, with the publication of Rachel Carson's *Silent Spring,* which demonstrated that the pesticide DDT was poisoning not only targeted insects, but birds and fish and even humans.

Between Earth and Sky describes both the spirit of early-twentieth-century invention that led to industrial "breakthroughs" like DDT and CFCs, and the evolving dissent from it, which coalesced in late-twentieth-century environmentalism. Health experts Alice Hamilton and Yandell Henderson were acting in the same progressive spirit that motivated Midgley and Kettering when they helped "invent" the field of occupational health in America, and when they opposed the sale of ethyl gas. By the mid-1960s, after *Silent Spring,* their prescient worry about the potential toxicity of industrial compounds was no longer derided as an eccentric preoccupation. Rachel Carson's stark message—that the modern concept of progress was, in some fundamental respects, at odds with nature—was widely accepted, and the environmentalist impulse to preserve and defend nature from human excesses broadened to include protection of an increasingly threatened landscape.

In the 1960s this impulse was institutionalized in a new, dynamic branch of jurisprudence, environmental law, whose roots include the effort by New York attorney Stephen Duggan and his wife, Beatrice "Smokey" Duggan, to save historic Storm King Mountain on the Hudson River from becoming the site of a Con Edison power plant. The principles forged at Storm King, and the public-interest law firm that grew out of that battle, the Natural Resources Defense Council, headed by Stephen Duggan and a corps of idealistic Yale Law School graduates, would later play a leading role in the defense of the ozone layer.

There was, over the course of the twentieth century, a kind of race between the industrial science that begat CFCs and academic science, which, during the same years, was enlarging its understanding of the atmosphere. CFCs were invented in 1928, but not until 1931 did British scientist Sydney Chapman delineate the chemical processes governing the ozone layer, demonstrating stratospheric ozone's importance in shielding earth from ultraviolet radiation.

From Chapman on, scientists recognized our utter dependence on the ozone layer, but few seriously considered the possibility that it could in fact be threatened, by either natural or man-made causes. University of Arizona physicist James McDonald and Berkeley chemist Harold

Johnston, who suggested in 1971 that exhaust from fleets of a new commercial aircraft, the supersonic transport, might diminish stratospheric ozone levels, were hooted down by the U.S. government and even by their own colleagues. By 1974, when F. Sherwood Rowland and Mario Molina of the University of California at Irvine discovered that the natural processes governing the ozone layer were subject to being drastically interrupted by relatively minute quantities of CFCs, industries worldwide had manufactured millions of tons of the offending chemicals, and were continuing to increase production. More disturbing knowledge arrived the next year when scientist Veerabhadran Ramanathan found that CFCs are also a highly efficient greenhouse gas, and thus contribute to global warming. Industry had, in effect, won the race for control of the atmosphere: by the time science was capable of understanding the threat CFCs posed, it was already far too late to prevent a great deal of damage.

Then the political battle began. The "Miracle Compound," as CFCs were called, was being used not only in refrigerators and car and home air conditioners, but had become integral to the aerosol, electronics manufacturing, and foam blowing industries, among others. Precisely because CFCs were ubiquitous, it was at first difficult for anyone to accept they could actually be harmful. And at the first sign of trouble, the huge industries that produced or relied on CFCs, led by the powerful Du Pont company, the world's largest CFC manufacturer, attempted to cast doubt on the scientists' theories, while vigorously fighting proposed governmental restrictions on the manufacture or use of CFCs. Then, in 1980, an American president was elected who was ideologically disinclined to take any action to prevent further damage to the ozone layer. Ronald Reagan rode into office in part on a wave of antienvironmental, antiregulatory sentiment, making it far more difficult for environmentalists and scientists to attain domestic or international pollution controls.

The theoretical threat of ozone depletion became a physical reality in the early 1980s, when it was discovered that stratospheric ozone over the Antarctic was severely depleted each austral springtime. Rather than resolve the debate, however, the new information only fueled the bitter controversy among the world's atmospheric scientists, who disagreed about whether the Antarctic ozone loss was caused by CFCs, or whether it could be accounted for by natural geophysical or climatic mechanisms. The continuing scientific disagreement was, of course, a gift to the recalcitrant CFC industry, for it promised to stall the regulatory process indefinitely. Corporate spokesmen had long contended that CFCs should be regarded "innocent until proven guilty," a legalistic-*sounding* standard of judgment that environmentalists and many scientists decried as wholly inappropriate, considering what was at stake. "What's the use of having developed a science well enough to make predictions," a discouraged Sherry Rowland asked, "if in the end all we're willing to do is stand around and wait for them to come true?"

Finally, a daring NASA airborne expedition into the ozone hole above the South Pole in September 1987 brought back irrefutable chemical evidence that CFCs were responsible for the ozone hole. That same month the world's major CFC-producing nations, meeting in Montreal, agreed to the first international environmental treaty restricting the production of CFCs. James Anderson, the Harvard researcher whose experiment aboard the NASA aircraft played a crucial role in resolving the question of what caused ozone depletion, spoke for the emerging scientific consensus when he commented, "It is time we stopped using the atmosphere as a test tube for global chemical experiments."

While efforts have continued since 1987 to halt the manufacture of CFCs and replace them with ozone-safe alternatives, even a dramatically accelerated phaseout will be inadequate to spare the world the consequences of a half century of unrestrained CFC use. Indeed, in 1992 scientists observed that severe ozone depletion was no longer occurring only above Antarctica, but over heavily populated portions of the northern hemisphere as well. Their conclusion—as this book goes to press—is that ozone depletion will certainly continue to worsen in the decades to come.

Like the sorcerer's apprentice who knows just enough magic to get into trouble, CFCs proved to be far more "miraculous" than their inventor could have imagined. They have changed the fundamental chemistry of the earth's atmosphere. This new, man-made atmosphere is not the one that life evolved in, and it seems increasingly clear that it is not one that is most conducive to life's continued well-being. All life on earth now dwells beneath a shattered sky.

Between Earth and Sky relates the rise and fall of an industrial compound that changed our world, in ways both expected and unexpected. From their birth in 1928, when CFCs represented a breakthrough for corporate science; to their adolescence as a starring player of mid-century industry; to their maturity as an unseen yet essential component of everyday life; and then through their decline, first accused, then proven to be an environmental hazard, the story of CFCs seems to us a parable of modern industrial times.

BETWEEN EARTH
AND SKY

PROLOGUE

ON SEPTEMBER 8, 1941, Thomas Midgley, Jr., the inventor of chlorinated fluorocarbons, traveled to Atlantic City to accept an award for his scientific accomplishments. The Priestley Prize, named for the eighteenth-century English theologian and chemist Joseph Priestley, was presented once every three years by the American Chemical Society to one of its members for outstanding creativity in chemical research. Although little known among the general public, the Priestley was considered by many scientists to be the American equivalent of the Nobel Prize in chemistry.

There was no question Midgley richly deserved the honor. The former General Motors researcher was already a celebrated hero of modern science, the force behind two of the century's most important achievements in industrial chemistry: the formulation of the lead-based anti-knock gasoline additive, ethyl, which had revolutionized the automobile industry by making possible the manufacture of larger, more efficient car engines, and the synthesis of the nontoxic, nonflammable, and inexpensive chlorofluorocarbons, known as CFCs or by their Du Pont trade name, Freon, which had made the refrigerator an affordable fixture in every American home.

Midgley, an amiable man who liked nothing better than the company of his fellow scientists, had long been prominent in the society's affairs.

Yet it had taken all his effort and determination to accomplish the journey by car and rail from his home near Columbus, Ohio, to Atlantic City. The previous winter, after a lifetime of scientific endeavor, extensive travel, and generally robust health, Midgley had been struck down by a case of poliomyelitis and was now paralyzed below the waist. He made a valiant effort to appear upbeat, but his doctors' failure to offer much hope for his recovery from the paralysis and a gnawing certainty that his powers of invention had begun to wane were devastating.

Seated to one side of the stage at the society's awards ceremony, confined to his wheelchair, Midgley listened to the words spoken in tribute to his many achievements and could not help but have the uneasy sensation he was hearing his own eulogy.

"Today we honor one whose accomplishments, in a very definite sense, speak for themselves," said ACS president William L. Evans. "Every chemist knows their significance. But today the layman as well . . . will testify to our indebtedness to one who has contributed so greatly to more pleasant and efficient living. Today's recipient has made science a liberator, and we are happy to know that he has had the great satisfaction of seeing, with his own eyes, the fruits of his labors. Posterity will acknowledge their permanent value."

As Evans stepped back from the podium, Midgley was wheeled forward. Next to him was an odd-looking contraption: a motor with two glass fuel tanks mounted on top. One of the tanks contained white-colored fuel, the other red. Midgley said nothing, but waited for the audience to grow totally silent; then he leaned over and flicked a switch on the apparatus. With a shudder the engine came to life, a light bulb on top indicating that the engine was operating on the white fuel. It ran poorly and at a slightly accelerated rate, emitting the loud "ping, ping, ping" that every person in the auditorium recognized, the hiccuping "engine knock" of an old jalopy. After a minute or so, Midgley flicked another switch and the engine changed over to the red fuel. The sound instantly quieted to a smooth hum. As one member of the audience later recalled, the engine's "cries of anguish subsided" until "it purred like a kitten full of cream."

Only now that he would not have to raise his voice over the roar of the engine did Midgley speak. Since he had discussed his life's work in industrial chemistry four years earlier in his talk to the society entitled "From the Periodic Table to Production," and since he had recently been occupied by executive duties instead of new scientific undertakings in the lab, he announced that he would present a series of demonstrations rather than deliver a traditional acceptance speech. This may have seemed like a rather casual way to acknowledge a prestigious award, but it was characteristic of Midgley, who was known for his irreverence toward scientific canon and his delight in "Barnumizing" scientific audiences. When, in the 1920s, a panic broke out over the safety of the lead-based gasoline additive Midgley had invented and that the Ethyl Corporation was putting on the market, Midgley quelled people's fears by traveling to New York City to preside at a press conference where, before reporters and government health officials, he cheerfully washed his hands and face with the feared substance.

Now, with the help of his longtime friend and associate Thomas A. "Tabby" Boyd, Midgley proceeded to demonstrate the other discoveries that had distinguished his career. They screened a short film called *The Magic Key* about a method Midgley—along with his mentor Charles Kettering, vice president of the General Motors Research Corporation—had pioneered for extracting bromine from sea water. He and Boyd then demonstrated a procedure he had devised for approximating the vulcanization of rubber. For the climactic finale of his performance, Midgley restaged a favorite demonstration involving chlorofluorocarbons, the so-called miracle compound he had invented with Kettering's encouragement in 1928. He leaned over and inhaled a substantial quantity of Freon from a small, shallow dish, held the gas in his lungs for several seconds, then exhaled through a tube to extinguish a burning candle—definitive proof that chlorinated fluorocarbons were completely safe for everyday use. Smiling broadly, Midgley was wheeled from the stage to sustained applause.

Thirty-three years later, in September 1974, when by coincidence the American Chemical Society once again convened in Atlantic City, it was the duty of ACS news manager Dorothy Smith to review the presentations being planned for the meeting and flag those papers that might interest the general public and the press. Major metropolitan dailies didn't usually cover ACS conventions, but the wire services, as well as chemical-industry and scientific journals did, and of the 1,840 presentations accepted for the conference, perhaps a dozen would be brought to the reporters' attention. Two of the presentation abstracts that caught Smith's eye had been submitted by a chemistry professor from the University of California at Irvine, F. Sherwood Rowland, and his postdoctoral assistant, Mario Molina. They were entitled "Photodissociation of CF_2Cl_2 and $CFCl_2$ in the Earth's Stratosphere" and "ClOx Chain-Catalyzed Removal of Ozone from the Earth's Stratosphere Following Solar Photodissociation of Chlorofluoromethanes."

While a nonscientist could stare long and hard at such headings and see nothing alarming about them, Smith recognized the chemical names in the titles as belonging to two very commonly used industrial compounds, the chlorinated fluorocarbons. She also knew that "photodissociation" referred to the process by which solar energy breaks molecules apart. As the abstracts explained, the Irvine scientists had found that chlorine released from these "dissociated" chlorinated fluorocarbons could, by means of a rapid catalytic reaction, erode the earth's protective shield of stratospheric ozone. Smith did not routinely contact the society's members to quiz them about their presentations, and F. Sherwood Rowland was no less than the chairman of the ACS Division of Physical Chemistry for the convention, but given the extremely wide use of chlorinated fluorocarbons, the claim the abstract made was serious business indeed.

"You mean Freon, don't you?" Smith inquired, when she got Rowland on the phone.

Yes, Rowland said, that was what he and Molina meant, although he pointed out that CFCs were manufactured by other companies as well as Du Pont and marketed under names other than Freon. Rowland explained that CFCs were especially prized by industry because they were not only extremely useful, but were also chemically inert. They did not break down or interact with other chemicals, which made them both nontoxic and nonflammable. Indeed, CFCs had proved themselves remarkably adaptable to a variety of industrial needs—in refrigeration, home and automobile air-conditioning, aerosol propellants, the production of Styrofoam, and the manufacture of electronic parts.

Rowland and Molina theorized, however, that while nothing whatsoever breaks down CFCs in the earth's lower atmosphere, over a period of decades they drift up to the stratosphere. There, the CFCs finally encounter something capable of breaking their chemical bonds: short waves of ultraviolet light, which do not usually reach the earth's surface but are prevalent at stratospheric altitudes. Once they split apart, CFCs produce a free chlorine atom that enters into a chemical reaction with ozone, dramatically reducing the concentration of ozone molecules and depleting the ozone layer.

Rowland and Molina had published their disturbing theory in the British scientific journal *Nature* in June 1974. "It seems quite clear that the atmosphere has only a finite capacity for absorbing chlorine atoms produced in the atmosphere," they had written. Rowland told Smith he intended to draw the obvious inference at the ACS meeting and call for a stop to the production of the offending chemicals.

Smith recognized that the theory was something worthy of a press release. She knew CFCs were ubiquitous; the manufacture of these useful chemical compounds was a billion-dollar industry, and a number of other billion-dollar industries relied upon them. Now along came a well-thought-of but not particularly prominent chemistry professor saying it all would have to come to an abrupt halt!

Rowland and Molina's claim would be startling in any public arena, but nowhere more so than at a convention of the ACS, a professional organization whose members included both the university-based researchers who studied atmospheric pollutants and the industrial chemists who created them. Not surprisingly, when Smith's news release on the Rowland-Molina presentation went out, a Du Pont representative phoned to protest her use of the Freon trade name. Next, a Du Pont press agent called, asking why she had scheduled a press conference to follow the presentation of such a speculative hypothesis. "I wouldn't call it pressuring," Smith later said. "He was leaning a little bit, but it was lightly done." The Du Pont agent reminded Smith that there was absolutely no proof to support the theory that CFCs depleted the ozone layer.

Smith took Du Pont's complaints seriously enough to look into the subject more deeply, and she phoned several scientists at the National Oceanic and Atmospheric Administration (NOAA) laboratories in Boulder, Colorado. They assured her that what was already becoming known in the atmospheric sciences as "the Rowland-Molina theory" was the result of sound, creative theoretical research.

The ACS meeting held in Atlantic City the week of September 9, 1974, at the Dennis and Shelburne-Empress hotels and the Boardwalk's Convention Center, resembled in many ways the organization's conference there in 1941. Chemists, ID badges pinned to their jackets, roamed the Boardwalk and visited the hotel conference rooms, chatting with old friends or renewing professional acquaintances, hastening off occasionally to catch a presentation whose description in the program had caught their interest. Rowland and Molina gave their presentation in the Garden Lounge on the main floor of the Hotel Dennis starting a little after two-thirty on the afternoon of Tuesday, September 10.

Rowland, who was in his mid-forties, was a large, powerful-looking man well over six feet tall, a former star basketball player at Ohio Wesleyan; Molina, smaller, younger, with a neatly trimmed dark beard, seemed the personification of scholarly precision and reserve. Each man spoke for about twenty minutes. Molina went first, laying out the chemical basis of how chlorofluorocarbons were dissociated, or broken down by sunlight at stratospheric altitudes; then Rowland described how chlorine monoxide, a by-product of this dissociation, entered into a catalytic chain reaction that removed ozone.

Dorothy Smith had arranged for the press conference concerning the ozone-depletion question to be held later that afternoon in the ACS News Service and Press Room in the penthouse of the Shelburne-Empress. There Rowland and Molina were joined by John W. Swinnerton of the Naval Research Laboratory in Washington, who had led several shipboard expeditions to measure chlorofluorocarbons, using a device invented by British scientist James Lovelock. In 1972, Swinnerton had found CFCs in significant quantities in the atmosphere between Los Angeles and Antarctica; two years later he had located them in even greater abundance above Spitsbergen, Norway, in the Arctic Circle. "This highly biostable chemical," Swinnerton told the reporters, "has apparently been traveling, invisible and unnoticed, on circulating air currents to virtually all portions of the globe."

Rowland came next, reporting his and Molina's calculations that if CFC production rose at the then-current rate of 10 percent a year until 1990, and then leveled off, up to 50 percent of the ozone layer would be destroyed by the year 2050. Even a 10 percent depletion, he said, could cause as many as 80,000 additional cases of skin cancer each year in the United States alone, along with genetic mutations, crop damage, and possibly even drastic changes in the world's climate. "There does not seem to be any natural trap for this type of substance," Rowland said of CFCs. "They are not absorbed in the oceans or caught in the soil, so virtually the entire amount—800,000 tons per year—must ultimately end up floating around in the air." Finally, Rowland voiced the obvious conclusion to be drawn from their study: chlorofluorocarbons ought to be banned.

The press conference marked the first time the Irvine scientists were challenged directly by spokesmen of the Du Pont company. The Du Pont men reminded the reporters that Rowland and Molina's assertion that the ozone layer had already been eroded 1 percent due to CFCs was pure conjecture, unsupported by a shred of experimental evidence. CFCs, they conceded, had been found in the lower atmosphere and in the oceans (Du Pont had even sponsored some of the research that had discovered them there), but the chemicals had never been detected in the stratosphere, which begins at about nine miles above the earth's surface; thus, it was pure speculation to suggest they arrived there at all, much more to say that they interacted with stratospheric ozone in the way Rowland and Molina said they did.

Rowland acknowledged that his and Molina's work had been theoretical, but insisted that "there is enough information available to persuade us that the eventual risk is large and that all aspects of the problem should be examined on a broad scale." Weighing the admitted benefits of aerosol sprays and refrigerants against the potential risks to biological systems and the world climate, he added, "my own opinion is that the advantages of the former are not worth the risks of the latter."

The opening shots had been fired in what was to become an epic political and scientific battle over protection of the earth's ozone layer. The story of the Rowland-Molina theory of ozone depletion broke the next day, September 11, 1974, appearing as a midsized wire-service article in the inner pages of hundreds of U.S. newspapers. The front pages of the nation's press that week were devoted almost exclusively to news of President Gerald Ford's controversial full pardon (on September 9) of former President Richard Nixon, who had resigned in August because of his role in the Watergate cover-up.

The two scientists had to wait until September 26 for the story to hit the front page of the *New York Times* under the headline TESTS SHOW AEROSOL GASES MAY POSE THREAT TO EARTH. The article was written by the paper's chief science reporter, Walter Sullivan, who had not attended the Atlantic City press conference but had followed up on the reports of Rowland and Molina's announcement. Curiously, Sullivan's article mostly described the work of other atmospheric chemists—especially Michael McElroy and Steven Wofsy at Harvard, who had confirmed Rowland and Molina's finding—and mentioned the theory's founders only in passing.

The Christian Science Monitor headlined its story, NOT WITH A BANG, BUT A PSSSST! DO AEROSOL CANS SPELL ENVIRONMENTAL DOOMSDAY? while *Science News* began its report on the discovery, "A fascinating paradox has surfaced regarding man, ozone and the atmosphere that adds an ironic twist to the story of technological advancement."

An ironic twist, indeed! The technological achievements of the early twentieth century had abundantly fulfilled beyond anyone's wildest imaginings an ideal that mankind had nurtured since the Enlightenment— that reason could vastly improve the human condition. The pace had been swift and assured, and further advancement through technology had seemed limitless. Pollution had come to be regarded as a nuisance; an unfortunate but inevitable by-product of progress, but certainly not a fatal impediment. One could at least conceive of a potential solution to the worst imaginable crisis. Waste sites could be cleaned up, smokestacks shut down, the dumping of industrial refuse in rivers and harbors stopped.

Now, for the first time, an absolute and unyielding limit to progress had been clearly sighted, a global environmental catastrophe without any conceivable solution. Even if the immediate halt to CFC production that Rowland and Molina had called for were somehow possible, there were already so many CFCs in the atmosphere that a significant amount of ozone depletion was inevitable. Progress, it appeared, might not after all march unswervingly in the direction of a more pleasant and productive future; it could instead bring the world back to a state far less comfortable than the one mankind had grown accustomed to, perhaps even to a world that would be uninhabitable by human beings.

1.

THE FORTUNATE VALLEY

OM MIDGLEY COULD NEVER leave off trying to fix the world. His friends and associates witnessed it dozens of times—a kind of involuntary reaction. While he was riding along the middle of High Street on the Columbus–Delaware Interurban, teeing up a golf ball, or chatting with his lab assistants, Midgley's gaze would momentarily come to rest on something in the middle distance; then he would look around at whomever he happened to be with and, with slight astonishment, declare, "I've just made an invention."

These spontaneous discoveries could have to do with anything from a variation on an industrial refrigerant to a way of getting salt into popcorn before it was popped, from a refinement in the manufacture of rubber tires to a method of treating the contents of a swimming pool to enable a person to swim farther underwater. For years he was interested in the possibility of creating a "long-distance golf ball" that would travel a mile or more off the tee, and only gave up the notion when friends pointed out such an invention would necessitate golf courses the size of Rhode Island.

"He could generate ten ideas in a minute," an associate, Carroll Hochwalt, later recalled. "Nine of the ten would probably be screwy, but the tenth would be a lulu." The trick, Midgley's subordinates discovered, was to keep him from wasting his and everyone else's time on the nine "screwy" ideas without discouraging him from thinking up the tenth.

Midgley's undisciplined brilliance was at times a source of concern to the corporations that paid him to develop commercially useful products, but it became evident early in his career that his eccentricities went hand in hand with a genius for solving difficult problems. While he was working for Ohio industrialist Edward Deeds during World War I on methods to improve the performance of aviation fuel for the Liberty engine, the plug in a hydrogen tank blew out, splattering Midgley in the face with pieces of the tank's metal safety diaphragm. Some of the metal particles became embedded in the cornea of his right eye. A physician was able to pluck out the larger ones, but almost fifty specks proved intractable, seriously impairing his vision.

Determined to regain his eyesight, Midgley made a risky presumption based on his knowledge of metallurgy: mercury was known for its ability to amalgamate readily with other metals; therefore, it was possible that liquid mercury, introduced into the eye, would form amalgams with the remaining metal particles, making them larger, so they might wash out or be more easily removed. Mercury compounds were used for their amalgamative properties in the making of dental fillings, and highly toxic mercuric chloride was used in very diluted form as an antiseptic, but no one had ever used mercury as an eyewash. Midgley, with his doctor's approval, used an eye dropper to administer a bath of purified mercury to his right eye. After repeated applications over a period of two weeks, the bath thoroughly cleansed the eye of all the remaining particles. The feat inspired the first of numerous articles that would be written about Midgley in scientific trade journals. "Can you point to an experience, either in fiction or real life, which shows more ingenuity in a pinch?" marveled the September 1919 issue of *Industrial and Engineering Chemistry.*

Midgley recognized his scientific bent as a birthright. His father, Thomas Midgley, Sr., was born in England in 1861 and emigrated to the United States in his teens. After serving an apprenticeship in a New England machine shop, he became an industrial manager and an inventor in the emerging field of processing rubber for bicycle and automobile tires. The creator of a detachable-rim rubber tire, he was acquainted with Harvey Firestone, Thomas Edison, and Henry Ford, among other "shed" inventors. Midgley's grandfather on his mother Hattie's side was James Emerson, inventor of the inserted tooth saw. An Emerson ancestor had worked alongside the Scottish scientist James Watt, father of the steam engine and originator of the term "horsepower"; another relation, one Richard Midgley, a native of Yorkshire, had been a prominent eighteenth-century London clockmaker.

Born in 1889 in Beaver Falls, Pennsylvania, young Tom Midgley grew up and attended public school in Columbus, Ohio, where his father had taken over the management of a bicycle factory. At age sixteen, he was sent to the Betts Academy, a college preparatory school in Stamford, Connecticut. He caused a stir during his senior year at Betts, when he took issue with a chemistry instructor's contention that the regular arrangement of the elements in the periodic table was proof of the existence of God. Midgley said it indicated only that—from one element to the next—the atoms were made up of still smaller particles.

In 1907, Midgley went on to the Sibley College of Engineering at Cornell University, where he majored in mechanical engineering. "Midgley's undergraduate work and his inexactitude as regards attendance were such that he would probably be 'busted out' if he were an undergraduate now," faculty advisor W. N. Barnard later said. "He was, however, keenly interested in research and he would chase up some loss of energy in a problem to the exclusion of the rest of his work. There were enough professors who appreciated his ability so that he was allowed to graduate, fortunately."

He seems to have been something of a recluse at Cornell. Midgley neither pledged to a fraternity nor went out for athletics, as he had in high school, and his photograph does not appear in any of his class yearbooks. The 1911 *Cornellian* cites his name only once, listing him as president and cofounder of the Cornell Aero Club, an organization devoted to discussing the new field of aviation, and even then the editors somehow managed to misspell his name.

The school's administrators made no such mistake that spring, however, when F. O. Clements, a recruiter from the National Cash Register Company in Dayton, Ohio, wrote seeking to know the identity of the school's most promising engineering graduates. In reply, Clements received not the list he had expected but a letter containing only one name: Thomas Midgley, Jr.

The first corporation in the United States to actively recruit talent from the graduating classes of the nation's top schools, National Cash Register was, under the autocratic presidency of founder John Patterson, one of the most progressive companies in America. Thomas Midgley was interested in NCR's job offer because of yet another of its innovations, an "Inventions Department," a version of the research-and-development divisions that had recently been established by other technology-based corporations like General Electric and Bell Telephone.

In order to lure top scientists from universities, these corporations strove to re-create an "academic" environment in the labs, to foster as best they could an illusion of relative freedom from the pressures of commercial enterprise. Even more persuasive were the generous starting salaries the corporations offered, often three or four times what a tenured university professor could demand. Corporate labs soon received glowing testimonials from those who tested the waters. "There is no evidence on the part of the officers of the Company, of impatience or a wish to interfere at all in my work," wrote Willis R. Whitney, an MIT chemistry instructor who gave up a promising teaching career to head the GE lab, to his former academic colleagues in 1901. "The only thing I want now is to accomplish some great thing for the 'General Electric.' "

Ten years later, when Midgley graduated from college, the pathway from the engineering classroom to the corporate research division was well marked, and having grown up in a household in which the safety bicycle, detachable tire rims, and other workaday marvels were regularly acclaimed, Midgley would have had few reservations about donning a work apron in a company lab. He would later cite "the Dayton address of National Cash and a bigger salary than I could have ever hoped for" as his reasons for accepting NCR's offer of a job. He was so eager to get started, he left Cornell without bothering to attend his own graduation.

In the summer of 1911 there was no better destination than Dayton for an ambitious young engineer. One of the new, liberated meccas of midwestern commerce and manufacturing, Dayton was home to the burgeoning bicycle, aviation, and automotive industries that since 1890 had transformed Ohio and southern Michigan into the Silicon Valley of the day. It was also the hometown of Orville and Wilbur Wright, inventors of the first successful flying machine, who, despite their worldwide fame, still lived and worked there.

Dayton stood at the confluence of the Mad, Stillwater, and Great Miami rivers, in a fertile area of rich bottomland farmers called the Fortunate Valley. Midway between the coalfields of Kentucky, the iron-shipping lanes of the Great Lakes, and the vast timber stands of Michigan, the city was perfectly located to exploit the Midwest's abundant natural resources and dense railroad network. Dayton enjoyed yet another advantage: there was little "old money" in the region and few ties to the eastern establishment interests that dominated American business, making the atmosphere conducive to the ascent of fresh ideas.

Dayton had grown rapidly in the last years of the nineteenth century as industrious German and Hungarian immigrants joined the descendants of the original New Englanders who had settled the area in the early 1800s. The population doubled from 25,000 to 50,000 between 1870 and 1880, increased to 80,000 in 1896, and reached 120,000 by 1910. That year the city led the world in the annual manufacture of cash registers, sewing machines, railroad cars ("enough for a train 100 miles in length"), automatic toys, and golf clubs, and was strong in bicycles, streetcar parts, paper bags, and folding ice-cream boxes.

The crowning glory of Dayton technology was the Wright brothers' airplane; yet the city's stature as an industrial capital was due to the mass production of another, far less glamorous local invention: the cash register. The machine's originators were two well-known Dayton restaurateurs, brothers John and James Ritty. James ran a restaurant at 10 South Main Street that had been known alternately as No. 10, the Empire, or —in less fashionable times—the Pony Room. In the early 1870s he became concerned because, although the café was frequently full of patrons, he seemed to be losing money. He suspected his cashiers were dipping into the till, but short of catching them red-handed, he had no way to prove it.

To help distract Ritty from his worries, a Dayton friend, a celebrated marksman named "Captain" Bogardus, who was to give shooting exhibitions on the Continent, invited the restaurateur to accompany him on his European trip. During the Atlantic crossing, Ritty's love of machinery drew him to the ship's engine room, where an idea came to him as he stood watching the automatic mechanism that counted the revolutions of the ship's propeller. "If the movements of a ship's propeller can be recorded," Ritty is said to have declared, "there is no reason why the movement of sales in a store cannot be recorded."

Back in Dayton, James and John Ritty built a similar clocklike "remembering device" to record store sales, patenting it in November 1879 as Ritty's Incorruptible Cashier. Within two years they were supervising ten workers and filling catalog orders for the machine from as far away as Bangor, Maine. But the device, despite some improvements, remained a kind of grandiose novelty item, and retailers hesitated to buy a machine that did something a clerk could do with a two-cent pencil and a scrap of paper. In 1885 the Rittys returned to the restaurant business, selling all their cash-register patents and production facilities for six thousand dollars to John Patterson, the owner of a general store, who had purchased one of the Incorruptible Cashiers and been impressed by the reforming effect it had on his employees.

Patterson established his factory to build the registers on a piece of farmland along the east bank of the Great Miami River, a few miles south of downtown Dayton. He nurtured a powerful vision of the cash register's future: with a faith typical of America's Progressive Era, he believed that by discouraging cashier "manipulations" the register could become a force for civic good. A new trend in retailing also favored the device. Across the country during the 1890s the number of large department stores and chain five-and-dimes was growing, and it was in these businesses, where direct owner supervision of employees was impossible, that the cash register would prove most essential. By 1901, only sixteen years after Patterson had started business, more than 7,000 workers were turning out 100,000 cash registers a year at National Cash Register. That year "the Cash" surpassed the Barney & Smith Car Company, a maker of plush railroad and trolley cars, to become Dayton's leading manufacturer.

The company owed much of its success to the innovative management and sales techniques improvised by its president. Patterson pioneered many business practices that later became routine in American corporations, including direct-mail advertising, the canned sales pitch, promotional brochures, protected territories with quotas, formal classes in the art of selling, and the annual sales convention.

In an era of notorious labor-related strife characterized by the Haymarket Riot and the Pullman strike, Patterson also helped define the modern corporate attitude of benign paternalism toward company employees. "An employer owes more to his employees than mere wages," he said. This approach, he contended, not only made union antagonism unnecessary, but benefited NCR interests in the long run because satisfied, healthy employees were more loyal and efficient workers, and there would be less turnover of the skilled machinists vital to the plant's operation. His reforms included employee cafeterias, health benefits, an infirmary, and daily exercise and recreation periods. Decrying the dark, grimy conditions that prevailed in industries back east, Patterson ordered that all new NCR buildings be walled with glass, where possible, to create "daylight" factories. He arranged for the female employees' shift changes to occur at different hours from the men's, so that the women could arrive and depart the factory without "unpleasantness and danger." The company also sponsored a "House of Usefulness" where local children could learn wood carving, drawing, and other skills, and even a special activity club for neighborhood boys who had been caught vandalizing the premises. For adult workers, there were cooking lessons, indoor archery, music societies, and night courses in everything from salesmanship to bait casting.

Patterson was not content to see his progressive ideas stop at the walls of the Cash. In 1914 he succeeded in convincing Dayton voters to adopt a new form of municipal government known as the city-manager or commission-manager system, in which a nonpartisan urban administrator was chosen by a board of local businessmen and civic leaders. Advocates of the city-manager method believed that a transformed technological society, with all its new complexity, would be poorly served by politics as usual and the political machines that ran most cities; what was required was "scientific government." Dayton was one of the first U.S. cities to adopt city-manager style of government, and the "Dayton Model" became a keystone of urban reform in early-twentieth-century America.

One of Patterson's best-known corporate innovations was the first extensive use of promotional photography. NCR sales brochures featured not only handsome photographs of cash registers, but also pictures of the firm's orderly machine shops, windowed factory rooms, classrooms, and activity areas, as well as its contented workers. When Thomas Midgley reported to work at the Cash in the summer of 1911, Patterson had recently purchased a rare and expensive novelty—a movie camera. One afternoon shortly after Midgley's arrival, he arranged for a member of the Wright Exhibition Team to fly an airplane in from the Wrights' field at Huffman Prairie, northeast of Dayton, and land in a pasture just south of the factory so that he could make a motion picture of the spectacle. Midgley, the former president of the Cornell Aero Club, had never actually seen an airplane in flight, and he was among the hundreds of other NCR workers that afternoon who spilled out of the factory buildings and watched in awe as the pilot executed a broad circle over the Great Miami River, then lowered the flying machine gently down to the field.

John Patterson's efforts at NCR and in Dayton were an expression of a powerful enlightenment taking place in America: progressivism. The historian Frederick Jackson Turner, speaking to a gathering of the newly formed American Historical Association at the Chicago World's Fair of 1893, had declared that, with the settling of the West, the American frontier was closed, and warned that with its loss a new emptiness, an ennui, would possess the American people and damage the national character. But within a decade of Turner's pronouncement, a new school of American intellectuals, led by the historian Charles Beard, were correcting Turner's appraisal as hasty; the old frontier might have closed, Beard and his followers acknowledged, but another, even grander frontier had opened, the frontier of technological progress.

This new frontier was abundant with promise: technology would rebuild the country, provide work, strengthen democracy; it would make possible new modes of transportation, better health care and nutrition, and would foster a host of technical innovations no one could presume to foresee. The pursuit of happiness no longer led west along a rutted wagon trail, but to the modern assembly line, the forge, and the production schedule.

Nothing inspired this faith more fully than the appearance of the airplane in the sky above American cities in the years 1909 through 1912. The airplane, invented by the Wrights in 1903, and popularized by them and others between 1904 and 1908, was, as historian Joseph Corn has observed, "a mechanical messiah whose coming would wondrously transform life and society," its arrival comparable to the appearance of the Star of Bethlehem two millennia earlier signaling the birth of Jesus. Fulfilling mankind's long-held dream of flight, the flying machine inspired expectations of unlimited technological progress. It was impossible to watch an airplane soar above Dayton and not recognize that the greatest glory of America must still lie ahead.

Thomas Midgley was not the first bright engineering graduate NCR attracted to its Inventions Department. In 1904 the company had brought on board a promising young electrical engineer from Ohio State University named Charles Kettering, and had asked him to take a leading role in a project designated a top priority by NCR's president: the electrification of the cash register. As John Patterson had complained to his research men, electricity was illuminating the skylines of big cities and powering whole interurban railways, yet the standard NCR machine was still cranked by hand.

Electrifying the register was under the supervision of NCR executive Edward Deeds, like Kettering the product of an Ohio farm boyhood. Deeds also shared with Kettering a great enthusiasm for the future of electricity. But electrifying small machines like cash registers was a daunting task because fractional horsepower motors for doing small jobs had not yet been perfected. In the case of the register, the problem was compounded by the need for the workings of the machine to return to exactly the same position after each "ringing up," and by the need to match the small motor to all types of potential electrical power sources, since the NCR registers were sold all over the world. Kettering nonetheless assured Deeds, "Of course we can do it. You don't need a big motor. You don't need efficiency. What you want is a spasm of quick-turning power. What you want is torque."

"A lanky, Lincoln-like fellow," a colleague once described Kettering, "[he was] an unusually tall stalk of corn, towering above those around it in the field." The comparison to Lincoln was understandable. Born in 1876 and raised in Loudonville, Ohio, Kettering attended a one-room schoolhouse and pursued his two boyhood passions, reading and tinkering, in the stolen moments between chores on the family farm. At his graduation from high school, he enjoyed the reputation of "having read more books than any boy in the history of Loudonville"; he used all of the fourteen dollars he earned helping to bring in a neighbor's wheat harvest to buy a telephone so he could tear the newfangled device apart and see what made it work.

With his twangy voice and country mannerisms, his homemade clothes and boyish enthusiasm for science, Kettering could not help but seem like a hayseed at NCR, where the style for young engineers was decidedly buttoned-down. But Patterson came to appreciate his new recruit's genius, particularly when Kettering began making headway in the electrification of the cash register. By 1906, Kettering's efforts had resulted in a small electric motor with a few interchangeable parts. In 1907 an improved version, the "Class 1000" register, went on the market; it would dominate the cash-register business for the next forty years. Kettering also designed a machine specifically for department stores. The stores' floor managers had complained of having to hurry from counter to counter to approve individual customers' credit charges. Kettering's "O.K. Charge Phone," a system that combined the electric cash register with the telephone and allowed cashiers to ring a central office for credit approval, alleviated this problem. A precursor to the credit card, the O.K. Charge completed the popularization of the cash register.

Patterson's style of aggressive promotion and systematized marketing rubbed off on Kettering, leading him to an important understanding: an invention was practically worthless if it was not vigorously promoted to the public; it became an *innovation* only if it was widely used. Kettering discovered that he enjoyed promoting his own inventions, and with Patterson's encouragement, he personally led the NCR campaign to convince Wanamaker's department store in Philadelphia to install the first O.K. system.

In 1909 he also started to apply the principles learned at the Cash to an independent venture. His friend and colleague Edward Deeds was building a do-it-yourself Packard "kit car" in the barn at the rear of his home on Central Avenue in Dayton, and he had requested Kettering's help with the automobile's electrical system. As they worked together on the Packard, the two engineers discussed the young, flourishing automobile market in southeastern Michigan, and the possibility of developing an electrical component that would be of value to carmakers. Electricity had revolutionized the cash register, among other machines: why not the automobile?

Deeds urged Kettering, "There is a river of gold running past us. Why can't we throw out a little dam and sluice some of it our way?"

The two men shook hands on an agreement to "put something on a car."

The automobile business, then barely ten years old, was in happy if tumultuous circumstances. Frank and Charles Duryea had built the first car powered by a gasoline engine in 1892; the first automaker, the Olds Motor Works, had been incorporated in Detroit in 1899; and by 1909 almost one hundred car manufacturers—many of them small one-garage operations employing fewer than a dozen workmen and mechanics—were spread across the Midwest from Pennsylvania to Illinois, competing to survive the initial stages of development and acceptance. The car itself remained so primitive that automobile owners of later generations would hardly have recognized it. The first manufacturers—Oldsmobile, Buick, Packard, among others—had essentially put a motor on a horse buggy; a few early automobiles even came equipped with a whipsocket. Meanwhile, the tires, chassis, and axles designed for a carriage proved inadequate to support the weight and vibration of a motor, and for years travel by auto over farm roads and city cobblestones remained hardly preferable to a buggy ride.

In 1907, however, Ford began its huge expansion with the introduction of the mass-assembled Model T. In response, Buick, Cadillac, Oldsmobile, and Oakland (later, Pontiac) merged to form a corporation called United (later, General Motors). If Ford intended to focus on manufacturing the all-purpose, reasonably priced Model T, GM would appeal to all segments of the car-buying public with models ranging from the utilitarian Oldsmobile to the luxurious Cadillac.

The organizing force behind General Motors was W. C. "Billy" Durant, partner in a sprawling Flint carriage-making business. As in Dayton, carriage-making in Flint had evolved logically from the region's vast lumber resources and was an obvious antecedent to the automobile industry. The success of Dort & Durant Carriage Company was due to Durant's innovative concept of component assembly. Rather than conduct manufacturing under one roof, Durant established smaller factories to make individual buggy parts—axles, bodies, wheels, springs, seats—and an assembly plant to bring all the pieces together.

Ford, with single-plant mass production, and General Motors, with component assembly, rushed to systematize automobile manufacturing, but at the cost of failing to solve some of the car's basic technical deficiencies. The industry was severely undercapitalized, in-house automotive research efforts were almost unheard of, and carmakers were wide open to technological improvements offered by independent shed inventors like Deeds and Kettering.

The two partners arranged the Deeds barn so that their guinea pig—first Deeds's Packard, later a Cadillac roadster—occupied most of the main floor. A lathe, drill press, and other tools were located upstairs in a hayloft, and the two floors were connected by a narrow spiral staircase that Kettering flew up and down a hundred times a day. Deeds generally took charge of the partnership's business affairs, the "white shirt stuff," as Kettering termed it, while a handful of moonlighting NCR engineers and mechanics—"the Barn Gang"—served as helpers for "Boss Ket."

Kettering's experience with electrifying the cash register spoke directly to one of the car industry's most critical needs, a consistent and dependable system of ignition for the motor. Engines in the early cars ran with either a magneto or a dry-cell-battery operation. The magneto-powered cars did not start reliably, ran poorly at slow speeds, and often stalled and had to be restarted, while dry-cell batteries, somewhat more reliable, had no efficient means of delivering their power to the motor. If a driver was lucky, a set of dry cells might last three hundred miles. These systems were so primitive that the headlights had to be operated separately. A canister of acetylene on the car's running board provided "headlamp" fuel; at dusk the motorist pulled over to the side of the road and lit the headlights with a match. When Kettering and the Barn Gang developed an electrical single-spark ignition in 1909, Cadillac's founder, Henry Leland, eagerly placed an order for eight thousand of the units.

But Deeds and Kettering, focusing on research, had given little thought to fulfilling a large manufacturing order for one of their inventions. Hastily incorporating as the Dayton Engineering Laboratories Company, the two men arranged for a Chicago manufacturer to assemble the ignitions according to Kettering's specifications, while Deeds secured a start-up loan of $150,000. One of the Barn Gang, a Spanish-American War veteran named Bill Chryst, inspired by the National Biscuit Company's acronym, Nabisco, suggested calling the new firm "Delco," an idea Deeds and Kettering instantly liked. Within days, the Barn Gang had become Delco, a fledgling automotive electrical firm, and Kettering resigned from NCR to devote himself exclusively to automotive work.

Then, in December 1909, a bizarre accident that would have a decisive effect on the fortunes of the new company occurred in Detroit.

Byron T. Carter, founder of the Cartercar Company, was driving across the Belle Isle Bridge when he saw a woman struggling to crank her stalled Buick. He pulled over to help. When he stooped to turn the crank, however, the motor kicked it violently back around the other way, striking the elderly Carter in the face and knocking him to the ground. He was hospitalized with a broken jaw and facial lacerations, and died of gangrene a few weeks later without having left his hospital bed. Cadillac's Henry Leland was moved by his friend's death to remark, "I'm sorry I ever built an automobile," and he vowed to rid the car once and for all of its hand crank.

Leland was the oldest of the automotive pioneers, a distinguished-looking man with a starch-white Vandyke beard and spectacles, who personified the link between the Detroit automotive revolution and the New England machine shop. Born in 1843 in Vermont, he had apprenticed during the Civil War as a gunsmith at the Federal Arsenal in Springfield, Massachusetts. Leland founded the Cadillac Automobile Company in 1902, and by 1909—largely because of his ability to design Detroit's most powerful and reliable car engines—Cadillac held the town's reputation for superior all-around quality and innovation. Cadillac, for instance, had been the first to introduce the steering wheel, replacing the tiller stick as a means of controlling the automobile.

Now, with the industry buzzing about "Uncle" Henry's demand for replacement of the hand crank, Earl C. Howard, Cadillac assistant sales manager and a former NCR salesman, recalled that Kettering had done something similar for the cash register. He mentioned it to Leland, who summoned Kettering to Detroit in early 1910 and encouraged him to build an electrical self-starter that would render the crank obsolete. "Something must be done," Leland told Kettering. "I am breaking arms all over the country and it has got to stop."

Back in Dayton, Boss Ket and the men of Delco established that an electrical charge could turn their Cadillac test engine over. But the apparatus needed to do so was much too large to fit under the hood of a car. Kettering got around the problem by applying a lesson from his work on the cash register: a strong surge of electricity was required only for an instant to start the car; once the motor was operating, far less electrical power was needed. Thus, a large electrical source was not necessary, just a compact one that could—for an instant—be mechanically amplified to turn the engine over. Kettering's crucial insight was that the problem of the hand crank was part of a larger problem. Existing power systems for cars, which treated each electrical need under the hood separately, often failed because they were only as strong as their weakest component. He set out to design a single system that would provide all the automobile's electrical needs, including starting. The system was composed of four 6-volt batteries, which could be linked in series or used individually. To start the car, all 24 volts were needed; once the car was operating, however, fewer were required to replenish the battery or operate the headlights and other accessories.

One of the first persons to enjoy a ride in a crankless car was Kettering's old NCR colleague Thomas Watson, Jr., later the founder of NCR's competitor, International Business Machines (IBM), whom Kettering met by chance one evening in February 1911 at the Dayton train station. He offered Watson a ride, and the two men climbed into the automobile Kettering was driving; Watson, thinking his absentminded friend had forgotten to crank the car, was about to say something when Kettering pulled a lever near the steering column and, to his passenger's amazement, the engine roared to life.

Kettering's self-starter made him a hero to the infant automobile industry and also brought him wide public acclaim, for the device hastened an important social revolution. As Malcolm Bingay, editor of the *Detroit Free Press,* noted of the elimination of the hand crank, "Kettering has done more to emancipate women than Susan B. Anthony or Mrs. Pankhurst or all the other valiant gals who got the credit he deserves."

2.

"IF GOD MADE GASOLINE KNOCK..."

N THE SUMMER OF 1916, when Kettering opened a small research lab in Dayton, Bill Chryst suggested that he hire Tom Midgley, whom Chryst knew from the Cash, as a research associate. Midgley had never met Kettering, though he was familiar with his achievements, for his work in the Inventions Department at NCR had involved refining the electrified cash registers Kettering had left behind when he moved on to found Delco.

The chance to join Kettering's team was an opportunity that would have been coveted by any young engineer. Boss Ket oversaw not only Delco, which manufactured the automobile self-starter he had invented, but also the Dayton Metal Products Company, which he, Deeds, and their financial partners had started to manufacture pumps and refrigeration accessories. The Domestic Engineering Company, the lab in which Midgley was offered employment, was Kettering's own in-house "inventions" division.

In Midgley, Kettering found a partner who shared both his disdain for normal lab routine and his exuberant love of scientific discovery. "He was the most unconventional worker in the world," Kettering said approvingly. Boss Ket always delighted in the bewildered looks on the faces of his listeners when he described—in his rapid-fire country twang—some new theory or solution to a scientific problem. But Midgley was not easily intimidated by the technological bull sessions Kettering was accustomed to dominating, the arguing and wondering out loud about things that science might make possible. If Boss Ket "spun out a little yarn," Midgley might just roll it out a little further.

Midgley respected Kettering, who was thirteen years his senior, as a mentor, and would often offer his own conclusions simply as a means of eliciting Kettering's "take" on a particular problem. "Midge would open the subject, then drink in Ket's thoughts," one Delco colleague later recalled. But Boss Ket was not infallible. Once, when Midgley spoke enthusiastically about the potential of the emerging technology of radio broadcasting, Kettering cut him off, saying: "Hell, Midge, radio broadcasting will never amount to anything. It's just a fad!" Midgley was still teasing Kettering about this proclamation twenty years later, long after Kettering himself had become a household name via a series of nationally broadcast radio talks.

Midgley's first job for Kettering was to finish the development of a hydrometer to indicate the degree of charge in the storage battery of a Delco-Light farm-lighting set. The Farm-Lights were a pet project of Kettering's, whose family still lived on a farm back in Loudonville. He believed fervently that farmers should not be denied the electric conveniences enjoyed by city dwellers. "Kettering," Tabby Boyd later explained, "thought he ought to be able to give his mother on the farm [this] luxury. He wanted to set her free of the kerosene lamp with its dim light and its need to be tended each day, of the outside well with its hand-operated pump, of the hand-power churn, and of other age-old contrivances which took so much of her time and strength."

Despite Kettering's affinity for rural folk, Delco salesmen marketing the Farm-Light kit were admonished to be aggressive. One proven strategy for clinching a sale was for the Delco man to call on a family farm in the evening, after the day's chores were done, and ask to set the Farm-Light up for a free demonstration. After the generator was operating, and the farmer and his family were beginning to get accustomed to the wonders of electricity, the salesman would quietly drift back to his car and abruptly shut the system off, plunging the farm back into total darkness. By 1916, Delco was selling more than forty thousand of the units per year.

None of John Patterson's protégés had learned better than Kettering that an invention was valuable only when it became an innovation that people bought and used. Kettering took this view a step further: he came to think of himself as working in partnership with his customers, and he looked to their reaction to help force the improvements in the design of a device that would make it even more useful. He believed in a kind of Darwinian obsolescence of bad machines, that in technology, as in nature, an improved species would always supersede an inferior one. Thus, when Delco Farm-Light owners began grumbling that the small engines at times emitted a loud knocking sound, Kettering responded not by defending the product but by becoming obsessed with identifying and correcting the problem.

"The noisy bugbear of knock," as Kettering called it, greatly inhibited the efficiency of all internal-combustion engines, and was a hindrance not only to the Delco-Light, which operated on kerosene, but also to the gasoline-run automobile. Automotive scientists knew that knock occurred when the fuel farthest from the spark plug became excited under pressure and exploded prematurely, before the combusting flame had reached it. But the phenomenon was imperfectly understood and had been blamed on the carburetor, the battery, even on Kettering's self-starter. One Detroit car dealer had gone so far as to name the horrible racket "Kettering knock," infuriating Boss Ket, who suspected the fuel was to blame but was unable to prove his theory.

Gasoline had not been an automatic choice of fuel for the car. Many experimental self-propelled vehicles in the nineteenth century were steam-powered. But to auto-industry mavericks like Ransom Olds, who tried adapting steam power to the car in the 1880s before turning to the internal-combustion engine, the drawbacks of steam quickly became evident. The coal that was used as fuel combusted so slowly it gave no "pickup" to the engine, making the vehicle trudge along at a smooth but slow pace; and for a trip of any distance so much coal was necessary that there was no room in the car for passengers or cargo.

When the Duryea brothers built their car in 1892, they used the internal-combustion engine, developed in 1876 by German inventor Nikolaus Otto, and fueled the engine with gasoline, then a by-product of kerosene production. Ransom Olds had adopted the gas-run car by 1897, and other nascent automakers followed suit. The gasoline engine delivered far more power, proportionate to its weight and bulk. Moreover, gasoline was cheap and in seemingly limitless supply, and could be sold to motorists at any country store.

A notable dissenter was Thomas Edison, who experimented between 1901 and 1907 with cars powered by electric storage batteries. In Edison's vehicles electricity made for a smooth, quiet ride, but the battery was bulky and required frequent and lengthy periods of recharging. Like the steam-powered car, the electric car also failed to deliver sufficient forward thrust. With the unqualified success of Henry Ford's gas-powered Model T in 1907, public and scientific interest in Edison's electric car waned, and a short time later Edison announced his retirement from the field of commercial invention.

Kettering was one of the first automotive engineers to give serious thought to gasoline and its relation to engine efficiency. In his view cars were designed around their motors, while the motors were built around the fuel they ran on. Therefore, he believed, the key to building more powerful cars was to improve the efficiency of gasoline, raising the engine's compression ratio by maximizing the combustion of air and gasoline in the cylinder. This meant solving once and for all the riddle of what caused motors to knock.

Kettering called Midgley into his office one day in 1916. "I want you to go over to my office in the old Delco plant and get a box," he instructed him. "And I want you to open that box up. You'll find some instruments in there and some old greasy papers and so forth . . ." Kettering had previously imported from England a Dobbie-McInnes Indicator, a manometer that recorded varying levels of pressure in the cylinder of an internal-combustion engine. The expensive device had wound up in a closet, unused and almost forgotten, a casualty of Kettering's busy schedule.

"I spent a whole Saturday afternoon," Kettering later said, "selling Midge on the idea that this was quite an important project." He cautioned the younger man against falling prey to existing dogma. "Remember," he warned Midgley, "everything is known about knock. You can go to a bookcase and there are twenty-five or thirty volumes in it that tell you exactly what will happen. It's all known and written down. Well, I don't believe there is a word of truth in that library. Everything that's in the books and everything that everybody thinks about this thing is wrong."

Like most of Kettering's opinions, his dim view of "experts" came with a corresponding anecdote: He had once mentioned to a colleague that he could complete the journey from Detroit to Dayton by car in four and a half hours. The man told Kettering that no one could do it that fast, so Kettering asked him to be his traveling companion that Friday afternoon when he returned to Dayton. When they arrived at their destination on schedule, the other man exclaimed, "My God, no wonder you can make it in four and a half hours. You don't stay on Route 25!" Thus, "Get off Route 25!" became a succinct expression of Kettering's homespun philosophy.

Midgley's first decision after agreeing to undertake the antiknock project was very much in the spirit of "getting off Route 25." He told

Kettering the manometer would not suffice for his investigation, and that the method he had devised would be more empirical: he wanted to watch the actual workings of an internal-combustion engine. To do this Midgley bored a two-inch-wide hole in the top of a small engine and inserted a narrow quartz window extending all the way across the engine's combustion chamber along the cylinder head. The window commanded the whole sweep of internal combustion starting from the spark plug and ending at the far side of the chamber. Midgley and Kettering then rigged up a primitive "movie-making" apparatus, using a camera with a fast, accurate shutter and an old tomato can as a drum for rotating the customized, extralong roll of film.

The resulting photographs depicted a miniature apocalypse—the bright flame dashing from the spark plug to the opposite end of the combustion chamber. The flame burned evenly when the engine operated normally, but jerked when the engine knocked. The Dobbie-McInnes manometer recorded an increase in engine pressure accompanying the knock. In testing the engine, Midgley observed that kerosene knocked worse than gasoline. This seemed to confirm Kettering's hypothesis that fuel, not ignition, was the source of knock. Hearing Midgley's results, Kettering suggested that perhaps kerosene did not vaporize and mix with air as readily as gasoline.

"When I was a boy on the farm," Kettering told Midgley, "I used to watch every spring for the first flower in the woods. The trailing arbutus. I used to wonder why the arbutus blooms so early, even before the snow was gone from the ground. I think it's because the red color in the leaves helps it use the sun's rays better than green-leaved plants do. Now do you suppose that if we colored the fuel red, it might absorb the heat better, thus stepping up the rate of vaporization?"

Midgley granted the idea had merit. It was a weekend, however, and the local chemical-supply house was closed. Unable to obtain any oil-soluble dye, Midgley added a handful of iodine crystals to a flask of kerosene, knowing it would turn the fuel reddish purple. The engine knocking decreased immediately. Afraid his ears were playing tricks on him, Midgley tried the experiment again—with the same results. Kettering's hunch about coloring the fuel appeared to have been correct. But on Monday morning, when Midgley obtained some red, orange, and yellow oil-soluble dyes and placed them in the engine, the engine knock did not decrease. He could only conclude that in his original experiment Saturday afternoon the iodine—not the red color—had suppressed the knock.

Iodine was scarce, and formed metallic iodides in a combustion cylinder that would destroy an engine in a few days. However, Kettering's idea about the arbutus—and fate, since no dyes had been at hand and iodine had been substituted—had allowed for an important break-through: a chemical additive would inhibit engine knock.

Midgley was giddy with his easy success. One afternoon soon after, when Kettering brought Henry Ford through the Dayton lab, Midgley decided to have some sport with the stern, no-nonsense industrialist. He saturated his handkerchief with iodine and stuffed it in the pocket of his suitcoat, then, when Kettering and his distinguished guest came by, he turned on a test engine. With the engine knocking violently, Midgley dipped his hand into his pocket and—with a magician's flourish—made several passes with his hand over the engine's air intake. As Ford watched in amazement, the engine breathed in enough of the iodine to stop knocking completely.

Kettering, encouraged by the quick results from iodine, insisted that Midgley head a search for other antiknocks. Iodine could not be the only one; there must be others. "If God made gasoline knock," Kettering declared, "he certainly made something to prevent it from knocking!"

Midgley was willing to share Kettering's optimism, but considered himself the last person to pursue an exhaustive chemical search. He told Kettering he had gone as far in gasoline research as his limited chemical expertise would allow, and reminded him that he had earned a degree in mechanical, not chemical, engineering. What the lab needed, Midgley advised, was "a top chemistry man" for the job; if Kettering didn't mind, he preferred to be assigned to something else.

Kettering minded a great deal. "What do I want a chemist for?" Boss Ket demanded. "He doesn't know any more about it than we do." He assured Midgley that he wanted him to undertake the project, because if "experts" came in, they would only try to make the problem conform to known facts. Kettering would much prefer to take his chances on Midg-ley's resourcefulness and ingenuity.

"[We are] like a group of fellows who are going on a long trip," he explained to his hapless protégé, "and don't want to start out with packs on their backs which contain a lot of things they will not use. Let's you and me go up and survey the road first without any packs on our backs."

By 1916, American involvement in the First World War appeared un-avoidable. One impact on the home front was a merger between Dayton's burgeoning aviation industry and the U.S. military. Kettering, Deeds, Orville Wright, and other businessmen—distracted from their peacetime endeavors—formed the Dayton-Wright Corporation to provide planes, engines, and aviation fuel for the war effort.

But it was changes taking shape during the war hundreds of miles from Dayton, along the Brandywine Creek in Wilmington, Delaware, home of E. I. Du Pont de Nemours & Company, that were to have the greatest impact on Kettering's and Midgley's affairs.

Du Pont—an American family company whose origins dated back to Jeffersonian times—had provided gunpowder for virtually every international conflict since the War of 1812. The company's profits always mushroomed in times of war, but the take from World War I was staggering—from $5 million a year before the hostilities to $59 million the year the war ended. The corporation's leadership—its young president, Pierre Du Pont, and his chief aide-de-camp and financial wizard, Jacob Raskob—had cause to worry over this enrichment, for the firm had been suffering what executives of a later generation might term "public-relations difficulties." Their profits had been so huge and the slaughter of Verdun and the Somme and Gallipoli so ghastly, that the League of Nations, the press outside Delaware, and even the governments who bought and used the powder were all denouncing Du Pont as a war profiteer. Before the war the company had been the target of gunpowder antitrust initiatives by Washington; more would surely follow. Over the long haul, the Du Ponts recognized, dominance of the market for any single product, particularly gunpowder, was not a viable base for a modern corporation.

The solution devised by the firm's leadership was a broad diversification program away from the company's traditional interests in gunpowder and into chemicals, dyes, and synthetic fabrics. This change in direction would be financed by the controversial war profits and facilitated by America's wartime seizure of German chemical and dyestuff patents, some three hundred of which were purchased from the U.S. government by Du Pont.

In early 1914, Jacob Raskob had given Pierre Du Pont some valuable advice: the price of shares of common stock in General Motors, then the nation's second-leading automaker, had dipped to $82 per share, a decline Raskob predicted would be temporary. Pierre bought 2,000 shares of GM common stock in February, and by December 1915 they were valued at $558 per share. Du Pont purchases of GM stock continued; by mid-1919 Du Pont's investment totaled $47 million, giving Du Pont 33 percent of all GM stock. Although in retrospect Du Pont's pattern of investment in GM appears entirely reasonable, even shrewd, at the time so large an investment in an automaker was considered quite reckless.

Most of the financial backing for the young auto industry had come from midwestern sources; eastern bankers and "old money" families like the Du Ponts had largely stayed aloof from so chaotic and unpredictable a business.

By the end of the war, Du Pont's holdings of GM stock allowed it to take control of the company. Billy Durant had proved himself incapable of managing the sprawling corporation, more than once driving it close to bankruptcy. In March 1920, Pierre Du Pont became chairman of the board of GM, and after another Durant financial stumble in November of that year, he replaced Durant as president as well. At the same time, GM bought out Charles Kettering's research firm, Domestic Engineering, appointing Kettering vice president for research in charge of the new General Motors Research Corporation. Kettering accepted on the condition the research operation be allowed to remain in Dayton.

For Pierre Du Pont and Jacob Raskob the car industry represented a double roll of the dice: not only were they backing a fledgling industry, they hoped that automobiles would present the ideal market for Du Pont leatherworks, dyes, synthetic fabrics, paints, and varnishes. As Raskob pointed out to Pierre, Du Pont control of General Motors would be a boon to Du Pont researchers, affording "many opportunities to keep our important men occupied with big things after the war." Beyond these practical stratagems, the two young men simply liked the idea of getting involved with automobiles. Commuting to Detroit, they thrilled to meet such celebrities as the burly, mustachioed French race car driver Louis Chevrolet, who had become a car designer; Walter Chrysler, the well-known builder of cars and locomotives; and Charles Kettering, the Ohio farm boy turned inventor who was, it was said, developing an antiknock fuel additive that would make cars *fly*.

Midgley's elation at his early triumph with the trailing red arbutus and iodine had proven fleeting. During and immediately after the war he had continued testing other substances with little success. Lacking a concrete research method, Midgley merely set about combing through various compounds on a hunch, like a bloodhound who had lost the trail, trying everything on the laboratory shelf. This was known as "hunt and try" or, with some unfairness to its namesake, "the Edisonian method"; it was associated with independent "wizard" inventors and considered outmoded in the modern research lab. No one could completely dismiss "hunt and try" or the part dumb luck sometimes played in lab work, and Kettering at first defended the technique, saying, "Why don't they call it the 'trial-and-success' method? That's what it really is." But soon even he tried to move Midgley toward developing some more exact methodology.

"How many substances have you tried now?" he demanded of Midgley shortly after the war ended.

"Nearly a hundred."

"Have you any idea how many different chemicals there are in the world?"

Midgley replied that there were about half a million listed in chemical catalogs.

"What disturbs me," said Kettering, "is that we don't know what we're doing. When we found iodine, we had a theory—an incorrect theory, to be sure, but it led us to iodine. Now we haven't even a theory."

Midgley and his staff were given a week to find a better antiknock than iodine. "We thought we had worked hard up to this day," Midgley later recalled, "but our work was mere idleness compared to the feverish activity that we crowded into the next seven days."

On January 30, 1919, Midgley, Tabby Boyd, and Carroll Hochwalt discovered the knock-suppressing qualities of aniline, a brownish substance with an "earthy" smell often used in the vulcanization of rubber. For the next several months their efforts centered on developing aniline for use as an antiknock. Kettering became involved, personally road-testing several of the aniline compounds, which Midgley estimated gave the test car twice its usual power and 40 percent better gas mileage. Aniline's undoing, officially, was its failure to prevent knock at high speeds, although Midgley privately observed, "I don't think humanity would put up with this smell, even if it meant twice as much gasoline mileage."

Once aniline had been abandoned, the researchers returned to a more or less random search of the elements, the meticulous Boyd maintaining a log of all the substances tried, entering the team's findings—"Knock Inducer," "No Effect," "Slight Knock Suppressant," "Antiknock"—next to the name of each test compound. During the summer of 1919 chemistry professors from Ohio State and Denison University brought Midgley suitcases full of different chemicals for trial. Midgley later described this period as being "like something from the Arabian Nights," a hunt for the "Open, Sesame" that would unlock the mystery. They tried everything: "from melted butter and camphor to ethyl acetate and aluminum chloride," Midgley later recollected, "and most of them had no more effect than spitting in the Great Lakes." One General Motors executive visiting the lab, thinking no one was watching, even tried pouring a little of Midgley's shaving powder into a test engine's intake. He was mortified to suddenly find Boss Ket standing at his side, but Kettering, far from being upset, merely inquired as to the experiment's results.

Kettering was not always so indulgent. "Ket did raise hell with us," Hochwalt later recounted. "He said, 'By God, if you don't come up with something within the next three to six months, you're all fired!' " Nor was Midgley immune to feelings of hopelessness. When aniline was finally judged unusable in December 1920, he confronted Kettering, reminding Boss Ket that he was not a chemist and that he didn't want to devote his entire career to seeking a knock suppressor that didn't exist. Kettering in turn reminded Midgley that "a good research man fails every time except the last one.

"If you fail nine hundred and ninety-nine times, it doesn't matter. The thousandth time when you win is what counts."

"I have failed nearly three thousand times," Midgley replied. "Let's quit this work while we're still young enough to get into something else."

"Midge would be the last one to say he knew any chemistry," Hochwalt said later, explaining Midgley's frustration. "And he didn't. Certainly not in those days. Ket had made him head of this unit to work on antiknock fuels. Hell, he learned a lot of chemistry then. He started doing it. In those days we didn't do market surveys as to whether there might be a market for the end-product. We did it on this philosophy expressed by Ket: 'If God made gasoline knock, he certainly made something to prevent it from knocking.' "

Kettering, on a train trip to New York in early 1921, read a newspaper item about a new "universal solvent" made of selenium oxychloride that had been synthesized by a professor at the University of Wisconsin. The item caught Kettering's eye because the notion seemed so unlikely, but on returning to Dayton he suggested that Midgley's crew try selenium oxychloride. The antiknock attributes of the compound, it turned out, were impressive, although selenium eroded a motor's spark plugs virtually on contact. For the first time, however, Midgley and his assistants started to test metallic compounds. No one, to Midgley's knowledge, had ever tried adding a metallic compound to an oil-solution fuel such as gasoline.

Once they had homed in on metallic compounds, Midgley and Boyd abandoned "hunt and try" in favor of taking a close look at the periodic table, which grouped all the known elements by their atomic weights. A recent upheaval in the study of chemical structure, promoted by Irving Langmuir, a physicist at the GE lab in Schenectady, had produced a popular new variation of the periodic table, in which the elements were arranged not by atomic weight but by their chemical valence, or the number of electrons in their outer shell. If an atom has more than two electrons, the additional electrons occupy spheres of activity outside the first. This second shell has room for only eight electrons, a third may possess between eight and eighteen, and a fourth may contain as many as thirty-two. Elements with completely filled outer shells—such as the inert gases—do not combine with other atoms, but those whose outer shells are incomplete seek stable structures by gaining, losing, or sharing electrons with other elements. The propensity of certain atoms, incomplete in their outer shell, to form molecules with the atoms of other elements, is stated as their valence, and is a measure of an element's combining power.

Langmuir's work represented an important breakthrough: whereas nineteenth-century chemistry had been largely concerned with understanding the composition of individual chemical elements, the new arrangement of the periodic table dealt with dynamics—how different elements behave when they react to one another or join together. His talk on the subject at a meeting of the American Chemical Society in Buffalo in 1919 was so enthusiastically received, Langmuir was called back to the podium to repeat it the very next day, an unprecedented occurrence in the annals of the society. The focus on valence was especially useful to an industrial scientist like Midgley, for it enabled him to more fully appreciate the possibilities of individual chemicals functioning together in chemical compounds. Using Langmuir's approach, Midgley and Boyd saw immediately that all of the metallic antiknock agents they had found so far by random selection actually had similar valence numbers and were grouped tightly together on the revised periodic chart. If an ideal antiknock existed, Midgley recognized, it would probably be found here.

On December 9, 1921, using the periodic table arranged according to the Langmuir theory, Midgley came to the end of the long antiknock search with the discovery of the knock-silencing attributes of tetraethyl lead. TEL demonstrated by far the best antiknock characteristics of all the metallic compounds. At a ratio of 1:1,300 mixture of lead to gasoline, test engines showed increased engine compression and greater fuel economy, as well as a 25 percent increase in horsepower. TEL, it appeared, would also be easy and inexpensive to manufacture.

But, as Midgley himself would later explain, "The popular idea might be that when we found tetraethyl lead we shouted hosannas for it, and all marched in to ask the boss for a raise. Actually, there wasn't a pause in the program." Eager to get the additive into the gas tanks of the nation's motorists, Kettering devised a marketing scheme that granted the new product an immediate identity. He named it "ethyl" and instructed his engineers to dye it so that the motoring public could differentiate it from other motor fuels. Midgley suggested the new product be dyed red—in honor of the trailing arbutus.

To market ethyl, General Motors and the Standard Oil Company of New Jersey formed the Ethyl Corporation with Kettering as president and Midgley as vice president and general manager. Standard Oil of New Jersey became the first major oil company to agree to sell ethyl gas at its pumps, while Du Pont received the contract to provide the tetraethyl lead. Du Pont would ship diluted tetraethyl lead in small bottles called "ethylizers," a term Midgley coined, directly to the gas station, along with easy-to-follow directions for adding it to a tankful of gasoline. For Du Pont the investment in the General Motors Research Corporation had paid off spectacularly. The potential financial gain from manufacturing TEL was immense, for an estimated 60 million pounds of TEL would be required to treat the gasoline consumed each year in the United States alone.

In January 1922, Midgley was informed that he had won the Nichols Award for his work on the antiknock, and he made plans to attend the award ceremony in New York in March, stopping off at Cornell en route to visit friends. He also planned a six-week vacation, for in the course of his research he had developed the symptoms of lead poisoning. Hochwalt had suffered from it, too, the previous fall, but a lengthy vacation had proved an effective cure. On January 22, Midgley wired his father that he planned to spend most of February in Miami "for my health."

To Wilder D. Bancroft, editor of the *Journal of Physical Chemistry* at Cornell, Midgley wrote a short time later, "I find that my researches in lead have been retroactive and that I contain a pair of lead-lined lungs. Symptoms being almost identical to the . . . second stage of tuberculosis except in one detail, sub-normal temperature instead of abnormal temperature. I find myself 2½ degrees shy at times, and if not for my health, simply out of self-respect, I feel that I must overcome this slight error or I shall soon be classified as a cold-blooded reptile. The cure for said ailment is not only extremely simple but quite delightful. It means to pack up, climb a train and search for a suitable golf course in the state named Florida. . . . One of the boys at Du Pont having gone through an exactly similar experience . . . he was 100 percent in health in five weeks."

Although he himself had been poisoned, Midgley believed that TEL was safe in the diluted form in which it was to be sold to the public. He had no experimental data to back up this opinion, but defended the theory when the surgeon general of the U.S. Public Health Service, Hugh Cumming, began making inquiries into the matter in late 1922. The PHS, headquartered in Washington, had asked one of its staff surgeons, Dr. Norman Roberts, to attend a talk Midgley gave at a meeting of the American Chemical Society in New York City on November 10, 1922, entitled "Gaseous Detonation and Control with Reference to Lead." Meeting with Midgley afterward, Roberts learned that most of the lead used in ethyl-burning test engines actually remained inside the motor. Once a process of filtering lead out of exhaust was developed, Midgley explained, it would pose virtually no risk at all to human beings. Experiments preliminary to the construction of the Lower Manhattan–Jersey City vehicular tunnels (later, the Holland Tunnel) had concluded that the highest safe level of carbon monoxide in air breathed by people was .01 percent; since lead was less toxic than carbon monoxide, Midgely argued, it followed that any tunnel or street deemed safe for motorcars would also be safe for leaded gasoline.

Midgley acknowledged that no safety testing of ethyl had been done, but he reassured Roberts he would be glad to cooperate with a thorough study. Roberts, in his report to the surgeon general, suggested that such an investigation was indeed necessary, because the rate of absorption of lead by the human body was unknown. "If Midgley's work is commercially successful," Roberts wrote, "as seems likely considering its nature and the financial standing of the parties interested, large quantities of lead-containing gasoline will soon begin to be used as motor fuel. . . ."

Roberts also learned from Midgley that Du Pont was the company most interested in developing TEL, prompting Surgeon General Cumming to write directly to Pierre Du Pont on December 20, 1922. "Since lead poisoning in human beings is of the cumulative type resulting frequently from the daily intake of minute quantities," Cumming wrote, "it seems pertinent to inquire whether there might not be a decided health hazard associated with the extensive use of lead tetra ethyl in engines." Cumming asked for any experimental data Du Pont had collected on the subject.

Rather than respond directly, Pierre Du Pont forwarded the surgeon general's letter to Midgley, who in a written reply gave Cumming the same assurances he had provided Roberts in New York the month before. People working in the vehicular tunnels between New York and New Jersey—who, Midgley and other automotive engineers assumed, would experience the greatest exposure to exhaust fumes imaginable—would probably absorb "a very small part" of one milligram of lead per day, while "the average congested street will probably be so free from lead that it will be impossible to detect it." Midgley was even more explicit in a response to a letter from a professional acquaintance, G. A. Round, an engineer with the Vacuum Oil Company of New York City, who had written questioning TEL's safety. "My dear Round," Midgley replied. "Poisoning is almost impossible, as no one will repeatedly get their hands covered with gasoline containing tetraethyl lead, [as] it stings and burns and is quite unsatisfactory for all other uses . . . except as a motor fuel. The exhaust does not contain enough lead to worry about, but no one knows what legislation might come into existence fostered by competition and fanatical health cranks."

The campaign to launch ethyl in a test market began on the morning of February 2, 1923, when the fuel went on sale at a Refiners Oil Company station on Main Street in downtown Dayton, only a few blocks from where Midgley and Kettering had first discussed the theory of the red trailing arbutus eight years earlier. A man driving a Buick touring car who gave his name as F. M. "Mike" Redelle had the distinction of purchasing the first historic tankful of leaded gasoline.

Midgley was apparently not dissuaded from his sanguine appraisal of TEL's potential danger by a letter he received from a German chemist, Dr. E. Krause, shortly after ethyl went on sale in Dayton. Krause, who had worked with TEL in nonautomotive contexts, cautioned that several of his coworkers had died from what he believed to be organic lead poisoning. He informed Midgley, "The compounds seem to possess, even in very reduced doses, malicious and creeping poisonous effects. . . . [However,] they do not produce the typical symptoms of lead poisoning . . . but a slow weakening and enfeebling of the whole body, which ultimately results in death."

"I have used every possible means of precaution," Krause concluded. "Nevertheless, I think that I have severely damaged my health."

In October 1923, concerned that fears about TEL's safety might influence efforts to market ethyl, Midgley and Kettering commissioned a study of TEL to be headed by R. R. Sayers of the U.S. Bureau of Mines and funded by General Motors and the Ethyl Corporation. From the start the study came under fire from occupational-health experts and the surgeon general's office. The Bureau of Mines was known to be strongly influenced by corporate concerns and had no record of providing unbiased studies in the public interest.

The haste to market ethyl before commissioning the report—much less awaiting its results—was symptomatic of the era's technological over-confidence. On a more personal level, it resulted from Kettering's distrust of government arbiters, as well as his eagerness to see a decade-long scientific development come to fruition. He seemed not to appreciate that his practice of relying on consumer reaction to validate a new product was unsuited to the nationwide sale of lead-doped gasoline. Midgley, for his part, believed after his long "scientific fox hunt" that he thoroughly understood the relative dangers and benefits of TEL and the other substances he had so laboriously tested.

For whatever combination of these reasons, General Motors and the Ethyl Corporation focused their efforts during 1923 and 1924 not on testing the safety of ethyl gasoline but on impressing auto dealers and gas-station owners with its superiority as a motor fuel. In special demonstrations key automotive and gasoline retailers were "hijacked" from their place of work in special GM test cars and made to experience for themselves the remarkable acceleration ethyl made possible. After a barreling high-speed ride through open country, up steep hills, and along city boulevards, it was hard not to be sold on the potential of the new super fuel. The ultimate "demonstration" came in May 1924, when ethyl-fueled race cars took first, second, and third places at the Indianapolis 500.

3.

HOUSE OF THE BUTTERFLIES

MEDIEVAL ALCHEMISTS thought of lead as the father of all metals. Common, easily mined, malleable enough to be smelted by the heat of a campfire, it had, by the twentieth century, been in widespread use for nearly ten thousand years. The Romans originated the first wide use of lead in pipes for transporting water. They called the soft metal that was so readily formed into pipes *plumbum*, the origin of the word for those who work with pipes: *plumbers*. In addition to pipes, Rome used lead to make pewter and colored glass. Rome's conquest of Britain was in part motivated by her reliance on lead, which was also used for coins and jewelry. The sites of voracious Roman lead scavenging in the earth are still visible in Britain after two millennia.

Lead was surrounded by a degree of superstition and prejudice, partly because it was used to line burial vaults, but also because it was known to have properties injurious to human health. Lead poisoning, which results from breathing lead-smelting fumes or ingesting lead-contaminated liquids or foods, manifests itself in disturbances of mind and vision, insomnia, fainting, stomach pains, loss of appetite, nausea, inflamed abdomen, convulsions, and paralysis. Widespread outbreaks of lead poisoning, which occurred in Europe throughout the Middle Ages, were called "colics," for the severe abdominal pains the poisoning induced, and were sometimes traced to lead used in wine and cider presses. The Romans knew of the dangers; Pliny the Elder writes of a "disease of slaves" believed to originate with the drinking of wine fermented in lead containers. The sociologist S. C. Gilfillan stirred up a scholarly controversy in this century by advancing the theory that creeping lead poisoning caused by lead aqueducts and pipes had contributed to the fall of the Roman Empire.

In America the first lead colics occurred in Colonial New England. Benjamin Franklin's diaries discuss the effects of lead poisoning in the printing trades, and nineteenth-century potters and painters were aware of the risks, but the lack of systematic medical observations and the resemblance of lead poisoning's symptoms to other diseases made it difficult to pinpont potentially dangerous lead industries.

The first comprehensive understanding of the dangers of lead poisoning in the United States came about in the early twentieth century through the pioneering efforts of Dr. Alice Hamilton, a reformer and perhaps America's first industrial toxicologist. Raised in a large, prominent Indiana family, Hamilton attended the University of Michigan Medical School in the 1890s, at a time when women medical students and physicians were almost unheard of. In 1897, she joined the staff of Hull House, the settlement house opened in 1889 by Jane Addams and Ellen Gates Starr among the sprawling tenements and sweatshops of Chicago's West Side.

Settlement houses offered a challenging alternative to the traditional middle-class response of charity, providing motivated individuals from the middle and upper classes an opportunity to work directly with the poor, helping to make education, health, and other needed services available. Bright, college-educated women—the doors of most other professions closed to them—were particularly active in the settlement-house movement.

At Hull House, Alice Hamilton supervised a well-baby clinic, researched the causes of typhoid, and rather intrepidly helped investigate the local cocaine traffic. But she increasingly became concerned about the devastating health problems that afflicted the poor factory workers, mostly immigrants, who populated the West Side. In a Chicago medical library she read English reformer Thomas Oliver's account of his investigations into occupational disease among British workers, *Dangerous Trades*. Hamilton became convinced that "the industrial poisons which Oliver described and the damage they were doing to working people must be as common in America as in Europe."

Continuing her research, she was troubled to find that all the literature on the subject of occupational disease came from European sources, and described conditions in European workplaces. There was not so much as a single monograph of American origin. "In those countries industrialized medicine was a recognized branch of the medical sciences," Hamilton later wrote; "in my own country it did not exist. When I talked to my medical friends about the strange silence on this subject in American medical magazines and textbooks, I gained the impression that here was a subject tainted with Socialism or with feminine sentimentality for the poor. The American Medical Association had never had a meeting devoted to this subject."

In September 1908, at age thirty-nine, Hamilton authored one of the first articles in America on the subject of occupational health in the magazine *Charities and the Commons,* in which she urged that serious consideration be given immediately to the problem of industrial disease.

The article's appearance helped encourage the creation of the Illinois Commission on Occupational Diseases, established in December 1908 by the reform governor of Illinois, Charles S. Deneen. The commission's charter was to catalog occupational health hazards related to the trades involving lead, brass, arsenic, carbon monoxide, turpentine, and cyanide. Hamilton, appointed to the commission by Governor Deneen, played a dominant role in the study, supervising the investigation of the more than one hundred trades that constituted the lead industries. In seventy-seven of them she discovered an above-average morbidity rate among workers. She found scores of men who continued working, even when they knew they were suffering from lead poisoning, because they could not afford to quit. One hospital she visited received so many patients complaining of work-related disease, the chief nurse had ordered a stamp made up bearing the name of the offending factory, to save her staff the repetition of entering it on hospital forms.

Despite her status as a member of the Deneen commission, Hamilton was forced to proceed cautiously with her investigations. The relationship between employer and employee at the time contained no actual or implied contract protecting workers from injury or disease. Employees were paid for their work and were responsible for their own safety; most employers would have found the suggestion ludicrous that they were in any way responsible for a worker's health. "In those early days," Hamilton wrote, "I met men who employed foreign-born labor because it was cheap and submissive, and then washed their hands of all responsibility for accidents and sickness in the plant, because, as they would say: 'What can you do with a lot of ignorant Dagoes, Wops, Hunkies, Greasers? You couldn't make them wash if you took a shotgun to them.' " The first compensation laws for disabling work-related injuries came into effect in 1910, but, far from reflecting an enlightened corporate attitude, the legislation was sponsored by industries eager to limit their liability in workplace-injury lawsuits. And these laws dealt exclusively with bodily injury, not work-related disease.

Hamilton's style remained pointedly nonconfrontational. She attempted to present an employer with the facts of her investigation and appeal to his decency and sense of fairness. She disapproved of public accusations and muckraking. Like other progressives, Hamilton combined a pride in the achievements of American industry with the faith that society could be improved by the exposure of its failings. Even factory bosses were given credit for possessing the capacity for constructive change. She had expressed the belief, in her 1908 article, that American captains of industry would willingly comply with health and safety codes in their workplaces once industrial dangers were made known to them, and that such safeguards would not have to be regulated by law, as had been the case in Europe. But while she was always willing to acknowledge "our best side," as she called it, Hamilton grew increasingly disturbed about "another side" of American industry, "where there is a back door and a cellar and a garbage pail and a cesspool."

"So long as the health, safety and contentment of the working class are left largely to the goodwill of the employing class," she would reluctantly concede in the 1920s, "there will always be dark spots of neglect and ignorance and callousness."

However, Alice Hamilton's patient efforts to illuminate those "dark spots" with the bright light of reform could not influence public opinion as dramatically as a single notorious catastrophe linked to industrial neglect.

The Triangle Shirtwaist Company, a Manhattan manufacturer of women's undergarments, was a typical big-city sweatshop. Located on the eighth, ninth, and tenth floors of the ten-story Asch Building, a block east of Washington Square, the firm employed hundreds of young European immigrants from the Lower East Side, mostly women. When a flash fire broke out on the afternoon of Friday, March 25, 1911, engulfing the building's upper floors, hundreds of the workers were trapped. Several of the exits had been locked to inhibit workers from stealing fabric or leaving before quitting time. Many jumped from windows to their deaths in the street below, while some died at the bottom of a gnarled iron fire escape that reached only halfway to the ground. Others, who spoke no English, perished because they were unable to comprehend shouted instructions from firefighters. The 145 fatalities stirred public outrage, especially after it was reported that a strike at Triangle in 1909, brutally put down by owners and police, had protested some of the very safety hazards that had contributed to the tragedy.

New York City remained in a state of numbed bereavement for days following the fire, the tenement blocks of the Lower East Side draped in black. The public funerals of the victims inspired dramatic outpourings of public grief—grief that turned to anger at the factory owners and the sweatshop system.

"Merciful God," the Reverend R. S. MacArthur intoned at one of the emotional "town meetings" held in the wake of the disaster, "teach employers of labor the duties which they owe to those under their care in the proper construction of factories. . . ."

Suffragist Dr. Anna Shaw informed a crowded lecture hall at Cooper Union, "There was a time when a woman worked in the home with her weaving, her sewing, her candlemaking. All that has been changed. Now she can no longer regulate her own conditions, her own hours of labor. She has been driven into the market with no voice in the laws and powerless to defend herself."

"The old Inquisition had its rack and its thumbscrews and its instruments of torture with iron teeth," declared Rose Schneiderman, one of the survivors of the fire. "We know what these things are today: the iron teeth are our necessities, the thumbscrews are the high-powered and swift machinery close to which we must work, and the rack is here in the firetrap structures that will destroy us the minute they catch fire."

The Triangle Shirtwaist Fire was a turning point, motivating greater scrutiny of industrial practices and demands for closer monitoring of workplace safety conditions. Outraged editorials in the city's newspapers and the volatile public meetings (it came to light at one that New York State had more game wardens than factory inspectors) led to the establishment of the New York State Factory Investigating Commission, which was staffed chiefly by women with backgrounds in labor reform and the settlement-house movement. "To the business man capital and labor are both abstractions," reformer Rheta Childe Dorr had written. "[But] to women, labor is a purely human proposition, a thing of flesh and blood."

If a sweatshop fire could arouse fierce debate about the devaluation of workers' lives, the First World War, with its overwhelming demonstration of the murderous capabilities of technological warfare, contributed to a more widespread concern about where the new age of the assembly line, the automobile, and the flying machine might be leading. The influenza epidemic of 1918 provoked an increased awareness of contagious disease, and the postwar era saw an invigorated interest in public health on the part of academia and state and federal government, including a broader acknowledgment of occupational-health issues. The government's concern may have been prompted in part by the discovery that large numbers of American men had been so physically depleted by factory work that they were unfit for combat. One result of this concern was the opening, in the years following the war, of the first clinics specializing in the study and treatment of work-related disease.

Staffing such institutions proved difficult. The field of industrial medicine was so new that when Harvard University sought to fill a professorship in the discipline in 1919, its trustees were forced to appoint Alice Hamilton, making her the first woman professor at Harvard, a remarkable concession considering that Harvard Medical School would not even accept women as students until 1945. Hamilton, in accepting the job, had to mollify outraged male faculty members by agreeing to forgo membership in the Harvard Club and other routine faculty perks such as tickets to home football games.

In 1921, Grace Burnham, the widow of an heir to the I. W. Harper bourbon fortune and a member of the New York State Factory Investigating Commission, and Harriet Silverman, of the factory inspection team of the International Ladies' Garment Workers' Union Health Clinic, joined forces to start an independent organization dedicated to protecting workers' health against industrial disease. The Workers' Health Bureau (WHB) offered free medical checkups for workers at a walk-in clinic in the old St. Denis Hotel at Eleventh Street and Broadway, not far from the site of the Triangle Shirtwaist tragedy. In their promotional literature, Burnham and Silverman described the WHB as an institution "organized in the belief that the elimination and control of trade dangers and the protection of workers from the ravages of occupational diseases are an inseparable part of the trade union struggle."

During the seven years of its existence, from 1921 to 1928, the bureau published numerous cautionary pamphlets on a wide range of industrial diseases, and sponsored the first-ever national conference on the subject of occupational health in Cleveland in June 1927. Unlike Alice Hamilton, who was one of the WHB's advisors, the bureau was highly skeptical of industry's willingness to assume responsibility for industrial disease or of government's ability to enforce necessary regulations, and believed it was up to the American labor movement to educate workers to occupational-health risks. Only in the WHB's last days, when its outspoken female leadership had lost the favor and support of the male-dominated American Federation of Labor, did Burnham and Silverman call for the creation of an exclusive federal agency to monitor industrial disease in the United States. (Their plea went unanswered until 1970, when Congress passed the Occupational Health and Safety Act, creating the Occupational Safety and Health Administration [OSHA] in the U.S. Department of Labor and the National Institute of Occupational Safety and Health [NIOSH] in the Department of Health, Education, and Welfare.)

Lack of a government agency to deal with problems of industrial disease, and widespread ignorance of industrial-health dangers, forced Burnham, Silverman, and colleague Charlotte Todes to improvise methods of reform. They were at their most creative in solving a health problem that plagued thousands of workers in the Northeast's hat industry. Mercury compounds used in the manufacture of felt hats were known to cause neurological disorders and even dementia in hat-factory workers—the origin of the expression "mad as a hatter." Yale University professor Yandell Henderson, an advisor to the WHB, wrote Burnham in March 1925 suggesting she petition a Danbury, Connecticut, hat factory "for the privilege of allowing the unions to send a committee composed of industrial hygienists through the Danbury hat shops." Granted permission to enter the plant, the bureau discovered that "boys 20 and 21 years old are already so badly poisoned that their hands shake continually, while many of the men who have served longer at the trade cannot even feed themselves." Burnham, having heard that in Russia a nonpoisonous substitute for mercury had been developed, traveled to Moscow and obtained a copy of the formula. Back in New York, she arranged for tests to be made on animal pelts to see if the Russian substance could successfully be used. Once she was satisfied that the substitute could effectively replace mercury, Burnham convinced one of the Danbury shops to try the new method. The results of the trial were satisfactory, the threat to workers' health was removed, and as Burnham wrote, "We have at last reached the point where we can make a campaign for the entire removal of nitrate of mercury in the felt hatting industry." The mercury substitute was eventually adopted nationwide.

Another of the bureau's chief areas of concern was in identifying and combating lead-related disease. The bureau issued pamphlets alerting workers to the signs of lead poisoning—"loss of weight, headache, constipation, pains in the joints, general weakness, dizzy spells, cramps"—and advised them that the best way to avoid lead contamination was to eat a good breakfast, keep fingernails clean, and have a daily bowel movement.

Despite new concern for the excesses of industry, the 1920s were not an easy time for reform causes. When the decade opened, the Socialist Party's candidate for president, Eugene Debs, was in a penitentiary for opposing American intervention in the world war and U.S. Attorney General A. Mitchell Palmer had launched an all-out assault on European-bred "agitators," later known as "the Palmer Raids," deporting thousands of immigrant political and labor leaders as subversives. The drama of Sacco and Vanzetti, anarchists convicted of murdering a paymaster and bank guard during a robbery in Massachusetts in 1921 and executed over great public protest in 1927, helped define a decade in which government was not only unsympathetic but could be openly hostile to the idea of labor concerns' infringing on industrial progress. Those who spoke out for increased vigilance against industrial disease did so with the assurance that they would be stigmatized as anarchists or "health cranks."

Occupational-health reformers Hamilton, Burnham, and Silverman were, in a sense, direct counterparts to industrial scientists Midgley and Kettering, equally part of the Progressive Era. In 1923, when ethyl gas went on the market, the research divisions at General Motors and Du Pont were racing pell-mell to discover as many new, profitable applications for the new chemical compounds they formulated as they could possibly find; the pioneers of industrial medicine, meanwhile, their discipline barely ten years old, were doing their utmost to keep pace, to examine the same substances, catalog their findings, and immediately inform workers and the public of any potential dangers.

On October 21, 1924, Standard Oil of New Jersey research worker Ernest Oelgert startled fellow employees by shrieking that three figures were "coming at him." Oelgert, who worked at Standard's Bayway plant near Elizabeth, New Jersey, where a pilot program to develop a commercial technique for manufacturing tetraethyl lead was underway, was having trouble breathing. He appeared panic-stricken, fighting off the first aid some of his colleagues offered as he gasped for air. He was taken by ambulance to the industrial-disease clinic at Reconstruction Hospital in New York City.

In the next two days several other Bayway workers exhibited symptoms of delirium and extreme paranoia similar to Oelgert's and were either hospitalized or placed under observation at their homes. On Saturday, October 25, Oelgert died, and on Monday, October 27, the *New York Times* ran a page-one article headlined ODD GAS KILLS ONE, MAKES FOUR INSANE. That evening one of the stricken workers, William McSweeney, threatened his sister with violence and had to be removed from his home in a straitjacket. A third worker, William Kresge, hurled himself out of a second-floor window, was taken by ambulance to a hospital, and later died. Walter Dymock died "violently insane" at Reconstruction Hospital and by Wednesday, October 29, McSweeney had died as well, bringing the total number of fatalities to four; thirty-one others remained under observation.

Autopsies revealed that tetraethyl lead had saturated the bloodstreams of the four victims, leading to congestion of the brain, delirium, and death. This differed from the lead poisoning that was known to afflict workers in the painting and typesetting trades, and the doctor who attended Ernest Oelgert—at a loss to fully describe what had killed his patient—officially listed the cause of death as "chemical psychosis." Ernest Oelgert, Sr., the victim's father, told reporters his son had been concerned about the early symptoms of his condition before October 21. "Ernest was told by the doctors at the plant that working in the lab wouldn't hurt him. Otherwise he would have quit. They said he'd have to get used to it."

M. D. Mann, head of the Research Division at the Bayway plant, denied that the dead or hospitalized men had in any way been affected by TEL. He acknowledged that the work being carried out was potentially dangerous, but noted that the men were paid a generous bonus for volunteering for it, and that they were issued gas masks for their protection. In a statement issued the day after Oelgert's death, Mann suggested that "these men probably went insane because they worked too hard." Mann himself was soon found to be suffering from TEL poisoning.

The newspapers dubbed TEL "Loony Gas," a name apparently used by the Bayway workers, and with news of the Bayway deaths, sales of ethyl fell off sharply at the approximately ten thousand service stations where the fuel was sold. Much of the scare could be traced to the widely printed assertions of Dr. Yandell Henderson of Yale University, who on October 27 had sharply questioned Standard Oil's assertion that the deaths of the workers were due to "unknown and unexpected results of chemical experiments." Henderson had been one of the designers of the gas mask U.S. troops wore in World War I, but had resigned his position with the Army's Chemical Warfare Service in disgust before the end of the war, publicly proclaiming himself a pacifist.

"Two years ago I warned representatives of General Motors that this substance is not fit for use by the general public," Henderson told the *New York World,* "[and] that lead poisoning is certain to result, not only in garage workers, but in all persons using automobiles."

General Motors officials in Detroit responded that TEL was entirely safe and observed that to prove its safety "the inventor frequently bathed in it."

On October 30, the *World* quoted an unidentified "expert chemist" —in all likelihood Henderson—who asked rhetorically: "What becomes of the lead? Some undoubtedly is retained in the [automobile engine] cylinders; but it is ridiculous to say none comes out of the exhaust pipe. It must come out in the form of a powder, and the deposit of this in congested places would be very dangerous."

Henderson, who had helped determine the ventilation requirements for the Holland Tunnel, estimated that automobile and truck traffic along Fifth Avenue between Twenty-third Street and the Plaza Hotel at Fifty-ninth Street would leave approximately three hundred pounds of lead dust per day if the vehicles were run on ethyl fuel. Thomas Midgley responded for the Ethyl Corporation, assuring a reporter that the amount would be closer to sixty-five pounds, that rain would wash most of it down the sewer, and that "it won't even kill the fish in the Lower Bay."

Thus far, the only individuals hurt or killed by TEL had been men working directly with the substance, yet with the efforts of Henderson, other health experts, and the press, it quickly came to represent a nascent "environmental" threat—the direct exposure of the general public to poisonous chemicals carried in automobile exhaust. At no time more than in the years following the First World War did the word "gas" connote panic and mass suffering, and most newspapers, informed by the expert opinion of Henderson and others, did not hesitate to express the potential danger of TEL in alarming images of gas attacks and stricken multitudes crumpling to the sidewalk along Fifth Avenue. "Dr. Henderson [does] not disguise the fact," the *World* commented, "that the mental pictures which he carried with him in wartime of the havoc his gases would play with the German Army have made him acutely sensible of the possibility of mass poisoning, and eager to protest against it." The newspaper warned that ethyl gas on one's hands would lower blood pressure and cause unconsciousness and death within minutes, and that exposure to TEL exhaust fumes could cause premature hardening of the arteries, kidney trouble, Bright's disease, arthritis, and, in women, the inability to bear normal children.

Ethyl gas was, at the time of the Loony Gas panic, available commercially only in the Midwest and parts of the South, so inhabitants of East Coast cities, not having had any firsthand experience with the new product, were particularly susceptible to the scare stories. Public-health officials, not entirely sure who or what to believe, were forced to act to quell the growing public alarm: within ten days of the death of Ernest Oelgert, the New York City Board of Health and local boards of health in New Jersey and Pennsylvania banned any future sale of ethyl gas.

Charles Kettering was traveling in Europe when the crisis erupted and did not at first grasp its implications. "[Kettering] is very upset," wrote GM patents executive James McEvoy, who had accompanied Kettering, to GM president Alfred Sloan. "Neither he nor I can understand how the Standard allowed this matter to obtain such broad publicity."

With the charismatic Boss Ket unavailable, Standard Oil executives called for TEL's creator, Thomas Midgley, to help deflate the crisis. At a press conference in Standard's New York offices on October 30, 1924, Midgley expressed regret about the Bayway deaths; he also confirmed a rumor that two workers at the GM Research Corporation in Dayton had died in the spring of 1924 after working with TEL, while forty others there had been placed under observation with "symptoms of mania." Midgley, however, said he agreed with an official GM statement made regarding the Dayton deaths that "without desiring to attach any blame to the employees," it had been "very difficult to get the men to make use of the safety devices provided for their protection by the company," and that the men in the Dayton facility had failed to observe proper procedures for cleaning up after working with tetraethyl lead.

Midgley then plied the kind of public relations he knew best, providing the assembled reporters with a demonstration of ethyl's harmlessness. "In proof of his argument, he produced a bottle of the Ethyl," the *Herald Tribune* reported the next morning. "Pouring it into his palms, [he] washed his hands with it and held the bottle to his nostrils for more than a minute. He insisted that the fumes could have no such effect as was observed in the victims if inhaled for only a short time."

Midgley, after discussing Standard's and General Motors' problems with TEL, reminded the reporters, "the Du Ponts have been having trouble, too." Indeed, the giant Wilmington firm was experiencing a Loony Gas crisis of its own—"secret" deaths and injuries at Du Pont's TEL manufacturing facility in Deepwater, New Jersey. Du Pont, when the story began to leak out, had immediately issued a preemptive statement:

> Tetraethyl lead is dangerous, and its manufacture involves risk, but no
> more so than many chemicals manufactured and used in enormously
> greater amounts. . . . The Du Pont Company, during the
> experimental period, experienced much trouble with men becoming
> poisoned, even to the extent of fatalities. . . . During the past year of
> production, when more than one hundred men have been employed

continuously, the difficulty has diminished steadily. In the past several months, under full production, only slight difficulties have been encountered.

Du Pont's fatalistic attitude toward the inevitability of worker deaths was a conditioned one. During a century of gunpowder manufacture dozens of workers and even a few Du Ponts themselves had "gone across the river," a company euphemism for being blown across the Brandywine Creek by the force of a powder explosion, the literal manner in which many Du Pont employees had died. Still, there was deceit in Du Pont's account. The Deepwater plant, the company claimed, had been shut down "for improvements." In fact, it had been closed by the New Jersey Labor Commission. And the "slight difficulties" the statement made reference to were actually recent fatalities. Between July and October 1924, four workers had died at Deepwater, where, according to one Du Pont worker, TEL was carried about in open buckets; an earlier death was traced back to September 1923. Their hallucinations so often took the form of flying insects that the workers called the Du Pont TEL facility "the House of the Butterflies," and as at Bayway, the mental and neurological symptoms of TEL poisoning progressed until the workers had to be hospitalized as raving lunatics.

The Deepwater story, as it was slowly unraveled by the press, was even more disturbing than the Bayway deaths because it revealed a chilling proclivity on Du Pont's part to completely isolate its vast chemical manufacturing enterprise and fully control the lives of its workers.

The six-square-mile town of Deepwater, across the Delaware River from Wilmington, turned out to be not much of a town at all. It had no mayor, no city council, no newspaper, no post office, nor did it appear on any map. Since all three newspapers in Wilmington, the nearest city, were owned by the Du Ponts, and the hospital where the men had died was operated under a Du Pont subsidy, anything that took place in Deepwater could remain forever Du Pont's secret. The story leaked out only when one of the stricken workers showed up at another New Jersey hospital.

In March 1925 the Bureau of Mines released the results of its study of TEL, which had consisted of exposing test animals to leaded exhaust in a Pittsburgh garage. To hardly anyone's surprise, the report completely exonerated TEL. Yandell Henderson immediately criticized the study's methodology and the Ethyl Corporation's complicity in it, terming the continued marketing of TEL "the greatest experiment in virtual race suicide ever carried out." Alice Hamilton wrote on behalf of the Workers'

Health Bureau and other union organizations to remind Surgeon General Hugh Cumming that the Ethyl Corporation had financed the Bureau of Mines study. She suggested that "an impartial investigation of this public health hazard be made by the U.S. Public Health Service . . . an investigation made by a public body which will be beyond suspicion and whose findings will be accepted as impartial and trustworthy."

In the 1920s, there was no federal agency empowered to regulate or even officially investigate private industry with regard to product safety. The only agency that came close to fulfilling this role was the U.S. Public Health Service, a subsidiary of the Treasury Department. Originally known as the Marine Hospital Service because its chief function was the supervision of quarantine facilities in U.S. port cities, the PHS's attention had first been directed toward industrial hygiene only as recently as 1915, as part of the heightened regard in the medical community for the deadly potency of communicable disease. The service could and did investigate specific industrial-health scares and communicate its concern, if necessary, to the firm responsible, usually via correspondence from the surgeon general; but it possessed no regulatory powers. It could issue warnings to the public, and sponsor conferences at which there would be a thorough airing of views. The surgeon general could then appoint a smaller investigatory panel to consider the subject in light of what had been said at the conference, and issue a recommendation based on the panel's conclusions.

The conference system was the most aggressive check on big business then available; however, the conferences were often dominated by the very industries whose activities were under scrutiny. Corporate interests could always claim greater knowledge of chemical compounds or manufacturing processes they themselves had invented; and there was, overall, a sense that progress would eventually iron out any glitches, that the difficulties at the plant would prove temporary. Most significant, the burden of proof lay with the party who had raised the question of whether a threat existed; industry frequently emerged victorious from a conference, its product "innocent," after no conclusive evidence of an industrial or public-health threat could be shown.

Kettering and Midgley were among more than seventy individuals representing industry, federal, state, and city health agencies, and labor interests who assembled when Surgeon General Cumming's inquiry into the safety of ethyl gasoline came to order in Washington on May 20, 1925. For Kettering the production stoppage and the state and city bans on ethyl had been painful to bear. It rankled that the breakthrough he and his researchers had worked for a decade to achieve could be rescinded by bureaucrats and headline writers. He knew that a vital distinction had been lost on the public: the men who had been killed had died of exposure to concentrated tetraethyl lead, not even diluted TEL, and certainly not automobile exhaust from cars burning ethyl fuel. Lead-treated ethyl gasoline contained only 1:1,300 parts of tetraethyl lead, and after two years on the market more than 200 million gallons of ethyl gas had been consumed by an estimated 1 million motorists without a single case of lead poisoning reported among them.

At the request of Surgeon General Cumming, Kettering began the proceedings by presenting a brief history of the development of the anti-knock substance. He described how Midgley had tested thirty-three thousand chemical compounds before hitting upon tetraethyl lead. Midgley then rose to explain that the system of distributing "ethylizers" containing pure TEL to service stations had been abandoned in favor of shipping the antiknock in a safer, less concentrated form. Dr. Robert Kehoe of the University of Cincinnati, medical director of the Ethyl Corporation, and R. R. Sayers of the Bureau of Mines, presented the findings from the bureau's disputed study. Sayers said his tests had exposed rabbits, dogs, sheep, ducks, and rats for several hours a day to the diluted exhaust from an engine running on ethyl gas. After months of experiments, no indication whatsoever of lead poisoning had been found; one of the dogs had even given birth to five healthy puppies during the testing period. Researchers, Sayers added, had named them "the Ethyl Gas Hounds."

In a related test sponsored by the GM Research Corporation in Dayton, Kehoe and Sayers explained, a four-cylinder engine was run on leaded gasoline for over a hundred hours, with its exhaust gases filtered through distilled water to catch any lead compounds they might contain. The quantity of lead captured was "negligible," according to the report. In another test, floor sweepings from a garage where vehicles using leaded gasoline operated were gathered and analyzed. After thirty days the amount of lead in the dust was so small, researchers estimated, that a man would have to "gobble down a full handful of floor dust" to put himself in danger of lead poisoning.

This testimony was immediately challenged by Yandell Henderson, who dismissed the investigations as wholly nonobjective. He again accused GM and the Ethyl Corporation of refusing to submit the question of TEL's safety to an unbiased study. Henderson was no stranger to such commission hearings, and he spoke bluntly: "The men engaged in industry, chemists and engineers," he said, looking across the room at Kettering and Midgley, "take it as a matter of course that a little thing like industrial poisoning should not be allowed to stand in the way of a great industrial advance." He cited the calamitous potential of such a policy—the tremendous unknown consequence of mass-producing a known industrial killer. "Leaded gasoline," he predicted, "will be in nearly universal use before the public and the government awaken to the situation." Henderson concluded his remarks by lamenting the lack of a government agency whose sole purpose would be to closely monitor such threats to the public health.

Alice Hamilton, in her testimony, recalled the reaction of the British government and industry to a similar crisis in 1916. After twelve British airplane factory laborers died from exposure to the solvent tetrachloroethane, she explained, Parliament directed the Ministry of Munitions to immediately develop a substitute, despite the fact that the country was at war. By 1917 one had been found and the deadly tetrachloroethane removed from the workplace. "Now we can not say that we in the U.S. are up against any emergency like that," Hamilton said. "And yet we have already equalled their death rate." Hamilton acknowledged that lead-using industries would probably never be completely free of lead-related disease, but as to what effect the potent cocktail of lead and carbon monoxide mixed in automobile exhaust might have on the public at large, she could only fearfully speculate.

Frank Howard, a spokesman for the Ethyl Corporation, spoke directly to this point. "Our continued development of motor fuels is essential in our civilization," he stated. "We have this apparent gift of God, tetraethyl lead, which can be produced at a low figure, and which will permit that gallon of gasoline which we have recovered from the earth to go fifty percent further, one hundred percent further in the long run. What is our duty under the circumstances? . . . Because some animals die and some do not die in some experiments, shall we give this thing up entirely?"

Howard urged the conference to consider all that was at stake before passing judgment. "It must be not fears, but facts, that we are guided by," he concluded. "This development must be stopped, if it is to be stopped at all, by proof of the facts."

There was a stir at the table where the representatives of the Workers' Health Bureau were seated, as Grace Burnham retorted: "This 'gift of God' was not a gift of God when those eleven men were killed or those 149 were poisoned." Gesturing to her colleagues from organized labor, who were seated nearby, she told the commission: "The thing we are

interested in in the long run is not mechanics or machinery, but men."
A. L. Berres, a union spokesman, seconded Burnham's thought, saying,
"I appreciate what it means to take the knock out of a motor. But we are
more concerned about taking and keeping the knock out of the human
being."

Frank Howard's presentation, though, had had a persuasive effect on
many in the room. The Ethyl Corporation's statements, as historians
David Rosner and Gerald Markowitz point out, "put the opposition on
the defensive, making them appear to be reactionaries whose limited
vision of the country's future could permanently retard progress and
harm future generations. . . . The stark portrayal of tetraethyl lead as a
key to the industrial future of the nation led naturally into industry's
argument that any great advance required some sacrifice."

The animosity of Grace Burnham's exchange with Frank Howard
carried over into the afternoon session, when Dr. M. Nicoll, Jr., commissioner of health of the State of New York, suggested that a resolution the
conference was attempting to draft read, in part: "It is the sense of this
conference that the Surgeon General appoint a committee of recognized
authorities to present to him—by January 1st next—a statement as to
the health hazards involved in the retail distribution of tetraethyl lead
gasoline, and that until such time distribution of this substance be discon-
tinued."

The corporate representatives quickly objected. The Ethyl Corporation had already stopped distribution voluntarily, and they wanted this
acknowledged more clearly. They insisted the end of the statement be
changed to read: ". . . and that this conference endorses as wise the decision of the corporation to discontinue temporarily the sale of tetraethyl gasoline."

Industry's tiny victory with the statement's wording anticipated the
conference's ultimate exoneration of TEL. The U.S. Public Health Service did conduct its own impartial study, although it did so in Dayton, a
curious setting for an unbiased investigation of ethyl gasoline. Authorities tested a group of 252 men that included ordinary car owners as well
as employees of the Dayton Municipal Garage and other "automotive
enterprises." After routinely examining the men for several months, physicians concurred with what Midgley and other industry spokesmen had
said all along, that tetraethyl lead was dangerous only in concentrated
form and that it posed no risk to motorists or the public under normal
conditions.

The surgeon general's report was released on schedule in January
1926. While tetraethyl lead did pose safety problems in production, it

concluded, the levels of toxic lead released by auto exhaust were tolerable provided the ethyl content of gasoline was limited. The Workers' Health Bureau, Alice Hamilton, Yandell Henderson, and others argued that the report was flawed, and studies in the 1960s would convincingly reverse the report's sanguine conclusions on the public-health risks of lead in auto exhaust, but for the time being the issue was buried. Despite the public hue and cry of the Loony Gas scandal, corporate technological leaders such as General Motors, Du Pont, Ethyl, and Standard Oil had come to embody progress itself, and progress, despite occasional admonishments to behave itself, could after all only go forward, and could not be turned back. As the Du Pont annual report for 1936 concluded, with a decade's hindsight, the TEL worker deaths at its Deepwater facility were "no sudden holocaust, due to the neglect of precautions," but the "slow and gradual toll which humanity has always paid, and perhaps must always pay, for the conquest of new and dangerous ground."

That the conclusions of the 1925 surgeon general's conference on lead in gasoline stood as gospel for forty years was due in no small measure to the continuing influence of Robert Kehoe of the University of Cincinnati. Kehoe amassed a substantial body of work on lead poisoning and became a thoroughly intimidating authority on the subject. He outlived old antagonists like Yandell Henderson and old friends like Thomas Midgley, and managed to sit on and dominate countless forums, panels, boards, and associations whose function it was to monitor the lead industry. For four decades, like a faithful watchdog of Kettering's and Midgley's legacy, Kehoe vigilantly defended the continued use of ethyl, singlehandedly refuting all efforts to prove the harmful effects of lead dispersed by car exhaust. Well past retirement age he was still adamantly facing down prying reformers, bureaucrats, and "health cranks," any and all who dared call into question the integrity of "this gift of God" —leaded gasoline.

Not until 1966, during a time of rising national concern about air pollution, were renewed attempts made to define lead in gasoline as an environmental hazard. Federal restrictions governing the lead content of motor fuels did not come into effect until the 1970s.

4.

THE GOOD OLD NOSE TEST

I N STATUARY HALL in the Capitol rotunda in Washington, D.C., each of the fifty United States is allotted space for a statue of its most distinguished citizen. There, among noted legislators, soldiers, and statesmen, stands one of the room's lesser-known figures, the entry from Florida, Dr. John Gorrie, Father of the Refrigerator.

Gorrie lived in the Florida Gulf Coast city of Apalachicola, where he was a physician from 1833 until his death in 1855. The town, located at the mouth of the Apalachicola River, was before the Civil War the third-largest U.S. cotton port on the Gulf of Mexico, after New Orleans and Mobile. Numerous problems thwarted the community's growth, however—roads that became impassable when it rained, a lack of housing, a shortage of fresh water—obstacles the local mercantile interests were eager to alleviate. Gorrie contributed to the effort by taking on another, more deadly regional threat: malaria.

In Gorrie's time, before the connection between malaria and the mosquito was known, physicians believed individuals contracted malaria by inhaling "vapors" of the oil of decomposing vegetable and animal matter; warm, muggy conditions, like those common in Apalachicola much of the year, were known to be conducive to the spread of the disease. Gorrie observed that the citizens of Apalachicola were most susceptible to malaria during the height of the warm Gulf summer, and that the disease seemed to travel inland at night. This led him to theorize that one way to protect people from its ravages would be to isolate them from the outside air while they slept. Local residents were accustomed to sleeping with windows and even doors wide open in summertime, so to keep the malaria out yet maintain an environment comfortable enough to sleep in, Gorrie envisioned a primitive system of air-conditioning—a windowless "sleeping room" whose only openings would be a "chimney" in the ceiling and a vent in the floor. A large block of ice would be rigged into place near the ceiling, and as it melted, a draft of chilled air would circulate in the room, creating a comfortable, "malaria-free" atmosphere.

Gorrie's scheme, however, relied on there being a sufficient supply of ice. Until the late nineteenth century, ice was a seasonal commodity, cut from frozen lakes and rivers up north in January and February, packed with sawdust, and shipped south. By June Apalachicola's precious supply was usually exhausted.

Gorrie decided to make his own ice. Guided by the established scientific principle that the sudden expansion of compressed air produced a cooling effect, he built an ice-making machine in which air was rapidly compressed by a steam-powered pump, then reexpanded in an engine cylinder. In this way, heat was absorbed, lowering the temperature inside a small, closed cabinet to 0°C, cold enough to freeze a tray of water. Gorrie kept his experiments with the machine during the spring and early summer of 1851 a secret from most of his acquaintances, then surprised them by showing up at a Bastille Day celebration at the home of the French consul with eight-by-ten-inch slabs of freshly made ice long after the town's regular supply had given out.

Ice from the machine was used to construct one of the sleeping units Gorrie had envisioned at a local hospital. He filed for and obtained the first U.S. patent granted for a system of mechanical refrigeration. But he failed in his effort to attract an investor to underwrite the costs of producing his invention on a larger scale. He died a disappointed man in 1855; however, his system of a locked cycle of compression and expansion, absorbing heat within a confined, airtight space, nonetheless contained the founding principle of the modern refrigerator. As a eulogist observed at an official remembrance staged in Apalachicola by the Southern Ice Exchange a half century after his death: "Physics speak of Gorrie's machine, if the encyclopedias do not."

This belated acknowledgment of Gorrie's efforts coincided with the first stirrings of the household refrigeration industry in America in the early years of the twentieth century. The steam-powered air-cycle system of refrigeration that Gorrie had devised gave way to other means, including the use of electricity to more efficiently maintain the compression cycle, and the use of chemical refrigerants such as ammonia, methyl chloride, and sulphur dioxide. These chemicals, changed by compression from a liquid into a gas, and back again, absorbed heat through vaporization, the same principle that cools a person's fingers when he or she wets them and waves them in the air.

Manufacturers of early household refrigerators struggled to make the refrigeration cycle work cleanly and effectively in a large wooden cabinet. But the first models were so cumbersome and prone to leakage that the families who bought them generally refused to keep the units in the house, relegating them to the porch or garage. Ammonia, the most efficient gas refrigerant known at the time, was popular in household units because it was nonflammable; ammonia was toxic if breathed in large quantities, however, and possessed a sharp, stinging odor that made it extremely objectionable even in cases of mild leakage. When it leaked, the gas not only fouled the air but spoiled the contents of the refrigerator.

Despite these difficulties, the commercial promise of household refrigeration tantalized Charles Kettering and General Motors' Billy Durant. The refrigerator, like the automobile, they believed, would appeal to an almost unlimited market if it could be made efficient, safe, and affordable. In June 1918, General Motors entered the refrigeration business by purchasing the Guardian Frigerator Company, a small Detroit manufacturer owned by engineer Alfred Mellowes.

To make the Guardians resemble something people would want to have inside their homes, Mellowes designed his refrigerators to look like a large piece of household furniture—a wooden wardrobe closet or chest of drawers. But only the well-to-do could afford the $714 price tag. After two years of production Mellowes had been able to sell only about a dozen of the machines.

Durant renamed the Mellowes company "Frigidaire." He succeeded in streamlining production and increasing sales, but complaints of leaks, breakdowns, and spoiled food remained so numerous that the GM engineers Durant had commissioned to transform the refrigerator into a reliable home appliance wound up spending most of their time making repair calls. Moreover, the new GM ownership was unable to improve much on Guardian's exorbitant price, and Durant disliked not being able to sell the Frigidaire as an affordable consumer item. By 1920, disenchanted with the refrigerator, Durant was poised to write off the Frigidaire as a failed experiment.

Kettering, who that year became vice president of the GM Research Corporation, convinced Durant not to sell Frigidaire, saying he wanted his researchers in Dayton to have a crack at solving the refrigerator's technical problems. Kettering began by seeking to rectify the appliance's chief shortcoming—size. The Frigidaire had to be made to fit inside the average American kitchen. His first innovation was to eliminate the brine tank and water-cooled compressor, which maintained the chill in the refrigerator during breakdowns of the regular cooling system. Kettering believed that the primary system, functioning properly, should be completely adequate; there should be no need for a backup system, particularly one that added weight and girth to the already bulky unit. To further reduce the refrigerator's size he ordered a change of materials, replacing the wooden "clothes closet" look with the first metal, porcelain-coated cabinet.

Frigidaire launched this basic design change in the mid-1920s with a series of magazine and newspaper advertisements emphasizing the new model's attractiveness and its place in the modern kitchen. Other refrigerator manufacturers followed Frigidaire's lead, streamlining their products, underscoring cleanliness, safety, and convenience in their sales efforts. The consumer response was encouraging. Throughout the late 1920s, yearly sales increases of between 25 and 75 percent were common among Frigidaire, Westinghouse, Kelvinator, and as many as twenty other refrigerator manufacturers. Through mass production and volume sales, the average unit cost entered a free-fall: from $600 in 1920 to $275 in 1930, to $165 in 1935 and $155 by 1940. One of the Frigidaire models, the Moraine, named after the site of the Dayton Frigidaire factory, sold in the 1930s for as little as $99.50. In 1925, 75,000 refrigerators were sold in the United States; by 1930 the annual sales reached 850,000, and the ascent continued even during the Depression.

Frigidaire's leading role in helping to develop the home-refrigeration market was crowned in 1930 with the company's participation in the introduction of an innovation designed expressly for the modern refrigerator—frozen food. This revolutionary development in food storage and preparation had been led by Clarence Birdseye, an Amherst graduate who served from 1912 to 1917 in remote Labrador as a member of the U.S. Biological Survey. There he had become intrigued by the Eskimos' ability to store meat and fish for weeks, even months or years, without a loss of flavor.

Seeking a scientific explanation for the phenomenon, Birdseye examined thin slices of frozen fish under a microscope. He concluded that the Eskimos' method of quick-freezing fish or meat immediately after it was killed prevented ice crystals from forming, as opposed to less rapid freezing, which allowed ice crystals to rupture food cells.

During the 1920s, Birdseye attempted to mechanically duplicate the quick-freeze method for use in the seafood industry. For ten years he experimented with buckets, brine, and ice, trying to emulate the trick the Eskimos managed easily in their subzero climate. Birdseye settled on a method known as multiplate freezing: calcium chloride brine, at a temperature of −40°C, was circulated inside hollow plates, which, brought into contact with packets of food product, froze them instantly. Birdseye's early multiplate freezers were mounted on trucks, so that food could be collected and frozen where it was freshest—at fruit harvests, fish houses, or meat slaughterhouses. Finally, in 1929, after nearly a decade of efforts that more than once brought him to the edge of bankruptcy, Birdseye lived out every inventor's dream by selling his quick-freezing patent to the Postum Company (soon renamed General Foods) for $22 million, one of the largest sums ever paid for a patent in the United States.

That same year Birdseye, now a General Foods consultant, approached Frigidaire with a special request. His fast-frozen foods required a new style of display case, one that would maintain frozen temperatures while remaining open at the top so customers could easily view and select the merchandise within. Frigidaire responded by designing and manufacturing the Kleer-Kool, the prototype of the sectional open-top freezer that would become a feature of the modern supermarket.

In a further collaboration, the Birdseye Division of General Foods and Frigidaire joined forces to stage a huge promotional event to officially introduce frozen foods to the American public. Springfield, Massachusetts, was selected as the "test" community. Full-page ads in newspapers up and down the eastern seaboard heralded March 6, 1930, as the first day of a special ten-day introductory period in which Springfield shoppers would be able to purchase frozen steaks, fish, fruit, and vegetables. Nearly ten thousand people visited the stores where the frozen products went on sale. "The first day's sales included quite a number of curiosity buyers," an internal Frigidaire memorandum reported, "but was far in excess of the fondest hopes of the General Foods organization . . . people were heard to make complimentary remarks about the product." After a few days it was necessary to order additional stocks of raspberries and the higher-priced cuts of meat from Boston, as these had proven to be the most popular items even though they sold at prices 10 percent above that charged for fresh. The report added:

[O]ne man, who apparently was employed as a mechanic, came in and purchased two pounds of sirloin steak at $1.08 per pound. The demonstrator asked him what he thought of the product. This man replied that he had purchased a sirloin steak the day before and had found it very delicious and much superior to the fresh product, which he had been buying at around 95 cents per pound. He also stated that although his position did not warrant his purchasing meats of this price every day, [his family] thought so well of the product that they were going to have these frozen steaks quite frequently.

Once again, it seemed, nature had been improved upon.

The late 1920s was an exultant era for the home refrigerator business, but manufacturers like Kettering still did not sleep soundly at night, for the industry had a dirty secret: none of the refrigerants used in the coils of household refrigerators was completely safe. Ammonia's awful smell and toxicity remained a serious concern. Methyl chloride, also toxic, was doubly lethal because it was odorless: a methyl chloride leak could kill the occupants of a small apartment in a few minutes, before the victims would realize the danger. Between August 1928 and July 1929 alone, the Cook County, Illinois, coroner reported to the American Medical Association no fewer than twenty-nine cases of methyl chloride poisoning from refrigeration leaks. Sulphur dioxide, which Frigidaire favored, gave off a skunklike odor, warning users of a potential problem, but even a small leak spoiled all the food in the refrigerator, while a major leak could be deadly if the poisonous gas spread quickly. The dangers of methyl chloride were made tragically clear on May 15, 1929, when 125 patients and employees at a Cleveland hospital, including several physicians, were asphyxiated by methyl chloride fumes that escaped following an explosion in an X-ray clinic. The vivid horror of the incident shocked the nation: carried instantaneously through the building's corridors and ventilation system by the force of the explosion, the fumes had overcome victims suddenly and without warning, allowing them no chance to flee. "Never in the history of medical science anywhere in the world," noted a reporter who visited the scene, "has such a strange disaster demolished an institution of mercy."

One of the chief watchdogs of the household-refrigeration business, constantly reminding the public of the fallibility of the commonly used refrigerant gases, was a group sponsored by the makers of home iceboxes. A venerable nineteenth-century industry troubled by the swift technological advances of the twentieth, icebox makers fought desperately in the 1920s to stave off the extinction they saw written in each year's mounting refrigerator sales. Aside from lobbying the public as to the dangers of refrigeration through their Household Refrigeration Bureau, they also sought to remain competitive by addressing a major shortcoming of their own product, introducing a method of balsa-wood insulation that extended the life of a block of ice in an icebox from two to seven days. The Household Refrigeration Bureau's actions helped maintain public anxiety about refrigerant gases, not too difficult a chore in the era of LOONY GAS headlines; in some cities health authorities began insisting that refrigerator manufacturers affix warning labels to their products, cautioning users about the gases the refrigerator contained.

The idea that such official cautions would be required greatly agitated Kettering. It was wholly unacceptable that Frigidaire, or any refrigerator manufacturer, should have to settle for selling a household appliance that was life-threatening. But Frigidaire was forced to admit just that, at least privately, when the U.S. Navy purchased Frigidaire cooling mechanisms for installation in newly built submarines. While Frigidaire executives could rationalize that, because of its smell, sulphur dioxide was a relatively safe household refrigerant, the prospect of a poisonous leak from a Frigidaire system in the confined quarters of a submarine, claiming the lives of American servicemen, was too disturbing to contemplate.

In the fall of 1928, Kettering and Frigidaire general manager Elmer G. Biechler agreed to step up the search for a new, safe refrigerant. Biechler suggested that a European refrigeration specialist would have to be brought in.

"What do you want to do that for?" Kettering demanded. "We have the best fellow right here at home."

Biechler asked who Kettering had in mind.

"Midge," answered Kettering.

"No, we won't have Midgley around," Biechler replied. "He is the most disorganized fellow there is in the world. He is a very high grade, intelligent fellow, but he gets an idea, he comes to work at three o'clock in the morning, and he will get a cot and sleep in the laboratory all night. He will get Jack [Gibbons, a wholesale plumber in Dayton] out of bed at two in the morning to get some valves and pipes, and then boggle up all the [requisition] records."

Kettering defended Midgley, suggesting a special arrangement that would allow Midgley to work at the Moraine facility without disrupting the plant's routine. "We will give Midge a place just outside the fence," Kettering told Biechler, "and we can run under the fence the electric light, gas, water, steam and what have you, so that he will have all the services but he will not have to go inside the Frigidaire lot at all."

Biechler relented. Kettering immediately telephoned Midgley. The "Father of Ethyl Gas" had been immersed of late in an extremely difficult research program, trying to find a method of manufacturing synthetic rubber. Midgley having had little success, Kettering was eager to get his star researcher focused on something else. "We must have a nontoxic, nonflammable, cheap refrigerating agent, quick!" he told him.

Kettering arranged for Midgley to meet with Frigidaire chief engineer Lester Kielholtz, who was traveling to Dayton from Detroit on the overnight train. Midgley went to see Kielholtz at his hotel the next morning, then returned to the laboratory where his assistants, Albert Henne and Robert McNary, were waiting to have lunch with him. It was a Saturday, normally their day off, but Midgley had told them something important was up. Henne, a native of Belgium, was a recent and particularly valuable addition to Midgley's research staff. He had come to the United States on an MIT fellowship following a distinguished academic career at the University of Brussels, and his role was to advise and correct Midgley on more intricate matters of theoretical chemistry.

Over lunch Midgley described their new research project: a quest for a new, completely safe, and noncorrosive refrigerant. Using the arrangement of the periodic table based on the Langmuir theory, which emphasized the elements' bonding characteristics according to their chemical valence, Midgley observed that all the elements whose boiling point—at which they would transform from a liquid into a gas—made them generally acceptable for a refrigeration cycle, were grouped on the right side of the chart. Of these, he dismissed boron, silicon, phosphorus, arsenic, antimony, bismuth, selenium, tellurium, and iodine as being too unstable; and the inert gases—neon, argon, krypton, helium, xenon, and radon—were rather low in boiling point. This left only those elements already commonly used in making refrigerants: sulphur, chlorine, ammonia, carbon—and fluorine, which no one had ever put in a refrigeration cycle because it was known for extreme toxicity and corrosiveness. Fluorine's chief industrial application was as sodium fluoride, a heavy-duty insecticide.

As Midgley and Henne had previously discussed, however, one of Henne's countrymen, Professor Frederic Swarts, had recently theorized that fluorine's toxicity *could* be negated in a chemical compound. With seven electrons and one vacant space in its outer shell, fluorine's valence structure was "incomplete," according to Langmuir's octet theory of molecular structure, meaning it would bond well with other chemicals that had complementary valences. If the bonding was strong enough, Swarts had asserted, the fluorine would be rendered harmless.

Midgley then had what Henne later characterized as "a stroke of genius." In discussing one of the few known fluorine compounds, carbon tetrafluoride, whose boiling point was listed in chemical tables as $-15°C$, Midgley suddenly blurted out that he thought this figure seemed too high, that the actual boiling point of carbon tetrafluoride would be closer to $-130°C$. If Midgley's hunch was correct, this lower boiling point suggested that a fluorine refrigerant would not only be more efficient in a refrigeration cycle than anyone would have previously thought possible, but would offer itself to many more formulaic variations. Midgley's insight was the first glimpse of the amazing utility of fluorine refrigerant compounds—the versatility that would become the hallmark of the extended "family" of chlorofluorocarbons.

The next day Kettering joined the theoretical discussion about fluorine in the old Victorian house Midgley used as a laboratory. For the benefit of Boss Ket, Midgley repeated his observations about fluorine's place in the periodic table according to the Langmuir theory. "We took the wallpaper off the old dining-room wall and put white paper over it," Kettering later said, "and we drew the coordinates in there of the critical pressures and temperatures of all the known gases used in refrigerators."

As Midgley, Henne, and McNary had found the day before, eliminating all the elements that were unacceptable for a refrigeration cycle for reasons of toxicity, stability, or volatility, left only one: fluorine. But the researchers were worried about fluorine's reputation for corrosiveness. "Everyone was horrified," Kettering recalled. "They said, 'You certainly wouldn't put [a fluorine compound] in a refrigeration machine . . . because it would eat it up.' 'I don't know,' I said, 'I think we ought to try it.' And so we did, and it didn't [corrode the metal parts of the refrigerator]. [Fluorine] was one of the nicest, most accommodating gases in the world."

The researchers then explored various methods of preparing a stable refrigeration compound based on carbon tetrafluoride. They had no experience synthesizing fluorine compounds in the lab. Midgley later described the process: "Plottings of boiling points, hunting for data, corrections, slide rules, log paper, eraser dirt, pencil shavings, and all the rest of the paraphernalia that takes the place of tea leaves and crystal spheres in the life of the scientific clairvoyant were brought into play." He suggested that chlorine might be effective as a bonding element in a fluorine compound because of its stable qualities. The first version they manufactured in the lab—two atoms of chlorine, one of fluorine, and one of carbon—was dichloromonofluoromethane, later known as CFC-

21. In a variation, they added another fluorine atom to synthesize dichlorodifluoromethane—later known as CFC-12.

Midgley and his assistants gave their new substance "the good old nose test" and, experiencing no dizziness or other ill effects, arranged to drive to Cincinnati the next day for a more scientific examination of the compound's toxicity at the laboratory of Ethyl Corporation medical director Robert Kehoe. Despite their initial success, fluorine's reputation had them worried. Would the molecular bonding really be adequate to render fluorine nontoxic?

In Kehoe's lab five guinea pigs were exposed to the compound. To the experimenters' delight, the first guinea pig placed under the bell jar reacted, as Midgley later said, by "running about almost merrily." The researchers' elation was short-lived, however, for the second guinea pig placed inside the jar instantly fell over and died. Midgley, bewildered at the two drastically different results, snatched up the remaining three bottles containing the test compound and sniffed them. They had been improperly prepared. In each he detected the unmistakable odor of carbonyl chloride, or phosgene, which had been used as a poison gas in the war and smelled like fresh-mown hay. The carbonyl chloride impurity, not the fluorine compound, had killed the second guinea pig.

Midgley saw the hand of Fate in this incident. "The chances were four to one against us," he later remarked, pointing out that, had the first guinea pig died, he and his colleagues would probably "have given up what would then have seemed a bum hunch."

"I still wonder if we would have been smart enough to have continued the investigation. Even if we had, the chances were still three to one against our using the one pure sample."

Far from a "bum hunch," the new refrigerant was soon the talk of the GM Research Corporation, and word of Midgley's latest triumph began to filter through Boss Ket to the highest levels of Frigidaire and General Motors management.

The Ethyl Corporation's nightmare with tetraethyl lead was still a recent memory, however, and Frigidaire executives advised caution and thorough testing of the new fluorine compound before a pilot manufacturing program was established. This was an unnerving period for Midgley and his colleagues: now that they had made a breakthrough with compounds of fluorine, the element's potential as a refrigerant seemed obvious; it was only a matter of weeks, maybe days, before someone else made the same discovery. While Frigidaire patented the formula for chlorofluorocarbons on December 31, 1928, and was given patent number 1,886,339, Midgley was forced to wait a full year—while manufacturing techniques for fluorine compounds were investigated at Du Pont—before an official announcement of his discovery could be made.

In April 1930, Midgley gave an arresting demonstration of the new safe refrigerant at an Atlanta meeting of the American Chemical Society. After lighting a candle and setting it in clear view of the audience, he poured liquid CFCs into a glass dish to the depth of one inch. Having come in contact with room temperature, the refrigerant instantly boiled. Midgley lowered his face over the dish, opened his mouth, and inhaled the cold steam. Then he slowly turned toward the candle and gently exhaled, his breath smothering the flame.

"This refrigerant," he explained to his peers, "is non-explosive and we believe non-poisonous. It has not harmed animals. I have breathed quantities of it without lasting bad effects."

Midgley reported that the fumes "produced a sort of intoxication."

"The best way I can describe this sensation is to say that it is deadening. Instead of exhilaration such as is credited to alcohol," he quipped, "these fumes do not rouse a desire to sing or recite poetry."

A few months later, on August 27, 1930, General Motors and Du Pont formed a joint stock corporation—the Kinetic Chemical Company, Inc.—to manufacture and market the family of fluorine refrigerant compounds. Midgley was rewarded for his essential role in the research with the position of vice president at Kinetic; the Products Division at Du Pont named the new wonder gas Freon.

In 1931, Frigidaire launched a $7 million advertising campaign to announce several innovations to the household refrigerator market: the "hydrator"—a separate compartment for storing vegetables—a sliding utility basket, an interior light, tall bottle space, and "Quickube," the metal "jerk" device for freeing ice cubes from their tray, which was promoted for its ability to "End Cube Struggle!" Freon soon topped the list of wonders, a "miracle" refrigerant whose combination of safety, cleanliness, and efficiency Frigidaire proudly trumpeted as "one of the most outstanding scientific achievements of our times." A debate over Freon's safety flared briefly, led chiefly by Frigidaire's competitors, who reminded the public that fluorine was toxic; a teaspoonful of the pesticide sodium fluoride, it was pointed out, would be fatal to a human being. Frigidaire, however, fended off these attacks—no one inside or outside the industry had reported any ill effects from handling or utilizing Freon (as had happened with tetraethyl lead)—and on November 16, 1931, the company released the results of a year-long study conducted by an independent Chicago chemical-testing firm and commissioned by Du Pont and

Kinetic. The tests concentrated on Freon-12's corrosive effects, its toxicity, and its flammability, and the report concluded:

> Dichlorodifluoromethane is a stable compound capable of undergoing, without decomposition, the physical changes to which it is commonly subjected in service, such as freezing, boiling and compression. The hazards to health resulting from exposure to dichlorodifluoromethane when used as a refrigerant are judged to be remote. Results of flammability tests indicate that mixtures of dichlorodifluoromethane vapor and air do not propagate flame either at ordinary or elevated temperatures upon application of electric sparks or gas flames.

The report gave a similarly approving account of the substance's non-corrosiveness.

Compared to the clamor over the sale of ethyl gas, there was virtually no large-scale public concern expressed about Freon's safety. Within a year even the flak generated by the competing appliance companies died down; everywhere, Freon was welcomed as the long-awaited replacement for the inferior and at times deadly refrigerant gases of the 1920s. By 1935, when 8 million new refrigerators were sold in the United States, virtually all of Frigidaire's competitors were purchasing Freon outright from the Kinetic Chemical Company or licensing the right to manufacture it. Chlorofluorocarbons had become the standard refrigerant in America's household refrigerators.

When Charles Kettering peered into the future, he invariably saw technology as a positive, transforming force in mankind's everyday affairs. He was among the first people to predict that air-conditioning, a technology made more feasible by the availability of Freon coolants, would totally transform daily life, and that huge demographic changes, such as the "Sunbelting" of the American South, would be the result.

In the spring of 1930, Kettering invited Willis Carrier, the inventor of air-conditioning, to visit Midgley's Dayton laboratory. Carrier, like Midgley a Cornell graduate, had invented air-conditioning as a young man before the First World War, and had proven its potential most convincingly by improving conditions in southern textile mills, formerly America's warmest and most unbearable factories, and in movie theaters, which previously had been unable to remain open during the warm summer months. He had capitalized splendidly on his success and was by 1930 the head of the Carrier Engineering Corporation of Syracuse, New York, and the acknowledged standard-bearer for this exciting new technology.

Kettering brought Carrier to Dayton because the lack of a safe, efficient all-around coolant was as much of a stumbling block to progress in the air-conditioning industry as it had been in refrigeration. Carrier had made great strides in theaters, factories, and office buildings, but small-unit and household air-conditioning awaited a refrigerant efficient enough to function in a smaller coil apparatus. Throughout the 1920s, Carrier had experimented with high-speed, lightweight centrifugal compressors to replace the large, bulky piston-operated compressors used in larger air conditioners, and had gone through a number of coolants—dichloromethane, dichlorethylene, and methylene chloride—all of which failed to provide the needed level of efficiency. Carrier came from Syracuse to see for himself the phenomenal new refrigerant synthesized by Midgley's lab.

In Carrier's presence, Midgley demonstrated his production method for several chlorinated fluorocarbons, including dichlorodifluoromethane, CFC-12. Carrier, however, was more interested in trichloromonofluoromethane, later named CFC-11, which contained one additional chlorine atom and one less fluorine atom. Carrier believed this compound was better suited to the needs of a small air-conditioning compressor, and was far superior to either of the refrigerants his small machines were currently using. "It could be compressed in two or three stages—instead of four, five or six as with methylene chloride," Carrier later explained. "This would reduce the cost of compression by half for any given capacity." Midgley didn't have the production information for trichloromonofluoromethane typed up, so he gave Carrier a photostat of his penciled notes and a liquid sample.

Carrier used the coolant in building the world's first self-contained home air-conditioning unit, the "Atmospheric Cabinet," which the Carrier Corporation put on the market in 1932. Because of its sparkling reputation for safety, Freon also soon came to be the preferred compressed gas in some of Carrier's large air-conditioning systems. In many cities public-health codes were revised, designating Freon the only air-conditioning coolant that could be used in cooling auditoriums, convention halls, and other places where large public gatherings were held.

Carrier had been born the same year as Kettering, 1876, and was, like Boss Ket, a "farm boy who heard about the Industrial Revolution and marched out and joined it." But unlike Kettering, who spread his energies out over countless projects, Carrier lived by the motto "One Faith, One Furrow," and from 1901, when he left Cornell with an engineering degree, until his death in 1957, he single-mindedly pursued his vision of a Carrier-cooled world. "The time is almost here," Carrier often said, "when men will no more let themselves and their families suffer from heat and humidity than they now permit them to suffer from cold and storm." His supreme fantasy, a vision he particularly cherished, was of air-conditioning an entire indoor city, a dream he saw partially realized in 1956 when America's first all-enclosed shopping mall, Southdale, opened in Edina, Minnesota.

Indoor malls, of course, proved just one part of the total transformation of the American landscape fostered by Carrier's invention. By the end of 1958, 90 percent of the theaters in the United States were air-conditioned, as were 40 percent of the restaurants and 25 percent of the hotel rooms. And as Kettering had foreseen, air-conditioning in homes, office buildings and skyscrapers, automobiles and buses, made possible the urbanization of entire regions of America—in Florida, Georgia, Texas, Southern California, and the Southwest. The 1960s were the decade of the Sunbelt—the flourishing of previously "uninhabitable" towns such as Atlanta and Houston—and of air-conditioning's proliferation into every aspect of American life, North and South. For all the apartments built between 1962 and 1966, air-conditioning was installed in 75 percent; by 1972, it was estimated that almost half of the home and apartment residences in the United States had some form of air-conditioning. In 1963, 15 percent of America's 6.5 million cars were air-conditioned; within eight years, by 1971, air-conditioned cars accounted for 58 percent of the 9.3 million cars on the road; and air-conditioning was common also in truck cabs, farm tractors, locomotives, even the cabins of moving cranes in factories. As one historian of refrigeration commented about the years 1961 to 1970, "It is possible to speak of this epoch as one in which there was a certain obsession, a madness, about air conditioning." The inevitability of air conditioning even led some shop owners, unfortunate enough not to be located in a mall, to air-condition the sidewalk outside their storefronts, in the hope of attracting customers inside.

5.

THE MOST BEAUTIFUL LAWN IN THE WORLD

EW PEOPLE, least of all Ronald Ross himself, would have imagined during his student days in London in the 1880s that he was destined to become one of the heroes of modern medicine. An aspiring poet and playwright, Ross had only grudgingly followed his father's wishes in attending medical school and he was, by his own account, profoundly unhappy the day he departed the lively London arts scene to accept a posting in the Indian Medical Service. Once Ross was stationed in the tropics, however, he was deeply affected by the terrible suffering of his patients, hundreds of whom were stricken by malaria. Researching the existing literature on the disease, he was astonished to learn how little was really known.

Man's dread of malaria was sustained for centuries by a fundamental misconception about how it spread. The Italians, who named the disease *mal aria*, "bad air," thought it was caused by breathing the air of swamps and dying vegetation, a belief shared by Apalachicola's John Gorrie and other doctors until almost the dawn of the twentieth century. A treatise written in the early 1800s by a Baltimore physician named John Crawford claimed that malaria and other swamp fevers were transmitted by mosquitoes, but Crawford's work was theoretical and had largely been ignored. While it was noted that the incidence of malaria decreased when swamps were drained or underbrush was burned, observers failed to make the connection that this was because such actions destroyed insect breeding grounds.

Back in London on furlough, Ross befriended Dr. Patrick Manson. Ross had read Manson's *British Medical Journal* article "On the Nature and Significance of the Crescentic and Flagellate Bodies in Malarial Blood," in which Manson described the first scientific research to support Crawford's theory about mosquitoes. A French Army doctor stationed in Algeria, Alphonse Laveran, had been able to detect microscopic parasites in the blood of malaria victims, parasites that could be the infectious agent transmitted by mosquitoes. When he returned to India, Ross set out to prove the Manson-Laveran theory by the difficult method of dissecting and cataloging hundreds of winged insects. On August 20, 1897, he successfully identified a parasite in the abdomen of an anopheles mosquito as closely resembling one that Laveran had found in the blood of human malaria patients. Later Ross matched malarial cysts in the mosquito's intestinal tract with cysts found in the bloodstreams of diseased birds.

As Ross's conclusions gained acceptance, eliminating malaria—and other swamp fevers such as dysentery and dengue fever—became synonymous with killing mosquitoes. One of the first major efforts to control malaria in this way took place in 1914 in Central America, where hundreds of U.S. engineers and workers were engaged in the construction of the Panama Canal. Endemic malaria had thwarted earlier canal-digging projects in the isthmus. The Americans poured kerosene on mosquito-nesting areas and succeeded in dramatically lowering the rate of malaria infection.

A more promising method of insect control was fumigation, developed in Germany in the years before World War I. The spraying of an insecticide by means of a hand-operated pump known as a flit gun soon became the preferred method of controlling not only malarial mosquitoes, but other insect pests as well. Farmers readily embraced the new technology, and began demanding increasingly more potent insecticides from chemical manufacturers.

The earliest insecticides were organic compounds of arsenic, copper, lead, manganese, and zinc. Around the time of the First World War, manufacturers turned from natural substances to far more potent synthetics. One of the first powerful synthetic insecticides was based on pyrethrum, which was made from the dried leaves of crysanthemums and had been used as a folk insecticide in Persia and in Europe in the nineteenth century. Manufacturers combined pyrethrum powder with glycerin, green soap, and diluted carbon tetrachloride. The resulting compound, pyrethrin, became one of the industry's best-selling "knock-down agents," the trade term for an insecticide with an especially fast "kill."

The most notorious technological "advancement" of the First World War, chemical warfare, directly influenced the development of powerful synthetic insecticides. Chemists often tested the compounds devised to kill human beings on insects. Certain compounds—chloropicrin, for example, a tear gas and vomiting agent developed and used by the Russians —were exceptionally effective insecticides, and at war's end, surplus stockpiles of chloropicrin and other chemical weapons were sold to insecticide manufacturers. (Twenty years later the Germans grotesquely reversed the pattern, ordering the Degesch Company, a leading German chemical firm, to make its insecticide Zyklon-B available for use in concentration camps. Zyklon-B, in its original form, was sold with a noxious odor added to warn human beings and other animals of its presence; at the Nazis' behest, Degesch removed the irritant.)

While powerful insecticides were giving mankind a foothold in the battle against malaria and other insect-borne diseases, entomologists were nurturing concern for another problem born of the modern age, "insect hitchhiking," or the ability of malarial or other disease-bearing insects to travel long distances by airplane or dirigible. For centuries seafarers had unwittingly provided transportation to vermin carrying illness and plague. But ships were relatively slow and epidemics could generally be contained. In the age of modern air travel, it was all too easy to imagine the disastrous consequences if disease-bearing insects were allowed to move freely and swiftly from continent to continent. A plane taking off from malarial West Africa in the morning could be discharging cargo and passengers in London that night; a flight from the Philippines would open its doors at Honolulu in a day, at San Francisco in two. An epidemic might easily spread to every corner of the globe before a quarantine could be imposed, even before a disease was recognized or diagnosed.

Among the first scientists to grasp the extent of the risk was entomologist William Sullivan of the U.S. Agriculture Department's Bureau of Entomology and Plant Quarantine in Beltsville, Maryland. Inspired by German entomologist Max Kisluik, who in 1928 collected and classified the insects that had traveled from Europe to America aboard the German dirigible *Graf Zeppelin,* Sullivan recognized airplane insect hitchhiking as an emerging field in which he could make his mark. In the 1930s he convinced his superiors to assign him the task of halting the spread of *Aëdes aegypti* mosquitoes to the United States and Europe aboard airplane flights originating in Africa. "Apparently my enthusiasm was catching," he later wrote of his early work on the project, for he soon had an eager partner in his endeavor, Agriculture Department chemist Lyle Goodhue.

Sullivan and Goodhue's objective was an efficient way to quickly disinsect the inside of a plane, ensuring that all insects aboard at takeoff would be dead by the time the plane reached its destination. To accomplish this, they would have to invent a method of dispersing an insecticide into an airplane so that its floor, walls, and ceiling would become thoroughly saturated. Flit-gun spray fumigation, still the most popular way to spread an insecticide, produced too large a droplet size to thoroughly coat all the narrow cracks and crevices inside a plane. As an alternative, Goodhue and Sullivan worked to develop pyrethrum-based insecticidal "smokes," dispersing chemicals by vaporizing them with heat, using either an internal-combustion engine or a hot plate. This process resulted in a fine particle mist known as an "aerosol." (The term would subsequently come to be popularly associated with household spray-can products, but scientists use it to describe any mist, such as fog or smoke, in which particles are suspended in air.) The vaporization method they used to create an aerosol had two shortcomings: the heat consumed too much of the insecticide, and what it did not consume it tended to disperse too randomly. Some of their methods of substance dispersal seem rather makeshift—such as hooking a vacuum cleaner to a hot plate and running it in reverse to spew out the insecticide. Indeed, their work was so inconclusive that when, in early 1941, they were ordered to appear at Department of Agriculture headquarters in Washington to describe their progress, they both feared they were about to lose their assignment.

On the drive into town the two scientists fell into a gloomy discussion about the likelihood that their research program would be terminated. Goodhue later recalled, "Then, since we were somewhat apprehensive about the future of our project, we decided to drag out my old idea recorded back in 1935."

Goodhue told Sullivan that six years earlier, while attempting to vaporize nicotine for greenhouse fumigation, he had considered creating an insecticidal aerosol using a gas maintained by pressure in its liquid form. Just as water vaporizes when sprayed on the surface of an extremely hot stove—the principle they had applied in their hot-plate experiments—so a liquid gas with a low-enough boiling point would vaporize when it was suddenly released to normal atmospheric pressure. This sudden release of the gas, Goodhue said, might effectively disperse a substance, such as an insecticide, with which it had been combined. Goodhue told

Sullivan he hadn't acted on the idea in 1935 because at the time he had doubted it would be possible to build a container that would safely hold both a liquid gas and a highly toxic substance like nicotine under pressure. But he had had the presence of mind to jot his idea down, and had asked a lab assistant to witness and sign it. One of the liquefied gases he had considered using, Goodhue added, was the refrigerant dichlorodi-fluoromethane—CFC-12.

With the official fate of his and Sullivan's research project still undecided, Lyle Goodhue returned to Washington on Saturday, April 12, 1941, and bought five pounds of Freon from a chemical supplier. The next day, Easter Sunday, Goodhue had Beltsville's South Building of Agriculture almost entirely to himself while most of his colleagues enjoyed the holiday with their families. He filled a large container with a mixture of pyrethrum and Freon-12 under pressure, added sesame oil as a lubricant, and fitted a nozzle onto the top. He then placed several adult cockroaches in a small glass fumigation case and, taking aim with America's first aerosol bug spray, opened fire. Accompanied by a hissing sound, the spray filled the fumigation case. "In less than ten minutes, all roaches were on their backs," Goodhue scribbled in his lab notebook, and added a personal comment: "Yelled with joy and excitement."

At the end of July 1941, after further experimentation, Goodhue and Sullivan filed for a public-service patent for their insecticide aerosol propelled by liquid gas. In both their patent application and in an article they wrote for the December 1942 issue of *Industrial and Engineering Chemistry*, Goodhue and Sullivan recommended Freon-12 as the most adaptable liquid-gas propellant, one that both vaporized easily and mixed effectively and harmlessly with the chemicals in insecticides.

That summer Sullivan arranged for the first public demonstration of the aerosol insecticide at a hangar at Washington's National Airport. He invited representatives of the armed forces, confident that a new, effective means of disinsecting aircraft would especially appeal to the military. After this impressive exhibition, Goodhue and Sullivan met with the surgeon general of the Army, Colonel W. S. Stone.

Stone listened with keen interest to Sullivan's description of the aerosol's portability, its amazing "kill," and unusual ability to penetrate insect "hiding places." In the summer of 1941, with U.S. entry into war zones in southern Europe, Asia, and Africa an increasingly likely possibility, Stone was looking for an effective delivery system for delousing powder. He introduced Goodhue and Sullivan to Colonel George Callender, commander of Walter Reed Hospital. A veteran of U.S. antimalaria efforts in Panama and an authority on tropical diseases, Callender became the aerosol's leading booster after watching Sullivan demonstrate its effectiveness in a cockroach-ridden staff dormitory at Walter Reed.

Sullivan had been promoting the aerosol's utility as an ideal airplane disinsector and Stone hoped it would work on lice, but Callender had another use in mind. Armies in the field, unable to maintain ordinary standards of hygiene, had historically suffered some of the worst ravages of insect-borne disease. Medical officers of Callender's generation had witnessed the devastation that typhoid and malaria had wreaked among American troops in European trenches during the First World War. Callender suggested that the primary virtue of a portable aerosol insecticide spray was that it could be carried by troops and used in rugged terrain, even in a combat zone.

Callender urged Sullivan to seek a commission in the Army Air Transport Command "Sanitary Corps," assuring him that he could best ensure military use of his invention if he were himself a medical officer. Callender also arranged for Sullivan's assignment to Wright-Patterson Field in Dayton, which, years after the Wright brothers had flown on the site, was still being used as an experimental air base. Here Sullivan continued and refined the aerosol tests, which culminated in the development of a three-pound aerosol container. He also wrote a regulation requiring that an insecticide aerosol be used to disinsect all Army Air Force aircraft traveling overseas.

Surgeon General Stone quickly ordered further tests of the three-pound prototype at the Army's Orlando, Florida, chemical research center. The tests proved more convincing than the Orlando researchers could have wished: their entire mosquito colony, maintained for test purposes and containing thousands of insects, was unintentionally wiped out by the aerosol's penetration, even though it was located three rooms away from the testing lab.

Freon-12 was the ideal liquefied gas for use in the new insecticide aerosol, and with war looming, the Army sought out representatives of the Du Pont Company to discuss a quick production buildup. Du Pont's Freon business had prospered during the thirties, but the company only manufactured the substance, and had little experience with methods of dispensing it under pressure. Du Pont referred the Army to Westinghouse, whose refrigeration technicians had been developing new methods of Freon packaging for refrigeration.

Since the American entry into the war in December 1941, Westinghouse had thrown itself into war-related work, manufacturing everything from binoculars to torpedoes. W. B. Anderson, assistant manager of Westinghouse's Springfield, Massachusetts, plant, had in peacetime designed a small, one-pound, five-by-three-inch container for charging Freon-12 into refrigerators, a device that was quickly adapted to hold the aerosol insecticide. It held ninety-three grams of Freon-12, five grams of purified pyrethrum, and two grams of sesame oil as a synergist. Westinghouse workers nicknamed it the "Bug Bomb."

Surgeon General Stone, shown a Bug Bomb, commented, "It's exactly what we want." Within a week, the design had been approved by the Army and an emergency production timetable set forth: pyrethrum concentrate would be provided by Dodge & Olcott Chemicals; Du Pont would supply the Freon-12; and the youth of the Civilian Conservation Corps would assist in the Mexican sesame harvest. It so happened that Westinghouse had surplus Freon containers on hand because of wartime restrictions on the sale of refrigerators. Upon hiring additional manpower, Westinghouse promised to assemble ten thousand aerosol bombs a day, an ambitious production goal, but one the company would actually exceed. The whole procedure, from the first production meetings to the delivery of aerosol bombs to U.S. troops stationed in the South Pacific, was accomplished in only three months.

The sense of urgency surrounding the rapid development of the aerosol was soon justified. The U.S. invasion of the Japanese-occupied Solomon Islands, the campaign known as "the Long Road Back," was launched in August 1942 at the chain's easternmost island, Guadalcanal. The humid jungles and swamps of the Solomon and Marshall islands were rife with malaria, dengue fever, and filariasis, and had historically proven deadly for nonnative "visitors." The first American troops to arrive were no exception. "For every man put out of action by the Japs, ten succumbed to the insects and the diseases they carried," one correspondent wrote. "We have had to fight a double battle on every beachhead." One U.S. Marine division saw nearly 8,000 of its 17,000 men contract some form of malaria in the first week of combat.

Sullivan, now a uniformed officer in the Sanitary Corps, helped train GIs in the use of the Bug Bomb. One bomb would spray for a total of twelve to fourteen minutes, but only thirty seconds' worth was needed to kill the mosquitoes and flies in a thousand-cubic-foot enclosure, such as a mess tent. For cockroaches a stiffer dose of pyrethrum was needed. There were problems: valves leaked or failed completely—Veteran Agriculture Department entomologist E. F. Knipling later estimated that as many as 25 percent of the bombs didn't work—and in hot, muggy Pacific battle zones, soldiers often preferred reverting the Freon to its original use as a refrigerant. Opening the bomb and tipping it upside down allowed the Freon to seep out, making the one-pound aerosol container a king-sized "ice cube" for chilling a pail of beer.

But the 75 percent of the aerosol bombs that did work performed as impressively as they had in Sullivan's demonstrations back in Washington, and historians of the war in the South Pacific credit them with helping to alter the difficult Pacific campaign. Stateside news accounts, in describing the Bug Bomb, commonly cited the role of Freon, "the miracle compound," and did not hesitate to heap praise on the inventor of the refrigerant–turned–aerosol propellant. Reported *Business Week*, "Midgley had no idea of discovering an agent for carrying bug-killing chemicals. But that's what he did. . . . Plant capacity, recently stepped up 60 percent with completion of a new plant at East Chicago, Indiana, has reached 5,500,000 pounds of Freon a month."

"A double delight is dichlorodifluoromethane, with its 13 consonants and ten vowels," observed the *New York Times*. "It brings death to disease-carrying insects and provides cool comfort to man when July and August suns bake city pavements. This wonder gas is popularly known as Freon-12."

Chlorine and carbon, the elements Thomas Midgley had combined with fluorine to synthesize Freon, were the key ingredients in the recipe for another "miracle compound" discovered in Switzerland in the late 1930s. Chemist Paul Müller, a researcher with the J. R. Geigy Company in Basel, was searching for a way to mothproof fabrics when he sprayed a test substance, dichlorodiphenyltrichloroethane, into a box containing a dozen flies. The test substance didn't seem to affect the flies, who kept buzzing around inside the box as if they had not been sprayed at all, but on a hunch, Müller decided to leave the experiment overnight.

When he returned in the morning, all the flies were dead. He removed them and put more flies in the box. Soon they were dead, too, so he tried a third batch, achieving the same results. Müller recorded in his lab notes that one spraying of the substance had killed three separate groups of flies—not a bad audition for a would-be insecticide.

Moving on with his work, Müller thoroughly scrubbed the box and used it for similar experiments with other test substances and new batches of insects. These other insecticides seemed promising, too, but a week later, when he tested them again in different containers, he was surprised to find that they were totally ineffectual. Was it possible that the original spraying of dichlorodiphenyltrichloroethane had killed not only all three test batches of flies, but the subsequent batches of flies as well, despite his vigorous scrubbing of the container? Müller soon confirmed that this was indeed what had happened. Running more tests, he matched the new compound against other insect test colonies—cockroaches, clothes moths, and potato bugs. It killed them all as effectively as it had the flies. It killed lice, too. It seemed to kill everything, and with such lasting and penetrating thoroughness that Müller was forced to conclude the new substance was the most powerful insecticide he had ever seen.

The substance's most pleasing virtue was its versatility. There had always been a large element of risk in the manufacture and sale of insecticides, because a specific insecticide was usually effective only against a particular pest. Insecticide manufacturers had at times faced bankruptcy when a certain bug infestation suddenly ceased to be a threat. Thus, insecticide developers always looked for "broad spectrum" poisons with the ability to destroy a wide range of insects.

Calling their new test product Gerasol Dust Insecticide, Geigy's New York office made a sample available to the U.S. Army's Orlando research station in November 1942. There the compound's name, dichlorodiphenyltrichloroethane, was shortened to DDT and routinely tested along with other insecticides. The Orlando scientists were most impressed by its effectiveness against lice: DDT powder killed all the lice on a human subject and gave three weeks' protection against reinfestation. In May 1943 Orlando recommended DDT for use by the U.S. armed forces, which in turn requested large quantities of it for combat troops in North Africa and in Italy, where the Sanitary Corps was battling an outbreak of typhus among Italian civilians. DDT was credited with halting the outbreak, and American GIs in southern Europe and the Mediterranean were deloused with DDT powder for the remainder of the war.

On the Pacific front, DDT was added with sensational results to the already powerful aerosol bombs using Freon as a propellant. Indeed, while the original aerosol bomb had been impressive, DDT's ability to wipe out insects exceeded all expectations. When it was sprayed on clothes, its bug-killing effect lasted an entire month; on screens and walls it lasted even longer. And when it was used in conjunction with pyrethrum as a quick-killing "knockdown agent," a jungle island teeming with flies, gnats, and mosquitoes could be completely "dusted" in less than ten minutes, and remain saturated for weeks. GIs who remembered the rough going earlier in the Pacific campaign now walked incredulously through jungle groves utterly devoid of insect life. One U.S. medical officer who had seen the new product in action later proclaimed the DDT-Freon aerosol "the atomic bomb of the insect world;" another described it as "the war's greatest contribution to the future health of the world."

The DDT-Freon bomb's transition from military use to the American consumer market was inevitable, and was facilitated by the large number of surplus aerosol bombs the military had on hand after the war. When soldiers who had seen the DDT-Freon combination in action returned home, the Bug Bomb became the subject of one of the most enthusiastic word-of-mouth promotions in history. "Most of the three to four million [aerosol bombs] made in 1946," Donald Davis, editor of the aerosol industry's leading trade periodical, *Aerosol Age*, later wrote, "were sold in hardware stores or Army-Navy outlets, probably to ex-GIs with good memories of how well they performed on some South Pacific atoll."

With the Bug Bomb, chlorofluorocarbons had convincingly shown that they no longer required their inventor to win new and profitable applications for themselves.

With two major discoveries to his credit, Midgley enjoyed a diverse career in the 1930s and early 1940s as researcher, educator, and government consultant, while serving on the board of directors of the Ethyl Corporation and Kinetic Chemical. He was on the go almost constantly in the decade before the Second World War, a frequently honored guest speaker at scientific conferences. Although he was now wealthy, enriched by his holdings in GM, Ethyl, and Kinetic, he had not lost his impetuousness. If there was research he wanted to conduct or someone he wanted to see, according to one friend, Midgley "would just get in his car and start driving west, even if there weren't any highways where he was going." His peers elected him repeatedly to various posts in the American Chemical Society, culminating with his election to the presidency in 1944. This was the crowning touch to the Midgley legend: that a man with no formal background in chemistry had, by dint of his own ingenuity, ascended to the presidency of America's leading professional chemists' organization. No one appreciated Midgley's unique accomplishment more than his friend Charles Kettering, who took to relating Midgley's story in many of his public appearances. The old inventor would begin by saying, "The greatest discovery I ever made was Tom Midgley."

Though not as famous as Kettering, Midgley enjoyed his celebrity. In an age when technology was revolutionizing the way Americans lived, people were especially receptive to the opinions and musings of the men who had brought this transformation about. Kettering served up folksy tales of the rewards of "getting off Route 25," and rhapsodized about the bright, glistening future. Midgley was fond of offering colorful descriptions of how technology would change daily life a hundred years in the future—"mood pills" and "wakefulness pills" so people could modulate their own need for rest, artificial-growth hormones to create "cows so big they will have to be milked from stepladders," and modes of telecommunication so efficient the inevitable result would be "the end of visiting."

Kettering was now working in Detroit and Midgley lived in Worthington, Ohio, a quaint, rural suburb of Columbus, but they remained close, the father-son relationship of the early Dayton years replaced in time by a more equal friendship as both became nationally renowned figures.

"They shared this incredible optimism about the future," a colleague later recalled. "They were two of the most optimistic people you ever saw." Midgley also stayed in touch with the old Dayton gang—Tabby Boyd, Edward Deeds, Robert McNary, Carroll Hochwalt, as well as Albert Henne, who had assisted in the discovery of Freon and was now on the faculty at nearby Ohio State—often welcoming them as guests at his Worthington home.

One of Midgley's pet projects until he became seriously ill in the early 1940s was keeping the grounds of his house lush green and impeccably manicured. He turned his three-and-a-half-acre lawn into a showplace for a fine grass known as Washington Bent, a deep-green strain, almost emerald, which grew with phenomenal uniformity of length, and had a soft, shiny texture. The lawn threatened to become as famous as its owner: soon the greens committee chairmen from golf courses throughout the Midwest were making the pilgrimage to Worthington to see Midgley's lawn and confer with its creator. The highest tribute came from the Scott Seed Company, which began to use a photograph of Midgley's white house and immaculate green lawn on the company letterhead.

Washington Bent was extremely delicate, however, and its proud owner went to great, some would say fanatical, lengths to protect it. When the grass proved vulnerable to the drying effect of the wind, Midgley installed an anemometer on the roof of the house and connected it to a small bell in his bedroom. Should a wind come up at night, the bell would alert him. He had linked control of the lawn sprinklers to the dial on his bedroom telephone, and by dialing a certain sequence of numbers, Midgley could start the sprinklers watering the lawn. When his gardeners informed him that worms were showing up in the grass, he modified the system so that the sprinklers could be changed over from water to a liquid insecticide. Midgley, who made a point in his travels of visiting famous estates and parks to inspect their greenery, liked to say he had the best lawn in the whole world—maybe not the biggest, but definitely the best.

One account of Midgley's later years asserts that he was taking vitamin B injections during the summer of 1940 because he feared he might be "precancerous." If Midgley felt anxious about cancer, it may have been because continual exposure to fluorine was known to affect one's liver; Albert Henne, Midgley's fluorine expert, would later die of liver cancer. Perhaps it was that fear, or some lingering doubt about his long-ago brush with lead poisoning, that first crossed his mind when, in September 1940, while attending an American Chemical Society meeting in Detroit, he suddenly began running a fever and complained of feeling weak. He returned immediately to Worthington, where he and his family were shocked by the doctor's diagnosis of acute poliomyelitis.

"I have been spending my spare moments in bed figuring out the statistical probabilities of a 51-year-old male catching poliomyelitis, as I have," Midgley explained to his colleagues soon afterward in an open letter in the trade journal *Industrial and Engineering Chemistry,* "and this comes out to be substantially equal to the chance of drawing a certain individual card from a stack of playing cards as high as the Empire State Building. It was my tough luck to draw it."

He did not at first curtail his many activities. Although bound to a wheelchair and requiring the assistance of a nurse, Midgley continued to travel and lecture widely. In Worthington he moved into the living room of his house, and there, surrounded by his favorite paintings and some group photographs from the General Motors years in Dayton, managed to conduct a large portion of his affairs over the telephone. He served as vice chairman of the wartime National Inventors Council, a group created by Secretary of Commerce Harry Hopkins in 1940—with Kettering as chairman—to help expedite worthy civilian inventions for military use.

Despite his characteristic optimism and his efforts to defy the limitations of his handicap, the polio increasingly took a psychological toll. The confinement of the wheelchair was sheer punishment to a man once accustomed to rushing clear across the country to demonstrate the harmlessness of his inventions or mingle with his admiring scientific brethren. Midgley had always been a good mixer, enlivening many an otherwise gray scientific gathering—telling stories and holding forth until all hours to a tableful of companions in the hotel bar. He liked nothing better than engaging them in what he referred to, euphemistically, as "the fundamentals of chemistry," and the excursions to distant scientific symposia provided him the freedom to indulge his taste for drink—away from the moderating influence of his wife and family. As Midgley's health waned in the early 1940s, it was to alcohol that he turned more frequently.

This growing despondency no doubt lay behind a curious speech he gave to the American Chemical Society in May 1944, a few months after becoming that organization's president. The talk, which he called "Accent on Youth," was pure Midgley, an odd blend of innovative research, self-aggrandizement, and off-the-wall speculation. In it he announced that he had concluded from examining statistics from the U.S. Patent Office that almost all "great" inventions had been made by men between the ages of twenty-five and forty-five. Citing these figures, Midgley called on all scientists older than age forty to remove themselves from positions requiring a high order of creativity. He suggested that, with their experience, they could best serve in administrative positions, thus leaving the nation's laboratory benches free for younger scientists.

Midgley cited his own career as an illustration: before the age of thirty he had discovered iodine as the first of the chemical antiknock agents; at age thirty-three he had made his famous breakthrough with tetraethyl lead, and just prior to turning forty he had discovered CFCs. He concluded his address by reciting a poem he had written:

When I feel old age approaching and it isn't any sport,
And my nerves are growing rotten and my breath is growing short,
And my eyes are growing dimmer and my hair is turning white,
And I lack the old ambitions when I wander out at night,
Then, though many men my senior may remain when I am gone,
I'll have no regrets to offer just because I'm passing on.
Let this epitaph be graven on my tomb in simple style,
"This one did a lot of living in a mighty little while."

He grew steadily weaker during the summer of 1944, then rallied to travel to New York in mid-September to preside over an ACS dinner at the Waldorf-Astoria Hotel. But by October, Midgley was too feeble to travel and had become a total invalid.

Despite his claims about the receding creative powers of middle-aged inventors, Midgley had recently brought his own talents to bear quite effectively. Annoyed that he had to call for his nurse or his wife, Carrie, each time he wanted to move from his bed into his wheelchair, he had devised a complex lifting mechanism involving a leather harness suspended over the bed by a rope and pulley, to allow him to accomplish the maneuver unassisted.

Sometime before dawn on November 2, 1944, Midgley apparently put the apparatus to an entirely different purpose. Entering his room later that morning with breakfast and the newspaper, Carrie Midgley found her husband hanging lifeless in the lifting device, the ropes tangled around his neck.

The newspapers reported Midgley's demise as a freakish accident, but the friends and family who had witnessed his recent suffering knew better. Columbus cemetery records list "Suicide by strangulation" as the official cause of death.

Telegrams of condolence began to arrive at the white house with the big, beautiful lawn in Worthington. One of the first came from Orville Wright, who wrote, "The world has lost a truly great citizen in Mr. Midgley's death. I have been proud to call him friend." Now seventy-three, statesmanlike in a dark suit, cane, and bowler hat, the hero of Kitty Hawk arrived from Dayton for the funeral on Monday, November 6, along with Kettering and a contingent of former Dayton colleagues, including Tabby Boyd and Carroll Hochwalt. Dozens of other prominent scientists and industrialists, representing the diverse arenas in which Midgley had been active, attended the service.

"He was one of the great geniuses on Earth," remarked James Boudreau, a colleague of Midgley's at the Ethyl Corporation.

An unusually quiet Boss Ket, sharing the backseat of a limousine on the ride back from the cemetery, made a similar observation. Kettering confided to Tabby Boyd that during the graveside service, when the minister had uttered the phrase "We bring nothing into this world, and it is certain we can carry nothing out," he had badly wanted to interrupt, and say, "In Midge's case, it seems appropriate to add, 'But we can at least leave a lot behind for the good of the world.'"

6.

THE PUSH-BUTTON AGE

T HE TWENTY-FIVE hundred Bug Bombs placed on sale at Gimbel's in New York City in September 1945, manufactured by Bridgeport Brass of Connecticut using the wartime DDT/pyrethrum/Freon formula, sold out in just two hours. Everywhere else they went on sale in late 1945 and early 1946, retailers reported that customers were sweeping the Bug Bomb—as well as Insect-o-Blitz and other spray insecticides—off the shelves almost as quickly as they could be stocked. American homeowners and gardeners, armed with the new aerosol sprays, began to score one-sided victories over bothersome insects of all shapes and sizes. Confidence in the powerful new bug killers was so great the maker of one, Real-Kill, publicly offered $25,000 to anyone who produced an insect able to crawl or fly away from a dousing of its aerosol insecticide.

The American packaging industry, meanwhile, was awakening to a singular realization: consumers would actually pay more for the convenience of a product that could be sprayed. A test survey of aerosol buyers provided a variety of revealing responses, including:

> You can follow flies around until you kill them. I feel commanding. I feel like a hunter.

I love to push the button. It amuses and amazes me. I feel as if I have
a gun in my hand, or a hand grenade.

It gives me a great deal of satisfaction from knocking them down, not
just eliminating them but killing them. I keep spraying until the fly is
dead.

The comments appeared in an issue of *Aerosol Age* containing an
advertisement that promised, "Whatever it does, your aerosol does it
better with Du Pont 'Freon' propellants."

Once aerosol manufacturers grasped that the success of aerosols was
related to convenience, they started to question their use of the bulky
"bombs," which weighed a full pound, and were therefore suited only to
insecticide or other nonpersonal uses. The breakout of the personal aerosol market—aerosols containing products like deodorant and hairspray
—awaited the development of a lightweight can that could safely contain
Freon under sufficient pressure to maintain it in liquid form.

Harry Peterson and Bill Palmer of the Continental Can Corporation
in Danville, Illinois, liked to brainstorm about products that might be
effectively packaged and sold in Continental's beer can. One night during
the war Peterson had wondered aloud whether Continental's cans could
house the high-pressure aerosol Bug Bomb used by the armed forces.
Palmer liked the idea, as did Peterson's boss, who asked him to look
into it.

Peterson found that the standard thin-walled Continental beer can
was not strong enough to contain the pressure of liquefied CFC-12, but
that it would hold an aerosol using a propellant combination of CFC-12
and CFC-11. The large Bug Bomb using CFC-12 had been packaged at
an average pressure of 70 pounds per square inch (psi). The "beer-can"
aerosol could not contain that much pressure, but the CFC-12–CFC-11
combination worked well at 40 psi. The problem was that the Interstate
Commerce Commission (ICC) outlawed the transport of beer-can containers with greater pressure than 25 psi, due to the risk that they might
leak or explode. In 1946 Peterson, with the support of his supervisors, a
competitor—Earl Graham of Crown Cork and Seal, a Philadelphia container firm—and William "Dusty" Rhodes, Du Pont's Freon sales manager, began to lobby for a change of ICC policy.

The nontoxicity and nonflammability of CFCs at normal temperatures gave Peterson and his cohorts a solid argument with which to
challenge the ICC rules. Du Pont scientists, who had published numerous technical papers detailing methods of preparing low-pressure aerosol

propellants with Freon, were delighted to find associates in the packaging industry willing to pursue the matter, and they couldn't help but have faith in Dusty Rhodes, who was known for getting results. Rhodes had almost single-handedly egged on the developmental work in personal aerosols during the war, personally seeing to it that small amounts of Freon, otherwise strictly allocated for war use, were made available to convenience-aerosol pioneers like Peterson.

In 1947 Rhodes, Peterson, and Graham made a presentation to the Aerosol Committee of the Compressed Gas Association, a professional group of packagers headquartered in New York City whose opinion would be a decisive factor in the eyes of the ICC. The low-pressure advocates met with tough resistance from the CGA committee, partly, they believed, because the group was dominated by men affiliated with high-pressure-container manufacturers, who knew too well what the requested change in rules would do to the high-pressure market. But with the strong-willed Rhodes leading the charge, the three men convinced the committee to approve the 40-psi resolution. The CGA reported its committee's decision to the Bureau of Explosives, a federal agency, which rubber-stamped its approval, and to the ICC, which in turn agreed to allow the exemption, permitting the interstate shipment of low-pressure aerosols at 40 psi.

In early 1947, Peterson left Continental Can to start his own company with Clarence F. Carter, an Illinois sportsman and former airplane barnstormer who had invented the "CarterVac," the world's most powerful aerosol filler, which was capable of filling 360 containers per minute. Earl Graham, meanwhile, led development at Crown Cork and Seal. Crown adapted a twelve-ounce beer can into "Spra-Tainer," and other low-pressure aerosol packages from Crown and Continental followed. Manufacturers like Bridgeport Brass, which were still offering the one-pound descendants of the war's Bug Bomb, were doomed the moment the beer cans hit the market. Insecticides packaged in Spra-Tainers sold, on the average, for about $1.50, while the heavier containers cost as much as $5.95.

Despite the breakthrough of the lightweight container, the aerosol still suffered from one significant failing. Wholesale aerosol-can salesmen were growing weary of hearing complaints from product packagers about leaky and nonfunctioning aerosol valves. Salesman John Baessler walked into the machine shop of his friend Robert Abplanalp on Gunhill Road in the Bronx one afternoon in the summer of 1949 carrying an armful of defective aerosol cans, and implored Abplanalp to look into the problem.

Abplanalp, an ex-GI, was familiar with the Bug Bomb, but had had little experience with aerosols, so he began by disassembling the defective aerosol cans. "The first thing in my head," Abplanalp later recalled, "was we had to get rid of the soldering." Early aerosol valves were soldered to the can, making them prone to leaks when the soldering began to soften or crack. The water in many cosmetic aerosols was especially hard on soldered valves.

Abplanalp realized that the simplest way to beat the problem was to develop a nonsoldered valve assembly, a "crimp and clinch" method in which the valve would physically lock onto the can. In order to increase the gripping ability of the assembly, he widened the can's top opening to one inch, and created a valve, actuator button, and stem assembly that could be set into the one-inch opening in one piece and locked, or "crimped," into place. His design had other advantages: soldering had precluded the use of aluminum, which was desirable for lightweight containers, and the new valve assembly permitted bottom-filling of aerosol cans, which was faster than pouring the contents in through a narrow hole at the top.

In September 1949, Abplanalp filed for a patent on the clinch-valve assembly and one-inch can opening—soon the standard for the entire aerosol industry—and with Baessler and another partner founded the Precision Valve Corporation.

"Bob Abplanalp's position in the aerosol industry is analogous to Henry Ford's in the auto industry," valve designer Walter Beard later said. "He introduced a cheap, easy-to-assemble valve with fewer parts and a means of mass production."

The combination of Harry Peterson's low-pressure, lightweight can and Robert Abplanalp's cheap, reliable valve permitted rapid diversification in the aerosol industry. To compensate for a drastic fall-off in receipts during the winter months, insecticide manufacturers introduced room deodorizers—Aer-o-Sol and Good-Aire were two of the first—and in 1950 "decorative snowflakes," the first item developed expressly for low-pressure aerosol technology. The flakes, named Christmas Snow and Make-It-Snow, sold an astounding 8 million units a year in 1951 and 1952. Another of the first "beer-can" aerosol products to win broad and immediate popular acceptance was Reddi Whip whipping cream.

From eight aerosol-related companies in the late forties, the industry grew to more than one hundred just a few years later. "The aerosol industry," *Aerosol Age* observed, "is a remarkable example of the effect of free enterprise and American ingenuity. Rarely has a more disorganized, sprawling, confused, disjointed, widely divergent, unplanned and unguided development program ever been set in motion . . . yet this illegitimate wedding of the refrigeration business and the tin can industry has grown from 8 million dollars in 1947 to almost 250 million dollars eight years later."

The prevailing sentiment among entrepreneurs entering the market during this happy boom period, Beard later recalled, was "You can't go too far wrong. Take anything, put Freon-12 in it, and spray." Aerosol manufacturers began to do just that. Aside from a few oddities the buying public resoundingly rejected, such as aerosol soft drinks and a dual-purpose toothpaste/shave cream, everything from oven cleaner, hairspray, car wax, shoe polish, cologne, and spot remover, to deodorant, diaper freshener, hand lotion, lens cleaner, allergy spray, and rust-inhibitor sold well in aerosol cans.

Along the way a change in terminology was adopted. " 'Bomb' tends to be associated with dangerous, explosive articles," an article in *Aerosol Age* pointed out in 1956, "[and] 'pressurized' and 'aerosol' mean absolutely nothing to almost 70 percent of the population. On the other hand, 'push-button' immediately means something tangible to almost anyone—even to children. 'Push-button' warfare is currently a headline newspaper subject, and there are more 'push-button' shift automobiles being made every day.

" 'Push-button' implies everything modern, and people like the idea. They can understand it quite readily without even wondering about technical terms they don't care a hoot about anyway."

The column encouraged those in the aerosol trade to "pick up the telephone now and call your local newspaper, and ask the editor if he is interested in a feature news story of considerable public appeal. Suggest that it might be entitled something like 'The Push-Button Age Is Here' and ask him to send a reporter out to cover the story."

The breakout years for CFC-propelled aerosols, 1947 and 1948, saw important changes in the city where chlorofluorocarbons had been invented—the death, at age seventy-seven, of Dayton's most beloved citizen, Orville Wright (Wilbur Wright had died of typhoid in 1912), and the retirement of Charles Kettering as vice president of the General Motors Research Corporation.

Wright, like most aviators of his generation, disapproved of the increasing use of the airplane as a weapon, and was greatly concerned in the last years of his life by the development of monstrous killing machines like the giant B-17 Flying Fortress used in World War II. He retained his faith in the technology he had helped father, however, even amid the horrors of the war. "I feel about the airplane much the same as I do in regard to fire," Orville confided to his friend and biographer, Fred Kelly, in 1943. "That is, I regret all the terrible damage caused by fire. But I think it is good for the human race that someone discovered how to start fires."

When Kettering retired in 1947 at the age of seventy-one, his scientific genius and homespun faith in the future and the importance of individual effort had made him a living legend. He embodied to millions of Americans the aspirations of the generation that had come of age during what historian Thomas P. Hughes has called "the era of technological enthusiasm." In January 1933, the "Prophet of Progress" had even been featured on the cover of *Time* magazine. The caption under his picture, the beginning of one of his own maxims, read, "A man must have a certain amount of intelligent ignorance. . . ."

In the early 1940s he was a guest each Sunday afternoon on the *General Motors Symphony of the Air,* giving five-minute talks on science and invention. So many people requested reprints of the talks that GM published the most popular ones in booklet form. The foremost theme in Kettering's public addresses was his certainty that the challenges of the present, met with creativity and intelligence, would foster a better future. History, he said, was, after all, merely "the laboratory results of what has happened"; it was crucial that the past be regarded as "a guidepost, not a hitching post."

Kettering practiced what he preached. His complete lack of a scientific background in medicine, for example, did not deter him from acting on his belief that the eradication of deadly disease was one of the primary objectives of science, a challenge to be met head on. Cancer, in particular, fascinated him, because it was said to be "incurable." It was another "hopeless" situation, the kind he loved to try to resolve, and the problem unexpectedly took on personal significance for him in the mid-1940s after his sister Emma and his wife, Olive, both died of the disease. In 1945 Kettering joined with GM president Alfred Sloan to fund a clinic to specialize in cancer research at New York's Memorial Hospital, the Sloan-Kettering Institute.

An early advocate of harnessing solar energy, Kettering had, since the First World War, also funded research into the secrets of photosynthesis, a preoccupation he referred to as "trying to find out why the grass is green." The farm boy–turned–engineer who had been inspired by the heat-absorbing capabilities of the trailing arbutus, Kettering was fascinated by the ease with which nature solved complex chemical and engineering problems. "Look around you in any large factory where materials are changed by chemical manipulation," he suggested to one scientific group. "You see blazing furnaces, boiling vats and high pressure at work. Look at nature and you see far more difficult processes carried out at ordinary temperatures and pressures. Chemists have to batter down gates . . . nature opens them with a key."

Boss Ket was not universally beloved. Always tantrum-prone and quick with an oath, Kettering developed a hair-trigger temper in the last decade of his life; his overbearing personality and impatience made him an unwelcome visitor even at the academic institutions, among them Ohio State and Antioch, he had helped endow. " 'If you can't make it in a bucket, it's not worth making' . . . that was his attitude," an OSU chemistry instructor later recalled. "He honestly thought you could solve any problem simply by rolling up your sleeves. It got so that the theoreticians didn't like to see him coming, didn't want him relating to the students. They were afraid he'd hold chemistry back for a century."

Kettering's biographer, Stuart Leslie, has pointed out that Boss Ket was born in 1876, the same year as the internal-combustion engine, while his death from a stroke in November 1958 coincided with the zenith of American automotive confidence and excess, when large V-8 engines, whitewall tires, chrome trim, and enormous space-age fins represented everything desirable in an automobile. Thus, the old "wrench-and-pliers scientist" never lived to know the concerns for auto safety, fuel efficiency, and air pollution that began to assail the automotive industry in the early 1960s.

Nor did he witness the outbreak of riots in Dayton's black community in 1968, or hear the subsequent analysis that decades of emphasis on business and technology in "the Fortunate Valley" had bred a harmful neglect of many of the city's people, and that now the bill had at long last come due.

Neither was he ever confronted with the news that one of the other innovations he had done so much to bring about, chlorofluorocarbons, were suspected of threatening the global environment—although his reaction is not difficult to imagine. Kettering always believed that technology held the power to solve man's problems, even the thornier problems progress itself created, and in doing so to transform the conditions of life for the better.

As he liked to demand of academic researchers, the "pure" scientists who tried to slip out the back door of the laboratory when they heard him come in the front, "But how will you apply your theoretical research to man's needs?"

7.

SCENIC HUDSON

N 1962, Rachel Carson, an acclaimed nature writer and former marine biologist with the U.S. Fish and Wildlife Service, published a book with an alarming argument: that the indiscriminate use of pesticides and herbicides, and particularly of DDT, was a threat to all living things. Carson's book, *Silent Spring,* was a rude jolt to a postwar American society infatuated with technological and scientific progress. *Silent Spring* became an immediate bestseller, and the storm of controversy that accompanied the book's publication marked the birth of modern American environmentalism.

Rachel Carson was well suited to her influential role. She was an academically trained biologist-turned-writer, a naturalist in the tradition of Henry David Thoreau and John Muir, for whom a personal involvement with nature was of paramount importance. "My real preoccupation is not with 'pure' or abstract science," she once wrote to her editor, Paul Brooks. "I am the sort who wants above all to get out and enjoy the beauty and wonder of the natural world, and who resorts only secondarily to the laboratory and library for explanations." Her books prior to *Silent Spring* were hymns to the interrelatedness of living things, or "the web of life," as she often called it. Before the earnings from her books enabled her to become a full-time author, she worked as a writer and editor with the Bureau of Fisheries in the Department of Commerce, which later merged with the Department of Agriculture's Biological Survey to form the Fish and Wildlife Service in the Department of the Interior. Over the years she wrote many government articles and pamphlets, including a series of booklets entitled *Conservation in Action* about various national wildlife refuges. She was also an avid bird-watcher and a member of the Audubon Society. But her first love was the sea, perhaps in part because it was less spoiled by man than the land. Her breakthrough book in 1951, *The Sea Around Us,* was on the *New York Times* bestseller list for eighty-six weeks.

In *The Sea Around Us* and in two other books, *Under the Sea Wind* (1941) and *The Edge of the Sea* (1955), Carson summarized what was known about the ocean in evocative prose, always stressing the "delicate balance" of nature, and the remarkable adaptability of life to sometimes harsh natural forces of tide, current, and climate. Though she did not use the word much, hers was fundamentally an *ecological* perspective. She wrote about entire ecosystems more than about individual species, and often noted how easily man's activities could disrupt and even destroy nature's balance. In *The Sea Around Us,* for instance, in a chapter on islands, she described the Pacific island of Laysan, "a far outrider of the Hawaiian chain," which once "supported a forest of sandalwood and fanleaf palms and had five land birds, all peculiar to Laysan alone." Then, in the late 1880s, rabbits had been introduced onto Laysan by man. With no natural predators to control their population, the rabbits quickly overran the island, reducing it to a sandy desert and driving its unique wildlife to extinction, including the Laysan rail, "a charming gnomelike creature no more than six inches high, with wings that seemed too small (and were never used as wings), and feet that seemed too large, and a voice like distant, tinkling bells."

This disapproval of man's insensitivity to nature permeates Carson's writing prior to *Silent Spring*. Her admonishment is more implied than stated, as if she knows the most effective way to impart her message is to eloquently share her own love for the subject. Carson's certainty that humans are part of nature and must live within its bounds pervades all her early work.

Though her writings are grounded in science, they encourage an appreciation of the aesthetic and spiritual rewards of nature. In this sense, Rachel Carson was the latest in a distinguished line of nature essayists dating back at least as far as the eighteenth-century English naturalist Gilbert White, whose posthumously published book, *The Natural History and Antiquities of Selborne* (1789), was a detailed account of his observations of the natural flora and fauna in and around the Hampshire town where he was born and served as parson. White's holistic view of nature, and his sense that the natural order is an expression of God's grace, powerfully influenced admirers such as British naturalist Charles Darwin and the American transcendentalist Henry David Thoreau.

For Darwin the inspiration helped produce the theory of evolution. Darwin was an untrained scientist when, at the age of twenty-two, he took a job as ship's naturalist aboard the HMS *Beagle,* which sailed on a scientific expedition to study the Pacific coast of South America and the Pacific islands in December 1831. Darwin's direct observations of nature on the five-year voyage, particularly those he made on the Galápagos Islands off the coast of Ecuador, led to his seminal work, *On the Origin of Species,* published in 1859. In striking contrast to earlier religious and scientific doctrine, which held that human beings were created by God, and that the natural world was created by God on their behalf, Darwin concluded that man was a product of nature. The simple idea that humans are close biological cousins of the apes has surely proven one of the most profoundly disturbing concepts of the modern age, and even many people who accept Darwin's theory of evolution have difficulty with its implications, which seem to bind human beings so inextricably to natural earthly processes.

Thoreau, along with the American Romantic writers Nathaniel Hawthorne and James Fenimore Cooper, developed his spiritual view of nature in reaction to the clang and clamor of the Industrial Revolution. To classical science—the science of Copernicus, Newton, Descartes, and Bacon—industrial technology represented the flowering of humankind's divinely endowed right to exploit, control, and ultimately dominate nature. "For the whole world works together in the service of man," Bacon wrote in *De Sapientia Veterum* (The Wisdom of the Ancients). Thoreau and the Romantics took an opposite view, rejecting the vulgar materialism of an increasingly mercantile civilization and embracing subjective feelings and emotions that classical science had rejected as "irrational"— intuition, fantasy, passion, imagination, inner truth. In the United States the Romantic impulse ran counter not only to the encroachments of the industrial age, but also to the "frontier ethic," which perceived nature as an obstacle to civilization and human progress. Indeed, the conquest of the western wilderness was the dominant preoccupation of nineteenth-century America, firmly rooting feelings of man's superiority over nature in the national psyche. To the vast majority of Americans of the mid-nineteenth century, Thoreau's now-famous dictum "In wildness is the preservation of the world" would have seemed nonsensical, so completely did it contradict both the frontier ethic and "rational" scientific thought.

Thoreau's most famous and influential work, *Walden,* covered the years between 1845 and 1847 when he lived alone in a modest cabin he built on the shore of Walden Pond, near his hometown of Concord, Massachusetts. Not only did Thoreau immerse himself in the natural world, he offered satirical commentary on the lives of his neighbors, the mercantile and agricultural citizens of Concord who were, in Thoreau's view, cut off from nature and consequently from their own human natures as well. The years that Thoreau lived and wrote in Concord were years of tremendous change in the ecology of New England, as the Yankee economy grew and industrialism spread. He witnessed the destruction of the natural systems he had come to know and love, in particular the clearing of the ancient New England forest. Though he saw folly in his neighbors' wanton destruction of the forest, he was more impressed by nature's fecundity and power of rejuvenation. He ultimately concluded that man could never fully destroy nature.

John Muir shared no such optimism. Like Thoreau, Muir was a wandering naturalist, largely self-taught, who sought and found spiritual fulfillment in forests and mountains. But by the time Muir embarked on his famous "thousand-mile walk" in the summer of 1867 at the age of twenty-nine, large swaths of the formerly wild American landscape had already been desecrated. Muir's walk took him from his home in Wisconsin across the American South, recently devastated by the Civil War. But it was the following year, in the spectacular Yosemite Valley in California's Sierra Nevada Mountains, that Muir found his own Walden Pond, a landscape that inspired his most passionate writing, and with which he is most strongly identified.

Where Thoreau assumed that nature would ultimately take care of itself, Muir was compelled to political activism to preserve some small remnant of wilderness. After he became a well-known essayist in the early 1870s, the spokesman for a growing nature cult which had also revived Thoreau, he attempted to convert others to his religion, or at least "gain a hearing on behalf of Nature." He wrote with a growing sense of urgency. In the few short years he had been exploring the Sierras, Muir had witnessed the loss of hundreds of thousands of acres of beloved meadows and woods to sheep ranchers and loggers, and could anticipate a day when there would be no ancient sequoia trees—the largest and oldest living things on earth—left standing. In 1889, Muir joined forces with other preservationists to lobby in Washington for the creation of Yosemite National Park, following the precedent of Yellowstone National Park, which had been established in 1872. The effort succeeded in 1890, thanks in large part to Muir's eloquence. In 1892 some of the men who had been active in the Yosemite campaign joined together to form an association to defend the integrity of the new park. John Muir was the unanimous choice for president of the newly incorporated Sierra Club.

Darwin, Thoreau, and Muir represent a reaction against the classical science of Descartes and Bacon, a diametrically opposed belief about the relationship between man and nature. This fundamental opposition carries through to present-day conflicts between environmentalism and industrial science. Historian T. O'Riordan has described these opposing philosophies as, respectively, *technocentrism* and *ecocentrism*. The technocentrist view holds that nature exists for the benefit of man, and that man can and should control the forces of nature to its own ends. The ecocentrist believes that man is part of nature, dependent upon it for his existence, and must live within nature's limits if he is to survive at all. There are numerous shadings within each school of thought, and most people are likely to embrace ideas with intellectual roots in both camps, vacillating between perspectives, sometimes from issue to issue. Although the technocentric philosophy is grounded in classical science and the ecocentric philosophy has roots in Romanticism, neither school has an exclusive claim on science. The rise of ecology as a legitimate scientific discipline has provided strong scientific arguments to the ecocentric camp by demonstrating both the fragility of ecosystems and humanity's ultimate dependence upon them.

Rachel Carson fits comfortably into the ecocentrist line stretching from Gilbert White to Darwin, Thoreau, and Muir. Like her predecessors, she is associated with a specific landscape—the rugged Maine coast, where she built and maintained a summer home. And as it was for Thoreau and Muir, it was the desecration of her "personal" environment, a clear and present threat to the "web of life" she so vigorously celebrated, that stirred her to action. But the massive introduction of synthetic industrial chemicals into the biosphere gave her a far more insidious and menacing theme to tackle than the mere greed and wastefulness of men that had so incensed the nineteenth-century naturalists. In another sense Carson's task was easier, for the modern environmentalist would not have to argue the question of whether or not one's soul suffered for lack of a relationship with nature—a mystical and subjective argument advanced by Thoreau and Muir—but could focus instead on whether man could survive at all if he continued to poison his own habitat.

Rachel Carson was not the first scientist to worry that DDT and other synthetic pesticides introduced during and after World War II could have a serious environmental impact. In 1945, the *New Yorker* editorialized against the War Production Board's decision to permit the first civilian use of DDT, quoting Edwin Way Teale, former president of the New York Entomological Society, who said, "A spray as indiscriminate as DDT can upset the economy of nature as much as a revolution upsets social economy. Ninety percent of all insects are good, and if they are killed, things go out of kilter right away." During the same period, two of Carson's associates at the Fish and Wildlife Service, Clarence Cottam and Elmer Higgens, wrote scientific papers on the dangers of DDT, and Carson herself tried and failed to interest the *Reader's Digest* in an article on the subject. Thirteen years elapsed before she returned to the issue, during which time pesticide production and use increased dramatically, to the growing alarm of many scientists. In 1958 Carson again wrote to the editor of the *Reader's Digest* inquiring if the magazine might be interested in an article on the dangers of DDT, and again she was rebuffed. Nor was Carson's literary agent able to arouse interest in the subject at several other magazines for whom Carson had previously written.

The reluctance of any popular magazine to assign the article to a writer as famous as Rachel Carson suggests how sensitive and controversial a subject pesticide use would be. Later, after she had embarked on the more ambitious project of a full-length book on the subject, and during the four years it took her to research and write it, Carson had numerous indications that her thesis would be greeted by a howl of protest from the chemical industry and the various government agencies that had used or encouraged the use of pesticides. Many of her sources at the U.S. Department of Agriculture, which sponsored various pest "eradication" programs, requested anonymity before they would consent to be interviewed; some refused to talk to her at all. Carson's old friend Clarence Cottam had served on the National Academy of Sciences/National Resource Council Committee on Pest Control and Wildlife Relationships that was established in 1960 in response to a public clamor over charges that the USDA Fire Ant Eradication Program had resulted in large wildlife kills in the South. Cottam had found himself in an isolated minority on the committee, surrounded by scientists with strong chemical-industry or government affiliations. In 1962, as *Silent Spring* was being readied for the press, the committee issued its report, which, over Cottam's objections, offered a reassuring assessment of then-current pesticide use. His experience on the NAS committee led Cottam to warn Carson that when *Silent Spring* was published she would be "subjected to ridicule and condemnation by a few. Facts will not stand in the way of some confirmed pest control workers and those who are receiving substantial subsidies from pesticide manufacturers."

Carson responded to the anticipated controversy by composing a work as tightly reasoned as a lawyer's brief. In a letter she wrote to Paul Brooks, reporting her progress at the midway point, she said, "I have a comforting feeling that what I shall now be able to achieve is a synthesis of widely scattered facts, that have not heretofore been considered in relation to each other. It is now possible to build up, step by step, a really damning case against the use of these chemicals as they are now inflicted upon us." By the time she was finished, *Silent Spring* was documented with fifty-five pages of source notes; in her acknowledgments Carson cited the dozen or so "experts" who had reviewed the manuscript prior to publication. She was armored, as much as possible, for the inevitable counterattack.

In laying out the argument against DDT, then the most widely used synthetic insecticide, Carson described how the chemical entered the food chain and accumulated in the fatty tissues of animals, including human beings. She noted the pesticide's lack of discrimination between pests and "good" insects and other forms of wildlife, and demonstrated how some insect populations had already developed an immunity to DDT. DDT became popular partly because it was effective and cheap, but primarily because it was persistent in the environment. A single application on a crop would kill insects for weeks and months, and would remain toxic even after it had been diluted in the environment for decades. This very virtue of DDT—its chemical stability—was especially worrisome since the longer a toxin, or any pollutant, remains in the environment and the more widely it is disseminated, the more it accumulates and the more damage it can do. Research cited by Carson in *Silent Spring* indicated that as of the mid-1950s, DDT contaminated virtually the entire food supply. "To find a diet free from DDT and related chemicals," Carson wrote, "it seems one must go to a remote and primitive land, still lacking the amenities of civilization."

First serialized in the *New Yorker* starting the week of June 16, 1962, *Silent Spring* drew instant fire from the chemical industry and its spokesmen. Dr. Robert White-Stevens of the American Cyanamid Company, who undertook a lecture tour at the end of 1962 in defense of pesticides, offered a succinct rebuttal popular with the book's critics: "If man were to faithfully follow the teachings of Miss Carson," he said, "we would return to the Dark Ages, and the insects and diseases and vermin would once again inherit the earth." *Silent Spring,* he added, "was littered with crass assumptions and gross misinterpretations." The Nutrition Foundation—composed of fifty-four companies in the food, chemical, and allied industries—put out a "Fact Kit" on the subject of *Silent Spring.* Wrote foundation president C. G. King in a cover letter, "The problem [of distortion] is magnified in that publicists and the author's adherents among the food faddists, health quacks, and special interest groups are promoting her book as if it were scientifically irreproachable and written by a scientist." The Monsanto Chemical Company produced a lengthy parody entitled "The Desolate Year," which related the devastating inconvenience of a world where famine, disease, and insects ran amuck because chemical pesticides had been banned. Monsanto distributed five thousand copies of "The Desolate Year" to newspaper editors and book reviewers across the country.

For all the invective, however, and despite the best efforts of its paid consultants and public-relations heavies, the chemical industry did not succeed in discrediting Rachel Carson. Too many eminent scientists rose to the defense of *Silent Spring*. President John F. Kennedy ordered the President's Science Advisory Committee to look into the issue, and its report, *Use of Pesticides,* issued on May 15, 1963, was, according to the journal *Science,* a "fairly thorough-going vindication of Rachel Carson's *Silent Spring* thesis." As a result, pesticide use came under much closer government scrutiny and control; DDT was eventually banned. The terms of debate changed from *whether* pesticides might be dangerous to *which* pesticides were dangerous, and the burden of proof shifted largely from the opponents of unrestrained pesticide use to the chemicals' manufacturers. The otherwise booming aerosol business charted for the first time a precipitate decline in the sale of the very product that had launched it.

But the most important legacy of *Silent Spring* was a new public awareness that nature was vulnerable to human intervention. Rachel Carson had made a radical proposal: that, at times, technological progress is so fundamentally at odds with natural processes that it must be curtailed. Few people rejoiced in the existence of the wilderness, as had Thoreau and Muir; most hardly noticed or cared when some more of it disappeared; but the threats that Carson had outlined—the contamination of the food chain, cancer, genetic damage, the deaths of entire species— were too frightening to ignore. For the first time the need to regulate industry in order to protect the environment became widely accepted: environmentalism was born.

Industry's reaction to *Silent Spring* was vehement because the chemical makers recognized in Carson's words a threat not simply to a single family of products. They knew that what she had written of one synthetic chemical could be true about any synthetic chemical, for who could predict what a chemical might do once it was loose in the environment, especially over long periods of time? There was no way anyone could know for certain, and it would be impossible to prove conclusively the safety of each and every chemical compound before marketing it, particularly with respect to long-term, cumulative environmental harm.

Carson was well aware of the larger implications in her work. Appearing on a *CBS Reports* special entitled "The Silent Spring of Rachel Carson" in April 1963, she said:

> We still talk in terms of conquest. We still haven't become mature enough to think of ourselves as only a tiny part of a vast and incredible universe. Man's attitude toward nature is today critically important simply because we have now acquired a fateful power to alter and destroy nature. But man is a part of nature, and his war against nature is inevitably a war against himself. . . . Now I truly believe that we in this generation must come to terms with nature, and I think we're challenged as mankind has never been challenged before to prove our maturity and our mastery, not of nature, but of ourselves.

Thus, industry's fears were hardly misplaced if it chose to read the challenge to pesticides as an ominous portent. Clearly, no one concerned about restoring balance to nature would long confine his or her interest to pesticides. Thus, business as usual could proceed only if Rachel Carson's entire ecocentric position was resisted. Nature could not possibly be vulnerable to man, if it was man's destiny to control nature.

John Muir was years ahead of his time in arguing that nature had as much right as humans to exist. "Any fool can destroy trees, they cannot run away," he wrote in 1897, "and if they could, they would still be destroyed—chased and hunted down as long as fun or a dollar could be got out of their bark hides, branching horns, or magnificent bole backbones. . . . God has cared for these trees, saved them from drought, disease, avalanches, and a thousand straining, leveling tempests and floods; but he cannot save them from fools."

Muir was surely the best propagandist that trees ever had, but it was a contemporary of Muir's who also loved forests, Gifford Pinchot, who would lobby more successfully for government protection of trees by citing the patriotic need to husband and replenish natural resources for America's future use. Equally zealous, but far more moderate in his aims than Muir, Pinchot devised the government policies that controlled American land-management practices well into the twentieth century.

The two men met in 1896, when Muir was the legendary Old Man of the Sierras and Pinchot, at the age of thirty-one, had just been appointed secretary of a National Academy of Sciences commission designated by the Department of the Interior to inspect and report on the condition of the nation's forest lands. The first national park, Yellowstone, had been established in 1872; in 1885 New York State set aside some 3 million acres in the Adirondacks primarily to protect watersheds; and in 1891 an act of Congress gave the president the authority to set aside public lands covered by forest or undergrowth. President Benjamin Harrison immediately established some 13 million acres of forest reserves. The new reserves marked the first step away from earlier government land-use policies, which had chiefly consisted of giving land away and encouraging its settlement and exploitation. Yet the establishment of the reserves launched a debate about how they ought to be managed, and sparked a fierce competition among preservationists and cattlemen, tourist promoters and lumber and mining interests. Pinchot, who had studied European forest-management practices at the French École Nationale Forestière in Nancy, would provide a strong voice on the Forestry Commission in favor of resolving the dispute over public lands with a policy of "multiple use" and "practical forestry."

Muir and Pinchot became acquainted when the NAS Forestry Commission reached Montana in July 1896. Muir, Pinchot wrote in his memoirs, *Breaking New Ground,* was "in his late fifties, tall, thin, cordial, and a most fascinating talker. I took to him at once. It amazed me to learn that he never carried even a fishhook with him on his solitary explorations. He said fishing wasted too much time." Later, when the commission reached the Grand Canyon, Muir and Pinchot "spent an unforgettable day on the rim of the prodigious chasm, letting it soak in. I remember that at first we mistook for rocks the waves of rapids in the mud-laden Colorado, a mile below us. And when we came across a tarantula he wouldn't let me kill it. He said it had as much right there as we did." The two men decided to spend the night on the canyon rim, making their beds of cedar boughs. "It was such an evening as I never had before or since," Pinchot wrote, choosing not to mention that he and Muir had stood on their heads to make the canyon colors seem even more vivid—a practice Muir advocated—and had burned some cedar as an incense offering to the gods.

The fundamental differences between Muir and Pinchot were momentarily masked, perhaps by the sheer force of Muir's personality. But they would quickly emerge. In 1897, Pinchot was appointed "confidential forest agent" in the Interior Department. On a tour of the West to lobby for federal management of forest reserves, Pinchot remarked to a group of shepherds that he had no objection to allowing sheep to graze in national forest preserves. Muir, who had written that sheep were "hooved locusts," happened to be staying in the same Seattle hotel at the time, and he angrily confronted Pinchot in the hotel lobby, asking Pinchot if he had been correctly quoted in a Seattle newspaper. When Pinchot confirmed that he had, Muir exclaimed, "Then I want nothing more to do with you." Although Pinchot later wrote that Muir had been right in his characterization of sheep, the rupture between the two men proved to be permanent.

Muir's unwillingness to even consider compromise helped Pinchot position himself as the reasonable moderate on issues of national resource management. Most of his energies went to defending the forests against encroachment by private interests, but first and foremost, Pinchot believed in the forests' utility; forestry, he often said, was tree farming, and forests should be managed to obtain the maximum sustained yield of lumber. Complete preservation of forests, to Pinchot's way of thinking, was as wrongheaded as clear-cutting with no thought for the forests' regeneration. Not surprisingly, he opposed the creation of national parks.

Pinchot was appointed chief of the Forestry Division in the Department of Agriculture in 1898. His period of greatest influence commenced in 1901, when Theodore Roosevelt, a famous outdoorsman, ascended to the presidency upon the assassination of President William McKinley. Though his rank was below that of a cabinet officer, Pinchot was one of the most powerful men in the Roosevelt administration, particularly after 1905 when Congress agreed to withdraw the forest reserves from the Department of the Interior and transfer them to Pinchot's Forestry Division, which was renamed the U.S. Forest Service. Pinchot moved quickly to rename the reserves "national forests"—to get away from the preservationist connotations of the word "reserves."

Pinchot won the support of the nation's timber interests by pointing out that forest preservation was in their own long-term interest, and with the president of the United States as his political patron, he was able to implement his ideas about forestry—namely to develop and *use* the forests—on a colossal scale. In 1907, when he was at the height of his power, Pinchot consolidated his thinking under a single rubric. It occurred to Pinchot that there was "one question instead of many, one gigantic single problem that must be solved if the generations, as they came and went, were to live civilized, happy, useful lives in the lands which the Lord their God had given them." This idea was the *conservation* of natural resources, for "a constant and sufficient supply of natural resources is the basic human problem."

Encompassing as the concept seemed to be, conservation could not satisfy all the competing interests in the forests; in particular, it made no allowance for wilderness. The deep rift between Pinchot's brand of conservation and John Muir's advocacy of wilderness preservation had widened in 1906 when Pinchot supported a proposal by the city of San Francisco to build a dam in the Hetch Hetchy Valley in Yosemite National Park. For Muir the project represented an intolerable desecration of God's finest work. "Dam Hetch Hetchy!" he wrote in 1912. "As well dam for water tanks the people's cathedrals and churches, for no holier temple has ever been consecrated by the heart of man." But for Pinchot the question was "whether the advantage of leaving this valley in a state of nature is greater than . . . using it for the benefit of the city of San Francisco." "The fundamental principle of the whole conservation policy is that of use," he explained in testimony before the House Committee on the Public Lands, "to take every part of the land and its resources and put it to that use in which it will serve the most people." The issue was not entirely clear-cut even among many progressive members of the San Francisco–based Sierra Club, especially in light of the fact that Hetch Hetchy was, by most accounts, the lesser of Yosemite's two spectacular alpine valleys. Many supported the reservoir proposal as an acceptable sacrifice in the interest of liberating the city from water monopolies and placing public utilities under public ownership. Muir was derided as an old crackpot who, as San Francisco Mayor James D. Phelan testified, would "sacrifice his own family for the preservation of beauty." Congress voted in 1913 to permit the damming of Hetch Hetchy.

"There are just two things on this material earth," Pinchot wrote in *Breaking New Ground*, "people and natural resources," thus giving explicit voice to his basic underlying assumption that humankind exists somehow outside of nature. This was the commonsense view. To believe otherwise was to risk being labeled foolish or impractical. Still, as historian Roderick Nash has pointed out, it was highly significant that Hetch Hetchy provoked a controversy in the first place. "One hundred or even fifty years earlier," he noted in *Wilderness and the American Mind*, "a proposal to dam a wilderness river would not have occasioned the slightest ripple of public protest. Traditional American assumptions about the use of undeveloped countryside did not include reserving it in national parks for its recreational, aesthetic, and inspirational values. The emphasis was all the other way—on civilizing it in the name of progress and prosperity."

John Muir contracted pneumonia and died the year after Hetch Hetchy was lost. He was seventy-six, but according to some of his followers, he died of a broken heart. The myth of the great man's martyrdom has endured as a kind of shrine to the eternal and perhaps unresolvable quarrel between Muir's ecocentric philosophy of "preservation" and Pinchot's technocentric philosophy of "conservation." When the issue broadened in the 1960s to include the use of toxic pesticides and herbicides, and the various problems associated with polluted water and air, the underlying question remained the same: whether humans ought to impinge upon nature, or whether it is in their ultimate best interest to preserve some elements of nature in the "wild" state.

Around the time Rachel Carson's *Silent Spring* was awakening public consciousness to an environment threatened by pesticides, a land-use fight was taking shape that would help spark fundamental changes in the law, altering the way Americans thought about their environmental responsibility. This pivotal campaign began quietly enough on September 27, 1962, when the Consolidated Edison Company of New York announced plans—reported on the front page of the *New York Times*—to build a $162 million hydroelectric pumped-storage plant at Storm King Mountain on the west bank of the Hudson River, some forty miles north of New York City. The plant was to be of unusual design; it would pump water out of the Hudson to a reservoir atop Storm King Mountain during periods of ample power supply, then release the water in the reservoir, permitting it to flow back through the plant's turbines to generate electricity during times of peak usage.

The intention was to help the utility meet exceptional surges in demand for power. With the proliferation of air-conditioning, Con Edison had fallen far behind in its ability to meet the electricity needs of the New York metropolitan area. The utility promised that the Storm King plant, acting as a "storage battery," would put an end to the power "brownouts" that routinely afflicted the region.

Storm King, the surrounding Hudson Highlands, and indeed the entire Hudson River Valley, held a special place in American culture as the distinctively American wilderness venerated by the nation's earliest writers—James Fenimore Cooper, Nathaniel Hawthorne, and Washington Irving—as well as the Hudson Valley School of landscape artists, including Thomas Cole, Asher Durand, George Inness, and Frederic Church. For the writers and artists, part of the area's appeal was its proximity to New York City, where their work was patronized. This proximity remains part of the Hudson River Valley's appeal today. Thus, the threat to Storm King offended a historic legacy of particular relevance to both preservationists and city-dwelling nature lovers.

The east side of the Hudson was mansion country, home to New York's most elite citizens since Dutch times, where the baronial homes of the Roosevelts, Vanderbilts, and Goulds looked out commandingly over the wide Hudson and the near slopes of the Catskills. The west side of the river had long been considered "Indian country," but a second wave of affluent homesteaders in the early nineteenth century had claimed the best real estate on the western shore, including the picturesque neighboring communities of Cornwall and Cornwall-on-Hudson at Storm King Mountain.

Opposition to Con Edison's plans for Storm King was slow to organize. There was substantial public support for modernizing Con Edison's aging facilities and no precedent of opposition to large-scale public-utilities projects. The mayor of Cornwall-on-Hudson, Michael Donahue, supported the project as a boon to the local economy, despite the fact that his town's reservoir would be drained and excavated if it went ahead. (Con Ed had promised to replace it.) Even the Hudson River Conservation Society, adhering to the principle of multiple use, favored the Storm King plant, objecting only to the proposed power lines across the gorge, which would carry the plant's electricity to New York City. Con Edison agreed in response to use underwater cables at an added cost of $6 million. When, in March and April 1963, the Federal Power Commission (FPC) first invited public comment on Con Edison's license application to build the plant, no objections were raised.

Unlike the Hetch Hetchy Valley, Storm King Mountain was not protected as part of a national park, and although some areas of the mountain fell within state park boundaries and privately owned reserves, Con Edison had already acquired the land it needed to build the power plant and associated reservoir and tunnels. Nor was Storm King an unspoiled wilderness. In 1876, the Storm King Highway, an engineering marvel of its day, was chiseled into the flank of the mountain between the village of Cornwall and West Point—site of the United States Military Academy—five miles south. Most of the land in the Storm King vicinity was in fact privately owned, the best of it by some twenty wealthy families whose ancestors had built country estates on the mountain. Initially, the controversy over Storm King pitted this landed gentry against the local population of Cornwall and other decaying river towns: the rich, who wanted to protect their view of the Hudson Highlands, against the working people, like Mayor Donahue, who favored economic development. Among the earliest and most vocal opponents of Storm King were Wall Street attorney Stephen P. Duggan and his wife, Beatrice "Smokey" Duggan, whose mother had donated to the town of Cornwall the pond that served as the town's water supply, and which was now threatened with destruction.

Stephen Duggan was an influential figure in the New York legal community, a partner in the prestigious firm of Simpson, Thacher & Bartlett, and not intimidated by the powerful interests who wanted to build the Storm King plant. He was fiercely loyal to the Highlands, a region whose blue, rolling mountains and splendid river vistas he knew to be "more beautiful than anything in the Rhine Valley." Duggan had a good idea how to defend Storm King. In the late 1950s he had represented a consortium of oil companies looking to construct a refinery in Rhode Island, not far from the lavish summer homes of Newport. To the complete surprise of Duggan and the consortium, the summer residents in the area formed a committee, hired one of Rhode Island's most fearsome litigators, Cornelius Moore, who was known respectfully in New England legal circles as "the Old Fox," and proceeded to blast Duggan and his client out of court with a parade of "expert" witnesses who linked the planned refinery with all sorts of anticipated environmental and biological damage to Narragansett Bay. By the end of the trial, Duggan later recalled, even the presiding judge had grown hostile to the idea of the refinery. Duggan never forgot this particular comeuppance, and having once been on the receiving end of aroused public opposition, he had a healthy regard for its use.

The Duggans and other early opponents of the Storm King plant got an unexpected boost in April 1963, when Con Edison released an "artistic rendering" of what the finished plant would look like. In the drawing the pumped-storage facility was not drawn to scale but appeared much larger than it would actually be relative to the surroundings. After the drawing was published, the Duggans began to hear from many of their alarmed neighbors, and in November 1963 the Duggans and a dozen others organized to wage a legal and public relations campaign against Con Edison. They called themselves the Scenic Hudson Preservation Conference.

The parochial interests of wealthy landowners did not at first engender much sympathy in Cornwall. In a referendum held in the summer of 1963, the residents voted 499 to 25 to sell their reservoir to Con Edison, and Duggan found himself shunned by acquaintances and storekeepers in town once word got out that he and his wife were attempting to orchestrate opposition. But in the spring of 1964, Scenic Hudson broadened its base of regional support when it joined forces with Walter Boardman, director of the Nature Conservancy, and Leopold Rothschild, an elderly New York attorney who was president of the New York–New

Jersey Trail Conference and who had independently begun to campaign against the plant. This was not Rothschild's first conservation battle along the Hudson; in the 1930s he led an unsuccessful effort to halt the construction of the George Washington Bridge linking Upper Manhattan with historic Fort Lee, New Jersey, and the spectacular river bluffs known as the Palisades.

Something new was happening. Landowners had for decades fought the invasion of highways, railroads, and suburbia into their privileged domains, while nature lovers like Rothschild mounted crusades to save particular scenic or wilderness areas. But the Storm King controversy forged a new alliance between blue bloods wielding money and influence and populist, mainstream conservationists. This coalition would propel Storm King from the obscure jurisdiction of the Federal Power Commission—where such matters were traditionally resolved with little fuss—to the front pages of the New York newspapers.

The struggle, at first, was heavily tilted in Con Edison's favor. The issues before the FPC were largely technical in nature: Was the plant needed? Was Con Edison capable of building and running it? And so on. Aesthetic considerations were irrelevant. Although Scenic Hudson testified in opposition to Con Edison's license application at several preliminary hearings—Hudson River historian Carl Carmer assuring the power commissioners, "We believe that ugliness begets ugliness and that nature's beauty, once destroyed, may never be restored by the artifice of man"—the Federal Power Commission nonetheless voted in March 1965 to grant Con Edison its license. Scenic Hudson attorney Lloyd Garrison immediately planned an appeal.

There was little precedent for the federal judiciary to overrule decisions made by regulatory agencies like the Federal Power Commission, and judges were traditionally reluctant to involve themselves in technical matters outside their expertise. Faced with this impediment, Duggan, former FPC attorney Dale Doty, Garrison, and Duggan's law partner Whitney North "Mike" Seymour, Jr., devised a novel strategy. Rather than question the merits of the Storm King power plant, Garrison argued in *Scenic Hudson Preservation Conference* v. *Federal Power Commission,* filed before the Federal Circuit Court of Appeals in New York in August 1965, that the Federal Power Commission had failed to protect the public interest in accordance with its congressional mandate under the Federal Power Act (1920), by not adequately considering all the factors that were of interest to the public, namely, the beauty and historic significance of Storm King Mountain.

Given their unprecedented strategy, Scenic Hudson members were not terribly optimistic. Duggan and another Scenic Hudson attorney, Albert Butzel, later credited Lloyd Garrison's well-written brief and his dignified standing in the eyes of the circuit court judges for improving their chances. Garrison, then in his sixties, was the great-great-grandson of the famed nineteenth-century Boston abolitionist William Lloyd Garrison. He had had a distinguished career as an administrator at the National Labor Relations Board and in July 1965 had been elected president of the New York City Board of Education. His was an eminent name associated with civil liberties and the public good.

At the circuit court hearing, Butzel recalled, Garrison was "quiet but passionate," while Con Edison attorney Randall LeBoeuf offended the judges with a show of arrogance, once even referring to the Scenic Hudson litigators as "bird-watchers." When LeBoeuf stated that the plant Con Edison had designed would actually improve the beauty of Storm King Mountain, the court was incredulous. On December 29, 1965, it ruled in favor of Scenic Hudson, setting aside Con Edison's license and ordering the FPC to hold new hearings. Scenic Hudson, the court ruled, had "standing to sue" in the case. "In order to insure that the Federal Power Commission will adequately protect the public interest in the esthetic, conservational, and recreational aspects of power development," the court said, "those who by their activities and conduct have exhibited a special interest in such areas, must be held to be included in the class of 'aggrieved' parties."

The decision was a legal landmark. For the first time, a conservation group had been permitted to sue to protect the public interest. Although Scenic Hudson had no personal or economic interest in Storm King— the usual basis for standing—the court ruled that it nonetheless could be construed to be an "injured party" and was entitled to judicial review of an agency ruling. The Federal Power Commission's renewed proceedings, the court said, "must include as a basic concern the preservation of natural beauty and of national historic shrines, keeping in mind that, in our affluent society, the cost of a project is only one of several factors to be considered."

The Storm King battle would be fought for another decade before Con Edison was finally forced to abandon plans for the plant. The 1965 circuit court ruling remained the significant legal precedent, however, helping to establish the legitimacy of environmental issues and opening the way for lawyers and the courts to play a highly significant role in all manner of land-use and environmental battles.

8.

THE HIGHEST USE OF THE COURTROOM

STEPHEN DUGGAN, Lloyd Garrison, and David Sive of the Sierra Club had relished their pioneering role in the Scenic Hudson Company. Forging new case law and establishing precedents, and forcing issues onto the nation's legislative agenda, was a political and intellectual challenge. For lawyers like Sive, who had long had a personal interest in conservation matters, it was especially gratifying to stop despoilers of the environment before they could rev up their bulldozers.

The Storm King experience had shown that while dramatic progress through the courts was possible, it was extremely expensive to take on an entrenched, powerful interest like Con Edison. "We were amateurs," Duggan later reflected, "licking stamps and dragging our wives and kids in to stuff envelopes." Riding along Manhattan's West Side Highway in a taxi one afternoon in the fall of 1969, Duggan exclaimed to law partner Mike Seymour, "This is no way to run a railroad. If we're going to capture this issue and make some sense of it, we've got to get more professional." Duggan began to envision a new type of law firm that would advance the cause of environmental law by representing selected plaintiffs in environmental battles across the country.

*　　*　　*

The spirit of legal activism that motivated attorneys like Duggan, Sive, and Seymour was richly nourished by the social and political activism of the sixties. Civil rights attorneys demonstrated in the late fifties and early sixties that the courts could be a major force for social change in the area of race relations. It was the NAACP Legal Defense and Educational Fund (NAACP/LDF) that developed the concept of "test-case law" and pursued the strategy of filing the lawsuits that led up to the 1954 Supreme Court ruling, *Brown* v. *Board of Education of Topeka, Kansas,* which found racially segregated schools unconstitutional and thus helped spark the civil rights movement. Then, in the summer of 1964, some four hundred lawyers and law students joined the Mississippi Summer Project, volunteering critically needed legal support to civil rights workers struggling to win basic civil rights, including the right to vote, for black Mississippians. Unlike traditional lawyers who waited for clients to come to them with a legal problem, the lawyers who went to Mississippi assumed an active political role; many returned north with a new faith in their ability as lawyers to help foster nonviolent social change. To others the Mississippi veterans presented an inspirational example of lawyers devoting themselves to the public interest. Indeed, the phrase "public-interest law," and the idea that this sort of legal practice might be a separate branch of law with particular relevance to modern social needs like environmental protection, dates from this same period of the mid-1960s.

Historically, the provision of free legal services to the poor and disenfranchised dates back much further, at least to 1876, when the first legal-aid society was formed by the German Society of New York to provide legal assistance to recent German immigrants to the United States. As distinct from *pro bono publico* work, which individual lawyers might occasionally undertake as a personal charity, the legal-aid society was conceived as an ongoing, independent institution staffed by full-time lawyers. The legal-aid movement—providing legal representation, as a matter of democratic principle, to those who could not provide it for themselves—spread to over fifty cities by 1940.

Another antecedent to the public-interest law of the 1960s and 1970s, the American Civil Liberties Union (ACLU), was founded in 1917 as a citizens' lobby to defend the First Amendment rights of pacifists and conscientious objectors during World War I. Unlike a legal-aid society, the ACLU depended on volunteer lawyers to file *amicus curiae* (friend of the court) briefs, in selected lawsuits. Rather than represent individual clients, the ACLU sought to defend large principles and serve as a watchdog on the government, soliciting the general public for support. Lobbying was at least as important as litigation.

The NAACP/LDF, founded in 1939, combined the full-time, independently supported staff of the traditional legal-aid society with the ACLU's orientation toward constitutional principles, and then took on a long-term objective: the eventual overruling of the notorious 1896 Supreme Court ruling in *Plessy* v. *Ferguson,* which permitted the segregation of the races in "separate but equal" institutions. The fund's strategy was to seek court rulings in carefully selected test cases that would serve as precedents demonstrating that "separate" was inherently *unequal,* building step by step from the most egregious examples of inequality to the final case that would be appealed to the Supreme Court. Because the strategy paid off so spectacularly, the NAACP/LDF became the most influential model for the practice of public-interest law.

While the NAACP/LDF forged ahead in the establishment of legal rights for African Americans, it simultaneously created a need for those rights to be defended in practice as, for example, by the lawyers who went to Mississippi in the summer of 1964. Hence, the legal-aid movement was revitalized in the 1950s and 1960s, funded in part by private foundations that supported progress in race relations and in part by the federal government, which in 1966, as part of President Lyndon Johnson's War on Poverty, started to finance a Legal Services Program under the auspices of the Office of Economic Opportunity. Foundation and federal support provided what had always been the essential scarce ingredient—money—in the successful practice of public-interest law. Indeed, its reliance upon private or public subsidy is a defining characteristic of public-interest law, since its goal is to provide legal services precisely to those who cannot compete for them in the private market either because they are too poor or because, as in the case of consumers or environmentalists, their interests are "diffuse."

In law, then, as in many other spheres, the civil rights movement was the wellspring for subsequent sixties' movements. The anti–Vietnam War, student, feminist, gay, consumer, and environmental movements all took inspiration and borrowed tactics from it.

Perhaps the key figure was Ralph Nader, whose 1965 book, *Unsafe at Any Speed,* did for badly designed automobiles what *Silent Spring* had done for persistent pesticides. Nader, a 1958 graduate of Harvard Law School and the son of Lebanese immigrants, published his first article on auto safety in *The Nation* in April 1959. In 1964, at the age of thirty, he took a job in Washington as an aide to Assistant Secretary of Labor Daniel Patrick Moynihan. Like Nader, Moynihan was concerned about the high fatality rate on the nation's highways, the leading cause of death for people between the ages of five and thirty; he hired Nader to prepare a report—"The Context, Condition, and Recommended Direction of

Federal Activity in Highway Safety." Nader very soon became an auto-safety expert. In late 1965, when auto safety was the subject of obscure Senate subcommittee hearings under the chairmanship of Senator Abraham Ribicoff of Connecticut, Nader scooped the Congress with *Unsafe at Any Speed,* rendering his expertise in hard-hitting, detailed, and emotional prose. In Chapter 1, by way of launching his exposé, he took on General Motors' new Chevrolet Corvair, describing its design failures and their potentially fatal consequences in exacting detail, while terming GM's production and marketing of the Corvair "one of the greatest acts of industrial irresponsibility in the present century." "How many victims of Corvair tuck-under—those who survived—know why their vehicle suddenly went out of control?" Nader asked. "General Motors' Charles Chayne can say, with little fear of contradiction by consumers, that 'excellence of automotive engineering is almost taken for granted by the public.' Beggars at the trough have no alternative." Nader went on to thoroughly demolish the automobile industry's long-standing contention that bad drivers, not faulty cars, were the primary cause of car accidents.

Unsafe at Any Speed was not at first widely read, nor was it even widely reviewed. Nader and the issue of auto safety might have remained relatively unknown, at least for some years, if not for the intervention of General Motors, which hired private detectives to investigate Ralph Nader and find out "what makes him tick." Some two months after the publication of *Unsafe at Any Speed,* in early 1966, Nader noticed he was being followed. Twice, strange women propositioned him in public. His friends and family were questioned. The story was picked up in the press and GM President James Roche was forced to admit that the company had in fact conducted an investigation of Nader to ascertain whether there was a link between Nader and any of the 106 Corvair-related lawsuits that had been filed against the company. The entire affair was aired, much to GM's embarrassment, before the Ribicoff subcommittee.

The publicity propelled Nader's book to a much wider public. GM had tried to discredit him, but in failing to uncover any personal motive behind Nader's interest in auto safety had succeeded only in underscoring his unusual integrity and selfless dedication. Congress responded by passing the Traffic and Motor Vehicle Safety Act (1966), which established federal safety standards for automobiles—a remarkable victory for citizen-activist Nader. Of equal importance was Nader's arrival as an effective gadfly in the unofficial processes of government. Nader used most of the $60,000 in royalties he earned from *Unsafe at Any Speed* and an additional $425,000 he won in a 1970 out-of-court settlement of an invasion-of-privacy suit against GM to finance other efforts in consumer protection. He began by establishing the Center for Automobile Safety —in practice, if not in name, a public-interest law firm—to monitor the National Highway Traffic Safety Administration.

But Nader had quickly expanded his interests far beyond automobile safety. In the summer of 1968 he recruited a group of young, predominantly Ivy League law students to conduct an investigation of the Federal Trade Commission. Their study, which concluded that the FTC was ineffective, drew considerable publicity, and the young people who conducted it were dubbed "Nader's Raiders." That fall Nader obtained foundation grants to establish the Center for the Study of Responsive Law. Nader study groups at the center investigated air and water pollution, the health effects of smoking, pesticide misuse, and the Interstate Commerce Commission, among other subjects. By the summer of 1969 there were a hundred Nader's Raiders working on various projects in Washington; by the summer of 1970, there were two hundred. Despite the low, subsistence wages offered, thousands applied for the available positions. Nader's Raiders splintered into a number of interlocking organizations, including, in mid-1970, the Public Interest Research Group (PIRG), which was staffed by lawyers. By then, it seemed as if Nader had almost single-handedly created a new sixties-style reform movement—consumer advocacy—and had found dozens of justifications for public-interest law.

Environmental issues fell within Nader's consumer-oriented universe. (He had discussed the contribution automobiles made to the formation of smog in *Unsafe at Any Speed*.) Environmental pollution, he explained, was a form of "compulsory consumption," an unwanted cost forced upon the consumer. But by the late 1960s the environment had become a big enough issue to warrant the undivided attention of its own corps of legal activists, and its own branch of law. In 1967 the first law firm explicitly dedicated to environmental law was formed. The Environmental Defense Fund (EDF) was an outgrowth of a pioneering lawsuit filed in April 1966 by a group of Long Island scientists and citizens seeking to restrain the use of DDT by the Suffolk County Mosquito Control Commission. The suit began when Carol Yannacone of Patchogue, New York, learned there had been a fish kill at Yaphank Lake, where she had swum as a girl. Encouraged by the precedent of the *Scenic Hudson* case, Yannacone's husband, thirty-one-year-old attorney Victor Yannacone, filed a class-action suit on behalf of his wife and all the citizens of the county, whose environment was degraded by the use of persistent pesticides. In the course of preparing his case, Yannacone joined forces with a number of scientists affiliated with the nearby Stony Brook campus of the State University of New York and the Brookhaven National Laboratory, who served as expert witnesses in the November 1966 trial. Although the court eventually ruled that the state legislature, not the court, must determine appropriate pesticide-use policy, Yannacone and the scientists had so thoroughly enjoyed the experience of subjecting public officials to cross-examination, and were so encouraged by the publicity resulting from the suit, that in October 1967 they formally incorporated, with the avowed aim of litigating test cases and establishing legal precedents in environmental law. In November 1967, the EDF filed suit in Berrien County, Michigan, to prevent use of the pesticide dieldrin to control the Japanese beetle in fruit orchards. Again the EDF lost but generated publicity, and promptly filed a second Michigan suit to prevent the use of DDT to control Dutch elm disease in the Grand Rapids area.

Under the flamboyant and aggressive leadership of lawyer Yannacone, a classic sixties personality who, according to a close colleague, really thought he could "save the world," the EDF was perceived as a militant organization, even by fellow environmentalists. "Sue the bastards!" was the group's unofficial motto. But lawyers traditionally prefer the maxim that "bad cases make bad law," and believe that test litigation in particular ought not to be pursued recklessly, for if a case is poorly chosen or argued, or is brought before the wrong court, the resultant landmark ruling can easily go the other way and set the cause back. And although, in the first cases it brought, EDF won publicity, it lost rulings. "I think there needs to be more consultation with some people who are older and stuffier," commented David Brower, the plenty-militant director of the Sierra Club, in reference to the EDF's first outings.

In September 1969 some seventy-five lawyers interested in conservation gathered for a conference in Warrenton, Virginia, in an effort to orient themselves and consolidate their thinking. The lawyers debated strategies: whether legal reform should be sought by increments in common-law rulings or by seeking a broad Supreme Court ruling establishing a constitutional right to a clean and healthy environment, and whether their focus should be on the courts or on lobbying for new legislation. The EDF's Victor Yannacone spoke out for impatient radicalism and provocative litigation. "It's about time the legal profession got some ecological sophistication," he declared. "We have to invent causes of action. We have to find new legal rules to overcome traditional government secrecy. Administrative agencies are the abortive offspring of modern legislation. Every bit of progressive social legislation of the last 50 years has come about only after litigation. It's the highest use of the courtroom—even when we lose—to focus public attention and disseminate information about intolerable conditions."

*   *   *

The 1960s included both political movements with specific aims, like the civil rights, anti–Vietnam War, and feminist movements, and the revolution in lifestyle associated with the hippies, whose hallmark was a rejection of traditional social values, which for many included a back-to-the-land ethic. The environmental movement, cresting with the massive demonstrations of Earth Day, on April 22, 1970, in some ways represented a synthesis of the various sixties upheavals. For many veterans of the civil rights and antiwar movements, environmentalism arrived just as those earlier crusades lost their momentum. For their part, hippies gave environmentalism a less political, friendlier cast. Hippies embraced Mother Nature, or her emblems—wearing long hair and eating homemade whole-wheat bread, for example—in reaction to the prevailing technocentric direction of modern society. Just as Thoreau and Muir were antiurban, antimodern, and antimaterialistic, so were the hippies, and for the same reasons: because man's alienation from nature alienated man from himself, and a society alienated from nature was a lost society.

Environmentalism was big enough to embrace the sort of scientific alarm raised by Rachel Carson, the activist bent of sixties' political movements and the neo-Romantic sensibility of the hippies. On college campuses, by the late sixties, these various impulses had coalesced into a widespread belief that the abuse of nature by humans was wrong, and that something ought to be done about it. Indeed, student groups at campuses across the country were rapidly organizing to fight pollution and defend natural areas from overdevelopment, borrowing protest tactics from the civil rights and antiwar movements. It was in this spirit—and the concurrent spirit of legal activism—that in 1968 Gus Speth, a second-year student at Yale Law School, began to think about how his legal education might somehow be applied to environmental problems.

The son of a farm-machinery salesman in Orangeburg County, South Carolina, James Gustave Speth, Jr., grew up in a time and place where environmental problems were all but unheard of. Like most farm children, he learned to hunt and fish at an early age, and it never crossed his mind that the countryside surrounding his home could ever disappear. In college he developed a keen interest in public policy, and so had ended up at Yale Law School. Since the late 1920s, when future Supreme Court Justice William O. Douglas was one of the most prominent members of the faculty, Yale had cultivated a progressive reputation, as a school where law was taught not as a mere trade but instead was understood to be a fundamentally political institution, reflective of the larger moral and ethical pressures at work in society. In a reaction against the traditional case-method study of law with its emphasis on legal concepts, which was practiced at Harvard, scholars at Yale developed a jurisprudence of "legal realism," which put the emphasis on what courts and judges actually did in practice, as opposed to the principles they supposedly upheld in reaching their decisions. The Yale realists "pointed to the role of human idiosyncrasy in legal decision making, stressed the uselessness of legal rules and concepts, and emphasized the importance of greater efficiency and certainty in law administration," according to legal historian Laura Kalman. By education, then, as well as by inclination, Speth and his friends Richard Ayres, John Daum, and several others who along with them served on the staff of the *Yale Law Journal,* were primed, as their graduation day grew near, to act on their social impulses. They had believed, idealistically, that an Ivy League law degree would "open doors," but were beginning to realize that the doors most widely open to even a Yale graduate led straight to private practice with a big New York or Washington firm, or to a job in government.

Seeking a way out of this dilemma and inspired by the example of the NAACP Legal Defense and Educational Fund, Speth and the others began to discuss the possibility of founding a public-interest environmental law firm. However, one of their professors, Boris Bittker, was skeptical when in 1968 Speth, Ayres, Daum, and several others approached him with their idea of forming an Environmental Legal Defense Fund modeled after the NAACP/LDF.

Bittker was a popular professor with whom the students felt a special kinship, and he in turn admired the students' ambition, but he cautioned them that he didn't welcome the prospect of losing some of the best young legal minds he had ever encountered to what he feared would prove a futile endeavor; he believed their plan to use public-interest law to argue environmental causes would founder on the lack of legal precedents. Bittker did not accept the analogy with the NAACP/Legal Defense and Educational Fund, and he reminded Speth, Ayres, and the others that from the start the NAACP/LDF had had at its disposal the Fourteenth and Fifteenth Amendments to the Constitution, which guaranteed equal citizenship rights to blacks, as well as other Reconstruction-era civil rights statutes—laws that admittedly were not observed, but that at least were on the books to be cited by enterprising civil rights lawyers.

Aspiring environmental lawyers, on the other hand, Bittker said, would have meager tools to work with. Principles of common law—including nuisance, trespass, and strict liability—would be difficult to apply to modern environmental problems because they had evolved to protect individual property rather than broad public interests. While the costs of such common-law litigation would be high and the likelihood of winning small, the potential relief it could offer was generally inadequate and localized. As for statutory law, the sixties' popular awakening to environmental problems had not yet been translated into meaningful legislation, and it was difficult for Bittker, or for anyone in 1968, to foresee how environmental legislation might affect the law, if and when such legislation was enacted.

Bittker's realistic appraisal of the challenges they faced, however, did not deter the students from going ahead with their plan. Speth had already traveled to New York City to visit David Sive, who was one of the few lawyers in the country trying to make a living practicing environmental law. Sive had put Speth in touch with Frank Barry, a legal specialist with an economic research group established by the Ford Foundation, Resources for the Future (RFF). On November 12, 1968, Barry and Ford program officer William Felling visited the Yale campus to meet the other students.

In preparation for the meeting Speth composed a draft memorandum outlining the purpose, functions, and structure of the students' proposed Environmental Legal Defense Fund. Speth wrote:

> There is a growing awareness that decisive action is necessary if this country is going to save what remains of her natural heritage and reclaim any portion of what has been destroyed. A simple extrapolation of present trends suggests a frightening world with few if any natural areas, unpolluted streams, or fresh breezes. While the fight against these trends must go on on several fronts, we are convinced that private legal action can be an effective instrument for curbing an industrial civilization's abuse of nature.

The primary function of the ELDF, Speth continued, "would be to serve as counsel or assistant to counsel in hearings and litigation that further the conservation goals of the organization." Speth anticipated that "a considerable portion of the workload would probably involve work before federal agencies." He singled out air and water pollution and wilderness preservation as "areas of concern," and envisioned the ELDF as "an organization of about twenty full-time lawyers operating out of several offices across the country"; it would be a tax-exempt corporation, supported through charitable contributions.

The very notion that a group of students—no matter how brilliant— without a single hour of courtroom experience among them might gain

Ford Foundation support to pursue an innovative area of law was auda-
cious. By the reasonable standards of any other time, Ford might have
dismissed the students with a thank-you and a handshake. But the idea
of legal remedies to environmental issues was in the air, the students were
clearly committed to it, and were gifted, so the foundation men offered
to give them a serious hearing.

Ford's relatively enlightened position on environmental issues had
resulted largely from the efforts of another foundation program officer,
Gordon Harrison. A former editor and editorial writer for the *Detroit
News* and the *New York Herald Tribune,* Harrison had joined Ford in
1963 to help staff a new office called Policy and Planning, which was
established to provide an overview of the foundation's activities and particularly to evaluate its public-affairs program, which dealt with poverty
and the problems of the inner city. After completing a lengthy report on
the public-affairs program, Harrison was asked to evaluate the foundation's conservation efforts. Immersing himself in the subject, he came to
believe there were deep implications of environmental policy in America
that Ford had not adequately recognized. Harrison submitted a report to
the trustees arguing there was much more Ford could do in the area of
conservation. Resources for the Future, he pointed out, had evolved into
a research organization whose efforts ignored a whole range of nonre-
search problems. In response to Harrison's report, the trustees established a new Ford division called Resources and Environment, and put
Harrison in charge of it.

Harrison did not agree with the trustees' preferred approach to conservation, which involved simply purchasing threatened plots of land.
Purchasing land, Harrison believed, was a wildly inefficient use of money.
In 1965 he spoke out against a $1.5 million Save-the-Redwoods grant
the trustees were eager to approve. He found it preposterous that environmental programs for protecting birds or marsh life stood a far better
chance of being funded than less romantic and more socially oriented
studies of, say, urban waste management. He spoke out increasingly in
favor of investments that would have a "multiplier effect" on society,
such as scholarship programs or biological field stations that increased
human understanding of the environment.

"Philanthropically supported conservation has tended to raise its eyes
above human settlements and their complex socially based environmental
dilemmas to a simpler world of plants and animals," Harrison observed
to his Ford colleagues in one memorandum. "[T]hey have tended to
focus on saving a little something from the juggernaut of progress, such
as wildlife, rather than challenging the process."

By the time of the November 1968 meeting between the Yale students and Harrison's representatives, Resources and Environment was well on its way to becoming one of Ford's most prolific divisions, recommending a steadily increasing number of grants. (It recommended just one in 1965 and twenty-nine in 1970.) Several professors besides Bittker sat in on the meeting with Barry and Felling, including Charles Reich, who had advised Scenic Hudson and who the following year would publish a surprise bestseller, *The Greening of America,* a book whose theme was the alleged rejuvenation of the United States thanks to precisely the sort of instinct for bold reform shown by the proposed Environmental Legal Defense Fund. The meeting was not auspicious from the students' point of view, as the Ford representatives remained pointedly noncommital. As it drew to a close, however, Speth handed Barry a copy of his draft proposal, along with a summary of the students' sparkling curricula vitae, liberally salted with magna and summa cum laudes from Harvard, Princeton, Yale, and Stanford, numerous publishing credits, awards, and law-journal positions.

Fortunately for the students, the idea of an environmental legal-defense organization could not have appealed more to Harrison's bias. He had met with EDF's Victor Yannacone, and was inclined to agree that public-interest environmental law could have a profound impact, although he was put off by Yannacone's abrasive manner. The Yale group provided Harrison with an ideal alternative. The students' records, Harrison recalled, were "so extraordinary that they had to be looked into." "We have in mind an organization," Harrison memoed his superiors, "that would . . . provide direct and supportive service in defense of citizens' environment rights, analogous to the services in defense of civil rights provided by the NAACP and the ACLU." Harrison noted, however, that such a group would require the help of the foundation and many others as well, especially at first, because "while the right to a livable world may secure Constitutional standing in time, no court has yet recognized it."

Harrison's encouragement was enough to inspire the students to organize more formally, redraft their proposal, and provide Ford with a detailed budget. The foundation's biggest reservation remained the group's youth and lack of courtroom experience. At one point in the course of the discussions, foundation representatives suggested the students affiliate with an older, more established conservation group. The students opposed the idea, convinced they could not successfully share their agenda with anyone else, and particularly not with authority figures who would try to dominate them. Part of the appeal of the ELDF was that they would be their own bosses. Harrison appreciated the importance of this, and attempted to appease both the Ford higher-ups and the students by arranging for older "advisors" who would monitor the activities of the ELDF.

By early 1969, Ford appeared on the verge of funding the group. It looked as though the students would be able to graduate from law school and begin work to save the environment right away. But an unforeseen obstacle arose. In February 1969 the House Ways and Means Committee, under the chairmanship of Arkansas Democrat Wilbur Mills, launched a probing examination of tax-exempt organizations. Ford, by far the wealthiest foundation in the country, and one of the most liberal, was a prime target. Ford's support of civil rights activity disturbed segregationist southerners like Mills. Ford had also aroused the ire of Albert Shanker, the powerful president of the United Federation of Teachers, because a Ford-backed school-decentralization project in Brooklyn had led to a number of teachers being transferred or fired. Other controversial Ford Foundation grants included one to the Citizens Advocate Center, a watchdog group that scrutinized federal agencies responsible for making policy that affected poor people and minorities; travel and study grants to eight members of the late Senator Robert F. Kennedy's staff; and support of a Congress of Racial Equality–sponsored voter-registration drive in Cleveland, which was credited with helping elect Carl Stokes as the first black mayor of a major American city. The question before the Ways and Means Committee was whether the taxpayer—in the form of exemptions to nonprofit philanthropies like Ford—should subsidize such "political" activities. One of the first witnesses called before the investigating committee was Ford Foundation president McGeorge Bundy.

A former national security advisor with the Kennedy and Johnson administrations, Bundy had been appointed president of the Ford Foundation in 1966 with a mandate to involve the organization more deeply in social change. His first year in office he declared that "full equality for all American Negroes is now the most urgent domestic concern of this country," and said that Ford would play "its full part" in working to achieve it. He vigorously defended the Ford Foundation's activism before Congress and in public. "If you were to say that foundations should do nothing with public policy questions, you would have to say that foundations should do nothing," he told a New York press conference in March 1969. But after he was called to testify before the Ways and Means Committee and recognized that Mills and his political allies fully intended to impose sharp restrictions on foundation activity, he opted for the prudent course of avoiding any new social initiatives until after Congress had considered and passed its tax-reform bill and the controversy had abated. As Harrison later remembered, "Mr. Bundy got a letter from Chairman Mills asking why we were dealing with a bunch of students, and why we were considering support for a special firm of [public interest] lawyers while others had to make their own way. . . . The Trustees then began to worry about how much of this activity could be justified as really in the public interest."

Bundy called the Yale students into his office to break the bad news to them personally. Ford could not, under the present circumstances, award them a grant, he said. Environmental litigation was bound to be controversial, and Ford already had more than enough controversy to deal with. "If you are still interested after the hearings are over," he told the young men, "come see us again."

The Tax Reform Act of 1969, passed in December, contained new restrictions on tax-exempt foundations considerably less onerous than those the more conservative legislators had originally suggested, and in January 1970, Richard Ayres contacted Ford on behalf of the entire Yale group to report that, although they had taken other jobs, including several Supreme Court clerkships, the young attorneys were still interested in obtaining Ford funding.

Neither had Gordon Harrison lost his regard for the students' plan. Coincidentally, during the hiatus from active consideration of the Yale students' proposal, the group of Scenic Hudson veterans led by attorney Stephen Duggan had approached the foundation with a remarkably similar proposal. The Duggan group had already incorporated under the name of the Natural Resources Defense Council (NRDC) and had a distinguished board of trustees, but no staff. The Yale group had a staff but no board or corporate structure. "For God's sake, why don't you all get together," Harrison implored Duggan. "You apparently have the board and the leadership and the support of the bar that we feel is necessary; we have a staff for you and it's a very exceptional group of seven very bright young men."

The students were horrified. A merger with NRDC might win them generous Ford Foundation support, but it would also bring with it a governing board composed of establishment types. The NRDC was also apprehensive. "We thought they were just a starry-eyed bunch of kids who would only get us into trouble," Duggan said. "And of course they didn't want anything to do with some stuffy Wall Street lawyers."

Still, in early January 1970, four of the students, including Speth and Ayres, met with NRDC representative Mike Seymour, who had recently been appointed U.S. attorney for the Southern District of New York. Despite their differences in age and temperament, it was apparent that the two groups had arrived by separate paths at an identical commitment, and that a merger was in everybody's best interest.

The students set forth four conditions for a merger: a formal guarantee that they, as staff members, would participate in important policy decisions; the inclusion on the board of several of their associates, including Yale professors Bittker and Reich; the establishment of a Washington, D.C., office; and salaries in the $18,000 to $20,000 range. NRDC agreed to the conditions, the students agreed to merge with NRDC, and Ford happily granted $410,000 to the fledgling organization for a period of fifteen months beginning October 1, 1970.

Environmentalism was a cause that virtually every American could support. Nobody favored dirty water and dirty air. Still, the huge official and public support for Earth Day, April 22, 1970, came as a shock. Congress stood in special recess that day. Massive rallies took place in New York, Philadelphia, Chicago, Washington, and other large cities, along with more modestly scaled observances in thousands of other towns and on college campuses. Television networks and national magazines gave extensive coverage to environmental issues. According to a National Education Association estimate, at least 10 million public-school children participated in environmental "teach-in" activities. In New York City, Fifth Avenue was closed to traffic for two hours, and an "ecological carnival" took place along Fourteenth Street. Even the Consolidated Edison Company of Storm King infamy joined in the spirit of the day, draping orange-and-blue bunting on the lampposts. All told, an estimated 20 million Americans participated in Earth Day observances of one kind or another, and virtually nobody—certainly nobody in public office—was against it.

The magnitude and inclusiveness of the observance marked Earth Day as a cultural watershed, like the Woodstock Music Festival or the 1968 Democratic National Convention in Chicago, a signal happening of the times. Although the day's events had been carefully orchestrated, the feelings summoned forth on Earth Day seemed both spontaneous and deep. It was as if, after the bitter divisiveness of the civil rights era and the antiwar movement, Americans enjoyed discovering the unifying sensation of this one issue.

Of course, an issue that everyone can embrace is not much of an issue at all, and the feel-good temper of Earth Day masked the profound conflicts that would arise when costly solutions were sought to address pressing environmental problems. But Earth Day forced environmental issues to the top of the political agenda, demonstrating to politicians and public officials everywhere the broad new national consensus. On New Year's Day, 1970, President Richard Nixon signed into law the National Environmental Policy Act (NEPA). "The 1970s absolutely must be the years when America pays its debt to the past by reclaiming the purity of its air, its waters and our living environment," the president stated. "It is literally now or never." Although Nixon publicly embraced NEPA, the law had principally been written by Democratic Senator Henry Jackson of Washington, and had been ushered through Congress over administration opposition. Among its provisions, NEPA explicitly required all federal agencies to conduct a thorough assessment of the environmental impact of all major programs.

Whether Nixon embraced environmental issues out of a genuine personal interest, or was pushed by popular sentiment and the Democratic opposition, or, as his sharpest critics suggested, he supported environmentalism in order to deflect attention from his controversial policies in Vietnam, the Nixon years were nonetheless marked by precisely the flood of legislation that environmentalists had long called for. NEPA was only the start. In his State of the Union message, delivered before Congress on January 22, 1970, Nixon made an attack on pollution his top domestic priority, and proposed a $10 billion, five-year plan to clean up America's waters by building municipal water-treatment plants. "Restoring nature to its natural state is a cause beyond party and beyond factions," Nixon said. "It has become a common cause of all the people of America. It is a cause of particular concern to young Americans because they more than we will reap the grim consequences of our failure to act on programs which are needed now if we are to prevent disaster later."

Nixon may have found himself trapped by his own stirring rhetoric. Challenged by Senators Jackson and Edmund Muskie and others, who pointed out that his "$10 billion" plan actually committed the federal government to less annual spending than Congress had already appropriated for 1970, Nixon substantially upgraded his own program. On February 10, 1970, some three weeks after his State of the Union message, the president presented a package of major environmental legislation to Congress, concentrating on three major areas in addition to the enhanced water-treatment plan: air pollution controls on automobiles and industry, solid-waste disposal, and an increase in park and recreation lands.

The all-important details of setting standards and establishing enforcement mechanisms had yet to be worked out. Weak laws would accomplish nothing. Some Democrats resented Nixon's attempt to steal the environmental issue from them just prior to midterm congressional elections. But the president had at the very least in his February 10 speech raised environmentalism to the status of a national crusade, making a commitment as eloquent and significant as President Kennedy's pledge to put a man on the moon and President Johnson's vow to end poverty. In doing so, Nixon put the prestige of his office and the power of the federal government squarely behind the central, cherished aim of environmentalism: finding a harmonious relationship between man and nature.

"At the turn of the century, our chief environmental concern was to conserve what we had," Nixon said in his speech, "and out of this concern grew the often embattled but always determined 'conservation' movement. Today, 'conservation' is as important as ever—but no longer is it enough to conserve what we have; we must also restore what we have lost. We have to go beyond conservation to embrace restoration."

With the president's basic assent, and public opinion loudly and clearly expressed by the demonstrations of Earth Day, legislators in Washington and in state capitols and city halls across the nation in the early seventies passed thousands of new environmental laws and ordinances. At the federal level the most important of the new laws were: the National Environmental Policy Act, which formally declared in its preamble that it was now federal policy to "use all practicable means and measures" to "create and maintain conditions under which man and nature can exist in productive harmony"; the 1970 amendments to several older "clean air" enactments dating back to 1963—laws that collectively became known as the Clean Air Act; and the Federal Water Pollution Control Act (FWPCA) of 1972—commonly known as the Clean Water Act. From these laws there evolved a large body of environmental case law. Subsequent federal legislation—notably the Consumer Product Safety Act (1972), the Environmental Pesticide Control Act (1972), the Endangered Species Act (1973), the Toxic Substances Control Act (1976), and the Superfund legislation to clean up hazardous-waste sites (1980)—added to the edifice of what is now, some twenty years later, a major branch of American jurisprudence.

Along with the new statutes, the early 1970s also saw the establishment by President Nixon of the Environmental Protection Agency—another capitulation by the Republican president to a proposal that had initially been put forth by a Democratic rival, Senator Muskie. EPA began operations on December 2, 1970, taking over a number of existing federal environmental programs scattered throughout the government, including water-pollution responsibilities from the Department of the Interior, air and solid-waste management from the Department of Health, Education, and Welfare, and pesticide regulation from the Department of Agriculture. EPA boasted some fifty-eight hundred employees and an annual budget of $1.4 billion, making it an instant Goliath among government agencies.

Environmental lawyers who prior to 1970 had worried about the barrenness of the legal arsenal suddenly found themselves armed with an abundance of new statutory weapons. The challenge was no longer to adapt principles of common law to environmental issues or dust off old, little-used statutes, but rather to monitor the administration of new statutes by EPA and other executive agencies, and, when necessary, to prod the agencies and test the new laws by filing lawsuits. All of the arguments in favor of public-interest law gained new force, for if public-interest law firms did not meet the challenge of the new legal climate, who would? It was more evident than ever that the private bar could not hope to represent the diffuse public interest that environmental legislation was designed to protect.

Along with the Environmental Defense Fund, the Sierra Club, Friends of the Earth, and others, the legal staff of NRDC plunged into the work of implementing and extending the reach of environmental law. One of the best of the new legal tools was section 102(2)(C) of NEPA, which required all federal agencies to prepare a detailed, written statement of the environmental impact that proposed actions may have, including alternative actions and their impacts. Though it was a little-discussed provision of NEPA when the law was debated in Congress, it proved to be NEPA's most important, and controversial, innovation, precisely because environmental lawyers utilized it to great advantage. The potential value of requiring agencies to submit an environmental impact statement (EIS) prior to their taking an action was suggested by the successful use that attorneys in the Storm King case had made of a similar provision in the Federal Power Act that required the FPC to consider "other beneficial public uses, including recreational purposes" in deciding whether to license any dam or related project. In that case the Second District Court in New York had ruled that the Federal Power Commission could not merely pay lip service to environmental concerns, but would have to demonstrate that it had in fact permitted ample testimony from environmental interests and furthermore had taken this testimony into full account in reaching its decision to grant a license. Even more, the court ruled that the FPC had an "active and affirmative" responsibility to protect the environmental rights of the public. The

NRDC—whose progenitors had fought and won the Storm King case —was the plaintiff in a number of the key suits that were filed under NEPA in the early seventies, in which the courts enforced similarly strict compliance with section 102(2)(C) of NEPA on scores of other federal agencies.

One of the earliest and most important cases—which was handled by Tom Stoel and Ed Stohbehn at NRDC—was a challenge to an Interior Department plan, first announced in June 1971, to lease 380,000 acres in the Gulf of Mexico off the coast of Louisiana for offshore drilling. A notorious oil spill from a well off the scenic coast of Santa Barbara, California, in 1969 had been one of the main catalysts for the great environmental awakening of the early seventies. The Santa Barbara spill was an especially telegenic disaster, featuring oil-soaked seals and pelicans and miles of hideously fouled beaches, and it came to symbolize America's unhealthy thirst for petroleum. The oil crunch of 1971, though it was the direct result of a politically motivated embargo conducted by the Arab, oil-producing countries of the Middle East, only underscored the point. From the environmentalists' point of view America was dangerously addicted to oil. Offshore drilling posed an enormous risk to sensitive and productive marine ecosystems and recreational resources to satisfy an addiction that sooner or later would have to be given up anyway.

Stoel and Stohbehn argued that the issues—the true alternatives to drilling, such as energy conservation and the development of alternative, less environmentally damaging supplies—were not fully discussed in the Interior Department's environmental impact statement, as NEPA required. They won a preliminary injunction halting the lease sale on December 16, 1971. The government appealed. On January 13, 1972, the Court of Appeals for the District of Columbia Circuit ruled in favor of NRDC, and went on to issue a detailed landmark opinion that helped define some of the most essential requirements of an environmental impact statement. An EIS, the court ruled, must discuss all the practicable alternatives to a proposed action, including actions over which the agency concerned has no control, and even if the alternatives do not offer a complete solution to the problem.

There were other victories for NRDC in its first two years of active life, a heady period during which the organization engaged in over seventy legal actions. A series of lawsuits engineered by Dick Ayres and David Hawkins forced EPA to issue clean-air standards in accordance with the Clean Air Act amendments of 1970. One of these suits required EPA to restrict the use of lead in gasoline. Still other NRDC legal actions challenged the Atomic Energy Commission's program to develop a liquid-metal fast-breeder reactor, the Tennessee Valley Authority's use of strip-mined coal, and a U.S. Forest Service plan to drastically expand the volume of timber sales from the National Forests.

Within only a few years of its founding, the Natural Resources Defense Council could already lay claim to an illustrious history, although dramatic court actions were only part of what NRDC was about. Lawyers in the Washington office had also become involved in administrative and legislative processes, submitting testimony and comments before agency and congressional hearings. The NRDC also undertook public education, primarily through the publication and distribution of handbooks and manuals about various environmental issues, which instructed citizens in how they could become involved in local environmental efforts.

By 1974 much pioneering legal work had been accomplished, and the basic framework for environmental law had been constructed. It had become apparent during this process, however, that lawyers alone could not unravel all of the complex issues involved in environmental advocacy. Often, tricky and controversial scientific questions—rather than statutory ones—lay at the heart of a lawsuit or an administrative debate over appropriate regulations. The law, for instance, might plainly require that a substance be banned if proven hazardous, so the essential question under review was whether the substance was or was not hazardous. In 1974, NRDC hired several staff scientists, one of whom was thirty-five-year-old biochemist Karim Ahmed.

Ahmed had chaired the organizing committee for the Earth Day observations at the University of Minnesota, and later had cofounded and served as research director for the Minnesota Public Interest Research Group (MPIRG), the first community-oriented public-interest research task force in the country. He had moved on to the Consumers Union, where he had been involved in consumer-product testing, but he missed the intense political involvement of his MPIRG days in Minneapolis, and in August 1974 sought a job with the more activist Environmental Defense Fund in Washington. Two weeks before he was scheduled to begin work at EDF however, he received a call from NRDC, and after interviewing with senior NRDC staff members in New York, Ahmed was asked to fly to Washington for a second round of interviews on September 26, 1974. During his flight he read a front-page article in the *New York Times* describing a controversial new scientific theory.

"Two scientists have calculated that gases released by aerosol cans have already accumulated sufficiently in the upper air to begin depleting the ozone that protects the earth from lethal ultraviolet radiation," began the article, headlined TESTS SHOW AEROSOL GASES MAY POSE THREAT TO EARTH and written by the paper's science correspondent, Walter Sullivan. The story went on to describe recent work by Harvard scientists Michael B. McElroy and Steven C. Wofsy, who had confirmed earlier findings by Drs. F. Sherwood Rowland and Mario J. Molina at the University of California at Irvine that chlorofluorocarbons pose a "new and ominous threat to stability of the ozone layer." CFCs, the scientists had found, are stable in the lower atmosphere, but when they rise into the stratosphere where they are exposed to ultraviolet light, they break down and release chlorine. The chlorine, in turn, enters into a catalytic chemical reaction with ozone, rapidly destroying the ozone.

Ahmed, like virtually all environmentalists, knew that oxides of nitrogen had recently come under scientific scrutiny as ozone scavengers because scientists had reported that a proposed fleet of supersonic aircraft, SSTs, would produce oxides of nitrogen and release them in their exhaust into the stratosphere. Opponents of the plane had cited this threat to the ozone layer as one reason the SST should not be built. Walter Sullivan's *Times* article quoted Rowland and Molina's contention that CFCs would destroy ozone six times more effectively than oxides of nitrogen, while noting that as of 1971, 2 million tons of CFCs were being released into the atmosphere each year.

By training, Ahmed was a chemist, with degrees in both physical chemistry and biochemistry. Though the newly proposed ozone-depletion theory was complex, he was well equipped both by scientific background and political inclination to grasp its disturbing implications.

A week later NRDC cofounder Tom Stoel had an experience similar to Ahmed's. Idly flipping through the October 7, 1974, issue of *Time* magazine while sitting in his dentist's waiting room, he came across an article about the startling ozone-depletion theory proposed by Rowland and Molina. The hypothesis had received important scientific support, *Time* reported, from Drs. Ralph Cicerone and Richard Stolarski of the University of Michigan, who had estimated that even if the use of CFCs in aerosols were halted immediately, the ozone layer would suffer a 10 percent depletion by 1990; Harvard's McElroy and Wofsy had calculated that the projected 10 percent annual increase in CFC production would result in a 10 percent ozone reduction in twenty years and a 40 percent reduction by 2014. Depletions of this magnitude, reported *Time*, would permit increased levels of the sun's ultraviolet radiation, which is ordinarily filtered out by stratospheric ozone, to reach the earth's surface. This, in turn, would cause a greater incidence of skin cancer, might disrupt the food chain by interfering with photosynthesis in crops and plankton in the seas, and could severely affect the earth's weather patterns and climate because the presence of ozone in the upper air warms the stratosphere.

Recognizing the public-policy implications of the ozone-depletion theory, Stoel decided NRDC should become involved. He quickly got together with Karim Ahmed to establish an aerosol-ozone project within NRDC. Stoel and Ahmed agreed that the first step would be for Ahmed to assess the merits of the scientific claim that CFCs destroy stratospheric ozone. If he concluded that the threat was sufficient to justify legal action, he would help NRDC build the scientific argument to form the basis of a lawsuit, or to otherwise help persuade the appropriate government agencies or the Congress to act. Stoel, meanwhile, would evaluate the various legislative, legal, and regulatory options.

9.

COLUMBUS OF
THE STRATOSPHERE

STROLLING THROUGH CENTRAL LONDON one morning in 1666 during the Dutch War, Samuel Pepys came upon a small crowd of people in St. James's Park who appeared to be acting strangely. When he asked what they were doing, they told him they were listening to the sound of the British Fleet's guns firing in the English Channel. This struck Pepys as extraordinary, for the Channel was more than fifty miles away. The occurrence seemed stranger still when, after making inquiries, he learned that the residents of the town of Dover, on the banks of the Channel, had not heard the guns at all.

"This makes room for a great dispute in philosophy," Pepys wrote, "how we should hear it and they not, the same wind that brought it to us being the same that should bring it to them: but so it is." Pepys concluded that what he and the others in St. James's Park had witnessed was "a miraculous thing," and made no further attempt at an explanation.

The strange phenomenon was noted again at the time of Queen Victoria's funeral in London in 1901, when the sound of cannon fired in her honor along the Thames was heard distinctly in parts of Yorkshire, hundreds of miles to the north, but nowhere in the Midlands. By then meteorologists were well enough acquainted with the strange effect to have introduced a term for the pockets of remote countryside where the cannon were heard, "zones of abnormal audibility," but they were no more able than Samuel Pepys had been to explain what caused them. Some thought "high-velocity winds" were responsible; others cited a probable chemical imbalance in the upper atmosphere.

The first step toward explaining the riddle was taken the following year, in 1902, when a French meteorologist, Léon Philippe Teisserenc de Bort, made a startling presentation to the French Academy of Science. De Bort had left his post with the Central Meteorological Bureau of France in 1895 to conduct kite and unmanned sounding-balloon experiments from his observatory in Trappes, near Paris. In one experiment he sought to monitor upper-air currents over Europe by attaching stamped, self-addressed postcards to his balloons; each card bore a request printed in several languages asking that the finder fill in a couple of lines of information about where and when the card was found and then mail it back. De Bort received the completed cards from as far away as Sweden. Instead of winning scientific acclaim for his independent pursuits, however, De Bort earned only the hostility of many of his fellow Parisians when, in August 1899, the lines of one of his kites became tangled in the telegraph wires connecting Paris with Rennes, on the very afternoon the verdict of the second trial of Army officer Alfred Dreyfus was eagerly being awaited.

If De Bort was not paying sufficient attention to where his experimental kites were landing, it was most likely because his sounding balloons were telling him something very curious about the upper air—something he knew to be scientifically impossible. Balloon and kite measurements of the atmosphere had convinced meteorologists that air temperature decreased with distance from Earth's surface. It was a scientific "given" that temperature fell at a rate of one degree for every 360 feet, and scientists believed this rate of decrease continued until, at approximately 140,659 feet, it reached $-459.67°F$, or "absolute zero," the lowest temperature theoretically possible. At this point, it was thought, earth's atmosphere ended and outer space began.

De Bort's balloons, however, equipped with a timepiece and a smoked cylinder upon which a needle scratched information during an ascent, showed that at 25,000 feet the temperature not only stopped decreasing, but actually began to rise. Was there warm air high above the earth? De Bort found it hard to believe, despite his own experimental data. In a notable demonstration of scientific thoroughness, he proceeded to conduct no fewer than 236 separate balloon flights to verify these unlikely temperature measurements, before going to the French Academy with his astounding findings in 1902.

De Bort's discovery was confirmed two years later by an American, A. Lawrence Rotch, director of the Blue Hill Meteorological Observatory, ten miles south of Boston, near Milton, Massachusetts. Rotch was a wunderkind, having overseen the 1885 opening of Blue Hill while still an undergraduate at MIT. He was also one of the guiding spirits of a group of Boston-area scientists who combined meteorological experimentation involving kites with an active interest in aeronautics. Kites, at the time, were believed to be likely precursors to flying machines, and each new successful kite altitude record at Blue Hill—one ascent reached 9,000 feet!—represented a significant advance to aeronautical inventors. In 1901, Rotch became the first person to fly experimental meteorological kites from the deck of a ship in mid-ocean, a feat he accomplished during an Atlantic steamer crossing.

De Bort and Rotch knew each other, and like many of the world's prominent meteorologists, they recognized that the future of significant work in their field would require international cooperation. In this spirit, De Bort urged Rotch to verify his Paris findings of warm temperatures in the upper sky with a series of balloon flights in America. Rotch's soundings, launched from the 1904 World's Fair in St. Louis, were the first upper-atmosphere sounding-balloon measurements made in the United States. The resulting data confirmed the measurements gathered by De Bort over Paris: while a minimum temperature of $-90°F$ was recorded at 47,600 feet, it warmed to $-72°F$ at 54,100. Two days later, Rotch found, the temperature was $-80°F$ at 39,700 feet and $-69°F$ at 42,200 feet.

Their mutual fascination with this previously unknown layer of warm air led to De Bort and Rotch's sailing together during the summer of 1906 on a scientific expedition to the tropics. From the deck of a tramp steamer they flew kites and launched sounding balloons, and succeeded in monitoring the same warmer temperatures in the upper atmosphere that they had observed in Europe and North America. "While not presuming to offer an explanation of the isothermal or relatively warm stratum in the high atmosphere," Rotch concluded, "I desire to point out that it is probably a universal phenomenon, existing at some height all around the globe."

At first, Rotch and De Bort used the term "isothermal layer" to designate the layer of warm air they had found. In 1908, De Bort proposed calling the lower part of the atmosphere, from Earth's surface to an altitude of approximately 50,000 feet, the "troposphere," from the Greek word *trepein,* meaning "to turn over," a reference to convection, or the rising and falling of air currents, which is exclusive to the lower atmosphere and determines weather and climate. For the mysterious region above the troposphere he suggested the name "stratosphere," from *stratum*, "flat layer," because of the complete absence of convection.

Rotch and De Bort's theory that a warm layer of air blanketed the earth was of keen interest to Oxford physicist Gordon M. B. Dobson, who, along with colleague F. A. Lindemann, observed on clear nights in 1922 and 1923 the deceleration or "burning up" of meteors as they entered earth's atmosphere. Dobson knew, from balloon measurements, the density and temperature of the air up to the tropopause, and had assumed both factors would continue to decrease with altitude. But the prevalence of "shooting stars" above the tropopause suggested greater, not lesser, atmospheric density at those altitudes, and hence a region of warmer temperature.

Meanwhile, British scientists were making the first systematic investigations of the still unresolved question of the propagation of sound over great distances, the "zones of abnormal audibility." During the First World War the phenomenon was observed numerous times, as the sound of fighting in Belgium and northern France was heard on the English side of the Channel. But because the tremendously loud noises that caused the effect were almost always unplanned, the opportunities for precise scientific investigation were limited. When, two years after the Armistice, the British government announced its intention to detonate some of its surplus military-ammunition dumps, meteorologists seized the occasion to prove once and for all that the zones of abnormal audibility were no collective hallucination. With the exact schedule of the detonations in hand, British Navy observers stationed across Britain confirmed that the curious effect of "bouncing sound" actually occurred.

In 1926 and 1927, F. J. W. Whipple, superintendent of the Kew Observatory, used newly invented and extremely sensitive listening devices known as hot-wire microphones to further refine the data. The microphones were sensitive to sounds inaudible to the human ear, and could pick up traces of loud noises as far as 200 miles from their source. The British Navy again played a role in the experiments, ordering heavy shipboard guns in Shoeburyness, at the mouth of the Thames, to be fired on cue. The sound was heard at Cardiff, 167 miles to the west, but not at locations somewhat closer. Since he knew precisely how much time had elapsed between the detonation and the "arrival" of its sound, Whipple was able to calculate the degree of the angle that described the sound's trajectory. These angles strongly suggested that the sound rose to a point several miles high before curving back downward to earth.

Whipple knew that in cold temperatures air molecules are more tightly packed, so sound waves are more rapidly absorbed; in warm temperatures the molecules are farther apart, consequently sound waves have farther to go before they encounter a sufficient number of molecules to absorb them. Thus, sound travels faster in warm air. Whipple theorized that the sound waves he had monitored had left the earth's surface and traveled upward at about a forty-five-degree angle, then—encountering De Bort's layer of warmer air, the stratosphere—had leveled off and were refracted downward. This refraction occurs because sound is a wave phenomenon, and causes a wave pattern of vibration of molecules through the atmosphere. When sound travels into colder air at an angle, the top part of the wave, encountering the coldest air, travels more slowly than the bottom, causing the wave to refract upward. When the wave encounters the relatively warmer air in the stratosphere, however, the pattern reverses: the top part of the sound wave speeds up while the bottom part remains moving at a slower rate, and the sound wave is refracted back toward earth. Whipple determined that the sound of the Navy guns had actually traveled into the upper air and returned to earth not just once but twice, for when the returning sound waves encountered the ground, they bounced forward and upward once again; reaching the high, warmer air a second time, the waves again curved back to Earth. The trajectory of the sound waves was two progressive arcs, like two forward jumps by a frog.

Léon Philippe Teisserenc de Bort and A. Lawrence Rotch, Gordon M. B. Dobson and F. J. W. Whipple—all had, by various means, established the existence of a warm layer of air in the upper atmosphere. A scientific explanation was at last in hand for the enigma Pepys had observed nearly three centuries before. The ability to reflect sounds emanating from the earth and to cause the disintegration of shooting stars were among the first traits ascribed to De Bort's "stratosphere." Scientists were left to resolve the question of what combination of chemicals, gases, and other phenomena helped maintain this particular atmospheric region.

Scientific writings of the early eighteenth century mention a gas with an unpleasant metallic smell found in the air close to the ground following thunderstorms. The Swiss chemist Christian Schönbein in 1840 named the gas ozone, after *ozein*, Greek for "to smell." Schönbein also developed a primitive means of measuring it, a mixture of potassium iodide and starch that could be blotted onto paper and would change color in ozone's presence. Schönbein's "litmus test" for ozone enabled him to establish some of the attributes of ozone in the lower atmosphere, for example, that its concentration varies greatly from day to day and peaks in the springtime.

The first individuals to suspect that ozone might be found in significant amounts in the upper air, well away from Earth's surface, were not chemists like Schönbein, but spectroscopists, or observers of light spectra. One of the pioneers of spectroscopy was the nineteenth-century Swedish physicist Anders J. Ångström, for whom the basic unit of measurement of light wavelengths in various parts of the spectrum is named. An angstrom unit, represented by the symbol Å, equals one ten-billionth of a meter. As instruments for measuring sunlight became increasingly precise in the late nineteenth century, spectroscopists grew certain that something was preventing the shorter waves of ultraviolet sunlight— those measuring less than 2,900 Å—from reaching the earth's surface.

Marie-Alfred Cornu, a professor at the École Polytechnique in Paris, theorized in 1879 that this cutoff of natural UV was due to absorption of the light by a gas in the atmosphere. W. N. Hartley, professor of chemistry at the Royal College of Science for Ireland in Dublin concurred, and added that he suspected the gas in question was ozone, because light measured through ozone under controlled conditions showed a cutoff of UV light matching what appeared to happen naturally to sunlight passing through the atmosphere. After devoting his summer holiday in 1880 to experiments with ultraviolet light in the Irish countryside, Hartley in 1881 submitted a seminal paper on ozone to the Chemical Society of London. In it he concluded that because known, ground-level quantities of ozone did not suffice to account for the total UV absorption recorded in sunlight, ozone must exist in higher concentrations in the atmosphere above the earth's surface.

Hartley's theory was interesting but unprovable, and many scientists resisted it. Accepting the idea that ozone was concentrated away from the earth's surface was difficult because ozone had always been associated with lightning discharges, which occurred near the ground. When balloon measurements and mountaintop spectra readings confirmed Hartley's UV absorption data, proving that ground-level ozone was not a significant factor in determining which wavelengths of UV light reached earth, many scientists still refused to accept his theory. Some instead advanced an alternative hypothesis: that the ultraviolet limitation was occurring not in Earth's atmosphere at all, but in the atmosphere of the sun.

Charles Fabry, professor of physics at the University of Marseilles and an inventor and authority in the field of spectroscopy, agreed with Hartley that ozone in Earth's atmosphere was causing the cutoff of the shorter UV wavelengths. Using optical equipment he himself had developed that was far superior to any Hartley had used, Fabry established in 1913 that while an artificial source of ultraviolet light at ground level would transmit rays of UV as low as 2,500 Å, in natural sunlight no light waves shorter than 2,900 Å were allowed to reach Earth. "We must therefore conclude," Fabry wrote, "that the greatest part of the ozone lies in the very high atmosphere. . . .

"We arrive at the conclusion that this ozone lies in the high layers [of the atmosphere]," Fabry continued, "only because we do not find it in the lower layers. But it would be of great interest to locate it more definitely."

In the years following the First World War, Fabry continued his research. He was able, by measuring the attenuation of solar radiation at varying zenith distances, to confirm his hypothesis that ozone forms a layer somewhere high above the earth. He estimated that this "ozone layer" was located in the stratosphere at an altitude of twenty-five to thirty kilometers. With his knowledge of the UV-absorbing qualities of ozone, he was also able to estimate that the cumulative effective thickness of ozone in the upper atmosphere must be approximately .3 centimeter. Later measurements roughly confirmed both calculations.

The work of Hartley and Fabry initiated a lasting relationship between spectrophotometry and stratospheric ozone. In 1926, Gordon Dobson designed a prism spectrophotometer for making precise measurements of stratospheric ozone, and as part of an effort to demonstrate that the characteristics of the ozone layer were universal, he created the first global ozone-monitoring network, placing his machines in such far-flung locations as Christ Church, New Zealand; Cairo, Egypt; and Arosa, Switzerland. This first generation of Dobson spectrophotometers gathered strong evidence that stratospheric ozone was found everywhere around the globe, though at both lower and higher altitudes than Fabry had estimated.

It was left to yet another Englishman to fully describe the workings of the ozone layer. Geophysicist Sydney Chapman, in a lecture to the Royal Society of London on June 25, 1931, modestly entitled "Some Phenomena of the Upper Atmosphere," explained that when oxygen (O_2) in the stratosphere absorbs sunlight waves of less than 2,400 Å, the oxygen molecule is split and two oxygen atoms are freed. Like caroming billiard balls, the two oxygen atoms go their separate ways until one free oxygen atom (O) joins a whole oxygen molecule (O_2) to create a molecule of triatomic oxygen, or ozone (O_3). Ozone (O_3), itself being highly unstable, is quickly broken up by longer-wave sunlight of 2,900 Å or by colliding with another free oxygen atom. Thus, ozone molecules are always being made and destroyed at a more or less constant rate, Chapman said, so that a relatively fixed quantity of them are always present.

This condition is known as "steady state." To describe "steady state," scientists sometimes use the analogy of a bathtub with water entering at the faucet and leaving through a drain. If the amount of water entering and leaving the bathtub is constant, the level of water in the tub will also be constant: steady state. If the amount of water entering or leaving the bathtub changes to a new constant value, a new condition of steady state will be achieved, but the level of water in the bathtub will have changed.

The incessant exchange of gaseous molecules that maintained the ozone layer also warmed the stratosphere, Chapman explained, creating the rise in temperatures at stratospheric altitudes that had so intrigued De Bort and Rotch.

Chapman's comprehensive description of ozone chemistry, known thereafter as "the Chapman reactions" or "the Chapman mechanism," proved definitive, and also served to inspire the popular conception of the ozone layer as a vital atmospheric buffer protecting living organisms from deadly shortwave ultraviolet light.

"The effect of unlimited solar radiation would be fatal," the British science writer Dorothy Fisk wrote in 1933, "and this layer of ozone, no thicker than a wafer biscuit, is all that stands between us and speedy death."

Dr. Charles Abbot of the Smithsonian Institution, quoted in the *New York Times* on October 30, 1933, echoed Fisk's conclusion: "It is astonishing and even terrifying to contemplate the narrow margin of safety on which our lives thus depend. Were this trifling quantity of atmospheric ozone removed we should all perish."

The potential loss or depletion of this "trifling quantity of atmospheric ozone" was depicted in apocalyptic terms from the moment of the ozone layer's discovery, although at the time no one seriously entertained the idea that such a dark disaster could ever occur. Knowing how fine a thread safeguarded mankind did not inspire fear, but only increased one's awe and appreciation of nature's intricacies.

Chapman called the study of planetary atmospheres "aeronomy," a name that echoed the period's infatuation with aviation and seemed to imply that the upper regions of the earth's atmosphere were ripe for discovery. Indeed, as Chapman, Dobson, and others during the 1920s and 1930s investigated the stratosphere, other physicists, such as Jörgen Hals and Carl Størmer, were working to improve their knowledge of yet higher regions of the atmosphere, such as the ionosphere, where gaseous particles are broken apart, or ionized, by the sun, creating the high electrical conductivity responsible for returning radio waves to Earth. It was the stratosphere, however, closer to Earth, and becoming less mysterious with each new advance, that was now fashionably viewed as one of the next great workshops for science.

Man's first trip to the stratosphere was a death-defying adventure prompted by the search for the most elusive and least-known form of radiation, cosmic rays. The quest for knowledge about these mysterious atomic nuclei represented the glorious frontier of physics in 1930 when forty-seven-year-old Swiss scientist Auguste Piccard, professor of physics at the University of Brussels and an amateur balloonist, announced his intention to record their activity in the uppermost reaches of the sky. Piccard, like many physicists, was convinced that cosmic rays could hold the secret to harnessing the power of the atom for an efficient new form of energy. "Calculations show that the energy liberated from the modification of atoms contained in six drops of water," Piccard wrote, "would suffice to light up one of the world's great cities for several hours." Piccard did not believe the use of atomic power would begin soon, but rather that "later on, when our deposits of coal and oil are nearing exhaustion, humanity will, perhaps, find in the reactions now being discussed a means of saving our civilization."

What was known about cosmic rays could not help but inspire lofty expectations. X rays, discovered by Wilhelm Röntgen in 1895, passed through leather and human flesh, but not lead; cosmic rays could pass easily through many feet of lead, and seemed to bombard objects from everywhere at once. But where did they come from? Did they stream toward the earth from deep space? Did they originate within the sun? Or did they emanate from inside the earth itself? Balloon measurements using an electroscope, a precursor of the Geiger counter, had determined that the rays were more abundant high in the earth's atmosphere. In 1912, Austrian physicist Victor Hess became the first to measure the rays during a 17,500-foot balloon ascent; later manned balloon electroscope readings were made at 29,000 feet.

Professor Piccard wanted to go much higher. He believed the tropopause, the uppermost layer of the troposphere, shielded the earth from most of the "cosmic bullets," as he called the rays, and that they were weakened considerably and transmuted into "secondary cosmic rays" by the time they reached the earth's surface. Piccard was determined to study "the primitive ray as it exists in cosmic space" before it was absorbed by the earth's atmosphere. This meant ascending to an altitude of at least 50,000 feet, to the stratosphere, where no human had ever gone.

Piccard, with his large, high forehead, tufted hair, and gold wire-rim glasses, looked the part of the scientific eccentric, an impression he reinforced by making some curious preparations for the trip. To be certain the tiny lead shot he intended to use as ballast on the flight would not harm anyone when he dropped it to increase altitude, he had an assistant throw some down onto his head from the chimney of the school's heating plant. Such procedures only contributed to the murmuring among his scientific colleagues that Piccard's scheme for reaching the stratosphere was quite impossible. Manned scientific balloon flights, after all, were mostly obsolete; the sounding balloon, capable of collecting data at heights up to 75,000 feet, had largely replaced it. Manned ascents had come to be seen as an almost quaint form of popular recreation, an entertainment associated with carnivals and fairgrounds.

Certainly, ballooning's allure had diminished considerably since its origins in France in the 1780s. Then, the celebrated ascents of the Montgolfier brothers brought astonished multitudes to Versailles, the Tuileries, or the Champ de Mars to witness so amazing an event as a human being departing Earth and soaring into the sky.

These early balloon voyages rarely went higher than 10,000 feet, but as technique and equipment improved, balloonists began to reach greater altitudes. They also began to encounter the lethal dangers of oxygen deprivation and prolonged exposure to subzero temperatures. The most celebrated balloon adventure of the nineteenth century was the ascent on September 5, 1862, by the British aeronauts James Glaisher and Henry Coxwell. Rising high above the English countryside in a plain wicker basket with no oxygen apparatus or thermal clothing, Glaisher lost consciousness as the balloon neared 35,000 feet. Coxwell managed to climb into the balloon's rigging but found he couldn't open the descent valve because his hands were so badly frostbitten. In desperation, he pulled at the valve with his teeth, managing to open it moments before he, too, lost consciousness and tumbled down into the basket beside Glaisher. Both men miraculously survived, their ascent establishing a world height record that went unchallenged for decades. In Britain, Glaisher and Coxwell became national heroes, lithographs and popular illustrations immortalizing their triumph over the elements.

Thereafter, balloonists seeking new altitude records equipped themselves with oxygen, heaters, and layers of warm clothes, although even with the most elaborate preparation and on-board equipment, many were not as lucky as Glaisher and Coxwell. One such doomed ascent was that of Captain Hawthorne Gray of the U.S. Army Air Corps, who went aloft in a hydrogen balloon from Belleville, Illinois, in November 1927. Gray was an experienced balloon pilot with several high-altitude flights to his credit, including an ascent to 28,510 feet the previous March, and he was determined to reach the stratosphere. Instead, his balloon drifted hundreds of miles to the east, apparently out of control, before coming to rest in a wooded area near Sparta, Tennessee. A boy who saw the balloon land in a tree climbed up its branches and discovered Captain Gray lying dead in the bottom of the basket. The flight's logbook indicated Gray had suffered acute oxygen deprivation and delirium—one cryptic entry read, "Hair pulling out belly, vacuum in mouth"—and he had apparently lived only long enough to pull the descent valve. The barograph reported his final altitude at 44,000 feet—a new world's record, but the achievement could not be officially acknowledged because Gray hadn't returned to earth alive.

Not wanting to rely on an oxygen bag, as had Captain Gray, Piccard conceived of building a sealed gondola that would carry its own supply of oxygen—an idea Piccard admitted came straight from the pages of Jules Verne's novel *20,000 Leagues Under the Sea*. The gondola, welded airtight and with a radius of seven feet, was constructed of a new .138-inch-thick aluminum that had been developed recently in the European manufacture of aluminum beer vats. The tiny cabin was outfitted with two manholes, eight portholes, and an apparatus that absorbed carbon dioxide and was capable of circulating twenty gallons of regenerated air, to maintain Piccard and his twenty-seven-year-old assistant, Charles Kipfer. As the professor remarked, "When you face the possibility of shutting two men up in an airtight space of such small dimensions, you must study very carefully the problem of their respiration."

Piccard's fellow European balloonists made a rather jaundiced appraisal of his "space capsule." The professor, they said, would never be able to fit enough ballast inside the gondola to break the balloon's speed of descent on the way back to Earth, particularly since he intended to travel with an assistant and several scientific experiments. And with only small portholes on each side of the gondola, there would be no sure way to guide the balloon to its landing. The press, taking its cue from the experts, also voiced skepticism, and ridiculed Piccard when his first attempt at a stratospheric ascent in September 1930 had to be scrubbed because of a sudden shift in the wind direction. Piccard resented the attempt to make him a laughingstock. "They concluded that I was the typical absent-minded professor," he later complained. "What happened, they explained, was quite natural: the absent-minded professor had made an error in his calculation, and consequently the balloon, instead of ascending ten miles, rose only ten feet!" Piccard unwittingly played into the hands of his detractors by permitting photographs to be taken of him and Kipfer modeling the protective headgear he had designed for the flight. The hats looked like upturned wicker baskets stuffed with pillows, which was more or less what they were. Newspapers published the photos with relish.

Gusting winds again threatened to force a postponement on May 27, 1931, when Piccard and Kipfer readied for their ascent at an airfield in Augsburg, Germany. But this time Piccard refused to delay his flight. He moved back the scheduled 5 A.M. lift-off and gave the order that the balloon be filled. At 3:30 A.M. he and Kipfer entered the gondola. Despite the hour, a crowd had gathered. "Many among the hundreds of spectators wept," a reporter noted, "to see the father of five children embark upon so perilous a voyage." Suddenly, Piccard's ground crew heard the professor's stern command, "Let go everything!" The men on the ground scrambled to untie the knotted grounding ropes, and a moment later the big yellow balloon emblazoned with the red and white Swiss flag sailed straight upward into the sky, trailing the gondola behind.

Piccard's first visit to the stratosphere began under somewhat mysterious circumstances, for he denied ever giving the order for the balloon to be released. While busy inside the gondola making their final preparations for the launch, he later explained, Kipfer had happened to look out one of the portholes, and immediately cried: "There is the smokestack of a factory beneath us!" Piccard rushed to see for himself. Aghast, he realized the crew had cut them loose prematurely. Both men then had to hurry to make the gondola airtight as it ascended into oxygen-thin altitudes. The whole flight rested on the concept of a pressurized cabin. "I had to get an electrostatic sounding instrument into this hole," Piccard related, "an operation that could not be carried out while we were on the ground, for the hole was in the bottom of the cabin." But the professor had intended to do so while the balloon was still tethered to the ground. Meanwhile, above the distressing sound of air whistling through the opening, Kipfer shouted to Piccard that they were already at 15,000 feet, which Piccard verified with a glance at the altimeter. "There was my beautiful airtight cabin absolutely of no use!" he later recalled. "We would have been quite as well off in a gondola of wickerwork."

Piccard informed Kipfer that if he couldn't stop the leak he would have no choice but to pull the descent rope and return them to earth. Nearly a half hour elapsed before the professor managed to plug the hole in the bottom of the cabin with pharmaceutical jelly and wadded cotton.

No sooner was this crisis resolved, however, than the aeronauts learned that the mechanism that operated the descent valve had been damaged in the abrupt lift-off, eliminating the option of returning the balloon to earth. "The winch revolves without pulling the line," Piccard dashed with a pen in his logbook. "I discovered the severed end of the line dangling outside. We are prisoners of the air."

The Piccard ascent came almost four years to the day after the historic solo transatlantic flight of Charles Lindbergh in the *Spirit of St. Louis*. Ballooning lacked the glamour of aviation, but by the early 1930s the press and the public had developed a keen appetite for flying stories and aeronautical adventures of all kinds, particularly when they involved endurance or altitude records and pitted aviators (or aeronauts) against seemingly impossible odds. Piccard's objective, the stratosphere, gave his mission a significance even the most thrilling airplane yarn could not touch. Once reporters on the ground at Augsburg confirmed that they had watched Piccard disappear into the dark predawn sky, newspapers around the world began tracking the flight.

At midmorning inside the gondola, 45,000 feet up and drifting toward Switzerland, the occupants were battling yet another equipment malfunction. Piccard had painted the gondola half black and half white, and devised a means of rotating it, so he could turn its position relative to the sun to either warm or cool the interior. The crank that operated this device had failed, however, leaving the gondola permanently stuck with its black side facing the sun, raising the temperature inside the gondola to 106 degrees. "What heat! What thirst! What uncertainty!" Piccard entered in the log. Trapped 8½ miles above the ground, unable to descend, he and Kipfer struggled in vain with the broken crank as the winds began carrying the balloon to the southeast.

Piccard's supporters on the ground had the first inkling something had gone wrong when noon, the hour at which Piccard had announced he would descend, came and went, and the balloon remained aloft above the Bavarian Alps, headed toward Italy. The gondola was known to contain only ten hours' worth of oxygen. The balloonists could reduce the supply, thereby buying themselves some extra time, but with each passing minute it became less and less likely Piccard and Kipfer could still be alive. Late in the afternoon a plane was sent up from a Munich airfield. The pilot managed to locate the balloon, floating over the valley of the Inn River in Austria, "unguided and apparently caught in a pocket of dead air," but the plane could not fly above 35,000 feet, and the pilot reported that the balloon was much higher up—too high for him to attempt to make contact with Piccard.

Engineers at the Reidlinger balloon factory in Augsburg, where the Piccard balloon had been built, were unable to say why the professor had not descended, and were at first reluctant to make any comments about his chances of survival under the circumstances. At last, as dusk settled over Europe, one factory official conceded, "It is assumed the craft is no longer under human control." As the *New York Times* would report the next morning, "Wrapped in silence and mystery, shrouded in the folds of night, the Piccard stratosphere balloon is floating aimlessly over the glaciers of the Tyrolean Alps, out of control and occupied only by the dead."

A radio broadcast announcing the death of the two balloonists was heard by George Schreiber, an innkeeper in the remote alpine village of Obergurgl, 6,300 feet up in the Austrian Tyrol. Since about 6 P.M. he had been watching a strange object drifting in the sky above the nearby mountain peaks. Sometime after 9 P.M. he saw it come over a neighboring mountain and sink gently toward a glacier above the town. Believing it might be the Piccard balloon, Schreiber began organizing a search party of men from the village. At daybreak, led by the local ski champion, Hermann Falkner, the search party began the hike up onto the glacier. The innkeeper had told the men they would probably find the balloonists dead in the wreck of the gondola, so it was with great surprise that the search party, on its way up the glacier, encountered a fit-looking Piccard and Kipfer making their way down. The aeronauts cordially greeted their rescuers, reporting that the only calamity they had suffered was that Kipfer, in the excitement of the balloon's descent, had split his trousers wide up the seam. "There is no doubt whatever that we reached the stratosphere," Piccard assured them. When Falkner told Piccard that they had not expected to find him and Kipfer alive, the professor implored him to use his skis to hurry back to the village ahead of the others and phone Mme. Piccard in Brussels to let her know he was safe.

Schreiber's wife, meanwhile, had already used the village's single telephone to alert the outside world that the Piccard stratospheric balloon had landed above the town, and a corps of newsmen began arriving in Obergurgl not long after Piccard and Kipfer themselves were led down the mountain to the hotel.

Instrument readings proved that Piccard and Kipfer's eighteen-hour flight had taken them to a height of 51,775 feet, or 9.81 miles, the farthest trip away from the earth's surface ever made by man. "At an altitude of ten miles, the Earth is a marvelous sight," the professor reported. "Yet it is terrifying, too. As we rose the Earth seemed at times like a huge disk, with an upturned edge, rather than the globe that it really is. The bluish mist of the atmosphere grew red-tinged, and the

Earth seemed to go into a copper-colored cloud. Then it all but disappeared in a haze."

He recounted the various difficulties he and Kipfer had met. By reducing their own intake of oxygen, Piccard explained, they had been able to remain alive until late afternoon, when the sun began to set and the hydrogen in the balloon contracted, lowering them back into the troposphere. The depletion of the balloon then freed the tangled descent line, permitting them for the first time to direct their return toward the earth. Reaching 10,000 feet, they threw open the porthole and desperately inhaled fresh air. "We were very near the end of our rope," Piccard said. "Two hours more and the oxygen supply would have been exhausted, and we would have been dead men." By then it was dark and they were over the mountains, and both knew they would not be likely to survive a crash landing on one of the steep mountain slopes. After hovering precariously for several hours, trying to glimpse a spot to land, Piccard had sighted the glacier at Obergurgl, illuminated by moonlight, apparently the smoothest, most level surface for many miles, and he pulled the descent valve for a landing. They spent the night on the glacier, enjoying a supper of melted snow mixed with Nestlé's chocolate powder, then fell asleep in the gondola. Next morning, sighting the chimneys of the village, the first men to visit and safely return from the stratosphere had roped themselves together and begun the hike down.

"The cosmic rays are rattling down on my gondola!" read one entry in Piccard's log of the flight. Piccard, who had stressed cosmic-ray research as the scientific rationale for his flight, had found the rays extremely active at high altitudes, as he had anticipated. (Since Piccard's time, cosmic rays have been shown to emanate from deep space and from the sun.) However, in the aftermath of his and Kipfer's dramatic flight, it was not cosmic rays but the successful use of a pressurized cabin and his poetic descriptions of the tranquil stratosphere, where "the sky is beautiful . . . bluish purple, a deep violet shade . . . ten times darker than on Earth," that most fired the public's imagination.

"[He] has made his mark by rising higher above this planet than any other human being," noted the *Literary Digest* in a lengthy tribute entitled "The Columbus of the Stratosphere." Back at the University of Brussels, the professor was given a ride across campus on the shoulders of his students. The now-famous gondola, which remained behind on the glacier at Obergurgl (the glacier was later renamed for Piccard), became an informal shrine to the flight, and for several months before it could be moved, it was a favorite stopping place for skiers and hikers in the vicinity, who used pocketknives and other implements to scratch their names and messages into the blackened side of the great aluminum ball. When the gondola was eventually towed down the mountain to Innsbruck on the flatbed of a truck, it was surrounded by townspeople, everyone wanting to see and touch the now heavily graffitied capsule that had traveled to the stratosphere and back again.

Piccard altered and improved the design of a second gondola, which he used to make a second stratospheric ascent from Zurich with Max Cosyns in August 1932, besting his own altitude record with a new one of 53,153 feet.

He responded to the interest in his method of pressurizing a cabin for safe travel by emphasizing the potential of stratospheric flight. "Our ascensions demonstrated the practical possibilities of the air-tight cabin for future rapid travel through the stratosphere," he told reporters who met him and his family when their boat docked in New York in January 1933, at the beginning of a U.S. lecture tour. Piccard predicted that one day a stratospheric "superhighway" would open, with a "crossing from New York to Paris [that] will take only from six to eight hours," making "next-door neighbors" of Europe and America. "As a result of his sky jaunt," commented the Literary Digest, "Professor Piccard visualizes airplane trips across the Atlantic in a few hours . . . for in the stratosphere, he says, planes would be capable of 400-mile-an-hour speed."

For the National Geographic, Piccard prepared a scenario of this speedy new means of travel. "Visualize a New York business man seated in his dining room at breakfast time reading the morning paper," the professor wrote.

The telephone bell rings. It is a friend in Paris asking him to drop in for dinner a few hours later. The New Yorker rushes to the airdrome and takes the stratoplane that carries him rapidly to the upper atmosphere.

'Do you think we will have a good crossing?' the passenger asks a porter.

'Without any doubt. All crossings via the stratosphere are good. You will soon see the sky dark blue, but the weather up there is always fair. There is no snow, no rain, or fog, or frost.'

With majestic calm the stratoplane pursues its course high above all fogs and tempests. Fifty thousand feet below, a mighty transatlantic steamer battles against a terrific gale. By radio its passengers are notified that the stratoplane is passing overhead.

'Next time I shall travel by stratoplane,' affirms a man on board the ship. 'Steamers for rapid traveling are a thing of the past.'

And he will be right. The stratosphere is the superhighway of future intercontinental transport.

"[Piccard] gives us to understand that the journey will be both speedy and placid," Dorothy Fisk wrote, "accomplished in flawless sunshine and remote from the storms and tempests that prevail nearer to the earth.

"No wonder that the very word 'stratosphere' has a pleasant sound!"

There were some dissenters. The *New York Herald Tribune* worried that while Piccard's balloon had not been affected by the "electrification" of the upper air, motorized aircraft would be. The writer noted that "the stratosphere lacks . . . the thick blanket of lower air which shields us surface dwellers from powerful and penetrating rays of sunlight, some of which are known to be harmful . . . while others are under suspicion. Perhaps these dangerous rays can be kept out of the cabins [of stratosphere planes], perhaps not."

The *Palm Beach Post* voiced concern over the social implications of Piccard's discoveries. "The world has shrunk too rapidly for our prejudices and our social habits to adjust themselves," read an editorial. "We have hardly begun to learn that we are next-door neighbors to all the nations of the Earth; we are still trying to operate a compact and highly integrated world by a system devised when each nation was isolated." Powerful new forms of energy derived from cosmic rays and stratospheric flight, the article concluded, would make industrial methods of that time look like "an ox cart beside a motor car . . . and unfortunately we can't even drive the ox cart intelligently."

Piccard's vision of a "superhighway of intercontinental transport" between Europe and the United States was realized in the 1950s, when commercial airplanes with pressurized cabins began flying extensive North Atlantic routes. Then, in November 1962, within months of the professor's death, France and England gave particular credence to Piccard's ideas by agreeing to jointly design and construct the world's first high-altitude passenger plane, the Concorde.

The French-British alliance was born of necessity, for the development of the Concorde would be very expensive, but the cooperation agreement represented something else: a banding together by two European powers frustrated by U.S. domination of world commercial aviation.

Consistently, and to the great embarrassment of the British and the

French, European efforts in jet technology had either failed outright or been readily surpassed by the Americans. Though the British had distinguished themselves by introducing wartime technologies such as radar and the jet engine itself, their first foray into commercial jet aviation after the war, the De Havilland Comet, was a dismal failure. It was American-made jets, the Boeing 707 and the McDonnell Douglas DC-8, that revolutionized air travel in the 1950s. Ceding the long-range 707 market to the Americans, the British and the French attempted to build a niche for themselves with the short-range Britannia and Caravelle planes, but the United States successfully countered with the Boeing 727 and the McDonnell Douglas DC-9. These commercial jets flew generally at altitudes of between 25,000 and 40,000 feet, and at top speeds of 400 to 600 miles per hour. The British and French designers called the Concorde they envisioned a "supersonic transport," or SST, because it was expected to travel at speeds exceeding the speed of sound, which was 760 miles per hour at sea level, denoted as Mach 1 (after the Austrian physicist Ernst Mach), and cruise at stratospheric altitudes well above 45,000 feet. The European aircraft establishment eagerly embraced the Concorde project in 1962 not only because supersonic jet speeds and stratospheric flight appeared inevitable, but because by successfully developing the Concorde, the Europeans hoped to leapfrog over the United States into an emerging commercial aviation technology.

The Concorde partnership caught American industry by surprise, although U.S. aviation experts remained confident of superior American know-how. In 1947 the Bell XS-1 test plane piloted by Chuck Yeager had been the first aircraft to break the sound barrier, the same year Britain's first supersonic test plane, the De Havilland Swallow, broke apart over the Thames Estuary. And the United States had followed the "X-planes" with other supersonic military craft, such as the Hustler fighter and the B-58 bomber, while the British and French had lagged behind. As one Boeing executive observed, "We can develop hell out of anything. We may not be original, but we know how to put it into production."

The British and French engineers, when they got down to work on the Concorde, were perplexed by the technical demands supersonic flight imposed. Commercial-sized aircraft capable of attaining Mach 1 would require huge engines and staggering amounts of fuel; after incorporating wings, motors, and fuel, the designers couldn't improve much on a drawing-board SST that, on a route between London and New York, would carry only fifteen passengers, hardly an incentive for airlines to order a fleet of the planes.

The designers were not dissuaded by these initial difficulties, but retained their faith in the inevitability of the superior form of aviation the SST appeared to represent.

The growing conviction that the SST represented the future of aviation compelled many Americans to wonder if the United States, too, should launch a supersonic program. President John F. Kennedy was at first uncertain whether to back such a commitment. The technology of the SST was wondrous to contemplate but, as the Europeans were finding, it was not yet practical, and the costs of research and design would be considerable. It was also unclear to Kennedy what percentage of the necessary funds the private sector could be expected to invest, and in the United States there was no precedent for the government's financing the development of a commercial airplane, as there was in Britain and France. But there were also strong arguments that favored development. Kennedy envisioned commercial supersonics as a logical supplement to his ambitious space program, and he took pleasure in imagining American SSTs crossing the Atlantic at the same time U.S. astronauts were landing on the moon. Vice President Lyndon Johnson, whom Kennedy assigned to head a committee to investigate the SST, was favorably disposed toward the plane; as a senator, Johnson had led the Cold War hue and cry against the United States' failure to match the launching of the Soviet Sputnik satellites in the fall of 1957, and he was not inclined to concede America's ability to compete in any vital new technology, especially when he and other administration officials learned that the Soviets, too, were initiating development of an SST. In January 1963 a Federal Aviation Administration (FAA) advisory group seconded the vice president's enthusiasm, recommending that the United States proceed with an SST program.

Johnson had an influential ally at the FAA in Najeeb Halaby, the charismatic new chief of the agency and a former test pilot. "For me," Halaby once noted, "flight has always evoked the biblical Genesis, in which God gave man dominion over the Earth and over every creeping thing upon the face of the Earth." Halaby viewed the SST as "inevitable . . . the logical expression of faith in aviation's progress," and he helped foster in President Kennedy and other government officials the notion that the United States had a "manifest destiny" to pioneer and dominate the supersonic industry.

Before Kennedy had fully decided upon a course of action, Juan Trippe, president of Pan American Airlines, forced the government's hand by announcing that he had placed an order for six of the European-made Concordes. Kennedy was irate because he felt the Pan Am chief was trying to frighten the other U.S. airlines and at the same time bully the government into going forward with the SST. Pan Am had been the first airline to introduce Boeing 707s on the highly profitable North Atlantic routes in 1958, forcing other airlines to invest in all-new jet fleets or risk bankruptcy. No one wished to see a second such panic, particularly one that would result in U.S. carriers' rushing to buy foreign-built planes. The next day, June 5, 1963, Kennedy used the occasion of a commencement speech at the Air Force Academy in Colorado Springs to announce plans for an American SST program, asking Congress to immediately approve $60 million in funding so that basic design research could begin.

While there was broad public approval of the president's commitment, most U.S. airlines were apprehensive. They had not forgotten the premature obsolescence of huge fleets of propeller planes, perfectly fine DC-7s and Super-Constellations with thousands of commercial flying hours left in them, which had been more or less mandated by the introduction of the Boeing 707. That had been only five years before, and some airlines still had not recovered financially from the transition. An SST that became available too soon, forcing them to hurriedly replace their jet fleets, would pose all kinds of hardship.

The airlines were not alone in their predicament, for the SST held out to all the same inducement: it asked the government, the public, and industry to act on an idea, the idea of technological progress, and to do so on faith, with no assurance that this particular technological dream was feasible, or what the consequences of realizing it might be.

10.

THE SOUND OF FREEDOM

Proponents of the sst routinely described a future in which most commercial air travel would be supersonic. By 1970 or 1980, they suggested, thousands of SSTs would cross the skies each day in all the world's major air corridors, reducing long transcontinental and transoceanic flights to only two or three hours; by the year 2000 even more powerful planes, hypersonic aircraft capable of flying at altitudes of 150,000 feet, would whisk travelers to their destinations at Mach 5 speeds of nearly 4,000 miles per hour. The hypersonic New York–to–London flight would last only fifty minutes.

It was, ironically, precisely this assured vision of the bustling supersonic future that awakened the first meaningful opposition to the SST. The criticism, voiced by a handful of private citizens and congressmen, focused on the sonic boom, a thunderlike sound that millions of Americans had first heard in the 1950s and early 1960s as a result of military jets flying overhead. An ordinary commercial jet like a Boeing 727 moves at a speed that allows the air in front of its nose to part and flow back around the plane. When a supersonic jet attains Mach 1, the air cannot move out of its path in time; the nose of the plane compresses the air, creating a shock wave that spreads out behind the plane and reaches the ground with occasionally destructive impact, smashing windows, cracking building foundations, causing roof cave-ins and startling people and animals. The shock wave is produced not only when the plane first reaches the speed of sound, but continuously, and travels along the ground behind it for as long as the plane maintains supersonic speed. Anyone who took the promoters of the SST at their word was left to contemplate a "supersonic future" that would be at least as loud as it was fast.

Americans had complained about the nuisance and damage caused by military sonic booms in the mid-1950s, although during the height of the Cold War the government and the Air Force deflected criticism by citing their military necessity, characterizing the booms in public-relations briefings as "the sound of freedom." As one U.S. senator assured his constituents, "It is far better to listen to the sonic booms, than listen to the shrill, deadly screech of falling bombs." Air Force Major General Jewel C. Maxwell, later the director of the U.S. SST program, liked to remind reporters, "During the Berlin Airlift, when coal and food were being flown in, no one around Tempelhof Airfield complained about the noise. They asked for *more* noise—more airplanes—loaded heavier." However, formal complaints from citizens about sonic booms rose steadily, from 36 in 1956, the year military supersonics were introduced, to 6,481 in 1962.

A government survey conducted in St. Louis in 1961 and 1962 following 150 military supersonic test flights revealed a rapid decline in public support when a population test group was subjected to continuous sonic booms. During the first week of tests, residents appeared willing to put up with "the sound of freedom," but as the sonic booms continued, thousands of complaints about noise and property damage were received. The government ultimately paid 825 damage claims totaling $58,684. Three years later, after the government had thrown its support behind the U.S. SST program, the FAA, the Air Force, and the National Aeronautics and Space Administration (NASA) staged their largest test of public tolerance levels, Operation Bongo, in which military jets intentionally boomed Oklahoma City eight times a day for five months to simulate the anticipated supersonic air traffic of commercial flights. Oklahoma City had agreed to host the tests because its town fathers nurtured the hope that the community might become an "SST city," its Will Rogers World Airport an inland port for the high-flying planes. "The whole project, happily, should help establish our image firmly in international aviation circles," wrote the *Oklahoma City Times* before the first actual test boom had been heard, and before the first of nearly 16,000 complaints was phoned in to authorities. As a result of Operation Bongo, almost 5,000 Oklahoma City residents sued the Air Force for damage to their homes and property.

In 1966, the year Boeing received the government contract to design and build America's SST, the tenets of the emerging opposition to the plane were set forth in a *Harper's* magazine piece written by John E. Gibson, dean of engineering at Oakland University in Michigan. Gibson detailed the folly of mass-producing an expensive and impractical airplane, particularly one capable of causing so much damage, and chastised the government and the American aviation industry for its blind devotion to progress. "Something about new means of transportation seems to bring to the surface the latent gullibility in the best of us," Gibson wrote. He cited nineteenth-century examples of American technological excess —four thousand miles of unprofitable canals, three unnecessary transcontinental railroads—and termed the present enthusiasm for the SST "the latest of such imbroglios which stretch far back into American history."

Gibson's magazine piece marked a turning point. That same year other articles began to crop up voicing opposition to the SST—the *Wall Street Journal* published one entitled SUPERSONIC SNOW-JOB—and the *New York Times* published a flurry of letters to the editor on the subject. "The lack of public discussion of the SST, and the evident desire of many people in our government to proceed in secrecy, are most disturbing," wrote Harvard biology professor John T. Edsall. "Our engineers might well develop a plane that is a technological marvel, and is at the same time an economic failure and a human disaster—in short, a dud."

Gibson, Edsall, and a few others had fired the opening salvo in the battle over the SST, but it was William Shurcliff, a senior research associate at the Cambridge Electron Accelerator of Harvard University, who led the movement that would most seriously challenge the American SST program. A veteran author of scientific reports—he had coedited *The Smythe Report,* the official U.S. account of the development of the atom bomb—Shurcliff was keenly sensitive to manipulations of words and shifts of emphasis in such documents, and was offended when he read the reports pertaining to the development of the SST. One such report was a March 1965 study conducted for NASA by the Cambridge acoustical engineering firm of Bolt, Beranek & Newman, entitled "Laboratory Tests of Subjective Reactions to Sonic Boom." Two-thirds of the Harvard and MIT students tested described the simulated sonic boom they heard as "extremely annoying" and one-third showed a sharp increase in heart rate when subjected to a series of "booms," yet the report's abstract ignored these findings and concluded simply that the boom's "startle factor" did not appear to be "significant."

Shurcliff then learned through his correspondence with the FAA that the agency had no intention of limiting SST flights to ocean routes, as it had previously implied, but planned to permit the jets to fly overland, even over large metropolitan areas. Shurcliff calculated that 150 SST flights a day over the continental United States would create no fewer than 75 million square miles of "boom carpet." Since the whole country contained only 3 million square miles, each American could expect to be "boomed" an average of twenty-five times a day.

Decades of reflexive faith in technology, Shurcliff believed, had rendered otherwise intelligent and scrupulous men of science suddenly blind, making it impossible for them to perceive the real significance and danger of the supersonics. "Money, jobs, aviation, science, the future—these were all tied together by the monolithic voice of the government and the aviation industry," he later recalled. "If Boeing, the Air Force, and others had bribed the report writers to gloss over the boom, the bias could hardly have been greater."

Shurcliff's first impulse was to find an existing group working against the SST to whom he could quietly donate support. "I have amassed a large file on the subject," he wrote to the National Parks Association in late 1966, "and am now looking for some group that plans to attack the sonic boom threat vigorously."

No such group existed, but in writing to others to discover if it did, Shurcliff increasingly became the de facto leader of the gathering opposition, a one-man clearinghouse for information about the SST. With the assistance of his Harvard colleague, John Edsall, and Bo Lundberg, a former Swedish test pilot and director of the Aeronautical Research Institute of Sweden in Stockholm, he had assembled a modest but influential network of concerned individuals in the United States, including Mrs. Katherine Embree and her friend Elizabeth Borish; Dr. William Vogy, secretary of the Conservation Foundation; Robert Baron, president of a New York group called Citizens for a Quieter Community; and Wisconsin senator William Proxmire. Borish had authored two letters to the editor of the *New York Times* and had enlisted Embree to write another one. Lundberg was known in Europe as the "Father of All Opposition to the SST." One of the few aeronautics professionals to publicly find fault with supersonics, he had been rising before avionics conferences since the early 1960s to ask, "Do people really wish to be shot through the air, rather than flown?" Lundberg helped arm Shurcliff with expert information on the sonic boom and the SST. He told his American protégé, "We are in the unique position of having still a chance—for the first time in history—to prevent an utterly disastrous development in advance rather than to have to counteract or bring a stop to its harmful side effects after the activity has become extensive." He also assured Shurcliff that he was not alone: an anti-Concorde campaign led by a retired schoolteacher, Richard Wiggs, was well under way in Britain; West Germany and Sweden were working on restrictions of SST flights; and in mountainous Switzerland a strong anti-SST movement was seeking an absolute ban on the planes for fear they would trigger avalanches.

On February 24, 1967, Shurcliff jotted a note to Edsall announcing his intention of starting the Citizens League Against the Sonic Boom. He then sent out several dozen invitations to the league's first meeting, to be held on March 9 in the living room of his home off Brattle Street in Cambridge. At the meeting the new members in attendance (others joined and stayed in touch with the CLASB by mail) discussed a variety of approaches to fighting the sonic boom, among them letter writing, congressional lobbying, and the possibility of bringing some sort of legal action against the Air Force, the FAA, the Boeing Corporation, or even individual airlines, once commercial SSTs actually took to the air. It was agreed that lobbying Congress prematurely was risky, because without public support, the powerful senators and congressmen from the Seattle area, where Boeing was headquartered, could squelch their campaign. For the time being, the group decided to stick to a letter-writing campaign. Shurcliff himself was already averaging between twenty and thirty letters per day, which he produced on a portable typewriter ("I type fast and I think like a lawyer," he later said), and the league took it to be an encouraging sign when it learned a few weeks later that the FAA had assigned a senior staff member the sole job of researching and refuting Shurcliff's claims.

Shurcliff had closely followed the court case of Bailey Smith, an Oklahoma City man whose house had been badly damaged during Operation Bongo. Smith had won $10,000 from his insurance company in a disputed case, despite the FAA's hostile testimony. Shurcliff believed the Smith case indicated that complainants would be able to successfully prosecute such claims against the government, although Senator Proxmire, after consulting with the general counsel of the FAA, advised Shurcliff that such suits were impractical. In Oklahoma City, an official Air Force test was underway at the time of the damage to Smith's house, but the average citizen who suffered injury from a sonic boom would be hard put to prove which plane and pilot had done the actual damage, information that would be essential to the success of a legal action. While Shurcliff continued to entertain various legal options, he increasingly relied on his letter writing, maintaining a wide network of contacts and providing an incessant flow of facts and figures about the SST to news organizations, politicians, and interested citizens. "I tried to win people over by working the press," Shurcliff explained later, "and that was the beginning of our victory, winning over the papers, the *New York Times* and the *Washington Post.*"

In his correspondence Shurcliff made public virtually every report of substantial sonic-boom damage collected since supersonic aircraft had come into use, from the smashed windows and collapsed roof of the Uplands air terminal in Ottawa in 1959, to the August 2, 1967, sonic boom over the French countryside that caused a barn to cave in, killing three people. A favorite story concerned Gordon Bains, director of the nation's SST program, who invited journalists in January 1965 to attend low-altitude demonstrations of military supersonics at the White Sands Missile Range in New Mexico. The FAA had set up a movie-set village of empty houses and shops in the middle of the desert to show the harmless nature of the booms. The demonstration went as expected, but when photographers asked Bains if an F-104 could come closer for one last pass, the plane came in too low at supersonic speed. Bains was at that precise moment standing before a group of newsmen explaining that the public's fears of the boom were exaggerated. "I believe there's a great deal of psychology in this," Bains remarked, as the F-104 shattered the sound barrier directly overhead. The shock wave blew out two enormous plate-glass windows nearby, and dislodged a ten-pound window screen that hit an FAA official on the head. Bains resigned from his position a short time later.

CLASB membership grew so quickly that by October 1967, only seven months after its first meeting in Shurcliff's living room, the group boasted 1,700 members and a treasury of $4,000 in contributions. An average of thirty messages of support were being received each day, many with cash donations.

The response suggested the sea change that was taking place in public sentiment. What in the 1950s had passed as "the sound of freedom" was now more likely to be considered, according to the title of a 1967 television documentary, "Noise: The New Pollutant." Previously, the sound of the neighbor's lawnmower, of kids playing, of an ambulance screaming by in the night, even sounds of traffic or a nearby factory, had been considered a nuisance—but a nuisance that emanated from a specific and recognizable source, and could be traced back to another person or persons. The concept of noise pollution implied something entirely different, an anonymous technological phenomenon that could not be readily identified, isolated, and switched off. *Noise* was an irritant limited to a particular place and time; *noise pollution* permeated the environment, causing anxiety and long-term physical harm. "There is a great tendency these days to conserve water, conserve park lands, etc.," Shurcliff noted in one of his letters. "What about conserving peace and quiet?"

*   *   *

When not fending off the Citizens League Against the Sonic Boom and the nation's editorial writers, the pro-SST forces had to reckon with mounting opposition on Capitol Hill. Led by Senator Proxmire, legislators had begun to question not only whether SST technology was feasible, but whether a private firm, Boeing, deserved $700 million of the taxpayers' money to find out. Economist Walter Heller spoke for a growing number of concerned Americans, both inside and outside the capital, when he asked, "If the SST is such a profitable undertaking, why does the U.S. government . . . have to put up 80 to 90 percent of the development costs?"

Lyndon Johnson, as vice president and then as president, had consistently supported America's SST program. His successor, President Richard Nixon, upon taking office in January 1969, ordered the Transportation Department to "investigate all aspects" of SST development, and appointed a special Ad Hoc Review Committee to conduct hearings and recommend a course of action. The need for a clear-cut decision on the American SST was urgent: France and England were about to test-fly the first Concordes, and the Russians had already successfully flown their supersonic, the Tupolev Tu-144. The Boeing program still had not produced a functioning prototype, despite the large federal subsidy.

The committee's findings, delivered to the president on March 16, 1969, strongly advised against carrying on with the project. Describing the SST's operating costs as "excessive," the report suggested that the government had been forced to shoulder the financial burden of the SST because it was "unattractive to private financing." Committee members also saw "substantial uncertainty regarding the range and payload and the environmental effects of a production aircraft flowing from the present prototype development program," and concluded, "We feel the prestige associated with a U.S. SST does not warrant the expenditure involved."

Nixon, it seemed, could not abide the threat to national pride inherent in the committee's frank recommendations, and he suppressed the report all that summer. In late September 1969 he publicly urged continuation of the SST project, and asked Congress for additional funding; when the committee report was released in October, after the funding had been approved, pushing the total government subsidy to almost $1 billion, many legislators were outraged by the president's subterfuge.

In this volatile atmosphere, the efforts of the anti-SST movement began to pay off. Shurcliff's Citizens League joined with the Sierra Club, the National Wildlife Federation, the Wilderness Society, Zero Population Growth, and Friends of the Earth to form the Coalition Against the SST, and in anticipation of Earth Day, scheduled for April 1970, Shurcliff assembled the sonic-boom data and anti-SST evidence he had been disseminating for years to create the *SST and Sonic Boom Handbook*. Published as an inexpensive paperback, the book became part of a sudden burst of pop techno/environmental literature flooding college campuses, along with such essential tomes as *The Population Bomb* by Paul Ehrlich, *The Frail Ocean* by Wesley Marx, and R. Buckminster Fuller's *Operating Manual for Spaceship Earth*.

It was no longer only "bird-watchers" or "health cranks" advocating caution; after Earth Day, April 22, 1970, every politician from the president on down and every social commentator was citing the environment as one of the major issues facing the country. Even Charles Lindbergh confided to Najeeb Halaby that he thought the SST was an example of excessive technology.

Lindbergh's defection was only one more annoyance for the FAA chief. "Hardly a day went by without the news media disseminating some new SST horror story," he later recounted. "The plane would destroy the mating habits of minks, kill all the fish in the ocean with sonic booms, shatter millions of windows on every transcontinental flight. . . ." While hyperbole did surface in some tabloid press accounts—CONCORDE TO MELT ICECAPS, read a headline in one London daily—what most alarmed the pro-SST crowd was that there seemed to be no quick fix to halt the steady erosion of support for the plane.

On December 4, 1970, Proxmire's forces in the Senate, for the first time in seven years, turned back a proposed SST appropriation of $290 million. Asked why he had switched his position on the SST, Senator Clinton Anderson, Democrat of New Mexico, replied: "I read my mail."

The president, Halaby, and others reacted furiously to the setback. They had grossly underestimated the ability of "cranks and lunatics" to organize and win a public-relations war. Nixon urged the House, where the appropriation bill would go next, to reverse the Senate's "devastating mistake" that would waste the millions of dollars already spent and deal a "mortal blow" to the aerospace industry, while relegating the United States to second place in aviation.

The vehemence with which the administration fought for the SST expressed an anxiety that went deeper than the concern for jobs and national prestige. As Halaby worried in a letter to Proxmire, "The whole anti-SST movement [is] not without its dangers. One of the terrifying things to one who is dependent on technology is that there seems to be abroad a feeling of anti-technology—[that] technology is the devil that has caused every problem that we have in the U.S. today."

Frightened by the implications of this strange turnabout in traditional American values, the president's forces managed to delay the final House showdown on the SST appropriation until March, but now faced the distinct possibility the American SST would never leave the ground.

Anyone who saw Dr. James McDonald making his way through the halls of the Capitol the first week of March 1971, his battered, overstuffed briefcase under his arm, could have identified him instantly as yet another scientific expert come to testify before Congress about the SST.

The fifty-one-year-old senior physicist at the University of Arizona's Institute of Atmospheric Physics in Tucson had been asked by the National Academy of Sciences in 1966 to investigate the possibility that global climate could be affected by the hydrogen oxides, or water vapor, emitted by SST exhaust into the upper atmosphere. Scientists had suggested it was possible that the exhaust from hundreds of supersonic aircraft would add so much water vapor to the upper atmosphere that huge, almost permanent contrails would result. In the calm air of the stratosphere, these contrails would linger and, like so many additional clouds, blot out the sun and possibly alter the climatic patterns of the earth. After thoroughly reviewing the question, McDonald concluded that the amount of water vapor put into the stratosphere by supersonic planes would be insufficient to create the massive, climate-altering contrails some scientists feared. But when the debate over the SST became more pitched in 1970, the NAS asked McDonald to reexamine the water-vapor question.

This time McDonald enlarged the scope of his investigation and researched the possibility that water vapor could interfere with stratospheric ozone levels.

Sydney Chapman's basic model of ozone creation and destruction by photodissociation had been a mainstay of atmospheric science since 1931, but scientists had subsequently realized that the Chapman mechanism was not the sole chemical reaction governing the ozone layer. Measurements made in the late 1950s by American high-altitude U-2 jets found three times less ozone than the mechanism could account for. Something other than the interplay of oxygen and ultraviolet light clearly must destroy ozone. Scientists suspected that trace gases in the upper atmosphere might be responsible because they could scavenge ozone by means of a catalytic chain reaction, a chemical sequence in which one molecule species destroys another without being destroyed itself. In this way the minuscule, almost "invisible" quantities of a naturally occurring trace gas could account for the disappearance of large amounts of ozone.

One species of trace substance already known for its catalytic properties with regard to ozone was hydrogen oxides. In the years after World War II, two English chemists, Ronald Norrish and George Porter, had developed a technique known as flash spectroscopy at their Cambridge laboratory for measuring very fast gas-phase chemical reactions. Gases were inserted into a large cylinder made of quartz, flanked by two electronic flash tubes; a pulse of ultraviolet light from the tubes brought the chemicals to their photoreactive state, then a second flash recorded the effect on the jar's contents. In tests with ozone Norrish and Porter found that the quantum efficiency of the Chapman process—the ratio of the number of ozone molecules destroyed to the number of photons of ultraviolet light absorbed—was 2. But when, accidentally, oxides of hydrogen formed in the cylinder, the quantum efficiency jumped to 100.

In 1965 an English scientist named John Hampson, who had worked in the Norrish-Porter lab, was researching the reentry into the upper atmosphere of intercontinental ballistic missiles (ICBMs) for the Canadian Armaments Research and Development Establishment. Recalling the results of the flash-spectroscopy apparatus in Cambridge, he suggested in an in-house report that hydrogen oxides might be the catalyst responsible for the discrepancy between ozone concentrations predicted by Chapman and ozone levels measured by U-2s in the stratosphere. Hampson noted in his memorandum that large numbers of SSTs spewing water vapor into the upper air would probably affect the ozone layer. At that time, however, no one was suggesting that SSTs caused ozone depletion, and Hampson's theory was not published anywhere, so the possibility remained unknown and undiscussed. The following year, however, an Australian weapons researcher named B. G. Hunt, who was also considering what conditions ICBMs would encounter during their reentry into the atmosphere, worked out some of the same calculations of ozone equilibrium from hydrogen catalysis as Hampson, and published them in the prestigious *Journal of Geophysical Research*.

Ironically, one of the first American scientists to take up the question raised by Hampson and Hunt was a young staff photochemist at the Boeing Science Research Laboratories in Seattle, Halstead "Ted" Harrison. He estimated that the global ozone depletion from water vapor produced by hundreds of SSTs in daily use would amount to about 1 percent.

By law, since the SST was being publicly financed, any company "document" related to it had to be released to other government agencies, such as the Air Force; an "in-house memorandum," on the other hand, which Boeing dubbed Harrison's study, did not. The work on SST emissions and ozone was, at this juncture, highly theoretical, and given the myriad other complaints against the SST already straining Boeing's public-relations capability, the company was no doubt eager to avoid acknowledging any new problems.

"Emotion was very high at Boeing," Harrison reflected later. "People thought the SST was the most beautiful airplane that had ever been built, and they couldn't understand the link between tiny amounts of water vapor and a problem with stratospheric ozone. It just didn't register. After all, to appreciate the threat posed by a trace gas is, in a way, counterintuitive. Common sense tells you that something that small can't possibly make a difference to all that volume up there."

Boeing and Harrison arrived at an agreement that would keep the water-vapor story out of the headlines for the time being, yet not compromise Harrison's scientific integrity. Harrison agreed that it was not, after all, his job to offer advice on important policy decisions affecting the company, and that his calculations should rightly be considered an "in-house memo of a worst case scenario"; for its part, Boeing assured the House Appropriations Subcommittee for Transportation—to whom word of Harrison's discovery had leaked—that a full and thorough investigation of the matter would be undertaken, headed by Harrison, and that the results would appear in a peer-reviewed article published in a prominent scientific journal.

In the article, "Stratospheric Ozone with Added Water Vapor: Influence of High Altitude Aircraft," which ran in the November 13, 1970, issue of *Science,* Harrison estimated that a 3.8 percent decrease in global ozone would occur from the oxides of hydrogen created by the exhaust of 500 American SSTs and 350 foreign SSTs. He warned, however, that "this result should be treated cautiously. Indeed, natural variations in water, temperature, and ozone profiles will make all of the estimates of this study extraordinarily difficult to observe." When Senator Proxmire invited him to testify before the House committee considering the refunding of the SST, Harrison demurred. "The scientific uncertainty was too large to make a public statement on the subject," he later explained.

Harrison felt he tried his best under difficult circumstances to "play it straight," balancing his loyalties to science and to his employer, and he was deeply offended when John Swihart, Boeing's chief engineer for the SST, wrote a letter to *Aviation Week and Space Technology* labeling Harrison and several other atmospheric scientists who had expressed concern with the SST "scientifically dishonest if not treasonous."

One of those also singled out by Swihart was James McDonald. The Arizona physicist had at first found his study of water vapor and ozone to be in line with Harrison's seemingly modest 3.8 percent estimate. "Then I did a double take," he later told the House Appropriations Subcommittee for Transportation, the panel before which Harrison had declined to appear. "[I] realized there is this gradient of skin cancer from north to south which will be altered systematically, and I said to myself, maybe the numbers will be significant. I examined them . . . and I was rather startled by the numbers."

Shurcliff, in his *SST and Sonic Boom Handbook,* had cautioned that the health risk relative to stratospheric ozone was that it might leak into the cabin of a high-flying SST, endangering passengers. McDonald, after checking and rechecking his calculations, believed he saw the real threat: increased ultraviolet light entering the troposphere because of ozone loss would cause tens of thousands of additional cases of skin cancer each year in the United States alone, a risk that dwarfed the other environmental hazards associated with the SST, including the sonic boom.

"When you go to changes in the ecologic sense," McDonald explained, "then these seemingly tiny changes, two-tenths of a degree, three-tenths, and so on, which look negligible compared to day-to-day weather changes, are known in fact to be of very significant proportions when averaged over a good many years."

Prior to his appearance before the House Appropriations Subcommittee, McDonald interviewed medical authorities and read the available literature on melanoma and other forms of skin cancer. "He spent a great deal of time in the library of the College of Medicine," a colleague, former Institute of Atmospheric Physics director Richard Kassander, later recollected. "My guess is that he knew more about epidermatology than most of the physicians at the College of Medicine, even those who were specializing in it." McDonald was known for being as aggressive in presenting his point of view as he was tireless in assembling massive amounts of documentation. He was, by the time he took the witness chair at the start of the subcommittee's afternoon session on March 1, 1971, a man with a paramount objective: to alert the country's policymakers to the imminent and far-reaching dangers of SSTs, water vapor in the upper air, and the depletion of stratospheric ozone. If only they would listen to him.

He had good reason to fear they might not, for McDonald was well known for his interest in the study of unidentified flying objects (UFOs). When a wave of UFO sightings swept the nation in 1965, McDonald was one of a handful of scientists to attempt to make an informed response to the public concern. "I believe this is a problem of the first order of scientific importance," he had told a reporter at the time. "It has been neglected and misrepresented and it is crying out for high-caliber attention."

UFO studies were then largely governed by two distinct schools of thought. Dr. Donald H. Menzel of the Harvard Observatory, representing one, had dismissed all UFO sightings as either hallucinations or atmospheric phenomena, while Dr. J. Allen Hynek, former chief Air Force astronomy consultant, led a small group of scientists who thought that unexplained UFO cases warranted more serious study. McDonald believed that in the case of UFOs, science had failed to live up to its usual standards of candid, objective investigation, and that the official Air Force studies so far conducted—"Project Sign," "Project Grudge," and "Project Bluebook"—were "almost meaningless."

Congress, meanwhile, had called for an official account of the phenomenon, appointing a committee headed by University of Colorado scientist Edward Condon. The Air Force was by now receiving a thousand new sighting reports per year, membership in UFO and "contactee" clubs had swelled, and in addition to a steady stream of magazine articles, more than two dozen books were published between 1966 and 1968 dealing with the subject.

The much-awaited Condon report to Congress on the UFO question, released in January 1969, concluded that all UFO sightings could be rationally explained as hoaxes or natural phenomena, and decreed that there was no scientific justification for any further investigations. McDonald denounced the Condon report as a whitewash, citing the group's shoddy investigative procedures and pointing out that its conclusions failed to jibe with its own admission of a significant percentage of unexplained sightings. The report's "scientific padding," McDonald wrote, "cannot conceal from anyone who studies it closely that it examines only a tiny fraction of the really puzzling UFO reports and that its scientific argumentation is often unsatisfactory." McDonald told *Time* magazine the Condon group had "wasted an unprecedented opportunity" to make a thorough scientific study of the UFO problem.

Fed up with the Air Force and the Condon committee, McDonald increased his own investigations of UFO sightings and his lecture appearances. His strident positions and habit of overwhelming opponents with relentless argument and reams of data, however, increasingly brought him into direct personal conflict with others in the UFO field. He remained a highly regarded scientist despite the controversy, but having allowed himself, in the defense of scientific principle, to become stigmatized as a UFO "nut," he knew that any data or conclusions he presented to Congress on the already contentious subject of the SST would surely be held up to harsh scrutiny.

*   *   *

"It is my present estimate," McDonald testified before the House Appropriations Subcommittee for Transportation on Monday, March 1, 1971, "that the operation of SSTs at the now-estimated fleet levels predicted for 1980–85 could so increase transmission of solar ultraviolet radiation as to cause something on the order of 5–10,000 additional skin cancer cases per year in just the U.S. alone." The subcommittee, chaired by Representative John J. McFall of California, routinely examined legislation pertaining to mass transit, highways, railroads, ferries, interstate buses, and commercial aviation; the committee members, like most people, knew little or nothing about the ozone layer. McDonald tried to excite the congressmen's interest by describing potential stratospheric ozone depletion from SST exhaust as "a good example of a subtle and initially unrecognized environmental hazard now calling for the most searching scrutiny." He cited the high-flying SST as "a new technology in a region of our total environment which—though it is a long way up —has very definite effects on us. We know much less about it than we should."

McDonald believed the projected level of SST flights might deplete as much as 5 percent of the ozone layer, but in presenting his data to the committee he used the figure of 1 percent, a depletion he calculated would cause a 10 percent increase in various skin cancers in the northern hemisphere.

"The purely biological and evolutionary evidence that we, as well as all other life forms, have evolved in ways leaving us only marginally protected from highly adverse effects of ultraviolet radiation is essentially incontrovertible," he testified. "We just can't stand that ultraviolet, and the whole history of evolution, it is becoming clearer and clearer, has been a battle with ultraviolet. We have always just barely won. . . ."

Congressman Sidney R. Yates of Illinois interrupted to ask McDonald to speak a little more slowly and indicate more clearly how what he was saying related to the SST. Compared to ozone depletion, the sonic boom had been a far easier threat for the layman to grasp, and the congressmen were almost totally uncomprehending, despite McDonald's best attempts to compress a short course in atmospheric chemistry into his presentation.

Representative Silvio Conte of Massachusetts reminded his fellow legislators that the witness had appeared on Capitol Hill before, in 1968, to testify on the subject of UFOs. Conte asked McDonald whether he still believed a statement he had made then to the effect that power failures in New York were caused by flying saucers. McDonald corrected the congressman, saying he had only observed at the time that there was a possible connection between UFO sightings in the area and power outages, and that this possibility had not been sufficiently investigated. Some people in the audience and even a few of the congressmen laughed when McDonald said this. Conte asked McDonald if he expected him to relate the SST–skin cancer hypothesis to other members of the House of Representatives without mentioning that the person who had presented it to the committee had a reputation as a UFO expert. "It is not entirely clear," McDonald retorted, "that there is a relationship between SSTs and UFOs."

But Conte had gained the offensive. "A man who comes here and tells me that the SST flying in the stratosphere is going to cause thousands of skin cancers has to back up his theory that there are little men flying around the sky. I think this is very important."

At Conte's insistence, part of McDonald's 1968 testimony, in which the physicist had stated that human contact with beings from outer space may have at some point taken place, was read into the *Congressional Record*. McDonald sounded angry when he was allowed to return to the subject of ozone depletion. "It is not 'kooky,' it is not 'nutty,' " he asserted, "it is not ecological extremism! It is physics and chemistry, photochemistry, cell biochemistry, atmospheric physics!

"Who thought DDT would do some of the things it does?" he said. "Who would have thought that various technologies would put mercury in codfish . . . who would have thought that antiknock, which was such a boon to driving cars from 1920 onward, in fact put lead in our environment to an extent that we may already have gone beyond the safe point? There are many examples of this."

McDonald couldn't be certain how fully Conte had damaged his credibility, nullifying the importance of what he had to say about ozone, or even if the committee had been able to understand his presentation. Most press accounts gave the day to Conte. An article in the *New York Times* concluded that the weight of the Arizona scientist's findings "was sharply discounted after he acknowledged, under questioning, that he had earlier testified before Congress to his serious concern about unidentified flying objects and the possibility that 'flying saucers' may have been related to power failures in New York City." William Kellogg, associate director of the National Center for Atmospheric Research, who had also testified, described McDonald's appearance in his notes of the session as "angry and finger-wagging, clouding the real issues by constantly implying that others who have looked at it are either ignorant or dishonest . . . he presents the case with too much emotion and a rather transparent hostility to the whole idea of the SST." But during his own turn in the witness chair, Kellogg assured the congressmen that McDonald was "a very distinguished atmospheric physicist," and noted that "each of the points he has raised deserves careful consideration by the scientists who can help clarify the situation. Jim McDonald would not have raised these worries without having some good arguments to back him up."

Eager to exploit any scientific finding that might help discredit the SST, Senator Proxmire asked Gio Gori, associate scientific director of the National Cancer Institute, for an evaluation of McDonald's skin-cancer estimates. Gori, to Proxmire's surprise, not only substantiated McDonald's report, but turned in a higher estimate of projected skin-cancer cases. Gori calculated that 800 daily SST flights in the United States—if they resulted in as much ozone depletion as McDonald said they would —would cause as many as 103,000 additional adult cases of skin cancer each year. He also pointed out that skin cancer might well prove to be only one of the health effects of having tampered with the ozone layer, and not necessarily the worst.

Also on hand at the Transportation Subcommittee hearing was Joseph Hirschfelder, a veteran of the Los Alamos Atomic Bomb Laboratory and a chemistry professor at the University of Wisconsin. Like Proxmire, Gori, and a few others, he had heard enough of McDonald's presentation to be alarmed. Hirschfelder was a member of the Department of Commerce's Technical Advisory Board, which was planning to convene a meeting soon on the environmental aspects of the SST; after listening to McDonald's testimony, he arranged for a separate emergency hearing to be held expressly to consider the new evidence McDonald had presented, and to be attended not by uncomprehending legislators and reporters but by those best suited to judge what he had to say, McDonald's peers—the nation's top atmospheric scientists and public-health officials.

Leading Hirschfelder's list of invited experts was Harold Johnston of the University of California at Berkeley. Johnston, the author of several books on atmospheric chemistry and an expert on atmospheric pollutants, was known for making rigorous and sometimes blunt evaluations of new hypotheses that emerged in his area of expertise.

It had been Johnston's good fortune to participate, as a graduate student at Cal Tech in 1948, in one of the era's great scientific breakthroughs in atmospheric science. During the Second World War, Southern Californians had complained of irritating, dirty-looking air near factories involved in the war effort. Apparently similar "smogs" caused by a mixture of coal smoke and fog had plagued London since the turn of the century. Professor A. J. Haagen-Smit, whom Johnston worked under, successfully proved that the Southern California "smog" was not a mixture of smoke and fog, but was composed largely of ozone, and that it was being formed photochemically as sunlight reacted with oxygen and the hydrocarbons and nitrogen oxide produced by the combustion of gasoline and other petroleum products. "People had been looking to see which factories should be closed down," Johnston later recalled. "Suddenly, it turned out everyone's *car* was doing it."

Haagen-Smit proved his assertion that smog contained large concentrations of ozone by devising what Johnston proudly remembers as the "cheapest lab proof ever to lead to a major scientific discovery," exposing common rubber bands to laboratory "smog" conditions. Ozone weakens rubber, so Haagan-Smit could measure its concentration in a smog sample by studying how easily and how far the rubber bands could be stretched. Unlike stratospheric ozone, which is beneficial to human beings in that it prevents the sun's ultraviolet radiation from reaching the earth's surface, ozone in smog is a health hazard. Haagen-Smit's work defined an environmental problem that would profoundly influence the politics and culture of Southern California, particularly the traffic-snarled Los Angeles area.

Johnston arrived at Hirschfelder's SST meeting in Boulder, Colorado, on March 18, 1971, and heard James McDonald repeat the presentation he had made in Washington. Some of the atmospheric scientists present attacked McDonald for introducing an emotional issue like skin cancer into what they felt should be strictly a discussion of stratospheric chemistry. Arnold Goldburg, meanwhile, the outspoken chief scientist of Boeing's SST division, repeatedly interrupted McDonald, contesting nearly every one of his findings. After years of defending Boeing and the SST program from relentless criticism, Goldburg was apparently determined to squash McDonald's theory before it had a chance to leave the room, and he subjected him to what others later characterized as a cross-examination. As Johnston noted, "I have never seen any person at any scientific meeting so abused as McDonald was during the course of presenting his paper."

Johnston himself felt McDonald's basic equation linking SST exhaust to ozone depletion to skin cancer was persuasive, but he took issue with some of McDonald's atmospheric chemistry. In his many studies of smog Johnston had worked and reworked equations showing how nitric oxide helps to create ozone in the troposphere below an altitude of 13 kilometers, so he was in a way perhaps ideally prepared to understand how nitric oxide could perform an opposite role. He suggested to the gathering, which had focused almost exclusively on oxides of hydrogen, that he suspected another category of trace substance found in SST exhaust—oxides of nitrogen—would be much more significant ozone-destroying catalysts.

Although Johnston and most of the other scientists present had not seen it, a Dutch meteorologist named Paul Crutzen working at the Clarendon Laboratory at Oxford University had only the year before published a hypothesis describing how oxides of nitrogen function as ozone scavengers. Crutzen theorized that as an inert by-product of the natural nitrogen cycle, nitrous oxide rises into the stratosphere, where it is disassociated by ultraviolet radiation to form oxides of nitrogen. While he recognized that oxides of hydrogen were an ozone-destroying catalyst, Crutzen's calculations indicated that they alone could not adequately explain observations of ozone levels at altitudes between 30 and 35 kilometers. The oxides of nitrogen, Crutzen suggested, were actually far more significant than oxides of hydrogen in their overall impact.

At the Boulder conference Johnston independently arrived at the same conclusion as Crutzen, but unlike Crutzen, Johnston now knew of a potential man-made source of nitrous oxide in the stratosphere—the SST. His deduction did not meet with much approval, however. "The next day when I made a formal motion that the conference inform the Secretary of Commerce that oxides of nitrogen were not 'negligible' in harming ozone, as had previously been believed, I got the same treatment as McDonald," Johnston later said. "Politics were so polarized and bitter at that time over the SST, one could not make a scientific argument without being branded, one way or the other, anti-progress. [My] formal motion was strongly defeated, the wording voted down."

Returning to Berkeley, Johnston sat down to chart his own estimates of stratospheric ozone loss due to nitric oxide in SST exhaust. Though his analysis differed from McDonald's, he soon understood the reason for his colleague's alarm. Using a sample of 500 SSTs operating in or near the stratosphere 7 hours a day, 365 days a year, Johnston concluded that average global ozone reductions would range from 3 to 23 percent, with 50 percent local reductions near zones of high SST activity.

Given the seriousness of his findings, Johnston felt he could do no less than get word to the highest authority: he placed a call to President Nixon's science advisor, Edward David. A member of David's staff returned Johnston's call, and after hearing what the chemistry professor had to say, politely informed him that the White House wasn't interested in hearing any more scientific warnings about the SST, and that in any case the House had just voted down the latest funding measure, effectively killing the U.S.-Boeing SST program.

The House had decided on March 17, 1971, by a vote of 215 to 204, not to continue funding the SST, and Nixon, for whom the issue of national pride had always been paramount, was not taking the news well. "What is involved here is not just the 150,000 jobs which will be lost," the president told newsmen, "but the fact that the United States of America, which has been first in the world of commercial aviation from the time of the Wright brothers, decides not just to be second, but not even to show." The president's words, however, were drowned out by a chorus of approval for the House vote. Remarked *Newsweek* of Nixon's lament, "In the wised-up seventies, that sort of appeal to national pride may be losing its old magic. [There is] a growing feeling that America needs to rethink its national priorities and that the technological adventures it has funded unquestionably in the past may be one good place to begin."

The House defeat was the end of the road for the American SST, and worldwide supersonic jet travel has yet to materialize. Besides the economic and environmental factors that beleaguered the SST's development, it was ultimately the appeal of another, far less glamorous airplane, the jumbo jet, that proved its undoing. The jumbo jet "wide-bodies" of the early 1970s—the Boeing 747, the McDonnell Douglas DC-10, and Lockheed's L-1011—could carry a payload constituting 20 percent of their weight, as opposed to the SST's 7 percent, and because jumbo jets flew chiefly in the troposphere and at subsonic speeds, they created no sonic booms. Built for comfort, not speed, and introduced in an era of spiraling fuel prices, the relatively economical wide-bodies were immediately popular with airlines and the flying public alike. In 1973 Pan Am and TWA canceled their orders for Concordes, leaving only British Airways and Air France flying daily Concordes on the North Atlantic routes. Even in London and Paris, resistance to landing and takeoff noise from the plane soured patriotic enthusiasms for the inauguration of service. In suburban Washington similar concern kept the Concorde from using Dulles Airport until 1976, while New Yorkers opposed to the SST stalled the Concorde's arrival at John F. Kennedy Airport until the fall of 1977.

11.

PURE SCIENCE

WHEN THE SST CONTROVERSY was finally resolved, atmospheric scientists were left to ponder the troubling implication that human activities could introduce enough additional quantities of a trace gas into the atmosphere to significantly alter the natural processes whereby stratospheric ozone is created and destroyed. The Department of Transportation's official response to this worry had been to fund a $21 million study of the SST's potential to modify climate, weather, and the chemistry of the upper air. Utilizing a thousand scientists from ten nations over a three-year period beginning in 1971, the Climatic Impact Assessment Program (CIAP) focused scientific interest on the stratosphere and pumped millions of research dollars into the atmospheric sciences. The SST controversy also gave wide publicity, for the first time, to the harsh consequences that any significant thinning of the ozone layer could have for life on earth. Depleted ozone, the public was told, would allow increased levels of ultraviolet light to enter the troposphere, where it could inhibit photosynthesis, harm essential sea plankton, and cause a host of medical problems for human beings, including various forms of skin cancer. But since the SSTs were not built in the large numbers once envisioned (the French and British ultimately produced only thirteen Concordes), as of the early 1970s the threat to the ozone layer remained largely hypothetical.

Twentieth-century atmospheric chemistry was something of an orphan of science, falling in between the more mainstream disciplines of meteorology, which concentrated on outdoor phenomena, and chemistry, primarily a laboratory pursuit. It had been invigorated, however, by the tremendous investment in nuclear-weapons research during the 1940s and 1950s. Atom- and hydrogen-bomb tests introduced radioactive elements into the atmosphere, and accurately measuring the by-products of nuclear detonations was essential so that the United States might know the full impact of its own weapons experiments and might monitor the Soviet competition. Samples of nuclear fallout could tell scientists precisely what a bomb was made of. But after atmospheric bomb testing was banned by international treaty in 1963, financial support for atmospheric chemistry was cut and interest in the field began to wane. In 1971 the Atomic Energy Commission, mindful, perhaps, that the test ban might not last forever, sponsored the first in a series of annual workshops bringing meteorologists and chemists together in an effort to reinvigorate the discipline.

One of the first hints that the issue of ozone depletion would once again become a matter of serious concern came in a presentation given by Lester Machta of the National Oceanic and Atmospheric Administration (NOAA) during one of the AEC workshops held in Fort Lauderdale, Florida, in January 1972. Among the participants at the conference was F. Sherwood "Sherry" Rowland, professor of chemistry at the University of California at Irvine. In the talk Machta revealed that, thanks to sensitive new instruments, measurable amounts of chlorofluorocarbons had been detected in the atmosphere. This announcement itself was not unusual, for atmospheric chemistry was still a young enough discipline that new discoveries about trace gases and the chemical interactions that take place in the atmosphere occurred with some frequency.

In 1972, CFCs were widely used as coolants in refrigerators and air conditioners, as a propellant in aerosol sprays, as a blowing agent in the manufacture of styrofoam and other plastics, and it had just been introduced as a solvent in the manufacture of computer chips—an industry expected to boom in the coming decades. Perhaps no industrial chemical compound more fully represented the slogan—"Better Living Through Chemistry"—that the Du Pont corporation had adopted in the midst of the Great Depression to suggest the power modern chemistry had to transform everyday life. (By 1970 the connotations associated with the word "chemistry" had changed, and the company had seen fit to drop its classic slogan and substitute a new one: "There's a World of Things We're Doing Something About.") Since their arrival as miracle refrigerants in the thirties and their adoption by the aerosol industry in the late forties, CFCs had retained their reputation as being among the most versatile and benign of all industrial compounds, posing no known danger to man or the environment. And due to their massive commercial proliferation they were quite literally everywhere on earth: in factories and in countless homes, cars, and places of work, in the air and in the oceans.

Lester Machta's presentation about CFCs at the 1972 conference discussed the as-yet-unpublished results of work by the maverick British scientist James Lovelock, who had succeeded in measuring CFC-11 in the atmosphere in concentrations roughly equal to the quantities that had been produced since its invention. Lovelock, who worked as a freelance scientist out of his home in Wiltshire, England, had been responsible for a major breakthrough in the atmospheric sciences, the invention of the electron-capture detector for gas chromatography, which made it possible for the first time for scientists to measure gases in the atmosphere in minute concentrations as small as 1 part per trillion. Before Lovelock's invention, chemists had barely been able to detect 1 part in a million. It was in the process of making observations with this instrument that Lovelock found CFC-11—in concentrations of approximately 70 parts per trillion in the northern hemisphere and 40 parts per trillion in the southern hemisphere. Machta reported Lovelock's suggestion that CFCs could be a potentially useful "tracer" of air motions in the atmosphere.

Following Machta's formal presentation, Rowland found himself in an informal discussion with several of the other workshop participants. He agreed that CFCs could be used as tracers, but he wondered aloud what eventually became of them. One of Rowland's specialties was photochemistry, or the study of how various molecules react when they are exposed to light or ultraviolet radiation. A decade before, when he was at the University of Kansas, he had worked with both fluorine and chlorine, constituent elements of CFC compounds, and one of his graduate students had conducted experiments with CFCs. Rowland knew enough about the photochemistry of the elements involved to deduce that while the CFC molecules Lovelock had measured in the atmosphere were stable in the lower atmosphere, they would almost certainly decompose if and when they drifted up as far as the stratosphere, where they would be exposed to short-wavelength ultraviolet light. Rowland also knew that chlorine had been shown in laboratory experiments to destroy ozone. And, having twice invited Harold Johnston to present seminars on the hydrogen-oxide and nitrogen-oxide chains, he recognized that catalytic reactions involving ozone were important.

To many of the scientists who attended the Fort Lauderdale workshop, CFC molecules were terribly complex. To a physical chemist like Sherry Rowland, however, CFCs, which in most forms contain only five atoms, are simple compounds. And while it was easy for the meteorologists to accept that CFCs were chemically inert and let it go at that, Rowland recognized what this assumption missed: that "there had to be chemistry involved" in their lingering presence in the environment.

Rowland felt strongly that the most interesting breakthroughs in science occurred "on the fringe," in places others might not be looking, and he was always alert to intriguing new research possibilities, but his wondering about the chemistry of CFCs in the atmosphere was at the time more a chemist's curiosity than a necessarily promising line of investigation. He knew Lovelock was wrong to assume that CFCs remained inert in the atmosphere, but thought it unlikely that they were present in sufficient concentrations to pose any serious environmental hazard.

Born in Delaware, Ohio, in June 1927, the second son of a mathematics professor at Ohio Wesleyan University, Sherry Rowland knew the name of Thomas Midgley, Jr., as a child. Midgley's home was only fourteen miles down the road in Worthington. Although Rowland's father, Sidney, was an academic, he had worked for General Electric before Rowland was born, and had a deep respect for the scientist-inventors of the early twentieth century and their life-enhancing achievements.

When Sherry Rowland graduated from Delaware High School in the summer of 1943 at the age of sixteen—too young to enlist in the service —he enrolled at Ohio Wesleyan, whose campus was only four blocks from his home, because as the son of a tenured professor, he could attend tuition-free. The war effort had decimated the university, leaving it particularly bereft of men. With normal college life so attenuated and a somber mood dominating the campus, Rowland attended classes year-round, studying diligently and with few distractions, gravitating toward a career in chemistry. Just before his eighteenth birthday, in 1945, he enlisted in the Navy, and was in boot camp when the war ended.

The break from academia may have been propitious. When he returned to Ohio Wesleyan after a year away, Rowland abruptly slowed the pace of his education. He had developed other interests, particularly in athletics. At six feet five, he proved to be a natural on the basketball court. He started at forward and was a star performer with the school's varsity team during his senior year in 1947–48. In 1948, Rowland graduated from Ohio Wesleyan and entered graduate school at the University of Chicago, where he was assigned at random, like all new graduate students, to two advisors; one was the renowned radiochemist Willard Libby.

Like most eminent chemists and physicists of his generation, Libby was an alumnus of the Manhattan Project. While working at Oak Ridge, Tennessee, in the early 1940s, he had helped develop a method for separating uranium isotopes, a critical step in the development of the atom bomb. After the war, at the Institute for Nuclear Studies at the University of Chicago, his continuing work in radiation and "hot atom" chemistry led to a major scientific breakthrough, one with surprising applications to the seemingly unrelated discipline of archeology. Libby speculated that although the amount of energy received by the earth from cosmic radiation is minute, it must alter the earth's atmosphere in detectable ways. Based on laboratory observations, he surmised that the neutrons formed by cosmic radiation would interact with the abundant nitrogen in the air to produce radiocarbon, or carbon-14, and tritium. A search for radiocarbon and tritium in the atmosphere found them in roughly the amounts and concentrations Libby expected.

Libby calculated that the half-life of radiocarbon—or the length of time it would take for it to deteriorate by half—was 5,568 years, plus or minus thirty years (calculations that have since been refined), sufficient time for the radiocarbon produced by cosmic radiation to become distributed through the reservoir of all the carbon on earth, including the carbon contained in carbon dioxide. Since plants ingest carbon dioxide, and animals live off plants, Libby predicted that all living things would be rendered radioactive by cosmic radiation.

Living things ingest radiocarbon at a steady rate, just as radiocarbon decays at a steady rate. When a plant or an animal dies, however, it ceases to ingest radiocarbon, while the radiocarbon it contains in its tissues continues to decay. In other words, once living things die, they lose their radioactivity at a fixed rate. Libby had conceived of a way to accurately date organic material by measuring its radioactivity, a hypothesis he tested by carrying out experiments with organic samples of a known age. A panel of archeologists supplied Libby with samples such as wood from the deck of a funerary ship from the tomb of the Egyptian pharaoh Sesostris III; linen wrappings from the Dead Sea Scrolls; charcoal from the caves of Lascaux near Montignac in the Dordogne region of France; and a lump of beeswax associated with a smith's hoard of late Bronze Age objects found in England.

The samples were processed to remove the carbon from them, which then had to be converted to carbon dioxide, purified, reduced, and collected. The resulting carbon's radioactivity was so weak that it was enormously difficult to measure. Libby was forced to invent a sensitive new instrument, a type of Geiger counter that could block out ubiquitous background radiation and detect minute amounts of radioactivity. The results were conclusive. By 1955 some two thousand samples had been tested. The ages of many samples were corroborated by Libby's method; others were discovered to have been incorrectly dated by archeologists who had relied upon far less precise and indirect methods—such as the rate of accumulation of sediments—to determine their age. Libby's carbon-14 dating method forced the reexamination of many accepted ideas about archeological and geological chronology. He later won the Nobel Prize for his efforts.

Libby's approach to science made a lasting impression on his young graduate student, Sherry Rowland. Libby had started out by asking basic questions about cosmic radiation, questions of purely scientific interest, with no obvious or practical end in mind. He had applied knowledge gleaned from laboratory work with radiation to natural, if previously undetected, phenomena. When necessary, Libby had invented equipment or techniques to test his theories. The eventual outcome was a major scientific development with tremendous implications far beyond the confines in which the work had originally been conceived.

Libby's freedom from orthodoxy extended to his personal relationships with students who worked under him. Throughout graduate school, Rowland devoted himself more to sports than to chemistry, a distraction other advisors might not have tolerated. Since he had come to athletics late as an undergraduate, Rowland had several years of eligibility left in both basketball and baseball and he played with the University of Chicago's varsity teams in both sports. In 1949, Rowland was named Most Valuable Player in the AAU Chicago city basketball championship game. He was a good enough basketball player to toy briefly with the idea of accepting an invitation to tour with the Harlem Globetrotters.

To Rowland, Libby's easy acceptance of his sports career was consistent with Libby's gifts as a research scientist, the expression of a relaxed temperament and a willingness to allow the world to impinge upon one's life and work. Inspiration could come to a scientist from the most unexpected places, and it was the whole person, with a full range of enthusiasms, who did the most creative work in the lab.

In the summer of 1952, Rowland married, earned his Ph.D. from the University of Chicago, and took an instructorship at Princeton. He was hired to teach undergraduates, but also continued the research work he had begun with Libby, investigating the chemical reactions of radioactive atoms. Where Libby worked with carbon-14 and bromine, however, Rowland focused on tritium, the second isotope produced by the interaction of cosmic rays and nitrogen.

Rowland's work involved tritium produced in nuclear reactors under controlled circumstances in the lab. Many experiments involved the use of tritium as a tracer because tritium atoms are relatively easy to detect. An example with practical applications might be putting tritium tracers into a drug, then testing the drug on an animal and analyzing where the tritium tracers, and the drug, end up in the animal's body.

During the summers, Rowland's tritium studies took him to the Brookhaven National Laboratory on Long Island. In 1953, Rowland and a colleague at Brookhaven were attempting to measure the natural tritium content in atmospheric hydrogen when they found an unexpectedly high concentration of the isotope. After submitting their results for publication, they were asked by their superiors at Brookhaven to withdraw the paper. When the two scientists questioned the request, they were told that if they didn't withdraw the paper, it would be classified as secret government information. For an ambitious research scientist, the implications of having one's work classified are entirely negative. Such an action stifles all possible dissemination of specific scientific ideas, and thoroughly removes a scientist's data and conclusions from the larger discourse by which science progresses, thwarting the sharing of information and the give-and-take by which reputations are made and careers advance. Tritium is an essential component of hydrogen bombs, and Rowland later learned there had been a tritium spill at the Hanford plant in Washington State, which his measurements on Long Island had detected. It was eight years before the paper could be published. Such an experience, Rowland later recalled, "tends to discourage you from doing atmospheric chemistry."

Of course, the history of both radiochemistry and atmospheric chemistry was inextricably bound up with nuclear-weapons research and development, regardless of how purely scientific the motives behind the work of any individual scientist may have been. The political and military interest in turn generated money for research in particular areas, such as radiochemistry and high-energy physics. Those areas, nurtured by cash, tended to be where the most exciting scientific advances were made. Even scientists who were not interested in building bombs were attracted both to the excitement of the work being done in those particular fields and to the government money available for "pure" research in those same areas. Sherry Rowland was no exception. Beginning in 1956, the same year he left Princeton for a job at the University of Kansas, his work was funded by the Atomic Energy Commission.

Within the small community of radiochemists, Rowland was well known for his continuing work with tritium, but the course of his career was not remarkable. In 1962 he branched out into photochemistry, and two years later, at the age of thirty-six, was hired to found the chemistry department at the brand-new University of California campus at Irvine.

The planned community of Irvine, in Orange County, sixty miles south of Los Angeles, stood at the frontier of the booming Sunbelt. Most of the future campus was a muddy construction site carved out of pastureland, and the challenge for the twenty or so newly hired faculty members was to build a sound academic institution from the ground up. Boasting no tradition of scientific excellence, no community of Nobel laureates, it hardly seemed a promising home for an ambitious scientist. But Irvine gratified Sherry Rowland's disposition for "the fringe," for "getting away from the crowd." While attending to his teaching and administrative duties, Rowland quietly pursued his interests in gas-phase kinetics, radiochemistry, and photochemistry.

Rowland's daughter, Ingrid, was a high-school senior and his son, Jeff, a freshman when Earth Day, April 22, 1970, came to the Irvine campus. Ingrid, in particular, was caught up in the Earth Day movement, helping to organize a protest march at her school. The Rowlands talked about the issues of the day at dinner; friends and family would cheerfully join in what they called "the Saturday night fights," which were often instigated by the outspoken Joan Rowland. Joan loved her new home in Corona del Mar, on a hill with a spectacular view of the Pacific, just a few miles from the Irvine campus. Sherry had bought the house before she saw it, on his second trip to California from Kansas. All she had asked, when he called to say he had found a house he wanted to buy, was that he make certain the kitchen was sunlit and bright. It had since become a family joke. At odd times Sherry would look at Joan and ask if the kitchen was bright enough. It was. But since moving to Corona del Mar in 1964, Joan had been disturbed that her view from the kitchen window was increasingly occluded by the smog that had begun to creep down the Orange County coast from Los Angeles. As environmental issues topped the national agenda in the 1970s and the Rowland family and friends debated them over supper, Joan would look across the table to her husband and his colleagues and say, "You guys are 'superscientists'! Why don't you do something?"

Rowland took the challenge seriously. He had always acknowledged that his own scientific inclinations were symptomatic of a larger social problem: that "good" scientists were attracted to theoretical challenges and shunned mere technical problems. That was why, he believed, nuclear power had not been developed to function satisfactorily—because prestigious scientists had not been willing to work with "garbage" such as nuclear waste. Perhaps he was even guilty, to some degree, he couldn't help but think, of perpetuating environmental problems by remaining complacently in an ivory tower. Rowland resolved to apply his skills to a practical problem. He chose, for his first venture, one of the leading environmental scares of the day: the possibility of widespread mercury contamination, particularly in fish.

Although mercury had been known for centuries to cause serious neurological disorders, even death, when ingested, it was thought to be harmless when it was released into the environment because it is heavy, insoluble, and inert. Inorganic compounds of mercury were confidently used in industry, and in agriculture as pesticides. The first suggestion that this practice might be harmful was a sensational case of mercury poisoning that occurred among people residing on the shores of Minimata Bay in Japan. Between 1953 and 1960, more than a hundred people died or were disabled after eating fish taken from the bay, and twenty-two children were born severely retarded and suffering from convulsive seizures to mothers who had eaten contaminated fish. A Minimata plastics and chemical factory had, since 1953, discharged inorganic mercury into the bay, yet the fish of Minimata Bay were found to be contaminated not with inorganic mercury but with the organic compound methylmercury, which was even more toxic. The riddle of the Minimata fish was solved by Swedish scientists who, in the mid-sixties, were concerned about elevated levels of methylmercury in Swedish wild bird populations and in eggs, fish, and meat. The Swedes discovered that inorganic mercury could be converted by microorganisms in mud into methylmercury, which then entered the food chain, becoming highly concentrated in fish.

In early 1970 a Canadian scientist reported finding dangerous levels of methylmercury in fish caught in the Great Lakes, and during the summer and fall of that year, fishing was banned or restricted in parts of seventeen states in the Great Lakes region, New England, and the South. In December 1970 a chemist at the State University of New York at Binghamton reported that he had tested a can of tuna and had found it to contain .75 part per million of mercury, well above the Food and Drug Administration's maximum allowable concentration of .5 ppm in a daily diet. Eleven days later the FDA began a recall of tuna from grocers' shelves, and within weeks announced that up to 89 percent of swordfish on sale in the United States also contained impermissible levels of mercury. Pregnant women were advised to be especially careful about the fish they ate. Tuna and swordfish were believed to be particularly risky because they were large and predatory, higher on the food chain, and so more of the contaminant was concentrated in their flesh.

The insidiousness of mercury poisoning was profoundly disturbing. The possibility that man had polluted the entire globe to the extent that even deep-sea fishes were contaminated raised the prospect of one of the first truly global ecological crises. Peter and Katherine Montague, writing in the *Saturday Review,* went so far as to suggest that increased human exposure to mercury might even be responsible for modern man's "growing nervousness, irritability, skin ailments, insomnia, memory lapses, and emotional derangements."

Although the evidence was strong that some freshwater fish, and the fish taken from an identifiably polluted arm of the sea like Minimata Bay, were contaminated by man-made sources of mercury, it was less clear how wide-ranging, deep-water species like tuna and swordfish could have been contaminated, despite their place high in the food chain. Was it really possible that human beings had poisoned the vast oceans? In 1971, Rowland, along with two other Irvine faculty members and three students, decided to investigate this question by measuring the mercury content in fish that had been caught when the oceans were presumably far less contaminated. Seven tuna samples, caught between 1878 and 1909 and preserved in formaldehyde and alcohol, were obtained from the Smithsonian Institution. A swordfish specimen was found at the Museum of the California Academy of Sciences in San Francisco. The swordfish had been caught off the west coast of Baja California in 1946, and its head had been preserved due to a peculiar abnormality: the bill was deformed in such a way that it curved around and pierced the fish's own head. It turned out that there was no significant difference in the average levels of mercury contamination in the archival samples and samples of recently caught tuna and swordfish, which the scientists tested using the same methods. Rowland and his team had not proved that tuna and swordfish were safe to eat, but they had shown that the mercury these fishes contained was natural.

The results of the fish analysis were publicized, and although Vince Guinn, a forensic chemist, was the lead spokesman for the group, Rowland was nonetheless baptized into the highly emotional politics of environmental science when he and his colleagues were decried as apologists for polluters. One faculty colleague from another department sought

Rowland out to tell him he deplored his group's publicizing its results. It was wrong to minimize the overall danger of toxic pollutants, he told Rowland, by removing one from the list. To Rowland this was nonsense. In science, he replied, you have to let the chips fall where they may.

The episode, in any case, did nothing to discourage Rowland's curiosity about the environmental destiny of chlorofluorocarbons. He did not act on the matter immediately after the Fort Lauderdale conference, but he didn't forget it either, and in the summer of 1973, in his annual budget proposal to the Atomic Energy Commission, Rowland included a request for additional funding to study CFCs. The additional money was denied, but Rowland was granted permission to redirect some of his allotment for the study of radio- and photochemistry to CFCs if he wanted to. The CFC question thus remained marginal, potentially interesting, but far from urgent. Rowland might have let it go for another year or two if not for the arrival at Irvine that October of a postgraduate student named Mario Molina.

Mario Molina was born in Mexico City, and at the age of eleven had informed his family of his intention to become a research scientist. Recognizing that the Mexican educational system had little to offer their precocious and determined son, the Molinas sent him to a Swiss boarding school on the theory that since German was the international language of science, Mario would be well served by learning to speak it.

"I was very excited," Molina recalled later, "and then very disappointed, because the children in the boarding school were the same as those in Mexico. They had no particular interest in science."

Back home Molina still sometimes felt hopelessly out of step. In the privileged world of the Mexican upper class, a talent for science could almost feel like a curse. He had every opportunity, after all, people assured him, with his brains and family connections (his father served Mexico in a number of diplomatic posts, including that of ambassador to Australia), to pursue a lucrative career in law, business, or government. At the University of Mexico he studied chemical engineering—a field of applied technology that was the closest he could come to his true interest of conducting pure scientific research.

As a graduate student at the University of California at Berkeley, which he entered in 1968, Molina finally had the opportunity to pursue basic physical chemistry. His advisor, George Pimentel, was known for his work with chemical reactions that produce laser light without the addition of any other source of energy. The scientific motive behind

Pimentel's work with chemical lasers was to develop a new tool with which to observe the microscopic distribution of energy in elemental reactions, but the Air Force, which had provided Pimentel's funding, quickly recognized the potential defense applications of chemical lasers in hydrogen bombs and started classifying the research. For Pimentel and most of his research assistants, including Mario Molina, the military applications of chemical lasers were of little or no interest, and Pimentel's funding, although it was provided by the Defense Department, had been "clean," which is to say it was intended for pure research. Yet, at Berkeley in the sixties, he and Molina still had to be concerned that radical students might target them for protest, perhaps even by vandalizing the laboratory or destroying experiments and equipment.

Molina completed his Ph.D. thesis in 1973 on aspects of his and Pimentel's work with chemical lasers, then decided to pursue another area of physical chemistry. He opted for radiochemistry. Molina had met Sherry Rowland at a conference at Lake Arrowhead, California, in February 1973. A short time later Pimentel wrote to Rowland to recommend Molina for a job as Rowland's postdoc, and Rowland responded with an offer. When Molina arrived at the Irvine campus in early October 1973, Rowland asked him if he was interested in working on one of his established, ongoing projects in radiochemistry or photochemistry, or on something new. The something new that Rowland had in mind was the question of what happened to CFCs in the atmosphere.

For Molina the safe choice would have been to work in an area where Rowland's reputation was well known. Molina's immediate career objective was rather conservative, to add areas of expertise to his résumé, ideally by doing respected work whose results would be published and subsequently cited by other scientists in their own future work. Such citations, which are indexed by the *Science Citation Index,* provide a precise measure of a scientist's influence and the importance of his work. A large number of citations translates directly into prestige. The gamble in choosing the CFC option was that it could lead nowhere, or nowhere interesting, and Molina would have wasted his time. Worse, Rowland had little background in atmospheric chemistry, which meant that if the work turned tricky and Molina got stuck, Rowland might not be of much help. But Molina shared Rowland's intuition that the CFC question could prove interesting. He understood instantly, as Rowland had, that CFC molecules, while inert in the troposphere, would dissociate under the influence of ultraviolet light in the stratosphere, which meant that *something* would happen to their constituent atoms, something a chemist could understand. Like Rowland, he had kept abreast of the science that had emerged from the SST controversy, and he didn't mind the possibility of moving into the reinvigorated field of atmospheric chemistry.

"If there was anything about chlorofluorocarbons that caught my attention," Molina later said, "it was simply that it seemed like 'bad manners' for men to put a chemical into the atmosphere without knowing exactly what happens to it."

Rowland and Molina discussed methodology. Before they examined whether CFCs were broken down by sunlight in the stratosphere, as they had theorized, they decided they first needed to demonstrate that there were no other significant CFC "sinks"—other processes by which CFCs were being removed from the atmosphere.

For Molina this was the "boring" part of his work, his basic education in the natural processes of the atmosphere. Because chlorofluorocarbons are chemically inert, Rowland and Molina knew it was highly unlikely there would be any sinks. The intellectual exercise for Molina was to dream up possible sinks in order to discount them. He concluded, among other things, that CFCs—even though they might enter the oceans—did not dissolve there, nor were they washed out of the atmosphere by rain; and CFCs neither interacted with nor were they absorbed by plants or other living things. Within two months he and Rowland felt confident in concluding that the only significant CFC sink was the stratosphere, as they originally had surmised.

The next step was to measure the rates at which CFCs break down under the influence of ultraviolet light. Similar work had been done the previous year, by scientists funded by Du Pont. In 1972, in response to James Lovelock's discovery that CFCs were present in the atmosphere, Du Pont had sent out a notice that it would finance the study of CFCs. Some of the money went to Lovelock to fund further measurements, some to pollution studies, and the rest to physicists at the University of Montreal, who measured light-absorption cross sections for CFCs. Not being atmospheric scientists, however, they were unconcerned with whether CFCs dissociated when they absorbed ultraviolet light, much less whether CFCs actually came into contact with ultraviolet light in the environment. Rowland and Molina confirmed the Montreal scientists' basic measurements showing the rates at which CFCs absorb ultraviolet light; they then did additional work to show that CFC molecules would eventually drift up into the stratosphere, with their average lifetime growing shorter the higher they drifted, as short as fifteen hours at the upper levels of the stratosphere.

Rowland and Molina had answered the basic questions they originally set out to ask. They had determined that chlorofluorocarbons have a long life in the atmosphere—between 40 and 150 years—before they eventually drift into the stratosphere, where they are broken down by ultraviolet light. They had also determined that when CFC molecules do break down, a free chlorine atom is produced. They discussed publishing their findings, but then decided to ask one more question: what happened to the free chlorine atoms released by CFCs in the stratosphere? This was, for Rowland and Molina, a relatively easy question to tackle, a matter of the gas-phase chemistry they knew intimately. It entailed, for Molina, going back to his office and simply writing down a sequence of chemical reactions.

From that point, Rowland later recalled, it was only about seventy-two hours before "the bottom fell out."

The day after he started work on the calculations, Molina reported to Rowland that he had come upon something unexpected. Chlorine atoms freed from CFCs by ultraviolet dissociation readily interact with ozone molecules (O_3), breaking the ozone apart and producing oxygen (O_2) and chlorine monoxide (ClO). The chlorine compound in turn breaks down, freeing its chlorine atom, which finds another ozone molecule to break apart, and the process begins all over again. *Thus, a single chlorine atom in the stratosphere would destroy not just one ozone molecule, but tens or hundreds of thousands, in a catalytic chain.*

The implication of Molina's discovery of this chlorine catalysis, what chemists refer to as a "chlorine chain," was so alarming that his first reaction was to assume he had made some kind of mistake. Rowland's response was also to wonder if Molina might have erred. They agreed to do the calculations over, separately and using different methods, to see if they would come up with the same finding. Quickly, they both confirmed Molina's original results. The chlorine chain was irrefutable. Rowland still felt shaken when he returned home from the lab that evening. When Joan casually inquired how the work was going, Rowland heard himself reply, "The work is going very well, but it looks like the end of the world."

There was one final step Rowland and Molina took to determine the extent of the problem they had uncovered. The real question was not how much chlorine there was in the stratosphere then, in 1973, but how much there would be in the future, after sufficient time had elapsed for CFCs to drift up and reach the stratosphere at a rate that equaled their rate of production. This calculation would ascertain the eventual degree of ozone depletion at steady state. Assuming a constant rate of tion at the industry figures for 1972 (a deliberately conse since the rates of production were in fact rising annually), 1

Molina calculated that the ozone layer might be diminished by as much as 20 to 40 percent within about a hundred years.

Twenty to 40 percent. It was a far more frightening estimate than the relatively small 1 percent or 3.8 percent losses projected during the SST debate. Even if, by a miracle, CFC production were halted immediately, there were already enough CFCs in existence, by Rowland and Molina's reckoning, to shatter the ozone layer.

"The feeling was of an abyss opening up," Rowland later said. "We weren't sure where the bottom was. We only knew it was down there somewhere—out of sight."

Once he realized that he and Mario Molina had found a major removal process of stratospheric ozone, Sherry Rowland called Harold Johnston at Berkeley. There were important parallels between Johnston's work with SST exhaust and nitrogen oxides and Rowland and Molina's work with CFCs and chlorine. As Paul Crutzen had shown and Johnston had confirmed, nitrogen oxides at naturally occurring concentrations contribute to the processes that maintain ozone at steady state. There is a nitrogen oxide chain similar to the chlorine chain Rowland and Molina discovered—that is, molecules of nitrogen oxides destroy stratospheric ozone without themselves being destroyed in the process. The absorption cross sections for nitrous oxide and CFCs are similar, and the nitrogen chain is analogous, chemically, to the chlorine chain. For anyone who understood nitrogen-ozone chemistry, chlorine-ozone chemistry was instantly comprehensible.

For Johnston and other scientists who attempted to calculate the potential impact of the SST in the early 1970s, the key question had not been whether nitrogen oxides were ozone scavengers, but whether the planes' exhaust would introduce enough additional nitrogen oxides to significantly deplete ozone levels at steady state. For Rowland and Molina, the question about the chlorine chain, once they had found it, was not really whether the chlorine chain itself would stand up to scrutiny—that, to them, was a matter of basic chemistry. The more pressing question was whether the amount of chlorine introduced by CFCs was enough to compete with the natural processes of ozone removal. Their conclusion of a 20 to 40 percent ozone reduction was so incredible that it only seemed prudent—before they did anything else—to run it by one of the few scientists knowledgeable enough about the subject to tell them they weren't crazy. After all, Molina reminded Rowland, the problem they had uncovered was so enormous, it seemed inconceivable no one else had noticed it.

Rowland called Johnston in early December 1973. "We've found a chlorine chain and a source of chlorine," he said.

"Do you know about Cicerone and Stolarski?" Johnston asked.

"No."

"They talked about the chlorine chain at Kyoto."

Ralph Cicerone, an electrical engineer, and Richard Stolarski, a physicist, both at the University of Michigan, had been awarded a contract to study the potential stratospheric effect of space-shuttle exhaust. NASA's 1972 final environmental impact statement for the space shuttle had revealed that the shuttle's rockets would spew, among other effluents, significant quantities of hydrogen chloride—containing chlorine—into the atmosphere.

Shortly after Cicerone and Stolarski started work on the NASA assignment, a Michigan colleague told them that Michael Clyne, a British chemist, had measured the rate constants of the reaction between chlorine atoms and ozone. Cicerone wrote to Clyne, and Clyne provided Cicerone and Stolarski with the results of his work. A brilliant laboratory chemist, Clyne had halted his efforts in chlorine-ozone chemistry, possibly because he was handicapped with a severe stutter, when he realized there were likely to be environmental and public implications to the work.

Cicerone and Stolarski had quickly determined that hydrogen chloride was totally foreign to the stratosphere. Clearly, then, something might go awry by introducing it in space-shuttle exhaust. Although, thanks to Clyne, they knew that chlorine destroyed ozone, it took several months—since neither of them was a chemist—for them to discover that it did so in a catalytic chain reaction. Even then the chlorine effluent in shuttle exhaust did not seem to pose an immediate environmental threat because, by Cicerone and Stolarski's calculations, the space shuttle—the only source of stratospheric chlorine they knew about—would deplete the ozone layer by only .3 percent at a rate of fifty shuttle flights a year.

In June 1973, Cicerone and Stolarski submitted their findings to NASA. Space-agency officials strongly suggested to the two researchers that much more work needed to be done in the area before experimental data potentially damaging to the space-shuttle program would be published. Consequently, when Stolarski presented the results of his and Cicerone's work on the photochemistry of chlorine at a scientific meeting in Kyoto, Japan, in September 1973, he did not mention the space shuttle. Instead, he talked about trace amounts of hydrogen chloride released into the atmosphere by volcanic eruptions.

Stolarski and Cicerone were interlopers in stratospheric chemistry. At Kyoto their paper was immediately attacked by a scientist who was far more established in the field, Mike McElroy of Harvard, who said he and his colleague Steve Wofsy had looked into the impact of hydrogen chloride released by volcanoes, and did not believe volcanoes were a significant source of chlorine in the stratosphere. As it happened, McElroy and Wofsy had also found the chlorine chain and were about to publish a paper on their discovery. Neither Stolarski nor McElroy revealed, however, either to each other or to any of the other participants at the Kyoto conference, what both of them knew: that the real chlorine source they were talking about was NASA's proposed space shuttle.

Thus, the chlorine chain, while of academic interest, did not seem to be of overwhelming importance, since there was no significant natural source of chlorine in the stratosphere, and the potential man-made source —NASA's space shuttle—was not yet flying. There would be time for Cicerone and Stolarski and McElroy and Wofsy, and for NASA itself, to fully explore the problem before the shuttle's maiden flight, which was scheduled for the early 1980s. Alternative propellants could be devised for the shuttle booster rockets if necessary. For Cicerone and Stolarski the study of chlorine chemistry in the stratosphere had proven to be just the tonic they had sought for their careers: apart from a little professional sparring with McElroy and Wofsy and moderate unease on the part of their NASA sponsors, they had found a quiet corner of the stratosphere to investigate.

Even though the chlorine sources Stolarski and Cicerone were studying were small, Stolarski recognized that the potential importance of their work was that there could conceivably be larger sources they didn't know about. Yet Stolarski did not pick up on a clue he received in November 1973, when a young physical chemist named Chuck Kolb approached him at a NASA conference in Houston and asked if he had given any consideration to CFCs as a potential chlorine source. Kolb was a recent Ph.D. graduate of Princeton who had done his 1971 doctoral thesis on fluorine-atom reactions with Freon and other halocarbons. He had read the paper Lovelock published in *Nature* in 1973 reporting his finding that CFCs were ubiquitous in the atmosphere. Having worked with CFCs, Kolb, like Sherry Rowland, knew that Lovelock's contention that CFCs would have no conceivable environmental impact was ill founded. To the contrary, he knew CFCs would photodissociate in the stratosphere when they were exposed to ultraviolet radiation. After his graduation Kolb had been hired by a small, struggling research-and-development company outside Boston called Aerodyne Research, Inc. There his professional orbit crossed that of Harvard professor Mike McElroy—the guru of planetary atmospheres. Through that association Kolb learned that research was underway suggesting that chlorine emitted in space-shuttle exhaust might pose a threat to the ozone layer. He realized instantly that the amount of chlorine introduced into the atmosphere by the space shuttle was "like a pimple on an elephant" compared to the chlorine that would be introduced by CFCs.

Kolb mentioned his insight to a number of people, including McElroy and his boss at Aerodyne. He later said he thought McElroy may not have paid much attention because McElroy still thought of him as a grad student. Similarly, in Houston, Kolb mentioned CFCs to Stolarski, but the comment, Stolarski later recalled, "sailed over my head.

"I was naive about chemistry," he later explained. "I guess I figured if they gave it a name like 'chlorofluorocarbons,' it must be something horrible. I didn't know it was actually a very simple molecule."

Kolb attempted to follow up on his hunch by writing a proposal to NASA for Aerodyne to study the CFC question, but the proposal was not funded. In the face of so much discouragement, Kolb was instructed by his employer to drop the question of CFCs and go back to the work the firm paid him to do.

Thus, by late 1973, although there were several researchers who knew about the chlorine chain, or who had concerned themselves with the long lifetimes of CFCs in the atmosphere, and at least one scientist, Chuck Kolb, who had speculated that CFCs were a potential source of chlorine in the stratosphere, only Rowland and Molina had put the complete picture together.

The two Irvine scientists flew to Berkeley to meet with Harold Johnston during the week between Christmas and New Year's, 1973. Johnston quickly confirmed their basic premise. There were, at least, no *obvious* mistakes in their reasoning. Johnston told Rowland and Molina that Michael Clyne's latest laboratory measurements had demonstrated that at stratospheric temperatures chlorine atoms would destroy ozone six times more efficiently than the nitrogen oxides associated with the SST.

Rowland asked Johnston if he would take the lead in helping to publicize this new danger to the ozone layer. Johnston was, after all, already a respected figure in atmospheric chemistry, and could, perhaps, better communicate the urgency of the problem. But Johnston recognized that both the burdens and the glories ahead belonged rightfully to Rowland and Molina. Publicly suggesting a ban on the production of CFCs would be controversial; it was, after all, the sheer size of the CFC business, and the modern world's dependence on the chemicals, that made Rowland and Molina's own calculations so disturbing.

"Are you ready for the heat?" Johnston asked them. The CFC industry, fat and prosperous, had thrived for more than four decades without question or interference. If this contented giant was disturbed, who could tell for certain what it would do?

*   *   *

Sherry Rowland was scheduled to begin a long-planned sabbatical in Vienna just after New Year's, 1974. At first, he thought he would have to change his plans; however, as he and Molina discussed how they should proceed, they recognized that there was nothing to be gained by dramatically rearranging their affairs. They were in possession of the scientific scoop of the century, but if they were to be believed, they would have to assume a nonalarmist posture and publish their findings in an authoritative scientific paper subject to peer review. Shouting the news from the nearest rooftop, while certainly warranted, would only make them less credible, and the premature disclosure of the ozone-depletion theory could subject it to attack before its authors were fully armed for its defense.

With publication of the theory their obvious and best next step, Rowland and Molina agreed that despite their sense of urgency there was really no reason for Rowland to cancel his plans. He could write the paper in Europe and submit it for publication from there. Until it was published, there was little that either one of them could do and Rowland might as well enjoy his sabbatical. Molina, meanwhile, could handle anything unexpected that might come up back home in Irvine. Both of them could use the time to continue thinking about the CFC-ozone problem, conferring with selected colleagues to reassure themselves they had not overlooked anything significant.

Rowland wrote the paper his first week in Vienna, and sent it in early January to the prestigious British journal *Nature*. He chose *Nature* not only because it is held in high esteem, but also because it had a reputation for promptness in responding to submissions, a reputation Rowland seriously began to question after several weeks went by and he received no word from the editors. Impatiently awaiting the journal's decision on whether it would publish the paper, he phoned *Nature*'s editorial offices repeatedly to inquire about the delay. When he finally did speak with someone from the journal's staff on the phone, he heard a number of excuses for the delay, chiefly having to do with the peer review process. Before a scientific paper is published, it is sent to "referees" in the field to verify its basic scientific merit. *Nature* informed Rowland that it was not having an easy time finding qualified referees in the field of stratospheric chemistry; in addition, the journal was between editors; the former editor, it seemed, had left for a long weekend and had simply failed to return.

The anticipation made it difficult for Sherry or Joan Rowland to be at ease. They talked constantly about the terrifying implications of his discovery and about how their own lives would change when the word got out. Rowland was in constant touch with scientific colleagues around the world, scientists who appreciated what he was going through and who for the most part reassured him that they saw no significant or obvious errors in his theory. Rowland reflected on his relatively obscure past career. "You work hard," he told Joan, "and you find the work fascinating, and you publish it, and maybe two dozen people will read it." Now he had to anticipate that his work would be received with far greater interest and consternation.

In the meantime, within the small community of atmospheric scientists, word of the Rowland-Molina theory was slowly filtering out. In January 1974, Ralph Cicerone wrote Rowland in Vienna. Cicerone told Rowland about his and Stolarski's work on the chlorine chain and suggested an exchange of information. In response, Rowland sent Cicerone a copy of his paper. Having come up with the same chemical reactions independently of Rowland and Molina, Cicerone and Stolarski could fully grasp the theory's significance. CFCs were a further example of a phenomenon Rachel Carson had first observed—that inertness in chemistry, traditionally associated with safety, could instead portend long-term environmental problems with the potential to gather quiet strength before exploding. Carson had demonstrated how a man-made chemical found in trace quantities in the environment could become concentrated in the tissues of animals. Now, Rowland and Molina had shown how, by means of catalysis, a synthetic gas at trace concentrations could endanger humanity by affecting the chemistry of the stratosphere, a region long defined by its inaccessibility and very remoteness from man.

Slowly, the Rowland-Molina theory began to gain advocates and a hearing in scientific quarters. Harold Johnston couldn't resist mentioning it in January 1974 at a scientific workshop sponsored by NASA. In February the theory was outlined in a speech to the Swedish Academy of Sciences by meteorologist Paul Crutzen, who had seen a copy of Rowland and Molina's paper. The story was picked up by a Swedish newspaper, but went no further.

Rowland and Molina were in touch by mail throughout this difficult waiting period, keeping one another abreast of the work they were pursuing separately, especially refinements in their calculations and possible changes to the *Nature* manuscript, and exchanging news of their respective contacts with other scientists. In late January, Molina visited scientists at the University of California at Riverside who had been awarded Du Pont grants to study the "ecological effects" of CFCs. "But of course," Molina wrote Rowland, "they had only worried about the tro-posphere." The important news, Molina continued, was that the River-side scientists seemed to "corroborate strongly our conclusions about tropospheric stability." Moreover, Molina wrote, he had managed to glean this information from the Riverside scientists without divulging his and Rowland's discovery of the stratospheric problem. In February, Mo-lina visited the National Center for Atmospheric Research in Boulder, where he met with atmospheric chemist Dieter Ehhalt to request strato-spheric air samples from NCAR for future work he and Rowland wanted to carry out. Ehhalt had been at the Fort Lauderdale AEC conference with Rowland and understood their work implicitly. Molina told Ehhalt that he and Rowland had been working with CFCs, which were a source of stratospheric chlorine, that chlorine was a catalytic scavenger of ozone, and that they'd gone to steady state.

"Beautiful," Ehhalt responded, and agreed to assist the Irvine scien-tists in obtaining their air samples.

Rowland, meanwhile, gave a few talks on the CFC problem in Eu-rope, outings that he intended to use to test his and Molina's work. The first presentations in West Berlin and Paris were easy because they were before chemistry colloquia, and Rowland was confident of his chemistry. The real test was a talk at the prestigious Institute of Meteorology in Stockholm, with Paul Crutzen and other notable meteorologists in the audience. Meteorology was Rowland's weakness. As it happened, Crutzen and Rowland hit it off well, although Crutzen did pose ques-tions about the potential impact of a particular hydrogen chain species, HO_2, on Rowland's calculations, enough to give Rowland cause for concern. That night, when he and Joan returned to their Stockholm hotel, he started work with his calculator to resolve the question. Lying in bed, Joan heard the "click, click" of Sherry's calculator all night long. The next morning he looked more refreshed than tired. "We're right," he told Joan. Crutzen, it turned out, had been up all night too, and had independently reached the same conclusion.

In March 1974, Rowland and Molina finally received word that *Na-ture* had accepted their paper. After several more weeks of delay they learned it had been scheduled for publication in June. "To use some Watergate language," Molina wrote Rowland in response to the news, "in retrospect we should have sent our letter to *Science,* not to (expletive deleted) *Nature.*" A condition of publication was that news of the ozone-depletion theory had to be embargoed prior to the publication date. But the news had already begun to leak out. Harold Johnston told Molina that reporters had begun to call his Berkeley office, asking him about the possible connection between Freon and ozone depletion. Following an

American Chemical Society meeting in Los Angeles, a tiny item regarding the pending news appeared in an article in the *Chicago Tribune*. Molina was alarmed, while attending a scientific meeting in Berkeley in March, to overhear Raymond McCarthy, technical director of Du Pont's Freon Products Division, discussing rumors he had heard about a new ozone-depletion theory involving CFCs with another Du Pont researcher. Molina did not introduce himself. In response to the rumors, in May 1974, McCarthy expanded Du Pont's research program at UC-Riverside to analyze Freons in the stratosphere.

Rowland and Molina's seminal paper, entitled "Stratospheric Sink for Chlorofluoromethanes: Chlorine Atom-Catalyzed Destruction of Ozone," finally appeared in the June 28, 1974, issue of *Nature*. For all the anticipation, and Rowland and Molina's concern about a press leak and the public impact of the news, the article was greeted by a resounding silence. To the two scientists who had authored the paper, and to their colleagues who understood its implications, the silence was as ominous as it was unexpected. It was as if they had shouted "Fire!" in a crowded theater only to find their warning mistaken by the audience as part of the entertainment. A press release issued by the public-information office at the University of California at Irvine was ignored by the national media, with only a few articles appearing in California newspapers, including a page-three story in the *Los Angeles Times*.

Perhaps it should not have been surprising that even when it was spelled out, the ozone-depletion theory was difficult to recognize or accept at first. Like many epochal ideas, Rowland and Molina's theory was strikingly simple, so elegant that Rowland himself still sometimes suspected there must be something wrong with it. "From a physical point of view the theory was a neat idea," Rowland later said. "It was *too* clean and simple and it made you wonder if maybe nature isn't that clean and simple." In *Nature* the paper took up less than two pages. The most disturbing paragraph read:

> It seems quite clear that the atmosphere has only a finite capacity for absorbing Cl [chlorine] atoms produced in the stratosphere, and that important consequences may result. This capacity is probably not sufficient in steady state even for the present rate of introduction of chlorofluoromethanes. More accurate estimates of this absorptive capacity need to be made in the immediate future in order to ascertain the levels of possible onset of environmental problems.

How easy it would be to read those words and fail to comprehend their meaning! The very language intended to convey a sense of scientific detachment also tended to mask any sense of urgency. Rowland and Molina were probably right to launch the debate on this cautious note, but were still disappointed when their paper set off no fireworks. "We had been a little naive," Molina reflected later, "in thinking the press would immediately snatch the story up. Here we were concerned about a news leak. The problem seemed simple enough. It didn't occur to us that the whole subject was probably still too complicated for a nonscientist to understand." The inadequate response, however, charged them with a renewed sense of purpose. Too much was at stake to permit this debate to be hashed out in the pages of obscure scientific journals. If nobody else was going to bring the issue to public awareness, they would have to do it themselves.

"We realized there were no other spokesmen," Molina recalled. "As soon as that became clear, we never questioned the need to go public . . . we had a *responsibility* to go public."

12.

NOT WITH A BANG, BUT A PSSST!

THE STORY OF THE ROWLAND-MOLINA THEORY finally broke in the national media only after the two scientists presented their findings at a press conference at the September 1974 convention of the American Chemical Society in Atlantic City.

Rowland was busy in the weeks following the ACS meeting. The third week in September he was named, along with Harold Johnston and Mike McElroy, to an ad hoc committee appointed by the National Academy of Sciences to investigate the ozone-depletion theory and report back what action, if any, was required. The committee met for the first time on October 26, in Washington. Later that week the committee chairman, Dr. Donald M. Hunten of the Kitt Peak National Observatory in Tucson, told a news conference that there should be an immediate halt to the sale of aerosols containing CFCs, quickly adding that this was his personal opinion, and not necessarily a reflection of his committee's recommendations. Officially, the committee recommended that the National Academy of Sciences undertake a full-scale study and complete it within a year. Unless the study turned up new factors that might ameliorate their current assessment of the threat, the committee advised, "drastic action will probably be necessary because the effects mount rapidly with time."

Rowland also spoke with Karim Ahmed, science advisor of the Natural Resources Defense Council. Ahmed and his colleague Tom Stoel had been alerted to the threat posed by CFCs by the publicity following Rowland and Molina's press conference in Atlantic City, and had resolved to investigate the matter. After talking by phone with Rowland and Molina, Cicerone, Stolarski, McElroy, and Crutzen, Ahmed had been able to assure Stoel that the scientific support for the ozone-depletion theory was sound. In November 1974 Ahmed attended a meeting sponsored by the National Oceanic and Atmospheric Administration in Silver Spring, Maryland, and was struck by the unanimity of opinion among the atmospheric scientists who had studied the ozone-depletion problem. "There is an unprecedented consensus that the problem is extremely serious," he wrote in a December 1974 technical review for NRDC, "and that the highest priorities should be given to addressing the issue in the next year."

Although the CFCs used in refrigerators and air conditioners were every bit as damaging to stratospheric ozone, Ahmed and Stoel agreed with Rowland that it was advisable to first seek a ban on the CFC propellant used in aerosols. There were good reasons to target aerosols, unfair though it seemed to aerosol manufacturers. To begin with, aerosols accounted for over half of overall U.S. consumption of CFCs, and the United States dominated world consumption. In 1973, of some 5 billion aerosols produced worldwide, approximately 2.9 billion were manufactured in the United States. A ban on CFC-containing aerosols in the United States would thus have an immediate, dramatic effect on overall CFC emissions, particularly if other nations followed the American lead. Furthermore, unlike refrigerators and air conditioners, which contain CFCs in their pressurized coils and release them into the environment only when they leak or are junked, aerosols dispensed CFCs directly into the atmosphere each and every time they were used. While this rapid consumption of CFCs in aerosols had long represented a profitable boon for CFC manufacturers, to environmentalists such a product was a prime example of profligate waste in a consumer culture hooked on disposable goods.

The use of an environmentally hazardous agent in aerosols containing products such as underarm deodorant and hair spray was, upon reflection, astoundingly frivolous. There were many other ready means of dispensing these products, including other aerosol propellants. The CFC-propelled aerosol was a form of packaging, a convenience device. No one could seriously weigh the benefit of, say, easily applying body deodorant against the risk of possible damage to the ozone layer and arrive at a conclusion favorable to the aerosol industry.

Although the arguments for an aerosol ban seemed irrefutable, Ahmed and Stoel knew that no matter how trivial a product might be, there was in America a firm belief that "unwarranted" regulation was unfair to business and harmful to the economy. Indeed, environmental regulation was still a young and controversial idea in the United States. The National Environmental Policy Act was not yet five years old, while other landmark environmental legislation of the seventies—including the Clean Air and Clean Water acts—was newer still. The enthusiasm and political impact of the Earth Day movement had yet to be fully translated into a mechanism for implementing or enforcing environmental controls. Environmental law, as practiced by the NRDC when Stoel and Ahmed first began to develop an approach to the chlorofluorocarbon problem, thus required bold initiative and imagination. As they surveyed a landscape where government searched uneasily for its appropriate role in response to rising public concern, and industry staunchly defended business as usual as a God-given right, the NRDC strategists could anticipate a long, bruising fight to restrict CFCs.

There were three government agencies with jurisdiction over aerosol products. The Food and Drug Administration (FDA) had sole authority to regulate CFCs in food, drugs, and cosmetics. The Environmental Protection Agency (EPA) had the power to regulate pesticides. The Consumer Product Safety Commission (CPSC), established under the Federal Hazardous Substances Labeling Act of 1960, had jurisdiction over consumer products generally, including such items as waxes, polishes, and cleaners that were not covered by the other two agencies. "Interested persons" could petition any of the three agencies to request that a rule be formulated, but only the CPSC was required by law to rule on a petition within a set time period—120 days. Because of this time provision, and because the CPSC's jurisdiction seemed to be the most encompassing of the three potential targets, Stoel decided to begin there.

In a memo to the NRDC executive committee, Stoel noted that the CPSC had recently banned aerosols containing vinyl chloride as a propellant, in response to evidence that monomeric vinyl chloride caused angiocarcinoma, a rare form of liver cancer. While on the one hand this indicated the CPSC's willingness to act, Stoel noted that "preliminary inquiries indicate that the CPSC feels it has expended its political capital" by banning vinyl chloride aerosols, and "is unlikely to deal on its own initiative with the ozone hazard." Where the CPSC might have felt a political inhibition from acting, therefore, NRDC was prepared to step forward.

Sherry Rowland joined Tom Stoel, Karim Ahmed, and NRDC executive director John Adams at a press conference in New York on November 21, 1974, at which NRDC announced it had filed its petition with the Consumer Product Safety Commission. They revealed that new measurements of air samples gathered by the Atomic Energy Commission for NOAA showed the presence of CFCs in the lower stratosphere, decreasing at higher altitudes. Although Philip W. Krey of the AEC's Health and Safety Laboratories later noted that the falloff in CFCs at higher altitudes could be a result of their slow upward diffusion into that region, Rowland told reporters that he considered the AEC observations to be an important confirmation of his theory that ultraviolet light would destroy CFCs as they rose in the stratosphere.

Leaving the press conference, Rowland asked Ahmed, "What do you think will happen? Will we get these things banned in the next few years?"

"I don't know," Ahmed replied doubtfully. "I think it looks like a fifteen-year battle."

As it had when the safety of DDT was first questioned, the chemical industry responded to the allegations against its product by sharply challenging the quality of the science that implicated it. In late September the Manufacturing Chemists Association (MCA, later the Chemical Manufacturers Association), a trade organization based in Washington, announced that it was financing its own research into the ozone-depletion question. One scientist whose research was supported by the MCA, Dr. Oliver C. Taylor of the University of California at Riverside, questioned the basic premise that CFCs break down when exposed to ultraviolet light under stratospheric conditions, stating that the alleged breakdown was predicted on the basis of theory, and had not been tested. Dr. Taylor's challenge to the theory could not withstand much scrutiny, and soon enough even the most loyal industry scientist would have to concede that CFCs break down under exposure to ultraviolet light in the stratosphere. But Taylor's activities provided an early glimpse at the tactics industry would employ in fighting Rowland-Molina: sponsoring reputable scientists who would question every aspect of the ozone-depletion theory and thus provoke endless debate about its validity. Having done all it could to foster this "scientific disagreement," industry then insisted that its product had been falsely accused. "All we have are assumptions," Du Pont's Raymond L. McCarthy said in a statement released November 1, 1974, by the Aerosol Education Bureau, an industry-sponsored organization that had originally been formed to discourage teenagers from the dangerous practice of inhaling aerosols to get high, and now found itself confronted with a much larger mission. "Without experimental evidence, it would be an injustice if a few claims—which even the critics agree are hypotheses—were to be the basis of regulatory or consumer reaction."

In response, Sherry Rowland pointed out that industry's position was "just hypothetical, too." "They have a hypothesis that it is safe to release fluorocarbons," Rowland said, "but no data to back up their position. We have a hypothesis that it is unsafe, but we do have some scientific data, and are coming up with more."

Although the majority of independent scientists quickly sided with Rowland and Molina, to the public it appeared as if the entire question of CFCs and the ozone layer were a subject of sharp controversy within the scientific fraternity. When John Muir and Gifford Pinchot tangled over the issue of forest preservation, every citizen could weigh in with an opinion based on some personal feeling toward trees. Modern environmental threats like DDT or CFCs are not so readily understood, and, indeed, at first can seem utterly fantastic. The subject of the CFC debate, the ozone layer, was a thin veil of molecules high up in the stratosphere. No one could see the ozone layer or understand its critical role in protecting life on earth without reference to science. Science discovered the ozone layer, science invented CFCs, and now only science could ascertain whether one of its discoveries was at risk from one of its inventions.

Confronted by conflicting testimony from scientists, the safest course for politicians and government officials was to call for additional study before presuming to act. Dr. Russell Peterson, chairman of the Council on Environmental Quality, spearheaded one study by the federal Interagency Task Force on the Inadvertent Modification of the Stratosphere, which came to be known by its acronym, IMOS. IMOS, formed in January 1975 with representatives from seven cabinet departments and five agencies, was committed to submitting a report within four months.

At IMOS's first public meeting, held in Washington on February 27, 1975, NRDC representatives Stoel and Ahmed found themselves in rare agreement with representatives from the chemical industry that it was essential that responsibility for the CFC issue be delegated to a "lead agency" so that the matter could be resolved efficiently. But industry representatives also wanted to investigate the question for themselves and have a voice in the scientific fray. John W. Dickinson, Jr., vice president of consumer affairs at Gillette, took the opportunity to announce the formation of a new organization, the Council of Atmospheric Sciences (COAS), which would gather the "data necessary to form the technical basis for legislation and executive decisions in the public interest on the fluorocarbon issue . . . and to place such data on the record and in the hands of governmental decision makers." COAS was made up of representatives from all of the industries affected by the controversy: CFC producers, producers of aerosol cans and valves, aerosol-product fillers and marketers, the air-conditioning and refrigeration industries, and related trade associations. Belying its name, COAS was not a committee of scientists, but intended to draw upon the research programs administered by the Manufacturing Chemists Association.

Even some scientists who generally supported the CFC ozone-depletion theory did not take a firm stand in support of a prompt aerosol ban. Mike McElroy testified at the February IMOS meeting that there was enough uncertainty about his own rather alarming estimates of potential ozone depletion that a delay before implementing a ban would not be disastrous. "The world is not about to end," he said, "and we won't do inestimable harm to the environment within five years. Nor is it possible to say that x tons of Freon will reduce ozone by y percent. Uncertain chemical factors may throw off calculations by an increment of five." Sherry Rowland disagreed, seeing no justification for a delay in view of the fact that seven independent studies had agreed that the CFC ozone-depletion theory was essentially sound. "The quantitative amount [of predicted ozone depletion] is not the issue here," Rowland argued, "but whether or not the phenomenon occurs." It was just as likely, he added, that the then-current best estimates of likely ozone depletion were too low as it was that they were too high. Forging ahead with his testimony, and continuing to sound an individualistic note, McElroy pointed out that CFCs were not necessarily the only synthetic chemical with ozone-depleting potential. Bromides, which were used in plastics manufacturing and crop fumigation, were such an efficient ozone scavenger, he said, that they could be used as a devastating weapon in war if they were deliberately injected into the stratosphere over enemy territory. McElroy may have been inspired by the publicity surrounding a September 5, 1974, speech by Dr. Fred C. Iklé, director of the Arms Control and Disarmament Agency, who said that a nuclear war could produce oxides of nitrogen that would deplete enough stratospheric ozone to "shatter the ecological structure that permits man to remain alive on this planet."

While McElroy's imagined military threat from ozone scavengers was a distraction from more immediate concerns, and was clearly farfetched —for one thing, such a device would indiscriminately harm friend and foe alike—it was nonetheless a stark reminder of humanity's ultimate and utter dependence on the continued integrity of the ozone layer. Since

1971 at least five potential threats to the ozone layer had been identified: the SST, the space shuttle, nuclear war, bromides, and CFCs. As Dr. Thomas M. Donahue, chairman of the Department of Atmospheric and Oceanic Science at the University of Michigan, testified before a House of Representatives subcommittee in December 1974, "The horror is that we are not sure that we have exhausted the inventory." Before the SST scare, the public scarcely knew what the ozone layer was—even science knew precious little about it—and yet this formerly obscure natural feature of the stratosphere had come to assume the leading role in an unprecedented environmental emergency.

In the face of this crisis, scientists dickered and conducted in-depth studies. The government formed a committee and industry temporized. For its part, the Natural Resources Defense Council tried to force quick official action on the issue. While NRDC environmentalists realized that the petition they had filed in November 1974 with the Consumer Product Safety Commission seeking a ban on aerosols containing CFCs was unlikely to result in decisive action, they hoped at least to force the issue of who within the government had the jurisdiction to regulate the chemicals. But in March 1975 the CPSC decided to defer judgment on CFCs because the IMOS task force, which included CPSC representation, had been established in part to resolve this question of jurisdiction and the IMOS report was not scheduled for release until June. Tom Stoel was not convinced that IMOS would solve the problem, so on March 25, 1975, he sent a memorandum to the NRDC executive committee seeking approval of a lawsuit against the CPSC. "The jurisdictional dispute could drag on indefinitely and preclude effective action on this important issue," the memo read. "It will clear the air if the CPSC is compelled to decide whether it has jurisdiction, as its statute plainly requires. A decision either way would be better than the present situation." NRDC filed suit against the CPSC in May 1975.

On June 13, 1975, IMOS issued its report. "Thus far the validity of the [ozone-depletion] theory and the predicted amounts of ozone reduction have not been seriously challenged," the report stated on its first page. "More research is required and will be undertaken, but there seems to be a legitimate cause for concern." The report went on to recommend that, on the basis of then-available scientific evidence, aerosol sprays using CFC propellants should be banned by January 1978, a date chosen to "allow time for consideration of further research results and for the affected industries and consumers to initiate adjustments." If new evidence disproved the ozone-depletion theory or significantly changed the scope of predicted ozone losses, the proposed aerosol ban could be canceled or altered accordingly. In the meantime, the IMOS report noted, an in-depth study of the problem had been undertaken by a committee of the National Academy of Sciences and was due to be completed by April 1, 1976. If the NAS study confirmed their own assessment, IMOS said, the aerosol ban could then be imposed on foods, drugs, and cosmetics by the Food and Drug Administration, on pesticides by the EPA, and on other consumer products, including spray paints, by the CPSC, thus resolving the jurisdictional question. The report also urged passage of the Toxic Substances Control Act (TSCA), then pending in Congress, which would provide a mechanism for the regulation of CFCs in air-conditioning systems, refrigeration, and plastics manufacturing, should that step prove necessary.

Despite its basic endorsement of their own view that CFCs ought to be regulated, the IMOS report seemed to Stoel and Ahmed to be a cop-out. The federal rule-making process took at least a year anyway, which meant that actions initiated immediately could not result in rules going into effect until well after the NAS report was released. As IMOS itself pointed out, should the NAS report somehow exonerate CFCs, the rules could be suspended or modified. "The scientific evidence indicates that a year's delay will result in depletion of the ozone layer by an additional 0.2–0.3 percent," Stoel noted, "causing approximately 2,000 extra cases of skin cancer every year in the United States. The [IMOS] Task Force has cited no reason why the public should be exposed to this additional health risk." IMOS nonetheless set the course of government policy on the CFC question, in effect excusing individual agencies within the government from having to act on their own. On July 9, 1975, reacting in part to the NRDC lawsuit seeking to force a decision, the Consumer Product Safety Commission voted to deny the NRDC petition on aerosols by a vote of 3 to 2. Following IMOS's recommendation, the CPSC stated that it, too, would await the results of the NAS study before taking action on CFCs.

How much proof was necessary? To wait for the august National Academy of Sciences to back them up may have seemed only prudent to the government officials who sat on IMOS. By passing the buck, however, IMOS had turned the NAS Panel on Atmospheric Chemistry, which had been established in April 1975 at the recommendation of the ad hoc committee on which Rowland had served, into a court of last opinion. The panel members had originally intended to produce a report not unlike the IMOS report, summarizing and assessing the available knowledge about CFCs and the stratosphere, but now found themselves called upon to do much more, to resolve the conflict over the Rowland-

Molina theory, or at least to assign some kind of quantifiable measure to the doubts that remained so that lay persons, including congressmen, the president, state governors, and other officials could act with confidence against powerful business interests.

Industry, meanwhile, reacted to IMOS with howls of pain and indignation. IMOS's prediction that restrictions on CFC use would probably have to be imposed was, according to a Du Pont press release, "tantamount to pre-judging the results of the [ongoing] research and imposing a guilty-until-proven-innocent verdict." According to Du Pont's ideal timetable, it would take at least three years to conduct thorough research into the ozone-depletion problem. Cried *Aerosol Age*: "There is no justice in this threat. It destroys the concept of orderly research. It flaunts the ideal of being innocent until proved guilty. There has been no trial, there has been no jury." The Aerosol Education Bureau released a statement to emphasize the alleged scientific uncertainties of ozone depletion: "Recent and potential discoveries and measurements of natural chlorine compounds in the atmosphere may ultimately invalidate the theory that fluorocarbons may contribute to ozone depletion."

But despite industry's outrage, IMOS's decision to wait for additional assurance from the NAS before acting was, in fact, a major concession to industry, which had stressed the uncertainties in the ozone-depletion theory from the moment it was proposed and had demanded a greater degree of proof before it was forced to abandon a product that, according to Du Pont, contributed $8 billion to the U.S. economy and employed more than 200,000 workers in 1975. Additional study not only implied uncertainty; it would take time, and time favored industry, which profited every additional day it could manufacture and sell CFCs and avoid the cost of developing alternatives.

NRDC, meanwhile, kept up the pressure, filing a July 1975 petition to the FDA requesting a ban on foods, drugs, and cosmetics in aerosol containers using CFCs. On July 29, 1975, Stoel and NRDC lawyer Ruby Compton wrote to EPA administrator Russell Train to request a ban on CFC-propelled pesticides. In December 1975, NRDC filed a new petition with the CPSC. Mindful that the United States produced and used only about half of the CFCs worldwide, Stoel also met in 1975 with officials of the United Nations Environment Program to urge them to work for an international ban on aerosols. All this activity—filing petitions, lobbying, testifying before Congress and legislative committees in states where aerosol bans were contemplated, providing information to the press and other environmental groups, and proposing international action—reflected the growing sophistication of environmentalism in the seventies, an essential counterbalance to industry, which suffered from no shortage of financial resources in representing its point of view.

Some industry money went for advertisements, like Du Pont's full-page ads in major newspapers in late June 1975, in which the company described a controversy in which "claim meets counterclaim. Assumptions are challenged on both sides. And nothing is settled. Nor will there be any hard answers until some hard facts are produced. In the meantime, aerosol products suffer under a cloud of presumed guilt, and other fluorocarbon-dependent industries are seriously threatened. We believe this is unfair." The ad was signed by Du Pont chairman Irving S. Shapiro.

Industry's chief public-relations success was in creating the impression that a scientific battle was raging over the ozone-depletion issue, making it impossible for even the best corporate citizen to take action pending the unknown outcome of the debate. But in fact, as early as 1975, it had been difficult for the chemical companies to find independent scientists willing to attack the Rowland-Molina theory, and when they managed to find one, they went to great lengths to help him put his views across. One of these was Dr. Richard Scorer, a professor of theoretical mechanics at London's Imperial College of Science and Technology, whom the COAS imported in July 1975 for a six-week speaking tour of the United States. An expert on clouds and air motions, Scorer was not an atmospheric chemist, yet he had the confidence to denounce the CFC ozone-depletion theory as "utter nonsense." He cited the presence of naturally occurring chlorine in the atmosphere—for instance, methyl chloride, which had recently been measured in the lower stratosphere—and argued that since the ozone layer had for millions of years withstood this naturally occurring chlorine, the additional chlorine released by CFCs couldn't possibly be significant. Of course, Rowland and Molina and any scientist remotely familiar with the workings of the stratosphere knew that there were natural ozone-depleting processes, and the CFC ozone-depletion theory was based on the idea that chlorofluorocarbons did in fact introduce enough additional chlorine to compete with and even supersede the natural processes and reduce overall density of ozone at steady state. Still, the influence of naturally occurring chlorine continued to tantalize those who would debunk the Rowland-Molina theory.

The Scorer tour reached Los Angeles, and the backyard of Rowland and Molina, in late July 1975. "Scientists who widely promote 'scare' theories based on limited scientific evidence and legislators who overreact to those theories are threatening the jobs of thousands of American workers," he charged. "This particular theory [of ozone depletion], which originated with two University of California professors, F. S. Rowland and M. J. Molina, is scientifically debatable." Scorer repeated his assertion that chlorine is a common element in the environment that "nature has handled in the past and can handle in the future," and called Rowland and Molina "doomsayers."

"The gentleman is good at attacking," Rowland told a reporter from the *Santa Ana Register,* "but he has never published any scientific papers on the subject."

James Lovelock was less easily dismissed. The man who had invented the instrument capable of measuring CFCs in the atmosphere, whose work had in fact first piqued Sherry Rowland's curiosity about them, also denounced Rowland and Molina's views on ozone depletion. Lovelock —who received research funding from the Manufacturing Chemists Association—told the British journal *New Scientist* in June 1975 that the American reaction to the Rowland-Molina theory "means that scientific arguments no longer count." The impact of CFCs on the ozone layer, Lovelock said, had been grossly overestimated. He also doubted that increased levels of ultraviolet radiation would necessarily lead to increased incidence of skin cancer, pointing out that excess ozone in the troposphere—smog—might be a more serious health hazard. NRDC, Lovelock said, was a nongovernmental body made up of environmentally conscious lawyers, "like Ralph Nader, but not as responsible."

Lovelock clarified his feelings to a British newspaper reporter. "This is one of the more plausible of the doomsday theories, but it needs to be proved," he said. "The Americans tend to get into a wonderful state of panic over things like this. It's like the great panic over methyl mercury in fish. The Americans blamed industry until someone went to a museum and found a tuna fish from the last century with the same amount of methyl mercury in it." Lovelock was plainly unaware that Sherry Rowland was on the team of UC-Irvine scientists that had conducted the tuna research.

Perhaps Lovelock's indignation was nothing more than an Englishman's instinctive reaction to what he took to be a typical American brouhaha. Or perhaps his defensiveness was in reaction to the "invasion" of his scientific turf. CFCs in the atmosphere were his discovery, after all, and he had declared in the published results of his finding in 1973 that "the presence of these compounds constitutes no conceivable hazard." More fundamentally, however, the ozone-depletion theory was at odds with ideas he would later consolidate and call the Gaia hypothesis. This concept, as Lovelock described it in his book *Gaia: A New Look at Life on Earth,* was that the earth's biosphere, which he named Gaia, after the

Greek earth goddess, is "a self-regulating entity with the capacity to keep our planet healthy by controlling the chemical and physical environment." The earth itself, Lovelock believed, though not a sentient being, has many of the qualities of a living organism, and Gaia is the "largest living creature on Earth." Life, according to the Gaia hypothesis, did not evolve to adapt to the conditions of the planet; on the contrary, life itself has modified and continues to maintain the planet to suit its own needs, regulating, among other things, the climate and the chemical composition of the atmosphere. For instance, the earth's mean surface temperature has been relatively constant over the millennia, ideal to maintain life, despite an irregular output of energy from the sun; this, according to Lovelock, was analogous to a human being's constant body temperature of 98.6 degrees. "Life on this planet is a very tough, robust, and adaptable entity," Lovelock wrote. Even a nuclear war, which would cause "catastrophic local devastation," would "not much disturb Gaia."

While Lovelock recognized that "the complete or partial removal of the ozone layer could have unpleasant consequences for life as we know it," he doubted that Gaia would countenance such a disturbance in the first place. She would find some way to compensate for the impact of CFCs or SSTs. Even if ozone depletion were to occur, Gaia would survive. "A visitor viewing the earth from outer space and discovering aerosol-propellant gases in our atmosphere, would have no doubt whatever that our planet bore life, and probably intelligence of a kind as well," Lovelock commented in *Gaia*. "In our persistent self-imposed alienation from nature, we tend to think that our industrial products are not 'natural.' In fact, they are just as natural as all the other chemicals of the earth, for they have been made by us, who surely are living creatures." So man is part of Gaia, man creates and disseminates CFCs, and CFCs must therefore be natural to Gaia. But where is the assurance that man's continued well-being is part of Gaia's grand scheme? Perhaps, as Sherry Rowland once observed, Gaia is ill, infected by this single species, man, who has run amuck, overpopulating and polluting the earth. Perhaps chlorofluorocarbons are precisely the ingenious medicine, or feedback mechanism, that Gaia has devised to restore herself to good health by depleting the ozone layer just enough to eradicate the human microbe that has raised her temperature.

Several years into the CFC controversy, in the late seventies, Rowland and Lovelock and several other scientists had dinner together, following a scientific meeting in Washington. They talked informally about how the earth might appear in a thousand years. "I imagine that the world might look much as it does today," Rowland said, "full of green plants and life . . . but humans might not be present." Lovelock looked at him and blinked. "Oh, I see," he said as if he understood for the first time why Rowland had been so disturbed by the prospect of ozone depletion. "You're looking at it from the point of view of the human race."

As the April 1976 target date for the release of the NAS study of CFCs drew near, science was providing little comfort for industry. Air samples collected by the National Oceanic and Atmospheric Administration and the National Center for Atmospheric Research in June 1975 confirmed the data presented in late 1974 by Philip Krey of the AEC, which had shown a falloff in CFC-11 concentrations at higher altitudes, just as the ozone-depletion theory predicted. The NOAA–NCAR data were found to be in remarkably close agreement with the theoretical calculations made by Rowland and Molina over a year earlier. These results proved not only that CFCs were reaching the stratosphere in predicted amounts, but also, said Art Schmeltekopf, the NOAA physicist who headed the project, that "something is destroying the fluorocarbons as predicted and at the rates predicted by the theory."

Industry was forced to cling to the argument that nobody had yet been able to measure actual decreases in the amount of stratospheric ozone. Indeed, industry spokesmen repeatedly insisted that they would accept no lesser proof before voluntarily giving up CFC production. Rowland argued that such a standard of proof was absurd. "If an egg dropped from our lab roof breaks," he said, "we can safely assume an egg would also break if dropped from the Empire State Building." Obtaining evidence of actual damage to the ozone layer was particularly difficult because stratospheric ozone levels naturally fluctuate by as much as 10 percent at different times of day, seasonally, and in response to the eleven-year sunspot cycle. In fact, a report published in *Nature* in mid-1974 reported that ozone levels in the 1960s had actually been increasing, not decreasing as the Rowland-Molina theory would seem to suggest they should have. Of course, one key aspect of the theory was that there would be a delay of up to one hundred years between the time CFCs are released and their arrival in the stratosphere, and the CFC industry's exponential growth had begun only in the 1950s. The effect as of the sixties would have been minimal.

Industry spokesmen argued, in any case, that the predicted ozone losses due to CFCs—even if they were to occur—would fall within the range of natural fluctuations in ozone levels and were therefore unlikely to cause any harm, less harm to an individual than he might experience by moving from, say, New York to Miami, since ozone levels vary with latitude as well. But ozone depletion due to CFCs would take place on top of natural fluctuations and would raise the overall levels of ultraviolet radiation that reached the earth's surface, particularly during periods of minimal sunspot activity when ozone levels are naturally lowest. If, as most scientists believe, the evolution of life has been, in part, a battle against ultraviolet, then it stood to reason, as Stanford biologist Kendrick Smith said, that "many organisms may be living at the edge of their capability to protect themselves," one of them, perhaps, "a key link in the plant-animal food chain." Even slight increases in ultraviolet radiation could doom some living creatures. Plankton was a special worry because it has no protective skin, lives on the surface of the seas, and occupies a critical bottom rung of the food chain.

Natural fluctuations in ozone levels also meant that before damage due to CFCs could actually be measured, it would have to be substantial. If no ban was implemented until the damage was obvious, and growth in CFC production continued, then by the time a ban finally was put in place, there would be enough CFCs in the atmosphere to deplete the ozone layer by as much as 50 percent, according to some estimates. As Herbert Gutowsky, chairman of the NAS panel, testified before a Senate panel in September 1975, "This is a large risk for the world to take."

As of late 1975, in the brief time since the Rowland-Molina theory had been published, scientists had found strong evidence to support the first two steps of the CFC ozone-depletion process—measurements showing that CFCs were in fact reaching the stratosphere, and are dissociated by ultraviolet light under stratospheric conditions. And they had begun to look for evidence to support the third step in the theory: chemical proof that the dissociated fragments of CFCs in the stratosphere were reacting with ozone. Proof of CFCs' role in ozone depletion, many scientists believed, would be the direct measurement of chlorine monoxide, a by-product of the chlorine chain, in the stratosphere.

Forty-three million Americans watched the hit television show *All in the Family* on February 1, 1975, when the characters Mike and Gloria argued about having children. Mike declared he did not want to bring children into a rapidly deteriorating world. Things were getting better, Gloria pleaded. "Oh, yeah," Mike replied, picking up a can of her hair spray. "What about spray cans? Right here, this is a killer! . . . I read that there are gases inside these cans, Gloria, that shoot up in the air and destroy the ozone."

Although the scientific debate surrounding ozone depletion had often been hard for a layman to follow, the public increasingly understood that the risk to the ozone layer was being ventured on behalf of underarm deodorant and hair spray. In the face of bad publicity such as the *All in the Family* episode, and with the latest scientific research offering little in the way of encouragement, industry found it difficult to maintain a united front. On June 18, 1975, Johnson Wax became the first major company to break ranks, with the announcement that it would stop using chlorofluorocarbons in aerosol products it manufactured and marketed in the United States. The company ran large advertisements in the form of an "open letter" signed by Chairman Samuel C. Johnson. "We at Johnson Wax are taking this action in the interest of our customers and the public in general during a period of uncertainty and scientific inquiry," the letter read in part. Henceforth, Johnson Wax products would be labeled, "Use with confidence. Contains no Freon or other fluorocarbons claimed to harm the ozone layer."

By trumpeting its position as a good corporate citizen, Johnson Wax made its corporate brethren look bad. "What they've done is to try to gain marketing advantage out of a difficult situation," an unnamed industry source told *Rolling Stone*. "I know damn well that's what it is." Others pointed out that it was easy for Johnson to eliminate CFCs, since, by Johnson's own admission, they made up less than 5 percent of the total propellants used by the company. But there was growing evidence that it simply made good business sense to get away from CFC-propelled aerosols. Johnson's action, according to the company's public-relations department, "brought in the most significant response in our history . . . 99.999 percent favorable."

Only about half of the 3 billion aerosols produced each year used CFC propellants, principally personal-care products like hair sprays and deodorants, where the compounds' inertness and nonflammability were important. Products like shaving cream, which was so waterlogged that flammability wasn't a problem, and spray paint, which was so flammable that the use of a flammable propellant made little difference, generally used less-expensive propellants, such as hydrocarbons, propane, or carbon dioxide. Yet it was difficult for consumers to know which aerosols were accused of ozone depletion and which weren't, and so aerosols across the board were suffering from the controversy. Sales of aerosols for the first six months of 1975 were down about 25 percent. While some of the drop could be attributed to a recession, there was no doubt that the ozone controversy had hurt. Du Pont's sales of Freon in 1975 were 25 percent below 1974 levels; production at Precision Valve was down 40 percent in February and March 1975, enough to force the indefinite closure of its Yonkers headquarters plant for the first time since its 1949 founding. Industry's own market research showed that younger customers were especially aware of the ozone issue and were using aerosols less. Meanwhile, sales of pump sprays, roll-ons, and squeeze sprays were up. Following Johnson Wax's defection, other companies started to aggressively advertise alternatives to products that used CFCs. Bristol-Myers spent $6 million in the first three months of its promotion of Ban Basic nonaerosol antiperspirant. Mennen's ad campaign for its roll-on deodorant—featuring the slogan "Get Off the Can and On the Stick"— was deemed especially offensive by an editorialist at *Soap/Cosmetics/ Chemical Specialties*, who wrote, "What is most amazing about this crude performance is that it is sponsored by an old-line, highly respected and conservative company which, incidentally, has been a leading marketer of aerosols."

On June 16, 1975, Oregon became the first state to ban aerosols containing CFC propellants. "I'd rather err on the side of caution," said Governor Bob Straub when he signed the law, which was slated to go into effect on March 1, 1977. In May 1975 the New York Public Interest Research Group seized the occasion of hearings before a committee of the New York State legislature, which was considering an aerosol ban, to present surprise testimony detailing the findings of a research project that had found that aerosols cost substantially more than the same product sold in less exotic containers. Arrid Extra Dry, for example, was 357 percent more expensive in the aerosol than in the roll-on; the aerosol cost 2.5 cents an application compared to .7 cent for the roll-on. Similar price differences were found for Coppertone suntan oil, Bactine first-aid spray, and for various paints, waxes, and insecticides. Thus, Nader-style consumer activism heaped still more grief on the beleaguered aerosol. The New York law authorizing the commissioner of the environment to impose a ban on CFC-propelled aerosols in 1978 if they were found to pose a hazard was enacted in July 1975, and signed into law by the governor of the state on August 9.

While the aerosol industry was reeling, the air-conditioning and refrigeration industries, even more guilty of CFC dependency, seemed to be getting off scot-free on the theory that they used CFCs in closed, recycling systems that did not release as many of the compounds into the atmosphere. *Aerosol Age* sounded a plaintive cry for solidarity, pointing out that, as those who worked in air-conditioning and refrigeration clearly understood, "no systems are truly closed"; soon enough, the article warned, the overzealous government regulators would get around to them. It evidently hurt, too, that aerosols had been branded as frivolous compared to air-conditioning. "Sitting in on various hearings," the *Aerosol Age* editorialist wrote, "we've been made ill by the pious concern for the atmosphere by the inquisitors comfortable in their climate-controlled environments. Deliberately, they have cut off testimony from the air conditioning experts who try to explain the impact. It has been apparent —the investigators felt they could destroy aerosols and not endanger the comforts and benefits of cooling. The time is now for the industry to close ranks."

The persecuted tone that filled the letters columns and editorial pages of *Aerosol Age, Soap/Cosmetics/Chemical Specialties, Household and Personal Products Industry,* and *Drug and Cosmetic Industry* was a dismal echo of the ebullient voices of only a generation before, when aerosol spokesmen had quoted staggering sales figures and sung choruses of praise for the newly arrived "push-button age." The sudden downturn in the industry's fortunes in the seventies had proven every bit as steep as its rapid ascent during the fifties. Now the aerosol business was fighting for its life.

To a scientist schooled in aeronomy, many aspects of the ozone-depletion theory were quickly and intuitively grasped. To industry scientists and others suddenly confronted by the theory, much background information —a basic education in atmospheric science—was needed before they could even hope to discredit it. Often, when industry scientists argued that certain aspects of the theory were "not understood" or "not proven," they were referring to their own lack of understanding. Early in the controversy, atmospheric chemist Donald Hunten estimated there were perhaps only half a dozen people in the world "really qualified to have an opinion on this—certainly fewer than a dozen."

"We understood that we had a terrific responsibility," Sherry Rowland later explained, "because we did not see sufficient scientific competence in our opposition. If there were flaws in the theory, we would have to find them ourselves."

Rowland and Molina decided to begin this process by looking more closely at chlorine nitrate. Chlorine nitrate was one by-product of the decomposition of CFCs in the stratosphere—formed when the chlorine monoxide formed by a chlorine atom from a decomposing CFC molecule reacts with nitrogen oxides. Chlorine nitrate ties up atoms of chlorine and prevents them from reacting with ozone, and at the same time it breaks up nitrogen oxide, which also scavenges ozone as part of the naturally occurring nitrogen chain. Chlorine nitrate could thus inhibit ozone depletion on two counts. Rowland and Molina had considered chlorine nitrate in their calculations when they first developed the ozone-depletion theory, but had dismissed it as relatively unimportant because measurements done by German scientists in the 1950s had shown that it decomposed in a few minutes in sunlight.

Still, given its potential to interrupt both the chlorine and the nitrogen chains, chlorine nitrate was, in Rowland and Molina's view, a compound that demanded more study, and in September 1975 they remeasured the absorption cross-section rates for the compound. It is surprising that no other scientist had the same idea, and especially surprising that none in industry thought of it. Chlorine nitrate was a logical place to look for a flaw in the Rowland-Molina theory.

The two Irvine scientists were expert at gas-phase kinetics, or measuring the speeds at which gases react, but chlorine nitrate was a particularly difficult compound to work with. It took Molina and an associate, chemist John Spencer, four months just to learn how to handle the material. The difficulty was that chlorine nitrate reacts instantly with water, so all lab surfaces and equipment had to be absolutely dry. By early 1976, Rowland, Molina, and Spencer were able to calculate that chlorine nitrate was far more stable in the stratosphere than they had assumed. The rate of decay in sunlight varied depending on various factors, such as altitude and the angle of the sun, but in general the rate was on the order of a number of hours, not minutes, as they had presumed.

These dramatically slower rates of decay for chlorine nitrate would have to be included in calculations and computer models that attempted to predict total overall ozone losses. The estimated amount of overall stratospheric ozone depletion caused by CFCs would have to be revised downward, perhaps, Rowland and Molina calculated, by as much as 20 to 30 percent. But chlorine nitrate also introduced significant new perturbations with respect to ozone losses at different altitudes. At 40 kilometers, which is where the greatest ozone losses were predicted, chlorine nitrate would have little effect because it does decay rapidly when subjected to the intense ultraviolet at that altitude. At lower altitudes, however, chlorine nitrate has a much longer life and, by virtue of tying up nitrogen (as well as chlorine), might actually increase naturally occurring ozone levels.

Rowland and Molina's newly calculated cross sections for chlorine nitrate thus represented a significant refinement of scientific understanding of chlorine chemistry in the stratosphere. Rowland reported the findings at a conference on chlorine chemistry held at the Jet Propulsion Laboratory in Pasadena in early February 1976. Word spread quickly among the dozen scientists whose study for the NAS Panel on Atmospheric Chemistry was almost complete and was due to be released in April. One of them, mathematician Julius Chang of the Lawrence Livermore Laboratory, plugged the new chlorine nitrate figures into the NAS computer model he was developing. Prior to receiving this new input, the model had predicted a 14 percent ozone loss. Now, suddenly, the numbers changed so dramatically that the model actually showed an ozone gain of 5 percent. Chang recognized that the numbers were meaningless. The computer model had not been programmed to make adjustments for the particular complexities of chlorine nitrate.

Computer modeling, initiated in the years after World War II by John von Neumann at Princeton's Institute for Advanced Study and Jule Charney at MIT, was originally conceived as a means of speeding up and perfecting the science of mathematical weather forecasting, even—in von Neumann's case—of possibly gaining sufficient understanding to ultimately control the weather. Modeling subsequently had spread to numerous other applications—economic forecasting, urban development, agriculture, flood predictability, erosion, ecology, even gambling—anywhere a more accurate forecast of future conditions could assist planning and preparation, and maximize profits or safety.

Modeling, however, had not—could not—live up to the expectations once held for it, and by the mid-1970s it was particularly distrusted in the area of weather and climate-change prediction. Powerful supercomputers that could analyze data in gigaflops, or billions of calculations per second, for all their remarkable speed still fell short of being able to fully simulate reality. Even basic weather modeling proved capable of making reasonably accurate forecasts for only a few days in advance. The major reason for this was the inability of even a supercomputer to adequately "know" all the relevant factors for a given situation involving the natural world. An ozone-depletion model might contain highly accurate approximations of CFC production and the known rate constants for certain gas-phase reactions, but the effects of air transport, temperature, reactions with other trace gases, positive and negative feedback mechanisms, and solar activity affecting ultraviolet light were far less easy to include, not to mention innumerable other half-known or unknown factors.

According to Lydia Dotto and Harold Schiff in their book *The Ozone War*, the NAS panel was thrown into turmoil by their new computer-model estimates. The panel members had prepared a preliminary draft of their report, which indicated that the ozone-depletion theory was sufficiently proven to justify regulation of CFCs, and had begun to circulate it for prepublication scientific review. Now, suddenly, their careful calculations of estimated ozone depletion seemed irrelevant. One pesky compound, chlorine nitrate, had made a shambles of Chang's computer model, demonstrating again the unreliability of models when it came to predicting the workings of the atmosphere. With their confidence in their ability to forecast real ozone losses seriously shaken, the NAS decided to delay publication of the panel's report for several more months while they evaluated the new chlorine nitrate data.

Industry was elated. Scientists scrambling to feed chlorine nitrate into their own computer models came up with widely differing estimates of possible ozone depletion, ranging from only a slightly reduced ozone loss to an actual increase in ozone. The science behind the ozone-depletion theory was clearly, demonstrably fraught with uncertainty—or so industry argued. On May 12, 1976, COAS called a press conference in New York to claim that the new findings reduced the threat "nearly to zero." Citing not only Rowland and Molina's discoveries about chlorine nitrate, but also reports, later disproved, that another compound, hydrogen chloride, might tie up chlorine in the stratosphere, COAS science advisor James Lodge claimed that the industry position was vindicated. No decision to ban aerosols ought to be made until more was known. "We would like a fair trial, not a lynching party," Dr. Lodge said. But of course absolutely no evidence had been presented to show that CFCs did not dramatically perturb stratospheric ozone. If anything, chlorine nitrate only complicated the disturbance to the stratosphere, redistributing ozone from the upper to the lower stratosphere, and the only thing that had been called into question, really, was the wisdom of too much reliance on computer models.

Despite a flurry of favorable news reports—"rumor is running rampant again . . . the theory was wrong, industry was right, the ozone layer is saved, and fluorocarbons deserve an official reprieve," read a typical article in *Science News*—industry had unwittingly painted itself into a corner. To cheer the results of Rowland and Molina's latest research, it was necessary to concede implicitly that CFCs did in fact have a substantial impact on stratospheric ozone. Industry could argue only that the precise effect was unknown. But was any inadvertent alteration of the ozone layer acceptable? Did anyone really wish to argue that man could hope to regulate stratospheric ozone—or redistribute it—seizing the controls away from age-old natural systems and managing the skies the way people managed rivers, for example, by building dams, or forests by declaring them reserves? Man had not been notably successful in his stewardship of rivers and forests. Yet to permit uncontrolled emissions of CFCs would be, in effect, to assume responsibility for an enormous natural system, far larger and more complex than any river or forest, and with a far greater impact on the world's overall climate and the entire biosphere. Was this really what Du Pont wanted, to attempt artificial regulation of natural chemical cycles that they themselves had argued were so extraordinarily complex that science did not begin to comprehend them?

The long-awaited NAS report was finally issued on September 13, 1976. Mindful that there were, no doubt, other surprises like chlorine nitrate in store, the NAS panel qualified its conclusions. As IMOS had in its report the previous year, the NAS committee upheld the basic science behind the CFC ozone-depletion theory and called for a ban on aerosols within two years, allowing time for further research. "Selective regulation of fluorocarbon uses and releases is almost certain to be necessary at some time and to some degree of completeness," the report read. "Neither the needed timing nor the needed severity can be reasonably specified today." At the 1973 level of CFC production and taking into account the impact of chlorine nitrate, the panel concluded that the ultimate level of ozone depletion, decades hence, would be about 7 percent, although the range of possibilities was anywhere between 2 and 20 percent.

More important, perhaps, the NAS scientists had recognized that although estimates of eventual ozone depletion were subject to revision as research deepened scientific understanding and computer models were refined, the underlying issue was the presumption behind man's chemical alteration of the atmosphere. Sounding an ominous note, the NAS report pointed out that increased ultraviolet radiation on the earth's surface— the threat of "skin cancer," in the popular shorthand—was not the only threat from CFCs, and maybe not even the most serious threat. As a greenhouse gas in the lower atmosphere, CFCs could raise the earth's average temperature. The redistribution of ozone from the upper to the lower stratosphere could also alter the earth's climate. The possibility of rapid and drastic climate change was, needless to say, fraught with risk for humankind.

Two days after the NAS report was issued, on September 15, 1976, an international conference on threats to stratospheric ozone began at Utah State University in Logan, sponsored by NASA, the Jet Propulsion Laboratory, USU, and various national and international scientific associations. Participants discussed a number of research programs, some already underway, that were designed to resolve lingering uncertainties about the CFC ozone-depletion theory.

On the second day of the conference, Dr. James Anderson of the University of Michigan revealed that instruments aboard a balloon flight on July 28 had detected the presence of chlorine and chlorine monoxide, rising steadily in abundance up to an altitude of 42 kilometers. The presence of chlorine monoxide proved that chlorine was reacting with ozone in the stratosphere. But industry claimed that Anderson's findings still didn't prove that chlorine entered a catalytic chain and destroyed as much ozone as the Rowland-Molina theory indicated it would.

Impatience with industry's wearisome tactic of continually shifting the standard of proof it would accept was expressed by several speakers on the third day of the conference. Russell Peterson, then completing his tenure as chairman of the President's Council on Environmental Quality, urged industry to phase out its use of CFCs, noting that regulation was inevitable. "From the pure scientific perspective, there remain valid doubts about the effect of fluorocarbons on the ozone shield," he said. "From the public-policy standpoint, however, there remains no valid reason to postpone the start of regulatory procedures." Peterson's opinion carried clout. Not only was he a high government official and a sponsor of IMOS; he had worked for Du Pont for twenty-seven years before entering politics as the governor of Delaware. "I believe firmly that we cannot afford to give chemicals the same constitutional rights that we enjoy under the law," he concluded. "Chemicals are not innocent until proven guilty."

On September 21, 1976, the IMOS committee met in Washington. In its original report IMOS had said the federal government should await the report of the NAS committee before acting to restrict CFC use. The NAS report had been released, and although it, too, called for additional study, it fundamentally affirmed the validity of the ozone-depletion theory. Now IMOS followed through with its original proposition, voting unanimously to call for a commencement of the rule-making process to ban CFCs in aerosols. Since IMOS included representatives from all the government agencies that would be responsible for formulating and enforcing a ban—the EPA, the FDA, and the CPSC—the battle to save the aerosol was lost.

The FDA was the first agency to act, announcing on October 15, 1976, a proposed orderly phaseout of all nonessential uses of CFC propellants in food, drug, and cosmetic products, and an interim warning label on the same products in the meantime. "Given the effects on human health, even a two percent ozone depletion from 'unessential' uses of fluorocarbons is undesirable," commented FDA commissioner Dr. Alexander M. Schmidt. "It's a simple case of negligible benefit measured against possible catastrophic risk, both for individual citizens and for society. Our course of action seems clear beyond doubt." The FDA announcement was the first step in the rule-making process, to be followed up shortly with the publication of the proposed rules in the *Federal Register.*

Although Du Pont labeled the announcement "astonishing" in view of the fact that the NAS report had "clearly recommended against the kind of action the FDA is planning," the other agencies responsible for CFC regulation quickly followed suit. The following spring, a joint aerosol-policy committee composed of the FDA, the EPA, and the CPSC announced that spray cans containing CFCs would be phased out and banned within two years, with only a limited number of exemptions for asthma medication and a few other essential products. The phaseout would have three steps: The first would be a halt to all manufacture of CFC propellants for nonessential uses, to go into effect on October 21, 1978. Second, all companies would have to stop using existing supplies of CFC propellants by December 15, 1978. Finally, a ban on the interstate shipment of nonessential aerosol products containing CFCs would go into effect on April 15, 1979.

The spray-can war was over. They said it would ruin them, but now that a ban was at hand, industry displayed little bitterness. According to COAS, only about 30 percent of aerosols were still using CFC propellants. "Any impact would be very minimal since we've been working on the problem for some two and a half years," said a spokesman for Union Carbide. Robert Abplanalp actually appeared to rejoice at a press conference he called to introduce a new valve he had invented, designed to use butane, isobutane, or propane in place of CFCs. "We've managed to put together something with tried and true engineering principles that totally changes the nature of the aerosol business," he told a reporter.

"By year-end most of our products will be using nonaerosol propellants and the pricing is exactly the same," said John Vinton, chairman of Gillette's aerosol task force for the Personal Care Division.

Du Pont, industry heavyweight, leader in the holy crusade to save the aerosol, champion of economic growth, jobs, and scientific certainty, and enemy of the "rule of witchcraft where, by definition, the accusation proves the charge," seemed especially nonchalant. In 1976, Du Pont sold about $250 million in CFCs, of which "only" about $50 million worth was for use as an aerosol propellant, a company spokesman pointed out. "That means that fluorocarbons accounted for about three percent of Du Pont's total sales of $8.36 billion in 1976," the spokesman continued, "while the aerosol propellant business represented roughly 0.5 percent of total sales. It wasn't very significant."

13.

LIFE'S ONLY CRUCIBLE

THE UNITED STATES' BAN on aerosols was a hard-won victory in the battle to save the ozone layer and a high point of seventies environmentalism—a definitive triumph over a powerful and wealthy industry. To most people, including many of the government officials and environmental activists who had helped bring the aerosol ban about, the issue of a deteriorating ozone layer appeared to have been resolved. At the Natural Resources Defense Council, as elsewhere in Washington, including the EPA, ozone depletion went on the back burner, relegated to a less privileged status as just one of an increasing number of pressing environmental problems.

While politicians relaxed their concern and industry continued to manufacture CFCs, albeit at a reduced rate, scientists persevered in their efforts to understand the chemistry of the stratosphere; indeed, the ozone-depletion theory and the ensuing regulatory debate about CFCs in aerosols had attracted many researchers into stratospheric studies. One scientist whose curiosity had been piqued by the Rowland-Molina theory was Dr. Veerabhadran Ramanathan, a refrigeration-industry engineer–turned–physicist. As an engineer in his native India, Ramanathan had worked to solve the vexing and chronic problem of how to slow or stop the leakage of CFCs from sealed refrigerator coils.

After relocating to the United States to pursue academic physics at the State University of New York at Stony Brook, Ramanathan studied the heat-absorption characteristics of gases, including CFCs. Ramanathan knew from his years of working in industry that the infrared absorption characteristics of CFCs were important. In September 1975 he published his finding that CFCs not only were ozone depleters, but also constituted a significant greenhouse gas in the lower atmosphere.

If chlorofluorocarbons reached a concentration of 2 parts per billion in the atmosphere, Ramanathan said, as predicted for the end of the twentieth century at then-current production levels, the temperature on Earth would rise an average of about 1.6 degrees. This would be more than enough to cause disruptive climatic changes, including, possibly, a partial melting of the polar ice caps and a rise in sea levels that could flood populous coastal regions. And, of course, the warming caused by CFCs would be in addition to any greenhouse warming caused by other anthropogenic greenhouse gases. "The effect of chlorofluorocarbons and chlorocarbons on the chemical balance of the earth-atmosphere system is currently a subject of concern," Ramanathan concluded in the paper, "Greenhouse Effect Due to Chlorofluorocarbons: Climatic Implications," which appeared in the *Science* issue of October 3, 1975. "The major conclusion of this report is that their effect on the earth's thermal energy balance must also be given serious consideration."

The idea that the earth maintains its relative warmth by means of a "greenhouse" mechanism was first postulated in 1827 by the eminent French mathematical physicist Jean-Baptiste Fourier, who is best remembered for the mathematical techniques and theorems he devised to describe heat diffusion, including the so-called Fourier integrals and Fourier series. Fourier regarded the question of global temperatures to be "one of the most important and most difficult in all natural philosophy," and he theorized that the atmosphere allowed the visible rays and energy of the sun to warm the earth, while impeding the radiation of heat back to outer space, working something like the glass of a greenhouse. Just how this mechanism might work was a mystery, however, since neither nitrogen nor oxygen—which constitute 99 percent of the atmosphere—absorb sunlight. Fourier's theory went unsubstantiated until 1863, when British scientist John Tyndall was able to measure the heat-absorbing properties of two atmospheric trace gases, water vapor and carbon dioxide (CO_2). These gases, Tyndall found, do not absorb sunlight, but, rather, infrared radiation, or the heat produced when the sunlight that strikes the earth's surface is radiated back into the atmosphere. Fourier's metaphor of a greenhouse, it turned out, was imprecise. The glass of a greenhouse does not absorb radiant heat, but warms air by trapping it where it is exposed to sunlight, and then preventing it from mixing with the cooler air on the outside. Nonetheless, the term "greenhouse effect" has persisted as a shorthand description of the phenomenon whereby carbon dioxide, water vapor, and other atmospheric trace gases absorb radiant heat and help maintain the earth's warmth.

In 1896, in an effort to understand the cause of ice ages, the Swedish chemist Svante Arrhenius calculated that although their concentration in the atmosphere is minute, water vapor and carbon dioxide together absorb enough infrared radiation to warm the earth's atmosphere by nearly 60°F. These trace gases, Arrhenius observed, prevent the earth from being a frozen planet, and in effect make life possible. Arrhenius theorized that ice ages occur when there is less carbon dioxide in the atmosphere, and went on to predict that growing concentrations of carbon dioxide in the atmosphere—a consequence in part of increasing coal use during the Industrial Revolution—would eventually raise the earth's temperature. Doubling the amount of atmospheric carbon dioxide, Arrhenius calculated, would warm the globe some 7° to 10°F. Although his theory later proved essentially correct, Arrhenius's venture into climatology found little support. Until 1957 most scientists believed that the bulk of the carbon dioxide produced by human beings would simply be absorbed by the oceans. That year Roger Revelle and Hans E. Suess of the Scripps Institution of Oceanography, near San Diego, published a study suggesting that half of the carbon dioxide produced by man would not be absorbed by the oceans, but would remain in the atmosphere. "Mankind is now engaged in a great geophysical experiment," the Scripps report warned. Starting in 1958, Scripps researcher C. David Keeling began to monitor atmospheric concentrations of CO_2 in stations at the South Pole and in Hawaii, far from sources of pollution, and was able to record steadily and dramatically increasing levels.

The irrefutable evidence that CO_2 was increasing in the atmosphere led most scientists to agree as of the 1960s that the prospect of "global warming" was real and would be felt to some degree, at some point in the future, if nothing was done to reduce CO_2 emissions. But there were many complications that could mitigate warming, for instance increasing cloudiness as a result of rising temperatures, which would shield the earth's surface from the sun and cool the planet back down. Some scientists argued, as Arrhenius had, that global warming might actually benefit mankind by promoting plant growth, for example, or by forestalling an impending ice age, or that it would be so gradual that life would easily adapt to it, or that the oceans would absorb most of the heat produced by the greenhouse effect. The earth's climate is so complex that few scientists were comfortable making predictions. And so while "the greenhouse effect" entered the lexicon of problems that worried environmentalists in the 1970s—and a warmer planet of the future remained a staple of science fiction—there was little urgency associated with it. For one thing, the major source of carbon dioxide—the use of fossil fuels as modern civilization's primary source of energy—was already high on the environmentalist hit list since it was the major contributor to smog. Clean up smog, a much more visible and immediate symptom of environmental degradation than global warming, and, it seemed to follow, the greenhouse effect would be sharply mitigated.

Ramanathan's revelation that CFCs were a greenhouse gas, perhaps ten thousand times as efficient as carbon dioxide, demonstrated yet again that atmospheric chemistry was dauntingly complex. And just as the Rowland-Molina theory launched a period of intensive study of chlorine chemistry in the stratosphere, Ramanathan's observation renewed and intensified scientific thinking about the greenhouse effect. Scientists quickly postulated that human activities could be raising the levels of other greenhouse gases in addition to carbon dioxide and CFCs: for example, methane, known familiarly as "swamp gas" or "natural gas," which is produced by bacteria in the guts of cattle and other animals, and in landfills, rice paddies, and wetlands; nitrous oxide, produced by combustion and modern agricultural practices; and the ozone in tropospheric smog. The combined effect of these gases could be significant, perhaps equal to or even greater than the warming effect of carbon dioxide.

With ozone-layer perturbations intricately bound up with global warming, there were innumerable variables and endless feedback mechanisms to consider. For example, increasing methane concentrations would slow down the rate of ozone depletion, since methane in the stratosphere diverts chlorine and interrupts the chlorine chain. In 1978, following up on speculation that methane levels could indeed be rising, Sherry Rowland asked a new graduate student at Irvine named Edward Mayer to analyze air samples the Irvine group had been collecting since 1977 in both hemispheres in connection with other research. In 1982, Rowland and Mayer, et al., published their study showing increases in methane levels at seven different latitudes in both hemispheres. Methane is about twenty times as efficient a greenhouse gas as carbon dioxide. Furthermore, it may oxidize and form water vapor in both the lower and upper atmospheres, and it contributes to the formation of ground-level ozone—both greenhouse gases in their own right.

New findings like these only strengthened the view of the earth's atmosphere as a great geophysical experiment running recklessly out of control. Yet, it seemed, the new information only made it more difficult for scientists to come up with reasonable estimates of future conditions —specifically, estimates of future ozone levels or global temperatures. In the world of politics, with the fate of industries hanging in the balance, effects were far more important than causes. It wasn't enough for science to be able to state categorically that human activities were dramatically changing the chemistry of the atmosphere. What politics required of science was much more: proof that the changes would be an environmental detriment. Paradoxically, greater understanding of causes led to less certainty about effects, more doubts about appropriate actions, and more excuses not to act at all.

One small blue-green planet, adrift in the void of space; life's only crucible, so far as we know; a complex global ecosystem of interdependent parts: Gaia. This image of earth seen from space, fragile and precious, has captured the human imagination. But the earth is also large from an individual's perspective, and often appears resilient. Environmental ills have historically been local, or regional at worst, of concern to individual nations or, at times, to neighboring nations. The threat of ozone depletion, however, served to realize the image of one interdependent world. It was "the first truly global environmental problem affecting each person and ecosystem on this planet," EPA administrator Russell Train pointed out in an October 1975 address before NATO's Committee on the Challenges of Modern Society.

To Train and other Americans working to ban the aerosol in the United States, the need for global cooperation was obvious. Yet it was equally apparent that achieving worldwide action would be a daunting task. The threat of nuclear war had advanced international diplomacy to a certain point—sufficient to have so far avoided a nuclear holocaust— and an increasingly interdependent global economy had encouraged international cooperation on many issues. But no category of problem posed as complex a challenge to international diplomacy as the question of global environmental degradation.

Prior to World War II, international cooperation on environmental issues had been confined to agreements to protect migratory wildlife. The 1911 Fur Seal Treaty among the United States, Canada, the Soviet Union, and Japan was a notable success in preventing the extinction of a species endangered by overharvesting. International efforts to regulate whaling were less successful, largely because two of the major whaling nations, Russia and Japan, did not participate. After World War II various organizations within the United Nations, including the U.N. Economic and Social Council, the Food and Agriculture Organization (FAO), and the U.N. Educational, Scientific, and Cultural Organization (UNESCO), conducted programs with environmental aspects, such as research into soil conservation. The World Meteorological Organization (WMO) maintained a worldwide atmospheric-monitoring network, primarily concerned with weather forecasting, which gathered some data on pollution. Several nongovernmental organizations, notably the International Union for Conservation of Nature and Natural Resources (IUCN), struggled in poverty and obscurity to advance preservationist aims on an international scale. Growing threats to African wildlife led in 1961 to the foundation of the World Wildlife Fund (WWF). It was not until 1970, however, the year of the Earth Day movement in the United States, that environmentalism exploded as an international issue with a vocal and influential constituency.

The roots of the international movement were much the same as those in the United States, including the influence of *Silent Spring*; environmental disasters such as the mercury poisoning at Minimata, Japan, in the early 1960s, the huge oil spill from the tanker *Torrey Canyon* in March 1967 off the southwestern coast of England, and the Santa Barbara oil spill two years later; and, more generally, the spirit of sixties activism. In September 1968, UNESCO sponsored a scientific conference on the global environment, the so-called Biosphere Conference (the Intergovernmental Conference of Experts on the Scientific Basis for Rational Use and Conservation of the Resources of the Biosphere). Four years later, in June 1972, the United Nations organized a Conference on the Human Environment, in Stockholm, Sweden.

Stockholm marked the coming of age of international environmentalism, attracting worldwide media attention. A spirit of hope and optimism characterized an occasion many considered a historic turning point. The conference dealt with the entire panoply of environmental ills, including ozone depletion, which was then exclusively associated with the SST. The conference unanimously adopted a proposal to recommend the establishment, under the auspices of the World Meteorological Organization, of a global network of 110 stations to monitor changes in the atmosphere, including ozone levels. Other so-called "earthwatch" programs were recommended to monitor the oceans, radioactive wastes, food contamination, and wildlife populations. A Declaration of Environmental Principles was adopted. Finally, in what was regarded by many delegates as its most important achievement, the conference recommended the establishment of a permanent environmental unit in the United Nations—the United Nations Environment Program, or UNEP.

The Stockholm conference gave moral weight to the principle that nations must share responsibility for the environment, and in particular for the global commons: the atmosphere and oceans. But nothing the conference did was legally binding. As heartening as they were, general statements of environmental principle would prove to be far easier to adopt than specific restrictions on the economic activities of sovereign nations. And despite the apparent unanimity displayed at Stockholm, the conference also underscored the different perceptions dividing wealthy industrialized nations from developing nations of the third world. To nations struggling to raise living standards above a subsistence level, environmentalism could seem like a luxury. Not only did rich nations consume and pollute more than their fair share, they could better afford controls and regulations. During the conference it became increasingly clear that no international agreement could be reached on any environmental issue if the terms of the agreement would significantly hinder economic growth in less-developed countries. From the conflict between richer and poorer nations there gradually emerged a "new" environmental ideal of "sustainable development," a concept peculiarly reminiscent of Gifford Pinchot's brand of conservation.

The euphoria of Stockholm thus gave way quickly to the difficult realities of implementing real solutions to environmental problems. The U.N. General Assembly heeded the Stockholm conference's recommendation and established UNEP in December 1972. In a bow to the sensitivities of less-developed countries, the new organization was located in Nairobi, Kenya, the first major U.N. body to have its headquarters outside North America or Europe. From its inception UNEP was underfunded, and its early record of accomplishment was spotty. The agency's major success was in helping countries in ten different regions devise "action plans" to clean up and protect regional seas. Most notably, UNEP brokered the Barcelona Convention for the Protection of the Mediterranean Sea Against Pollution, which was adopted in 1975 and went into force in 1978.

In April 1975, NRDC's Tom Stoel met in Nairobi with Dr. Ramses Mikhail, the UNEP official responsible for the ozone issue, to request that UNEP take a leadership role on the matter. From that date forward NRDC kept Dr. Mikhail up to date on scientific and political developments. In March 1976, before the Fourth Session of UNEP's Governing Council, the NRDC presented a statement recommending that UNEP coordinate international ozone-depletion research efforts, taking care to avoid duplication of research already underway in the United States. Stoel believed UNEP could help form a "consensus among scientists of different nations on the gravity of the fluorocarbon problem," which was "probably the most important prerequisite to effective regulation world-wide."

In March 1977, UNEP sponsored the first international conference on CFCs. Held in Washington, the conference was attended by representatives of the European Economic Community (EEC) and representatives from thirty-three nations. The conference devised a World Plan of Action on the Ozone Layer. In response to the plan, UNEP set up a Coordinating Committee on the Ozone Layer (CCOL) to collect information about ongoing and planned research and publish brief summaries of it in the *Ozone Layer Bulletin*. The next month, the EPA, the FDA, and the CPSC, signaling perhaps a lack of complete confidence in UNEP, cohosted a second international conference on CFCs, attended by CFC-producing nations, including the Soviet Union, Canada, Japan, Great Britain, France, and Germany. The conference convened in Washington on April 26, 1977, just as plans for an aerosol ban in the United States were being finalized. The idea was that the United States might successfully lead by example, inducing other nations to announce aerosol bans of their own, thus avoiding the need for complicated international negotiations. Only Canada and Sweden joined the United States in an aerosol ban, however. Germany agreed to host a follow-up conference in December 1978 in Munich.

In preparation for the Munich conference the German sponsors decided to prepare a comparative review of the policies, laws, and regulations of various countries and international organizations that were relevant to CFC control. The issue was so new, particularly outside the United States, that there were few researchers prepared to write the report in the short amount of time—less than a year—before the conference was scheduled. The search for someone to do the study led eventually to Tom Stoel at NRDC. Stoel hired Alan S. Miller, a recent graduate of the University of Michigan Law School, to work under him. Working furiously, Miller and Stoel completed the study in six months, concluding that while many countries had adequate legal power to regulate CFCs, the issue had provoked widely differing responses. The United States, Canada, Sweden, and the Netherlands had moved quickly to regulate CFCs, while, at the other end of the spectrum, the Soviet Union, Australia, Japan, and Yugoslavia had not recognized the problem as meriting serious attention.

Miller and Stoel attended the Munich conference—"a tremendous education in international environmental diplomacy," in Miller's recollection; a "failure," according to Stoel. The American delegation was led by Barbara Blum, deputy administrator of the EPA, who delivered a talk in which she described the American experience with the aerosol ban as having been a tremendous success. CFC production had been dramatically cut, she noted, while industry had adapted with relative ease. Blum urged "a unified global approach to dealing with the health and environmental risks associated with CFC production and use." But she was immediately assailed by a French Revlon representative who argued that while a ban on CFCs in aerosols might have been feasible in the United States, such an action would never be tolerated in France because, he stated, as was well known in the cosmetics trade, American women accepted inferior products. In any case, European Economic Community agreements prevented any individual member of the alliance from restricting CFCs unilaterally; any action would have to be communitywide. Lacking a precedent for establishing international environmental regulations and not yet convinced that the threat to the ozone layer was real, the nations of the European Community easily brushed aside the American position and declined to pursue CFC restrictions. Many delegations in Munich favored voluntary agreements with industry, while others saw no reason to take any action at all. The Munich conference ultimately resolved simply to support further research on ozone depletion and the economic and trade consequences of international regulation, and to recommend a precautionary reduction in the global release of CFCs.

In 1979 the National Academy of Sciences published its second report on the CFC ozone-depletion theory, which estimated that at 1977 world production levels there would be a 16.5 percent depletion of stratospheric ozone by the late twenty-first century. The study warned bluntly that ozone levels decreased by this magnitude would result in sharply higher rates of skin cancer and in serious damage to the marine food chain and to crops. Concluding that a wait-and-see attitude was "clearly not a prudent strategy," the report urged the United States to lead a worldwide effort to control CFCs. Although industry seized upon a report issued the same year by the United Kingdom's Department of the Environment, which was not written by scientists but by British government officials, and which cautioned that due to scientific uncertainties and continuing doubts about the reliability of computer models it was still too soon to say if the ozone-depletion hypothesis was valid, more nations, notably West Germany and the Netherlands, had come around to the position that some form of CFC restrictions ought to be imposed. In March 1980, the Commission of the EEC asked its members to stop adding to its capacity to manufacture CFCs and to seek a 30 percent reduction in the use of CFC-propelled aerosols by June 1981. Then in April 1980, at a meeting hosted by the government of Norway in Oslo, representatives from the United States, Canada, Sweden, Norway, Denmark, West Germany, and the Netherlands called for immediate steps to reduce CFC emissions. The head of the U.S. delegation to the meeting, Barbara Blum, announced that the United States would freeze CFC production at the 1979 level of 551 million pounds per year, an action, she explained, that was "neither the first, nor the last, step to control chlorofluorocarbons." "The action . . . conveys the urgent and deep concern of the United States about the threat chlorofluorocarbons continue to pose," Blum said. "Our country is moving forward now because we believe that chlorofluorocarbons comprise one of the leading international environmental issues of the decade." The next essential step, Blum added, was "rapid, parallel actions by all chlorofluorocarbon producing nations." Blum followed the Oslo meeting with a series of meetings in London, Rome, Dublin, and Brussels, where she met with representatives of the EEC.

In the first week of October 1980 the EPA followed through on Blum's Oslo announcement by publishing in the *Federal Register* an advance notice of proposed rulemaking (ANPR) for Phase Two regulations —the aerosol ban had been Phase One—to phase out "nonessential" chlorofluorocarbons by one of two means, or by a combination of them. The first possibility was a cap on production, enforced by traditional mandatory controls and standards—for example, by banning particular uses of CFCs. The second approach, which the EPA favored, was to provide economic incentives to industry to develop alternatives to CFCs by restricting overall CFC production and establishing a system of permits allocated directly to producers and consumers of CFCs or auctioned off to the highest bidder. These "permits to pollute" could then be bought and sold on a free market.

The second of EPA's proposals marked an advance in the art of regulation. Economists and environmentalists had often theorized that economic incentives, including taxes or mechanisms like marketable permits, could be a viable alternative to traditional regulations. CFCs seemed to lend themselves especially well to such economic controls. First, the environmental problems associated with CFCs were not local, and so regulations to restrict them could and should be made applicable nationwide. More cumbersome traditional regulations, which take into account factors such as where a pollutant is produced and how it enters the environment, would be unnecessary to control CFCs. Second, different varieties of CFCs were used in so many different applications that a market mechanism seemed a more efficient way to allocate limited supplies. CFCs with different chemical compositions were not all equally destructive of ozone, depending on, for example, how much chlorine they contained and how rapidly they decomposed in the stratosphere. Rather than the EPA's having to make separate determinations as to which species of CFC and which CFC uses were permissible and to what degree, the agency could simply restrict production of various CFCs depending on their ozone-scavenging potential and let the marketplace decide how, where, and by whom the legally limited number of compounds would be used. In 1976 the EPA had commissioned the Rand Corporation to undertake an economic analysis to evaluate the costs and effectiveness of various regulatory options. The 1980 ANPR reflected Rand's conclusions that marketable permits could be a more efficient way to reduce CFC production and emissions, although it did not specify how the permits would be issued or allocated. Rather, it set forth several options and solicited public comment.

NRDC's comments on the ANPR were prepared by Alan Miller and submitted to the EPA by NRDC, along with the Sierra Club, the National Aubudon Society, and Friends of the Earth. Miller reviewed the state of scientific knowledge, including the potential impacts of ozone depletion, and analyzed the costs of CFC restrictions versus the potential effects of ozone depletion. He concluded that "the best scientific opinion is that CFCs will cause a ten percent depletion of ozone . . . if emissions are not substantially reduced." Noting that after seven years of research, with active industry participation, "no one can credibly argue that the issues have been decided hastily, or that promising scientific avenues have gone unexplored," Miller strongly urged the EPA to adopt its proposed market approach to regulations.

Including Miller's comments, the EPA received only four letters in support of its proposed regulations, clear evidence that among environmentalists and the general public interest in the CFC ozone-depletion issue had sharply waned. While the environmentalists' effort to control CFCs had lost momentum, however, industry had stepped up pressure on its end. Some twenty-three hundred letters were received by the EPA in opposition to the proposed Phase Two regulations, a flood of correspondence that was orchestrated by the Alliance for Responsible CFC Policy, a coalition of CFC users and producers that had been formed following Barbara Blum's alarming announcement in Oslo that production caps were imminent. The purpose of the alliance, a spokesman said, was "to convince the government—Congress, the White House, and anyone else —that EPA's proposal to restrict CFCs is ill-advised."

The EPA's proposed regulation is "unwarranted at this time," said Charles N. Masten, then director of Du Pont's Freon Products Division, since new evidence "raises questions about the validity of the ozone depletion theory." Moreover, Masten pointed out, the problem was global in nature and could not be solved by unilateral U.S. actions. There might be a short-term drop in overall global production levels if U.S. restrictions were imposed, but eventually growth in other nations would make up the difference, leaving the global problem unchanged while major American industries—air-conditioning, refrigeration, and electronics—were put at a significant disadvantage via-à-vis foreign competitors. Indeed, some industry representatives argued, the United States would maintain negotiating leverage with other nations only so long as America was a CFC producer. By a similar stroke of reasoning, American companies would be better able to introduce their customers to CFC substitutes, if and when the introduction of such substitutes proved necessary, if they kept their customers and did not drive them into the arms of their foreign competitors by being forced prematurely out of the market.

Despite Du Pont's vigorous public protest of the EPA's proposed regulations and its active sponsorship of the Alliance for Responsible CFC Policy, the company was actually not concerned that new CFC restrictions would be imposed. Four months before the publication of the proposed Phase Two regulations, in June 1980, Du Pont had quietly suspended research on CFC alternatives. Before then, Du Pont had the most ambitious research program in the CFC industry, and spent $3 million to $4 million a year in the late seventies seeking to identify CFC substitutes. Several promising CFC alternatives—hydrochlorofluorocarbons, or HCFCs, which would decompose before they reached the stratosphere, and other compounds containing no chlorine—had been found, but they cost between two and five times as much to manufacture as CFCs. Joseph M. Steed, who headed the Freon Products Division team responsible for scientific and governmental relations and public affairs policies, later explained the company's decision to halt the research. "We could have built a $100 million plant, filled our tanks and not sold any of it," Steed said. "There wasn't scientific or economic justification to proceed. How much do you trade a possible [environmental] risk for [a business risk] that is real?" According to another Du Pont manager, "There was obviously no interest in the marketplace to go to alternatives at three times the price" of existing compounds. Moreover, identifying potential substitutes had been the relatively easy and inexpensive part of developing CFC alternatives. Testing the new compounds for toxicity and safety to satisfy EPA requirements before they could be marketed would cost many millions more.

No doubt the managers of the Du Pont Freon Products Division made a sound business decision in halting research on CFC alternatives. The company had closely monitored the international discussions and knew that an international agreement to restrict CFCs was far off, if it was attainable at all. Stratospheric science was still subject to debate, which, from their point of view, was entirely legitimate. Most important, the political tides in the United States were turning. The Carter administration was in its last days. Ronald Reagan had campaigned vigorously against "excessive" government regulation of industry, and was famous for his contempt for environmentalism. "You know, a tree is a tree— how many more do you need to look at?" he once said with respect to redwood preservation when he first ran for governor of California. A long-time champion of unfettered capitalism and individual freedom, Reagan embodied, in demeanor as well as ideology, something quite opposite from environmentalism: a cowboy ethic indigenous to the open range of the American West. On election night, 1980, as Reagan won forty-four states to crush the incumbent president, Jimmy Carter, it appeared that the heyday of the environmental movement in the United States might be past.

14.

THE OPEN RANGE

AFTER THE GREAT BUFFALO HERDS had been destroyed and the Native American tribes were subdued and restricted to reservations, the vast range of the American West became home to the cowboy. The cowboy and the range created and shaped one another. It took a particular breed of man to survive on the expanses of semiarid western lands that were deemed of little value to anybody else— land the government couldn't sell or give away to railroads or homesteaders during the period of westward expansion, "reclaim" with irrigation projects during the era of conservation, or consider worthy of inclusion in national forests or parks. The range was bequeathed to cattle and the cowboys who drove them. Land containing water was the only valuable property on the range, so western ranchers bought only those select parcels, where they built homes and other facilities, and grazed their livestock on the adjacent, unfenced lands that nobody owned. Numerous elements of western legend, recounted in countless movies, television shows, and dime novels, evolved to suit the conditions of this "open" range, including brands to establish ownership of cattle, cattle drives to move livestock to fresh forage and to market across vast distances, range wars between cattlemen, and a system of justice that made cattle rustling a capital offense. By the 1970s, running cattle on federally owned rangeland, though a way of life for a relative handful, had nonetheless been sanctified by folklore and was tantamount to a cherished American tradition.

There was, however, a deep contradiction in the cowboy's soul. Fiercely independent, the very embodiment of rugged individualism, the modern cowboy was in fact heavily dependent on the minimally restricted use of public lands. Land policies that had been patched together over several generations had resulted in a significant federal subsidy to western stockmen. Part of the cost that the American taxpayer yielded to western ranchers—and to a taste for the low-cost beef they produced—was in the form of serious damage to overgrazed public lands, land that, in writer Edward Abbey's memorable phrase, was "cowburnt."

Conflict between the cowboy and a growing environmental movement was inevitable in the 1970s. The environmentalists won the early battles, but the cowboys had their revenge in 1980 with the election of Ronald Reagan, a western president who walked, talked, dressed, and acted like a cowboy, and who took refuge from the White House at his California ranch, Rancho del Cielo, where, according to his publicists, he enjoyed nothing more than clearing brush. Reagan appointed like-minded westerners to administer environmental programs: Anne Gorsuch of Colorado as administrator of the EPA and James Watt of Wyoming as secretary of the interior. For the eight years of Reagan's presidency, the grand edifice of progressive environmental law and federal regulation that had been built up in the 1970s was under the control of these individuals and others like them who shared the philosophy of the open range. Progress toward resolution of the ozone-layer crisis was, in effect, at the mercy of these cowboy-administrators. Following the aerosol ban, which had been imposed by the Carter administration, any additional domestic regulation of chlorofluorocarbons would be their responsibility, and they would have to carry forward any initiative the United States might undertake to attempt to restrict global CFC use.

Only government regulation could save the ozone layer, and yet regulation, and particularly environmental regulation, was completely at odds with the values of the open range. Reagan strode into office vowing to slash oppressive and costly federal "overregulation," which, he argued in campaign appearances, had not only stifled the economy but was incompatible with the American ideal of freedom. The environmental movement of the 1970s had won clean-air and -water legislation; it had won wilderness designations and had helped ban the aerosol; it had seen the institution of thousands of regulations and a bureaucracy to enforce them; but it had also inspired a powerful and resentful antienvironmentalism that rose up out of the West.

The Natural Resources Defense Council had certainly done its part to arouse and antagonize westerners. In 1972, largely so it could better address western land-use issues, NRDC opened a California office in Palo Alto. One of the first staff members hired was Yale Law School graduate Johanna Wald, who quickly focused on the issue of grazing policy on public lands. After talking to other national environmental organizations, local groups, and current and former employees of the Bureau of Land Management (BLM) and the Forest Service, she determined that the BLM was probably in violation of the National Environmental Protection Act in failing to produce environmental impact statements concerning its livestock-grazing-permit program. Before filing a lawsuit, Wald initiated discussions with the BLM, informing them of the likely violation, and seeking a remedy. The bureau's response was to file a single "programmatic" environmental impact statement to cover the entire BLM grazing program. The statement was so general that it was all but useless in describing the actual conditions on the range. At that point, in 1973, Wald and NRDC decided to sue.

The BLM managed over 171 million acres of public lands in the eleven far-western states, most of which—some 150 million acres—was leased to stockmen under the provisions of the Taylor Grazing Act of 1934. Fourteen percent of the livestock in the United States spent some part of their lives on BLM lands. The BLM itself had noted in various reports and studies that overgrazing had dramatically degraded the lands under its jurisdiction. One report in 1973 stated that 84 percent of BLM-managed grazing land was in fair, poor, or bad condition and only 16 percent was in good or excellent condition; overgrazing had turned meadows to brush, had destroyed wildlife habitat, had induced serious erosion, and had led, in extreme cases, to desertification. Nonetheless, the BLM asserted that its single "programmatic" environmental impact statement was adequate to cover its entire livestock-grazing program. The NRDC did not ask the court to halt or restrict grazing on BLM lands, but sought to require the BLM to prepare separate "site-specific" environmental impact statements on an appropriate district or geographic level. On December 30, 1974, the Federal District Court for the District of Columbia issued a ruling in favor of the NRDC.

The NRDC's victory in *NRDC* v. *Morton* was a direct threat to the interests of politically influential ranchers. The Taylor Grazing Act had established grazing districts on public lands, and a system of grazing leases and permits, administered by a new Division of Grazing, later known as the Grazing Service, in the Department of the Interior. In exchange for collecting fees from cattlemen, the Grazing Service assumed responsibility for conserving the range, including such measures as re-seeding degraded areas and maintaining water supplies. But the Taylor Grazing Act had been passed expressly in response to the needs of ranchers, and in practice the Grazing Service was dominated by ranchers who sat on "district advisory boards" and held tremendous sway over the allocation of leases. These same ranchers' forebears handily fought back various attempts by the Grazing Service in the 1930s and 1940s to reduce the numbers of cattle permitted on depleted rangelands and to raise grazing fees to levels closer to those imposed for grazing rights on private property. For the Grazing Service, the political price of attempting both to regulate and to serve the interests of ranchers proved fatal; with Nevada Senator Pat McCarran leading the charge, the agency was phased out of existence in 1946 and was merged with the General Land Office to form the Bureau of Land Management. Cattle grazing continued on the open range, unfettered as usual—until the 1974 NRDC courtroom victory forced the BLM to reconsider its livestock-grazing program.

For the first time a court had ruled that an ongoing government program was subject to the provisions of the National Environmental Policy Act. The case was a political as well as a legal landmark. Suddenly, the BLM had an enormous new mission, to produce 212 environmental impact statements, a task that would require the bureau to hire a large number of new employees, many of whom were trained in disciplines that had not been represented at the BLM before. Moreover, the BLM had a new constituency—environmentalists—who had a legally protected interest in its management of public lands.

The NRDC's legal breakthrough added pressure to an already tense situation on the range, with traditional users of public land finding themselves increasingly on the defensive. In 1964, Congress had responded to mounting and contradictory pressures to develop, sell, or protect the public lands by commissioning the Department of the Interior to conduct a study of the future of public lands. Six years later the Public Land Law Review Commission published its study, entitled *One Third of the Nation's Land*. The report recommended the permanent retention of the BLM lands and the imposition of "multiple-use" management policies, like those that had been implemented by Gifford Pinchot at the Forest Service. In 1976, several weeks after the ruling handed down in *NRDC* v. *Morton*, Congress passed the Federal Land Policy and Management Act, incorporating many of the commission's recommendations. Abruptly, after over a hundred years during which the government had done all it could to dispose of and encourage the exploitation of the public lands, drastically different policies were established. The new legislation balanced commercial and noncommercial uses of the land; required the protection of "scientific, scenic, historical, ecological, environmental, air and atmospheric, water resource and archeological values"; and called for the public to receive fair market value for minerals, timber, and other commodities extracted from the public lands. The BLM was given vast new powers and responsibilities to meet these objectives, and the new act—which was signed into law by Republican president Gerald Ford—took its place alongside the other landmark environmental legislation of the environmental decade.

To ranchers, whose grazing leases were a prized asset handed down from father to son, the demand for exhaustive analyses of the environmental impacts of the BLM grazing programs added up to more intolerable federal interference with their businesses—and a direct assault on their income. Their fury helped fuel a political movement in the West, the so-called Sagebrush Rebellion, renewing an old call first heard in the 1920s and again in the 1940s for the sale or granting of federal lands to private ownership or the states. The battle cry was "state's rights" or "local control," and environmentalism was made out to be an agent of big government, grasping bureaucracy, even encroaching socialism. In 1979, the Nevada legislature passed legislation asserting a legal and moral claim to the 49 million acres of public-domain lands within the state's boundaries. By August 1980 five other western states had passed similar legislation. Proudly declaring himself a Sagebrush Rebel, presidential candidate Ronald Reagan carried the Rocky Mountain West in the November election by 60.7 percent (to Jimmy Carter's 28.8 percent and independent John Anderson's 8.1 percent), a larger winning percentage than he tallied in any other region.

While the Federal Land Policy and Management Act of 1976 may have been the spark that set off the Sagebrush Rebellion, westerners understood that their grievance lay with environmentalism itself, a movement whose political base was primarily urban and largely eastern and yet nonetheless was making new claims on rural western lands. Wilderness designations, wildlife protection, and federally mandated environmental impact reviews all threatened to hamper western economies and "lock up" resources. Grazing leases remained an especially potent issue. The BLM spent millions of dollars to prepare the environmental impact statements ordered by the court in 1974—as much as $50 million in direct and indirect costs for the first nine statements prepared, according to a BLM study—far more than the grazing leases were worth. Although the NRDC successfully argued in court that the problem was BLM incompetence, the absurdity of government spending on paperwork so grotesquely out of proportion to the economic interests that were being regulated was trumpeted by conservatives as a classic example of over-zealous environmentalism and government "overregulation"—precisely the sort of waste that Ronald Reagan had vowed to stop.

In a larger sense, the reaction, beginning in the mid-seventies, against environmentalism and federal power at the expense of local interests was part of a wider reaction to sixties liberalism, a reaction that was soon dubbed the "New Right." It included a variety of institutes, think tanks, political-action committees, and, in the legal sphere—responding to the dramatic achievements of progressive public-interest law firms like the NRDC—public-interest law firms with a conservative, aggressively pro-business bent. The prototype for the right-wing public-interest law firm was the Pacific Legal Foundation (PLF), founded in early 1973 by several California industrialists, including J. Simon Fluor of the Fluor Corporation and Fred Hartley, president both of Union Oil and of the California Chamber of Commerce. (An early behind-the-scenes broker between these men and others was attorney William French Smith, whose clients also included then California governor Ronald Reagan, and who would later be appointed attorney general of the United States.) The purpose of the proposed legal foundation was frankly stated in an unpublished study: "to meet the challenge of those who have gone to the courts to seek change in public policy in areas which vitally affect private, industrial, business and agricultural interests." More succinctly, the idea was "to fight fire with fire."

Businessmen and conservatives simply had a different concept of "the public interest" than the practitioners of what they called "traditional" public-interest law. "Litigation purportedly brought in the public interest has not benefited the people," said Raymond Momboisse, one of the founding staff members of the PLF, in a 1982 interview. "It has deprived them of jobs, housing, food and medicine. It has increased costs. . . . By any test, the general public has not been well served by many of our self-proclaimed 'public interest' law groups."

Many of the founders of the PLF were former employees of Governor Reagan's administration, who had successfully defended court challenges to cutbacks in California's welfare system. They included Momboisse, who had been a deputy attorney general of California, and Ronald Zumbrun, formerly deputy director of legal affairs for California's Welfare Department. As much as they despised government handouts, these men hated environmentalism even more. In early cases the PLF defended the use of DDT to stop the spread of a moth epidemic, supported the construction of a dam and reservoir project, and argued for the use of herbicides in national forests. The PLF also intervened on behalf of the BLM in *NRDC* v. *Morton,* in defense of the BLM's grazing-lease policies.

The PLF quickly won admiration and financial support from members of the business community whose interests it defended. In 1973 the PLF received $250,510 in gifts, grants, and contributions, a figure that rose to over $2 million by 1981, most of which came in contributions from corporations and various business associations.

In 1975 the PLF concept was expanded. The National Legal Center for the Public Interest (NLCPI) was formed to "assist in the establishment of independent regional litigation foundations dedicated to a balanced view of the role of law in achieving economic and social progress." The intention was to promote "limited constitutional government, private property, the American free-enterprise system and individual initiative and freedom with responsibility." Environmentalism was a prime target. Within a year or so of its founding, NLCPI had helped found five regional and two Washington-based legal foundations.

Among them, none gained more renown or influence or was more active than the Mountain States Legal Foundation (MSLF), thanks largely to the talent of its first president, James G. Watt. Given its location in Denver, MSLF, which was founded in July 1977, was dedicated largely to environmental and land-use issues; indeed, it was born, according to an NLCPI fund-raising brochure, in response to an environmental movement that was "becoming an exercise in ideological fanaticism." An MSLF leaflet charged environmental groups with having cost American taxpayers billions of dollars through legal actions in opposition to offshore oil drilling, nuclear-power-plant construction, the Alaska pipeline, hydroelectric projects, and the use of DDT and other pesticides on crops and timberlands. Contributors to MSLF included major corporations, primarily mining, forestry, and energy companies, whose activities were coming under increasing challenge from environmentalists. In early cases under Watt's direction, MSLF went to court to fight wilderness designation for Wyoming's oil-bearing Overthrust Belt, and to argue that the EPA had exceeded its authority in penalizing Colorado for failing to implement an auto-pollution-control plan. Watt minced no words in expressing his feelings about environmentalism. "I fear that our states may be ravaged as a result of the actions of the environmentalists," he said, "the greatest threat to the ecology of the West."

Thus did James Watt stake out his credentials to be named president-elect Ronald Reagan's choice as secretary of the interior in December 1980.

To Reagan, environmental issues were not paramount. The weak

American economy and the nation's alleged loss of international influence and military might were the major campaign issues in 1980, and the environment was scarcely discussed. The one time Reagan did discuss the environment at any length, before a group of steel- and coal-company executives and community leaders in Steubenville, Ohio, he betrayed his complete ignorance of the issues. Reagan was preceded to the podium by several of his hosts, who denounced "environmental regulatory overkill" and "faceless bureaucrats" at the EPA, who had prevented the use of high-sulphur Ohio coal. When it came his turn to speak, Reagan picked up the theme.

"We are all today environmentalists," he began, "but we've got to realize that people are ecology too." Some officials in Washington, Reagan went on, had gone too far. "What they believe in is no growth. What they believe in is a return to a society in which there wouldn't be the need for the industrial concerns or more power plants and so forth. . . . I have flown twice over Mount St. Helens out on our West Coast. I'm not a scientist and I don't know the figures, but I just have a suspicion that that one little mountain out there in these past several months has probably released more sulphur dioxide into the atmosphere of the world than has been released in the last ten years of automobile driving or things of that kind that people are so concerned about." (In fact, Mount St. Helens produced 2,000 tons of sulphur dioxide a day compared to 81,000 tons produced daily by automobiles, and automobiles also produce harmful carbon monoxide, hydrocarbons, and nitric oxide.)

Reagan continued: "I know Teddy Kennedy had fun at the Democratic Convention when he said that I had said that trees and vegetation cause 80 percent of the air pollution in this country. Well, now he was a little wrong about what I said. First of all, I didn't say 80 percent, I said 92 percent, 93 percent, pardon me. And I didn't say air pollution, I said oxides of nitrogen. And I am right. Growing and decaying vegetation in this land are responsible for 93 percent of the oxides of nitrogen." The Great Smokies, Reagan claimed, are so named because of the prevalence there of oxides of nitrogen, which "some doctors" believe "might be beneficial to tubercular patients." (Reagan evidently confused harmless nitrous oxide produced by decaying plants with dangerous nitric oxide emitted from factory smokestacks.) The next day, when the campaign made a stop at an abandoned steel mill in Youngstown, Ohio, campaign aides handed out a report on regulatory reform that contained the statement that "air pollution has been substantially controlled." Reagan called for a major overhaul of the Clean Air Act on the grounds that clean-air regulations had caused unemployment in the steel industry.

Asked by a reporter the next day in St. Louis whether a record smog then besieging Los Angeles posed a contradiction to the statement that air pollution had been controlled, Reagan responded, "Fellows, I think all of this is, again, a little nit-picking trying to divert us from the real issues." "When I was governor," he continued, "we passed the strictest air pollution laws in California, even had to go to court against the federal government to do so. We had the cleanest water act that has ever been passed in the United States. There, I am for clean air."

When he was on his way home a few days later to Southern California, Reagan's flight was diverted from Hollywood-Burbank Airport, which had been closed due to the overwhelming smog. Later, at an appearance in nearby Pomona, he was greeted by protesters chanting "Smog, smog, smog" and a sign on a tree reading, CHOP ME DOWN BEFORE I KILL AGAIN.

Reagan's astounding capacity for both making and surviving outlandish statements would soon become all too familiar, but his misstatements on the environment posed only a momentary distraction to his election bid. Environmentalists were already against him; and he had the hapless incumbent Jimmy Carter on the ropes. Reagan's election represented the long-awaited, ardently sought political triumph of the American conservative movement. The overriding goal was to drastically shrink the size and limit the power of the federal government—with the notable exception of the military—by slashing taxes and budgets. This primary objective was consistent with a secondary goal: a smaller government would relieve American business of "excessive" and "burdensome" regulation, which was purported to have hurt the economy. All the regulatory functions of government were thus, within the Reagan administration, suspect, including civil rights enforcement, consumer protection, and the monitoring of workers' health and safety. Environmental regulation was near the top of the hit list.

Reagan started with the basic premise that government was too big and intrusive, and so he airily dismissed problems that called for ambitious government remedies. Such problems were inconvenient, whether they were environmental, such as acid rain and ozone depletion, or social, such as homelessness, AIDS, or racial discrimination. Reagan's politically most efficacious skill was to put his denials across with such dazzling ease that a good portion of the electorate failed to notice how utterly bizarre they often were.

As governor of California, Reagan actually did attempt to balance development and Pinchot-style conservation, as he claimed, favoring lumber interests when he fought to reduce the size of Redwood National Park on the one hand, and blocking a controversial dam that would have flooded the scenic Round Valley on the other. But captured by his own conservative presidential campaign, Reagan welcomed antienvironmental zealots into his administration. Following his election, the president ignored the "moderate" recommendations made by a transition task force on environmental policy, which included two former EPA administrators, William D. Ruckelshaus and Russell Train. The task force recommended that all the environmental laws passed in the seventies, including the Clean Air and Clean Water acts, be reexamined for possible changes, that the EPA be restructured, and that regulations be loosened in favor of a greater reliance on economic incentives. But the task force did not question the basic policy goals that had been established by both Republican and Democratic administrations since the sixties. Reagan, preoccupied with economic and defense issues, delegated responsibility for environmental policy to Nevada Senator Paul Laxalt, who in consultation with right-wing Colorado brewer Joseph Coors, urged James Watt's appointment to Interior.

Watt was as outspoken as he was zealous. "What is the real motive of the extreme environmentalists," he once asked, "who appear to be determined to accomplish their objectives at whatever cost to society? Is it simply to protect the environment? Is it to delay and deny energy development? Is it to weaken America?" Watt's implication that environmentalism was un-American, even subversive, was not entirely without foundation. Watt clearly understood that environmentalism did in fact challenge many fundamental American precepts; he recognized that environmentalism had evolved many of the characteristics of an ideology. And to Watt this ideology looked suspiciously socialistic. Like socialism, environmentalism asked individuals—and businesses—to sacrifice some of their individual freedoms for the larger public good. Starting with Rachel Carson, environmentalists, in the view of the rising antienvironmental movement, had resorted to alarmism and "doomsday scenarios" to advance their hidden socialist agenda; environmentalists had promoted "wilderness" and other statutory designations such as wild and scenic rivers as a tool for stopping economic activity; and environmentalists had confiscated private property from unwilling sellers for unworthy public parks. Environmentalism had resorted to increasing degrees of "coercion," an especially alarming tendency, in the view of conservatives, when coercion was used not merely to benefit society directly, but rather to benefit nature itself—to protect an endangered species, for example, or a wilderness. By their own admission, in their own writings, many environmentalists were proudly antitechnology, antiprogress, anticapitalism.

Author Ron Arnold, in his defense of James Watt, *At the Eye of the Storm: James Watt and the Environmentalists,* is able to quote dozens of statements by environmentalists to alarm any self-respecting conservative. He quotes, for example, Stewart Brand, creator of *The Whole Earth Catalogue*: "We have wished, we ecofreaks, for a disaster, or for dramatic social change to come and bomb us into the Stone Age, where we might live like Indians in our valley, with our localism, our Appropriate Technology, our gardens, and our homemade religion, guilt-free at last." Arnold points out that even many liberals have accused environmentalism of being antihumanity, since people cause pollution. Some so-called deep ecologists openly endorse the view that people are, indeed, a blight upon nature. Arnold quotes a Greenpeace founder, Paul Watson, as saying that as a child he "got the impression that instead of going out to shoot birds, I should go out and shoot the kids who shoot birds." Greenpeace has gained considerable fame (or notoriety) for acts of "ecotage," such as sinking whaling ships, and Arnold cites "ecoterrorism" as the ultimate proof of environmentalism's radical tendencies.

For Arnold and Watt theirs was nothing less than a battle to save America and industrial civilization from subversives, many of whom had been appointed to high office during the Carter years. "We have bit by bit," writes Arnold, "impaired our productivity with excessive and unwise restrictions on forest and rangelands, on water and agriculture, on construction and manufacture, on energy and minerals, *on every material value upon which our society is built*. Serious problems have arisen from a multitude of these restrictions. Most of the problems were unexpected side effects of genuine attempts to improve our quality of life. The impacts of this well-meaning but devastating movement are so widespread that even experts cannot calculate the ultimate economic destruction." Reciting the list of environmentalism's legislative achievements of the sixties and seventies, but describing them as a series of catastrophes, Arnold concluded that by 1976 "America had become a thoroughgoing Regulation State."

James Watt opposed environmentalism not on tactical grounds to protect this or that special interest—which is how most environmental battles are fought—but on ideological grounds. "The battleground," he said, "is not what our critics would like you to believe it is, protecting the environment. It is over ideology, over forms of government that lead to a centralized, socialized society." Watt believed nature had no inherent value; resources were put on earth for man's benefit. A self-described fundamentalist in matters "economic, social, spiritual and political," Watt was aggressively protechnology, proprogress, and procapitalism. With Watt leading the antienvironmentalist charge, the battle lines were, at least, sharply and clearly drawn.

As secretary of the interior, Watt quickly moved to address the simmering grievances of the Sagebrush Rebels and reorient department policies in favor of easier and more profitable resource extraction from public lands. "We will mine more, drill more, cut more timber to use our resources rather than keep them locked up," Watt vowed. Although he was a stalwart opponent of big government, and of government interference with individual freedom, Watt had actually devoted his career to public service—he had served in the Nixon Interior Department as deputy assistant secretary for water and power resources—and he knew precisely how to bend the bureaucracy to his will. He was especially adept in employing the Reagan administration strategy of using budget cuts and administrative "reorganizations"—which were justified on budgetary grounds—as the means to remake policy, and he did it openly. "We will use the budget system as the excuse to make major policy decisions," he said at a Conference of National Park Concessioners. Rather than seek a repeal or reform of the Surface Mining Control and Reclamation Act of 1977, which regulates strip mining, Watt simply slashed the budget and staff of the Office of Surface Mining, eliminating field enforcement offices and making it virtually impossible for the agency to enforce the law. With respect to "privatization"—the Sagebrush Rebels' battle cry—Watt announced plans to raise $4 billion a year by selling "surplus" federal lands. This goal proved impractical. The Federal Land Policy and Management Act made the sale of large plots of public lands subject to approval by Congress, where there was sufficient opposition to land sales to block most of them, and furthermore there were few buyers willing to pay "market value" for the land—least of all ranchers accustomed to paying low grazing fees for access to the same lands. But with the aid of Colorado rancher Robert Burford, whom Watt appointed to head the BLM, Watt easily resisted efforts to increase grazing fees or reduce grazing allotments.

Watt also moved to open up previously designated wilderness to mining and oil and gas exploration and to prevent additional wilderness designations by withdrawing hundreds of thousands of acres from wilderness consideration; he sought to offer vast new areas of the continental shelf for oil and gas leases, and to lease new coal fields; he halted government purchases of land for additions to the national park system, and even proposed deauthorizing parks near urban areas ("playgrounds," he called them), including Gateway National Seashore outside New York

and Golden Gate National Park outside San Francisco—on the grounds
that these areas, despite their heavy use, lacked the character of true
national parks. "My concept of stewardship is to invest," he explained,
"build a road, build a latrine, pump in running water so you can wash
dishes. Most people think that if you can drive in, walk 20 yards and
pitch a tent by the stream you've had a wilderness experience. Do we
have to buy enough land so that you can go backpacking and never see
anyone else?"

Watt was opposed in court, in Congress, and in the press, and was
able to accomplish only a fraction of what he attempted. One sure accomplishment was to inspire a dramatic increase in the membership rosters
of environmental groups—and an increased militancy on the part of
groups such as the Wilderness Society and the Audubon Society, which
had never been known for their political activism. Only four months into
Watt's tenure, Audubon president Russell Peterson, a Republican and
chairman of the Council on Environmental Quality under Nixon and
Ford, bluntly decried the "radical" changes in environmental policy under
the Reagan administration. "Most environmental leaders were concerned
about President Reagan's taking over because of his obvious lack of
enthusiasm for the environment," Peterson explained. "But I don't think
any of us realized how bad it was going to be. . . . The appointment of
Watt and [EPA administrator Anne] Gorsuch really means a deliberate
attempt to turn the clock back on environmental policy." Peterson vowed
to lead the Audubon Society in coalition with other environmental
groups to vigorously resist proposed cuts in the budgets for environmental agencies and parks and proposed leases to increase offshore oil drilling
and strip mining. In November 1981 the Sierra Club presented to Congress a petition bearing a million signatures, which demanded Watt's
removal from office. In terms of membership and fund-raising, 1981 was
the best year in Sierra Club history.

Watt's eagerness to confront, and even to bait his critics, made him a
darling of the Republican far right and the Republican Party's second-
best fund-raiser after Reagan himself. But he was a menacing caricature
to almost everyone else, and a literal caricature in the "Doonesbury"
comic strip. As he found himself increasingly the subject of controversy,
Watt's sense of righteousness seemed only to deepen. "This is not a
struggle over the environment," he told the *New York Times*. "It is not
about resources. This battle is over the form of government we will have
in America. We are battling over the future of America." His critics, he
said, were "political activists, a left-wing cult which seeks to bring down
the type of government I believe in." To a group of House Republicans

he said, "The specter of environmentalism haunts America by threatening to inhibit natural resource development and economic growth." Increasingly beleaguered, Watt became more arrogant, adding to his growing legions of political enemies. "I never use the words Republicans and Democrats—it's liberals and Americans," he said in a 1982 speech. By January 1983 he was comparing environmentalists to Nazis and Bolsheviks. Like the Nazis and Bolsheviks, Watt said, environmentalists were pursuing the "greater objective" of "centralized planning and control of society." ("Only James Watt could fail to see the difference between Hermann Göring and John Muir," retorted J. Michael McCloskey, executive director of the Sierra Club.) In 1983 Watt canceled a performance by the Beach Boys at a Fourth of July celebration on the Washington Mall, in favor of Wayne Newton, whom he deemed more "wholesome." Finally, in September of that year he made the ultimate gaffe, joking, in reference to a commission he had set up to study his controversial coal-leasing policies, "I have a Black. I have a woman, two Jews and a cripple." Watt never seemed to understand why the quip cost him his job.

Shortly after his own appointment as secretary of the interior, Watt successfully lobbied the Reagan administration's transition team for the appointment of Anne M. Gorsuch as administrator of the EPA. Like Watt, Gorsuch was a product of western resentment, a leader in the class of conservative Republicans elected to the Colorado legislature in 1976. Named both "best dressed" and "outstanding freshman legislator" her first year in the legislature, Gorsuch went on to establish a reputation for rigid opposition to government regulation and, especially, to environmentalism. She led battles against a state hazardous-waste law and against EPA impositions of sanctions on the state for failing to control smog in Denver. Self-described "legal brain" of the so-called crazies in the legislature, Gorsuch was immensely proud of her accomplishments in Colorado, recalling in her memoir, *Are You Tough Enough?*, "We did 'Reaganism' in the Colorado legislature before Reagan did it."

Gorsuch did not run for reelection in 1980. Instead, in the happy aftermath of Reagan's election, she actively sought an appointment at the EPA—where she could "really make a difference." She thought she might become deputy administrator. Her eventual nomination on February 21, 1981, as Reagan's choice as administrator testifies not only to Watt's influence, but also to the low priority Reagan assigned to the EPA, to the desirability of naming at least some women to upper-level administrative posts, and ultimately to Gorsuch's hard-line positions. She interviewed well with transition-team officials, including Budget Director

David Stockman, readily agreeing that she could slash the EPA budget by 50 percent.

Although Gorsuch was every bit the ideologue that James Watt was, she lacked his experience or skill as an administrator, and was aloof and frosty where he was affable. Yet hers was the more difficult assignment. To Reaganite ideologues, the EPA was more suspect than Interior since its mission was expressly regulatory. "In my opinion they are simply anti-industry and anti-business," Gorsuch later wrote in reference to the "liberals" who administered the EPA under Carter. "I believe that if they could, they would happily make regulations so costly that they would have the effect of cutting off all economic growth. They would be happy to deindustrialize the United States." Of Washington-based environmental lobbyists, who had been instrumental in bringing forth much of the legislation the EPA enforced, Gorsuch wrote, "Their main concern is seeing how much money they can raise for their organizations by scaring the American public half to death. The truth about the vast majority of them is that they are not interested in the environment at all. They are interested in power, political power, and the environment is just a platform for them."

In taking environmental groups like the NRDC out of the loop of policymaking and refusing to meet with them, Gorsuch effected a strange realignment. The NRDC had sued the EPA many times over its performance and interpretation of the law. But essentially the environmental lawyers of the NRDC and EPA officials were all working toward the same end: effective protection of the environment. Now, suddenly, environmentalists and EPA staff were allies in opposition to the new EPA administration, which seemed intent not on enforcing but on dismantling the law, even on dismantling the agency itself. In late January 1982, the NRDC took out a full-page advertisement in the *Washington Post,* an "open letter" to EPA staff that pleaded with them, "Don't Give Up." The letter read, in part:

> You joined the Environmental Protection Agency as dedicated professionals seeking to achieve a goal shared by millions of Americans—a safe, healthy environment for us and for our children.
>
> You have worked long and hard during the last decade, under three different administrations, to carry out the nation's environmental laws—laws passed to protect the public from poisons in the air, water and land. Those laws were passed because the public demanded them. Those laws have not been changed. . . .
>
> [N]ow a decade of environmental progress is in jeopardy.

New political bosses have come to EPA. They openly scorn the environmental laws Congress passed. They hold your achievements in contempt. To them, you are dangerous, because you care about your lawful responsibilities.

Many of you are being fired, transferred, demoted. You are being deprived of authority to act and ordered to disregard the laws and the facts. You are being publicly derided and shabbily treated by those for whom you work. Many of you are quitting in frustration and disgust.

We urge you to stick it out. If you are driven from the agency, it will be left an ineffectual shell, an illusion of protection. The most important work of all is still to be done. . . .

The letter was signed by "the lawyers and scientists of NRDC." An unnamed EPA official was quoted in the *Times* as dismissing the advertisement as "a fund-raising gimmick," which it may in fact have been— but it also was a telling reflection of a once-proud agency in disarray.

Gorsuch was forced from office even before Watt, resigning in March 1983 after she had been weakened by a seemingly endless series of controversies over EPA budget and personnel cuts, reorganizations, conflicts of interest, and enforcement procedures. She had also been caught up in scandals revolving around Rita Lavelle, the assistant administrator for solid waste and emergency response, who was charged with having ex parte communications with a former employer that was being sued by EPA.

Although Watt and Gorsuch drew environmentalists' fire during their brief time in office, in many ways they were scapegoats. The antienvironmentalism they embodied continued to hold sway long after they left the Reagan administration.

"The price of progress is trouble," inventor Charles Kettering (*far right*) liked to say, "and frankly I don't think the price is too high." With Kettering in 1914 were (*from left*) engineer J. B. Edwards, Delco engineer Bill Chryst, and Cadillac founder "Uncle" Henry Leland.

A leader in the effort to make Dayton, Ohio, an industrial mecca, National Cash Register's President John Patterson applied Progressive reasoning to his design of the factory floor. The large windows at "the Cash" were in stark contrast to the dark, grimy conditions typical of nineteenth-century factories.

In search of an antiknock. Thomas Midgley, Jr., the inventor of chlorofluorocarbons, with an early invention, the "optical gas engine indicator." Mounted on a single cylinder engine, the instrument allowed Midgley to observe the effects of different gasoline additives on engine combustion. The additive finally found to work, tetraethyl lead, was later marketed under the brand name ethyl.

The Refiners Oil Co. service station on Main Street in Dayton, Ohio, where ethyl gasoline first went on sale on February 2, 1923.

Alice Hamilton, one of the pioneers of industrial health in America and the first woman on the faculty of the Harvard Medical School, urged that "an impartial investigation" be conducted before allowing tetraethyl lead to be added to gasoline.

President Theodore Roosevelt with John Muir at Yosemite. Their differing philosophies—Roosevelt advocated the conservation and management of natural resources and Muir the preservation of nature—continue to characterize the debate over environmental issues.

Chlorofluorocarbons helped make the refrigerator a safe, affordable fixture in every American home. A Frigidaire promotional photo from the 1940s emphasizes the appliance's cleanliness and convenience.

The first men to reach the stratosphere. Balloonists Professor Auguste Piccard (*right*) and his assistant, Charles Kipfer, wear the unique protective headgear Piccard designed for their flight.

Piccard's balloon gondola, the first conveyance to transport human beings to the stratosphere and back, became an object of intense fascination, and was heavily marked with grafitti. Here the gondola is lowered from the Ober-Gurgl glacier to the town of Innsbruck, Austria, following Piccard and Kipfer's 1931 ascent.

Harvard physicist William Shurcliff calculated that 150 SST flights a day over the continental United States would create no fewer than 75 million square miles of "boom carpet." The Citizens League Against the Sonic Boom, which he founded in 1967, led the nation's fight to halt the plane's development.

"Something about new means of transportation seems to bring to the surface the latent gullibility in the best of us," wrote John E. Gibson in *Harper's Magazine* in 1966. Thought a technological dream to some, the Supersonic Transport was a costly nightmare to others.

F. Sherwood Rowland, professor of chemistry at the University of California at Irvine (*right*), and his postdoctoral associate Mario Molina, shown here in their lab at Irvine in 1974, were the first to theorize that CFCs destroyed stratospheric ozone. "If there was anything about chlorofluorocarbons that caught my attention," Molina later said, "it was simply that it seemed like 'bad manners' for men to put a chemical into the atmosphere without knowing exactly what happens to it."

To obtain conclusive proof that CFCs were responsible for ozone depletion above Antarctica, in 1987 NASA used its high-altitude research aircraft, the ER-2, for a dramatic series of flights into the ozone hole.

Coauthor of the theory that heterogeneous reactions on polar stratospheric clouds could explain the Antarctic ozone hole, NOAA scientist Susan Solomon, shown here in the Dry Valleys of Antarctica, headed the National Ozone Expedition to Antarctica in August 1986.

15.

ANPR

URING ITS FINAL DAYS the Carter EPA issued a series of regulations covering a variety of topics, an action the incoming Reagan administration regarded as an outrageous affront. Although the advance notice of proposed rulemaking to restrict CFCs had been published in October 1980, several weeks before the November election, and had been in the works for many months prior to that, it was still pending, and was lumped together with the so-called midnight regulations and placed in a special category of Carter-era guidelines—namely rules the incoming Reaganites were especially determined to scuttle. At the end of January 1981, specifically to negate the last-minute actions of the Carter administration, President Reagan issued an executive order freezing all proposed and pending regulations so the new administration could review them before allowing them to take effect.

On July 15, 1981, with Reagan's antiregulatory crusade in full swing, the chemical industry and the Alliance for Responsible CFC Policy on the offensive, and the environmental movement in retreat, a House subcommittee on small business held hearings on the EPA's proposal to cap CFC production. The subcommittee had caught a raging case of antiregulatory fever and the hearings were charged with indignation. Here, in the view of subcommittee chairman Thomas A. Luken of Ohio, was a prime example of the EPA run amuck, a proposal to cap production of "a vital product for major industries on the basis of mere suspicion." Many of Luken's fellow subcommittee members shared his open dislike of the agency. "In my opinion," said Congressman Lyle Williams of Ohio in the course of interrogating an EPA official, "the EPA has done more damage to this country, economically and probably environmentally, than any agency that is here.

"The problem isn't that we have too much CFCs or too many CFCs in the air," Williams added. "We have too much ink in Washington."

The EPA's proposals to regulate through the relatively novel use of issuing marketable permits for the manufacture of CFCs seemed to greatly inspire the opposition's vehemence. A dozen members of the Alliance for Responsible CFC Policy—small businessmen for whom CFCs were "essential"—testified before the Luken subcommittee that they would be devastated by the proposed regulations, priced out of the CFC market at the same time that larger firms, for whom CFCs were not necessarily essential, would monopolize all the supply.

"I implore you, don't put me out of business," testified William Jelin, executive vice president of NRG Barriers of Sanford, Maine, a producer of cellular plastic foam laminated to foil and plywood facing for use in roofing and sidewall applications. "We don't make anything but this product," he said. "Fluorocarbons are the active ingredient to this product. There is no substitute."

Linda Kohler, former owner of Florida Containers, Inc., of Sebring, Florida, which manufactured polystyrene egg cartons and sandwich containers, testified that she had sold the company partly due to her concern about the possible impact of the CFC production cap. She chose to testify anyway because, she said, she believed in "the cause" and "the free enterprise system," and thought that the CFC controversy was "a great example of some of the things that are wrong with the system today." "As I understand it," she explained, "and I am not an expert in the ozone theory . . . we don't know enough yet to know whether this really affects the ozone layer or not. I really do find it incredibly irresponsible and just truly unbelievable that a protective arm of the U.S. Government has proposed to regulate based solely on the theory that this chlorofluorocarbon may harm the ozone layer. . . . On top of that, part of my tax dollars are paying for these people to do this."

Following testimony from several equally indignant frozen-food processors and solvent packagers, as well as an air-conditioning service company president who said he would not be able to provide vital air-conditioning to hospitals and supermarkets without CFCs,

Edward A. Klein, director of the Chemical Control Division in EPA's Office of Pesticides and Toxic Substances, took the witness chair. After reviewing the history of the CFC controversy, Klein testified that an ANPR is "not a rule," or "even a statement by EPA that it will regulate CFCs now or in the future," but rather an "information-gathering tool." The EPA, he added, "is extremely sensitive to the needs of small businesses."

Responding to allegations that the EPA had failed to consider the economic cost of CFC regulations, Klein referred to an EPA-commissioned Rand Corporation analysis of the economic implications of regulating CFCs in nonaerosol applications. This study, he testified, had taken three years to complete and had concluded that a cap on CFC production would not harm many businesses because those industries that could find a substitute for CFCs would do so as prices rose in response to the cap, while those industries in which there was no obvious substitute—notably refrigeration and air-conditioning—were precisely the industries for which the cost of CFCs represented a small fraction of the total cost of the finished product. By 1990, according to the Rand study, a production cap at 1980 levels would cause the price of a home refrigerator to increase by $7, the price of a home freezer to increase by $9, and the price of a mobile air-conditioning unit to increase by $6, as expressed in constant 1976 dollars.

Further findings from the Rand study were equally reassuring: the flexible-foam industry could implement recovery and recycling technologies and switch to substitute chemicals; recovery and recycling could be used in the electronics industries that relied on CFCs as a solvent, and although the cost of solvent cleaning would be higher, it represented a small percentage of the overall cost in producing electronic goods. The rigid-foam industry would be severely affected by a CFC production cap, but nonfoam substitutes were readily available in producing egg cartons and fast-food packages.

Despite having demonstrated that the EPA had given detailed study to the question of potential economic impacts of proposed CFC regulations, Klein concluded with a bow to the prevailing antiregulatory climate. "Let me reiterate that the Agency has not yet decided whether to undertake rulemaking on nonaerosol uses of CFCs," he assured the congressmen. "Any such decision would occur after the Agency's Administrator and other new senior staff have had the opportunity to fully consider the available information and potential options."

Congressman Luken nonetheless subjected Klein to sharp questioning.

LUKEN: In your statement, you indicated that the ANPR—the
        advance notice of proposed rulemaking—is not a rule.
        I believe you say it is not even a statement that EPA will
        regulate CFCs. I would be almost tempted to say, what
        is it?

KLEIN: I think—

LUKEN: Since you have indicated what it isn't, is it nothing?

KLEIN: It is an information-gathering tool. As my testimony
        indicated, we got—

LUKEN: Well, you wouldn't issue it if you weren't thinking about
        it just slightly, would you?

KLEIN: Certainly it was being considered. But it is not the same
        thing as saying that it is a promise that EPA will go
        regulate.

In soft-pedaling the ANPR, repeatedly describing it as an "information-gathering tool," and by insisting that the EPA was still in the process
of analysis and had not reached a decision to regulate, Klein may have
hoped to placate the subcommittee, but in fact he opened the way for
Luken to challenge the propriety of the EPA's "threatening" industry
with possible actions it might not take. "You are not suggesting that
[businesses] haven't been threatened, are you?" Luken asked. "Well,"
Klein conceded, "I think that some businesses view any statement by a
federal agency as a promise to come forward and regulate."

The hearing reflected the tidal shift in Washington. Not only were
Congressmen Luken and Williams and the Alliance for Responsible CFC
Policy emboldened by the prospect of a new administration at EPA, but
an EPA official who plainly understood the full dimensions of the CFC
dilemma had been forced into strategic retreat. The subcommittee was so
sure of itself, it did not bother to hear from any scientific or environmental experts.

Alan Miller did submit a statement on behalf of NRDC, which appears as an addendum to the official record of the hearing. EPA's "commendable effort to obtain industry and public comment in advance of an
agency decision to regulate," Miller wrote, "has been characterized incorrectly as a regulatory proposal and made the target of an industry onslaught unprecedented since the Allies invaded Normandy." Industry
witnesses at the hearings had discussed "only the consequences of a production cap, as if that was the only possible form of regulation," and had
"assumed the absolute worst possible scenario, including no effort to
assure that small businesses would have fair access to the available supply.

. . . Rather than encourage and contribute to the evolution of a promising alternative to bans or technology-based controls," Miller's statement concluded, "industry has chosen obstructionist tactics."

The issue received a more balanced review a week later at hearings before a Senate subcommittee of the Committee on Environment and Public Works, where not only Miller but also Mario Molina and other scientists were given the opportunity to testify alongside industry representatives. Molina pointed out that "much of the uncertainty in the prediction of total ozone loss is due to the complicated nature of the chemistry in the lower stratosphere," in contrast to "large upper stratospheric perturbations" which had "undergone no significant revisions in the past 5 or 6 years." These upper-stratospheric perturbations, Molina explained, were "nontrivial" and were occurring, on a geological time scale, extremely rapidly. Indeed, these changes threatened to alter the very nature of the stratosphere, and could substantially affect the earth's climate.

Miller testified that CFCs would not be the last issue of scientific uncertainty that would come before the Congress. Making regulatory decisions in the face of significant scientific uncertainty would inevitably be necessary, he said. The risks of ozone depletion were real and the costs of waiting ten years to begin regulation would be high. The United States, he added, could have a great deal of influence internationally. "When the United States makes a decision to regulate . . . other governments want to know why," he said. "They become more interested themselves. . . . If in fact we take the opposite position, if we cut back and curtail our regulation, that will signal the exact opposite position to the rest of the world. . . . I think the U.S. efforts toward international cooperation have been commendable, and we hope the new administration will continue them."

But representatives of the Alliance for Responsible CFC Policy also testified, stressing the many uncertainties of ozone science, the economic hardships of further restrictions, the lack of viable substitutes, and the folly of unilateral U.S. action. Moreover, industry found in Lloyd Bentsen of Texas a Senate cosponsor for the proposed amendments to the 1970 Clean Air Act that Representative Luken had introduced in the House. These amendments would, in effect, rescind some of the provisions of the 1977 amendments that provided the EPA with much of its clout to regulate CFCs, prohibiting the EPA from issuing regulations unless there were either actual measurements of ozone depletion that could be directly attributed to CFCs or international agreements to control the chemicals. Senator Bentsen explained that his bill "revises the

current research efforts to focus on actual detection of ozone depletion."
Urging reason and balance, Bentsen explained that in his part of the
country CFCs in air-conditioning had "moved from the category of lux-
uries to the category of almost necessities."

Bentsen was the ideal legislator to speak in favor of extreme prudence
in the curtailment of CFCs. He hailed from the Lower Rio Grande
Valley, a region of Texas that was so humid and sweltering it made
Houston, whose summer heat was unbearable, seem almost moderate by
comparison. Bentsen did not exaggerate when he told his Senate colleagues that a modern way of life would be nearly impossible in the
Lower Rio Grande Valley without air-conditioning; the miracle of climate control had had a revolutionary impact on life in South Texas.

In an exchange of friendly questions and answers between Senator
Bentsen, John Norris of Lennox Industries, a Dallas air-conditioning
manufacturer, and Chuck Masten, director of Du Pont's Freon Products
Division, Bentsen had occasion to reflect that southerners once had a
reputation "for not only talking slow, but thinking slow. But I think
much of that was the heat," Bentsen said. "I can't help but remember
working in a southwest corner office on the second floor with no air-
conditioning and anyone who wore a coat and a tie was obviously a
salesman from out of town. You wore short-sleeved shirts and you tried
to work on a contract and do the signatures with the sweat of your arm
and try to think." Norris observed that although some people had predicted there would be between 800 and 1,000 deaths a year from skin
cancer due to ozone depletion, 1,200 Americans had died from the heat
in the summer of 1980 in just the eastern part of the United States alone.

For eight years industry had responded to the ozone-depletion theory
by calling for more research. In the late summer of 1981, with Luken
championing its cause in the House and Bentsen in the Senate, the CFC
industry stood a good chance of seeing its longstanding preference for
still more research—and a restraint on early regulation—written into
law.

At the end of March 1982, the National Academy of Sciences issued its
third report on stratospheric ozone. The report did not refute the ozone-
depletion theory, but it did present a revised estimate of eventual ozone
depletion that appeared to greatly reduce the situation's urgency. The
previous NAS report, issued in November 1979, had estimated ozone
depletion of 16.5 percent by late in the twenty-first century at the 1977
rate of CFC emissions. The new study lowered the estimate by 50 per-

cent, forecasting an eventual 5 to 9 percent depletion. At the same time, it noted that the link between ozone depletion and the most serious form of skin cancer, melanoma, was not sufficiently established to allow a "quantitative prediction about the increase of this disease associated with a decrease of ozone."

Thus, the 1982 NAS report arrived like a giant gift-wrapped present to the CFC industry. A government-sponsored panel of scientific experts had changed estimates of ozone depletion and reevaluated its probable consequences. Such a shift of opinion only underscored industry's contention that not enough was known about CFCs and ozone depletion to justify any regulation or restriction of their use.

The new NAS report did not minimize the harm that could come of a 5 to 9 percent loss of ozone, noting in particular that increased ultraviolet radiation could cause eye irritation and damage to the human immune system, yet the overall perception was that the ozone-depletion problem had been exaggerated, or that the aerosol ban had largely solved it, and that industry had been right in cautioning against premature restrictions. What was widely overlooked was that the NAS's latest estimate of a 5 to 9 percent loss fell within the range of Rowland and Molina's original 1974 estimate of eventual ozone depletion—7 to 13 percent—which had set off the alarm in the first place. The same week the NAS report was released, Sherry Rowland published findings based on actual atmospheric measurements which showed that, despite the aerosol ban, CFC concentrations in the atmosphere had tripled in the previous decade.

As it happened, no Clean Air Act amendments at all made it through Congress during the Reagan administration. This left the EPA's regulatory powers, as set forth in 1977, fully intact—not that the head of the EPA had any inclination whatsoever to exercise that authority.

Anne Gorsuch had the capacity to review the material on chlorofluorocarbons and ozone depletion that had been compiled by EPA staff, environmentalists, independent scientists, and industry, and comfortably conclude that no immediate action was warranted. At her confirmation hearings in 1981, Gorsuch had testified that in her view the ozone-depletion theory was "highly controversial," and that there was a "need for additional scientific data before the international community would be willing to accept it as a basis for additional government action." She probably revealed her ultimate assessment of CFCs in her memoir, in which she wrote by way of dismissing environmental "scare issues" in general, "Remember a few years back when the big news was fluorocarbons that supposedly threatened the ozone layer?"

Nor did Gorsuch feel much political pressure to act. Many environmentalists felt dissuaded from vigorously pursuing their most ambitious objectives in the early 1980s, given the hostility they knew awaited them in Washington, and they settled for targeting the administration mouthpieces. The environmentalist effort went almost entirely to questioning the overall direction of the Reagan administration's policy on the environment, and to defending against losing earlier environmental gains such as wilderness designations and clean-air and -water legislation, issues that were perceived to be more fundamental than ozone depletion.

With little prospect of curbing CFCs domestically, the best hope for protecting the ozone layer lay in the international arena. There, too, the Reagan administration proved wonderfully capable of obstruction. The United States had already done more than most other nations by banning aerosols, and so the Reagan administration took the position that other nations should at least catch up by banning aerosols before America took further unilateral actions.

The United States was the biggest financial contributor to the United Nations Environment Program. Even prior to the 1972 U.N. conference in Stockholm, which established UNEP, the United States had traditionally taken a leading role in seeking international cooperation on environmental issues. Presidents Johnson, Nixon, Ford, and Carter all supported U.S. sponsorship of numerous international treaties and protocols such as the Law of the Sea Treaty. Not only had the United States led the way in restricting CFCs in aerosols; under the Carter administration it had helped initiate the exhaustive diplomatic process leading toward a more comprehensive international ban.

During the Reagan administration, however, American initiative in international environmental affairs stopped altogether; indeed, many longstanding American policies were reversed. Reaganites regarded international organizations like the U.N. as being even less legitimate and possibly even more wasteful and bureaucratic than the bloated federal government. During the U.N. Conference on the Global Environment in Nairobi in May 1982 on the tenth anniversary of the Stockholm Conference, Gorsuch announced that the United States would be drastically reducing its $10-million-a-year contribution to UNEP, which represented 40 percent of the organization's budget, to $7.85 million. (The $7.85 million appropriated by Congress was considerably more than the administration had originally requested, which was zero.) In her address to the UNEP delegates, Gorsuch offered the same environmental nostrums she had attempted to apply at home. "Many of our actions have failed to take advantage of the natural corrective measures that can work through market forces, if governments allow them to operate," she told the assembly. "Too frequently, we responded with alarm to pessimistic projections—squandering scarce resources on inappropriate measures—rather than devoting those resources to the careful study of practical and effective ways in which we might improve our world." Gorsuch seemed unaware that few if any of UNEP's third-world member states could boast efficient market economies wherein corrective forces might be "allowed" to work.

Responding at a news conference, UNEP's founding executive director, Maurice F. Strong of Canada, said, "It is quite clear that the United States' role at this meeting is in stark contrast to its leadership role in Stockholm." Fortunately, Strong added, nongovernmental American groups, including the Audubon Society, the Sierra Club, and the NRDC, were "a very strong and positive force at this meeting."

The Reagan administration quickly became notorious in international environmental affairs. Besides reducing support for UNEP, the United States backed away from prior commitments to Canada to reduce emissions that contribute to acid rain, contending that more research was needed to resolve "scientific uncertainties" before expensive remedies could be pursued, and Reagan rescinded President Carter's executive order prohibiting the export of toxic and hazardous substances that were banned or restricted domestically. The reasons behind these actions were economic, a fear that the American economy would be hampered by new international regulations. A dramatic reversal had taken place since the early days of international environmentalism, for then it had been third-world countries with developing economies that had seen environmental efforts as a threat to growth.

Recognizing the decline of American commitment even before the Nairobi conference, UNEP had nonetheless established in May 1981 an Ad Hoc Working Group of Legal and Technical Experts to design a Global Framework Convention for the Protection of the Ozone Layer, modeled after UNEP's Regional Seas Program. The proposed convention would cover "monitoring, scientific research and the development of best available and economically feasible technologies to limit and gradually reduce emissions of ozone-depleting substances, as well as the development of appropriate strategies and policies." The group held its inaugural meeting in Stockholm in January 1982. By then the State Department, in consultation with the EPA, had taken the position that the process should be slowed down, and to that end sent a U.S. delegation with authority only to hold preliminary discussions. A good deal of debate at Stockholm was devoted to precisely how international agreements to protect the ozone layer should be structured. Fundamentally, it was agreed that a "framework convention" would establish a common objective and an agreement to cooperate in research, monitoring, and the exchange of information. Subsequent "protocols" and "annexes" would be required to impose specific controls. These subtreaties would, of course, be far more difficult to achieve than a framework convention. But there was considerable reluctance at the Stockholm meeting, much of it expressed by the American delegation, even to enter into a convention for fear that it would inevitably lead to future protocols that were unacceptable. For that reason, some delegations felt that it would be better to negotiate a convention and protocols simultaneously.

Even if the United States had taken a proactive stance, negotiating a convention to protect the ozone layer would necessarily be daunting in its complexity. There was little precedent in international environmental law with respect to atmospheric safeguards. The Partial Nuclear Test Ban Treaty of 1963 prohibited only nuclear explosions in the atmosphere. On the other hand, the Convention on Long-Range Transboundary Air Pollution, adopted in November 1979 among European nations, was an encouraging precedent, and Principle 21 of the 1972 Stockholm Declaration—which stipulates that nations have a duty not to cause damage to the environments of other nations or to areas beyond the limits of national jurisdiction—provided a sound legal basis for a convention to protect the ozone layer. Still, a convention would have to be global in scope, and to establish global quotas for the production and release of CFCs among nations with widely differing perspectives and economic needs would be a "mammoth task," as the UNEP secretariat noted in a report it prepared for the Stockholm meeting. Finally, the convention would have to be flexible, so it could readily accommodate constantly changing scientific knowledge. All this, along with the Reagan administration's opposition to an agreement that involved anything more than further research, guaranteed that the negotiations would be arduous and prolonged.

As much as the administration opposed the process, it could not keep it from advancing, and once international negotiations were underway, it was clearly in the United States' best interest to participate in them. Indeed, the Reagan administration itself had helped turn the focus to the international arena by declaring, in essence, that no further domestic U.S. action on CFCs would be taken pending international developments.

For Alan Miller and NRDC on the one hand, and for industry and the Alliance for Responsible CFC Policy on the other, the challenge was to exercise as much influence as possible over the American position at the international negotiating table. UNEP's Ad Hoc Working Group of Legal and Technical Experts held seven meetings from January 1982 to January 1985. Experts and observers from fifty countries and eleven intergovernmental and nongovernmental organizations participated in the process. The draft convention, with two technical annexes, was revised five times in six languages, and took into account written comments from nations that did not participate directly in the process. Throughout the lengthy negotiating period, whenever the State Department solicited public comment, both Miller and the alliance would oblige. Characteristically, the alliance suggested in response to a December 8, 1981, State Department request for comment, that the convention should provide for a "properly targeted, orderly, and internationally coordinated research program to obtain the needed scientific information to resolve the critical uncertainties in the ozone depletion theory." Miller argued to the contrary that "a convention will be of little benefit it if does no more than facilitate exchange of scientific information."

Meanwhile, the Reagan administration's formula for supporting industry and stonewalling the environmentalists was simple: new domestic controls had to await international action, while, at the same time, the United States—whose cooperation was essential to any meaningful international agreement on CFCs—opposed international controls. Given these conditions, industry could feel confident that there would be no new controls at all. The Pennwalt Corporation, for one, was so confident that it announced plans, in the spring of 1982, for a $10 million expansion of its CFC plant in Calvert City, Kentucky.

When Anne Gorsuch—newly named Anne Burford, following her February 20 marriage to a fellow Coloradan, Bureau of Land Management director Robert Burford—resigned as EPA administrator on March 9, 1983, there followed a brief period of euphoria within EPA and in the environmental community. Champagne was uncorked in offices throughout the labyrinthine EPA building, and Burford's successor, William D. Ruckelshaus, was greeted at a meeting in the EPA auditorium with a standing ovation. The NRDC board of directors shared in the celebratory spirit and voted to allow Ruckelshaus a brief grace period before proceeding with any of its many pending lawsuits, including one Alan Miller had been preparing to force the EPA to formally promulgate Phase Two regulations on CFCs. Ruckelshaus, the EPA's first administrator from 1970 to 1973, during the Nixon years, had been reappointed by President Reagan on March 21 in large part because he was respected by environmentalists, and could, it was hoped, douse the multiple fires that had been consuming the once-proud agency under Gorsuch's tenure. An added advantage Ruckelshaus brought to the job was an unassailable reputation for integrity, secured on the night of October 20, 1973, for his part in the so-called Saturday Night Massacre, when he had resigned as deputy attorney general rather than carry out President Nixon's order to fire Archibald Cox, the special prosecutor in the Watergate investigations.

The EPA changed quickly under Ruckelshaus. Before he accepted the EPA appointment, he had won a promise from President Reagan that he would enjoy both direct access to the president and considerable independence, including the freedom to appoint his own deputies. Once in office, he replaced Anne Gorsuch's assistant administrators with far less belligerent officials. In late April 1983, however, EPA policy on CFCs had not changed, as the United States responded negatively to a proposal put forward by Norway, Sweden, and Finland to impose an international ban on CFCs in aerosols. The United States was prepared to oppose the so-called Nordic Annex on the by-now-hallowed grounds that the scientific understanding was insufficient to justify it, and that, in any case, agreement on a convention on the protection of stratospheric ozone should precede any annex to it.

With Ruckelshaus obviously determined to reform the EPA, the circumstances seemed right for the NRDC to threaten a lawsuit to get the new EPA administrator's attention and encourage him to take action without the necessity of a court order. Would-be litigants are required under the Clean Air Act to give the EPA sixty days' notice of their intention to file a lawsuit. Miller filed the sixty-day letter announcing the NRDC's intention to sue on May 31, 1983; in the letter he outlined the NRDC's position that the EPA's refusal to regulate CFCs was in violation of the Clean Air Act.

"EPA has made no official statements concerning the issue [of ozone depletion due to CFC emissions] since releasing an Advance Notice of Proposed Rulemaking in October 1980," Miller wrote to Administrator Ruckelshaus. "We believe the Agency is legally obligated to take some regulatory action on the basis of the scientific conclusions stated in the ANPR or, in the alternative, to publicly state its reasons for concluding that a threat to human health and the environment no longer exists. Since the change in Administration, we have been told on several occasions that some official statement of policy was imminent. In every instance, the promised deadline passed with no comment by the Agency . . . ."

Section 157 of the Clean Air Act obligated the administrator of the EPA to propose regulations for the control of any substance, practice, process, or activity (or any combination thereof) which in his judgment may reasonably be anticipated to affect the stratosphere, especially ozone in the stratosphere, if such effect in the stratosphere may reasonably be anticipated to endanger public health or welfare.

Miller went on to summarize his previous two years of frustrating efforts to "move the Agency through less formal approaches"—including meetings and correspondence with EPA officials and participation in State Department and EPA briefings concerning the international negotiations.

"Based on my experience to date," he concluded, "I can only believe that EPA has in fact no plan to issue a proposed regulation following up the ANPR. Since the Agency has stated its determination that continued emissions of CFCs present a 'significant and increasing threat to human health and the environment,' EPA is obligated to act by Section 157 of the Clean Air Act. We hope it will not be necessary to enforce this obligation through the courts."

Alan Miller's threat to sue the EPA may not have had quite the effect he intended. In response, officials within the Office of Toxic Substances began to prepare a draft notice for publication in the *Federal Register* announcing the EPA's intent to withdraw the 1980 ANPR and its implied "finding" that CFCs pose a "significant and increasing threat to human health and the environment," removing the basis for Miller's lawsuit. The draft notice claimed that, due to an improved understanding of the science provided by a new NAS report, the agency no longer believed that CFCs were an environmental risk.

The NAS study, entitled *Causes and Effects of Changes in Stratospheric Ozone: Update 1983,* was the fourth the academy had issued on the subject. It revised ozone-depletion estimates down from 5 to 9 percent to 2 to 4 percent, the lowest numbers yet proposed in any scientific study. There were two primary reasons for the revision. First, lab studies had resulted in refined rate constants for many of the 192 chemical reactions and 48 photochemical processes then known to occur in the stratosphere. Some of these difficult-to-measure reactions were faster and some slower than had previously been believed. Second, the effects of rising levels of other trace gases, including methane, carbon dioxide, and nitrous oxide, were incorporated into computer models. The result of these two types of refinements was a prediction that while the photochemical processes first identified by Rowland and Molina could dramatically reduce ozone levels in the upper stratosphere, other processes could cause an equally dramatic increase in ozone levels in the lower stratosphere and troposphere. Under some scenarios the total amount of ozone overhead at any given spot—a measurement known as "total column ozone"—could even increase. This would all but eliminate the myriad threats posed by excessive ultraviolet radiation reaching the earth's surface, since ozone would filter out UV radiation regardless of its altitude. The report warned, however, that a number of the gases in question were greenhouse gases. It also pointed out that the rearrangement of ozone from the upper to the lower stratosphere had, in the words of a reviewer for *Science*, "the potential to become as troubling as a sharp depletion in stratospheric ozone might have been," with "potential hazards"—smog and climatic effects—that are "much more complicated than it would appear at first blush."

Although, as Mario Molina pointed out at the time, "a large perturbation of the ozone layer . . . is still a major disruption of a natural system," to many people all the years of excitement and worry over stratospheric ozone now seemed to have been overblown.

"People were exiting the stratosphere right and left, and getting into the troposphere," John Hoffman, director of the strategic studies staff in the Office of Policy and Resource Management, who was supervising the preparation of the EPA's first major report on global warming, later recalled.

The proposed notice to withdraw the ANPR on CFCs crossed Hoffman's desk in mid-1983. Hoffman possessed an ideal background for an EPA official: a master's degree in systems modeling from MIT, which combined course work in engineering, business, and urban planning with sophisticated computer programming. As a graduate student, he and a friend had developed a computer model to assist the Lawyers Committee for Civil Rights Under Law in an effort to prove that state political redistricting plans discriminated against racial minorities. After graduation he worked for consulting companies that designed models to evaluate urban transit systems.

Hoffman's first efforts at EPA were in the area of developing market-incentive regulations to help control air pollution. Then, beginning in the early 1980s, he grew interested in the problem of global warming, a "coming" environmental issue with vast public-policy implications, whose understanding and study relied almost entirely on computer modeling. He had assigned an intern to prepare a paper on the greenhouse effect, and in the fall of 1980 had attended a two-day interagency workshop where he had met many of the scientists who were working on greenhouse issues. Hoffman reported to his superior, Marty Wagner, that global warming was an important environmental problem that EPA ought to be involved with. Wagner agreed that in general it would be beneficial for the EPA to conduct "strategic studies" on where the agency's future emphases should lay, and Hoffman was named staff director of Strategic Studies.

The Strategic Studies staff started out small—Hoffman had only four people working under him—and thanks to the budget freeze that accompanied the Reagan inauguration, it stayed small. Despite the group's grandiose name, its focus was limited to global warming. Beginning with Veerabhadran Ramanathan's 1975 discovery that CFCs were a greenhouse gas and Sherry Rowland's subsequent finding that atmospheric methane levels were rising, scientists had identified a number of significant greenhouse gases in addition to carbon dioxide. Hoffman's group was among the first to construct a model in the early 1980s that included all the newly discovered gases working in concert, to ascertain their total cumulative effect.

It was in the course of this work that Hoffman had become knowledgeable about CFCs, and he believed the Office of Toxic Substances' draft proposal to withdraw the 1980 ANPR was flawed. The most serious flaw was its uncritical acceptance of industry's assertion that future CFC production would remain flat. In constructing his own model on global warming, Hoffman had assumed that future growth was likely, if not inevitable, after the then-current recession ended. According to calculations buried deep within the NAS report, even modest growth in CFC production would result in significant ozone depletion in excess of the study's own 2 to 4 percent estimate. Hoffman raised his concerns with Wagner, who agreed that the draft notice should be opposed.

Hoffman and Wagner were not alone in their misgivings about EPA's CFC policy. Jim Losey, a junior official in the Office of International Affairs, opposed another position paper that was being circulated for comment by the Office of Toxic Substances, this one outlining U.S. opposition to the Nordic Annex to the proposed ozone convention, which would regulate CFC-propelled aerosols internationally. Losey believed it would be absurd for the United States to oppose internationally a prudent measure it had imposed domestically in 1974. The position paper also drew the attention of Steve Weil, in the Office of Policy, Planning, and Evaluation. Weil had helped draft the 1980 ANPR while at the Office of Toxic Substances. He had left the EPA briefly between 1980 and 1983—neatly missing the Gorsuch years—but had remained involved with CFCs, helping to draft three reports on the subject during his tenure on the staff of the Organization for Economic Cooperation and Development in Paris. At the OECD, Weil had commissioned a computer run projecting the effects of rising CFC levels, the same run whose results, quietly cited in the NAS report, had caught Hoffman's eye.

Thus in mid-1983, with international negotiations pending and a potential lawsuit on its hands, the EPA's CFC policy was in disarray. Officials in the Office of Toxic Substances had been arguing for three years—under Gorsuch's administration—that the science was too uncertain to warrant going ahead with Phase Two regulations. An abrupt change of course now would be too naked an admission that politics, not science, had dictated EPA's course. Yet, emboldened by the changes in EPA administration, junior officials in the Office of Planning, Policy, and Evaluation and the Office of International Affairs were willing to take a strong position for a change in EPA policy.

Shortly after he was nominated by President Reagan to be the new administrator of the EPA, William Ruckelshaus began hearing from many sources—Congress, the environmental community, the White House, and even from within the agency—that Joe Cannon was one Gorsuch subordinate who ought to be kept on at the EPA. Cannon had been associate administrator for policy, planning, and evaluation under Gorsuch, and in this capacity he had been responsible for John Hoffman's Office of Strategic Studies. He was immensely popular within the agency and at the same time was respected by environmentalists and the White House. Ruckelshaus responded by naming Cannon assistant administrator for air and radiation. As it happened, this was the ideal position from which Cannon could involve himself with CFCs and ozone depletion.

The Office of Toxic Substances had been responsible for CFCs since the late 1970s under the authority of the Toxic Substances Control Act. But the 1977 Clear Air Act Amendments provided the legal basis for the Air office to take over. The Toxic Substances office was primarily concerned with the regulation and control of commercial chemicals, which CFCs were, but CFCs were also an emission. As the science of ozone depletion had become more technical, it had moved beyond the scope of Toxic Substances. The CFC ozone-depletion problem fell much more comfortably into the area in which Hoffman was developing expertise: global change.

In addition to pressing the jurisdictional argument that responsibility for CFCs should be handed over to the Air office, Cannon, Hoffman,

Weil, and Losey argued that the EPA would put itself in a favorable negotiating position with the NRDC (or any other potential litigant) by taking a proactive stance in the ongoing international negotiations to control CFCs. This point carried considerable weight with the EPA's Office of General Counsel.

Finally, Don Clay, acting assistant administrator for pesticides and toxic substances, stated that although he was not willing to change Toxic Substances' oft-pronounced position on CFCs, he was willing to wash his hands of the entire issue, provided that the Air office would relieve him of legal responsibility for it. Cannon agreed and Ruckelshaus approved the reorganization. Just days before it was scheduled for publication in September 1983, Toxic Substances' proposed withdrawal of the 1980 ANPR was killed.

With the EPA logjam finally broken, Jim Losey wrote the State Department, arguing that the United States at the very least ought to be willing to support Article One of the Nordic Annex, which would place a worldwide ban on nonessential, CFC-propelled aerosols.

In mid-October, the U.S. delegation to a UNEP meeting in Geneva was notified by cable of the change in the U.S. position. "Effects of ozone depletion and CFC emissions on climate are potentially serious," the cable read in part. "Given this state of affairs, the U.S. believes that it is prudent to seek international agreement on control of certain uses of CFCs. . . . The U.S. delegation should state that it supports the objective of Article One of the Nordic Proposal. . . ." to put into effect a worldwide ban on nonessential aerosol uses of CFCs.

Although the delegation was further instructed to oppose Article Two of the Nordic Annex—which would restrict nonaerosol uses of CFCs—United States' policy on CFCs, after three years in hibernation, had finally stirred.

Alan Miller was encouraged by the movement, which seemed to obviate the need for legal action. Beyond that, he was told by EPA staff that a lawsuit seeking to force the EPA to issue new domestic regulations could interfere with the revived international process. Even worse, political support for the EPA's policy change was weak within the agency and the administration at large. If pressed by a lawsuit, there was a real possibility that the forces of reaction would rise up and once again work to remove the basis for the lawsuit by withdrawing the 1980 ANPR. Miller and the NRDC decided to quietly back off, at least for the time being.

Meanwhile, Joe Cannon recruited John Hoffman to direct the new Stratospheric Protection Task Force within the Office of Air and Radiation. Although he had a negligible budget and a minuscule staff, Hoffman was confronted with an enormous docket of responsibilities. First, he would play a role in developing U.S. policy with respect to the ongoing international negotiations. Second, he and Cannon agreed, it was essential to document the scientific basis for their actions, internationally and domestically (should it become necessary to impose Phase Two regulations), by commissioning studies and publishing results. In essence, they agreed, they had to "put the issue on the map."

"Putting issues on the map" was something Cannon and Hoffman knew something about. Hoffman, along with his cohort Steve Seidel, had just completed their major study on global warming, *Can We Delay a Greenhouse Warming?,* and had seen it spark a media frenzy after Cannon sent it to reporter Philip Shabecoff at the *New York Times.* The report's impact was a testament to its scientific authority—it was thoroughly documented and peer-reviewed—and to its bluntness. To begin with, the report's answer to the question posed by its title was a resounding "No!" Global warming was inevitable, and the world should begin to prepare for the many consequences of living in a warming world, including "dramatic" changes in precipitation and storm patterns, and a rise in global average sea level. "A soberness and sense of urgency should underlie our response to a greenhouse warming," the study concluded.

"We are trying to get people to realize that changes are coming sooner than they expected," Hoffman explained to a reporter. "Major changes will be here by the years 1990 to 2000, and we have to learn how to live with them." The impact of Seidel's EPA study was underscored when, just three days later, the NAS released a report that agreed that global temperatures would sharply rise in the next century. The NAS had reached a dramatically different conclusion, however, expressing "concern, but not panic," at the prospect of global warming, prompting President Reagan's science advisor, George A. Keyworth III, to criticize the EPA report as "unwarranted and unnecessarily alarmist." The NAS panel suggested there was ample time, as much as twenty years, to refine scientific understanding of global warming before taking drastic actions. By itself the NAS report might have calmed fears about global warming, but instead it served as a foil for the more frightening EPA paper. Differing so dramatically in their assessment of the situation's severity, the two reports generated an intense media storm, with Hoffman and Cannon at its epicenter. Their findings and concerns appeared on the front page of newspapers and as the lead story of the evening news, and they were often surrounded by reporters when they stepped from their offices.

John Hoffman's efforts on ozone depletion and global warming were underfinanced, understaffed, and—to the degree that they were recognized at all—regarded in the wake of the global-warming contretemps with profound suspicion by powerful elements within the Reagan administration. Yet Hoffman and Seidel had a sense of duty. As tenuous as their position was, there was no one else in government better placed than they were to move U.S. policy on CFCs forward. Having won the internal battle to keep the CFC issue alive, they now had an opening: an opportunity to prepare an exhaustive and unassailable study of CFCs and ozone depletion, to tackle head-on the endlessly debated question of whether there was time to wait or whether international regulations of CFCs ought to be pursued aggressively and implemented as quickly as possible.

16.

ONE GOOD OBSERVATION

ORDON DOBSON, the Oxford physicist whose observations of the luminosity of meteors in the 1920s helped confirm the existence of the ozone layer, also presented science with its first modern apparatus for ozone measurement. Introduced in 1926, the Dobson spectrophotometer employs a small quartz prism to split solar radiation into its various light wavelengths. Because ozone absorbs only certain of those wavelengths, a Dobson spectrophotometer measures how much ozone solar radiation encounters as it travels earthward through the earth's atmosphere. The resulting quantity of ozone is known as a column ozone measurement and is expressed in Dobson units (DU).

Compared with other trace gases, which exist in even more minute quantities, ozone is relatively easy to measure from the ground, and the Dobson meter is technologically simple and straightforward to operate. A degree in optics or atmospheric science is not required to be able to take Dobson readings.

After nearly half a century of service, the Dobson spectrophotometer was still, as of the early 1980s, the most widely used means of measuring ozone levels. This was evidence not only of its designer's ingenuity, but of the unchanging nature of ozone science itself. The basic network of a dozen or so ozone stations established by Dobson in the thirties had broadened considerably in 1957–58 during the International Geophysical Year, a period of concentrated global geophysical and atmospheric research; and additional stations had opened since the early 1970s. By 1981, there were approximately sixty Dobson instrument stations in the northern hemisphere and ten in the southern hemisphere. These stations tracked daily and monthly ozone levels and, if they chose to, reported their readings to the International Ozone Commission, which had been established at the Stockholm conference, or to the Canadian Atmospheric Environment Service; both organizations compiled monthly averages and published their results in rectangular red ledgers known throughout the world aeronomy community as the "Red Books."

Though computer models had predicted large ozone decreases, and the ozone depletion issue was often in the news, on a daily basis there was probably no duller activity in all the earth sciences than paging through ozone data. Dobson levels, while subject to fluctuations due to season, sunspot activity, or volcanic eruptions, remained essentially consistent from year to year, and researchers who maintained an active interest in ozonometry, like Joseph Farman, head of the Geophysical Unit of the British Antarctic Survey (BAS), were a rare breed. By the early 1980s, Farman had been collecting ozone data from a remote BAS base at Halley Bay, Antarctica, for nearly twenty-five years. He was the first to admit there was something slightly perverse about his diligence: it was like a penchant for saving theater stubs or obsolete train schedules, and he was accustomed to having well-meaning friends question his dedication to so mundane a branch of scientific inquiry.

Farman's Halley Bay observations became suddenly less predictable in October 1981, however, when his Dobson meter began reporting a dramatic change in the ozone levels overhead—20 percent below the 300 DU normally reported over Antarctica during the austral springtime, when solar radiation returns to Antarctica after six months of polar darkness. Farman trusted the Dobson instrument, believing that "for something invented more than fifty years ago, it had stood the test of time rather well," but could only assume that something had gone wrong with his Halley Bay apparatus. He knew, of course, about the Rowland-Molina theory and the scientific debate over the relationship between man-made chemicals and ozone depletion, but the Dobson reading was simply too low to suggest anything but an instrument malfunction.

Farman ordered a brand-new Dobson, one recently calibrated against the UK Meteorological Office standard, to be shipped to Antarctica in October 1982. Rather than report that all was normal, however, the new instrument reported ozone levels very much like those from the year before.

"We were frankly baffled," Farman later explained. Was there some-

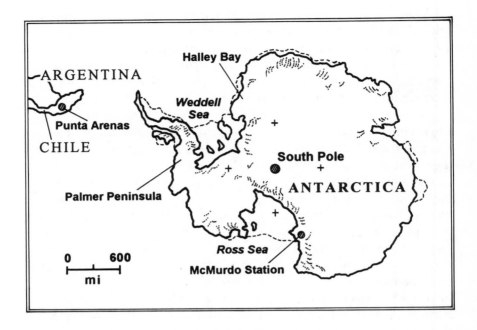

thing odd going on in the sky directly above the Halley Bay station, some electromagnetic interference, perhaps, that was distorting ground-based ozone observations?

Scientists knew that if ozone depletion was going to occur as the theories predicted, it was going to be difficult to identify against the natural background variation of ozone levels. Indeed, the sheer challenge of measuring ozone depletion had always figured prominently in the scientific and regulatory debate. Ozone levels were unpredictable and not thoroughly understood at any latitude. Over Antarctica, they were further complicated by extremely low levels of solar radiation—which meant that little or no stratospheric ozone was produced locally. Ozone over Antarctica arrived on air currents from warmer latitudes and then tended to collect above the South Pole.

Another factor was the polar vortex. Antarctica is surrounded by terrifically fierce winds that sweep almost unhindered around the pole at the high southern latitudes; nineteenth-century whalers called them the "Roaring Forties" and the "Furious Fifties," and used them for a quick trip around the bottom of the globe. These winds, caused by the sharp thermal contrast between the frigid Antarctic ice mass and the relatively warm waters of the Antarctic Ocean, create a vortex, an enclosed weather system that clamps shut over Antarctica during the austral winter, causing temperatures so cold they deflect the meteorological equator of the globe northward nearly 10 degrees latitude.

Researchers who had spent time in Antarctica knew the continent was as unpredictable as it was vast—a zone of outsized geophysical disturbances. It was a place where icebergs the size of Belgium calve from the main shelf and float away; where mysterious polynyas, warm-water holes that can grow as big as New England, open suddenly; where strange halos and configurations of light, produced by the sun's reflection and the unrelieved whiteness of the terrain, play against the sky; and where powerful natural phenomena sometimes beguile monitoring instruments.

Farman was not naive about the possible implications of the Dobson reports from Halley Bay. He knew from BAS studies of DDT levels in penguin blubber that Antarctica, however physically remote from civilization, was vulnerable to the intrusion of industrial chemicals, and because of his own prior studies of the slow transport of volcanic dust in the region, he knew that the insular polar vortex could work strange effects on the atmosphere. He also knew from measurements made in the 1970s that CFCs permeated the Antarctic atmosphere.

But Farman could not immediately conclude that the ozone loss he had measured over Antarctica was related to the current theories of ozone depletion. The dramatic seasonal ozone depletion he had found contradicted not only everything in his own experience, but also all the existing models of anticipated stratospheric ozone depletion. And he knew that publicizing the BAS findings could be risky. After a dozen years of argument, conflicting scientific estimates, and controversial regulatory efforts, news of a significant ozone depletion above Antarctica would be sure to agitate the world's atmospheric science community. Making this provocative finding known prematurely would, if it turned out to be wrong, reflect very poorly upon Farman's judgment and that of the British Antarctic Survey.

Furthermore, Farman's ozone project was run on a shoestring—about $18,000 a year—and he breathed a sigh of relief each year when his funding was renewed. In light of Britain's longstanding opposition to ozone-protection measures, supported by the skepticism of the British scientific establishment, it wasn't hard for Farman to imagine how members of Parliament would react if his program called attention to itself with a colossal scientific error.

Farman had first come to the Ice, as Antarctica was sometimes known, in 1956, to help prepare for Britain's participation in the International Geophysical Year, then the most ambitious global endeavor in the history of the physical sciences. The IGY, a worldwide program of coordinated studies, which ran from July 1, 1957, through December 31, 1958, involved sixty-six nations and represented the culmination of two hundred years of efforts to bring about global scientific cooperation. It allowed an opportunity for unprecedented widespread data-gathering and sharing of technology and information among countries, and in doing so helped inspire better-known 1960s "big science" undertakings like the Soviet and American space programs. The IGY also established the precedent for the brand of global scientific coordination that would prove crucial when ozone depletion and other global pollution crises arose a quarter of a century later.

"The single most significant peaceful activity of mankind since the Renaissance"—as Hugh Odishaw, director of the U.S. program, described the IGY—had its inspiration in Francis Bacon's seventeenth-century admonishment to men of learning to seek the truth about the natural world not from metaphysical argument, but in direct observations and scientific experiments. The influential European national scientific academies of the Enlightenment, such as Britain's Royal Society and the French Academy of Sciences, grew up around this Baconian ideal. Another of Bacon's concepts, that humankind would profit from scientific "experiments in concert" between nations, was first realized in the informal eighteenth-century practice of oceangoing ships from all countries sharing vital information about storms, sea currents, and trade winds.

In 1873, Karl Weyprecht, a lieutenant in the Austro-Hungarian Navy, approached the International Meteorological Organization, which was then in its infancy, with the idea for a unique scientific crusade—a 12-month period that would be set aside for concentrated Arctic and Antarctic studies conducted by many participating nations: a Polar Year. Much could be learned about earth's mysterious auroras and magnetic behavior, Weyprecht suggested, if observing stations were established around the poles and the nations involved pooled their collected data. No one country could mount so ambitious a program, he emphasized, so the cooperation of many would be required.

Weyprecht's idea appealed to the public imagination. While he downplayed the romantic side of polar exploration, it didn't hurt his cause that he was himself a famous *Nordpolforscher,* an Arctic explorer, who had played a leading role in the discovery of Franz Josef Land off northern Russia. Trips to the Arctic by the British, and later by the French and the Americans, had grown out of the search for the Northwest Passage and were to the mid-nineteenth century what space travel would be to the twentieth. But unlike space exploration, conducted by national space agencies, polar exploration was open to everyone. All manner of colorful characters, regardless of their qualifications, undertook ambitious voyages of polar discovery, and their adventures filled the columns of countless newspapers and "illustrateds" in Europe and America.

Weyprecht's efforts to organize a Polar Year were also abetted by the significant technological breakthroughs of the late 1870s—including the telephone, the phonograph, and the carbon filament bulb—which contributed to growing public expectations of science. Weyprecht's vision was fulfilled in the First Polar Year, which ran from August 1882 to August 1883. Hundreds of scientists and volunteers from the United States, Russia, and ten other countries participated in coordinated geophysical, geological, and meteorological experiments at thirteen bases in Greenland, the Arctic, and the Antarctic Ocean.

At the instigation of German meteorologist Johannes Georgi, a Second Polar Year took place fifty years later, in 1932. This second year was expected to make extensive use of the impressive new technologies of rocketry and radio waves, although the Depression almost caused its cancellation and greatly reduced the scope of most participating nations' activities. Experiments in Antarctica proved too difficult to mount altogether. Afterward, efforts to collate the research data were complicated by the international political tensions of the 1930s, and ultimately by the outbreak of the Second World War. The result was that thousands of scientific records were lost forever, and some of the program's data, collected at great expense and personal risk, was never published. An official report of the 1932 Polar Year could not be assembled and published until 1950.

In April 1950 a group of veterans of the unsatisfactory 1932 endeavor—prominent among them Oxford geophysicist Sydney Chapman, scientist and explorer Lloyd V. Berkner, and U.S. Navy rocket researcher James Van Allen—discussed the desirability of scheduling another year of international scientific cooperation. The official polar years were originally planned to occur every fifty years, placing the next one in 1982, but the Second Polar Year had been so disappointing, and technology had raced forward so dramatically since then, that a whole new range of scientific experiments could be contemplated. Berkner, an authority on geomagnetism, suggested an ideal year for a global scientific program would be 1957, when solar activity would be at a peak. This scientific opportunity, he pointed out, would not recur until 1970. In addition, he noted, Antarctica, though nominally included in the earlier polar exercises, had never really been given the scientific attention it deserved. Berkner's suggestion was widely embraced, particularly by Chapman, who became its most influential sponsor.

The objective of the sixty-six-nation IGY was eminently practical: to find out what the earth was really like. How round was the globe? How deep were the oceans? How high was the atmosphere? How old were the mountains? Participants in the program such as Joseph Farman made coordinated measurements of geomagnetic effects, cosmic-ray events, earthquakes, volcanic activity, and the auroras, using new data-gathering technologies—radar, rocketry, satellites, deep ice coring, and bathy-scaphic indicators.

The IGY's very spirit and purpose were put to a harsh test, however, on October 4, 1957, when the USSR launched the first man-made earth satellite, *Sputnik I*. The United States was angry and humiliated: America had previously announced *its* intention to launch an unmanned earth satellite during the IGY and apparently had no idea it was about to be upstaged. Americans had assumed that U.S. know-how and technology were inherently superior to the Russians' and that Soviet technological advances such as the jet engine and atom bomb had been copied or stolen outright from the United States. The Sputnik flights—*Sputnik I* was followed by *Sputnik II* on November 3, 1957—shattered that illusion. The United States suffered further humiliation on December 6, when the satellite rocket *Vanguard*, America's attempt to join the Russians in space, burned on the launching pad at Cape Canaveral. Finally, on January 31, 1958, a second American effort, *Explorer*, was successfully put into orbit.

Sputnik heightened the tensions of the Cold War and opened an era of intense scientific competition between the two superpowers. Yet the advent of the satellite only underscored the timeliness of the IGY's emphasis on global cooperation. As *New York Times* science reporter Walter Sullivan commented, "The provincialism of the pre-Sputnik era was dead forever. Science and scientists came out of the IGY as a potent influence in world affairs."

Joseph Farman joined the Falklands Dependencies Survey (later the British Antarctic Survey) in 1956, after having worked briefly in the British aerospace industry. He first set foot on the Ice that austral summer, joining some sixty other young scientists and graduate students who annually staffed Britain's eight scientific stations in the Antarctic Ocean. He managed to distinguish himself during that first year out, according to the British explorer Vivian Fuchs, as "a man of parts, whose erudition on many subjects often baffled us, with highbrow tastes in music and a connoisseur's judgment of wines." Evidently well thought of by the program's officers, Farman in 1957 was named base-camp director at the Falkland Islands station.

Though an international agreement was signed during the IGY, stipulating that no country could advance territorial claims in Antarctica, Farman and his countrymen, historically, had strong emotional ties to the region. The British had, since Captain James Cook's first sally onto the ice pack in 1775, compiled a notable record of Antarctic conquest, and had suffered more than their share of hardship, most notably the deaths of the explorer Robert Scott and his entire party on a journey to the South Pole in 1911–12.

By the time Joseph Farman got there, scientists were beginning to appreciate that in isolated Antarctica's 5 million square miles of stark wasteland, its vast snowy plateaus and mountain ranges, dead volcanoes, and crevasses of unknown depth, its crystalline atmosphere and frozen seas, lay one of the most enticing opportunities in the history of human curiosity: the chance to use advanced technology to study an entire continent that had come down to the modern age virtually untouched by civilization. Most of Antarctica's interior was not seen by humans until after World War II, when a United States airborne project, Operation High Jump, surveyed it from above. Even then, after Britain, the United States, the Soviet Union, and other nations began financing long-range scientific missions to Antarctica, few researchers ventured far into the interior or remained on the Ice after the beginning of the austral winter in April, when the entire continent was plunged into frozen darkness until September.

The first British research stations in Antarctica had been established in 1943 on the narrow Palmer Land Peninsula, the most accessible part of Antarctica, which, geologically, is a continuation of the Andes Mountains and appears, in maps, to be attempting to reach back up toward Tierra del Fuego, the southernmost tip of South America, in an effort to reconnect itself. Seeking to broaden their network of Antarctic research stations in the mid-1950s, the British constructed a new base on a remote, little-explored shoreline of the Antarctic mainland at Halley Bay on the Weddell Sea. Conditions at Halley Bay were so harsh that most of the base had to be built underground, and it was assumed the site would be abandoned at the conclusion of the IGY in 1958. But Halley Bay proved to be situated directly beneath a belt of maximum auroral activity, and rather than dismantle it, the British later converted it into a permanent research installation.

Soon after the Halley Bay station opened, Farman was named chief of the BAS Geophysical Unit at Halley Bay, responsible for experiments and long-term measurements in geomagnetism, solar radiation, seismology, and ozonometry. Ozone studies were included because scientists hoped local ozone levels would tell them something about the Antarctic's wind and weather patterns, and might help explain a phenomenon known as "tropopause holes," in which serene stratospheric air enters the more turbulent troposphere.

Farman knew that none of the models of ozone depletion based on water vapor, nitrogen oxides, CFCs, or any combination thereof, called for the dramatic reductions in ozone he began monitoring in the 1980s. Such substantial reductions were predicted only in worst-case scenarios, and even then were not supposed to occur until late in the next century. Assuming that his data *must* be incorrect, Farman was forced to consider all the possible explanations. Dobson spectrophotometers only measure ozone directly overhead; therefore, he reasoned, some unknown factor could be influencing the data-gathering above Halley Bay and nowhere else. He decided to reposition the Dobson at another British station a thousand miles away, and compare measurements when austral spring returned the following year.

Given that he had not previously been involved in the ozone debate, Farman believed it was essential that any scientific claims he made be fully supported. "We were fed up with hearing all the various theories and arguments about ozone," he later said. If the BAS was going to get involved in the ozone fray, it would join in only when it was armed with solid data and a compelling hypothesis. There would be no premature leaks of the data, or rumors circulated, if Farman could help it. When, in 1983, one of his graduate students attempted to include the 1982 Halley Bay readings in his doctoral dissertation, Farman used his authority to quash its publication.

One important technical fact colored all of these considerations: Farman's Dobson readings were markedly inferior in scope and sophistication to the ozone measurements being made by NASA's *Nimbus 7* satellite, which had been orbiting overhead since 1978. *Nimbus* carried two new computerized ozone-monitoring devices, the solar backscattered ultraviolet experiment (SBUV) and the total ozone mapping spectrometer (TOMS), and Farman felt confident that, were there anything seriously amiss in the stratosphere, the instruments aboard *Nimbus* would surely have spotted it.

Indeed, the SBUV and TOMS had already recorded the severe ozone depletion Farman had observed, but the computers that logged the satellite data had been programmed to identify such impossibly low ozone numbers as erroneous, thus had disregarded them.

*   *   *

It is characteristic of the rapid pace of technological progress in the twentieth century that less than forty years after aviation pioneers ventured aloft in canvas-winged biplanes to take the first crude aerial photographs, scientists had mastered the ability to scan the earth from outer space. Satellites fulfilled a centuries-old dream of meteorologists and physicists by providing scientific observation "platforms" away from the earth's surface from which the planet can be observed over extended periods of time.

The earth-viewing capability of satellites was revolutionary. Until April 1, 1960, when the Television and Infrared Observation Satellite (TIROS I), the world's first weather satellite, began transmitting photographs back down to NASA after launch from Cape Canaveral, no more than 15 percent of the earth's surface was covered by routine weather observation, namely, those areas occupied by nations with well-developed weather services. Although TIROS I functioned for only seventy-eight days, in that time it transmitted an astounding twenty thousand photos of earth's weather patterns and cloud systems, assuring NASA of the system's potential.

The reality of fully utilizing TIROS, however, proved frustrating. Even when functioning properly, the optical resolution of the camera on TIROS was poor, no better than about ten kilometers, and because the satellite's rotation during orbit made it impossible to keep the lens pointing squarely back at Earth, meteorologists studying TIROS photos grew exasperated trying to distinguish what kinds of clouds they were looking at, and from what angles the pictures had been taken. Sometimes they found themselves literally unable to determine up from down, and without more precision and coordinating data, the photos were tantalizing but not really useful. A story that made the rounds during the early days of satellite imaging was that of the researcher who had attained generous funding for what seemed a most enviable project—assembling the first map of global cloud cover, based on TIROS data. It was expected he would complete his analysis in a few months. More than a year later he was still deeply immersed in the project, desperately trying to make sense of the TIROS data, his research funds totally exhausted. As the National Center for Atmospheric Research's Quarterly Report commented, "Understandably, a good many people who had been enthusiastic about the possibilities of using satellite data lost interest when they encountered such problems." From these early difficulties with instrument calibration arose lingering doubts about the trustworthiness of satellite data and the ability of satellite-program scientists to fully comprehend it.

One of the young physicists concerned with the urgent need for improvement in satellite instrumentation in the early 1960s was Donald Heath, who had recently earned a Ph.D. in physics at Johns Hopkins University, studying under William G. Fastie, a pioneer in rocket measurements of ultraviolet light, auroras, and air glow, and one of the first scientists to develop and apply spectroscopic techniques to space exploration. Heath started to work at NASA's Goddard Space Flight Center in Greenbelt, Maryland, just outside Washington, D.C., on August 28, 1964, the very day, coincidentally, that NASA put a weather satellite named *Nimbus 1,* a successor to *TIROS,* into orbit.

For Heath the appeal of satellite instrumentation was its rigorously demanding precision combined with the Jules Verne–like adventure of putting a scientific observing platform into outer space. Sophisticated satellite observation promised to provide reams of experimental data to science, ending its total reliance on ground-based observations, lab work, and theoretical models. Theories, certainly, were essential, but even the most convincing required some form of physical substantiation, an ideal expressed neatly in an axiom Heath first heard from University of Maryland climatologist Helmut Landsberg: "One good observation is worth a thousand models, and a million speculations."

The Nimbus series was originally conceived to improve weather forecasting. *Nimbus 1* made a smashing debut by photo-imaging Hurricane Cleo on its first day in orbit, August 28, 1964, and though it functioned for only one month, it advanced satellite technology by providing more than twenty-seven thousand infrared images of nighttime cloud cover, the first ever made. *Nimbus 2,* launched in May 1966, carried a device to measure the earth's albedo, or the sunlight reflected by the earth back into space, inspiring Heath, his Goddard unit director William Nordberg, and others at NASA to consider using *Nimbus* to make earth-science measurements in addition to those directly related to weather forecasting. With Nordberg's encouragement, Heath began working on plans to put an ozone-measuring device on an upcoming *Nimbus* shot. Such an instrument seemed perfect for *Nimbus,* for though it was an atmospheric-monitoring instrument, it also provided useful data to meteorologists, because falling or rising stratospheric ozone levels could serve as another integer to weather prediction. Areas of high pressure were known to produce low ozone readings, while storms and areas of low pressure were generally accompanied by high ozone levels. The first scientists to describe the desirability of satellite ozone measurements, University of Maryland physicists S. F. Singer and R. C. Wentworth, had had in mind just such a meteorological purpose. In a paper published in the *Journal of Geophysical Research* in 1957, they pointed out that since ozone moved about in the stratosphere on both lateral and vertical air currents, an understanding of ozone transport could assist weather forecasters. To know the altitude profile of ozone, not just its column measurement, would require a "nadir-looking" or downward-looking instrument situated on an orbiting satellite.

Heath's plan called for just such a device—a "backscatter" instrument that would measure total column ozone and give its altitude profile. The term "backscattering" refers to the phenomenon whereby solar radiation bounces off atomic particles and molecules and "scatters" in the atmosphere. The backscatter instrument compares the scattering of "outgoing" infrared light in the earth's albedo on a particular type of molecule, such as ozone, with the effect caused by "incoming" or scattered ultraviolet solar radiance on that same molecule.

NASA's official response to Heath's idea, unfortunately, was not encouraging. "It's an excellent proposal," one NASA scientist consoled Heath as the project was being rejected. "But once you've measured ozone, why would you want to do it again and again?"

Heath soon gained a valuable ally among the ranks of junior scientists at Goddard, an aeronomer named Arlin Krueger. Krueger was a veteran of the high-altitude ballooning program at the University of Minnesota which, under the leadership of physicists Edward Ney and John Winkler in the 1950s, had helped reinvigorate scientific ballooning. Auguste Piccard's generation of balloon scientists had used rubberized cotton to construct their balloons, but using polyethylene, a tough, adaptable new plastic developed during the war, made it possible for Ney, Winkler, Krueger, and others working from a suburban airport near Minneapolis, to send small balloons as high as 145,000 feet. These balloons were called "vertical probes," for they went straight up, but another innovation in ballooning, automatic ballasting systems, allowed unmanned "horizontal" balloons to sustain their drift time for as long as two weeks. Some managed to completely circumnavigate the globe. Thus, there was nothing unusual about Krueger's dual interest in balloons and satellites: long-drifting "horizontal" sounding balloons were direct forerunners to orbiting satellites. With balloon technology becoming increasingly sophisticated, many scientists believed that some combination of satellites and horizontal balloons—electronically "interrogating" one another for data—would constitute the future system of global atmospheric monitoring.

With Krueger's support, Heath was finally able to convince NASA to put a backscatter ultraviolet instrument aboard *Nimbus 4,* launched in

April 1970. The BUV made a promising showing of its potential by helping substantiate Paul Crutzen's theory about the sun's role in nitric oxide's catalytic destruction of ozone.

Krueger later recollected: "Crutzen, who knew of the BUV instrument on *Nimbus,* called one day in August 1972, very excited, asking 'Did you see that event?'" Crutzen was referring to a "proton event," a rare burst of powerful solar energy, which had occurred the day before. Such a powerful release of protons into earth's atmosphere breaks down nitrogen into nitric oxide, which Crutzen had theorized would catalytically scavenge ozone. "When Heath and I looked at the data, we saw that there had been a twenty percent drop in ozone, but only at the geomagnetic latitudes—the polar regions where protons enter the atmosphere—and no significant change at the equator. So the BUV proved that Crutzen's theory worked. This was the kind of observation only a satellite instrument could accomplish, and of course it was a major step up the ladder in terms of validating the capability of the BUV."

The instrument performed less impressively, however, when NASA lab technicians in Houston looked to Heath and Krueger to confirm theories about the depletion of ozone by chlorine put into the atmosphere by early space-shuttle flights. The chlorine-related depletions, believed to be only about .5 percent, were too small to be accurately monitored by the BUV.

Krueger and Heath aimed to alleviate this shortcoming with the introduction of Krueger's total ozone mapping spectrometer, or TOMS. The BUV on *Nimbus 4* provided global coverage of column ozone and altitude profile, but TOMS, which flew on *Nimbus 7,* launched in October 1978, was fitted with a sequential optical apparatus and could make hundreds of wavelength observations every few seconds. *Nimbus 7*'s orbit was sun-synchronous, meaning it ascended across the equator on one side of the earth at local noon, went over the North Pole and then descended at local midnight on the other side, and came up and around again from the South Pole headed toward the equator, varying a degree or two in longitude with each pass. With the satellite traveling 600 miles above the earth at a speed of 4 miles a second, completing its full orbit of the globe in 104 minutes, the result was an exquisite coordination of image and motion. TOMS measured column ozone and altitude profile, as well as the spatial distribution of ozone, or levels of ozone at a specific time across broad geographic areas. In effect, it took pictures of the "total" ozone layer over the entire globe.

The satellite, shaped like an ocean buoy, was only ten feet tall and, besides a refined BUV device known as the SBUV, and the TOMS, carried instruments to measure the earth's albedo, ocean salinity, wind patterns, cloud cover, and polar stratospheric clouds—each expensive, highly sensitive device the technological darling of an Arlin Krueger or a Donald Heath, who closely monitored its performance from the Goddard Space Flight Center. On each of its 104-minute orbits, this instrument-laden satellite told Goddard investigators more about the earth's atmosphere than earlier generations of scientists could have imagined possible.

In 1981, Heath became convinced *Nimbus 7* was telling him that there had been global decrease in ozone. He had been announcing, within NASA and at scientific symposia as early as 1975, that BUV data from *Nimbus 4*'s first two years in orbit, 1970 to 1972—the period in a satellite's life when its instrument calibration is most dependable— showed lower ozone values than those being reported by ground-based Dobson stations. By 1981, with the confirmation of data from *Nimbus 7*, he felt certain enough to submit a paper to *Science* concluding that during the 1970s global ozone had been depleted by 1 percent. He suspected, because the largest and most persistent depletion was taking place at an altitude of 35 to 45 kilometers, where chlorine scavenges ozone most effectively, that CFCs might be to blame. "There is no way that can happen fortuitously," he later recalled explaining to an editor at *Science*. "Something real has happened in the atmosphere." *Science* distributed Heath's paper for peer review but rejected it, citing the unreliability of conclusions based on combined data from two different satellites, *Nimbus 4* and *Nimbus 7*. In particular, *Science* doubted the reliability of the SBUV's diffuser plate, which scatters sunlight into the instrument. The effect of sunlight on this plate is to eventually dull it, limiting its efficiency by about 50 percent, but Heath claimed his calculations could account for the diffuser-plate degradation. "People didn't want to acknowledge what I could pull out of my satellite data," Heath later said with some bitterness, "because it contradicted the models, and the article's reviewers were modelers, not experimentalists."

In the meantime, with *Nimbus 7*'s incredible range, speed, and altitude, the SBUV and TOMS instruments were generating an overwhelming amount of data, much more than could be analyzed and assimilated by NASA technicians. To more efficiently process the information, NASA scientists programmed the computers that cataloged the data to analyze only the ozone data that fell between 180 and 650 Dobson units, bounds well outside what were considered to be realistic ozone variables. Though the data falling outside the parameters were assumed to be the result of instrument malfunction, they were not discarded. On July 31,

1984, a technician named David Lee at ST Systems, Inc., NASA's chief contractor for TOMS, was glancing through the previous year's ozone data when he came across some of the aberrantly low readings. He brought them to the attention of his supervisor, Dr. Pawan K. Bhartia. As Bhartia later told the *Atlanta Constitution,* "Our initial reaction was that it was a problem with the instrument. A reading of 180 DU had never been seen by anyone anywhere on the globe." Bhartia mentioned Lee's finding at the next meeting of project scientists at Goddard, but, he later recounted, "everybody agreed it was an instrument problem."

Bhartia and Heath did include the data in a scientific paper they were writing, although they were put off publicizing the incident more widely both by Heath's unhappy experience with *Science* and by the lack of corroboration elsewhere in the ozone-measuring community. "We right away checked the Red Books," Heath later said, "but seeing no corroboration there from any ground-based station, we held off." It so happened that Joseph Farman was not then submitting his data to the Red Books.

17.

A HOLE YOU COULD SEE FROM MARS

F OR MANY YEARS, Sherry Rowland had argued that stratospheric chemistry was not as simple as one-dimensional, steady-state models suggested. CFCs would not necessarily deplete ozone uniformly at all altitudes and latitudes and at all times of the year, he said. In fact, it was unlikely ozone depletion would occur in a tidy linear fashion, with x increase of CFC emissions leading to y more ozone depletion, globally averaged. Models that attempted to average out total column ozone at steady state, Rowland believed, were thus fundamentally flawed.

The notion that ozone depletion might not be linear received a strong endorsement in June 1984, when data were presented at a conference in Munich describing a new model developed by Dr. Michael J. Prather of NASA's Goddard Institute for Space Studies, along with Harvard's Michael McElroy and Steven Wofsy. Prather's model predicted possible ozone depletion of 15 percent or more by the middle of the twenty-first century if CFC use grew by 3 percent annually. But what was more startling was the suggestion that ozone depletion might suddenly accelerate when chlorine concentrations reached a level of around 10 parts per billion, approaching the concentration of nitrogen oxides. When there isn't enough nitrogen oxide to neutralize all the chlorine as chlorine nitrate, Prather explained, "we find out fairly dramatic things happen to the ozone column." In the Prather model, a hypothetical doubling of CFC production based on 1980 levels did not simply double the amount of ozone that would be depleted, it increased it by a factor of between four and six—a "chlorine catastrophe."

Prather's finding that there was a threshold level of chlorine concentrations beyond which ozone depletion might increase abruptly and dramatically strongly refuted industry's longstanding argument that ozone depletion, were it to occur at all, would be so gradual that there would be ample time to do additional research before regulating.

The Prather model also seemed to refute the conclusions reached by the 1983 NASA report and to vindicate John Hoffman's efforts to save the CFC-control program within the EPA. Shortly after assuming responsibility for the EPA's Stratospheric Protection Task Force, Hoffman had met with Prather and other scientists to urge them to conduct new studies based on an assumption that the rate of CFC emissions would increase, not remain flat or decrease as industry had claimed they would. The result was a number of new models predicting future potential ozone losses, with Prather's the "kinkiest" among them. Although as of July 1984, in response to Prather's findings, the EPA had "reached no conclusion as to what, if any, further domestic regulatory action is necessary" (as Administrator Ruckelshaus wrote in a letter to Representatives Edward Madigan of Illinois and Thomas Luken of Ohio), the EPA was reconsidering the domestic production cap proposed in its 1980 ANPR. Industry, however, was not impressed. One representative at the Munich meeting dismissed Prather's work as something he wouldn't want to "carry outside the laboratory." At a "scoping meeting" called jointly by the EPA and the State Department in August 1984 to gather public comment for preparation of a draft environmental impact statement, Donald Stroback of Du Pont reiterated the industry line, saying, "There is no immediate, imminent threat and harm to the ozone layer, and with that there is no need for a regulatory protocol at this time."

The European Economic Community, which in UNEP negotiations had strongly resisted the idea of a worldwide aerosol ban, was similarly unmoved. The EEC had taken the familiar position that more convincing scientific evidence was necessary before any costly regulatory measures were put into effect, and had only grudgingly accepted the concept of a production cap on CFCs. But they had set the cap at a level well in excess of their existing production capacity—in effect paying lip service to the problem of ozone depletion without taking any serious measures to prevent it. The United States, the Nordic countries, and Canada—in an alliance known as the Toronto Group (named after the city where they had their initial meeting)—supported the proposed Nordic Annex to an international convention governing CFCs, which would impose a global aerosol ban. The Toronto Group proposed several options for implementing restrictions on nonessential aerosols at a negotiating session in Geneva between October 22 and 26, 1984, which were countered by an EEC proposal to cap CFC production capacity and cut aerosol uses by 30 percent from 1976 levels within two years. Although this represented a softening of the initial European position, this too was unacceptable to the United States, since the member nations of the EEC were only producing at 50 to 60 percent of capacity, as compared to U.S. companies, which were near or at capacity. It would thus take as long as twenty years for the cap to become binding on the Europeans.

Suggesting a need for greater urgency, Prather's results (published in the November 15, 1984, issue of *Nature*) were cited by U.S. ambassador Richard Benedick—who had taken over as head of the American delegation in late 1984—at a negotiating session in Geneva in late January 1985. The Prather study, Benedick said, suggested that "the ozone layer appears to be highly sensitive to even relatively minute changes in emissions of CFCs and other gases over time—as little as one or two percentage points in annual growth rates can make an enormous difference in ozone depletion. This means that the margin of error between complacency and catastrophe is too small for comfort." The Europeans dismissed Benedick's warning as "scare-mongering."

Over the two-and-a-half-year course of the UNEP negotiations, delegates had been able to agree on the terms of a general-framework convention to cooperate on matters of scientific research and the exchange of information, and, more important, on a schedule for continuing discussions to hammer out specific regulatory mechanisms in future protocols to the convention. But the question of how to write a protocol that would begin to make actual cuts in global CFC production had degenerated into a fruitless debate between the Toronto Group and the European Community over an international aerosol ban versus a production-capacity cap, with neither side willing to compromise and each insisting that its approach would better avert an environmental catastrophe.

An agreement adopted at a meeting in Vienna on March 22, 1985, incorporating the measures that had thus far been agreed to, was a significant achievement in the annals of international environmental diplomacy. UNEP executive director Mostafa K. Tolba noted that the so-called Vienna Convention was "the first global convention to address an issue that for the time being seems far in the future and is of unknown proportions"; it is, he said, "the essence of the anticipatory response so many environmental issues call for—to deal with the threat of the problem before we have to deal with the problem itself. . . . It is hard enough to cope with the permanent disappearance of a species, or the death of a lake, or the turning of fertile lands into desert. But in the case of ozone depletion, who could forgive us if we reacted too late?"

And yet the Vienna Convention did not begin to resolve the problem of ozone depletion. The convention would not enter into force until ninety days after twenty countries had ratified it, a process that would be likely to take several years at best, and once ratified, its only agreed-upon provisions involved exchanges of information, research, and data, and the establishment of new permanent international institutions, including a secretariat, to coordinate the exchanges and to elaborate more specific rules.

In the meantime, although the appearance of the Prather article had failed to move the European Community and the Toronto Group toward agreement on an international protocol, the idea that ozone depletion might not be linear was having a significant impact on the domestic front: it provoked the NRDC to finally file its long-pending lawsuit against the EPA, seeking to force the agency to impose domestic restrictions on CFCs in accordance with the requirements of the Clean Air Act Amendments of 1977.

Alan Miller had left the NRDC in early 1984 to take a job at the World Resources Institute, handing the CFC file over to a friend and colleague at NRDC, David Doniger. Doniger was more abrupt in manner than Miller, more confrontational in nature, and possibly more inclined to litigate. Doniger's first letter to the EPA threatening a lawsuit was dated August 3, 1984, and was addressed to Administrator Ruckelshaus. Receiving no response, the NRDC filed suit in Federal District Court in Washington on November 27, 1984, asking that the EPA be required to issue rules within six months to limit further emissions of CFCs. John Hoffman responded that the EPA was involved in a broad program to deal with the ozone problem, but said he did not think it would be feasible to come up with rules limiting CFCs within six months.

The next day, November 28, though his action was in no way related to the NRDC's suit, Ruckelshaus announced his resignation from the EPA, effective January 5, 1985. Even his most severe critics, including NRDC attorney Jonathan Lash, noted that Ruckelshaus had been able to restore morale and public trust to the EPA, even if he had failed to change the basic thrust of the Reagan administration's environmental policy. Lash and others worried that the EPA could now regress to the way it had been under Gorsuch. The skeptics were only somewhat relieved when, on November 29, the president nominated forty-year-old Lee Thomas, a former deputy director of the Federal Emergency Management Agency (FEMA) who had replaced Rita Lavelle as assistant administrator for toxic wastes, to replace Ruckelshaus. "They have chosen a good soldier instead of a general to lead the EPA," Lash said.

Almost immediately upon being nominated as EPA administrator, Thomas was confronted with the issues of CFC regulation, ozone depletion, and the NRDC lawsuit. By his own admission, Thomas was familiar only with the EPA's toxic-waste programs. But detailed briefings with John Hoffman quickly convinced him that "ozone depletion was a big issue that the EPA ought to be dealing with," despite ongoing efforts by the Office of Management and Budget to cut CFC-related funding from the EPA budget. Moreover, Thomas did not believe it would be difficult to reach a settlement with the NRDC, because he did not disagree fundamentally with the environmentalists' goal of "a systematic approach to the problem of ozone depletion, with a timetable to move forward."

On January 7, 1985, just a few days after Thomas officially took office, the NRDC and the EPA advised the district court of the possibility of an out-of-court settlement. A few weeks later, on February 5, 1985, the Alliance for Responsible CFC Policy moved for leave to intervene as defendant, a motion that was unopposed and was granted by the court on March 1. Negotiations among the three parties to reach a settlement lasted for the better part of a year. With Lee Thomas's full consent, and with John Hoffman in charge of the program, the EPA agreed "to continue a multi-faceted work plan of study, scientific review, document development, and regulatory analysis" that would lead to a final agency decision on the control of CFCs by a set date. The biggest sticking point in the negotiations was timing. The EPA wanted the pace of international negotiations to set the pace for domestic action. Doniger insisted that the EPA should be required to issue domestic regulations regardless of how international negotiations proceeded.

There were three primary elements in the agreed-upon Stratospheric Ozone Protection Plan, devised by Steve Seidel: research and analysis aimed at narrowing economic and scientific uncertainties; participation in a series of domestic and international workshops and conferences; and, most important, a commitment to decide by May 1, 1987, whether additional domestic regulation of CFCs was warranted, "based on the information gained during the period of study." Final rules regulating CFCs would then have to be promulgated—or an official announcement published in the *Federal Register* indicating that no action would be taken —no later than November 1, 1987.

*   *   *

Since John Hoffman had taken charge of the EPA's ozone-protection program in 1983, scientific and public awareness of the problem of ozone depletion had rebounded dramatically, as a result of a stream of substantial studies and reports. Several studies Hoffman had commissioned concluded in mid-1985 that total worldwide CFC production would increase by about 3 percent a year for at least the next ten years. A working paper Hoffman's office prepared for the Vienna Convention and released in April 1985 predicted that the ozone layer would be depleted by as much as 60 percent by the middle of the next century if CFC production grew by 4.5 percent annually, and would be depleted by as much as 26 percent even if the growth rate dropped to 2.5 percent a year. A 133-page advance draft of a NASA–WMO report, released in mid-January 1986, projected average ozone depletions between 4.9 percent and 9.4 percent by the mid–twenty-first century, at 1980 rates of CFC production—a deliberately conservative assumption, since CFC production rates had already increased significantly since 1980. "Given what we know about the ozone and trace gas–chemistry–climate problems," the NASA report said, "we should recognize that we are conducting one giant experiment on a global scale by increasing the concentrations of trace gases in the atmosphere without knowing the environmental consequences." The reiteration of this haunting image, suggesting that mankind's contamination of the atmosphere was tantamount to an uncontrolled "experiment," coming as it did in a prestigious report, was widely cited in the coming months and years. But the major impetus by far to renewed concern was the May 1985 publication in *Nature* of Joseph Farman's paper describing his findings of seasonal ozone depletion over Antarctica.

As Donald Heath and other NASA scientists had been discouraged at times from publicizing their aberrant satellite measurements of ozone depletion, so had Farman been reluctant to rule out the possibility of instrument error or some other technical factor to explain the low-ozone data his team had recorded in Antarctica. The BAS was a far smaller, simpler organization than NASA, and Farman's dilemma was less a bureaucratic complexity than a difficult private decision. "My politics were what you might call 'vaguely Green,'" he later said. "And if anyone had told me beforehand that someday I would be standing up and making a lot of speeches about anything, I would have thought they were crazy."

In the fall of 1984, however, after reading Prather's paper in *Nature* about nonlinear ozone depletion, and studying his October readings from Halley Bay and also from Argentine Island, a British station a thousand miles away, Farman decided it was time to come forward. With the help of three BAS colleagues, Brian Gardiner, Bob Murgatoyd, and J. D. Shanklin, he wrote an article describing the 30 to 40 percent annual loss in ozone they had observed. Because of the BAS's relatively long history of ozone measurement, Farman was able to cite continuous statistics for Antarctic ozone as far back as 1957, and conclude that the recent depletion was a distinct anomaly. The paper, which appeared in *Nature* on May 16, 1985, began decisively:

> [A]ssessments of the effect of human activities on stratospheric ozone using one-dimensional models . . . have suggested that perturbations of total ozone will remain small for at least the next decade. Results from such models are often accepted by default as global estimates. The inadequacy of this approach is here made evident by observations that the spring values of total O_3 in Antarctica have now fallen considerably . . . possible chemical causes must be considered.

Since the early 1970s, as part of its routine atmospheric monitoring, the BAS had also been measuring anthropogenic trace gases, including chlorofluorocarbons. These measurements, along with known values of worldwide CFC production, enabled Farman to report a rise in CFCs over Antarctica corresponding to the local loss of ozone. "The present-day atmosphere," he pointed out, "differs most prominently from that of previous decades in the higher concentrations of [CFCs]." The paper went on to suggest that the loss of ozone might be linked not only to CFCs but to the unique attributes of the polar vortex. He surmised that the intense cold and darkness of the stratosphere above Antarctica during the austral winter could make the region "uniquely sensitive to the growth of inorganic chlorine" by creating chlorine reservoirs that hold vast amounts of atomic chlorine until the austral springtime, when it is released to destroy ozone in the catalytic chain reaction Rowland and Molina had described.

Farman's article citing an observed ozone depletion of 30 to 40 percent stunned the world's atmospheric-science community. The recent NASA–WMO report had predicted ozone losses in the 5 to 9 percent range or less by the middle of the twenty-first century. Moreover, Antarctica was the last place on earth anyone had thought there would be large regional decreases in ozone, particularly during the austral winter, when, given the complete absence of solar radiation, it was assumed ozone-depletion mechanisms would be inactive. Farman, by suggesting that reservoir molecules might store chlorine until the daybreak of austral spring, had challenged this safe assumption. "All the models put the atmospheric chemistry to sleep at night," one of his colleagues later explained. "Only Farman had worried about goings-on in the polar night-time. The [*Nature* paper's] reviewers couldn't shoot Joe down, because no one else really knew enough about it."

Sherry Rowland and Mario Molina were as surprised as anyone else when they opened their copies of the May 16 issue of *Nature*. Like most of their peers, they had never heard of Joseph Farman. Yet the paper seemed well grounded, and Rowland had always felt an immense debt of gratitude to researchers like Farman who doggedly maintained records of stratospheric ozone; now, it appeared, one of these unsung heroes of atmospheric science, quietly compiling ozone data at the bottom of the world since 1957, had made a critical observation. To Rowland and many others, Farman's long track record of ozone measurement and his obvious restraint and humility in bringing his disturbing findings to light only after patient, careful investigation, made for impressive science and lent additional credence to his stated conclusions. Rowland became further convinced of the merit of Farman's work when he met one of the paper's coauthors, Brian Gardiner, at a conference in Hawaii during the summer of 1985 and was strongly impressed by Gardiner personally.

In Switzerland later that summer, at another scientific meeting, Rowland found that many of his colleagues were skeptical of Farman's claims. Farman, after all, some said, was only a geophysicist who maintained ground-based records. If a depletion the size he had described really had occurred, why hadn't computer models anticipated it, and most of all, why hadn't it turned up on NASA's satellite data?

Indeed, while Farman's *Nature* paper had become a topic of intense discussion wherever atmospheric scientists gathered in the summer and fall of 1985, a far more heated discourse was taking place at NASA's Goddard Space Flight Center, where, according to Donald Heath, "Headquarters was extremely upset." Heath, Arlin Krueger, and their colleagues, after reading Farman's *Nature* article, had immediately begun to plow back through their BUV, SBUV, and TOMS data, carefully searching for data that would refute or corroborate Farman's report. Krueger couldn't help but wonder, a bit angrily, why the British had kept their information secret for so long. "If Farman had publicly archived data from the early 1980s [i.e., put it in the Red Books], it might have been a different story," he said. Krueger was not alone in questioning Farman's motives.

For the NASA scientists the initial embarrassment of having missed something so significant was tempered by having the world atmospheric-science community now look to the satellite data to verify Farman's observations. In findings formally reported in the August 1986 issue of *Nature,* Krueger, Richard Stolarski, and a team of four other NASA scientists announced that the *Nimbus* data from as far back as 1978 fully confirmed Farman's measurements. The average minimum level of ozone above Antarctica during the austral spring between 1979 and 1984 had decreased 40 percent, while the average maximum had fallen by 20 percent. From a minimum of 240 Dobson units in 1970, the low average springtime ozone level had, by 1984, dropped to 162 DU; the maximum was down from a 1970 reading of 484 DU to a 1984 measurement of 446 DU.

NASA's verdict was conclusive. The seasonal ozone depletion over Antarctica was on a scale totally unanticipated. It had created a hole in the stratosphere 18.8 million square kilometers in size, larger than the surface area of Antarctica and twice the size of the continental United States, a "croissant-shaped patch of stratosphere" according to the *Atlantic Monthly,* an "ozone hole."

Ozone hole. To most people the phrase sounded like something from *Star Trek* or an old Flash Gordon serial, and even some scientists at first said they doubted whether such a thing could really exist. But others recalled Michael Prather's hypothesis that ozone depletion might not always be linear, that it would under certain conditions occur suddenly, with catastrophic effect, and they could not help but feel a chill, for they were reminded of the kind of total breakdown of a natural system that modern environmentalists like Rachel Carson had warned of for so long.

Before publishing Joseph Farman's article describing the Antarctic ozone hole, the editors of *Nature* had distributed several copies in manuscript form for scientific peer review. One copy was sent to Susan Solomon of the NOAA Aeronomy Lab in Boulder. Solomon was regarded as something of a prodigy by her fellow scientists. After completing her graduate work under two of the world's most respected atmospheric scientists, chemist Harold Johnston at Berkeley and meteorologist Paul Crutzen at NCAR, she had authored a textbook on atmospheric chemistry and had won the prestigious McElwane Award of the American Geophysical Union, all before turning thirty. While the process by which the Farman paper had come to her was more or less random, she was ideally qualified to appreciate its contents, for her twin specialties were atmospheric chemistry and dynamics, the science of air motions. Since joining the NOAA lab she had worked primarily in an area known as "coupling"—modeling interactions between chemical and dynamical mechanisms in the atmosphere.

Sitting in her office leafing through the Farman paper, Solomon later said, she had no premonition that the dozen or so pages she held in her hands were destined to change her life. "The possibility that the stratospheric ozone layer could be depleted by half at certain latitudes and seasons," she explained, "would have been deemed a preposterous and alarmist suggestion in the early 1980s.

"The idea was so incredible, I think my first response was to wonder 'Who are these people, are they crazy?' But what was so convincing was the good job they had done. Their theory cited a very specific seasonal variation, and they had years of good data and measurements from two ground locations."

The paper's disturbing message was still much on her mind after it appeared in print in May 1985, and when Solomon spoke by phone with Sherry Rowland, they shared their impression that Farman's observation was important. Solomon had met Rowland the previous summer at a scientific conference in Feldafing, West Germany, where Rowland, following up on the work he and Molina had performed in 1976 with chlorine nitrate reservoirs, had presented (with Don Wuebbles of the Lawrence Livermore Laboratory and Haruo Sato of UC-Irvine) a paper suggesting that reservoir chemistry involving molecules of hydrogen chlorine and chlorine nitrate could deplete ozone by 32 percent. This astounding depletion rate was explained by "heterogeneous" chemistry, in which chemical processes that ordinarily take place in gas phase are sped up by the presence of a surface on which they can occur. The natural processes of ozone destruction and regeneration described in the Chapman mechanism, as well as all the various ozone-depleting catalytic chains involving chlorine, nitrogen, and hydrogen, are "homogeneous" reactions. In their gaseous state, molecules bounce around and eventually may or may not collide with one another—*homogeneous reactions*. But the introduction of a relatively stationary surface can drastically speed up these reactions because there is much less random molecular movement involved—*heterogeneous reactions*.

With NCAR scientist Rolando Garcia, Solomon had attempted to see if they could computer-model the Antarctic ozone loss Farman had described. Their results could not completely account for the reported depletion. "Everyone tweaked their models hard to see if they would chew up ozone," Michael Prather later recalled. "Not that their mechanisms didn't work, but most models could only account for about ten to twenty percent of the large reported loss." When Solomon plugged in Rowland, Wuebbles, and Sato's data on heterogeneous reactions with hydrogen chloride and chlorine nitrate, however, the results began to conform to the drastic Antarctic depletion.

Heterogeneous chemistry, it appeared, might be playing a role in that depletion. But what surface was involved? Rowland and Wuebbles's swift heterogeneous reactions had occurred on the glass wall of the laboratory reactor vessel. There were no glass beakers floating around in the stratosphere. It was possible that volcanic particles were responsible. In April 1982 the Mexican volcano El Chichón had erupted, strewing volcanic debris into the atmosphere and creating the ideal conditions for ozone-depleting heterogeneous reactions to occur. Rowland, Wuebbles, and Sato had cited this in their 1984 paper, explaining that the surfaces of the sulphuric particles from El Chichón were behaving as a template for the accelerated release of atomic chlorine. However, it was doubtful that volcanic particles alone could explain a perturbation as severe or localized as the ozone hole.

By the fall of 1985, Susan Solomon was convinced that heterogeneous chemistry was contributing to the perturbation of ozone above Antarctica in the austral spring, but her inability to identify a surface on which the heterogeneous reactions were occurring rendered the theory all but useless. Then, at a meeting of the American Geophysical Union in San Francisco in early December, she heard a presentation on the topic of polar stratospheric clouds by University of Wyoming aeronomer Dave Hofmann, a veteran atmospheric balloonist with many seasons of experience in Antarctica.

PSCs, as the clouds are known, form at altitudes of 10 to 20 kilometers. They thrive in the extreme cold of the polar stratosphere, beginning as a haze of liquid droplets of nitrogen compounds and water, which freeze as temperatures plummet. The colder the temperatures, the larger the ice particles that form the clouds. There are more PSCs over Antarctica than over the Arctic, Hofmann reported to the San Francisco conference, because the polar vortex in the south is stronger, and it creates colder conditions at stratospheric altitudes.

The clouds had been observed since the early days of Antarctic exploration. Located at such a tremendous altitude that they reflect the sun's light even when the sun is well below the horizon, they were first mentioned in the logs of nineteenth-century sailing vessels as mysterious "illuminated objects" high in the night polar sky. They were often confused with stars or bursts of light from the aurora, and were considered just one more scientific oddity peculiar to the Antarctic region. Serious scientific consideration of PSCs did not begin until 1982, when NASA scientist M. Patrick McCormick started compiling systematic observations using an instrument positioned on *Nimbus 7*, the stratospheric aerosol measurement (SAM).

McCormick's satellite data demonstrated that PSCs remain in the stratosphere above Antarctica all through the long, dark, austral winter. As Hofmann later explained, "Prior to that, we didn't see them all the time, so we couldn't assume they were there all the time." One of Hofmann's charts at the AGU meeting showed the vertical profile of PSCs, which increase dramatically between 10 and 25 kilometers. Solomon noted that the vertical profile of the clouds correlated almost exactly with the vertical profile of ozone depletion reported in satellite data. "Suddenly," Solomon later said, "it all just clicked into place."

Solomon immediately phoned Rowland to report her germ of a theory that heterogeneous reactions on PSCs could be the cause of the ozone hole. At around the same time, NASA officially reported that El Chichón's effects on the Antarctic atmosphere had begun to diminish after 1983, and could not be considered a major factor in the current observed ozone loss over Antarctica. After further consultation with Dave Hofmann, Solomon organized the authorship of a scientific paper, later published in *Nature*, in collaboration with Rowland, Don Wuebbles, and Rolando Garcia, describing PSCs as the reservoir for rapid chlorine chain reactions leading to ozone depletion in the Antarctic stratosphere.

One key piece of evidence the paper cited was that the austral spring ozone depletions were occurring at an altitude between 10 and 20 kilometers. Homogeneous chemistry could not account for such a large depletion at this altitude because the bulk of chlorine in the stratosphere is normally located much higher up. It would be found in the 10-to-20-kilometer range only if it had become tied up in some kind of reservoir. During the austral winter, according to the theory Solomon and her colleagues proposed, the PSCs "froze" the chlorine reservoirs of hydrogen chloride and chlorine nitrate at temperatures as low as $-120°F$. At the first sunlight of austral spring in late September, as temperatures rose to about $-80°F$, the sun's rays caused chlorine dioxide to dissociate and produce two atoms of chlorine. This rapid heterogeneous reaction freed huge amounts of atomic chlorine to scavenge ozone, causing the large, sudden depletion Farman had charted each year at that precise time. Not until early November, when air from the mid-latitudes finally broke down the polar vortex, did additional ozone arrive and restore a kind of equilibrium. By then, of course, a major removal of ozone had occurred.

This comprehensive explanation—accompanied by one from Harvard's Mike McElroy, Steve Wofsy, Ross Salawitch, and Jennifer Logan, which focused on heterogeneous reactions involving bromine compounds—became the basis for what became known as the chemical or photochemical theory of Antarctic ozone depletion. But as thorough as the Solomon and McElroy papers may have been, their central hypothesis was not universally accepted. Many scientists did not believe chemistry alone could account for the ozone hole. Heterogeneous chemistry in general was suspected in many quarters of being a convenient catchall, a kind of "theory of last resort" that researchers turned to in desperation when no other plausible explanation came to hand. Additionally, chlorine catalysis was known to work most effectively at altitudes of 35 to 45 kilometers, so to many the suggestion that chlorine chemistry was causing the severe perturbation in the lower Antarctic stratosphere (10 to 20 kilometers) seemed highly unlikely.

The interdisciplinary nature of atmospheric science was never more evident than when physicists, spectroscopists, chemists, meteorologists, and aeronomers began debating the cause of the ozone hole. Many researchers became convinced that the solution must lay in the work *they* had been pursuing for years, and the high public profile of the problem exacerbated professional jealousies. Physicists, for instance, felt that to explain ozone depletion in the polar nighttime would require a solar or geomagnetic theory of some kind, while meteorologists believed it was possible that the winds and plunging temperatures of the polar vortex were simply moving the ozone around, not depleting it. There was, among some, a disapproving belief that Rowland (a photochemist) and Solomon (a modeler of atmospheric chemistry) had, because of their own predispositions, rushed to the conclusion that there must be a chemical explanation for the hole.

Linwood B. Callis of NASA's research center at Langley, Virginia, was the most prominent among a small group of scientists who linked the reported fluctuations in Antarctic ozone levels to changes in solar activity. Since the ozone layer can be depleted by active nitrogen compounds, Callis theorized that abnormally high levels of these molecules were being produced in the atmosphere by blasts of energetic particles from the sun. These solar particles zoom in on the poles because of earth's magnetic field, and are drawn into the stratosphere by the powerful polar vortex winds. The odd nitrogen, as this species of sun-created active nitrogen compound is called, can remain in the polar stratosphere for five years. As Callis pointed out, 1979 had seen one of the most intense periods of solar activity in centuries, creating sufficient quantities of odd nitrogen to promote the continuing depletion of ozone above Antarctica.

Callis's conclusions had some historical basis, for after a burst of solar activity in 1958 there had been a drop in global ozone levels. Hal Johnston had theorized that the real depth of the ozone losses in 1958 had probably been obscured by a sudden rise in the amount of ozone caused by the cessation of atmospheric nuclear testing in the early 1960s. Thus, it appeared possible that there had been an "ozone hole" at least once before due to solar activity, although its presence had not been fully measured.

This linking of odd nitrogen with large-scale destruction of ozone was at the heart of two other controversial theories. In the early 1970s, a group including Paul Crutzen contributed a paper to *Nature* suggesting that the extinction of the dinosaurs 65 million years ago may have been caused by sun-flare activity and a subsequent buildup of odd nitrogen; this drastic change in the atmospheric nitrogen budget resulted in massive ozone depletion and higher levels of ultraviolet light, to which the dinosaurs and other species could not adapt. John Hampson, the British scientist who had helped identify the hydrogen chain, was the author of a second frightening theory involving nitrogen. In 1974 he suggested the oxides of nitrogen released by a nuclear explosion would deplete the ozone layer to the extent that the damage to earth's UV shield would dwarf even the more immediate destruction from a nuclear war. After Hampson's paper appeared, Harvard's Michael McElroy and other atmospheric scientists became concerned about the threat, and the NAS convened a conference on the subject in January 1975. Its panel of experts confirmed Hampson's theory: if half the world's 1974 stockpile of weapons were exploded, about ten thousand megatons, the ozone over the northern hemisphere would be reduced by between 30 and 70 percent; over the southern hemisphere, where fewer people lived and there were fewer potential nuclear targets, depletion would reach 20 to 40 percent. Such percentages would have certainly sufficed to bring an end to the dinosaurs, and would likely do so again to other species, including humans.

Another theory put forward to explain the ozone hole involved the Antarctic vortex. The "dynamics theory" originated with Mark Schoeberl, a NASA scientist who had been asked by Richard Stolarski to draw up a computerized "movie" of the depletion based on the agency's satellite data. In early 1986 Schoeberl uncovered data indicating that not only ozone levels but also temperatures had been dropping above the southern polar cap since 1979. To Schoeberl this suggested that a powerful movement of air into the "depleted" area might be the cause of the ozone hole, for if temperatures high in the atmosphere were very cold, it meant warmer air from the troposphere would then be drawn upward, what dynamicists called an "upwelling." This upwelling would displace, not deplete, stratospheric ozone. Other scientists who weighed in on the side of the dynamics explanation included TOMS designer Arlin Krueger, Princeton meteorologist Jerry Mahlman, and a newcomer to the ozone debate, Ka Kit Tung of the State University of New York at Potsdam.

The growing controversy about the cause of the ozone hole represented more than just differing scientific interpretations of existing data. It reflected the diverse instinctual responses among scientists and policy-makers to the threat of large-scale ecological change. As one scientist had remarked of the odd-nitrogen theory, "It's kind of nice because it's a natural solution." A faith in nature's benevolence or, conversely, the conviction that the environment was highly vulnerable to manmade changes, could not help but influence the debate and directly contribute to the formulation of scientific theory. While this was not atypical of how science works, to Sherry Rowland the pace was excruciatingly slow. Was it really necessary to hear every argument and collect each last bit of data before acting to limit the production of CFCs? Such deliberation, Rowland felt, was an undue courtesy to CFC manufacturers, and the cost of delay was much too high. "Industry always said that we'd have plenty of advance warning of any ozone problems," he commented bitterly in August 1986, "but now we've got a hole in our atmosphere that you could see from Mars."

18.

THE NATIONAL OZONE EXPEDITION

I N MARCH 1986, a NASA-sponsored scientific meeting in Boulder to discuss ground-based methods of ozone measurement turned into a contentious debate on the Antarctic ozone hole. The topic had been thrust onto the agenda by Susan Solomon; her paper describing the role of polar stratospheric clouds in the Antarctic depletion had not yet been published, but she insisted on speaking about the subject, and Mike McElroy and Dave Hofmann made related presentations. Debate ensued, prompted by scientists who favored a dynamical or odd-nitrogen explanation for the ozone hole. That did not surprise Solomon, McElroy, and Hofmann, although they were incredulous that, ten months after Joseph Farman's *Nature* article had appeared, so many of their colleagues still were unwilling to accept Farman's data or acknowledge the significance of his discovery. "The chance of it being a goof with Joe Farman was very small," NOAA Aeronomy Lab director Daniel Albritton, who attended the conference, later recalled, "although the possibility remained that it was a local Halley Bay phenomenon."

Robert Watson, head of NASA's atmospheric sciences program, chaired the meeting, and reacted to the discord by suggesting that the answer might be to send a scientific team to Antarctica to carry out balloon and ground-based observations of the ozone hole. This was a startling proposal, for any such expedition would have to be in place on the Ice by August in order to capture readings of the large depletion in the austral spring, and August was only five months away, hardly enough time for the extensive preparation that would be necessary. Hofmann, however, had already announced his intention to go to Antarctica in August on a "win-fly"—a special Navy flight into the U.S. base at McMurdo Sound before the "daybreak" of austral spring—to resume the Antarctic balloon research he had pursued since 1972. A handful of other scientists at the meeting expressed interest in going along. Most had never been to Antarctica. Watson suggested that the larger expedition could be built around Hofmann's plans.

Like NASA's Arlin Krueger, Dave Hofmann was an alumnus of the pioneering balloon program at the University of Minnesota. From Minnesota, Hofmann had moved on to the University of Wyoming at Laramie, which, to his delight, proved an even better location for upper-air balloon research than Minneapolis. The vast, nearly treeless Great Plains lay to the east of Laramie, and the prevailing winds always carried his sounding balloons in that direction. "There was nothing to it," Hofmann later explained. "You just had to follow the balloon in an aircraft and, when it descended, talk a truck in by radio." In over five hundred flights from Laramie, Hofmann and his colleagues never lost a single balloon.

Hofmann's specialty was stratospheric aerosols, the layer of particles in the lower stratosphere, emanating from a variety of sources—plant and animal decomposition, volcanoes, meteors—that had been discovered in 1962 by Christian Junge at the University of Mainz in West Germany. Aerosols in the so-called Junge layer are mostly sulphuric, but also can include trace amounts of nitric acid, chlorine, and bromine. These constituents are sometimes referred to as "natural pollutants," and the study of their behavior in the atmosphere is analogous to the observation of man-made trace gases.

Hofmann had resisted joining the rush away from balloon science to satellites in the 1970s. "I'm just an *in situ* man," he reflected later. "When everyone else went into satellites, I thought, 'Hell, someone's got to stick around and do the ground truth.'" In 1972 he conducted some of the first high-altitude balloon research ever based in Antarctica.

With his background in natural atmospheric pollutants, including chlorine, Hofmann was intrigued by the Rowland-Molina theory, and in 1976, two years after its publication, he confirmed through high-altitude balloon testing a tenet central to the theory: chlorofluorocarbon molecules in the atmosphere were broken apart by the shorter waves of UV light. Following the eruption of El Chichón in 1982, he measured the higher chlorine levels the volcano had introduced into the atmosphere, but did not investigate heterogeneous surface reactions that took place on the surfaces of the volcanic material. Neither did Hofmann at first suspect that the polar stratospheric clouds he was studying played a role in ozone depletion, but a week after hearing him describe PSCs in San Francisco, Susan Solomon called to ask if he would mind stopping in at her office at NOAA the next time he came through Boulder. "I have an idea about particles," she told him.

When Hofmann returned to Boulder for the NASA meeting in early 1986, he brought his own Antarctic data, gathered in October 1985, which showed severe ozone depletion. Listening to the general discussion, he realized that the odd-nitrogen theory had little or no support, and that if the controversy came down to a chemical versus a dynamical explanation, his balloon measurements could provide the answer. If the upwelling or "fountain effect" of air the dynamicists described was taking place, his instruments would be able to detect it.

Returning to Washington from Boulder, Robert Watson leapt to the task of assembling scientists for an Antarctic expedition. Within days he had compiled a short list of obvious names to be invited to take part: in addition to Dave Hofmann, Crofton "Barney" Farmer of NASA's Jet Propulsion Lab in Pasadena had done infrared balloon measurements of ozone and other trace gases and had put a solar viewing instrument aboard the space shuttle *Challenger*; Philip Solomon and Bob De Zafra from the State University of New York at Stony Brook had a ground-based microwave device that measured chlorine monoxide, the decomposition product of ozone depletion; at Boulder's NOAA Aeronomy Lab, Art Schmeltekopf had an instrument that measured nitrogen dioxide but could be converted to measure chlorine monoxide.

Watson's confidence the project could be organized quickly stemmed partly from the fact that NASA, alone among government science agencies, maintained no review program for experimental proposals. His approval alone would be enough to get the various experiments funded. There was one change made, however, in the lineup of scientific personnel. When Schmeltekopf said he wouldn't be available to make the trip to Antarctica, Susan Solomon surprised everyone by volunteering to go in his place. She was a computer modeler, with no expertise whatsoever in making ground-based measurements, but she knew Schmeltekopf's instrument was, as she later explained, "so easy to operate, even a monkey could do it—literally." NOAA aeronomy lab chief Albritton not only welcomed Solomon's decision, he recommended that Solomon be designated the expedition leader, citing her dual background in dynamics and chemistry, as well as her natural leadership abilities.

The instrument Solomon's team would be using had been designed by Schmeltekopf and another NOAA scientist, named John Noxon, and originally had measured nitrogen dioxide at twilight using the Umkehr effect. *Umkehr* in German means "to bend back," and the Umkehr effect refers to the low angle of the sun at twilight as its absorption bands of light bend and widen, allowing scientists a more detailed view of molecules in the atmosphere. Noxon was fascinated by the connection between solar "proton events"—the bursts of powerful energy occasionally released by the sun—and the production of oxides of nitrogen in the upper atmosphere, the same mechanism Crutzen, Heath, and Krueger had charted in 1972. Whenever significant solar activity was reported, NOAA colleagues later recalled, Noxon would load the instrument he and Schmeltekopf had designed into his pickup truck and head north toward Canada, where the higher latitude provided a longer twilight and enhanced Umkehr readings.

Noxon also took a great interest in the polar vortex, and in the rapid chemical changes that occur in the atmosphere when the vortex breaks up in the spring. Years before the report of the ozone hole, he had observed that nitrogen dioxide became suppressed in the high polar atmosphere during winter, a tendency neither he nor other NOAA researchers could explain. Only later did Susan Solomon and others realize that Noxon had actually discovered a natural process related to the seasonal ozone loss—nitrogen being removed from the polar atmosphere to form chlorine nitrate reservoirs. Had Noxon's observation been more thoroughly investigated at the time, Solomon later explained, NOAA scientists might have come much earlier to an understanding of the chemistry that was ultimately shown to cause the ozone hole. Indeed, Noxon's expertise and knowledge of the vortex would have been ideally suited to the challenge his NOAA colleagues faced in Antarctica, a fact that only compounded the tragedy of his suicide in Boulder in early 1985, just weeks before the Farman paper crossed Solomon's desk.

For SUNY–Stony Brook scientist Philip Solomon (no relation to Susan), Watson's invitation to take part in the expedition to Antarctica was a fitting reward for a career decision made in the mid-1970s. A pioneer in radio astronomy, or the study of the radio-frequency radiation emitted by celestial bodies, Solomon had been working with giant molecular clouds, the most massive objects in the galaxy, when he heard from a friend at Harvard about the Rowland-Molina theory. His colleague suggested to Solomon that radio astronomy could be adapted to detect the presence of molecules like chlorine monoxide in the upper atmosphere.

Solomon was intrigued. "Astronomy, as pure science, is more exciting than environmental science," he later explained, "but environmental science seemed to offer a chance to do something useful. And frankly, that's where the action and the money were, the research money to build an instrument capable of detecting a fine trace gas like chlorine. So I got involved, and began to build up a group at Stony Brook."

NASA, to whom Solomon turned first for funding, however, was not interested in funding a radio, or microwave, device because in general the agency favored airborne, not ground-based, experiments. In addition, there seemed to be some doubt that the technology Solomon's proposal described would work. All molecules rotate and give off characteristic radio-frequency signals that can be used to identify them, but the detection of chlorine by microwave would be difficult because of the very faint signal molecular chlorine emits and its relative sparsity in the atmosphere. Ozone, at 1 part per million, is fairly easy to locate using the method; chlorine, however, is present at natural levels of only 1 part per billion, and accordingly is a thousand times harder to find. Indeed, the use of microwave technology in the stratosphere, first suggested in 1962 and carried out in experiments throughout the late 1960s, was almost always limited to detecting trace quantities of ozone, carbon monoxide, and water vapor, all of which are relatively abundant in the upper air and all of which produce strong signals.

Solomon had better luck when he approached the Chemical Manufacturers Association (CMA, formerly the Manufacturing Chemists Association). The CMA's sympathies were, of course, biased, but its Fluorocarbon Program Panel had, in Solomon's opinion, "many respected scientists on it." The CMA made no secret of its hope that Solomon's investigation, when finished, would help prove that CFCs were *not* responsible for ozone depletion, but Solomon was satisfied the CMA would not attempt to interfere with his conclusions.

When Bob Watson phoned in March 1986, Phil Solomon had been making chlorine measurements with the microwave instrument he had built for nearly six years, and he eagerly accepted the invitation to go to Antarctica.

Barney Farmer of Pasadena's Jet Propulsion Lab had followed a route somewhat similar to Phil Solomon's, from astrophysics to atmospheric physics, and had been drawn into the search for chlorine in Earth's atmosphere during the Climatic Impact Assessment Program. His first efforts in chlorine detection convinced him of the chlorine chain's potential for rapid ozone destruction. Following up work done by Richard Stolarski on chlorine emissions from the space shuttle, Farmer used a sensing device on board a high-altitude U-2 aircraft to measure trace molecules in the wake of space-bound rockets, and found that the large chlorine-spewing rockets totally removed ozone from their path as they passed through the stratosphere.

Farmer was a veteran of an earlier Watson-run atmospheric science program, the Balloon Intercomparison Campaign (BIC), which NASA conducted in 1983 at the National Science Balloon Facility near Palestine, Texas. BIC's objective was to use a large number of diverse balloon-borne measuring instruments to simultaneously measure key molecules and observe how the different instruments functioned in relation to one another when conditions and study objectives were the same. BIC was, in Farmer's esteem, "a nice piece of science," calling for simultaneous balloon launches of multiple-instrument balloons. This logistical challenge, combined with the technical difficulties imposed by a shortage of high-quality balloon material, wreaked havoc at the launch facility. "We had balloons falling all over the sky," Farmer later explained.

Farmer was destined to suffer the greatest calamity of the BIC campaign. On the afternoon of June 21, 1983, a balloon carrying five instruments, including an expensive infrared device of Farmer's, and weighing about four thousand pounds, began to drift from its course. NASA officials, concerned that it might drift into commercial air-traffic lanes, ordered the balloon to be "cut down," its flight terminated by radio control. Its payload was then to fall gently back to earth by parachute. Because of the balloon's great altitude, however, there was not enough air pressure to open the parachute, and the heavily laden gondola free-fell for several thousand feet before sufficient pressure forced the chute open. By that time the speed of the descent was so great, nearly two hundred miles per hour, that the swivel piece connecting the chute to the gondola snapped off and the two tons of valuable scientific cargo plunged down toward the West Texas prairie like an incoming meteor. "When it went up, there was eighteen feet of scientific instrumentation on that gondola," Farmer later recalled. "It looked like a small apartment building. But when we found it, it was only three feet tall."

In the early summer of 1986, as Farmer, Hofmann, and the two Solomons readied their instruments, Watson's NASA associate James Margitan addressed the considerable question of logistical support for the Antarctic operation, which was now being called the National Ozone Expedition (NOZE). Putting a scientific program into Antarctica on such short notice would not be easy. Fortunately for NASA, Peter Wilkniss, director of the National Science Foundation's Office of Polar Programs, which directs all American Antarctic research, was completely sympathetic to the expedition's purpose. Wilkniss thought it terribly ironic that the ozone hole had been spotted "not by the multi-million-dollar fancy stuff we have up in the sky" but by the Dobson spectrophotometer, "a thousand-dollar instrument using technology from the 1920s."

Wilkniss had extensive research experience in Antarctica, working in the little-known field of chemical oceanography, or the study of trace molecules in the ocean and lower atmosphere. In 1972 he had been part of a Navy research group that had experimented with James Lovelock's CFC-measuring device in tests in the Antarctic Ocean. Lovelock himself had trained the Navy group in the use of the instrument. As in the lower atmosphere, CFCs make good tracers of ocean currents because of their stability and well-known production history. In water, CFCs are even more durable than in the air; Wilkness and the chemical oceanographers estimated that CFCs could take as long as a thousand years to travel from the equator to one of the earth's poles. The scientists also used the CFCs to date sea-bottom water masses, much the way glaciologists use the layers of volcanic ash residue in deep ice cores.

"The Lovelock machine weighed only a couple of pounds," Wilkniss later recalled, "yet it was so fine in measuring concentration levels it was unbelievable." One of the experiments called for the Navy team to gauge to what extent waterborne CFCs used in industrial nations to the north were making their way down toward the South Pole. Like most polar scientists, Wilkniss thought of Antarctica as one of nature's last unspoiled treasures, and he was troubled when the experiment showed that CFCs were present in the polar seas. This was nothing compared to the indignation he felt when the Farman paper appeared in 1985. "It was like a bombshell," Wilkniss remembered. "We were completely overwhelmed. A place which had never produced a single CFC, had never even used CFCs, had become the first place to suffer from them."

The NOZE expedition would not represent the first time a group of Americans had rushed off to Antarctica in an effort to explain a scientific enigma. Congress and the Navy had, ironically, launched U.S. Antarctic science in the early nineteenth century in response to a similar public and scientific concern about a supposed "hole at the pole."

The scientific fascination with the Antarctic terra incognita was sparked in April 1818, when Ohio naturalist John Cleves Symmes, Jr., a decorated veteran of the War of 1812, announced in a prominent broadside:

[T]he Earth is hollow and habitable within, containing a number of solid concentric spheres, one within the other and . . . it is open at the poles twelve or sixteen degrees. I pledge my life in support of this truth and am ready to explore the hollow, if the World will support and aid me in the undertaking. . . .

Symmes's claim was an elaboration of a belief common among early polar explorers, such as William Edward Parry and Benjamin Morrell, Jr., that there were warm, ice-free open seas around the north and south poles. Sir John Barrow, who presided over England's prolific exploration of the Arctic in the early 1800s, was particularly influential. So trusting were the British of Sir John, some polar expeditions did not even bother to bring warm clothes. The American, Symmes, took the "Open Polar Sea" concept quite a bit further, predicting that the warm poles themselves were openings in the earth approximately two thousand miles in diameter, the one at the South Pole being slightly larger. "Symmes's holes," they were called.

Beginning in 1820, Symmes toured the country extensively to lecture on his theory, his travels financed by a young Ohio newspaper editor named Jeremiah N. Reynolds, who touted Symmes as "the American Newton." With Reynolds as his advocate, Symmes and his theory proved far more durable than many would have believed possible. By the time his followers forwarded a petition to Congress in 1822 demanding that the United States send an expedition to investigate Symmes's claim, it bore the signatures of no fewer than fifty members of the Pennsylvania legislature.

The acceptance of so absurd an idea, and the popularity of the "Hollow Earth Movement," as it was termed, was nourished by the country's emerging nationalism and a related desire to believe in the potential of American, as opposed to European, scientific genius. Even those who most loudly criticized Symmes's homegrown thesis could not help but support his efforts to mount a polar expedition. One critic agreed to donate the proceeds from the sale of a printed attack on the hollow-earth theory in order to help fund Symmes's cause.

When in the mid-1820s Symmes tired of the lecture circuit, Reynolds became the movement's standard-bearer. He stood in front of audiences holding a model of Symmes's hollow world and, diluting Symmes's original hypothesis somewhat by conceding the inner earth was probably not habitable, argued with great reasonableness that no one would ever know whether the hollow-earth theory was correct until an expedition was launched to find out. The idea was particularly attractive to the New

England whalers and sealers who knew the southern latitudes to be potentially lucrative hunting grounds. By the early 1830s an alliance of public, scientific, and mercantile interests, led by Reynolds, demanded of Congress that the bottom of the world—be it land, sea, ice, or hole—be explored by an American party.

In 1836 Congress allocated $300,000 for a United States Southern Exploring Expedition to visit the Antarctic Ocean under the command of career naval officer Lieutenant Charles Wilkes. The Wilkes expedition, which sailed from Norfolk, Virginia, on August 18, 1838, with 325 men, including naturalists, mapmakers, artists, botanists, and other observers, was one of the first large government-sponsored scientific undertakings in American history.

Unfortunately, the expedition did not go smoothly. The six reconditioned ships Wilkes had been given were inadequate for the task of venturing amid the ice floes of Antarctica. One vessel was lost with all hands. The rigors of the voyage, and the stormy demeanor of Wilkes, a stern authoritarian not even popular with his fellow officers, led to near-mutinous conditions. The pressure on the expedition to attain some tangible sign of success was increased by the presence in the Antarctic Ocean of competing French and British discovery expeditions. Wilkes sighted Antarctica in mid-January 1840 and charted its coastline for several days before sailing to New Zealand. Leaving New Zealand, he traversed the Pacific, surveyed the North American coast along what is now Oregon and Washington, then recrossed the Pacific to the Philippines, eventually returning to New York around the Cape of Good Hope in June 1842.

The homecoming the returning seafarers received was perhaps the most indifferent in the annals of nineteenth-century exploration. Not one official of the government that had dispatched the expedition bothered to attend when the ships docked in New York Harbor, and Wilkes, making his way to Washington a few days later, was received coldly by the new president, John Tyler. Political sympathy for the expedition had soured in its absence, and the venture was being cited by Tyler's Whig administration as typical of the wastefulness of the previous Democratic president Andrew Jackson. Worse still, the British explorer James Clark Ross had charged that Wilkes had falsified his sightings of land in Antarctica, and complaints about excessive corporal punishment on board ship had led Secretary of the Navy A. P. Upshur to bring court-martial charges against Wilkes.

The ensuing inquiry found Wilkes guilty of excessive and illegal punishments. Although the government chose to wash its hands of Wilkes and his troubled enterprise, the far-ranging voyage—the first U.S. expedition to circumnavigate the globe—actually produced a large number of scientific achievements. Apart from making the first official U.S. visit to Antarctica, it increased the number of ocean depth soundings, a great help to the designation of mercantile sea-lanes, charted nearly three hundred Pacific islands, and after inland exploration of the Northwest, described likely overland routes for settlers to follow into the Oregon Territory. Meanwhile, the collection of zoological specimens the naturalists who accompanied Wilkes had collected became the basis for the country's first museum of natural history. And in 1947 an airborne U.S. surveying program confirmed the accuracy of Wilkes's disputed 1840 landfall sighting.

The Wilkes expedition was equally a scientific and cultural milestone, establishing a beachhead for American exploration in Antarctica while stimulating American literary and artistic fascination with the high seas and the terra incognita of the southern polar region. For a place where no one lived, and where few had even set foot, Antarctica and the South Seas developed a substantial literary tradition by the mid-nineteenth century. A reader could choose between gripping factual narratives by explorers such as James Cook, George Shelvocke, and Edmund Fanning; fictionalized adaptations by Jeremiah Reynolds; the science fiction of Edgar Allan Poe; or even the bizarre *Symzonia: A Voyage of Discovery,* written in 1820 by "Adam Seaborn"—possibly Symmes himself—and describing an imaginary civilization inside the earth entered from the open South Pole. And Herman Melville's pitiless, obsessed sea captain, Ahab, was thought by many to have been modeled after Charles Wilkes.

The earliest travels to Antarctica were motivated by curiosity and a desire for knowledge, yet the prevailing cultural image of Antarctica perpetuated by popular literature and poetry, notably that of the English poet Samuel Taylor Coleridge and Poe, was that the bottom of the world contained horrors best left undisturbed.

This tradition probably began with Coleridge, who used Cook's narrative and an incident described in Shelvocke's *Voyage Round the World, by the Way of the Great South Sea,* as the basis for his epic poem *The Rime of the Ancient Mariner,* written in 1798. In Coleridge's story of a seafarer who kills an albatross and suffers a doomed Antarctic voyage, Antarctica —complete with mists and whirlpools—becomes a zone beyond human rationality, where the familiar is turned inside out and the physical world appears fantastic or grotesque. Poe invoked this same Antarctica in the short story "MS. Found in a Bottle," again in "The Unparalleled Adventure of One Hans Pfaall," and ultimately in his only novel-length work, *The Narrative of Arthur Gordon Pym of Nantucket.*

The story begins with the teenaged Pym, pining to go to sea, encouraged by his friend Augustus to stow away on a whaling ship captained by Augustus's father. After a series of incredible disasters, including murder, shipwreck, starvation, and cannibalism, Pym and a sole companion drift in a canoe into the frigid Antarctic Ocean, then enter the warm polar sea of Antarctica. "White ashy material" begins to fall around them; then, records Pym, "we rushed into the embraces of a cataract, where a chasm threw itself open to receive us. But there arose in our pathway a shrouded human figure, very far larger in its proportions than any dweller among men. And the hue of the skin of the figure was of the perfect whiteness of the snow." Here the saga of Arthur Gordon Pym abruptly and mysteriously ends.

One hundred and fifty years after Poe's strange novella enthralled readers, Antarctica had lost little of its obscurity or incoherence, even for scientists, as they confronted the menacing ozone hole above the South Pole. "Atmospheric scientists are struggling to explain one of the strangest mysteries ever to confront them," reported the *New York Times* at the end of July 1986, a "sudden, highly localized hemorrhaging." The article quoted NASA's Mark Schoeberl, who warned: "Just as an earthquake precedes volcanic eruptions, this could be a signal of something worse. It could be the leading edge of something more detrimental. It could expand outward to more populated areas. We just don't know right now."

Susan Solomon and the other specialists who traveled south to Antarctica in 1986 stood at a historic crossroads. Despite the sophistication of its methods—its satellites, spectrometers, and super-computer modeling—science had awakened suddenly to find an ominous environmental disaster unfolding in a cold, uninhabitable place man had never fully understood.

19.

THE SPIRIT OF LEESBURG

THE DISCOVERY OF A HOLE in the ozone layer over Antarctica was not enough to convince the CFC industry that further controls on CFCs were finally warranted. To the contrary, in anticipation of renewed regulatory efforts, industry went on the offensive. In a speech before a March 6, 1986, EPA workshop, Alliance for Responsible CFC Policy chairman Richard Barnett called it "disconcerting" that "before the ink was dry on [the Vienna] Convention to Protect the Ozone Layer"—which the alliance had supported because it stopped short of mandatory controls—"the call was out to begin to regulate." For years industry had argued that atmospheric models were insufficiently reliable to be the basis for regulation. Now Barnett went on to say something quite different: "Atmospheric model calculations of all substances thought to affect ozone continue to suggest that no significant change in total ozone will occur through the next several decades." In the next breath he discounted concern about the ozone hole, arguing that "no plausible mechanism has been proposed to explain this phenomenon." Since the models hadn't predicted the ozone hole, there was no basis for assuming it was CFC-related. To be sure, some atmospheric scientists questioned the possible link between CFCs and the ozone hole for precisely the same reason. But it was striking that given a choice between the reality of the ozone hole and the projections offered by computer models, industry suddenly preferred the comfort of the models.

Many participants in the international and domestic regulation process took a similar approach. Given the lack of consensus among atmospheric scientists as to the cause of the ozone hole, and pending the results of NASA's National Ozone Expedition, scheduled to reach Antarctica in late August 1986, government and industry representatives tacitly agreed to leave the Antarctic perturbation out of their discussions. It was understood that if science eventually proved CFCs were to blame for the ozone hole, the argument for swift and comprehensive regulations would be greatly strengthened. But the advocates of regulation also knew there was a risk in citing the ozone hole to further their cause: if they won new guidelines on that basis, and it later turned out they were wrong, their victory would likely be overturned and their further efforts discredited.

Thus, each side in the debate preferred to argue theoretical ozone depletion, even though a catastrophic example of the real thing now appeared to exist.

Faced with these constraints, and new to international diplomacy, the EPA's John Hoffman and Steve Seidel entered the fray at the first of two scheduled UNEP workshops in Rome at the end of May 1986. The workshop, hosted by the European Community and chaired by Britain, was supposed to be devoted to the future demand for CFCs and the feasibility of technical controls, but it quickly degenerated into the old argument between the Toronto Group, which championed an international aerosol ban, and the European Community, which favored a production-capacity cap. Delegates to the workshop strongly disagreed on reports of then-current CFC production figures, and could not even begin to agree on the projections for future rates of growth, or the costs and effects of the hypothetical controls that had been suggested. Failure to achieve consensus on the past and present rendered all discussion of the future meaningless.

"We were devastated," Hoffman later said, recalling his and Seidel's disappointment with their first experience at an international CFC conference. "I realized that in aggressively pursuing an international aerosol ban we were pursuing a policy that was absolutely suicidal. The Europeans had come to Rome prepared to defend their proposal for a production-capacity cap and oppose an aerosol ban to the bitter end. When we talked about an aerosol ban, they thought we were reopening prior negotiations. I came away from the meeting convinced that we were dead if we didn't change our approach."

There had been only one evening during the Rome workshop when the delegates weren't at one another's throats. That was at a dinner held in a villa just outside the city where the participants relaxed and got to talk about something other than CFCs. Hoffman resolved to use the experience as a model for the second international workshop, which the United States was scheduled to host in Washington in September 1986. The subject of the workshop was supposed to be alternative regulatory strategies for international control of CFCs, but so far as Hoffman was concerned the issue had become more basic than that. The challenge was "to change the character of how the people involved in the meetings were relating to each other."

Hoffman and Richard Benedick, who was the State Department's chief negotiator in the ozone talks, booked the September CFC workshop into the Xerox Corporation's conference facility in rural Leesburg, Virginia, and scheduled numerous informal events, including a barbecue and square dance, to help create a mood of congeniality. Their most strategic maneuver, however, was to announce on the first day of the workshop that the United States no longer believed an international aerosol ban was a viable control policy. Deprived of the issue that had been the focus of their resistance, the Europeans were left with no option but to approach the issue from a fresh perspective. The shift in the U.S. position and the relaxed mood of the conference succeeded in creating a new, less confrontational atmosphere for future negotiations. Ambassador Benedick, in his closing address to the participants, dubbed it "the spirit of Leesburg."

In his talk Benedick cited the emergence of "broad areas of agreement" at the conference, including the fundamental agreement that "the ozone layer has been, is being, and will continue to be adversely affected by the long-lived chlorine molecules which stem from *all* CFC products." Moreover, he concluded, the risks of ozone depletion were now "considered by virtually all countries as sufficiently serious as to warrant control actions."

The new international consensus achieved at Leesburg ended the debate between advocates of a global aerosol ban and advocates of a production-capacity cap; it shifted the negotiations toward more fruitful discussions of appropriate limits of global CFC emissions and equity among nations. For the first time since the UNEP negotiations had begun, some kind of binding international protocol to restrict CFC production appeared to be within reach. On September 16, 1986, just after the international workshop adjourned, the Alliance for Responsible CFC Policy bowed to this likelihood and issued a surprise announcement, calling on the U.S. government to "work in cooperation with the world community under the auspices of the United Nations Environment Program to consider establishing a reasonable global limit on the future rate of growth of fully halogenated CFC production capacity."

In addition to the changing tides of international opinion, another factor behind the alliance's change of heart was a chorus of negative publicity the industry had received following the publication in the June 9, 1986, issue of the *New Yorker* of an article by Paul Brodeur. The story was Brodeur's second on ozone depletion for the magazine—the first, published in April 1975, described the aerosol-ban controversy in the United States. Revisiting the issue over a decade later, and reviewing the long history of industry's resistance to CFC controls, Brodeur did not mask his dismay that the production of CFCs had continued unabated. He quoted a weary and disgusted Sherry Rowland at length. Rowland cited many reasons for what Brodeur called "a failure on the part of society to come to grips with an issue whose consequences were less than certain," including "indecisiveness on the part of the scientific community, timidity on the part of the regulatory agencies, ignorance on the part of the public, inconsistency on the part of the press, indifference on the part of other nations, and obstruction and obfuscation on the part of industry."

"Chemists," Rowland said, "have tended to feel stigmatized by all the adverse publicity that has surrounded their profession in recent years. Their reaction to environmental problems caused by chemicals—whether it's the pollution of Love Canal, the contamination of ground water, or the destruction of the ozone layer—is frequently a defensive withdrawal from public involvement. Many of them are convinced that such problems are either nonexistent or grossly exaggerated. . . . Over the past eight years I have probably been to more than a hundred scientific meetings about the ozone problem—meetings that were attended by at least half of the thousand or so atmospheric scientists who are conversant with this problem—and I have never failed to wonder at how completely the sheer technical aspects of stratospheric science dominate such gatherings, and how little discussion, either formal or informal, is given to the implications of ozone depletion upon plants, crops, fish, weather, or, for that matter, human health."

Rowland also cited the influence upon science of research funding from industry, which, he said, may have discouraged scientists from speaking out in favor of regulatory action. Rowland said that assumptions as to what level of ozone depletion was acceptable were not based upon science, but represented "guesswork, crossed fingers, and wishful thinking."

Reminding Brodeur of a commitment Du Pont made in 1974 to cease production of CFCs if it was shown that they posed a threat to human health, Rowland said, "These days, the chlorofluorocarbon industry appears to have decided that it does not intend to consider any evidence credible as long as there is the slightest doubt about the validity of any part of the ozone-depletion hypothesis." Since uncertainty was inherent in the measurement of atmospheric change, and there would "always be discrepancies in mathematical models," Rowland said, "one can expect industry to keep on asking for more time. . . .

"What's the use of having developed a science well enough to make predictions," Rowland asked, "if in the end all we're willing to do is stand around and wait for them to come true?"

With the discovery of the ozone hole, his most dire prediction seemed to have come true. But he hardly felt vindicated. "It is pointless to waste time estimating what the production of chlorofluorocarbons will be in the year 2050," Rowland said, in reference to the arguments that had dominated a recent EPA workshop on the future demand for CFCs, "because the environmental consequences of their use will have long since overtaken us . . . the hole in the ozone layer above Antarctica is, unfortunately, just the beginning."

The industry response to the Brodeur piece was harsh and immediate. *Air Conditioning, Heating and Refrigeration News* headlined an editorial blasting the writer's reputation, REFRIGERANT MANUFACTURERS GET MUGGED IN "NEW YORKER" ARTICLE. "Not for nothing," the editorial fumed, had Brodeur been dubbed "the Toxic Journalist" by the *Wall Street Journal*. Evidence of the writer's alleged bias included his failure to mention "how CFCs have helped to raise the standard of living around the world" and his identification of the Alliance for Responsible CFC Policy as a "lobby," compared to his description of NRDC as "an organization."

But neither Brodeur nor Rowland was easily discredited. In October, within a few weeks of the alliance's announcement, Du Pont issued its own statement calling for "the development and adoption of a protocol under the United Nations Vienna Convention for the Protection of the Ozone Layer to limit worldwide CFC emissions."

Explaining the reasons behind the company's abrupt change of heart in a letter to Freon customers, Freon Products Division director Joseph P. Glas allowed the possibility that the Antarctic ozone hole and satellite measurements of total ozone depletion at higher latitudes could involve CFCs, and he noted that CFCs were possibly a greenhouse gas as well, raising new scientific questions and uncertainties. He acknowledged that CFC use worldwide was growing, and that all of the existing models predicted that sustained growth of the chemicals would result in significant ozone depletion.

"Because of the new questions and concerns," Glas wrote, "the inability of science to define a safe, sustainable emissions growth rate for CFCs, and the fact that resolution of these and other uncertainties is not likely in the near term, we have concluded that it would now be prudent to take further precautionary measures to limit CFCs worldwide while science works to provide policymakers with better guidance."

Du Pont's statement marked a complete turnabout in the corporation's position. The year before, the company had announced a major expansion of its CFC production capacity in Japan. For over a decade Du Pont had argued vehemently that until science was certain, regulations of CFCs would be inappropriate and unfair. Now, suddenly, Glas was willing to cite scientific uncertainty as the primary justification for implementing controls. Even more significant was the company's simultaneous announcement that environmentally acceptable and commercially viable alternatives to CFCs were within reach. All that stood between these alternatives and the marketplace were incentives in the form of regulatory policy. "If the necessary incentives were provided," Glas wrote in the letter to Freon customers, "we believe alternates could be introduced in volume in a time frame of roughly five years."

NRDC issued a press release hailing the company for its "act of corporate responsibility." "This announcement by Du Pont represents the biggest breakthrough on these vitally important global issues since the United States banned ozone-depleting aerosol sprays in 1978," the release stated, quoting NRDC cofounder Tom Stoel.

While both Du Pont and the alliance still insisted that, based on current theory, "no significant modification of the ozone layer is expected during the next few decades" and therefore there was "no imminent threat to human health and the environment," and industry lobbyists continued to oppose unilateral U.S. regulations of CFCs, which would "injure U.S. industry to the benefit of international competition" and "undermine efforts to obtain an international resolution," the bottom line was a painful if belated acceptance that CFCs would have to be regulated and eventually replaced. This proud industry—so prodigious in its youth, so beleaguered in middle age—was facing a future of sharp limits and inevitable decline. As alliance executive director Kevin Faye later reflected, "A business with no growth potential is a lousy business to be."

Now the arguments would turn to how the regulations should be structured, and how soon CFC production could be curtailed.

*　　　*　　　*

There remained ample room for disagreement. Industry had called for "a reasonable global limit on the future rate of growth" of CFCs, which was widely understood to mean a production "cap" or, at worst, if the science warranted it, a "freeze." Industry believed, moreover, that in accepting a production cap, it had come a lengthy distance. David Doniger of NRDC, on the other hand, after praising Du Pont for coming as far as it had, called for an 80 percent cut in the production of stratospheric ozone depleters over five years, and a full phaseout within ten years. But Doniger's proposal was regarded as "radical," and therefore unsupportable, just another example of environmentalists' staking out an extreme position. It seemed clear that an international protocol was attainable, and that while it would probably go beyond the freeze industry supported, it would also fall well short of Doniger's phaseout. There was plenty of room in the middle where moderates could feel at home.

To find that moderate position and establish it as the official U.S. thrust for the upcoming negotiations was now the responsibility of John Hoffman's Stratospheric Protection Task Force. Taking into account the latest science, the most recent economic projections for the impact of CFC reductions, and factoring in both domestic and international political pressures, what percentage in CFC emissions ought to be cut back? And on what timetable? A plan first proposed by Canada—to establish a global emission limit, which would be periodically reviewed in light of new scientific understanding—was a good starting point, but allocating national emission limits based on population and GNP, as the Canadians suggested, would be difficult to negotiate. At the same time, models were indicating that, because of CFCs' long atmospheric lifetime, cuts in emissions of 85 percent would be necessary just to stabilize then-current chlorine concentrations in the atmosphere. But that was tantamount to a phaseout.

The more David Doniger reflected on these hard facts, the more he firmly believed that a complete phaseout of ozone-depleting chemicals was the only defensible position. On October 20, 1986, the NRDC issued a press release calling for a phaseout in five years or less. "Even without the Antarctic hole, the case for a rapid phase-out of these gases [is] overwhelming," the release quoted Doniger. "If the Antarctic hole is linked to chlorine," he added, "or if the NASA satellite data are confirmed, then we will be facing an emergency that will make Chernobyl look like a trash fire at the county dump. Then even a five-year phase-out will be too slow, and CFCs will have to be cut immediately." If it proved impossible for the United States to attain international agreement for a phaseout during the upcoming negotiations, Doniger said, then the government should ban the chemicals domestically and terminate imports of foreign products that used them.

A number of influential congressmen had agreed to sponsor legislation to make Doniger's proposition law. On October 6, 1986, eight members of the Senate Committee on the Environment and Public Works wrote a letter to Secretary of State George Shultz urging that the United States negotiate a global phaseout of CFCs. If such negotiations failed, the letter threatened, domestic legislation would be passed to ban the chemicals as well as the importing of products that failed to meet the standards and requirements applicable to products produced in America. The State Department's Richard Benedick set a deadline of Halloween 1986 for agreement on the United States' international position in preparation for the resumption of talks, scheduled for December 1, 1986, in Geneva.

Thus, the pressure was on as Hoffman, Seidel, and other senior EPA staff met with Administrator Lee Thomas near the end of October 1986 to formulate the agency's position. Their own, 1,600-page, five-volume study, *Assessing the Risks of Trace Gases That Can Modify the Stratosphere,* was in draft form and ready for evaluation by EPA's independent Science Advisory Board. Although it was subject to revision prior to official publication, the risk assessment estimated that unless chemical emissions were curbed, increased levels of ultraviolet radiation would cause 40 million additional skin cancers over the next eighty-eight years, 800,000 of them fatal, 12 million eye cataracts, and a growing number of immune-system dysfunctions. Crops, forests, and aquatic communities would also be adversely impacted, and photochemical smog—itself an environmental hazard—would increase. Global warming, the report warned, would accompany ozone depletion and the consequent melting of polar ice would cause sea levels to rise dramatically, putting coastal areas at risk.

Despite having produced the gloomiest and most thoroughly documented prediction yet of damage expected to be caused by ozone depletion, Hoffman's group did not enter the meeting with Thomas prepared to call for a phaseout. They knew the Europeans would vehemently oppose a phaseout, so they had devoted their efforts to devising equitable formulas for a freeze along the lines proposed by the Canadians, by balancing national populations and GNP, and by allowing for an interim treaty that could be periodically updated as science and politics changed. Thomas, however, took his staff members by surprise.

"It came through the discussion," Thomas later remembered, "that from a regulatory point of view we needed a more clear-cut goal to work toward. From a scientific point of view a phaseout was the correct goal because these were offending chemicals. All this discussion they were having about a freeze seemed to blur the fact that this was the ultimate goal. . . . I felt a phaseout was something we could defend better than what they were coming up with."

"Nobody came to Lee with this alternative," Hoffman later explained. "We were talking about problems in achieving a freeze, and going for a phaseout had never occurred to me. But Lee had an insight that changed the basis of the debate. He cut right through the Gordian knot."

By Halloween, Benedick had the EPA position he was to take to Geneva, and on November 5, 1986, a cable went out to American embassies apprising them of it. The United States favored a two-step process —a near-term freeze at or near current production levels for both CFCs and halons (a second class of ozone-depleting compounds containing bromine and used in fire extinguishers), followed by a scheduled long-term phaseout of the chemicals, over a time period to be negotiated, and subject to periodic review. The United States also advocated limited trade sanctions against countries that did not agree to abandon CFCs. A key part of the plan was the idea that the certainty of an impending phaseout would provide the necessary incentive to CFC producers to come up with substitutes.

In adopting the concept of a phaseout of ozone-depleting chemicals, Lee Thomas had not only leapfrogged over his own staff; he had left industry in the lurch. The CFC producers' own recent acceptance of a freeze suddenly appeared much less noble; indeed, industry spokesmen once again found themselves in the role of obstructionists. "We do not believe the scientific information demonstrates any actual risk from current CFC use or emissions," CFC Alliance chairman Richard Barnett announced, and in an op-ed piece in the *New York Times,* Barnett defended industry's preferred solution of a production cap, arguing that a cap "would eliminate the worst-case scenarios that are based on a large, future growth in emissions." He went on to urge U.S. officials to "resist efforts to attempt to force an international agreement by threatening unilateral domestic action under the guise of global leadership. This approach failed when we banned most aerosols in the 1970s, and other nations have made it clear that it will also fail now."

The NRDC, for its part, cheered the government's new policy, but urged a quick timetable for the proposed phaseout: at least a 30 percent emissions reduction within eighteen months of the adoption of a protocol and a complete ban on emissions by the end of 1992. "Any more protracted schedule would be unacceptable," Doniger and NRDC attorney David Wirth wrote Seidel and State Department official Suzanne Butcher on November 25, 1986. "As it is," they added, "new information about ozone depletion at high latitudes and the thinning of the ozone layer over Antarctica suggests that reductions over an even shorter time frame may be necessary."

The National Ozone Expedition led by Susan Solomon arrived at the U.S. research base, McMurdo Station, on August 21, 1986, to investigate the Antarctic ozone hole. McMurdo was located on Ross Island, not far from the site the American explorer Richard Byrd had used as a staging area for his 1929 flight to the South Pole. Byrd had named his base camp Little America, partly with the idea that someday it would be the site for a utopian community for the first Antarctic "settlers." But when U.S. Navy Seabees located it in 1955 during preparations for the International Geophysical Year, hoping it might be serviceable as a site for a new U.S. research station, they found Byrd's former headquarters, which had been constructed on the edge of the Ross Ice Shelf, looking anything but utopian: most of the original base had calved off into the iceberg-choked sea.

The Seabees moved on to adjacent Ross Island, an atoll of bare volcanic rock populated on three sides with swarming penguin rookeries, and set to work building laboratories, dormitories, stores, warehouses, a power plant, a wharf, and a landing strip. Named for Lieutenant Archibald McMurdo of James Clark Ross's 1841 British exploratory expedition, the new post was the largest permanent research station in Antarctica. It can house twelve hundred U.S. scientists and technicians, and beginning with the IGY, it has been the center of all U.S. polar science activity in the southern hemisphere.

When the big Navy C-130 carrying the NOZE expedition members touched down on its skis at McMurdo following a nine-hour flight from New Zealand, the temperature was −47°F. The flight had been scheduled to land at local noon so the pilots could take advantage of the little sunlight available at midday in the austral winter. The plane stopped on the packed-snow landing strip only long enough for the passengers and cargo to be dumped, then hurriedly taxied and departed, leaving the U.S. scientists and their precious equipment in a heap by the side of the runway. The new arrivals spent the next twelve hours storing their instruments and gear away from the subzero cold, before dropping into their beds exhausted. Waking groggily the next morning, the Antarctic greenhorns glanced out the window for their first look at their new home, only to see veteran Dave Hofmann and his balloon team already on the ice in goggles and full Antarctic gear, happily sending up vertical probes.

Although Robert Watson and Peter Wilkniss had assured the NOZE team members that it was unlikely they would solve the ozone hole question on their first mission to Antarctica, the researchers couldn't help but feel the pressure to pick up the sluggish pace of routine scientific investigation and come up, heroically, with conclusive results.

"The work was tough," Susan Solomon later explained, "because of three things: we had to do our work publicly, complete it very rapidly, and announce our results without the benefit of peer review. This is not the way science usually works, and not the way we as scientists were accustomed to functioning. For me the resolution of the ozone-layer issue was the first environmental issue that raised the question: can science adjust to the need to work in a fishbowl?"

Watson would later concur. "There was a great deal of pressure on NOZE I. Conditions in Antarctica make experimentation very difficult, and these instruments were complex. I thought Dave Hofmann, who had worked there before, might get readings, but I wasn't so sure about the others. I felt that we might only come away having learned which instruments worked and which didn't, then we would go back the next year and get our hard data."

It was also a distinct challenge for the scientists to maintain their objectivity. As Barney Farmer recalled, "We had already seen that chlorine had increased due to man's activities, and all of us certainly knew that chlorine scavenged ozone. This led to what could be considered a rather obvious supposition about chlorine and the hole. Yet you had to stay open-minded about it, and not prejudge the data."

The data soon spoke for itself. The Schmeltekopf-Noxon instrument Susan Solomon had brought could detect the atmospheric presence of chlorine dioxide, a sign of chlorine catalysis, as well as nitrogen dioxide, an indicator that the solar or odd-nitrogen theory of ozone depletion might be at work. "The nitrogen dioxide abundances inside the ozone hole," Solomon was able to report by mid-September, "are the lowest we have observed anywhere in the world." Solomon was well qualified to conclude that such a finding virtually eliminated the odd-nitrogen theory as an explanation for the hole: her Ph.D. thesis had examined the transport of reactive nitrogen from the mesophere and the thermosphere to the stratosphere, precisely the transport the NOAA instrument would have spotted if indeed odd nitrogen were to blame. In addition, the device showed that trace chemicals did not appear to be rising in the polar vortex, which seemed to discount the dynamicists' theory that an upwelling of air was responsible for pushing ozone out of the area.

Meanwhile, working with their microwave apparatus, Philip Solomon and Stony Brook cohort Bob De Zafra found chlorine monoxide, usually present in the stratosphere in a quantity of .01 part per billion by volume (ppb), in abundances of between .5 and 2.0 ppb. Their readings also confirmed that a great proportion of the chlorine in the stratosphere above McMurdo was in the active form of chlorine monoxide, the decomposition product of the chlorine chain. They considered this to be convincing evidence that unusual destruction of ozone was occurring.

Some of the most powerful raw data came from Dave Hofmann in the form of altitude profiles. In measurements taken from 33 balloon launches, he found that 35 percent of the ozone layer between 7.5 and 12.5 miles up was missing, and that in a pocket between 8 and 11.5 miles the depletion was 70 percent. One balloon sent into the center of this latter region reported that an astounding 90 percent of local ozone had disappeared.

The readings represented a turning point for the Antarctic veteran. "Until '86 I was skeptical about the chemical explanation," Hofmann later reflected. "Of course, I didn't believe the dynamicists, either. I thought maybe it was some combination of natural phenomena. But when I saw that severe depletion myself in '86, localized at various altitudes, I knew then that it was chemical."

Barney Farmer had brought a version of a device that had flown on the space shuttle *Challenger,* known as an atmospheric trace molecule spectrometer, which measures a wide range of molecules in the infrared spectrum. The three-hundred-kilometer-high shuttle flight—the last the *Challenger* would make before it exploded in a launch from Cape Canaveral in January 1986—had fulfilled a long-held dream of Farmer's to measure the sun's infrared spectrum with no interference from the earth's atmosphere. In Antarctica, Farmer and his crew were delayed in getting usable data by temperatures of $-60°F$ that inhibited the optical mechanism on the spectrometer. When on-site adjustments succeeded in getting it working, the device tracked thirty or forty trace gases in the infrared spectrum, including huge amounts of chlorine nitrate, the notorious CFC-reservoir molecule.

Farmer and Philip Solomon waited until they returned to their home labs to complete the analysis of their data, but even based on their preliminary findings and the information Susan Solomon and Hofmann had gathered, there was strong evidence that the atmospheric chemistry over Antarctica had been perturbed and that the two nonchemical theories for the hole should be discarded. Yet the scientists felt constrained. Farmer later admitted, "We argued about it—about what to say. The problem was not unanimity, but that even if we all said it was a chemical process at fault, we still didn't know how it worked, and this was the real handicap. If you can't say how something works, then you don't have much of a case. Most scientists are extremely wary of not having a theory to go along with what they observe."

Knowing full well the import their words could have on the regulatory and scientific debates raging at home, and with the evidence so overwhelming in favor of a chemical explanation, the group arranged for a special satellite press conference in mid-October to relate their findings to reporters gathered at NSF headquarters in Washington. If they could not yet say for sure what particular chemical mechanisms were depleting ozone, or even if Susan Solomon's own theory about polar stratospheric clouds was involved, they could at least announce what they were certain of. On October 20, Solomon read a prepared statement agreed upon by all the NOZE researchers announcing that the expedition had found severe ozone loss at altitudes between 12 and 20 kilometers. "We suspect," she said, that "a chemical process is fundamentally responsible for the formation of the hole." Acknowledging that an exact chemical mechanism to explain the process had not yet been fully modeled, she admitted that "what's happening is more complicated than what has been proposed so far."

The dynamicists and odd-nitrogen theorists, none of whom had participated in NOZE, were indignant. "The press conference was a circus," NASA's Mark Schoeberl charged. Angered by their exclusion from the project, he and other dynamicists pointed out that Susan Solomon had coauthored a paper citing chemical reactions before setting foot on Antarctica. "You send chemists to the South Pole," Schoeberl said, "and of course they denounce dynamics." Linwood Callis, who had put forward the odd-nitrogen theory, joined in the criticism. "Their suggestion that the solar cycle is not playing a role in this is wrong," Callis said. "And even if it is not wrong, it's certainly premature."

While some atmospheric scientists, most notably the NSF's John Lynch, have frequently credited the prescience of Rowland and Molina's original theory for the scientific community's ability, a decade later, to grasp relatively quickly the significance of the ozone hole, others held an antithetical view: that the prominence of the Rowland-Molina theory had stifled debate by predisposing people to a chemical explanation and inhibiting the consideration of alternatives. Schoeberl told a reporter he thought the rush to claim a chemical cause for the ozone hole was evidence of "how much people have lost their scientific objectivity because of political and funding pressures." The dynamicists argued further that McMurdo Station, altogether on one side of Antarctica, was situated at the edge of the ozone hole, which roughly conformed to the shape of the Antarctic continent. If NOZE had been serious about giving the dynamical theories a fair test, they protested, observations should have been made from a number of Antarctica sites.

The dynamicists had their turn at bat in November 1986, just after the NOZE project had ended, when the influential journal *Geophysical Research Letters* published a special supplement containing a number of papers on the subject. Edited by two leading dynamicists, Schoeberl and Arlin Krueger, the issue reflected a decidedly prodynamics, antichemical bias. Everywhere ozone was being depleted, the dynamicists pointed out, temperatures were also dropping, proving—to the dynamicists, at least —that some fundamental atmospheric shift was taking place. Ka Kit Tung of the State University of New York at Potsdam and Princeton's Jerry Mahlman were among several others who proposed that atmospheric waves that carry heat and ozone to the Antarctic had been getting weaker and that some general change in global wave motion had occurred, with Antarctic stratospheric ozone levels the first indicator.

"The origin of the ozone change may be a weak climatic shift in the troposphere that is being felt in the stratosphere first, because the stratosphere's got very little mass," Schoeberl explained. "It's like the tail on the dog. The dog shakes itself a little and the tail goes all over the place."

The actual explanation of the correlation between ozone loss and the colder temperatures was far more ominous than most of the dynamicists guessed, and was accurately described by only one contributor to the *Geophysical Research Letters* supplement, Keith Shine of Oxford University. Subsequent research in Antarctica would show that colder temperatures were not causing lower ozone levels, but rather it was the other way around—the stratospheric warming mechanism explained by the Chapman reactions was inactive in the absence of ozone.

The appearance of the supplement, along with the seemingly endless griping about the way in which NOZE had been carried out, caused a tremor in the atmospheric-science community, worrying chemists and government officials alike that the NOZE press conference had been too hasty. Far from settling the issue, the evidence NOZE had gathered directly beneath the ozone hole seemed only to have stirred up greater rancor and dispute among scientists—just the kind of debate the CFC industry had always found most comforting. Dave Hofmann, who knew how hard his team and others had worked to obtain their data under arduous conditions, couldn't help but feel disillusioned. "You could talk about it all you wanted," Hofmann said. "No one was willing to be convinced on the basis of the data."

"In retrospect," Barney Farmer later said, "we were probably too timid. We didn't want to say it was CFCs. We were all scared at being labeled sensationalists. Ordinarily, you take years, longer than any legal case, to bring in a scientific judgment, and we were being asked to say what was and what wasn't in six weeks."

As Susan Solomon had noted, the ozone-hole crisis—by challenging researchers to quickly get to the root of a major global environmental catastrophe—implied nothing less than the need for scientists to redefine their own roles in society. Warnings from environmentalists, dire forecasts based on sophisticated computer models—these were not sufficient. Nor were the results of a NASA-sponsored mission, if those results did not first bring consensus to the scientific community. Prolonged disagreement, even if scientifically justified, could be a form of paralysis. The CFC industry could go on forever defending its own refusal to change by simply pointing to the controversy among those who were supposed to be experts.

There was in all this a powerful paradox: science had for centuries advanced by rigorous experimentation and the establishment of cause and effect, by the careful pursuit of knowledge and open-ended theoretical discussion and debate. Now, if one took the threat of ozone depletion seriously, it seemed imperative that the discussion be silenced, the debate cut off, and that the pursuit come to an end—in short, that the scientific method adapt to new circumstances.

Bob Watson saw that there was no alternative. A second expedition would have to be assembled to return to Antarctica in August 1987, the next time the ozone hole would reappear.

20.

HATS, SHADES, AND SUNSCREEN

UROPEAN INTRANSIGENCE CONTINUED to thwart American efforts to curtail global CFC emissions. At a meeting in Geneva in early December 1986, the United States formally introduced a draft protocol containing proposals to freeze CFC production in the near term and cut back in the long term. The Nordic countries responded by calling for immediate cuts, while the European Community, joined by the Soviet Union and Japan, retreated to their old position favoring a production-capacity cap. The EC opposed the U.S. and Nordic ideas in part because its industries maintained they were at least a decade behind American industry in developing alternatives to CFCs. Japan wanted to exclude CFC-113, used extensively in its electronics industry, from the protocol. The Soviets were reluctant to yield a technology with significant military applications. But the EC was the most resistant. Announcing that it had authority to negotiate nothing more than a production-capacity cap, the EC delegation also proposed a postponement of the next scheduled round of negotiations. When the plenary session rejected the move, the heads of the delegations from the United Kingdom and the EC left Geneva prematurely.

As Ambassador Benedick later noted, one reason for the European attitude was that the issue had "not caught the imagination of the general public [in Europe]," as it had in the United States in the 1970s. To remedy this problem the United States Information Agency organized programs and broadcasts in five European cities so that NASA officials and scientists could present the case for CFC controls. The State Department and EPA also initiated numerous meetings with representatives of the European governments. At the same time, the NRDC and other American environmental groups stepped up their contacts with European environmentalists.

In January 1987, David Doniger told Congress that he and other environmentalists remained "uncertain" where EPA was headed. "The U.S. should be proposing a domestic phase-out," Doniger testified, "and to do that would strengthen our hand in the international negotiations, because other countries would see that if they don't negotiate a deal with us, they are going to not be able to bring their cars and their computers and other products into our country. If the negotiations still fail, they would have to follow suit, based on the fact that those markets are much more important to them than making an adjustment in how they use CFCs." Within a few weeks of Doniger's appearance, Republican Senator John H. Chafee of Rhode Island and Democrat Max Baucus of Montana introduced separate but similar bills that would do what the NRDC attorney had proposed.

When international negotiations resumed in Vienna on February 23, 1987, Canada and the Nordic nations formally embraced the U.S. proposal, and a number of other countries, including Egypt, Mexico, New Zealand, and Switzerland also lent their support. Although the EC delegation budged slightly—informally offering a 10 or even a 20 percent reduction—any such reductions would have to be postponed for nearly a decade.

The U.S. reaction was sharp. The European position was "totally unacceptable" and "simply ridiculous," Ambassador Benedick told members of the press when the negotiating session adjourned. "Some participants at these negotiations seem to be concentrating more on short-term profits than on our common responsibility to conserve the environment for future generations," he explained in a thinly veiled reference to France and Britain. "Unfortunately, after two difficult sessions in Geneva last December and this week in Vienna, the hardest work still remains to be done."

The Americans could take some measure of hope in growing indications that the member nations of the EC were starting to disagree with one another. West Germany, the Netherlands, and Denmark were reportedly putting pressure on Britain and France to move in the Americans' direction. The Germans advocated a first-step cut of 50 percent. It was anticipated that the March meeting of the EC Council of Environment Ministers would produce agreement on a common policy of CFC reductions. "Given the amount of international pressure," an unnamed EC source was quoted in the *Guardian* of London as saying, "I do not believe that even Britain would dare to block everything by using its veto." At the same time, the Japanese were reportedly greatly impressed by the threat of U.S. trade sanctions and were reconsidering their stubborn defense of CFC-113.

As the Europeans and Japanese were moving toward a compromise, however, back home, industry forces and antiregulatory ideologues in the Reagan administration were gathering for a mighty last effort at reversing the official U.S. negotiating position.

One powerful source of industry support was Michigan congressman John D. Dingell, the powerful chairman of the House Committee on Energy and Commerce. A longtime friend of the automobile industry, which was heavily reliant on CFCs in automobile air conditioners, Dingell charged at hearings of the House Subcommittee on Health and the Environment on March 9, 1987, that Ambassador Benedick and his EPA support staff were "negotiating on a seat-of-the-pants basis" lacking "adequate technical and policy support within the administration" and that they were "trying to bow too far toward those seeking stringent reductions now without a full understanding of economic, technical, and the scientific problems and concerns that exist with regard to action there."

The accusations were quickly taken up by others. The conservative journal *Human Events* summarized the antiprotocol tack in a June 1987 article. The EPA and the State Department were trying to pull a fast one and "sneak through" an unwarranted and "radical negotiating program for international controls on CFCs . . . largely out of sight of the Administration," the magazine reported. The argument carried all the more weight in view of the fact that for Benedick, *Human Events* said, "out-of-sight maneuverings were hardly new." This was the man, the magazine reminded its readers, who, "on the eve of an international conference on population control in Mexico City . . . organized opposition to the official White House policy of withholding all funds for international organizations that encourage abortion as a means of population control."

Rebecca Norton Dunlop, who was a senior aide at the Department of the Interior at the time—and who had crossed swords with Benedick over the population issue when she worked on the White House staff and he was coordinator for population affairs at the State Department—

later said of his handling of the CFC issue: "Benedick did not do his job properly. He got clearance for his position, but who did he get it from? From career federal employees. We investigated and found out that the Circular 175 [a document that authorized the U.S. negotiating position] had not been signed by anyone at a policy level at any department or agency except for EPA and State. He had a responsibility when dealing with something of this magnitude to ensure it was circulated at a higher level around the government."

Benedick was particularly stung by these charges because he had obtained formal clearance of the Circular 175 in November 1986, from the Departments of State, Commerce, and Energy, the Council on Environmental Quality, the EPA, NASA, NOAA, the Office of Management and Budget, the U.S. trade representative, and the White House Domestic Policy Council (DPC).

Officials at the Departments of the Interior, Commerce, Energy, and Agriculture, the Office of Science and Technology Policy, and the Office of Management and Budget were readily persuaded that the CFC policy was so far-reaching that it ought to have been cleared at the cabinet level. As a result, David Gibbons, deputy associate director of the Natural Resources Division of the OMB, established an interagency working group of the Domestic Policy Council to reexamine U.S. CFC policy. In March and April 1987, Gibbons convened a series of briefings at which EPA and State Department officials were invited to defend their policy before senior officials from other branches of the administration. At the first of these interagency meetings, on March 27, 1987, Gibbons announced that U.S. policy on CFCs would henceforth be made by the Domestic Policy Council, and that the U.S. delegation to the next session of UNEP negotiations, set for April 27–30 in Geneva, was to advocate nothing more than a freeze.

David Doniger likened the ensuing briefings, which commenced at the end of the working day for a period of three or four weeks, and sometimes ran late into the night, to a "star chamber." Even industry found itself outflanked on the right by Gibbons and other administration conservatives who opposed the protocol, the EPA–State Department position in the negotiations, Richard Benedick personally, the way policy had been decided generally, and who even seemed to believe that industry itself had caved in and taken a weak position.

"As we got closer to a protocol," Lee Thomas recalled, "the entire issue was raised to a higher level within the administration. I believe it happened for a couple of reasons. To begin with, industry got exercised because I had taken this thing farther than they wanted to go. Then, State had the responsibility for coordinating with other agencies. In hindsight, they did a poor job. The 'Circular 175' treated this as low-level process. Plus, EPA was suspect and there were people who felt it was always necessary to moderate our position. We ended up having to go through the entire cabinet process, all the way to the president."

Benedick speculates that one reason for the "unexpected onslaught" was that "senior officials who would normally as a matter of principle have opposed environmental regulations simply had not been paying attention when the 'Circular 175' had been developed and approved several months previously."

In any case, once the siege began, the task before John Hoffman, Steve Seidel, and their immediate superior, Eileen Claussen, was to present the findings of their massive risk-assessment study and demonstrate that it had been reviewed and endorsed by reputable independent scientists. The underlying basis for the EPA's policy choices—the five-volume risk-assessment study—could not be dismissed out of hand. "We had done our homework," Hoffman said, "and a blue-ribbon panel had given it high marks."

The chair of that panel, Dr. Margaret Kripke, head of the Department of Immunology at the University of Texas Cancer Center in Houston, was especially effective. She was unusual in her willingness to take an active role in defending a study she had not written, but had only been asked to review. EPA's risk-assessment document had gone through a number of revisions at her committee's recommendation, and was, she believed, an "up-to-date document that accurately and fairly assessed the state of knowledge" about CFCs and ozone depletion. She attended one of the early DPC meetings on April 13 at the invitation of NASA's Robert Watson, who had been invited to make a scientific presentation on CFCs and ozone depletion. "I had never been to a meeting like that before," Kripke said. "I was most taken aback by the hostility of the audience and the nature of the questioning." Since she had not been on the briefing's official agenda, Kripke simply observed most of the meeting. In the last five minutes or so, almost as an afterthought, her area of expertise—skin cancer—was addressed. Kripke was "incensed," she recalled, to find herself being "badgered by one of the people in the audience [Gibbons] with a question suggesting that skin cancer was a self-inflicted disease" because sunbathers choose to lie in the sun or live in the South, and therefore the government should not be expected to undertake expensive remedies to mitigate it.

Kripke began to rebut the suggestion that skin cancer was a self-inflicted disease, but then, spontaneously, added that in any case she did not believe skin cancer was the area of greatest concern. Skin cancer had received most of the attention, she allowed, because it was "spectacular" and because it was the area of concern about which there was the greatest amount of scientific documentation. But there were other concerns related to ozone depletion with far greater global consequences, she believed, notably the potential impact on the global food supply and the possibility that ozone depletion would lead to widespread outbreaks of disease due to the effects of ultraviolet radiation on the human immune system. If these areas had received less attention than skin cancer, she observed, perhaps it would be wise to devote more scientific research dollars to them.

The assertion by a cancer expert that the threat of skin cancer, though grave, was far from the most serious possible consequence of ozone depletion, brought that particular DPC meeting to a sober close.

Kripke later wrote Gibbons to elaborate on her response to his suggestion that skin cancer might be "self-inflicted," since, she said, she had been "caught unprepared for this line of reasoning."

"The majority of cancers we see . . . cannot be characterized as belonging to the leisure or sun-worshiping sets," Kripke wrote. "Most of our patients with skin cancer are farmers, ranchers, oil field workers and people who work on offshore oil rigs. . . . I feel that I am doing our patients a great disservice by leaving uncontested the impression that skin cancer is a problem limited to suntan seekers. This is clearly not the case." Later introduced into the official record at a congressional hearing, Kripke's letter rebutting so glib an attempt to refute the EPA's risk-assessment study helped render the study all the more credible.

The way the Clean Air Act was written, risks to human health are the principal justification for regulations, so EPA's risk assessment focused on health issues related to ozone depletion. One could argue that CFCs were not conclusively proven to lead to ozone depletion—as industry had indeed argued for years—but as that line of defense began to weaken following the NOZE findings in Antarctica, opponents of regulation assumed a fallback position, suggesting instead that the consequences of ozone depletion had been greatly exaggerated, or that potential harm could be avoided simply by staying out of the sun. But the forces opposed to CFC control found little comfort when the regulatory debate shifted away from atmospheric scientists to health experts like Kripke.

In May 1987, several months after the longstanding assumption that ozone depletion was hazardous to human health had first been challenged, the Senate Subcommittee on Hazardous Wastes and Toxic Substances chaired by Senator Baucus convened to hear testimony on ozone depletion from some of the nation's leading medical authorities.

"Skin cancer" had been the dreaded buzzword associated with ozone depletion since the days of the SST controversy. Exposure to high levels of shortwave ultraviolet light was known to result in or contribute to three kinds of skin cancer—either squamous or basal cell carcinoma, which are disfiguring but rarely fatal, and cutaneous malignant melanoma, which is fatal in about 20 percent of cases.

"We are speaking about a special kind of UV which is invisible," Thomas B. Fitzpatrick, chief dermatologist at Massachusetts General Hospital and chairman of the Department of Dermatology at the Harvard Medical School, explained to Baucus and other senators. "This invisibility makes it very tricky, because it is not only invisible but it is not perceptible; it is unlike heat. It doesn't give any warning signal."

There are three kinds of ultraviolet light—UV-A, which is harmless to humans and is a component in visible sunlight; and UV-B and UV-C, the shorter wavelengths of ultraviolet light, which are screened by ozone. The longer-wave UV-B will brown or "tan" human skin, but the shorter rays of UV-B penetrate on contact and are absorbed by the chemical bonds in human DNA. This impact snaps or tangles the bonds, creating the distorted messages that cause cancer. The damage occurs instantly, although it may take decades before it results in illness.

Carcinomas are sometimes referred to as a "lifestyle" cancer, because they have increased as human beings have come to possess more leisure time, and changing styles of clothing and different attitudes about the enhancing effects of a suntan have led people to expose more of their bodies to the sun's rays. Malignant melanomas can often be traced to a particularly harsh incidence of sunburn in youth. Melanoma has also increased as individuals with pigmentation and UV sensitivity more suited to the mid- or high-northern hemisphere have relocated to sunny, equatorial latitudes. An acute example of the syndrome was observed in Scandinavia, where a statistical linkage was found between an outbreak of skin cancer and the popularity of bargain charter flights from Stockholm to the south of Spain.

As Dr. Kripke told the Baucus committee, the same principle is at work in Australia, which has the highest melanoma rates in the world and which she described as "nature's experiment of taking a white, susceptible population and moving them to a tropical environment and then having them be outside all the time."

Societal and lifestyle changes greatly complicate the efforts by scientists to determine what impact ozone depletion may have already had on human health. While the mortality rate from melanoma has stabilized at about 20 percent, the number of new cases per year in the United States doubled between 1980 and 1989. A child born in 1930, around the time CFCs were invented, had a 1-in-1,500 chance of developing malignant melanoma; by 1988 the risk was 1 in 135. One of the most disturbing demographic statistics came from Dr. Fitzpatrick. Between 1975 and 1985, the Boston specialist told the senators, researchers had seen an astonishing 340 percent increase in cases of melanoma in the southwestern United States. He also called the legislators' attention to some "astounding data" published in the *New England Journal of Medicine* in the fall of 1986, which showed melanoma to be the second-most-prevalent tumor in males ages thirty to forty-nine and the fourth-most-prevalent in those ages fifty to fifty-nine.

Fitzpatrick concluded his testimony by pointing out that decreased ozone would undoubtedly increase future skin cancers, and he termed the pollution of the stratosphere with ozone-depleting chemicals "an act of destruction causing [human] death and disfigurement of major proportions." Were the ozone shield at mid-northern latitudes to become badly reduced, he said, "You are going to have radiation in Boston that is equivalent to what is [currently] present in Miami." The EPA had earlier made a similar correlation, estimating that each 1 percent depletion in ozone would cause an approximate 2 to 3 percent increase in UV-B light and a 5 percent increase in skin cancer, including a 1 percent increase in malignant melanomas.

Dr. Stanley Lerman, professor of ophthalmology at Emory University, also appeared before the Baucus committee to testify that, unlike the skin-cancer threat, "the ultraviolet doesn't discriminate as to color or creed" when it comes to the potential harm the sun can do to people's eyes. On a short-term basis, ultraviolet in the shorter wavelengths causes momentary blindness, which almost all people experience from time to time, but even the longer waves of ultraviolet, not just the UV-B, but the UV-A, can reach the interior of the eye and cause permanent damage. These rays, Lerman explained, penetrate through the cornea and intrude on the eye's ocular lens, the last line of defense in guarding the retina.

"The cornea can be replaced," he commented. "The ocular lens can be removed . . . [but] the retina, once it is destroyed, assures blindness. There is nothing we can do about the retina once you destroy it."

As with skin cancer, the risk factor for retinal damage would correlate with higher levels of global or regional ozone depletion. Ophthalmologists received a dramatic demonstration of this during the summer of 1987, when Dr. Lawrence A. Yannuzzi, a physician at Columbia Presbyterian Medical Center in New York, saw six patients with solar retinitis —retinal sunburn. The condition usually occurs when people stare at the sun, as while viewing a solar eclipse, but Yannuzzi's patients suffered a different type of exposure. All six had been sunbathing on the afternoon of March 29, 1987, an unseasonably warm day that had sent people across the Northeast out of doors to parks, backyards, and beaches. What none realized, or could have known, was that the balmy weather was accompanied by an "ozone hole" stretching from Michigan to New England. Yannuzzi's six patients all had damaged their retinas gazing up at an ozone-depleted sky through which high levels of UV light were pouring in.

The danger to human health from exposure to ultraviolet radiation, while not completely understood, has been fairly well established. Not as well known are the risks to plants and other living things. Photosynthesis is the most essential link in the earth's biosphere—literally the basis of all life—and researchers cannot help but fear that this fundamental process by which plants utilize sunlight to fuel their growth will be affected by increasing levels of ultraviolet light. Dr. Alan H. Teramura, of the Department of Botany at the University of Maryland, who appeared at the May 1987 hearing, testified that the potential of UV to damage crops and plants was indisputable. "To date the scientific community has screened roughly 200 or so species of plants and different varieties of plants," Teramura said, "and alarmingly, they found that two out of every three of these seem to show some degree of sensitivity to ultraviolet radiation."

Teramura described the results of a six-year study in which artificial UV simulating a 25 percent ozone depletion caused a 20 percent reduction in the total dry weight of beans. "To put this 20 percent reduction in yield into some sort of perspective for you," Teramura told the senators, "today in the United States, weeds account for roughly 17 percent loss of our gross soybean harvest. Diseases account for about 12 to 14 percent. We lose about 10 percent due to mechanical harvesting losses and insects account for about 3 percent of our yield losses." A related problem is that increased UV *produces* tropospheric ozone—the major component in smog—which also inhibits crop growth.

Perhaps the most worrisome consequences of excessive levels of UV light, however, will be those that occur among the lower echelons of the food chain. Too much UV can be a severe and usually fatal "stress" on aquatic life. "UV-B radiation causes damage to the larval and juvenile stages of fish," Dr. Robert C. Worrest of Oregon State University told the Baucus committee, creating "a more unstable ecosystem. A decrease in column ozone would diminish the near-surface feeding season of small invertebrate animals. Whether this population could endure a significant shortening of the surface season is unknown."

Worrest described a laboratory test which had found that a 20 percent increase in UV radiation resulted in the death of 100 percent of anchovy larvae within fifteen days of exposure.

Mortality among lower-level marine creatures such as phytoplankton would have immense consequences. In Antarctica, for instance, a large-scale destruction of phytoplankton would cause major upheaval: the krill, which feed on the photyplankton, would die, as would all the creatures that rely on the krill—the squid, shrimp, whales, seals, and penguins. Some creatures would perish from direct exposure to the harsh UV light, others from lack of food, some from the combination of these two effects, and others would be so weakened that they would not be able to compete for the reduced food supply. Many organisms, such as zooplankton, shrimp, and crab larvae, simply lack the ability to react to or escape increases in UV-B. "If some things are poorly adapted, others are going to substitute for them," John Calkins of the University of Kentucky said in concluding his presentation before the 1987 hearings. "The problem is, are we going to be happy with the changes that are going to take place?"

"Is there a threshold level, an acceptable level of ozone depletion?" Senator John Chafee asked the medical and biological scientists assembled at the Baucus hearing. The panelists hesitated for a second, unsure whom the question was directed to, then replied in chorus: "No."

If the eleventh-hour opponents of the U.S. negotiating position on the ozone protocol were on shaky scientific ground, the NRDC's David Doniger knew that politically they were no more secure. At the one interagency meeting that environmentalists were invited to attend, in April 1987, Doniger saw an opening when an OMB official casually observed that their purpose was to seek a policy on CFCs. Doniger interrupted to point out that the United States had a policy on CFCs—a policy to phase them out—which had been approved through all the proper administration channels, had wide bipartisan support in Congress, and had been publicly proclaimed and aggressively pursued at international forums. The OMB meeting, in Doniger's view, was therefore not about seeking a policy but about changing one.

After the meeting Doniger said: "I did something I hadn't done since high school. I wrote out a script for a phone call. I called the people who'd been at the meeting and read them the script. It went something like this. 'We've tried very conscientiously to work this issue from the inside, but the United States has a policy, and you're talking about changing it. If you change this policy we will make it publicly known who did it and why.'

"A day later I got word that my calls had made a difference. They were backing off. . . ."

Finding it difficult to reverse U.S. policy in the middle of ongoing negotiations—an action that would have had to contradict the compelling EPA risk-assessment analysis and incur large political consequences—the interagency group met on April 23, 1987, just prior to the resumption of negotiations in Geneva, and did not attempt to change the U.S. delegation's negotiating instructions. However, they appointed representatives of the Interior and Commerce departments to the delegation. Although these delegates managed to blunt the U.S. leadership role in Geneva, Benedick was able to conduct negotiations without revealing there was any question as to the depth of commitment behind the U.S. position. Indeed, in his plenary statement in Geneva, Benedick somewhat slyly alluded to the internal conflict at home, suggesting that the involvement of eighteen different departments and agencies "in detailed scrutiny of all aspects of the protocol which we together are trying to construct" was an indication not of disarray but of the degree of "seriousness" with which the United States government regarded the negotiations.

With the United States maintaining the appearance of strength in its resolve to see CFCs phased out, pressure on the reluctant parties at Geneva to compromise their position grew stronger. The most significant development, in Benedick's view, was the direct participation in the negotiations, for the first time, of UNEP executive director Mostafa Tolba. In an opening address to the delegates Tolba discussed the conclusions of a scientific meeting organized by UNEP in Würzburg, West Germany, in early April. The workshop had been called in an effort to review EPA model projections presented at the February negotiating meeting and to finally achieve some consensus in the scientific community. Scientists from eight nations were asked to apply different scenarios of CFC control to their models. The results from eight models were in close agreement, all showing that only significant reductions in CFC emissions would prevent serious ozone depletion, and that CFC-113 and halons would have to be covered by any effective regulatory action. Tolba drew the obvious conclusions:

No longer can those who oppose action to regulate CFC release hide behind scientific dissent. I might add that line was always a charade. Scientific debate and disagreement has always—and will always be—a normal part of the quest for knowledge. . . . Our course of action should be clear.

Tolba convened closed meetings with delegation heads and was able to produce an unofficial draft protocol. In the agreement, which included CFC-113 and halons, the delegates backed a freeze at 1986 levels of production beginning in 1990 and a 20 percent reduction in production and consumption within two years after that, with options for a further 30 percent reduction to be negotiated later.

When the U.S. negotiating team returned home to Washington from Geneva in early May 1987, it could point to tangible success in moving the European Community and Japan closer to the U.S. position. But far from being hailed for its accomplishments, the EPA–State Department team found itself under attack from both sides. The NRDC described the outcome of the Geneva meetings as a "failure" because it fell far short of the original U.S. position calling for a 95 percent cut in global emissions of six ozone-depleting chemicals within ten to fourteen years. To environmentalists it seemed the United States was retreating just when there were encouraging signs that other countries had begun to understand the seriousness of ozone depletion. This U.S. weakness, Doniger wrote in an NRDC press release, was "directly traceable to the actions of junior administration officials with a long history of hard-line opposition to environmental protection." Anticipating there would soon be hard scientific evidence linking the Antarctic ozone hole to CFCs, Doniger said that the agreement hammered out in Geneva, if ratified, "may be out of date literally a month after it is signed."

Meanwhile, the court-approved deadline for EPA to issue proposals for domestic controls of CFCs was pushed back by mutual consent of the NRDC and the EPA from May 1, 1987, first to May 11 and then to December 1. Doniger agreed to the postponements, not because he wavered in his belief that domestic rules were in order, but because conservatives within the Reagan administration had not abandoned their belief that the EPA and the State Department had gone too far in pushing for anything more than the freeze on CFC production. The issue was kicked upstairs from the interagency working group convened by David Gibbons of the OMB, and was put on the agenda of a May 20, 1987, meeting of the Domestic Policy Council, composed of Attorney General Edwin Meese and selected cabinet secretaries. For Doniger to force EPA to propose unilateral domestic regulations at this precise moment would only inflame the opposition.

The fate of the ozone layer had, in effect, reached the White House. In May 1987, President Reagan's popularity was at its lowest ebb, in the wake of the disclosure that the White House had not only traded arms to Iran in exchange for hostages but had then taken the proceeds from these transactions and illegally transferred them to the contras fighting Nicaragua's communist government. Reagan, according to Donald Regan, his outgoing chief of staff, was "in the grip of lassitude" during this unusual period of public disapproval, displaying little of his usual humor or political combativeness.

Although it was always difficult to know how political decisions were reached in the Reagan White House, certain influences on Reagan vis-à-vis ozone are clearly discernible. Secretary of State George Shultz, whose staff had negotiated the ozone policy under review, was at a particular zenith of influence. Shultz was on the record as having opposed both arms sales to Iran and covert aid to the contras. Meanwhile, the State Department as well as EPA were telling high-placed members of the administration including Attorney General Edwin Meese, that the Clean Air Act required the United States to issue domestic regulations on CFCs irrespective of international developments. The law was clear on this point. This country therefore stood to gain nothing by blocking an international protocol if, in the end, domestic regulations would be imposed anyway. On the contrary, the United States stood to lose a great deal if its CFC industry were forced to shut down while the CFC industry abroad remained unfettered. Meese was reportedly convinced by this line of reasoning of the importance of supporting a meaningful international treaty.

There was also mounting pressure from the nation's environmental lobby. On May 21, 1987, the day after the first Domestic Policy Council meeting to review U.S. CFC policy had ended without agreement, the leaders of the ten major environmental organizations in the country, including the NRDC, the Sierra Club, and the Audubon Society, published a letter they had sent to Reagan, stating, "We urge that you lend your personal support to the position developed by the EPA." These very same organizations had branded Reagan an enemy of the environment, yet they had proven their political clout in helping to drive his first secretary of the interior, James Watt, and his first EPA administrator, Anne Gorsuch, from office.

Last, but not to be discounted, was Reagan's personal connection to the health risks related to ozone depletion—risks being described that same month in Senate hearings on Capitol Hill. The president had spent a lifetime in the sun, and relished the image of himself as an outdoorsman —a fit-looking Reagan on horseback was an essential part of his public persona. However, he had had cancerous basal cell epitheliomas removed from his nose twice in 1985, and would have a third removed in July. When polyps were removed from his colon in 1985, he had sounded blasé in explaining to a reporter, "I didn't have cancer, I had something inside of me that had cancer in it and it was removed." But after his third experience with epithelioma, it is doubtful he appreciated the argument that skin cancer was a self-induced illness. A few days after he had undergone surgery, Reagan remarked to a group visiting the White House that the bandage on his nose should be considered a billboard, reading STAY OUT OF THE SUN.

Perhaps the most straightforward description of the Reagan White House policy decision on ozone depletion was provided by the EPA's Lee Thomas. "We had several cabinet sessions with the president, where we talked through the issues," the former administrator said. "Representatives from other agencies also expressed their views. There were particularly strong views from Interior, Commerce, OMB, and the Council of Economic Advisors. The president's science advisor [William Graham] put forward other positions. I felt we had to—at a minimum—establish an overall goal without a time frame for a phaseout, with at least a fifty percent cutback in ozone-depleting chemicals committed to. I felt this was the minimum that would be required to force industry to develop substitutes and get a market in substitutes established. I felt that they could achieve thirty percent through good housekeeping, such as recycling and so forth, so we needed at least fifty percent. Other issues that were discussed were the timing of the cutbacks, breadth in terms of which ozone-depleting chemicals should be included, and threshold, meaning what percentage of producing nations had to sign on before the protocol would become effective.

"Over the course of several meetings, some of the others who had initially disagreed with us came around. Typically with President Reagan what happened was that at the end of the meetings, he was presented with an option paper written by the White House staff, reflecting all of the options that had been discussed during the course of the meetings. Each cabinet officer had the opportunity to review the options paper before it went in to the president. And then the president signs the option he wants us to go with."

One of the options being considered by the Domestic Policy Council, however, was a rogue proposal advanced primarily by Secretary of the Interior Donald Hodel, and it was so idiotic it was about to explode like a gigantic public-relations booby trap on an administration already in deep trouble with its image. Interior justified its interest in the matter of ozone depletion on the premise that, as the largest landowner in the United States, it would be more affected by increased levels of ultraviolet radiation than anyone else. Visitors to national parks, for instance, would be at risk. Possibly heedless of the president's own medical history, Hodel also promoted the theory that skin cancer was self-inflicted. Moreover, Hodel believed the president ought to be presented with options other than regulatory ones, options more in keeping with his own antiregulatory philosophy.

When David Doniger heard that the Domestic Policy Council was giving serious consideration to Secretary Hodel's program of "personal protection"—the use of hats, sunglasses, and sunscreen as an alternative to restricting CFCs—he immediately called reporters he knew from the *Atlanta Constitution,* the *Washington Post,* and the *Wall Street Journal.* Hodel's plan was so flagrantly unrealistic that the writers at first assumed Doniger was joking or exaggerating. Certainly, they said, they couldn't run with the story based solely on Doniger's hearsay. Doniger suggested they call Hodel's office to ask directly about the proposed policy. Not only did Hodel's aides confirm the story; so did White House spokesman Albert R. Brashear and Science Advisor William Graham.

The story broke on May 28, 1987, in a page 18 story in the *Atlanta Constitution.* Graham and Hodel were said to "have made lengthy arguments against the United States' agreeing to the treaty," because of, according to Graham, "very significant uncertainties in our understanding of the atmospheric processes that both produce and remove ozone." Moreover, the *Constitution* reported, Graham or Hodel or both had supported David Gibbons's argument that the government should not be responsible for protecting people from self-inflicted disease.

The next day the story appeared in other papers. ADMINISTRATION OZONE POLICY MAY FAVOR SUNGLASSES, HATS, read the page 1 headline in the *Washington Post.* In the *Wall Street Journal,* it was ADVICE ON OZONE MAY BE: "WEAR HATS AND STAND IN THE SHADE." Expressing doubt about predictions of a million cancer deaths over time due to ozone depletion, Hodel told the *Journal,* "People who don't stand out in the sun—it doesn't affect them."

The arrant foolishness of Hodel's position was immediately obvious, and within a few days administration officials who had supported his alternative policy began to decline comment. Reagan made no public comment on the matter. Meanwhile, his beleaguered secretary of the interior was busy trying to back out of the predicament, claiming that he had been misunderstood and that the policy he had proposed was merely a fallback if no international agreement was possible. But the damage was already done.

Dubbing Hodel's proposal "the Ray-Ban Plan," Doniger told the *Washington Post,* "If it costs people $25 to buy glasses that filter out ultraviolet radiation, plus a hat and two bottles of sunscreen at $5 each, that's $40 a person. Take that times 200 million people and you get $8 billion a year. Obviously, you cannot protect crops or the marine environment by personal protection. It's very hard to get fish to wear sunscreen."

Members of Congress were indignant. "This is neither the time nor the place to let the rhetoric over regulation obscure the facts," said Senator Chafee, while Senator Baucus, who had recently chaired the hearing into the health risks of ozone loss, dismissed Hodel's proposal out of hand. "This approach to environmental protection," Baucus pointed out, "is akin to throwing away the air pollution control on your automobile and wearing a gas mask, or turning off the sewage treatment plant and putting a water distillation facility in every household."

Not content to merely criticize the secretary of the interior in remarks to reporters, Congressman Thomas J. Downey of New York showed up for work on the House floor on June 1 wearing an enormous sun hat and dark glasses. The next day Congressman James H. Scheuer of Brooklyn and Congresswoman Patricia Schroeder of Colorado, wearing hats and shades, posed with a display they had created of cardboard cutouts of animals decked out in custom-fitted hats and sunglasses.

While environmentalists wearing hats, shades, and sunscreen gleefully called for the resignation of a secretary of the interior who clearly did not understand the potentially disastrous effects of increased UV, Lee Thomas found he had a renewed license to affirm the administration's ability to talk sensibly about the environment. Thomas confirmed that the United States was still seeking a 95 percent reduction in CFC emissions over the next decade. "We are continuing our negotiations," he said, "and I believe an international agreement can be completed over the next several months." Secretary of State George Shultz also, for the first time, publicly proclaimed his support for the international protocol, and reportedly admonished Meese, saying that the Domestic Policy Council had been an inappropriate forum for attempting to change an international position the United States had taken. He and his staff would continue their pursuit of an international agreement, Shultz said, unless the president personally instructed him to do otherwise.

As the *Washington Post* concluded, "The grown-ups have taken back control of administration ozone policy."

Hodel backed far away from hats and sunglasses. Representing himself as a victim of the press, he wrote to Senator Timothy Wirth of Colorado in response to a request to explain his position on CFCs. "I have not suggested and do not believe that the complex issues concerning effects of stratospheric ozone depletion should be or could be solved by some simplistic approach such as sunglasses, hats and locations," Hodel wrote. On the contrary, Hodel claimed, his only concern was that any proposal backed by the United States be workable. Meanwhile, the interior secretary's allies within the administration could only lie low, some convinced that the EPA and the State Department had leaked the story about Hodel's "alternative policy," and had misrepresented it in the bargain.

"They leaked it because they realized they were losing," Rebecca Norton Dunlop later said. "They realized they were not effectively answering the questions put to them. The decision might well have been made to delay signing the Montreal Protocol until after there were more conclusive scientific results from Bob Watson's expedition to Antarctica. They realized if they could destroy Hodel's credibility, they could win."

Once the story was leaked, Dunlop recalled, "everybody ran for cover. Some of us kept up the fight within the administration, but we knew we had lost. We'd look at each other and shrug and say, 'Let's pack this one in.'"

With Hodel forced by ridicule into a strategic retreat, perhaps it was inevitable that the president would sign off on the far more defensible position favored by his secretary of state and the EPA administrator. But even after the hats-and-sunglasses debacle, it wasn't clear to the U.S. negotiating team how the issue would finally be resolved at a decisive Domestic Policy Council meeting with the president scheduled for June 18. Indeed, Benedick only received official instructions after he had arrived at an international meeting in Brussels, on the day before negotiations were scheduled to begin. Reagan had approved precisely the formulation the EPA and the State Department had outlined: the United States would continue to fight for a 95 percent cutback in CFC emissions in its public pronouncements, but would settle for 50 percent. At last, the way to Montreal was clear.

*   *   *

The debate on CFCs within the United States during the spring and summer of 1987 had done nothing to encourage a compromise from the European Community. Unsure of the depth of the American commitment to a strong position, the EC and the United Kingdom "showed unexpected intransigence" at Brussels and at a follow-up meeting of legal experts at The Hague later in July. As a result, the parties went to Montreal on September 8 for a final round of negotiations prior to the start of a diplomatic conference on September 14 with more than the optimum number of brackets—indicating areas still subject to negotiation—in the draft text of the protocol. There were, in fact, enough areas of disagreement that the prospects for achieving a protocol were far from certain.

The final impasse to be overcome between the European Community and the United States concerned whether under the terms of the protocol the EC would be counted as twelve separate nations or as a single bloc. The EC—rapidly evolving toward a single market—wanted to be treated as a single unit for purposes of determining compliance with the terms of the treaty, yet could not guarantee that it could enforce compliance by its sovereign member states, nor would it relinquish the separate votes each of its member states enjoyed as individual parties to the protocol. At the same time, the United States and other parties opposed allowing EC members to swap production quotas under the protocol, so that a production decrease by one nation would allow an increase by another. Fearful that the dispute could undermine the entire treaty, the U.S. team orchestrated a one-on-one private meeting between Lee Thomas and EC delegation head Laurens Brinkhorst. Over breakfast the two negotiators were able to reach agreement on a compromise initially proposed by New Zealand, that the EC would be treated as a single unit for purposes of consumption, but not for purposes of production.

The greatest obstacle to the protocol was a last-minute change of position by the United States regarding the provisions that would put the protocol into effect. The draft protocol called for ratification by at least eleven countries responsible for 60 percent of CFC production. At Montreal the United States proposed instead that countries representing 90 percent of CFC production be required to ratify the protocol. The administration's rationale for the 90 percent threshold was that it would avoid a situation in which a major producer nation could refuse to sign the protocol—which had gone into effect nonetheless because enough others had ratified it—and thus corner the world market. An unnamed source told a reporter from the *Boston Globe* that the proposal was the initiative of "probusiness elements" in the Reagan administration, who hoped to delay the onset of regulations by five, ten, or fifteen years. That is exactly how environmentalists viewed the late change in the U.S. position.

"This is really a backdoor attempt to undercut the protocol and keep it from coming into force," charged NRDC attorney David Wirth. The administration's reasoning was "preposterous," he added. "The way to enforce the treaty is to have strong trade provisions."

Moreover, environmentalists and a number of other nations pointed out that the U.S. proposal would allow either the Soviet Union or Japan —each of which produced slightly more than 10 percent of the world's CFCs—to block the protocol's entry into force. Those two nations plus the United States and the EC would all have to ratify the protocol for it to become effective under the terms of the 90-percent-threshold proposal.

The proposal may indeed have been a last-minute display of muscle by American industry and administration conservatives, but only the Soviet Union backed it. The United States retreated after "a decent interval," according to Benedick, while U.S. negotiators absorbed "criticism from both allied governments and environmentalists, in order to remove any lingering doubts in Washington that the position was fundamentally untenable." American negotiators finally accepted a compromise requiring ratification by at least eleven parties, whose production of controlled ozone-depleting substances equaled at least two-thirds of global production as of 1986.

The Montreal Protocol on Substances That Deplete the Ozone Layer was adopted on September 16, 1987. Representatives of twenty-four nations signed it that day, including the United States, Japan, and members of the EC—enough signatories to put the treaty into force once those same nations had also ratified it. Although the Soviet Union did not sign, its chief delegate indicated that it would, after the document could be reviewed in Moscow.

"This is perhaps the most historically significant international environmental agreement," Richard Benedick declared after the signing. "For the first time the international community has initiated controls on production of an economically valuable commodity before there was tangible evidence of damage . . . it shows that the world community can sit down and engage in international risk assessment and risk management."

Kevin Faye, of the CFC Alliance, agreed that the protocol was a "significant step," although he worried that the schedule for compliance was "too tight," and that it might not offer U.S. industry a "level playing field" in world markets. Because the protocol went further than industry thought necessary, costs would also go higher. Nonetheless, Joseph Steed of Du Pont said the company would urge ratification of the treaty by the U.S. Senate, and in other countries where Du Pont operated.

Environmentalists, too, were reserved in their praise. "Lee Thomas and the United States deserve a lot of credit for proposing this agreement and for following up with measures that got the agreement here," said NRDC's David Wirth. But, he added, the protocol did not go far enough. More restrictions would be needed, he said, to avert ozone depletion. "The treaty is an important first step because it is a precedent for further action," Doniger explained. "But it is really only a half step in controlling the ozone problem."

In its final form the protocol imposed a freeze on CFCs at 1986 levels of production starting in 1989, followed by two reductions: 20 percent by 1994 and another 30 percent by 1999. Halons were to be frozen at 1986 levels by 1994. The freeze and cuts applied to industrially developed countries. Developing countries were permitted to increase their annual production of CFCs by as much as 10 percent a year over the following ten years, a concession that had been necessary to win their participation in the protocol and was, in the view of most nations, only fair. Even so, it seemed doubtful that India or China, for whom the development of modern refrigeration industries was an important national goal, would join in the treaty. The Soviet Union, too, was permitted to exempt CFC plants under construction in its current five-year plan from some of the protocol terms. As a result of the exemptions, CFC production was projected to fall by only 35 percent under the terms of the protocol. If it was not nearly enough to halt ozone depletion, the protocol would at least put a dent in the rate of ozone depletion and would spur development of CFC alternatives.

The adoption of the Montreal Protocol, said Mostafa Tolba, "proves that we can act when our scientists tell us that we are facing a distant threat; it proves that we can move before the full magnitude of the disaster is upon us."

But the researchers who had first described the threat remained distinctly concerned. Sherry Rowland and Mario Molina, like most of the world's atmospheric scientists, had been watching with great interest events in Antarctica, where the second NASA expedition to study the ozone hole—the Antarctic Airborne Ozone Experiment—was underway. "We have to go for a 95 percent cutback, and soon," stated Rowland the week following the adoption of the Montreal Protocol, while Molina anticipated that "in the near future, we'll have a stronger case for much more severe restrictions."

That very month, both Rowland and Molina knew, the lowest ozone levels ever recorded had been monitored over Antarctica. Between mid-August and mid-September 1987—even while the nations of the world were meeting in Montreal to sign their unprecedented accord—a reduction of 50 percent was measured, compared to 40 percent only the year before. In describing his latest readings from Halley Bay, Joseph Farman did not mince words. "Above the Antarctic," he wrote, "the layer of ozone which screens all life on Earth from the harmful effects of the Sun's ultraviolet radiation is shattered."

21.

INTO THE OZONE HOLE

IVEN THE EXTREME DIFFICULTY of conducting scientific observations in Antarctica, Robert Watson had not expected the National Ozone Expedition to unravel the ozone-hole mystery on its first visit to Antarctica in 1986; but having witnessed the skepticism with which the NOZE results had been greeted, he now knew that a second expedition would have to prove beyond a shadow of a doubt the link between industrial chemicals and ozone loss.

As its critics had been quick to point out, the limitation of NOZE was that its observations were ground-based and had been made from a single location at McMurdo Station. Watson knew that more conclusive evidence could be obtained only by staging a more ambitious program, orchestrating an "ensemble of measurements," including data from the total ozone mapping spectrometer aboard *Nimbus 7*, many more ground-based readings covering a wider geographic area, and in situ measurements made from aircraft flying into the ozone hole itself at the altitude from which ozone was most rapidly disappearing.

Watson appreciated the irony underlying the elaborate new mission. He shared Sherry Rowland's sense that the demand for physical proof of the involvement of CFCs in ozone depletion rendered pointless the highly sophisticated science of computer models and satellite observation. But Watson also recognized that the computer models and the satellite observations had missed the ozone hole.

The airborne measurements Watson had in mind would resemble those taken by the Stratosphere-Troposphere Exchange Project (STEP), a NASA-sponsored upper-atmosphere program begun in Australia in January 1987. STEP's purpose was to study the vertical mixing between layers of the upper atmosphere, which occurs chiefly in giant thunderclouds. These clouds, known as convective plumes, are so large they often extend up through the troposphere into the stratosphere, where their anvil-shaped tops serve as a funnel through which atmospheric gases ascend. To monitor which tropospheric gases were traveling into the stratosphere in this way, NASA used a special high-altitude research aircraft, the Lockheed ER-2.

The ER-2 was a direct descendant of the first aircraft ever to fly in the stratosphere, the legendary Cold War spy plane, the U-2. The U-2 could fly undetected at great altitude and cover an enormous range due to its gliderlike weight, which dramatically lessened its fuel requirements. The plane could, for instance, cross a land mass as large as the Soviet Union without refueling. Although by the late 1960s satellites and a new, faster aircraft, the SR-71 Blackbird, had replaced the U-2 for reconnaissance purposes, it was increasingly used by NASA for high-altitude atmospheric research because all the newer planes capable of stratospheric flight were supersonic, and mach-level speeds did not permit the capture of air samples in flight. The U-2 was the only plane that flew in the stratosphere at subsonic speeds. With its new scientific mission in mind, Lockheed designers improved and slightly enlarged the plane, dubbing it the ER-2. The first model was delivered to the NASA Ames Research Center at Moffett Field near San Francisco in 1981. This plane and the two that followed (only three exist) were all based at Ames, flown by Lockheed pilots, and used extensively for high-altitude photography, laser examination of thunderstorms, and the sampling of volcanic dust. The ER-2 quickly established an impressive track record—collecting the first sample of intergalactic "cosmic" dust, photo-mapping Alaska in its entirety, and snapping color infrared photos of hardwood forests of the Northeast with such accurate resolution scientists could use them to determine the extent of gypsy moth infestation.

Watson's call to the Ames Research Center to request the use of an ER-2 above Antarctica nevertheless surprised the NASA operations managers. No one had ever flown a high-altitude research plane over Antarctica, in part because lightweight planes are extremely sensitive to winds in takeoff and landing, and require a smooth runway. There are no real runways at all in Antarctica, and it is the last place in the world a pilot of any aircraft can expect a routine takeoff or landing. Watson was adamant, though, that he needed the plane, and he managed to persuade them that the scientific basis for the expedition was crucial, not just "a bunch of scientists off on a lark."

He explained that over Antarctica the ER-2 would be carrying some of the same instruments it was using in the STEP mission, as well as a special instrument to measure chlorine monoxide. The whole world would be watching the outcome of the experiment, for it would help establish once and for all the cause of the ozone hole. The Ames crew agreed to conduct an analysis of the Antarctic mission's potential hazards, and within a matter of days they got back to Watson: so long as the ER-2 could take off and land on a paved runway, they would take on the assignment.

NASA would have to convince a southern-latitude country to host the Antarctic Airborne Ozone Experiment. In the past, such negotiations hadn't always gone smoothly; two full years had been required to arrange for the STEP program to be based in Darwin, Australia. This time, however, the task was simpler because officials in the southern-latitude countries, particularly Argentina and Chile, were very concerned about the local depletion of ozone—El Agujero (The Hole), as it was dubbed by newspapers in Buenos Aires. Chileans and Argentinians needed only to glimpse a copy of the TOMS satellite photograph of the depletion, with its most garish colors depicting the areas of greatest ozone loss, to recognize their own vulnerability. "South Americans were worried. Some became angry," a writer noted in the *American Scientist*. "Soccer and ozone. For a while, nothing else seemed to matter."

In Punta Arenas, Chile, the southernmost city in the world, local property values had declined by nearly a third since the discovery of the ozone hole. City officials there were prompt to offer the use of the local Presidente Ibáñez Airport as the staging site for the ER-2 flights. Winter at Punta Arenas, located on the Strait of Magellan, is severe, with cold rain and winds so strong they had been known to blow trains off their tracks. But the airport had three runways and a hangar big enough to store an ER-2, and some of the control-tower personnel spoke English. The key taxiway leading from the hangar area to the runway was full of potholes, so NASA agreed to shoulder the cost of repaving it prior to the ER-2's arrival.

While the research plane would carry aloft a number of trace-gas-measuring instruments, the most critical would be the one designed to measure chlorine monoxide. In May 1987, with planning well advanced for the airborne project, now only four months away, this device still existed only on paper. Watson could feel reasonably comfortable with such brinkmanship only because the individual he had commissioned to construct the device, Harvard University's James Anderson, had more experience building airborne chlorine-monoxide-reading equipment than anyone in the world. "Jim was the only person who had any hope of making that measurement," Watson later observed. "He was the only person in the world who had made sensitive measurements of ClO. He was one of the best experimenters in the world, and he had a unique balance of scientific and engineering know-how. It so happened he also had a very good team around him, people like Bill Brune, who had been with him for eight or ten years, and some brilliant postdocs."

The previous summer, Watson had tracked down Anderson while he was on vacation with his family in Idaho. Watson explained the project's urgency, telling Anderson, "We've got to do something about it and rather quickly. I want you to build an aircraft-based instrument to measure chlorine monoxide and bromine."

Anderson reminded Watson that although he had built a number of trace-gas-measuring devices for balloons and rockets, he had never before built an aircraft-based instrument, and he rated the chance of successfully completing it in a year as "a long shot." Usually two years were required to put a scientific device on the ER-2. Watson conceded that the job would have to be done under pressure, but urged Anderson to try.

To Anderson, NASA's request was a distinct challenge, but a satisfying one, for he had an old grudge to settle with chlorine monoxide. In the summer of 1977, when he was at the University of Michigan, something strange had happened while he was measuring ClO. In seven balloon flights from Palestine, Texas, he recorded levels of chlorine monoxide at 2 parts per billion. An eighth flight, on July 14, 1977, showed an incredible reading of 8 ppb! The measurement was so high that other researchers were unsure whether to treat it as a "spike" of a severe chemical perturbation in the upper atmosphere, confirming the trend Anderson's experiments had already detected, or a flub, which would throw Anderson's methods and all of his data into question. Had he achieved a major breakthrough, or had he simply screwed up? One rumor that made the rounds in the atmospheric-science community was that Anderson's technicians had cleaned the anomalous probe with chlorine-containing solvents, then had been afraid to confess their mistake to Anderson. Although he had been the first scientist to detect chlorine monoxide in the stratosphere, proving an essential link in the ozone-depletion theory, the 8 ppb incident was never resolved, and gave Anderson what he considered to be "black sheep" status in the atmospheric sciences.

The instrument Watson wanted Anderson to design for the ER-2 had several demanding specifications. There was room in an ER-2 for only one person, the pilot, who could not be expected to both fly the plane and operate a collection of complex experiments, so the instrument would have to be computer-automated. It also had to be capable of detecting .1 part per trillion of chlorine monoxide—a difficult reading in any situation, but here, unlike one of Anderson's balloon-based instruments, it would have to reckon with the rapid air flow caused by a plane.

This was where Anderson's lack of experience with aircraft measurements created the most formidable problem. Anderson's method, known as "representative sampling," called for a parcel of air to be taken, undisturbed, from the environment. The chemicals involved could not be allowed to react with any surface. And since the molecules Anderson needed to measure would be destroyed by a collision with the measuring instrument's entry duct at high speeds, he would have to "correct" for the crushing airflow in his data, which would put the overall accuracy of the experiment at risk.

After conferring with Art Schmeltekopf at NOAA and exchanging no fewer than five hundred drawings with Lockheed Aircraft, Anderson developed a device that would ride beneath the wing of the ER-2 and would measure chlorine monoxide using a technique known as resonance fluorescence. Paul Soderman, an aerodynamicist at Ames and a friend of Anderson's, designed a duct system that would slow the airflow passing into the entry duct from 200 to 20 meters per second. An air sample would then pass by a window illuminated by a fluorescent plasma lamp, which emitted a frequency of light that only chlorine monoxide absorbed. In a process known as "side-scattering," which one of Anderson's postdocs, Darin Toohey, compared to "kicking up the dust in your basement and shining a flashlight on it," the lamp would "read" the amount of chlorine monoxide in the air sample.

Anderson's team had the instrument ready on paper by spring, but prepared to assemble it for the first time only as field trials of experiments scheduled to ride on the ER-2 got underway at Moffett Field on May 20, 1987. The ER-2, with all the necessary scientific instruments on board, was scheduled to report to the staging site at Punta Arenas by mid-August. Meanwhile, the press converged on Moffett Field, to the occasional discomfort of some of the scientists, who were under mounting pressure to get their equipment up and running. "What do you mean 'How's the instrument working'?" Anderson demanded irritably when asked about the new experiment that was so vital to the Airborne mission. "The instrument has never worked. It has just been converted from a basket of parts!"

*   *   *

Never in NASA's history, with the exception of manned space launches from Cape Canaveral, had the space agency coordinated so many special arrangements for a program as for the Antarctic Airborne Ozone Expedition. The program's chief component was the dispatching of an ER-2 research plane across the Antarctic ozone hole to capture in situ evidence of the depletion; however, because the ER-2 had a flying range of only thirty-five hundred miles and would not be able to get very far out over Antarctica, operations managers would have to be able to guide the plane directly into the hole. To do this, flight-plan data would have to be dead-on. This was where NASA's *Nimbus 7* satellite was expected to help. Under ordinary circumstances, the NASA satellite data was not processed for months, but for the ER-2 flights, it was processed immediately, and faxed from NASA's Goddard Space Flight Center in Maryland to Punta Arenas. TOMS could provide ozone-spatial-distribution data from a particular *Nimbus* orbital swath within four hours and for the full southern hemisphere within twenty-four hours, allowing NASA researchers to track the daily fluctuations of the hole's boundaries and then guide the ER-2 directly into it. The TOMS spatial-ozone reports were accompanied by satellite updates on the location and altitude of polar stratospheric clouds and, twice daily, by forecasts from the British Meterological Office, which had the best observational weather system in the region.

Consistent with this real-time preparation for the ER-2 flights, program scientists with experiments on the research plane were expected to perform corresponding real-time analysis of their in situ data. This was part of a concerted effort to avoid the confusion and dissension that had followed NOZE. The scientists were given only six hours from the ER-2's return, or what the Ames operations staff referred to with intimidating precision as "wheels touch down," to reach their conclusions; those with atmospheric observational experiments aboard a larger participating research aircraft, a converted DC-8, were given twenty-four hours.

"The emphasis on real-time analysis was to come up with accurate statements," Operations Manager Estelle Condon later said. "We wanted consensus, if possible, because the press were crawling all over us. We didn't want the results to change upon further scrutiny, when scientists went back to their home labs. This was very difficult to coordinate and had, as far as I know, only been done once before, in STEP, and that was with none of the media pressure that attended the Antarctic expedition."

Anderson was not so much concerned about rapidly processing his data as he was simply hopeful his resonance-fluorescence instrument would function in the Antarctic cold. In a test flight at Moffett Field in May, the device had handled the problem of airflow and had demonstrated that it could successfully detect chlorine monoxide. But it remained a question whether it would function as well in the subzero stratosphere over Antarctica. Meanwhile, NASA had upped the ante by assigning the resonance-fluorescence device "Go/No Go" status, meaning Anderson's unproven instrument was so central to the mission that if it was not functioning properly, the ER-2 flights would be scrubbed.

While Anderson and the other scientists fretted over every imaginable scenario for malfunction of their experiments, those taking the largest personal risk, the ER-2 pilots, weighed every contingency for their upcoming flights. No plane had ever flown in the Antarctic stratosphere, so there was no past experience to draw on, but since Antarctica was the coldest place on earth, it could only be assumed that the stratosphere overhead would present the coldest conditions the ER-2 had yet encountered. If forced to ditch, the pilots knew they were as good as dead. No one lost in Antarctica would survive without survival gear, and given the small cockpit of the ER-2 and the need to conserve every ounce of weight on the mission, none could be carried along.

The pilots qualified to fly the ER-2 were all Vietnam combat veterans, chosen because their background with the F-105 jet fighter during the war had provided them with experience in handling a single-seat, single-pilot, manually operated aircraft—an unusual and specialized skill in the world of modern, high-tech "systems" aviation. The ER-2 pilots were cowboys, jet jockeys, combat-hardened veterans who relied on their own skill and savvy to fly an expensive research aircraft into the stratosphere and return it to earth. But they weren't daredevils, and they considered the risks of running experiments up into the stratosphere over Antarctica very carefully. "We've had the ER-2 for five years and all the time it's flown like a dream," pilot Doyle Krumrey told a reporter on the eve of the Antarctica mission. "It's extremely dependable in all environments. However, the chances of us recovering if we have to eject from the plane are very, very slim." NASA's James Margitan solemnly agreed. "It's very cold down there, very windy; wave heights are quite often fifty feet or so. The pilots realize they probably can't survive in the water for more than a few minutes."

As the plane's pilots were something of a throwback to an earlier, more heroic age of aviation, so the aircraft itself was also an anachronism—a single-engine, single-pilot flying machine with no backup systems that flew "like an albatross" at low altitudes and on landing bumped awkwardly along the ground. To save weight the ER-2 dispenses with the hydraulic landing-gear system standard on most planes, and uses disposable "pogo" wheels on the wings that fall away at takeoff. This is a tremendous weight-saving feature, but on landing the plane has only a set of small wheels in place along the fuselage, and the pilot must balance it carefully down the landing strip like a bicycle. The ER-2 on a wobbly, white-knuckle landing approach was an unmistakable reminder of even stratospheric aviation's link to the 1909 Wright Flyer.

In the two and a half years since Joseph Farman's paper had been submitted to *Nature,* scientists had pondered and speculated endlessly about the aberrations Farman had reported in the Antarctic stratosphere. On August 17, 1987, it was the ER-2's turn to encounter them firsthand. Pilot Ron Williams, who was to fly the first mission, arrived at the ER-2 hangar at Punta Arenas a few hours before takeoff. The hangar was kept no warmer than −10°F, so the pilots could get accustomed to the chill they would experience once airborne. One hour before the flight, Williams was assisted into his pressurized suit and helmet, and about forty-five minutes ahead of takeoff began breathing 100 percent oxygen, which rids the bloodstream of nitrogen so a high-altitude pilot will not get the bends. While Williams prepared in the hangar, another pilot who would not fly that day entered the cockpit of the ER-2 to perform the preflight test, so that Williams could remain on pure oxygen. The engine was started only at the last minute, in order to save fuel.

Finally, Williams emerged from the hangar, crossed the tarmac, and took the other pilot's place in the cockpit. Again to conserve fuel, he wasted little time maneuvering the plane into position for takeoff. He made one last voice check with the control tower, then aimed the ER-2 down the runway and pulled back on the throttle.

Leaving his pogo wheels behind on the runway, Williams pushed the plane through its takeoff ascent toward the open sky over Antarctica. "This mission is more dangerous than anything any of us ever flew over Vietnam," he had said earlier. "If you punch out over Antarctica, you are going to die . . . [but] this is probably going to be my last chance to make my mark in history."

Warned of "high winds aloft" before leaving Punta Arenas, Williams experienced little turbulence once he had cleared the runway and made his twenty-minute climb into the stratosphere. When he cleared 61,000 feet, however, he observed something strange: tiny ice particles—polar stratospheric clouds—racing back over the wings of the plane. Williams had flown high-altitude planes for twenty years but had never seen clouds above 60,000 feet. The PSCs were everywhere, in front, behind him, and off to either side. "They stretched across the sky," he later reported, and appeared to extend up to about 85,000 feet.

"Everywhere else in the world I had flown high-altitude research—and I had flown just about everywhere—I had been above the weather," Williams later said. "Even when those big thunderstorms come up in the Midwest, you can still ride right over them. In the Arctic you might see small patches of ice clouds, but I didn't believe Antarctica until I went into solid weather at 61,000 feet. I went into clouds at 61,000, and I didn't come out the whole time."

A more threatening development was the unexpectedly low stratospheric temperature. "Once you get into the stratosphere," Williams said later, "temperatures are fairly steady, usually around minus-55 to minus-70. From experience we thought we'd see something like that, but instead it was minus-130! Now, the ER-2 has no heaters on its fuel tanks, and naturally I was concerned the fuel tanks would freeze up."

Above normal land masses—for example, above Australia, where the ER-2 had participated in STEP the previous January—the pilot could always descend to warmer temperatures to thaw a frozen fuel line, and perhaps ascertain his position by sighting a ground beacon of some sort. But Antarctica offered no warmer altitude waiting below, and there were no navigational beacons to sight on. Williams had to descend back immediately toward Punta Arenas for fear his fuel might freeze.

Despite his difficulty with cold and clouds, Williams had managed to flick the switch that activated the airborne experiments. When the instruments were hurriedly taken from the plane and examined upon landing, it was the scientists' turn to be disappointed. James Anderson's resonance-fluorescence device had malfunctioned. His group had used only high-quality gold-plated connectors on the instrument, hoping to avoid low-temperature failure, but to Anderson it appeared the connectors had worked only before and after the ER-2 had flown in the very cold polar vortex, not in the vortex itself, where it counted. Before he had the problem fully diagnosed, NASA informed Anderson that it would attempt to fly the ER-2 again the next day and hope for better luck. Working swiftly, Anderson's team created a computer program to locate the faulty connector, and when NASA pilot Jim Barrilleaux took the ER-2 into the stratosphere for a second time the next day, August 18, the computer spotted the problem: a frozen connector in the communications line between the resonance-fluorescence instrument and the operating computer. After a third ER-2 flight went into the vortex and returned to Punta Arenas, Anderson quickly processed the instrument's data from the magnetic tape on which the computer stored it. He breathed a great sign of relief when he saw that, at last, results had been obtained. And what results they were: the instrument showed clearly that as the ER-2 had flown outside the ozone hole, levels of chlorine monoxide had been normal, even below normal, but that when the plane had entered the hole the ClO level had shot up to nearly three hundred times the levels usually observed at stratospheric altitudes. The main chemical constituent in the scientific case linking CFCs to ozone depletion had been caught red-handed.

In a total of twelve ER-2 flights, the Anderson instrument, although sensitive enough to measure chlorine monoxide at levels as small as .1 part per trillion, had found the trace gas in parts per billion within the polar vortex. Throughout the last week of August and the first week of September, ClO levels just outside the vortex varied between 5 and 30 parts per trillion, but within the vortex reached .7 part per billion, or nearly four hundred times normal levels. Meanwhile, the amount of ozone within the vortex continued to decrease. By mid-September a dramatic anticorrelation existed between ozone and ClO that was starkly visible at the "wall" of the vortex; within a few hundred feet, which the ER-2 passed through in one or two seconds, ozone dropped by a factor of three precisely where ClO increased by a factor of ten.

Meanwhile, ozone-measuring data from the ER-2 and from ground-based and balloon measurements provided more disturbing news: the ozone hole had deepened since the NOZE program a year before. Total column ozone concentrations between latitudes 70° and 80° were 15 percent lower than in 1985, down to less than 50 percent of normal levels. Over Joseph Farman's BAS base at Halley Bay, in one of the more frightening upper-atmosphere readings of the season, balloon flights on October 7 revealed that 97.5 percent of the ozone present at 10.3 miles altitude on August 15 was now missing altogether. "Ozone was virtually undetectable at this height," Farman noted in the *New Scientist*.

While chlorine levels measured by Anderson inside the perturbed region reaffirmed the NOZE expedition scientists' conviction that the basis for the ozone hole was chemical, not dynamic or meteorological, some large-scale changes in ozone were partly attributed to weather. The largest such event occurred on September 5 above the Palmer Peninsula. Over a twenty-four-hour period, total ozone as reported by the TOMS instrument aboard *Nimbus 7* dropped by 25 DU over an area of 3 million square miles. So rapid a decrease is hard to explain chemically, and was likely due to a sudden large transport of air from another part of the stratosphere or the troposphere. This odd meteorological "feature" drifted over the Weddell Sea and persisted until September 16.

At NASA's Goddard Space Flight Center in Greenbelt, Maryland, researchers continued to give the Antarctic project top priority, processing overnight data that ordinarily would take months to analyze. To avoid the controversy that had followed the pronouncement of the team's conclusions at the culmination of NOZE, Robert Watson had asked all the scientists involved in the 1987 mission to create a joint statement that would unambiguously present all the existing scientific evidence. Their response was the conclusion that half the ozone layer over Antarctica had disappeared during August and September 1987, and that all data indicated a decomposition product of CFCs was to blame.

At a press conference at Goddard on September 30, 1987, Watson told reporters "there is no longer debate" as to whether there is chlorine in "the perturbed region" of the stratosphere over Antarctica at "abundances sufficient to destroy ozone, if our current understanding of the chlorine ozone catalytic cycle is correct." He added that there was now twice as much chlorine in the Antarctic atmosphere as there had been in 1975, when the first measurements of the trace gas had been made, and, as NOAA's Dan Albritton explained, the intense cold of Antarctica seemed to be "moving at fast forward" chemical changes in the atmosphere that would occur elsewhere much more slowly. Nitrogen, which ordinarily in the gas phase would tie up chlorine in reservoirs, rendering it "passive," was itself frozen as nitric acid in PSCs, the scientists said; thus, when atomic chlorine escaped the PSCs in austral spring and reentered the gas phase, it found a denitrified atmosphere in which it could remain "active" with little chance of being sucked into a reservoir molecule.

Coordinated with in situ ozone measurements made from the fuselage of the ER-2 by Walter Starr of NASA and Michael Proffitt of the NOAA Aeronomy Lab, Anderson's resonance-fluorescence device data was the centerpiece of the Airborne expedition's results reported by Watson. The *Washington Post* echoed most of the news media in terming the expedition's findings "the first hard evidence that the critical environmental loss can be blamed on a man-made gas." As the *New Scientist* pointed out, "It is now very difficult to escape the conclusion that industrial production of CFCs is indeed to blame for the ozone depletion." NSF's Peter Wilkniss, appearing at a Senate hearing on October 27 on the implications of the Antarctic mission, assured the legislators that, given the proven link between ozone loss and skin cancer, he now feared for the health and safety of American researchers at McMurdo Station and elsewhere in Antarctica. Harvard's Michael McElroy, also present, called for moving forward the phaseout schedule described in the protocol just signed in Montreal. Sherry Rowland, recapping his efforts since 1974 in light of the recent findings above the South Pole, cautioned:

In 1974, when Molina and I first suggested there would be a chlorofluorocarbon effect on ozone, there was about 1.8 ppb of chlorine in the atmosphere. At that time, it was suggested that if only we had three more years of scientific research, we could get the answers. We are now 13 years into that three year period, and we now have 3.7 ppb of ClO in the atmosphere. . . .

I don't need any more [research] money to know that the chlorofluorocarbons have accumulated dangerously and that we ought to be limiting them.

In mid-October the ozone hole shared the cover of *Time* magazine with global warming. The article was entitled "The Heat Is On: How the Earth's Climate Is Changing, Why the Ozone Hole Is Growing" and consumed a dozen pages of the magazine. The piece discussed the history of the ozone-depletion issue, and made no attempt to offer false comfort.

"Humans are altering the Earth's surface and changing the atmosphere at such a rate that we have become a competitor with natural forces that maintain our climate," the magazine stated, quoting NCAR's Stephen Schneider. "What is new is the potential irreversibility of the changes that are now taking place."

Despite the widespread sense that the ozone issue had at last been resolved, Watson continued to caution that the expedition results were "inadequate for national or international policy making." While scientists now believed they knew the cause of the Antarctic depletion, they were still at a loss to explain its massive size. At first, some expedition scientists speculated there might well be some sort of dynamic transport of air, still not clearly understood, like the weird meteorological "feature" of early September, contributing to the ozone loss, or some aspect of heterogeneous chemistry they had not considered. The answer was to come from a scientist who, though he had never been to Antarctica, had not relinquished his efforts to understand the chlorine chain: Mario Molina.

In 1987, after Molina had relocated from UC-Irvine to the Jet Propulsion Lab in Pasadena, he had staged a lab simulation of the Antarctic ozone hole in order to study the PSC-chlorine reservoir mechanism described by Solomon, Rowland, Wuebbles, and Garcia. Rowland had shown in 1984 that chlorine nitrate and hydrogen chloride on surfaces released atomic chlorine rapidly when exposed to ultraviolet light, but critics of the mechanism contended that Rowland's experiment had used lab surfaces, and that PSCs would not offer so much surface area; they estimated that the efficiency of the reaction on the ice droplets of a PSC would be one in a million. Molina, in his 1987 experiment, used ice, not lab surfaces, and in doing so proved that the reaction efficiency was much greater—between one in ten and one in a hundred, not one in a million. And Molina found that these reactions took place in just a few thousandths of a second, much faster than Rowland had been able to prove, indicating that heterogeneous chemistry involving PSCs would produce chlorine rapidly enough and in sufficient volume to seriously deplete ozone.

"This particular reaction on the ice surface," Molina wrote, "could explain how chlorine can rapidly be released from the inactive reservoirs to its most active form, free atomic chlorine, since even the faint radiation over Antarctica in the spring can break chlorine molecules apart into their constituent chlorine atoms. Another important characteristic of the PSC-mediated reaction is that the other product, nitric acid, remains frozen in the ice. In this way, the nitrogen oxides are kept out of the gas phase and so cannot interfere with the chlorine cycles."

What was left unexplained was how the catalytic chain involving chlorine, which depended upon the presence of atomic oxygen, could work so efficiently in the cold, dry upper atmosphere above the South Pole, where—although molecular oxygen accounted for 21 percent of all molecules present—there was virtually no atomic oxygen.

Molina solved this last riddle as well. The chlorine chain, under normal circumstances, is triggered by a collision between atomic chlorine and an ozone molecule; this collision breaks apart the ozone molecule, leaving two new molecules in its place: atomic chlorine with one of the ozone molecule's released oxygen atoms attached, chlorine monoxide, and an oxygen molecule composed of the remaining two atoms of oxygen. The chlorine monoxide then collides with a single oxygen atom and surrenders its own oxygen atom to it, creating another oxygen molecule and freeing atomic chlorine to begin the process again.

Oxygen, in both molecular and atomic form, was essential to chlorine catalysis in gas phase. In the absence of atomic oxygen, Molina theorized, the only explanation for the cycle to work would be a type of bonding mechanism known as a "dimer," a reaction in which the electrovalence of a certain molecule permits its atomic elements to bond with its twin, another molecule bearing its exact atomic character. Dimers, like the similar but more intricate bonding mechanisms called polymers, were known for their usefulness in industrial chemistry but were rarely implicated in atmospheric gas-phase kinetics. Molina postulated, however, that the chlorine monoxide molecule, finding no available atom of oxygen, would resort to binding with another identical chlorine monoxide molecule; thus, the two oxygen atoms would bind to become an oxygen molecule, leaving *two* free atoms of chlorine to continue the chain reaction.

Thirteen years apart, but resembling elegant matching bookends, two of the most vital pieces of recent atmospheric science had been proposed by Mario Molina: first the original calculations of the devastating potential of the chlorine chain, and now the chemical explanation for the devastation of Antarctic ozone, and he had done it all in the lab. His lifelong ambition to perform "pure science" had taken him very far indeed.

In the fall of 1987, Molina received an interesting confirmation of his work; it arrived one day at his office rolled up inside a cardboard tube. James Anderson had drawn up a chart indicating the "anticorrelation" between falling ozone levels and rising chlorine levels in the ozone hole above Antarctica, and in tribute to the authors of the ozone-depletion theory, the Harvard scientist sent Rowland and Molina the first copies. The close correspondence of the two lines was startling. One line indicated the sudden decrease in ozone as the ER-2 flew into the Antarctic ozone hole; the other showed the equally sudden rise in chlorine monoxide.

Robert Watson also received a copy of the chart, and carried it with him to a conference in Berlin in early November. The Berlin workshop was a postmortem examination of the recently concluded effort at the bottom of the world. James Lovelock, Sherry Rowland, Paul Crutzen, Joseph Farman, Philip Solomon, Ralph Cicerone, Jerry Mahlman, and Watson were among those who gathered to weigh the newest evidence and to consider, yet again, all the alternative explanations for the Antarctic ozone loss. Every theory, every postulate, every wild idea and hypothesis was to be scrutinized and compared with the data now in hand, which pointed overwhelmingly toward a chemical explanation.

Watson reported the finding of a low level of actual CFCs in the polar vortex, which proved that a dynamic upwelling was not involved in the ozone hole because only a parcel of old air from the upper stratosphere could contain such a small quantity of CFCs. Crutzen described how PSCs form not just from water but from nitric acid and water, and how the resulting ice particles become so large they fall through the atmosphere to an altitude of six to fifteen miles, right where the largest depletion was seen. This process, explaining the denitrification of the stratosphere in the regions where PSCs formed, is important because low levels of nitric oxide create an environment that inhibits active ClO from reconverting to less harmful chlorine nitrate. Richard Turco of UCLA proposed that the Junge or particle layer of the atmosphere offered the opportunity for heterogeneous chemistry at latitudes other than Antarctica, which could create equally dangerous conditions for depleting ozone. Ralph Cicerone suggested that trace metals such as aluminum oxide thrown into the Junge layer by volcanoes could serve as surfaces for these heterogeneous reactions, compounding the threat to the ozone layer posed by volcanic activity, since volcanoes are also one of the few sources of natural chlorine.

Jerry Mahlman of Princeton laid out his theory of an expanding polar vortex: a depleted ozone layer would itself reduce stratospheric warming because less solar radiation would be absorbed by the stratosphere; in a cooler stratosphere there would be more PSCs, and with more PSCs, more heterogeneous chemistry and greater ozone depletion. After all the ozone in the polar vortex was destroyed and the air grew colder, the vortex and the ozone hole might begin to reach outward, into other latitudes. British scientist Jonathan Shanklin added a chill to Mahlman's presentation by reporting that, indeed, that winter the mass of cold air in the vortex had broken up much more slowly than usual, while James Lovelock provided an appropriate last word, a sober recantation of his own past optimism, confiding: "People sometimes have the attitude that Gaia will look after us. But that's wrong. If the concept means anything at all, Gaia will look after *herself*. And the best way for her to do that might well be to get rid of us."

As ever, the available data had prompted new conclusions and new speculation, but for the moment, at least a note of finality had been introduced by the Anderson anticorrelation chart. "One chart with just a few words of explanation," as Watson later described its unveiling at the Berlin workshop. "But as they say, it spoke volumes. Here was the ultimate 'proof' that industry and government had been conditioning their response to the crisis on for so long. Visibly it was very powerful. In fact, it sort of hit you in the face." Anderson had authorized Watson to show the chart but not to allow anyone to copy it, so the scientists and journalists present were forced to gather around for a look. The record of the severely damaged Antarctic ozone layer was a kind of Pietà of the martyred stratosphere. Journalist John Gribbin later described his first glimpse of the corresponding lines: "People talk of finding the 'smoking gun' that incriminates CFCs. This [was] more in the nature of a signed and witnessed confession."

"Miraculously" inert CFCs have far longer lifetimes than human beings, so while gazing at the results of Anderson's Antarctic data, it would not have been at all farfetched for someone to wonder if some of the atomic chlorine represented there had once belonged to the original CFC molecules produced by Thomas Midgley in his Dayton laboratory in 1928. In 1987, as today, there was no doubt that at least some of Midgley's first samples of what he called "di-chloro di-fluoro-methane" must still be floating around somewhere in our atmosphere. The same would be true of course for all the millions of tons of CFCs employed over the years in everything from "Kleer-Kool" store freezer cases, Alberto VO5 hairspray, and "climate-controlled" shopping malls, to Styrofoam burger packs and frozen fish sticks—the airborne sweepings of a streamlined half century of industrial progress and customer convenience down below.

The Anderson anticorrelation graph was hard proof that this era of faith in "miracle compounds" had come to an end. Already the four and a half decades in which CFCs had been allowed to slip quietly and unnoticed into the environment, 1931 to 1974, could be regarded as a period distinct from all others—a time of "chemical innocence." The thirteen years that followed and were occupied by the prolonged debate over CFCs and ozone could be forgiven, perhaps, as a necessarily troubled period of adjustment. Thirteen years for the world to agree to shut down a major industry might even be viewed, given the normal pace of international diplomacy, as breathtakingly fast. But by 1987, surely, there was not another year to spare. From that time forward, every ozone-depleting molecule produced by man was nothing less than a sign of willful neglect, or indifference, to the fate of the earth.

EPILOGUE

A DECADE AFTER the discovery of the Antarctic ozone hole, the ozone-depletion issue is ruled by a distinct irony. Levels of global ozone, our protective shield against dangerous forms of ultraviolet light, will continue to decline well into the next century. However, recent international phaseout agreements governing ozone-depleting substances, voluntary production stoppages announced by industry, and the development of promising CFC alternatives constitute an effective precedent for safeguarding the global environment.

The broad consensus of opinion on CFCs and ozone loss—which seemed impossible during the "ozone wars" of the 1970s and 1980s—began to form immediately in the wake of the 1987 Antarctic Airborne Ozone Expedition. On January 1, 1988, only two months after the unveiling of Harvard scientist James Anderson's anticorrelation data in Berlin, Dr. Kenneth P. Bowman of the University of Illinois published an analysis of *Nimbus 7* satellite data showing that global ozone levels dropped an average of 5 percent between 1979 and 1986. While the erosion was most severe at the two poles, Bowman's study estimated there had been ozone depletion of 6 to 7 percent in the earth's densely populated middle latitudes. Bowman's alarming findings were confirmed less than twenty-four hours after the Montreal Protocol was unanimously ratified by the U.S. Senate on March 14, 1988, by the release of a massive international assessment coordinated by NASA. The multiagency Ozone Trends Panel, composed of more than one hundred scientists, had been formed in 1986 to sift through virtually all the ozone data in the world, past and present, ground-based and satellite, and reanalyze the "trends" of total column and vertical profiles of ozone.

The Ozone Trends Panel's findings verified that global stratospheric ozone levels had dramatically decreased between 1978 and 1985. Ground-based Dobson data indicated losses in annual averages of total column ozone ranging from 1.7 percent in the latitudes from Florida to Pennsylvania, to as much as 3 percent in latitudes from Pennsylvania north to the middle of Canada, and as high as 6.2 percent in the extreme high-northern latitudes. Over Australia and New Zealand, in the vicinity of the ozone hole, average ozone depletion was estimated to be 4 percent. Indeed, NASA's 1985 prediction that at 1980 levels of CFC production, global ozone levels would decline by about 10 percent over the next century now appeared much too low. By 1988, the panel concluded, the world had already suffered more ozone depletion than had been forecast for the year 2050 by the scientific studies used as the basis for negotiating the terms of the Montreal Protocol.

The Ozone Trends Panel put an unmerciful end to any hope that the ozone problem was restricted to the South Pole. "This is not an Antarctic ozone hole," emphasized Sherry Rowland, who served on the panel. "This is ozone loss over the U.S. and over Western Europe . . . losses on the order of 15 to 20 Dobson units. That is 6 or 7 percent seen in some months at these individual [Dobson] stations. This means that we have a concern in the temperate zone. . . ."

Given a ratio of 2 percent of increased ultraviolet light reaching earth's surface for each 1 percent of the ozone layer that is depleted, the Ozone Trend Panel's findings suggested that UV increases as large as 25 percent could affect populated areas of the earth early in the next century.

The picture became even more bleak in April 1991, when the Ozone Trends Panel's estimates of ozone depletion were updated by NASA. EPA Administrator William Reilly announced that the new data showed that ozone loss over the United States since 1978 had amounted to 4 to 5 percent—8 percent at the northern latitudes of Sweden and Hudson Bay. In July 1991, British scientists confirmed that the ozone layer over Europe had been depleted 8 percent in the 1980s, twice the rate of ozone depletion in that region during the 1970s. Six months later James Anderson found the same chemical conditions present in the stratosphere above the Arctic Circle that had caused the ozone hole above Antarctica, portending a large removal of ozone from the populous northern hemisphere, depletions of as much as 40 percent over the northernmost parts of the United States, Canada, Europe, and Russia.

Reaction to these stark confirmations of the ozone-depletion threat has been swift. On March 24, 1988, nine days after the Ozone Trends Panel presented its results, the Du Pont Corporation announced that it had accepted the scientific evidence linking CFCs and ozone depletion and would join the international effort to phase out the chemicals. Although critics were heard to suggest that the company's surrender was merely an indication of its readiness to begin cornering the market for CFC alternatives, the capitulation of the world's largest CFC producer helped usher in a new era of global ozone politics. Since 1988, numerous companies, more often CFC users than CFC makers, including McDonald's, the General Electric Company, Nissan Motors, Honda, and AT&T, have announced phaseouts or cutbacks in their CFC use.

The drafting of the Montreal Protocol had purposefully ignored the ozone hole at the South Pole. The confirmation of a chemical basis for the Antarctic perturbation—coupled with the release a few months later of the Ozone Trends Panel's report—nonetheless stimulated calls for an accelerated phaseout of CFCs beyond the partial phaseout agreed to in Montreal. A provision of the Montreal Protocol allowed for just such a reopening of negotiations. In March 1989, representatives of 120 countries met in a nonbinding conference in London to take up the issue of toughening the protocol; the United States and the European Community indicated their intention to call for a total phaseout by the year 2000 (the original protocol had stipulated a 50 percent phaseout by 1998), and when 80 countries met in Helsinki two months later, they endorsed the U.S. and EC position. Thus the objective of a total phaseout by 2000 was well shared by the time the nations gathered formally in London in June 1990.

Fifty-seven nations had signed the Montreal Protocol in 1987. The 1990 London Agreements were signed by 93 nations, including for the first time China and India, whose nonparticipation in the Montreal accord was one of the protocol's weaknesses. The London Agreements, while calling for a total phaseout by 2000, allowed poorer countries until 2010, so they would have time to profit from existing technology and to develop non-CFC technology. In addition, a 14-nation committee was established to administer funds to poor nations to help them develop this alternative technology. The United States agreed to provide $40 to $60 million to the fund. The developing nations agreed that if "drop-in" alternatives were found relatively soon, they would consider joining the total phaseout in 2000.

The commitment made to this fund by U.S. negotiators in London caused an ugly policy scuffle back in Washington, however, when President George Bush announced that he would not honor it. Ironically, it was the CFC industry lobby that ultimately forced Bush's hand, pressuring the administration to contribute $25 million to the development fund —a remarkable indication of the seismic shift in ozone politics.

When James Anderson's northern hemisphere data became available in early 1992, the ozone crisis once again hit the front pages of U.S. newspapers and magazines. The Senate responded by voting unanimously to seek an end to U.S. CFC production by 1996 under the terms of the Clean Air Act of 1990, which called for an accelerated phaseout of CFCs if new scientific evidence indicated a greater threat to the ozone layer. As Senator Albert Gore, Jr., remarked: "Now that there's the prospect of a hole over Kennebunkport, perhaps President Bush will comply with the law." The president, after conferring with EPA chief Reilly, did just that, and ordered American manufacturers to end by December 31, 1995, virtually all production of chemicals that destroy ozone. Meeting in November 1992 in Copenhagen, delegates from 87 countries advanced the international phaseout agreed to in London only two years before from 2000 to 1996.

Responding to the increasingly tough new regulations, industry researchers have worked assiduously to reform the CFC market. Progress has been most encouraging in the electronics industry, where AT&T and other firms have replaced a large portion of their enormous diet of CFC-113 with a non-ozone-depleting formula called BioAct EC-7, made from terpenes found in the rind of citrus fruit. Meanwhile, researchers at Motorola and Northern Telecom, Ltd., of Canada were prompted by the imminent CFC ban to totally rethink CFC's role in electronics manufacture; rather than seek out a CFC substitute, they eliminated the use of the rosin-based soldering materials in circuit-board manufacture that made the CFC bath necessary in the first place. Solvent cleaning represents only about 20 percent of CFC use in the United States. Replacement materials for the other major CFC applications—in refrigeration and air-conditioning—have been more elusive. The two chief alternatives developed thus far are hydrochlorofluorocarbons (HCFCs) and hydrofluorocarbons (HFCs). Du Pont has promoted HCFCs and HFCs as "environmentally enlightened," and has created several variations— HFC-125 for refrigeration, HFC-134a for auto and residential air-conditioning, HFC-143a and HFC-152a for refrigeration, and HFC-123 for large commercial air-conditioning. HFCs do not contain chlorine and are no threat to the ozone layer. But both HCFCs and HFCs contribute to global warming: directly, because their infrared-absorption characteristics closely resemble those of CFCs, and indirectly, because they are less efficient in air conditioners and refrigerators than CFCs, and thus consume more energy. Some HFCs have five hundred times more global-warming impact per molecule than carbon dioxide. HCFCs, meanwhile, do contain chlorine and have some ozone-depleting capacity, but they also contain a hydrogen atom, so they are more prone to break down in the lower atmosphere, with fewer of them ever reaching the ozone layer.

Industry has argued that HCFCs and HFCs must be permitted as transitional chemicals for at least enough time for industry to recoup its substantial investment in developing the compounds and building plants to manufacture them. Environmentalists continue to push for the earliest possible phaseout for these less-than-ideal substitutes. According to the Copenhagen Agreements, HCFCs must be eliminated in stages starting in 2004 and ending in 2030.

Despite efforts to phase out CFCs and to begin using non-ozone-depleting substitutes, the accumulation and long lifetimes of CFCs guarantee increasing chlorine concentrations in the atmosphere well into the next century. Between 1974, when Rowland and Molina first called the world's attention to the problem, and 1988, when the Ozone Trends Panel report appeared, global atmospheric levels of chlorine rose from 1.8 parts per billion to 3.6 ppb. With the current phaseout agreements, it is believed chlorine levels will peak at around 4.5. ppb by the year 2000, then slowly decline to about 4 ppb by mid-century. Some scientists believe chlorine levels may go as high as 6 to 8 ppb. Although it is unclear what effect the introduction of CFC substitutes will have, for now we must expect a period of ever-increasing ozone-depletion levels before chlorine concentrations will ultimately begin to abate. Scientists estimate the ozone layer will, with a strict adherence to the CFC phaseout schedule now in place, begin to stabilize by about the middle of the next century. They admit, however, that it is impossible to rule out the occurrence of another unexpected ozone catastrophe, as the amount of chlorine in the atmosphere rises to levels never before experienced in earth's history.

The mechanisms that govern global ozone are still not completely understood. For example, are the large global decreases now being measured in temperate zones caused by "pools" of ozone-poor air drifting away from the ozone hole when the polar vortex breaks up each year? Or are other reactions responsible, perhaps involving particles other than the ice crystals in polar stratospheric clouds that are known to expedite ozone depletion? Dave Hofmann, now with the National Oceanic and Atmospheric Administration, has pointed out that while much of the sulphuric gas pumped into the atmosphere by humans and nature falls out in acid rain, some molecules penetrate the upper reaches of the sky and hover there at all latitudes. Volcanoes are a chief source of sulphuric gas, but Hofmann believes the 5 percent increase in northern latitudes during the past decade may be linked to jet exhaust from the increased number of commercial aircraft that now fly closer to the stratosphere.

Sulphuric particles have less ozone-depleting potential than the ice crystals in polar stratospheric clouds because they are smaller in mass and particle size. However, lab experiments have shown that the chemical reactions that occur on PSCs to create the Antarctic ozone hole can also occur on sulphuric acid droplets anywhere in the stratosphere. "The mechanisms may vary or may even be something we don't know about or haven't conceived of yet," NOZE scientist Philip Solomon explained, "but what we know now, based on our experience in Antarctica, is that chlorine monoxide destroys ozone, and when it finds a mechanism and starts to work, the results can be mind-boggling." One particularly worrisome scenario is that a large volcanic eruption, occurring early in the next century when global chlorine levels will be near their peak, could inject huge quantities of sulphuric acid particles into the atmosphere, providing the heterogeneous surfaces that could trigger a large-scale global depletion of ozone.

Pondering the likely effects of future ozone depletion is a luxury only the residents of the Northern Hemisphere can enjoy. For the populations of Australia, New Zealand, Chile, and Argentina, the future has already arrived. Each year after the breakup of the polar vortex, the ozone-poor air from the ozone hole spreads across the region, exposing local populations to greatly intensified UV levels. Despite a "good" year in 1988, when global wind patterns reduced the strength of the polar vortex, readings between 1989 and 1992 have continued to indicate serious depletions at the South Pole—from an average low of 115 DU in 1987 to approximately 123 DU in 1990. In 1990, Hofmann found absolutely no ozone at all in a layer of the atmosphere between 9.3 and 10.8 miles above Antarctica. In 1992, when the ozone hole was particularly severe, he reported his suspicion that sulphuric particles from the eruption of Mount Pinatubo in the Philippines had joined with PSCs to exacerbate the local hemorrhaging.

Sunblock, sunglasses, hats, and staying in the shade have become daily facts of life in many southern-latitude communities. In Punta Arenas some parents keep their children indoors between 10 A.M. and 3 P.M. Outdoor school activities like soccer practice are moved from mid- to late afternoon. In Australia, the government issues official warnings when exceptionally high levels of ultraviolet light are expected. No measurable increase in cancers or eye cataracts has shown up yet in Chile or New Zealand, but experts warn that these diseases often take years to develop.

In researching and writing *Between Earth and Sky* we talked to numerous scientists, environmentalists, lawyers, and industrialists about the related issues of ozone depletion and global climate change. Many of these people are proud of all they have accomplished in the past two decades. Scientists recognized an urgent environmental threat and identified its causes, while environmentalists and government officials brokered domestic regulations and created precedent-setting international agreements to mimimize ozone depletion and encourage the search for CFC alternatives. The international negotiations leading to the Montreal Protocol and the subsequent London and Copenhagen amendments are a landmark achievement, providing a workable framework for the world to use in addressing other global environmental problems, especially the prospect of global warming. The international consensus on CFCs encourages a sense of optimism that, as overwhelming as they sometimes seem, global environmental issues can be addressed.

Time and again in the course of researching this book we were struck by the powerful moral responses people had to the CFC issue, and the ease with which the discussion turned to the question of survival and of humankind's place in the cosmos. It was unsettling to discover that the most pessimistic voices on the subject of global change were often those of the atmospheric scientists, the very handful of men and women who best understand the myriad complexities of ozone depletion and global warming. To most of us, even when we are confronted with alarming news stories about an ozone hole over Antarctica, the environmental crisis of atmospheric change remains distant, at the periphery of our daily "universe" of seemingly larger problems involving our work or our families.

To Sherry Rowland or Mario Molina or Susan Solomon or James Anderson, however, what's happening in the atmosphere is completely tangible. Rising rates of chlorine in the stratosphere, and methane in the troposphere, are powerful evidence that humankind has fundamentally altered the chemistry of the atmosphere, probably irrevocably. They know that the harm that might accompany global warming is far less easy to predict or quantify than the harm associated with increased ultraviolet light reaching the earth's surface; and that monitoring ozone depletion was simple compared to the difficulties they face in obtaining conclusive proof of climate change. Knowing the immense damage that CFCs have caused, and the enormous obstacles that were overcome in regulating them, they recognize that international action to alleviate global warming will be even harder to achieve in the face of scientific uncertainty about its causes, and that it will be far more costly and complex to regulate greenhouse gasses than it has been to regulate CFCs. Every year of delay in implementing change compounds the problems associated with chemical contamination of the atmosphere. Ultimately, waiting for an "ozone hole"–like aberration to force swift action increases the likelihood of irreversible harm.

From the story of the rise and fall of CFCs emerge hard questions about human nature and our future on this earth. Can we rise to the challenge of preventing or even minimizing dramatic changes in our climate? Ultimately, will human nature prove adaptable to the kind of sacrifices and commitment that may be required? Can we find a new definition of progress?

ACKNOWLEDGMENTS

Between Earth and Sky could not have been written without the generous cooperation of the scientists, lawyers, government officials, environmentalists, and business people whose story it tells. We are especially grateful to F. Sherwood Rowland and Mario Molina, authors of the ozone-depletion theory, not only for making themselves accessible to us, but for opening their personal files for our use and providing invaluable advice and suggestions. Joan Rowland also contributed many insights and recollections of the "ozone war."

Numerous other atmospheric scientists made time to respond to our questions. We wish to thank Daniel Albritton, Ralph Cicerone, Paul Crutzen, Joseph Farman, Crofton "Barney" Farmer, Donald Heath, David Hofmann, Harold Johnston, Chuck Kolb, Arlin Krueger, Julius London, John Lynch, George Mount, Michael Prather, Veerabhadran Ramanathan, Philip Solomon, Susan Solomon, Richard Stolarski, Darin Toohey, and Robert Watson.

Current and former staff members of the Natural Resources Defense Council helped us tackle the history of NRDC and of environmental law. They include John Adams, Karim Ahmed, Richard Ayers, Boris Bittker, David Doniger, Stephen Duggan, Dick Hall, Angus MacBeth, Alan Miller, David Sive, Gustave Speth, Tom Stoel, and Johanna Wahl. We were also granted access to the NRDC Files, which proved to be an invaluable resource.

John Hoffman, Steve Seidel, and Eileen Claussen of the Environmental Protection Agency provided essential interviews, as did former EPA officials Barbara Blum, Joe Cannon, F. Alan "Tex" Harris, Jim Losey, George Semeniuk, Lee Thomas, John Topping, and Steve Weil.

We are also grateful to Kevin Faye of the Alliance for Responsible CFC Policy, Dr. Margaret Kripke of the University of Texas Cancer Center, and Gordon Harrison, formerly of the Ford Foundation, as well as former White House aide Rebecca Norton Dunlop and past State Department officials Suzanne Butcher, Scott Hajost, and especially Ambassador Richard Benedick. Curtis Moore, former staff member for the Senate Committee on Environment and Public Works, gave us insight into the workings of Congress and the environment lobby. Polly Penhale and Peter Wilkniss of the National Science Foundation's Division of Polar Programs illuminated many aspects of U.S. Antarctic research.

Aerosol-industry pioneers Robert Abplanalp, Walter Beard, Donald Davis, and Harry Peterson were forthcoming with their insights and recollections of the early days of "the push-button age," while Dora K. Hayes and E. F. Knipling of the U.S. Department of Agriculture graciously shared their memories of former colleagues Lyle Goodhue and William Sullivan.

Richard Scharchburg, curator of the Kettering Archives at the General Motors Institute, Mary Mathews of the Montgomery County Historical Society, Robert E. Daley of the Kettering Foundation, Jane Trucksas of the Worthington Historical Society, and Harold Schecter and A. B. Garrett of the Chemistry Department at Ohio State University answered many queries about the lives and scientific endeavors of Thomas Midgley, Jr., and Charles F. Kettering.

William Shurcliff generously shared the story of his battle to ground the SST and pointed the way to other sources of information, while Richard Kassander, formerly of the Institute of Atmospheric Physics at the University of Arizona, spoke with us about his friend and colleague Dr. James McDonald. We would like to thank particularly the helpful staff at the MIT Archives for providing access to the papers of the Citizens League Against the Sonic Boom.

We owe our gratitude also to Lawrence Novey, who suggested likely sources at the EPA; Melvin Dray, Alison Dray-Novey, Art Goodtimes, Lianne Smith, Dimitris Stevis, and Marta Tarbell, who read parts of the manuscript and offered advice and encouragement; Oscar Ackelsberg, who provided a knowledgeable technical reading; and Pantheon assistant editor Jennifer Trone, for her many intelligent and timely efforts on our behalf.

Finally, we would like to thank our agent, Amanda Urban, for her consistent support, and our editor, Linda Healey, whose diligence and thorough reading of the manuscript made her a third collaborator.

NOTES

PROLOGUE

p. 4 "Today we honor one": Priestley Prize to Thomas Midgley, Jr., *Chemical Manufacturing* (News Edition), vol. 19, no. 8, 1941. See also the *Columbus Sunday Dispatch Magazine,* December 23, 1951.

p. 4 "cries of anguish subsided": Harland Manchester, "The Magic of High-Octane Gas," *Harper's Magazine,* February 1942.

p. 6 "You mean Freon, don't you?": Author interviews with F. Sherwood Rowland and Mario Molina.

p. 6 "It seems quite clear": Mario J. Molina and F. Sherwood Rowland, "Stratospheric Sink for Chlorofluoromethanes: Chlorine Atom-Catalyzed Destruction of Ozone," *Nature,* June 28, 1974.

p. 7 "I wouldn't call it pressuring": Lydia Dotto and Harold Schiff, *The Ozone War* (Garden City, N.Y.: Doubleday, 1978), pp. 21–22.

p. 8 "This highly biostable chemical": *Arizona Republic,* September 11, 1974.

p. 8 "There does not seem": David Salisbury, "Not with a Bang, but a Pssst!" *Christian Science Monitor,* September 24, 1974.

p. 8 Rowland voiced the obvious conclusion: Paul Brodeur, "Annals of Chemistry: Inert," *New Yorker,* April 2, 1975. See also "Chlorofluorocarbons Threaten Ozone Layer," *Chemical and Engineering News,* September 23, 1974.

p. 9 "there is enough information": "Freon: Destroying the Ozone Layer?" *Science News,* September 21, 1974.

p. 9 "A fascinating paradox has surfaced": Ibid.

CHAPTER 1: THE FORTUNATE VALLEY

p. 11 "He could generate ten ideas": Carroll Hochwalt Oral History, audiotape in Kettering Foundation Library (cited hereafter as KFL), Dayton, Ohio. Additional information about Midgley: Albert Henne Oral History, Kettering Papers, General Motors Institute Alumni Foundation's Collection of Industrial History (GMI), Flint, Michigan. Also, author interview with Harold Schecter.

p. 12 "Can you point to an experience": *Industrial and Engineering Chemistry,* vol. 11, September 1919, p. 892.

p. 13 "Midgley's undergraduate work": Letter from Emerson Hinchliff to R. K. Scales, May 30, 1946, Cornell Alumni Association Papers, Cornell Library, Ithaca, N.Y.

p. 14 "There is no evidence": Thomas Hughes, *American Genesis* (New York: Viking, 1989), p. 163.

p. 14 "the Dayton address": Thomas A. Boyd, "Some Recollections of Thomas Midgley," MS in Thomas A. Boyd papers, Special Collections, Ohio State University Library, Columbus.

p. 15 Dayton had grown rapidly: Background information on Dayton, Ohio, is from Tom D. Crouch, *The Bishop's Boys: A Life of Wilbur and Orville Wright* (New York: Norton, 1989); and Charlotte Reeve Conover, *Dayton: An Intimate History* (New York: Lewis Historical Publishers, 1932). Historian Judith Sealander: "Dayton was a fascinating microcosm. Perhaps in no other area of the country did so many pioneering features of business progressivism emerge so quickly and receive so much national attention." (*Grand Plans: Business Progressivism and Social Change in Ohio's Miami Valley, 1890–1929* [Lexington, Ky.: University Press of Kentucky, 1988], p. 12). By World War I, reporters from as far away as New York and California were visiting Dayton to see for themselves how technological progress and civic cooperation could produce a model modern community. At a time of growing national concern for the management of cities, "the Dayton Model" represented an exemplary and highly functional union of human needs and technological aspiration.

p. 15 That year the city led the world: Conover, p. 215.

p. 15 "If the movements of a ship's propeller": Isaac F. Marcosson, *Wherever Men Trade: The Romance of the Cash Register* (New York: Dodd, Mead, 1945), p. 12.

p. 16 "An employer owes more": Conover, p. 217. There is additional information about Patterson's reforms at NCR in Samuel Crowther, *John H. Patterson: Pioneer in Industrial Welfare* (New York: Doubleday, Page, 1923). Along with a reputation for innovation, Patterson was known for out-and-out kookiness. Inspired by the example of President Theodore Roosevelt, he became a rabid physical-fitness enthusiast, and introduced to NCR such unheard-of perquisites as women's calisthenics classes and, for executives, mandatory morning horseback rides. "A man who cannot handle horses cannot handle men," Patterson decreed.

p. 16 Patterson was not content: An account of Patterson's advocacy of the city-manager system is found in Henry J. Allen, "Running a Modern Town," *Collier's,* October 16, 1915. After resisting Patterson's entreaties for more than a dozen years, even his threats to move NCR out of Dayton, the citizens of Dayton were convinced to accept the city-manager plan after March 1913, when a flood destroyed most of Dayton, claiming four hundred lives. In the tragedy's aftermath the mayor and the town's other elected officials were unable to respond; Patterson, turning his NCR plant into a refugee station, serving hundreds of hot meals and providing blankets and medical supplies, paying for the first relief trains to reach the stricken area, became the city's hero. Grateful voters threw out the politicians and gave Patterson the form of "business" government he wanted.

p. 17 a member of the Wright Exhibition Team: The anecdote is in a letter from

Thomas Midgley to Orville Wright, May 18, 1943, Wright Papers, Library of Congress.

p. 18 invented by the Wrights in 1903: Wilbur and Orville Wright were from Dayton's West Side, the sons of a local minister. They had first flown in Kitty Hawk, North Carolina, in 1903, but they had perfected the airplane at Huffman Prairie, a meadow northeast of Dayton, between 1904 and 1907. A local interurban railway brought Daytonians out to watch the test flights. After the demonstration of Wright aircraft in Europe and at Fort Myer, Virginia, Dayton gave the Wrights a heroes' welcome on June 17 and 18, 1909, the largest celebration the city had ever seen. When the brothers announced their intention to remain and work in their hometown, despite their worldwide fame, it reaffirmed what most Daytonians already knew: that there was something special and privileged about life in the Miami Valley, and that the atmosphere was particularly favorable to those engaged in technological adventure.

p. 18 "a mechanical messiah": Joseph Corn, *The Winged Gospel: America's Romance with Aviation, 1900–1950* (New York: Oxford University Press, 1983), p. 30.

p. 18 "Of course we can do it": *Kettering Digest* (Dayton, Ohio: Reflections Press, pp. 10–11.

p. 19 "A lanky, Lincoln-like fellow": Thomas A. Boyd Oral History, audiotape in KFL.

p. 20 "There is a river": Isaac Marcosson, *Colonel Deeds: Industrial Builder* (New York: Dodd, Mead, 1947), p. 114.

p. 20 The two men shook hands: *Kettering Digest*, p. 16.

p. 22 "I'm sorry I ever built an automobile": Mrs. Wilfrid Leland and Minnie Dobbs Millbrook, *Master of Precision: Henry Leland* (Detroit: Wayne State University Press, 1966), p. 129.

p. 22 "Something must be done": *Kettering Digest*, p. 19.

p. 23 One of the first persons: Stuart W. Leslie, *Boss Kettering: Wizard of General Motors* (New York: Columbia University Press, 1983), p. 49.

p. 23 "Kettering has done more": Thomas A. Boyd, *Professional Amateur: The Biography of Charles Franklin Kettering* (New York: Dutton, 1957), p. 82. The Delco self-starter made its debut as promised on the Cadillac, as well as on two other GM makes—the Olds and the Oakland. Most other car manufacturers quickly adopted the self-starter, with the notable exception of Henry Ford, who thought it an unneeded luxury and dismissed the notion of a car without a crank as "unmanly." Boss Ket could not comprehend Ford's indifference to the clear preference of the driving public. When he next encountered the older man in Detroit, he scolded him. "Mr. Ford," Kettering said, "[it] is something you yourself are not going to have anything to say about." (Boyd)

CHAPTER 2: "IF GOD MADE GASOLINE KNOCK . . ."

p. 24 "He was the most unconventional worker": Charles Kettering Oral History, Kettering Archives, General Motors Institute (GMI), Flint, Michigan.

p. 25 "Midge would open the subject": Richard K. Scales Oral History, Kettering Archives, GMI.

p. 25 "Hell, Midge": Ibid.

p. 25 "Kettering . . . thought": *Kettering Digest*, p. viii. Henry Ford, sharing Kettering's rural heritage and commitment to improving life on the farm, equipped the Ford Model T with a conversion kit so that the car could also be used as a tractor.

p. 27 Edison announced his retirement: Wyn Wachhorst, *Thomas Alva Edison: An American Myth* (Cambridge, Mass.: MIT Press, 1981), p. 99.

p. 27 Kettering called Midgley: *Running Errands for Ideas,* long-playing record of anecdotes and remarks by Charles Kettering, Kettering Foundation Library, Dayton, Ohio.

p. 27 "I spent a whole Saturday afternoon": Kettering Oral History, Kettering Archives, GMI.

p. 27 "Get off Route 25!": *Kettering Digest,* pp. 2–8; also cited in Boyd, *Professional Amateur,* and Leslie, *Boss Kettering..*

p. 28 "When I was a boy": Boyd, *Professional Amateur,* p. 100.

p. 29 Kettering brought Henry Ford: Anecdote recounted in T. A. Boyd, "Some Recollections of Thomas Midgley," MS, Special Collections, Ohio State University Library, Columbus.

p. 29 "If God made gasoline knock": Carroll Hochwalt Oral History, audiotape, KFL.

p. 29 "What do I want a chemist for?": Kettering, *Running Errands for Ideas,* KFL.

p. 30 formed the Dayton-Wright Corporation: One of the new firm's projects was one of the world's first "guided missiles," an "air torpedo" designed by Midgley and others, that could be armed and sent sailing over enemy lines. "The Messenger," soon renamed "The Bug" by engineers for its erratic behavior, was launched along a set of rail tracks. On October 4, 1918, in a test flight of the torpedo staged for visiting dignitaries from Washington, the unarmed prototype shot off on an uncontrolled flight over Dayton, crisscrossing the sky, "headed for Xenia." Kettering and a posse of engineers and soldiers gave chase, careening down country roads in their automobiles like so many Keystone Kops. They found it in a cornfield twenty-one miles away. No more than fifty of the forty thousand units ordered by the military were ever produced.

p. 30 America's wartime seizure: Gerald Colby, *Du Pont Dynasty* (Secaucus, N.J.: Lyle Stuart, 1984), pp. 210–11. See also David F. Noble, *America by Design: Science, Technology, and the Rise of Corporate Capitalism* (New York: Knopf, 1977), p. 16.

p. 30 an investment in an automaker: Durant, who frequently traveled to Boston and New York during GM's early years to seek backing, had once tried to assure George Perkins of the Morgan Guaranty Trust that American automakers would soon be producing as many as half a million cars a year—a modest estimate, as things turned out. Perkins's incredulous reply—"Really, Mr. Durant, if you're going to make such wild claims, no one will take you seriously!"—typified the eastern establishment's scorn for the "fad" of carmaking. (Author interview with Prof. Richard Scharchburg, General Motors Institute)

p. 31 affording "many opportunities": David Hounshell and John Kenly Smith, Jr., *Science and Corporate Strategy: Du Pont Research and Development, 1902–1980* (Cambridge: Cambridge University Press, 1988), p. 128.

p. 32 "How many substances": Arvid E. Roach, "Ket: America's Best-Loved Inventor," unpublished MS in Kettering Archives, GMI, 1943.

p. 32 "We thought we had worked hard": George B. Kauffman, "Midgley: Saint or Serpent?" *Chemtech,* December 1989.

p. 32 "I don't think humanity": *Columbus Sunday Dispatch Magazine,* December 23, 1951.

p. 32 "from melted butter and camphor": William Haynes, in *The Great Chemists,* ed. Eduard Farber (New York: Interscience, 1961), p. 1592.

p. 33 "Ket did raise hell with us": Carroll Hochwalt Oral History, GMI.

p. 34 "The popular idea might be": Kauffman, p. 719.

p. 35 He named it "ethyl": Boyd, *Professional Amateur,* p. 147.

p. 35 "a pair of lead-lined lungs": Letter from Thomas Midgley to Wilder D. Bancroft, January 19, 1923, in Midgley "Personal File," Kettering Archives, GMI.

p. 36 "If Midgley's work": Memorandum from Norman Roberts to Surgeon General Hugh Cumming, November 13, 1992, U.S. Public Health Service Files: Tetraethyl Lead; National Archives.

p. 36 "Since lead poisoning in human beings": Letter from Surgeon General Hugh Cumming to Pierre Du Pont, December 20, 1922, Public Health Service Files: Tetraethyl Lead; National Archives.

p. 37 "the average congested street": William Graebner, "Science, Engineering, and Lead Poisoning, 1900–1970," in *The Health and Safety of Workers,* ed. Ronald Bayer (N.Y.: Oxford University Press, 1988), p. 29.

p. 37 "My dear Round": Letter from Thomas Midgley to G. A. Round, February 14, 1923; Midgley "Personal File," Kettering Archives, GMI.

p. 37 "The compounds seem to possess": Hounshell and Smith, p. 152.

CHAPTER 3: HOUSE OF THE BUTTERFLIES

p. 40 "the industrial poisons": Alice Hamilton, *Industrial Medicine,* vol. 4, 1935, p. 427.

p. 41 "In those countries": Alice Hamilton, *Exploring the Dangerous Trades: The Autobiography of Alice Hamilton, M.D.* (Boston: Little, Brown, 1943), p. 115.

p. 41 "In those early days": Ibid., p. 5.

p. 42 Like other progressives: As *New Republic* editorialist Walter Lippmann described them, Alice Hamilton's generation of reformers were "born into a world in which the foundations of the older order survive only as habits or by default," and where all human beings were given credit for possessing the capacity for constructive change. (Thomas Bender, *New York Intellect: A History of Intellectual Life in New York City from 1750 to the Beginning of Our Time* [New York: Knopf, 1987], p. 230.)

p. 42 "a back door and a cellar": from "Nineteen Years in the Poisonous Trades" by Alice Hamilton in *Harper's Magazine,* October 1929.

p. 43 "Merciful God": Leon Stein, *The Triangle Fire* (Philadelphia: Lippincott, 1962), p. 134.

p. 43 "There was a time": Ibid., p. 139.

p. 43 "The old Inquisition": Ibid., pp. 144–45.

p. 44 "organized in the belief": Workers' Health Bureau fund-raising letter, September 1924, in WHB folder, Wagner Labor Archives, New York University Library, New York City.

p. 44 During the seven years of its existence: We are indebted for our discussion of the Workers' Health Bureau to David Rosner and Gerald Markowitz, "Safety and Health as a Class Issue: The Workers' Health Bureau of America during the 1920's" in *Dying for Work,* ed. Rosner and Markowitz (Bloomington, Ind.: University of Indiana Press, 1987), pp. 53–64.

p. 45 "boys 20 and 21 years old": From the Annual Report of the Administrative Staff to the Executive Committee of the Workers' Health Bureau of America, quoted in Rosner and Markowitz, p. 59.

p. 45 "We have at last": Letter from Grace Burnham to C. E. A. Winslow, March 30, 1928, C.E.A. Winslow Papers, Yale University Library.

p. 45 "loss of weight": Health Leaflet #1, Workers' Health Bureau, 1923, "Daily Health Rules for Protection Against Lead and Other Poisons," in WHB folder, Wagner Labor Archives, New York University Library.

p. 47 "Ernest was told": *New York Herald Tribune,* October 27, 1924. We are indebted for our account of the "Loony Gas" scare, based, in part, on David Rosner and Gerald Markowitz, " 'A Gift of God?' The Public Health Controversy over Leaded Gasoline in the 1920s"; and William Graebner, "Hegemony Through Science: Information Engineering and Lead Toxicology, 1925–1965." Both articles appear in *Dying for Work,* ed. Rosner and Markowitz.

p. 47 "these men probably went insane": Hounshell and Smith, p. 154.

p. 47 "Two years ago I warned": *New York World,* October 28, 1924.

p. 48 "What becomes of the lead?": *New York World,* October 30, 1924.

p. 48 "it won't even kill the fish": *New York World,* May 3, 1925.

p. 48 "Dr. Henderson [does] not disguise": *New York World,* May 3, 1925.

p. 49 "Neither he nor I": Hounshell and Smith, p. 154.

p. 49 "without desiring to attach": *New York Herald Tribune,* October 31, 1924.

p. 49 "In proof of his argument": *New York Herald Tribune,* October 31, 1924.

p. 50 Between July and October: Hounshell and Smith, p. 152.

p. 50 The Deepwater story: Editorialized *The Nation* (July 8, 1925): "It is a profitable going concern, the E. I. du Pont de Nemours, and Wilmington is its showplace. But only the cerebral ganglions of a complicated industrial and financial organism are to be found there. The dynamite plants and commodity factories are elsewhere. The poison factories are huddled in the propitious obscurity of Deepwater."

p. 51 "an impartial investigation": Letter from Alice Hamilton to Surgeon General Hugh Cumming, February 12, 1925, Public Health Service Files, National Archives.

p. 52 In a related test: Roach, *"Ket,* America's Best-Loved Inventor": Manuscript, 1943, Kettering Archives, GMI.

p. 52 "The men engaged in industry": Henderson's testimony, and all testimony before the Cumming inquiry, is derived from United States Public Health Service, *Proceedings of a Conference to Determine Whether or Not There Is a Public Health Question in the Manufacture, Distribution, or Use of Tetraethyl Lead Gasoline,* Public Health Bulletin #158 (Washington, D.C.: GPO, 1925).

p. 54 The Ethyl Corporation's statements: Rosner and Markowitz, p. 130.

CHAPTER 4: THE GOOD OLD NOSE TEST

p. 57 "Physics speak of Gorrie's machine": George H. Whiteside, "Dr. John Gorrie: Sketch of the Career of the Original Inventor of the Ice Machine," *Ice & Refrigeration Magazine,* May 1897.

p. 58 Durant renamed the Mellowes company: *Frigidaire History,* pamphlet in the Frigidaire Papers, GMI.

p. 60 Birdseye lived out every inventor's dream: *Time,* October 22, 1956.

p. 60 "The first day's sales": Memorandum from R. W. Sinks, National Users Dept., Frigidaire Corp., to P. K. Bates and others, March 13, 1930, in Frigidaire Papers, GMI.

p. 61 "Never in the history": *New York Times,* May 16, 1929.

p. 62 "What do you want to do that for?": Kettering Oral History, Kettering Archives, GMI.

p. 63 "We must have": William Haynes in *The Great Chemists,* ed. Eduard Farber (New York: Interscience, 1961), pp. 1589–97. Kettering was grateful for the chance to distract Midgley from the scientific investigation that had preoccupied him during the mid-1920s—the search for a synthetic replacement for rubber. Midgley had persevered despite his lack of success, often veering off into areas of research with little or no commercial potential, thereby straining his relationship with General Motors. (Leslie)

p. 63 It was a Saturday: The description of the invention of CFCs is based on the Albert Henne Oral History, Kettering Archives, GMI; Leslie, p. 223; Thomas Midgley, Jr., "From the Periodic Table to Production," *Journal of Industrial and Engineering Chemistry,* February 1937; and *Running Errands for Ideas,* KFL.

p. 66 "The best way": "Human Breath Converted into Fire Extinguisher by Cornellian Scientist," *Ithaca Journal News,* April 14, 1930.

p. 66 In 1931, Frigidaire launched: Freon-12 Refrigerant Demonstration script, Frigidaire Papers, GMI.

p. 67 "Dichlorodiflouromethane is a stable compound": *Freon: A Safe Refrigerant,* brochure published by Kinetic Chemicals Inc., 1931.

p. 67 He was among the first: Kettering told a reporter from *American City Magazine* in 1929, the year Frigidaire controlled 49 percent of the American market for mechanical refrigeration, "To the eye of the Lord I suppose a Mexican is a precious human soul, but what good is he to an American industrialist who has radios and washing machines and vacuum cleaners and automobiles to sell? He is almost zero. But what will this tropic man be, both as a competitor and as a purchaser, when he begins buying temperature just as he buys water and light? The possibility of this simple idea is so great that we can hardly begin to visualize the changes it will make." (John T. Flynn, "Big Changes Ahead": Interview with Charles Kettering, *American City Magazine,* January 1930)

p. 68 "It could be compressed": Alfred Lief, authorized biography of Willis Carrier, unpublished MS, Carrier Papers, Cornell University Library, Ithaca, N.Y. Our discussion of Willis Carrier and the invention of air-conditioning is indebted to Margaret Ingells, *Carrier: Father of Air Conditioning* (Garden City, N.Y.: Doubleday, 1952); and Cloud Wampler, "Dr. Willis H. Carrier: Father of Air Conditioning," speech delivered to the Newcomen Society, April 13, 1959, pamphlet in the New York Public Library.

p. 68 a "farm boy": "He Dries Air with Water and Cools It with Steam," *American Magazine,* February 1933.

p. 69 Carrier lived by the motto: Robert Friedman, "The Air-Conditioned Century," *American Heritage,* August–September 1984, p. 32. Carrier's first success with artificial cooling came in southern textile mills. Efforts to control temperature and humidity in the plants had been known as "yarn conditioning," the origin of the term "air-conditioning." Carrier air-conditioned a pharmaceutical manufacturer in Detroit in 1907, a celluloid film plant in New Jersey in 1908, and a tobacco warehouse in Kentucky in 1909. Although the original objective had been preservation of perishable goods, employees favored the air-conditioned sections of their workplaces, and thus Carrier's next market—comfort cooling—was obvious. One of the first major tests for comfort cooling was the Rivoli Theater at Forty-ninth Street and Broadway in New York. "I am sure no playwright and no cast ever worked with greater enthusiasm and determination for success," Carrier later recalled of preparations for air-conditioning's "Broadway debut." (Lief MS, Cornell Library) The opening was widely advertised for Memorial Day, 1925. The weather cooperated, as the temperature reached a high in the low nineties. A long line formed at the box office to see *The Little French Girl,* starring Alice Joyce and Neil Hamilton. Among the spectators was the film's coproducer, Adolph Zukor.

"The people filled all the seats and stood seven deep in the back of the theater," Carrier later recalled. "We had more than we had bargained for and were plenty worried. From the wings we watched in dismay as two thousand fans fluttered. When the film started, we felt that Mr. Zukor was watching the people instead of the picture—and saw all those waving fans! It takes time to pull down the temperature in a theater, and still longer in a packed house on an extremely hot day. But gradually the fans dropped into laps as the effects of the air conditioning system became evident. Only a few chronic fanners persisted, but soon they, too, ceased fanning. We had stopped them 'cold.' "

Zukor told Carrier, "The people are going to like it." Receipts at the Rivoli increased by $100,000 over the previous summer. (Friedman) Over the next several years air-conditioning was nearly universally adopted in theaters. Summer soon became the film industry's most profitable season, and going to the movies one of the most pleasurable ways of beating the heat.

p. 69 "It is possible to speak": R. Threvenot, *A History of Refrigeration Throughout the World* (Paris, 1979), p. 361.

CHAPTER 5: THE MOST BEAUTIFUL LAWN IN THE WORLD

p. 73 "Apparently my enthusiasm was catching": William N. Sullivan, Jr., "Research on Insecticidal Aerosols to Prevent the Transport of Insects on Common Carriers," thesis summary, University of Tokyo, 1977. Our description of the work of Goodhue and Sullivan and the development of the aerosol insecticide is based also on interviews with Drs. E. F. Knipling and Dora Hayes of the U.S. Department of Agriculture, Bureau of Entomology. Also, D. K. Hayes, E. J. Gerberg, and M. S. Schecter, "The History and Development of Pyrethroids," *Chemical Times and Trends*, vol. 2, no. 1 (October 1978); and E. F. Knipling, "Insect Control Investigations of the Orlando, Fla., Laboratory During World War II," *The Smithsonian Report for 1948*, pp. 331–48.

p. 73 "Then, since we are somewhat apprehensive": Lyle Goodhue, "How It All Began," *Aerosol Age*, May 1965.

p. 74 "In less than ten minutes": Ibid.

p. 74 In both their patent application: U.S. Patent #2,321,023, Method of Applying Parasiticides, L. D. Goodhue and W. N. Sullivan.

p. 74 Stone listened with keen interest: Lyle Goodhue, *Journal of Economic Entomology*, February 1942.

p. 75 Callendar urged Sullivan: William N. Sullivan, "The Coupling of Science and Technology in the Early Development of the World War II Aerosol Bomb," *Military Medicine*, February 1971.

p. 76 "It's exactly what we want": David O. Woodbury, *Battlefronts of Industry: Westinghouse in World War II* (New York: Wiley, 1948), p. 144.

p. 76 "For every man": "Science Develops New Chemicals for War Against Insects," *The Laboratory*, January 1945.

p. 77 "Midgley had no idea": "New Products: War on Bugs," *Business Week*, November 25, 1944.

p. 77 "A double delight": *New York Times*, June 17, 1945.

p. 77 when he sprayed a test substance: DDT had originally been synthesized in 1874 by German chemist Othmar Zeidler while in search of chlorinated compounds.

p. 78 "the atomic bomb": *The Laboratory*, January 1945.

p. 79 "Most of the three to four million": Donald Davis, quoted in *The Science and Technology of Aerosol Packaging*, ed. John J. Sciarra and Leonard Stoller (New York: Wiley, 1974), p. 10. Goodhue and Sullivan could not expect to gain financially from their invention. Because they were government researchers, all licensing royalties from their public service patent were assigned to the secretary of agriculture. Both men nonetheless remained active in encouraging further commercial development of their brainchild. In the June 23, 1944, issue of *Science* they reported that "the Freon gas now being used successfully in 'bombs' to fight mosquitos in tropical regions can [also] be used for fighting germs in the air of rooms. The nontoxic and nonflammable nature of [Freon] gas is responsible for the success of [the aerosol] method." In an enticing postscript they added, "Since the study of germicides is outside the field of research of the Bureau of Entomology and Plant Quarantine, the writers plan no further tests of this method and hope that others will be interested in exploring its possibilities."

After the war Goodhue left government service to finish his career with the Phillips Petroleum Company. Ironically, he helped that company develop propane and isobutane as aerosol propellants, substances that would be credited with saving the aerosol business when Freons were indicted for destruction of the ozone layer in the 1970s. (Author interview with Donald A. Davis) Sullivan returned to Beltsville to fulfill his ambition of becoming one of the country's leading authorities on airplane disinsection. Much as he had earlier pushed for military adoption of the aerosol, he began to hound NASA to include disinsection studies in the U.S. space program. His persistent efforts, in collaboration with Agriculture Department researcher Dora K. Hayes, culminated in the 1977 *Skylab 4* mission, which carried seven hundred gypsy moth eggs from one of his Beltsville test colonies into orbit around the earth. To Sullivan it had seemed extraordinary that men could head into outer space and expect to leave the insects behind. (*Science,* June 23, 1944; author interview with Dora K. Hayes)

p. 79 "CFCs had convincingly shown": Midgley did not envision the use of CFCs in convenience aerosols, but he did advocate their use as propellants in fire extinguishers. He also pursued the idea that CFCs might work as an anesthetic, although his experiments in this area were less than encouraging. In one test whose results he reported to Du Pont in the 1930s, two lab dogs remained "permanently anesthesized."

p. 79 Midgley "would just get in his car": Author interview with A. B. Garrett, former chairman of the Chemistry Department, Ohio State University.

p. 80 "They had this incredible optimism": Author interview with Harold Schecter, professor of chemistry, Ohio State University.

p. 80 One of Midgley's pet projects: The description of Midgley's endeavors with his lawn are from "Remarks by One of His Former Colleagues, R. K. Scales," made at the "Midgley Medal Dinner" in Detroit, January 12, 1965. Our thanks to Jane Trucksas of the Worthington Historical Society, who gave us a tour of Worthington and answered many questions about the community where Midgley lived.

p. 82 "When I feel old age approaching": T. A. Boyd, "Some Recollections of Thomas Midgley," MS, Special Collections, Ohio State University Library. The poem had originally been included in "Hobbies of 1926–1928," chapbooks of his own light verse that Midgley mailed to friends as Christmas greetings in the mid-1920s.

p. 83 "Suicide by strangulation": In deference to his standing in the community, perhaps, Midgley's death was reported as an accident in 1944. Later biographers found it hard to resist the irony that the inventor of such controversial items as ethyl and CFCs had died after becoming entangled in one of his own inventions. It was the coroner's verdict, however, that Midgley had taken his own life, and this appears to have been common knowledge among his friends. Albert Henne, called to the house by Carrie Midgley on the morning of November 2, later assured A. B. Garrett, head of Ohio State's Chemistry Department, "That was no accident." (Author interview with A. B. Garrett; Carroll Hochwalt Oral History)

p. 83 "The world has lost": Telegram from Orville Wright to Mrs. Thomas Midgley, Jr., November 2, 1944, in Wright Papers, Manuscript Division, Library of Congress.

p. 83 "He was one of the great geniuses": Joseph C. Robert, *Ethyl: A History of the Corporation and the People Who Made It* (Charlottesville: University Press of Virginia, 1983), p. 102.

p. 83 "We bring nothing into this world": Thomas A. Boyd, "Thomas Midgley, Jr.," *Journal of the American Chemical Society,* June 24, 1953.

CHAPTER 6: THE PUSH-BUTTON AGE

p. 84 "You can follow flies": Jordan, W. Alec, "Why They Buy Aerosols," *Aerosol Age,* December 1956.

p. 85 Harry Peterson and Bill Palmer: Author interview with Harry Peterson. Peterson's wife provides a lively account of his active role in the birth of the aerosol in Elaine Peterson, *Poof: The Aerosol Game* (New York: Carlton Press, 1989).

p. 86 Despite the breakthrough: Russell B. Stoddard, "Low Pressure Aerosols: Their Future Will Probably Be Determined in 1949," The weakness of the aerosol spray-can system was discussed in *Soap and Sanitary Chemicals,* July 1948. Also, author interviews with Harry Peterson, Walter Beard, Robert Abplanalp, and Donald Davis.

p. 87 "The first thing": Author interview with Robert Abplanalp.
p. 87 In September 1949: U.S. Patent #2,631,814, Robert Abplanalp; and author interview with Abplanalp.
p. 87 "Bob Abplanalp's position": Author interview with Walter Beard.
p. 87 "The aerosol industry": "Aerosols and Their Promise of a Billion Dollar Market by 1965," *Aerosol Age,* May 1956.
p. 88 The prevailing sentiment: Author interview with Walter Beard.
p. 88 " 'Bomb' tends to be associated": Editorial by Pete Clapp of Western Filling Corporation, in *Aerosol Age,* July 1957.
p. 89 "the laboratory results": Stuart W. Leslie, *Boss Kettering: Wizard of General Motors* (New York: Columbia University Press, 1983), p. 317.
p. 89 "Look around you": *Kettering Digest* (Dayton, Ohio: Reflections Press, 1982), p. 67.
p. 90 " 'If you can't make it' ": Author interview with Harold Schecter.
p. 90 "But how will you apply": Leslie, p. 335.

CHAPTER 7: SCENIC HUDSON

p. 91 "My real preoccupation": Paul Brooks, *The House of Life: Rachel Carson and Her Work* (Boston: Houghton Mifflin, 1972), p. 124.
p. 92 *New York Times* bestseller list: Ibid., p. 129.
p. 93 For Darwin the inspiration: We are indebted for the discussion of Darwin, Gilbert White, and Thoreau to David Worster, *Nature's Economy: The Roots of Ecology* (San Francisco: Sierra Club Books, 1977).
p. 93 in reaction to the clang and clamor: In the early years of the nineteenth century, many Americans, prominent among them Thomas Jefferson, believed that, due to the vastness of the land, the United States would long remain an agrarian nation. It was with a mixture of revulsion for the new and nostalgia for this lost vision of America that Thoreau and the other Romantics decried the coming of the mills and factories that in Britain had reduced human beings to cogs, and the railroads, the "machines in the garden," which shattered the tranquillity of America's rural life.
p. 93 "For the whole world works together": Francis Bacon, quoted in David Pepper, *The Roots of Modern Environmentalism* (London: Croom-Helm, 1984), p. 55.
p. 93 "In wildness is the preservation": Henry D. Thoreau, "Walking," reprinted in *The Selected Works of Thoreau,* Cambridge ed. (Boston: Houghton Mifflin, 1975), p. 672.
p. 94 "gain a hearing"; John Muir, "Wild Wool," quoted in Frederick Turner, *Rediscovering America; John Muir in His Time and Ours* (New York: Viking, 1985), p. 230.
p. 95 Historian T. O'Riordan: T. O'Riordan, *Environmentalism* (London: Pion, 1981).
p. 96 "A spray as indiscriminate": Edwin Teale quoted in Brooks, pp. 230–31.
p. 96 Many of her sources: Frank Graham, Jr., *Since Silent Spring* (Boston: Houghton Mifflin, 1970), p. 29.
p. 96 "subjected to ridicule": Brooks, p. 36.
p. 97 "I have a comforting feeling": Ibid., p. 244.
p. 97 "To find a diet": Carson, *Silent Spring,* p. 179. In its chemical stability, DDT had an essential quality in common with its related family of chemicals, the chlorofluorocarbons, which are also a form of chlorinated hydrocarbon, built by industrial chemists on the remarkably strong and versatile bond that can be formed between atoms of chlorine and atoms of carbon. Rachel Carson died of breast cancer in April 1964, two years after the publication of *Silent Spring* and a decade before Sherry Rowland and Mario Molina revealed that chlorofluorocarbons, too, pose a

significant threat to the environment. But Carson might not have been surprised to learn of the Rowland-Molina theory. There are suggestive parallels between DDT and CFCs—not only the chemical stability of the chlorinated hydrocarbon species, but the reckless volume in which both "miracle compounds" were disseminated.

p. 97 "If man were to faithfully follow": Brooks, p. 298.

p. 97 "littered with crass assumptions": Graham, p. 60.

p. 97 "The problem [of distortion]": Ibid., p. 59.

p. 98 a "fairly thorough-going vindication": Brooks, p. 306.

p. 98 who could predict: GM and Du Pont, for instance, in marketing Freon, had tested for corrosiveness, toxicity, and flammability, but no one had thought to consider the possibility that CFCs might damage stratospheric ozone—nor would they have been equipped to carry out such an investigation even if it had occurred to them. The science of atmospheric chemistry was still in its infancy, and there was neither the intellectual foundation nor the technical means available to trace CFCs in the atmosphere, much less to deduce their ultimate chemical fate.9

p. 99 "We still talk": Brooks, p. 319.

p. 99 "Any fool can destroy trees": John Muir, "The American Forests," *Atlantic Monthly,* August 1897.

p. 100 "in his late fifties": Gifford Pinchot, *Breaking New Ground* (New York: Harcourt, Brace, 1947), p. 100.

p. 100 "spent an unforgettable day": Ibid., p. 103.

p. 100 "It was such an evening": Turner, p. 302.

p. 100 On a tour of the West: Ibid., p. 312. See also Frank Graham, Jr., *Man's Dominion: The Story of Conservation in America* (New York: M. Evans, 1971), p. 98.

p. 101 Pinchot moved quickly: Stephen Fox, *The American Conservation Movement: John Muir and His Legacy* (Madison: University of Wisconsin Press, 1985), p. 130. Originally published by Little, Brown, 1981.

p. 101 Pinchot consolidated his thinking: Pinchot, pp. 322–26.

p. 102 "Dam Hetch Hetchy!": John Muir, *The Yosemite* (New York: Century, 1912), pp. 261–62.

p. 102 "whether the advantage": Roderick Nash, *Wilderness and the American Mind* (London and New Haven: Yale University Press, 1967), pp. 170–71.

p. 102 "sacrifice his own family": Graham, p. 342; Fox, p. 142.

p. 102 "There are just two things": Pinchot, p. 32.

p. 102 "One hundred or even fifty": Nash, p. 181.

p. 103 a special place in American culture: Barbara Babcock Lassiter, *American Wilderness: The Hudson River School of Painting* (Garden City, N.Y.: Doubleday, 1978).

p. 105 not intimidated by the powerful: Author interview with Stephen Duggan.

p. 106 "We believe that ugliness": W. M. Tucker, "Environmentalism and the Leisure Class," *Harper's Magazine,* December 1977.

p. 107 "quiet but passionate": Author interview with Albert Butzel.

p. 107 "In order to insure": Court ruling cited in Russell D. Butcher, "Conservationists Go to Court," *American Forests,* June 1971, and in Joseph L. Sax, *Defending the Environment* (New York: Knopf, 1970), p. 132.

CHAPTER 8: THE HIGHEST USE OF THE COURTROOM

p. 109 the provision of free legal services: The background of public-interest law is discussed in Nan Aron, *Liberty and Justice for All: Public Interest Law in the 1980s and Beyond* (Boulder and London: Westview Press, 1989); Council for Public Interest Law, *Balancing the Scales: Financing Public Interest Law in America,* 1976; and

Benjamin W. Heineman, Jr., "In Pursuit of the Public Interest," *Yale Law Journal,* November 1974.

p. 110 Moynihan was concerned: Jay Acton and Alan Lemond, *Ralph Nader: A Man and a Movement* (New York: Warner Paperback Library, 1972), p. 37.

p. 111 "one of the greatest acts": Ralph Nader, *Unsafe at Any Speed* (New York: Grossman, 1965), pp. 4–5.

p. 111 "General Motors' Charles Chayne": Ibid., pp. 42–43.

p. 111 "what makes him tick": Acton and Lemond, p. 62.

p. 111 James Roche was forced to admit: Robert F. Buckhorn, *Nader: The People's Lawyer* (Englewood Cliffs, N.J.: Prentice-Hall, 1972), p. 8.

p. 112 By the summer of 1969: Acton and Lemond, pp. 89–90.

p. 112 a form of "compulsory consumption": Buckhorn, p. 239.

p. 113 "save the world": Dr. Charles F. Wurster, Jr., quoted in Gilbert Rogin, "All He Wants to Save Is the World," *Sports Illustrated,* February 3, 1969.

p. 113 "I think there needs to be": Luther J. Carter, "Environmental Pollution: Scientists Go to Court," *Science,* December 22, 1967.

p. 113 "It's about time": *New York Times,* Sunday, September 14, 1969.

p. 115 The Yale realists: Laura Kalman, *Legal Realism at Yale, 1927–60* (Chapel Hill and London: University of North Carolina Press, 1986), p. 3.

p. 116 "There is a growing awareness": Gus Speth, "The Environmental Legal Defense Fund," first draft, November 6, 1968, Gus Speth personal files.

p. 117 Harrison did not agree: Author interview with Gordon Harrison.

p. 117 "Philanthropically supported conservation": Confidential in-house memorandum from Gordon Harrison, "Resources and Environment Review and Projections," Division of National Affairs, Ford Foundation, November 1969, Document #002866. "Man's relations with the environment," Harrison continued, "are economic, ecological and esthetic. From time to time men can, and do, act as if only one of these relationships really mattered . . . [and] America has long subordinated esthetic and ecological considerations almost entirely to economic ones. Pollution crises now upon us signify at once . . . that is wrong."

p. 118 The meeting was not auspicious: Memorandum from Gus Speth to Daum, Bryson, Ayres, Stohbehn, and Rosen, re: call from Frank Barry, November 22, 1968. (Gus Speth, personal files) Our discussion of the origins of the Yale students' role in the founding of the National Resources Defense Council is based on author interviews with Gus Speth, Stephen Duggan, Richard Ayres, Boris Bittker, Angus MacBeth, John Daum, Dick Hall, Gordon Harrison, and John Adams.

p. 118 "We have in mind": Confidential in-house memorandum from Gordon Harrison, Ford Foundation.

p. 118 The foundation's biggest reservation: "We agonized over funding such young men with no experience whatsoever," Harrison recalled. To provide ballast, friends on the Yale faculty sometimes accompanied the students to meetings with Harrison and others in New York. One such supporter, Charles Reich, reacted with horror when he arrived for the first time at the opulent Ford Foundation Building on East Forty-second Street—an obscene display of conspicuous luxury, he thought, for a philanthropic institution. Reich vowed never again to set foot inside the building, but for the students' sake he curbed his disgust during the meeting. (Author interview with Richard Ayres)

p. 119 "full equality for all": Richard Armstrong, "McGeorge Bundy Confronts the Teachers," *New York Times Magazine,* April 20, 1969.

p. 119 "If you were to say": *New York Times,* March 2, 1969.

p. 120 "Mr. Bundy got a letter": Gordon Harrison Oral History, Ford Foundation Archives.

p. 120 Bundy called the Yale students: Author interview with Richard Ayres.

p. 120 "For God's sake": Author interview with Stephen Duggan.

p. 120 "We thought they were": Ibid.

p. 120 Despite their differences in age: Ibid.

p. 121 The students set forth: Memorandum from Speth, Stoel, and Stohbehn to Ayres, Bryson, Daum, and Rosen, February, 1970, Gus Speth files.

p. 121 NRDC agreed to the conditions: Even though, for some time, the two generations of NRDC attorneys continued to sit on opposite sides of the table whenever they met, a feeling of mutual regard eventually developed. Duggan: "In the early days, when I'd hear one of them was going down to Washington to appear in court, I'd get a little nervous. I would call someone up and say, 'I want to read their brief,' or 'Have they studied everything on that?' Their briefs were almost always excellent, but it was still difficult for me to accept that these young kids were going to successfully take on corporate interests and agencies of the federal government. So I went along to Washington a few times, and I was amazed, because they were brilliant. And they'd never tried a case in their lives."

p. 122 "The 1970s absolutely": *New York Times,* January 2, 1970.

p. 122 "Restoring nature": *New York Times,* January 23, 1970.

p. 123 "At the turn of the century": *New York Times,* February 11, 1970.

p. 124 EPA boasted: *New York Times,* December 3, 1970.

p. 126 Ahmed had chaired: Author interview with Karim Ahmed.

p. 127 "Two scientists have calculated": *New York Times.* September 26, 1974.

p. 127 Stoel had an experience: Author interview with Tom Stoel.

CHAPTER 9: COLUMBUS OF THE STRATOSPHERE

p. 129 "This makes room": Samuel Pepys, quoted in Dorothy Fisk, *Exploring the Upper Atmosphere* (New York: Oxford University Press, 1934), p. 55. For our discussion of mankind's early efforts to understand the earth's upper atmosphere we are indebted to Richard A. Craig, *The Edge of Space: Exploring the Upper Atmosphere* (Garden City, N.Y.: Doubleday, 1968); and Frank A. Bower and Richard B. Ward, *Stratospheric Ozone and Man* (Boca Raton, Fla.: CRC Press, 1981); also A. L. Rotch, *Sounding the Ocean of Air* (London, 1900); and Alexander McAdie, *The Principles of Aerography* (Chicago: Rand McNally, 1917).

p. 131 "While not presuming": A. L. Rotch, "The Warm Stratum in the Atmosphere," *Nature,* May 7, 1908.

p. 134 Hartley in 1881: W. N. Hartley, "On the Absorption of Solar Rays by Atmospheric Ozone," *Journal of the Chemical Society* (London), 1881.

p. 135 "We must therefore conclude": Charles Fabry, "Ozone as an Absorbing Material for Radiations in the Atmosphere," *Journal of Mathematics and Physics,* vol. 4, no. 1 (January 1925). Our account of early ozone science and spectroscopy is also based on A. Khrgian, *The Physics of Atmospheric Ozone* (Jerusalem, 1975).

p. 135 S. Chapman, "Some Phenomena of the Upper Atmosphere," *Royal Society of London, Proceedings,* Series A. 132 (1931).

p. 136 "The effect of unlimited solar radiation": Fisk, pp. 82–83.

p. 136 "It is astonishing": *New York Times,* October 30, 1933.

p. 137 "Calculations show": The account of Piccard's ascent to the stratosphere is based primarily on Piccard's own description, which he rendered in detail in "Ballooning in the Stratosphere: Two Balloon Ascents to Ten-Mile Altitudes Presage New Mode of Aerial Travel," *National Geographic,* March 1933; and Auguste Piccard, *Between Earth and Sky* (London, 1950). Other sources of information on the Piccard flight are: "Piccard's Marvelous Plunge into the Blue," *Literary Digest,* June 13, 1931, and "Columbus of the Stratosphere and His Twin," January 28, 1933; *New York Times,*

May 28, 1931; and Jacques Piccard and Robert Dietz, *Seven Miles Down: The Story of the Bathyscaphe Trieste* (New York: Putnam, 1961). Also, author interview with Donald Piccard, Auguste's nephew and a balloonist in his own right.

p. 145 "[Piccard] gives us to understand": Fisk, p. 43. Piccard's last high-altitude balloon flight took place in 1937; he then devoted himself almost exclusively to the study of deep sea exploration. By the late 1940s he had invented the bathyscaphe, a self-propelled, untethered sphere designed on balloon principles and intended to withstand pressures of 12,000 pounds per square inch. In 1953 the vessel carried Piccard and his son Jacques to a depth of 10,168 feet—a world record. In January 1960, Jacques Piccard and Lt. Don Walsh of the U.S. Navy descended in the Piccard-built bathyscaphe *Trieste* to a depth of 35,800 feet in the Marianas Trench of the Pacific.

p. 145 "the stratosphere lacks": "Columbus of the Stratosphere and His Twin," *Herald Tribune* article quoted in *Literary Digest,* January 28, 1933.

p. 145 "The world has shrunk": *Palm Beach Post,* quoted in "Columbus of the Stratosphere and His Twin," *Literary Digest,* January 28, 1933.

p. 147 "For me, flight has always worked": Najeeb Halaby, *Crosswinds: An Airman's Memoir* (Garden City, N.Y.: Doubleday, 1979), p. 16.

CHAPTER 10: THE SOUND OF FREEDOM

p. 150 "It is far better": John Costello and Terry Hughes, *Concorde: The International Race for a Supersonic Passenger Transport* (London: Angus & Robertson, 1976), p. 125. Our discussion of the SST era is also based on Geoffrey Knight, *Concorde: The Inside Story* (London: Weidenfeld & Nicolson, 1976); Andrew Wilson and F. G. Clark, *The Concorde Fiasco* (Harmondsworth, Middesex: Penguin Books, 1973); and Arthur Gibson, *Concorde* (London: B.P.C. Publishing, 1976).

p. 150 "During the Berlin Airlift": *Wall Street Journal,* February 9, 1967.

p. 150 "The whole project": *Oklahoma City Times,* February 7, 1964.

p. 151 "Something about new means": John E. Gibson, "The Case Against the Supersonic Transport," *Harper's,* July 1966.

p. 151 "The lack of public discussion": Letter to the editor of the *New York Times,* August 31, 1966.

p. 151 In a March 1965 study: Author interview with William Shurcliff. See also CLASB Papers, MIT Archives, Cambridge, Mass.

p. 152 "Money, jobs, aviation": Author interview with William Shurcliff.

p. 152 "I have amassed": Letter from William Shurcliff to the National Parks Association, October 26, 1966, CLASB Papers, MIT Archives.

p. 152 "We are in the unique position": Letter from Bo Lundberg to William Shurcliff, November 9, 1966, CLASB Papers, MIT Archives.

p. 154 Shurcliff made public: "The Sound That Chills," *Mechanics Illustrated,* October 1965. Virtually all of William Shurcliff's data, anecdotes, and collected knowledge about SSTs and sonic booms appears in his book *SST and Sonic Boom Handbook* (New York: Ballantine, 1970).

p. 155 "If the SST": Quoted in "The House Falls in on the SST," *Newsweek,* March 29, 1971.

p. 155 Describing the SST's operating costs: Ad Hoc SST Review Committee Report, March 30, 1969.

p. 156 Even Charles Lindbergh: Halaby, p. 205.

p. 156 "Hardly a day went by": Ibid., p. 206.

p. 156 "I read my mail": "No to SST," *New Republic,* April 3, 1971.

p. 156 "The whole anti-SST movement": Costello and Hughes, p. 187. Halaby's fear was echoed in a widely read study commissioned by the National Academy of Sciences in 1969, which concluded, "The future holds great peril whether from the uncontrolled effects of technology itself or from an unreasoned political reaction against all technological innovation." (National Academy of Sciences, "Technology— Processes of Assessment and Choice," July 1969)

p. 157 Measurements made in the late 1950s: Author interview with Harold Johnston.

p. 158 Ironically, one of the first: Our discussion of Halstead "Ted" Harrison's work on the link between ozone depletion and water vapor is based on the authors' interviews with Harrison, as well as on Halstead Harrison, "Stratospheric Ozone with Added Water Vapor: Influence of High Altitude Aircraft," *Science*, November 13, 1970. See also Dotto and Schiff.

p. 159 "scientifically dishonest": Swihart quoted in Dotto and Schiff, p. 48.

p. 160 "Then I did a double take": James McDonald's testimony before Congress (which is quoted throughout this chapter) is from U.S. Congress, "Civil Supersonic Aircraft Development (SST)," hearings before the Transportation Subcommittee of the House Committee on Appropriations, 92nd Cong., 1st sess., March 1–4, 1971, p. 339.

p. 160 Shurcliff, in his: Shurcliff had written to McDonald in the fall of 1970 for information about his theory that SST exhaust could deplete stratospheric ozone. McDonald, in turn, sent Shurcliff a copy of the report he had prepared for the NAS. Shurcliff was impressed, and in McDonald's detailed consideration of the problem he could not help but recognize a kindred scientific spirit. "Very clear. Not overdone, not underdone. Just right," Shurcliff commented in a note to McDonald, adding: "Pro-SST forces counterattacking heavily. Don't know how the vote will come out." (Letter from William Shurcliff to James McDonald, March 10, 1971, CLASB Papers, MIT Archives)

p. 160 "He spent a great deal of time": Author interview with Dr. Richard Kassander.

p. 160 "I believe this is a problem": *New York Times*, October 21, 1966.

p. 161 McDonald believed: James McDonald, "Science in Default: Twenty-two Years of Inadequate UFO Investigations," in *UFO's: A Scientific Debate*, ed. Carl Sagan and Thornton Page (Ithaca, N.Y.: Cornell University Press, 1972), pp. 52–55.

p. 161 "scientific padding": Ibid., p. 54.

p. 161 "wasted an unprecedented opportunity": "Saucers' End," *Time*, January 17, 1969.

p. 163 "But Conte had gained": David M. Jacobs, *The UFO Controversy in America* (Bloomington: Indiana University Press, 1975), p. 261.

p. 163 "was sharply discounted": *New York Times*, March 2 1971.

p. 163 "angry and finger-wagging": Dotto and Schiff, p. 43.

p. 164 Gori calculated: Mel Horwitch, *Clipped Wings* (Cambridge, Mass.: MIT Press, 1982), p. 322.

p. 164 It had been Johnston's good fortune: Author interview with Harold Johnston.

p. 165 "I have never seen": Dotto and Schiff, p. 47. On April 9, 1971, a few weeks after returning to Tucson from the Boulder conference, McDonald tried to commit suicide. He shot himself in the head, but botched the attempt, nearly blinding himself. Treated at the local VA hospital, he was released on June 10 and returned to work at his office at the University of Arizona. The following day he purchased a used .38-caliber revolver from a pawnbroker for $58, and was last seen walking down a narrow desert trail that led through some low grass and shrubs into an area known as Canyon del Oro. There, two days later, his body was found. Fastidious to the last detail, McDonald had written a note, to be found on his body, addressed to a local police deputy he knew. In the note he said that he had taken his own life due to marital problems. (*Arizona Republic*, June 15, 1971)

p. 166 a hypothesis describing: Author interviews with Paul Crutzen and Harold

Johnston; also H. S. Johnston, *The Atmospheric Effects of Stratospheric Aircraft: A Personal Perspective*, NASA Reference Publication #1247, September 1990, p. 6; also Dotto and Schiff, p. 46; and P. Crutzen, "The Influence of Nitrogen Oxides on Atmospheric Ozone Content," *Quarterly Journal of the Royal Meteorological Society*, vol. 96 (1970), pp. 320–25.

p. 166 "The next day": Author interview with Harold Johnston.

p. 167 "What is involved here": Costello and Hughes, p. 186.

p. 167 "In the wised-up seventies": *Newsweek*, "The House Falls in on the SST," March 29, 1971.

CHAPTER 11: PURE SCIENCE

p. 168 Climate Impact Assessment Program: National Research Council, Climatic Impact Committee, *Climate Impact Assessment Program (CIAP): Environmental Impact of Stratospheric Flight: Biological and Climatic Effects of Aircraft Emissions in the Stratosphere*, National Academy of Sciences, Washington, D.C., 1975. On January 21, 1975, CIAP issued a report that concluded that "an increase in the number of stratospheric airplanes with present engines will diminish the amount of ozone in the stratosphere and consequently will increase the intensity of UV light at ground level." But by then the SST had lost its urgency, as the number of SSTs expected to fly in the stratosphere had been greatly reduced. Even if the phenomenally large SST fleets once predicted ever did become a reality, the report said, atmospheric levels of the inert industrial compounds known as chlorofluorocarbons—recently investigated by California researchers F. Sherwood Rowland and Mario Molina—threatened to deplete atmospheric ozone six times more efficiently than oxides of nitrogen. (After all the storm and fury over the SST, it was in the end the common aerosol can that most seriously threatened life on earth.)

p. 170 Lovelock found CFC-11: *New York Times Magazine*, December 21, 1975; author interview with F. Sherwood Rowland.

p. 170 Rowland found himself: Author interview with F. Sherwood Rowland. The account in this chapter of Rowland's early interest in CFCs and the ozone layer is largely based on our interviews with Rowland.

p. 175 "You guys are 'superscientists'!": Author interview with Joan Rowland.

p. 177 "growing nervousness": Peter and Katherine Montague, "Mercury: How Much Are We Eating?" *Saturday Review*, February 6, 1971.

p. 177 In 1971, Rowland: G. E. Miller et al., "Mercury Concentrations in Museum Specimens of Tuna and Swordfish," *Science*, March 10, 1972, pp. 1121–22.

p. 178 Mario Molina was born: Author interview with Mario Molina. All dialogue attributed to Molina throughout this chapter is from author interviews.

p. 181 "The work is going very well": Shari Roan, "The Man Who Saw the End of the World," *Orange County Register*, June 5, 1988.

p. 183 "They talked about the chlorine": Our discussion of the exchange of scientific information concerning the chlorine chain in the early 1970s is based on author interviews with Harold Johnston, Ralph Cicerone, Richard Stolarski, and F. Sherwood Rowland.

p. 185 "like a pimple on an elephant": Author interview with Chuck Kolb.

p. 185 Clyne's latest laboratory measurements: Paul Brodeur, "Annals of Chemistry: Inert," *New Yorker*, April 2, 1975.

p. 187 "You work hard": Author interview with Joan Rowland.

p. 187 Harold Johnston couldn't resist: Dotto and Schiff, p. 134.

p. 187 The story was picked up: Ibid., p. 19.

p. 187 "But of course": Letter from Molina to Rowland, January 24, 1974 (provided to the authors by Mario Molina).

p. 188 "Beautiful," Ehhalt responded: Rowland interview.

p. 188 "We're right": Author interviews with Joan Rowland and Paul Crutzen.

p. 188 "To use some Watergate language": Letter from Molina to Rowland, May 19, 1974 (provided to the authors by Mario Molina).

p. 189 Molina was alarmed: Dotto and Schiff, p. 20.

p. 189 "It seems quite clear": Mario Molina and F. S. Rowland, "Stratospheric Sink for Chlorofluoromethanes: Chlorine Atom-Catalyzed Destruction of Ozone," *Nature*, June 28, 1974.

CHAPTER 12: NOT WITH A BANG, BUT A PSSST!

p. 191 "drastic action will probably be necessary": Dotto and Schiff, p. 199.

p. 192 "There is an unprecedented consensus": Karim Ahmed, "The Effects of Fluorocarbons on Atmospheric Ozone: A Technical Review," NRDC Files, December 1974, p. 23.

p. 192 In 1973: Ibid., p. 12.

p. 193 Ahmed and Stoel knew: Author interviews with Ahmed and Stoel.

p. 193 "preliminary inquiries indicate": Tom Stoel, "Memorandum to NRDC Executive Committee," October 31, 1974, NRDC Files.

p. 194 the fall off in CFCs: *New York Times*, November 21, 1974.

p. 194 "What do you think": Author interview with Karim Ahmed.

p. 194 Dr. Oliver C. Taylor: *New York Times*, September 27, 1974.

p. 194 "All we have are assumptions": *New York Times*, November 2, 1974.

p. 195 In response, Sherry Rowland: "NAS Launches Study on Fluorocarbons," *Science News*, November 30, 1974.

p. 195 John W. Dickinson, Jr.: Ling-gee Gibney, "Federal Task Force Probes Ozone Issue," *Chemical and Engineering News*, March 10, 1975.

p. 196 "The world is not about to end": McElroy and Rowland testimony from "Ozone Depletion: IMOS Proceedings on Propellants Are Sidetracked by Bromine Issue," *Drug and Cosmetic Industry*, April 1975; Ling-gee Gibney, "Federal Task Force Probes Ozone Issue," *Chemical and Engineering News*, March 10, 1975; *New York Times*, February 28, 1975.

p. 196 "shatter the ecological structure": *New York Times*, November 12, 1974.

p. 197 "The horror is that": *New York Times*, December 11, 1974.

p. 197 Tom Stoel was not convinced: Memorandum from Tom Stoel, David Michelman, and Ruby Compton to NRDC Executive Committee, "Proposed Ozone Depletion Suit," March 25, 1975, NRDC Files.

p. 197 On June 13, 1975: *New York Times*, June 13, 1975. See also Council on Environmental Quality and Federal Council for Science and Technology, *Fluorocarbons and the Environment: Report of the Federal Task Force on Inadvertent Modifications of the Stratosphere (IMOS)* (Washington, D.C.: U.S. Government Printing Office, 1975).

p. 198 "The scientific evidence indicates": NRDC press release, "Environmentalists Criticize Ozone Task Force," June 11, 1975, NRDC Files.

p. 198 The panel members: Dotto and Schiff, pp. 204–5.

p. 199 "tantamount to pre-judging": *Chemical and Engineering News*, June 16, 1975.

p. 199 "There is no justice": "Allied's Orfeo Stresses Uncertainty in Ozone Theory," *Aerosol Age*, June 1975.

p. 199 "Recent and potential discoveries": "Fluorocarbon Harming Ozone?: IMOS Sees 'Cause for Concern,' Recommends Aerosol Labeling," *Chemical Marketing Reporter*, June 16, 1975.

p. 199 contributed $8 billion: *New York Times*, March 31, 1975.

p. 199 On July 29, 1975: Letter from Tom Stoel and Ruby Compton to Russell Train, July 29, 1975, NRDC Files.

p. 200 "claim meets counterclaim": *New York Times,* June 30, 1975; *Los Angeles Times,* June 30, 1975.

p. 200 the confidence to denounce: *New York Times,* July 8, 1975.

p. 200 Still, the influence: *New York Times,* October 1, 1975. In October 1975, Dr. James P. Lodge, formerly chairman of the Colorado Air Pollution Commission, and then the newly appointed "science advisor" to COAS, eagerly monitored an Alaskan volcano that threatened to erupt and throw large quantities of seawater containing chlorides into the stratosphere. The eruption, Dr. Lodge predicted, would prove that the ozone layer could withstand the introduction of chlorine without being seriously depleted. The volcano did erupt in January 1976, but Lodge's observations were inconclusive. (*New York Times,* October 1, 1975)

p. 200 "Scientists who widely promote": *Santa Ana* (Calif.) *Register,* July 27, 1975.

p. 201 "The gentleman is good": Ibid., August 1, 1975.

p. 201 "scientific arguments no longer count": "Hysteria Ousts Science from Halocarbon Controversy," *New Scientist,* June 19, 1975.

p. 201 "one of the more plausible": *Yorkshire Post* (Leeds, England), December 18, 1974. "I think we need a bit of British caution on this," Lovelock continued. "If the scare about Freons had happened four years ago, and Freons had been banned, manufacturers could have replaced it [*sic*] with a gas called vinyl chlorine. Vinyl chlorine was known as 'nontoxic' and decomposes quickly, but two years ago it was discovered that it was a violent producer of cancer. I respect Professor Rowland as a chemist but I wish he wouldn't act like a missionary. I don't like his statement about 40,000 extra cases of skin cancer in the United States. That's pure conjecture about something very emotive, and it's just as unscientific as publicity handouts from aerosol manufacturers saying aerosols are good for you. I think the theory should be investigated. We have a few years and that's what we should be doing. . . ."

p. 201 "the presence of these compounds": Quoted in John Gribbin, *The Hole in the Sky: Man's Threat to the Ozone Layer* (New York: Bantam Books, 1988), p. 43.

p. 202 "a self-regulating entity": James E. Lovelock, *Gaia: A New Look at Life on Earth* (Oxford: Oxford University Press, 1979), p. xii.

p. 202 "largest living creature": Ibid., p. 1.

p. 202 "Life on this planet": Ibid., pp. 40–41.

p. 202 "the complete or partial removal": Ibid., p. 40.

p. 202 "In our persistent self-imposed alienation": Ibid., p. 80.

p. 202 "I imagine that the world": Author interview with F. Sherwood Rowland.

p. 203 "something is destroying": *Wall Street Journal,* December 3, 1975.

p. 203 "If an egg dropped": Michael Drosnin, "Not with a Bang, but with a Pssssst!" *New Times,* March 7, 1975.

p. 203 a report published in *Nature:* Dotto and Schiff, p. 211.

p. 204 "many organisms may be living": Drosnin.

p. 204 "This is a large risk": *New York Times,* September 10, 1975.

p. 204 Proof of CFCs' role: The catalytic chain reaction between chlorine and ozone was, according to a Du Pont brochure, the "most speculative and most critical aspect of the theory" and "the most difficult area to research." (Dotto and Schiff, p. 227)

p. 205 "We at Johnson Wax": Johnson Wax ad, *New York Times,* June 20, 1975; *Los Angeles Times,* June 20, 1975.

p. 205 "What they've done": Michael Rogers, "Spray Away Layers of Ugly Ozone Fast, Fast, Fast," *Rolling Stone,* December 4, 1975.

p. 205 "the most significant response": Ibid.

p. 205 production at Precision Valve: Robert Abplanalp declared that the move was made "to reduce overhead costs, particularly the price of power in the Yonkers area," where "the powerful ecology lobby" had prevented the local utility, Consolidated Edison, from using lower-priced fuel oil, coal, and/or nuclear power. (*New York Times,* June 22, 1975)

By the early 1970s Abplanalp was known for being more than the "Henry Ford of the aerosol business"—he was also a close personal friend of President Richard Nixon. Abplanalp had met Nixon in 1960, when he'd contributed to Nixon's losing presidential campaign, and the two men and their families had vacationed together in Key Biscayne, Florida, or on Abplanalp's private island in the Bahamas, Grand Cay. As Abplanalp told *Life* magazine in 1971, he'd once called Nixon "Dick," but "now, it's strictly 'Mr. President'.

"The day he gets elected, there's something that happens—not to him, but to you." (*Life,* March 5, 1971)

p. 206 Industry's own market research: *Aerosol Age,* June 1975. These were, the magazine reported, "the young people of the sixties who reacted so violently to the Vietnam War and civil injustices," in the twenty-five-to-twenty-nine age category.

p. 206 Bristol-Myers spent $6 million: *New York Times,* May 12, 1976.

p. 206 "What is most amazing": "Scientist Sciarra Addresses Seminar," *Soap/Cosmetics/Chemical Specialties,* September 1975.

p. 206 "I'd rather err": *Portland Oregonian,* June 17, 1975. At the same time it was battling the CFC problem, the aerosol industry was fighting reports that had emerged out of Consumer Product Safety Commission hearings which indicated that aerosols were responsible for 125 deaths a year among teenagers who sniffed them to get high. (*New York Times,* May 10, 1975) While sniffing CFCs was admittedly a deliberate abuse of aerosols, injuries and deaths that resulted from it nonetheless suggested that lesser, incidental doses of CFCs inhaled by people who used aerosols properly might also endanger health. Medical research indicated that CFCs depressed the heart's ability to contract and caused arrhythmia, lowered blood pressure in animals, and was suspected of causing various lung diseases, leading Consumers Union to warn people with known heart and lung ailments to avoid the use of aerosols altogether, or at least to use them in a well-ventilated room. (*Philadelphia Inquirer,* December 8, 1974) The CPSC also considered charges that aerosols could misfire their contents, particularly if they found their way into the hands of children, and were subject to exploding when exposed to heat. Those filled with flammable products could, when accidentally ignited, turn into deadly blowtorches. All told, aerosols were responsible for five thousand trips to emergency rooms each year.

Freon-113 has been blamed for causing numerous deaths due to heart arrhythmias between the late 1960s and the present day. The victims are usually individuals working with large concentrations of the CFCs as a cleaner or degreaser. One of the first such accidental deaths linked to Freon-113 occurred at Du Pont itself when, in a study named "Project Delilah," engineers tested methods of using Freon-113 in an application that would remove the oil and dirt from women's hair without disturbing their hairstyles. Du Pont secretaries such as Beverly Mannering, forty-four and the mother of two, stayed after work and were paid $5 to serve as subjects for the experiments. Mannering died during her twenty-seventh exposure to Freon-113 on May 23, 1967. (See Merritt Wallick, "Du Pont Secretary Died in Test of Freon-113," *Wilmington News Journal,* August 30, 1991, and "Death Has Struck at Work and Play," *Wilmington News Journal,* August 25, 1991.

p. 206 *Aerosol Age* sounded: "Allied's Orfeo Stresses Uncertainty in Ozone Theory," *Aerosol Age,* June 1975.

p. 207 "really qualified to have": George Haber, "The Crumbling Shield," *The Sciences,* December 1974.

p. 207 "We understood that we had": Rowland interview. In the fall of 1974, Rowland was invited to give a talk at Du Pont. Rowland reviewed the basic underlying science, showing some fifty-two slides. The Du Pont scientists asked only one question when Rowland was done: what one experiment could they do to prove most directly that Rowland was wrong? "Look for the chlorine-oxygen radical in the upper atmosphere," Rowland replied. "If it's not there, you're OK. If you find it, you can shut down." Devising instruments that could detect the minute quantities of chlorine monoxide that Rowland's theory predicted would be present would probably take several years, however, longer than it was prudent to wait before regulating CFCs. Rowland later heard that the consensus among the audience at Du Pont was that his talk had been highly emotional, and that he had not offered any science to support his theory. The experience made Rowland realize that the Du Pont scientists were not competent to assess the ozone-depletion theory. They simply had not understood him. (Rowland interview) "I think there has to be a long educational process for industry as to what goes on in the atmosphere," he testified at the first public IMOS hearing, in February 1975, "and I don't think we have time to wait." (Bob Benchley, "Aerosols Under Fire," *Food and Drug Packaging*, March 27, 1975)

p. 210 "We would like a fair trial": *New York Times*, May 13, 1976.

p. 210 "rumor is running rampant again": Dotto and Schiff, p. 255.

p. 211 "Selective regulation": National Academy of Sciences, *Halocarbons: Effects on Stratospheric Ozone* (Washington, D.C.: National Academy of Sciences, 1976), quoted in *New York Times*, September 13, 1976.

p. 212 "From the pure scientific perspective": Dotto and Schiff, p. 283. Utah State University Conference covered in *New York Times*, September 18, 1976.

p. 212 "I believe firmly": *New York Times*, May 13, 1977.

p. 212 "Given the effects": U.S. Department of Health, Education, and Welfare press release, "New News," October 15, 1976, NRDC Files; also *New York Times*, October 16, 1976.

p. 213 "Any impact": *New York Times*, May 13, 1977.

p. 213 "We've managed"; "By year end": Ibid.

p. 213 "rule of witchcraft": Dotto and Schiff, p. 264.

p. 213 "That means that": *New York Times*, May 13, 1977.

CHAPTER 13: LIFE'S ONLY CRUCIBLE

p. 215 "The effect of chlorofluorocarbons": V. Ramanathan, "Greenhouse Effect Due to Chlorofluorocarbons: Climatic Implications," *Science*, October 3, 1975. See also *New York Times*, September 14, 1975; and *Science News*, "Propellants: New Actors in Troposphere," October 4, 1975.

p. 215 "one of the most important": Fourier, quoted by V. Ramanathan, "The Greenhouse Theory of Climate Change: A Test by an Inadvertent Global Experiment," *Science*, April 15, 1988. Originally: J. B. Fourier, *Mem. Acad. Sci. Inst. Fr. 7*, 569 (1827).

p. 216 Swedish chemist Svante Arrhenius: William R. Moomaw, "In Search of the Greenhouse Fingerprint," *Orion*, Winter 1989.

p. 216 "Mankind is now engaged": Michael Weisskopf, "Greenhouse Effect Fuels Policymakers," *Washington Post*, August 15, 1988.

p. 218 "the first truly global": "Statement by the honorable Russell E. Train, Administrator of the U.S. Environmental Protection Agency to the Environmental roundtable of the NATO committee on the challenges of modern society on international implications of the Freon-ozone issue. Tuesday, October 14, 1975," NRDC Files.

p. 218 Prior to World War II: For the history of international environmental cooperation and international environmentalism, we are indebted to Lynton K. Caldwell, *In Defense of Earth: International Protection of the Biosphere* (Bloomington and London: Indiana University Press, 1972), pp. 61–67; also John McCormick, *Reclaiming Paradise: The Global Environmental Movement* (Bloomington and Indianapolis: Indiana University Press, 1989).

p. 220 In April 1975: "Proposal for NRDC Aerosol/Ozone Project," NRDC document, undated, NRDC Files.

p. 220 NRDC presented a statement: "Statement of Position in Regard to UNEP's Ozone Depletion Research Program," NRDC document, March 1976.

p. 220 Stoel believed UNEP: Author interview with Thomas B. Stoel, Jr.

p. 221 The United States, Canada: "Regulation in Selected Countries and International Organizations," presentation by Thomas B. Stoel, Jr., at the Natural Resources Defense Council International Meeting on Chlorofluoromethanes, Munich, December 6–8, 1978, NRDC document.

p. 221 "a tremendous education": Author interview with Tom Stoel.

p. 221 a "failure": Author interview with Alan Miller.

p. 222 "a unified global approach": Environmental Protection Agency, "Report on the Progress of Regulations to Protect Stratospheric Ozone," report to Congress, August 1979.

p. 222 she was immediately assailed: Author interviews with Miller, Stoel, and Blum.

p. 222 The Munich conference ultimately resolved: Organization for Economic Cooperation and Development, "Environment Committee Report on Chlorofluorocarbons," Paris, 1982.

p. 223 "The action . . . conveys": "Prepared Statement of Barbara Blum, Deputy Administrator, U.S. Environmental Protection Agency, at International Meeting on Chlorofluorocarbons, Oslo, Norway, April 15, 1980." Reprinted in *EPA Proposed Rulemaking on Chlorofluorocarbons (CFCs) and Its Impact on Small Business,* hearing before the Subcommittee on Antitrust and Restraint of Trade Activities Affecting Small Business of the Committee on Small Business, House of Representatives, 97th Cong., 1st sess., July 15, 1981, pp. 58–59.; *EPA Journal,* October 1980, p. 16.

p. 223 the EPA followed through: "Ozone-Depleting Chlorofluorocarbons; Proposed Production Restriction. Advance notice of proposed rulemaking," *Federal Register,* October 7, 1980.

p. 224 the EPA had commissioned: Michael Shapiro and Ellen Warhit, "Marketable Permits: The Case of Chlorofluorocarbons," *Natural Resources Journal,* July 1983, pp. 577–91.

p. 224 "the best scientific opinion": Alan S. Miller, "Comments on the Advance Notice of Proposed Rulemaking by the Environmental Protection Agency: Ozone-Depleting Chlorofluorocarbons"; Proposed Reduction Restriction, 45 Federal Register 66726 (October 7, 1980), submitted by the Natural Resources Defense Council, Inc., Miller's personal files.

p. 224 a coalition of CFC users: Forest Reinhardt, "Du Pont Freon Products Division," National Wildlife Federation, 1989; author interview with Kevin Faye.

p. 225 "unwarranted at this time": *New York Times,* October 8, 1980.

p. 225 In June 1980, Du Pont: Reinhardt.

p. 225 "We could have built": Michael Weisskopf, "CFC's: Rise and Fall of Chemical 'Miracle,' " *Washington Post,* April 10, 1988.

p. 225 "There was obviously no interest": Reinhardt.

p. 226 "a tree is a tree": Quoted in Lou Cannon, *Reagan* (New York: Perigee Books, 1984), p. 351.

CHAPTER 14: THE OPEN RANGE

p. 229 Wald, who quickly focused: Author interview with Johanna Wald.

p. 229 a ruling in favor of NRDC: *Natural Resources Defense Council* v. *Morton, No. 1983-73, Environmental Law Review,* vol. 5, p. 20238.

p. 230 forebears handily fought back: Paul J. Culhane, *Public Lands Politics: Interest*

Group Influence on the Forest Service and the Bureau of Land Management (Baltimore and London: Resources for the Future/Johns Hopkins University Press, 1981), p. 87.

p. 231 far more than the grazing leases: Robert H. Nelson, "Economic Analysis in Public Rangeland Management," in *Western Public Lands: The Management of Natural Resources in a Time of Declining Federalism,* eds. John G. Francis and Richard Ganzel, (Totowa, NJ: Rowman & Allanheld, 1984), pp. 65–68.

p. 232 "to meet the challenge": Oliver A. Houk, "With Charity for All," *Yale Law Journal,* vol. 93, no. 8 (July 1984).

p. 232 "to fight fire with fire": Ernest Heuter, president of NLCPI, quoted in Karen O'Connor and Lee Epstein, "Rebalancing the Scales of Justice: Assessment of Public Interest Law," *Harvard Journal of Law and Public Policy,* vol. 7, no. 2 (Fall 1984).

p. 232 "Litigation purportedly brought": Momboisse, quoted in O'Connor and Epstein.

p. 233 In 1973 the PLF: Houk.

p. 233 "assist in the establishment": NCLPI, Articles of Incorporation, quoted in ibid.

p. 233 "limited constitutional government": *NLCPI, A Prospectus: National Legal Center for the Public Interest, Dedicated to a Balanced View of the Role of Law in Achieving Economic and Social Progress* (July 18, 1975), quoted in ibid.

p. 233 "becoming an exercise": Ibid.

p. 233 An MSLF leaflet: Timothy Lange, "New Tactic for the Right Wing: Public-Interest Legal Foundations, Just Like the Left Has," *Straight Creek Journal,* October 6, 1977.

p. 233 "I fear that our states": Houk.

p. 234 "We are all today": Reagan quoted in Cannon, pp. 287–89. See also Albert R. Hunt, "The Campaign and the Issues," in *The American Elections of 1980,* ed. Austin Ranney (Washington and London: American Enterprise Institute for Public Policy Research, 1981), p. 165; and Lawrence Mosher, "Talking Clean on the Hustings," *National Journal,* November 1, 1980.

p. 235 As governor of California: Cannon, p. 349.

p. 236 "What is the real motive": Jeffrey Klein, "Man Apart: James Watt and the Marketing of God's Green Acres," *Mother Jones,* August 1981.

p. 237 "We have wished": Brand, quoted in Ron Arnold, *At the Eye of the Storm: James Watt and the Environmentalists* (Chicago: Regnery Gateway, 1982), p. 36.

p. 237 "instead of going out to shoot birds": Quoted in ibid, p. 38.

p. 237 "We have bit by bit": Ibid., p. 123.

p. 237 "America had become": Ibid., p. 153.

p. 237 "The battleground": Ibid., p. 44.

p. 237 A self-described fundamentalist: Ibid., p. 3.

p. 238 "We will mine more": Cannon, p. 359.

p. 238 "We will use the budget system": Arnold, p. 136.

p. 239 "My concept of stewardship": *New York Times,* August 22, 1981.

p. 239 "Most environmental leaders": *New York Times,* April 19, 1981.

p. 239 1981 was the best year: *New York Times,* November 11, 1981.

p. 239 "This is not a struggle": *New York Times,* April 15, 1982.

p. 240 Like the Nazis: *New York Times,* January 21, 1983.

p. 240 "I have a Black": Quoted in Culhane.

p. 240 "We did 'Reaganism' ": Anne M. Burford with John Greenya, *Are You Tough Enough?* (New York: McGraw-Hill, 1986), p. 17.

p. 240 "really make a difference": Ibid., p. 9.

p. 240 She interviewed well: Jonathan Lash, with Katherine Gillman and David Sheridan, *A Season of Spoils: The Story of the Reagan Administration's Attack on the Environment* (New York: Pantheon Books, 1984), pp. 9–12.

p. 241 "In my opinion": Burford, p. 68.

p. 241 "Their main concern": Ibid., p. 98.

p. 241 "You joined the Environmental Protection Agency": *Washington Post,* January 28, 1982.

p. 242 "a fund-raising gimmick": *New York Times,* February 1, 1982.

CHAPTER 15: ANPR

p. 243 Reagan issued an order: In early 1981, even before Gorsuch was sworn in, the Presidential Task Force on Regulatory Relief, under the chairmanship of Vice President George Bush, recommended the suspension or revision of a number of EPA rules, including those regulating noise from garbage trucks, controlling hazardous waste, and requiring chemical companies to notify EPA prior to producing new and potentially dangerous substances. In an effort to offer quick relief to "small" refiners, the task force actually proposed loosening EPA's hard-won 1973 restrictions on lead in gasoline, heedlessly reviving the old controversy dating back to the days of Alice Hamilton, Yandell Henderson, and the Workers' Health Bureau. The proposal was later withdrawn in the face of evidence that the reduction of lead in gasoline was one of the EPA's incontrovertible successes: according to a March 1982 Centers for Disease Control report, average lead levels in blood dropped 36.7 percent nationwide between 1976 and 1980, a drop the report attributed directly to the reduction of lead in gasoline. The report noted that "although the decreases in mean blood-levels was dramatic, the problem of pediatric lead poisoning in the United States has not been solved," adding that further reductions in lead in gasoline would increase the "margin of safety" for children. (Lash, pp. 27–28, 139–44; *New York Times,* March 30, 1982)

p. 243 House subcommittee: "EPA Proposed Rulemaking on Chlorofluorocarbons (CFCs) and Its Impact on Small Business," hearing before the Subcommittee on Antitrust and Restraint of Trade Activities Affecting Small Business of the Committee on Small Business, House of Representatives, 97th Cong. 1st. sess., July 15, 1981. Luken and Williams commentary and witness testimony are derived from the transcript of this hearing.

p. 244 The EPA's proposals: In a postmortem memorandum, two EPA officials wrote that the agency had "grossly underestimated the difficulty of introducing and explaining the marketable permit concept to potentially affected parties. The ANPR, in the absence of other mechanisms for public information, was not a good vehicle for introducing the idea." (Michael Shapiro and Ellen Warhit, "Marketable Permits: The Case of Chlorofluorocarbons," *Natural Resources Journal,* July 1983)

p. 244 "I implore you": "The Effect of Chlorofluorocarbons on the Ozone Layer," testimony before the Senate Subcommittee on Toxic Substances and Environmental Oversight of the Committee on Environment and Public Works, 97th Cong., 1st sess., July 23, 1981. All commentary and testimony is from the official transcript of the hearing.

p. 249 "quantitative prediction"; National Academy of Sciences, *Causes and Effects of Stratospheric Ozone Reduction: An Update* (Washington, D.C.: National Academy of Sciences, 1982).

p. 249 Sherry Rowland published findings: *New York Times,* March 27, 1982.

p. 249 "Remember a few years back": Burford, p. 133.

p. 250 Gorsuch announced: Burford, p. 137. See also Caldwell, *In Defense of Earth,* p. 333.

p. 250 "Many of our actions": Gorsuch quoted in Caldwell, p. 321.

p. 251 "It is quite clear": *New York Times,* May 12, 1982.

p. 251 The proposed convention: Governing Council of UNEP, 9th sess., May 1981, decision 9/13 B, NRDC Files.

p. 251 By then the State Department: Author interview with former State Department attorney Scott Hajost.

p. 252 "mammoth task": UNEP Secretariat, "Towards an Ozone Convention: A Look at Some Issues," December 31, 1981.

p. 253 The draft convention: Peter H. Sand, "The Vienna Convention Is Adopted," *Environment*, vol. 27, no. 5 (June 1985).

p. 253 the convention should provide: Alliance for Responsible CFC Policy, "Summary of Critical Points Which Should Be Considered in the Formulation of the U.S. Position for the Global Framework Convention for the Protection of the Ozone Layer," December 21, 1981, Alan Miller files. Miller argued in comments responding to the December draft that "a convention will be of little benefit if it does no more than facilitate exchange of scientific information," since such exchanges were effectively taking place through existing institutions; nor, he added, should a convention retreat from previous international agreements which already endorsed the need for global reduction in the release of CFCs. The convention "must recognize the critical importance of caution when dealing with a risk of irreversible, catastrophic changes in a fundamental element of the ecosystem," and should not "imply that there is some clear period of time in which it is safe to wait to take action while research continues." Furthermore, "statements concerning remaining scientific uncertainties should not obscure the substantial scientific basis for the ozone depletion theory." ("Comments by Alan S. Miller, Natural Resources Defense Council, on the Draft Convention for the Protection of the Ozone Layer," Alan Miller files)

p. 253 The Pennwalt Corporation, for one: Paul Brodeur, "Annals of Chemistry: Inert," *New Yorker*, April 2, 1975.

p. 254 In late April 1983: Memorandum from Rob Blake to Alan Miller, Tom Stoel, Jessica Mathews, and Irving Mintzer, October 12, 1983.

p. 254 With Ruckelshaus obviously determined: Morale within the EPA had been "visibly and dramatically" restored by Ruckelshaus, reported Philip Shabecoff in the *New York Times* of March 27, 1983. Some EPA staff, proud and relieved to have survived the Gorsuch regime, took to wearing T-shirts (when they were off-duty) emblazoned with the words ACID REIGN on the back and with the names of Gorsuch and other departed officials on the front, crossed out, under the Gorsuch dictum DOING MORE WITH LESS. (*New York Times*, May 7, 1983)

p. 254 "EPA has made no official statements": Letter from Alan Miller to William Ruckelshaus, May 31, 1983, Alan Miller files.

p. 255 The NAS study: National Academy of Sciences, *Causes and Effects of Changes in Stratospheric Ozone: Update 1983* (Washington, D.C.: National Academy of Sciences, 1983).

p. 256 "the potential to become": Thomas H. Maugh II, "What Is the Risk from Chlorofluorocarbons?" *Science*, March 9, 1984.

p. 256 "a large perturbation": Roan, p. 111. Sherry Rowland echoed Molina's thoughts. "No one has yet succeeded in developing a scenario in which the increase of CFCs doesn't decrease upper stratospheric ozone," he noted. "But lots of scenarios that have been developed show this offsetting either in the troposphere or lower stratosphere, so that the calculations of how much total ozone would change have fluctuated wildly." Others, including Donald R. Strobach, manager of environmental programs of Du Pont's Freon Products Division, expressed satisfaction. "[The NAS report] shows we don't have an imminent crisis on our hands," he said. "What we have is time to research in a rational way." (Brodeur)

p. 256 "People were exiting": Author interview with John Hoffman.

p. 257 Hoffman and Wagner were not alone: Author interview with Jim Losey.

p. 257 The position paper: Author interview with Steve Weil.

p. 259 With the EPA logjam: Author interview with Jim Losey.

p. 259 "Effects of ozone depletion": U.S. Department of State cable, "Instructions to USDEL for UNEP Ozone-Layer Meeting, Geneva, October 17–21"; U.S. Department of State cable, "U.S. Reaction to Nordic Proposal at the Upcoming Meeting."

p. 259 Alan Miller was encouraged: Author interview with Alan Miller.

p. 259 Meanwhile, Joe Cannon: Author interviews with Cannon, Hoffman, and Topping.

p. 260 *Can We Delay:* Stephen Seidel and Dale Keyes, *Can We Delay a Greenhouse Warming? The Effectiveness and Feasibility of Options to Slow a Build-up of Carbon Dioxide in the Atmosphere* (Washington, D.C.: U.S. Environmental Protection Agency, Strategic Studies Staff, September 1983).

p. 260 "We are trying": *New York Times,* August 18, 1983.

p. 260 "unwarranted and unnecessarily alarmist": *New York Times,* August 21, 1983.

CHAPTER 16: ONE GOOD OBSERVATION

p. 263 Farman trusted the Dobson instrument: Author interview with Joseph Farman.

p. 263 but could only assume: Joseph Farman, "What Hope for the Ozone Layer Now?" *New Scientist,* November 12, 1987.

p. 264 Another factor was the polar vortex: For the discussion of Antarctic conditions we are indebted to Stephen J. Pyne, *The Ice: A Journey to Antarctica* (Iowa City: University of Iowa Press, 1986); Finn Ronne, *Antarctica, My Destiny* (New York: Hastings House, 1979); and Richard Byrd, *Alone* (New York: Putnam, 1938). Background information on the recent history of scientific research in Antarctica was provided, in part, by Drs. Peter Wilkniss, John Lynch, and Polly Penhale of the National Science Foundation's Division of Polar Programs, Washington, D.C.

p. 266 "The single most significant": Walter Sullivan, *Assault on the Unknown: The International Geophysical Year* (New York: McGraw-Hill, 1961), p. 4. The description of the IGY is based on Sullivan, Pyne, and also J. Tuzo Wilson, *IGY: The Year of the New Moons* (New York: Knopf, 1961).

p. 267 All manner of colorful characters: The best-known and certainly the longest-running polar melodrama of the nineteenth century was that of the Sir John Franklin Expedition, which vanished without trace in the Arctic in 1845. Beseeched by Lady Jane Franklin, the wife of the expedition's leader, more than fifty heroic rescue expeditions went north between 1848 and 1859, providing further grist for the newspapers but locating not one of the 128 missing men, nor even so much as a ship's plank. (More than a century later, modern researchers would discover enough scant physical evidence to theorize that the men of the Franklin Expedition had perished not on account of storm, cold, or hostile Eskimos, but rather had succumbed to lead poisoning caused by the tinned food carried in the ships' holds.)

p. 268 "The provincialism of the pre-Sputnik era": Sullivan, p. 415.

p. 268 "a man of parts": Vivian Fuchs, *Of Ice and Men: The Story of the British Antarctic Survey, 1943–73* (Shropshire, UK: A. Nelson, 1982).

p. 271 "Understandably, a good many people": "The Past and Future of Satellite Data," *NCAR Quarterly Report,* October 1965.

p. 272 "One good observation": Quoted by Donald Heath during author interview. Our account of the Nimbus satellite and satellite research in general is indebted to Dr. Heath and Dr. Arlin Krueger of NASA, as well as the following sources: Jon Erickson, *Exploring Earth from Space* (Blue Ridge Summit, PA.: TAB Books, 1989); Judith Viorst, *Projects: Space* (New York: Washington Square Press, 1962); and Hugh Odishaw, ed., *The Challenges of Space* (Chicago: University of Chicago Press, 1962).

p. 272 The first scientists: S. F. Singer and R. C. Wentworth, "A Method for the Determination of the Vertical Ozone Distribution from a Satellite," *Journal of Geophysical Research*, June 1957.

p. 273 Krueger was a veteran: Author interview with Arlin Krueger. Heath and Krueger's conviction that monitoring of the upper atmosphere was a suitable role for NASA satellites would be fully realized in September 1991, when NASA put in orbit the Upper Atmosphere Research Satellite (UARS), the world's first satellite devoted solely to making global measurements of the chemistry, dynamics, and energetics of the earth's atmosphere. UARS is part of a research program known, appropriately, as *Mission to Planet Earth*.

p. 274 "Crutzen, who knew": Ibid.

p. 274 The instrument performed: Ibid.

p. 275 In 1981, Heath became convinced: Author interview with Donald Heath.

p. 275 "There is no way": Roan, p. 49.

p. 275 In particular, *Science* doubted: Richard Kerr, "Stratospheric Ozone Is Decreasing," *Science*, March 25, 1988.

p. 275 "People didn't want to acknowledge": Author interview with Donald Heath.

p. 276 "Our initial reaction": *Atlanta Constitution*, July 9, 1989.

p. 276 "We right away checked": Author interview with Donald Heath.

CHAPTER 17: A HOLE YOU COULD SEE FROM MARS

p. 277 "we find out": *New York Times*, November 28, 1984.

p. 278 Hoffman had met with Prather: Author interview with John Hoffman.

p. 278 "carry outside the laboratory": "New Models Predict Greater Ozone Depletion from Increased CFC Emissions, Scientists Say," *International Environment Reporter*, July 11, 1984.

p. 278 "There is no immediate": "CFC Protocol to Draft Ozone Convention 'Premature,' Industry Representative Says," *International Environment Reporter*, September 12, 1984.

p. 279 Although this represented: "Several Options to Control CFC Emissions Developed for Protocol to Ozone Convention," *International Environment Reporter*, November 14, 1984.

p. 279 "the ozone layer appears": Richard E. Benedick, "Protecting the Ozone Layer," Public Information Series, United States Department of State, Bureau of Public Affairs, January 21, 1985.

p. 279 The Europeans dismissed: Richard E. Benedick, *Ozone Diplomacy: New Directions in Safeguarding the Planet* (Cambridge and London: Harvard University Press, 1991), p. 43.

p. 279 "the first global convention": Mostafa K. Tolba, "The Significance of the Convention," *Environment*, June 1985. See also Paul H. Sand, "The Vienna Convention Is Adopted," *Environment*, June 1985.

p. 280 John Hoffman responded: *New York Times*, November 28, 1984.

p. 280 Lash and others worried: *New York Times*, November 29, 1984; December 3, 1984.

p. 281 "They have chosen": *New York Times*, November 30, 1984.

p. 281 By his own admission: *New York Times*, November 30, 1983.

p. 281 "ozone depletion was a big issue": Author interview with Lee Thomas.

p. 281 EPA agreed "to continue": *Natural Resources Defense Council, Inc.* v. *Lee Thomas*, "Plaintiff's and Defendant's Joint Motion for Entry of Order," NRDC Files.

p. 281 There were three primary elements: *Federal Register*, January 10, 1986.

p. 282 "Given what we know": National Aeronautics and Space Administration, "Present State of Knowledge of the Upper Atmosphere: Processes That Control Ozone and other Climatically Important Trace Gases 18," 1986. See also Thomas H. Maugh II, "Studies Renew Anxiety About Fading Ozone," *Los Angeles Times,* February 2, 1986.

p. 282 "My politics were what": Author interview with Joseph Farman.

p. 283 "[A]ssessments of the effect": J. C. Farman, B. G. Gardiner, and J. D. Shanklin, "Large Losses of Total Ozone in Antarctica Reveal Seasonal ClOx/NOx Interaction," *Nature,* May 16, 1985.

p. 284 "All the models": Author interview with Arlin Krueger.

p. 284 as surprised as anyone: Author interviews with Rowland and Molina.

p. 284 "Headquarters was extremely upset": Author interview with Donald Heath.

p. 284 "If Farman had publicly archived": Author interview with Arlin Krueger.

p. 285 In findings formally reported: R. S. Stolarski et al., *"Nimbus 7* Satellite Measurements of the Springtime Antarctic Ozone Decrease," *Nature,* August 1986.

p. 285 NASA's verdict was conclusive: Mark R. Schoeberl, Arlin J. Krueger, and Paul A. Newman, "The Morphology of Antarctic Total Ozone as Seen by TOMS," *Geophysical Research Letters,* November Supplement, 1986.

p. 285 "croissant-shaped patch": Ellen Ruppel Shell, "Weather Versus Chemicals," *Atlantic Monthly,* May 1987.

p. 285 One who received a copy: Author interview with Susan Solomon.

p. 286 "The possibility that the stratospheric": Susan Solomon, "Progress Towards a Quantitative Understanding of Antarctic Ozone Depletion," *Nature,* September 27, 1990.

p. 286 "The idea was so incredible": Author interview with Susan Solomon.

p. 286 "Everyone tweaked their models": Author interview with Michael Prather.

p. 288 McCormick's satellite data: M. P. McCormick and C. R. Trepte, *"Sam II* Measurements of Antarctic PSCs and Aerosols," *Geophysical Research Letters,* November Supplement, 1986.

p. 288 "Prior to that": Author interview with David Hofmann.

p. 288 "it all just clicked": Author interview with Susan Solomon.

p. 288 Solomon organized the authorship: Susan Solomon et al., "On the Depletion of Antarctic Ozone," *Nature,* June 19, 1986.

p. 289 Many scientists did not believe: Author interview with Dave Hofmann.

p. 290 Thus, it appeared possible: Richard Rood, "Global Ozone Minima in the Historical Record," *Geophysical Research Letters,* November Supplement, 1986.

p. 290 two other controversial theories: Dotto and Schiff, pp. 31 and 32; John Gribbin, *The Hole in the Sky: Man's Threat to the Ozone Layer* (New York: Bantam, 1988), pp. 77–78.

p. 291 "It's kind of nice": Roan, p. 140.

p. 291 "Industry always said": *Wall Street Journal,* August 13, 1986.

CHAPTER 18: THE NATIONAL OZONE EXPEDITION

p. 292 "The chance of it being": Author interview with Daniel Albritton.

p. 293 "There was nothing to it": Author interview with Dave Hofmann.

p. 294 "I have an idea": Susan Solomon, quoted by Dave Hofmann in author interview with him.

p. 294 "so easy to operate": Author interview with Susan Solomon.

p. 295 another NOAA scientist: Author interviews with George Mount and Susan Solomon.

p. 295 "Astronomy, as pure science": Author interview with Philip Solomon.

p. 297 Farmer was a veteran: Author interview with Barney Farmer.

p. 298 Wilkniss thought it terribly ironic: Author interview with Peter Wilkniss.

p. 299 "[T]he Earth is hollow": Quoted in William Stanton, *The Great United States Exploring Expedition of 1838–1842* (Berkeley: University of California Press, 1975).

p. 302 "White ashy material": Edgar Allan Poe, *The Narrative of Arthur Gordon Pym of Nantucket* (London: Penguin, 1975), pp. 238–39.

p. 302 "Atmospheric scientists are struggling": *New York Times*, July 29, 1986.

CHAPTER 19: THE SPIRIT OF LEESBURG

p. 303 "before the ink was dry": "Remarks by Richard Barnett, Chairman, Alliance for Responsible CFC Policy to the Environmental Protection Agency Workshop Protecting the Ozone Layer, Workshop on Demand and Control Technologies," March 7, 1986. (NRDC Files)

p. 304 But the advocates of regulation: Benedick, *Ozone Diplomacy*, p. 56. Author interviews with Benedick, Losey, and Hoffman.

p. 304 "We were devastated": Author interview with John Hoffman.

p. 305 "the spirit of Leesburg": UNEP, "Report of the Second Part of the Workshop on the Control of Chlorofluorocarbons. Leesburg, USA, 08–12 September 1986."

p. 306 The story was Brodeur's second: Paul Brodeur, "Annals of Chemistry: In the Face of Doubt," *New Yorker*, June 9, 1986.

p. 307 Du Pont issued its own: Du Pont position statement on the Chlorofluorocarbon/Ozone/Greenhouse issues, September 1986, NRDC Files.

p. 308 "Because of the new questions": Letter from Joseph P. Glas, Freon Products Division Director, Du Pont, to "Freon customers," September 26, 1986, NRDC Files. Du Pont's reversal of position was startling in itself. But even more significant was the company's simultaneous announcement that environmentally acceptable and commercially viable alternatives to CFCs were within reach. All that stood between these alternatives and the marketplace was incentives in the form of regulatory policy. "If the necessary incentives were provided," Glas wrote, "we believe alternates could be introduced in volume in a time frame of roughly five years." Thus, Du Pont not only acquiesced to regulations; it actively sought them!

p. 308 The year before: Douglas G. Cogan, *Stones in a Glass House: CFCs and Ozone Depletion* (Washington, D.C.: Investor Responsibility Research Center, 1988), p. 46.

p. 308 NRDC issued a press release: NRDC news release, issued October 3, 1986, NRDC Files.

p. 308 "no significant modification": Alliance for Responsible CFC Policy, "Policy Statement," September 16, 1986, NRDC Files.

p. 308 "no growth potential": Author interview with Kevin Faye.

p. 309 "Even without the Antarctic hole": NRDC news release, October 20, 1986, NRDC Files.

p. 310 "It came through the discussion": Author interview with Lee Thomas.

p. 311 "Nobody came to Lee": Author interview with John Hoffman.

p. 311 "on November 5, 1986": U.S. Department of State, "Principles for an International Protocol on Stratospheric Ozone Protection," November 5, 1986, NRDC Files. See also *New York Times*, November 5, 1986; *Wall Street Journal*, November 6, 1986.

p. 311 "We do not believe": Mark Crawford, "United States Floats Proposal to Help Prevent Global Ozone Depletion," *Science*, November 21, 1986.

p. 311 Barnett defended industry's preferred solution: Richard Barnett, "The U.S. Can't Do the Job All Alone," *New York Times*, November 16, 1986.

p. 312 "As it is": Letter from David A. Wirth and David D. Doniger, NRDC, to

Suzanne Butcher, Office of Environment and Health, Department of State, and Steven Seidel, Office of Policy Analysis, EPA, November 25, 1986.

p. 312 McMurdo was located: The description of McMurdo and Ross Island comes from Charles Neider, *Edge of the World: Ross Island, Antarctica* (Garden City, N.Y.: Doubleday, 1974), p. 16. See also Peter Briggs, *Laboratory at the Bottom of the World* (New York: David McKay, 1970).

p. 313 "The work was tough": Author interview with Susan Solomon.

p. 313 "There was a great deal": Author interview with Robert Watson.

p. 313 "We had already seen": Author interview with Barney Farmer.

p. 313 "The nitrogen dioxide abundances": Pamela S. Zurer, "Complex Mission to Probe Origins of Antarctic Ozone Hole," *Chemical and Engineering News,* August 17, 1987.

p. 314 powerful raw data: Gribbin, *The Hole in the Sky,* p. 120.

p. 314 "Until '86 I was skeptical": Author interview with David Hofmann.

p. 315 "We argued about it": Author interview with Barney Farmer.

p. 315 "We suspect": Richard Kerr, "Taking Shots at Ozone Hole Theories," *Science,* November 14, 1986. "I had not talked to Susan the whole time she was down there, not until the press conference," Watson later explained, "so I wasn't certain what was coming. But she managed to observe the Golden Rule: only say what you can be sure of. Be able to recognize the differing levels of certainty. Don't say things you're later going to have to retract." (Author interview with Robert Watson)

p. 315 "You send chemists": Gary Taubes, "Made in the Shade? No Way," *Discover,* August 1987.

p. 315 "Their suggestion": S. Weisburd, "Pole's Ozone Hole: Who NOZE?" *Science News,* October 1986.

p. 316 "how much people have lost": Ellen Ruppel Shell, "Weather Versus Chemicals," *Atlantic Monthly,* May 1987.

p. 316 "The origin of the ozone change": Pamela S. Zurer, "Complex Mission Set to Probe Origins of Antarctic Ozone Hole," *Chemical and Engineering News,* August 17, 1987.

p. 317 "You could talk about it": Author interview with David Hofmann.

p. 317 "In retrospect": Author interview with Barney Farmer.

CHAPTER 20: HATS, SHADES, AND SUNSCREEN

p. 318 As Ambassador Benedick: U.S. Senate, "Ozone Depletion, the Greenhouse Effect, and Climate Change," joint hearing before the Subcommittees on Environmental Protection and Hazardous Wastes and Toxic Substances of the Committee on Environment and Public Works, 100th Cong., 1st sess., January 28, 1987, Pt. 2, p. 50.

p. 319 "totally unacceptable": *New York Times,* February 28, 1987.

p. 319 West Germany, the Netherlands: Benedick, *Ozone Diplomacy,* pp. 70–71.; *New York Times,* February 28, 1987.

p. 320 "Given the amount": *Guardian* (London), March 12, 1987.

p. 320 At the same time: Author interview with Lee Thomas. Testimony of David D. Doniger, senior attorney, NRDC, on protection of the stratospheric ozone layer, before the Subcommittee on Natural Resources, Agricultural Research, and Environment, House Committee on Science and Technology, March 12, 1987.

p. 320 Dingell charged: U.S. House of Representatives, Subcommittee on Health and the Environment of the Committee on Energy and Commerce, "Ozone Layer Depletion," 100th Cong., 1st sess., March 9, 1987, p. 7.

p. 320 pull a fast one: *Human Events,* June 20, 1987. As coordinator for population affairs at the State Department, Benedick had worked for five years, starting in the Carter administration, to promote family planning to control population growth. This was in accordance with established U.S. policy, but population affairs became a primary target of pro-life groups in the United States after those groups helped elect Ronald Reagan president.

In 1983, Benedick saw the culmination of a three-year effort to gain an audience with Pope John Paul II in the hope of persuading the pope to cease his attacks on the U.S. population program. The pope agreed. In 1982, Benedick successfully opposed an initiative by then–Undersecretary of State James L. Buckley to eliminate population affairs from the State Department budget. Secretary of State Alexander Haig sided with Benedick.

As a result of his effectiveness, Benedick was branded "the single most dangerous antilife official in the Reagan Administration" by the American Life Lobby (*New York Times,* August 16, 1984). That group and others who opposed abortion believed that the United States should withhold its sizable contribution to international population-control efforts from any organizations that "perform or actively promote abortion as a method of family planning." (James L. Buckley, *New York Times,* August 12, 1984) The issue came to a head in the weeks prior to the U.N.-sponsored International Conference on Population in Mexico City in August 1984, as conservatives inside and outside the administration succeeded in reversing U.S. policy.

The abrupt change in policy went against the tide of world opinion. Not only did the United States have a new antiabortion policy; it had a new theory of population growth, too, one that "reject[ed] the notion that we are caught up in a global population crisis." (*New York Times,* August 9, 1984) Ascendant conservative dogma held that population growth was a neutral or even a positive phenomenon that could be accommodated by free-market economies that fostered growth. To carry the new policy forward, Benedick's old State Department nemesis, James L. Buckley, was appointed head of the U.S. delegation to Mexico City. Benedick, who had worked for years to prepare for the conference and had attended every preparatory meeting since 1981, was booted off the delegation entirely.

Benedick wrote to Tufts University president Jean Mayter that he had been "the object of an inexplicable and vicious campaign." He viewed his defeat as "humiliating" and "a personal trauma." (*New York Times,* August 16, 1984)

Benedick's rehabilitation began slowly, after he was asked to temporarily cover the environment portfolio by the assistant secretary of state for oceans and international environmental and scientific affairs. The temporary appointment became permanent in the spring of 1985.

p. 321 "Benedick did not do his job": Author interview with Rebecca Norton Dunlop.

p. 321 Benedick was particularly stung: Author interview with Richard Benedick. "These people are dangerous to your health," he later reflected.

p. 321 on March 27, 1987: Memorandum, "International Negotiations to Protect the Ozone Layer," NRDC, March 30, 1987.

p. 321 "star chamber": Author interview with David Doniger.

p. 321 Even industry found: Author interview with Kevin Faye. "There were some meetings we felt good about," Faye later said, "but others where we felt like we were treated like socialists. Some folks in the administration seemed to think we had given away the farm."

p. 321 "As we got closer": Author interview with Lee Thomas.

p. 322 Benedick speculates: Benedick, *Ozone Diplomacy,* p. 58.

p. 322 In any case, once the siege: Author interviews with John Hoffman, Steve Seidel, and Eileen Claussen.

p. 322 "We had done our homework": Author interview with John Hoffman.

p. 322 "I had never been": Author interview with Margaret Kripke.

p. 323 "The majority of cancers": Letter from Margaret L. Kripke to David Gibbons, April 6, 1987. Reprinted in U.S. House of Representatives, Subcommittee on Health and the Environment of the Committee on Energy and Commerce, "Ozone Layer Depletion," 100th Cong., 1st sess., March 9, 1987, pp. 623–25.

p. 324 "We are speaking": U.S. Senate, "The Effect of Chlorofluorocarbons on Stratospheric Ozone, Health Effects of Ozone Depletion, and Substitutes for Ozone-Depleting Chemicals," joint hearings before the Subcommittees on Environmental Protection and Hazardous Wastes and Toxic Substances of the Committee on Environment and Public Works, 100th Cong., 1st sess., May 12–14, 1987, p. 44.

p. 326 Dr. Lawrence A. Yannuzzi: *Orion Magazine,* Winter 1989.

p. 328 "I did something": Author interview with David Doniger.

p. 328 Benedick somewhat slyly alluded: UNEP Conference on Protection of the Ozone Layer, Plenary Statement by Ambassador Richard E. Benedick, United States Representative, Geneva, April 27, 1987.

p. 328 The most significant development: Benedick, *Ozone Diplomacy,* pp. 71–72.

p. 328 Tolba drew the obvious conclusions: Mostafa Tolba, "Nowhere to Hide," Statement to the Ad Hoc Working Group of Legal and Technical Experts for the Preparation of a Protocol on CFCs to the Vienna Convention for the Protection of the Ozone Layer, 3rd sess., Geneva, April 27, 1987. Reprinted in U.S. Senate, "The Effect of Chlorofluorocarbons on Stratospheric Ozone, Health Effects of Ozone Depletion, and Substitutes for Ozone-Depleting Chemicals," joint hearings before the Subcommittees on Environmental Protection and Hazardous Wastes and Toxic Substances of the Committee on Environment and Public Works, 100th Cong., 1st sess., May 12–14, 1987, pp. 57–62.

p. 329 This U.S. weakness: NRDC news release, "U.S. Ozone Protection Policy Sabotaged," May 4, 1987, NRDC Files.

p. 329 Doniger agreed to the postponements: Author interview with David Doniger.

p. 330 Reagan, according to Donald Regan: Francis FitzGerald, "A Critic at Large: Memoirs of the Reagan Era," *New Yorker,* January 16, 1989.

p. 330 "We urge that you lend": Letter to President Ronald Reagan from John H. Adams, NRDC; Peter A. Berle, president, National Audubon Society; Michael S. Clark, president, Environmental Policy Institute; Michael Fischer, executive director, Sierra Club; George Frampton, president, The Wilderness Society; Jay D. Hair, executive vice president, National Wildlife Federation; Frederic D. Krupp, executive director, Environmental Defense Fund; Jack Lorenz, executive director, Izaak Walton League of America; Paul C. Pritchard, president, National Parks and Conservation Association; Cynthia Wilson, executive director, Friends of the Earth, May 21, 1987, NRDC Files.

p. 331 "I didn't have cancer": Bob Schieffer and Gary Paul Gates, *The Acting President* (New York: Dutton, 1989), p. 231.

p. 331 STAY OUT OF THE SUN: *New York Times,* July 31, 1987.

p. 331 "We had several cabinet sessions": Author interview with Lee Thomas.

p. 332 Interior justified its interest: Mark Crawford, "Ozone Plan Splits Administration," *Science,* May 1987.

p. 332 When David Doniger heard: Author interview with David Doniger.

p. 332 Graham and Hodel were said: *Atlanta Constitution,* May 28, 1987.

p. 332 "People who don't stand": *Wall Street Journal,* May 29, 1987.

p. 333 "the Ray-Ban Plan": *Washington Post,* May 29, 1987.

p. 333 "This is neither the time": *Atlanta Journal-Constitution,* May 30, 1987.

p. 333 "This approach": Ibid.

p. 333 Congressman Thomas J. Downey: *New York Times,* May 4, 1987.

p. 333 "We are continuing": *Los Angeles Times,* May 30, 1987.

p. 333 publicly proclaimed his support: *Washington Post,* June 15, 1987.

p. 334 "The grown-ups": *Washington Post*, June 7, 1987.

p. 334 "I have not suggested": Letter from Donald Hodel to Senator Timothy E. Wirth, June 4, 1987, NRDC Files.

p. 334 "They leaked it": Author interview with Rebecca Norton Dunlop.

p. 335 Unsure of the depth: Benedick, *Ozone Diplomacy*, p. 73.

p. 335 An unnamed source: *Boston Globe*, September 10, 1987.

p. 336 "a backdoor attempt": *Boston Globe*, September 10, 1987; *Denver Post*, September 6, 1987.

p. 336 "a decent interval": Benedick, *Ozone Diplomacy*, p. 89.

p. 336 "This is perhaps the most": *New York Times*, September 17, 1987.

p. 336 "significant step": Author interview with Kevin Faye.

p. 337 Joseph Steed of Du Pont: *Wall Street Journal*, September 17, 1987.

p. 337 "Lee Thomas and the United States": *New York Times*, September 17, 1987.

p. 337 "The treaty is an important first step": *Los Angeles Times*, September 20, 1987.

p. 337 "proves that we can act": *New York Times*, September 15, 1987.

p. 337 "We have to go": *Los Angeles Times*, September 20, 1987.

p. 337 "in the near future": Ibid.

p. 338 "Above the Antarctic": Joseph Farman, "What Hope for the Ozone Layer Now?" *New Scientist*, November 12, 1987.

CHAPTER 21: INTO THE OZONE HOLE

p. 339 unravel the ozone-hole mystery: Author interview with Robert Watson.

p. 339 a second expedition: Ibid.

p. 340 The ER-2 was a direct descendant: Prior to the advent of the U-2 in the late 1950s, the United States military had relied on captured World War II German aerial photos of the Soviet Union for much of its intelligence. Between 1956 and 1960, using infrared detectors, radar, and cameras, the U-2 mapped hundreds of thousands of square miles of Soviet territory, yielding new and highly reliable knowledge of Soviet military strength. "Today," *Time* magazine could boast by 1960, "the folders of Strategic Air Command bomber crews bulge with accurate pictures of potential enemy targets." (*Time*, May 30, 1960)

Ironically, when a U-2 went down over the Soviet Union in May 1960, President Dwight Eisenhower claimed the aircraft was an upper-atmosphere-research plane on a weather mission. Indeed, U-2s were sometimes used for atmospheric research, but not this time. Eisenhower's attempted subterfuge, revealed when the Soviets produced the captured pilot, Francis Gary Powers, damaged both U.S.-Soviet relations and Eisenhower's prestige.

p. 340 The ER-2 quickly established: NASA Information Bulletin, "High-Altitude Aircraft Program," December 1988.

p. 342 "Jim was the only person": Author interview with Robert Watson; and Roan, p. 183.

p. 342 "We've got to do something": Roan, p. 185.

p. 342 an old grudge to settle: Roan, p. 95; author interviews with Darin Toohey and F. Sherwood Rowland.

p. 343 "side-scattering": Author interview with Darin Toohey.

p. 343 "What do you mean": Roan, p. 187.

p. 344 "The emphasis on real-time": Author interview with Estelle Condon.

p. 345 "We've had the ER-2": Ellen Ruppel Shell, "Solo Flights into the Ozone Hole Reveal Its Causes," *Scientific American*, February 1988.

p. 345 "It's very cold": Pamela S. Zurer, "Mission Set to Probe Origins of Antarctic Ozone Hole," *Chemical and Engineering News*, August 17, 1987.

p. 347 "Everywhere else in the world": Michael D. Lemonick, "The Heat Is On," *Time*, October 19, 1987.

p. 347 "Once you get into the stratosphere": Author interview with Ron Williams.

p. 348 "Ozone was virtually undetectable": Gribbin, *The Hole in the Sky*, p. 128.

p. 348 The largest such event: NASA News Release No. 87-50, "Initial Findings from Punta Arenas, Chile," September 30, 1987.

p. 349 "there is no longer debate": *New York Times*, October 1, 1987.

p. 349 "moving at fast foward": Ibid.

p. 349 "the first hard evidence": *Washington Post*, October 1, 1987.

p. 349 "It is now very difficult": Christopher Joyce, "Chlorine Clears the Ozone Layer Down South," *New Scientist*, October 8, 1987.

p. 349 NSF's Peter Wilkniss: McElroy and Rowland testimony, joint hearings. Committee on Environment and Public Works, U.S. Senate, October 27, 1987.

p. 350 "Humans are altering": Michael D. Lemonick, "The Heat Is On," *Time*, October 19, 1987.

p. 350 Watson continued to caution: *New York Times*, October 1, 1987.

p. 351 "This particular reaction": Mario J. Molina, "The Antarctic Ozone Hole," *Oceanus*, vol. 31, no. 2 (Summer 1988).

p. 352 workshop was a postmortem: The Berlin workshop is described in Gribbin, *The Hole in the Sky*, pp. 130–31.

p. 353 Jonathan Shanklin added a chill: *New York Times*, December 19, 1987.

p. 353 "People sometimes have the attitude": Gribbin, p. 161.

p. 353 "One chart with just a few words": Author interview with Robert Watson.

p. 353 "People talk of finding": Gribbin, *The Hole in the Sky*, p. 133.

EPILOGUE

p. 355 Bowman's study estimated: *New York Times*, January 1, 1988; *Washington Post*, January 1, 1988.

p. 356 Over Australia and New Zealand: *Los Angeles Times*, March 16, 1988.

p. 356 By 1988, the panel concluded: David Doniger, "Global Emergency," *The Environmental Forum*, July/August 1988, p. 17.

p. 356 In July 1991, British scientists confirmed: Francesca Lyman, "As the Ozone Thins, the Plot Thickens," *The Amicus Journal*, Summer 1991.

p. 357 The developing nations agreed: *New York Times*, June 30, 1990.

p. 358 "Now that there's the prospect of a hole": Michael D. Lemonick, "The Ozone Vanishes," *Time*, February 17, 1992.

p. 359 HCFCs, meanwhile, do contain chlorine: *New York Times*, July 1, 1990.

p. 359 According to the Copenhagen Agreements: *New York Times*, January 11, 1990.

p. 359 Some scientists believe: *New York Times*, March 20, 1988.

p. 360 Hofmann believes the 5 percent increase: *New York Times*, May 29, 1990.

p. 360 "The mechanisms may vary": Author interview with Philip Solomon.

p. 360 In 1990, Hofmann found: *New York Times*, October 12, 1990.

p. 361 Sunblock, sunglasses, hats: Michael D. Lemonick, "The Ozone Vanishes," *Time*, February 17, 1992.

SELECTED BIBLIOGRAPHY

Acton, Jay, and Alan Lemond. *Ralph Nader: A Man and a Movement.* New York: Warner Paperback Library, 1972.

Allen, Frederick Lewis. *Only Yesterday: An Informal History of the Nineteen-Twenties.* New York: Harper, 1931.

Allyn, Stanley C. *My Half-Century with NCR.* New York: McGraw-Hill, 1967.

Anderson, Frederick R. *NEPA in the Courts: A Legal Analysis of the National Environmental Policy Act.* Washington, D.C.: Resources for the Future, 1973.

Arnold, Henry H. *Global Mission.* New York: Harper, 1949.

Arnold, Ron. *At the Eye of the Storm: James Watt and the Environmentalists.* Chicago: Regnery Gateway, 1982.

Aron, Nan. *Liberty and Justice for All: Public Interest Law in the 1980s and Beyond.* Boulder and London: Westview Press, 1989.

Barbour, Ian G. *Western Man and Environmental Ethics: Attitudes Toward Nature and Technology.* Reading, Mass.: Addison-Wesley, 1973.

Baum, Robert A. *Public Interest Law: Where Law Meets Social Action.* London, Rome, and New York: Oceana Publications, 1987.

Bender, Thomas. *New York Intellect: A History of Intellectual Life in New York City from 1750 to the Beginning of Our Time.* New York: Knopf, 1987.

Benedick, Richard E. *Ozone Diplomacy: New Directions in Safeguarding the Planet.* Cambridge and London: Harvard University Press, 1991.

Bergaust, Erik, and William Beller. *Satellite!* New York: Hanover House, 1956.

Berton, Pierre. *The Arctic Grail: The Quest for the Northwest Passage and the North Pole, 1818–1909.* New York: Viking Penguin, 1988.

Bogdanor, Vernon, ed. *Science and Politics: The Herbert Spencer Lectures 1982.* Oxford: Clarendon Press, 1984.

Bower, Frank A., and Richard B. Ward. *Stratospheric Ozone and Man.* Boca Raton, Fla.: CRC Press, 1981.

Boyd, Thomas A. *Professional Amateur: The Biography of Charles Franklin Kettering.* New York: Dutton, 1957.

———. ed. *Prophet of Progress: The Speeches of Charles F. Kettering.* New York: Dutton, 1961.

Boyle, Robert H. *The Hudson River: A Natural and Unnatural History.* New York: Norton, 1969.

Briggs, Peter. *Laboratory at the Bottom of the World.* New York: David McKay, 1970.

Brooks, Paul. *The House of Life: Rachel Carson at Work.* Boston: Houghton Mifflin, 1972.

Buckhorn, Robert F. *Nader: The People's Lawyer.* Englewood Cliffs, N.J.: Prentice-Hall, 1972.

Burford, Anne M., with John Greenya. *Are You Tough Enough?* New York: McGraw-Hill, 1986.

Byrd, Richard. *Alone.* New York: Putnam, 1938.

Caldwell, Lynton K. *In Defense of Earth: International Protection of the Biosphere.* Bloomington and London: Indiana University Press, 1972.

Cannon, Lou. *Reagan.* New York: Perigee Books, 1984.

Carr, William H. *The Du Ponts of Delaware.* New York: Dodd, Mead, 1964.

Carson, Rachel. *Under the Sea-Wind.* New York: Simon & Schuster, 1941.

———. *The Sea Around Us.* New York: Oxford University Press, 1951.

———. *Silent Spring.* Boston: Houghton Mifflin, 1962.

Chandler, Alfred D., and Stephen Salsbury. *Pierre S. Du Pont and the Making of the Modern Corporation.* New York: Harper & Row, 1971.

Clawson, Marion. *The Federal Lands Revisited.* Baltimore and London: Resources for the Future/Johns Hopkins University Press, 1983.

Cogan, Douglas G. *Stones in a Glass House: CFCs and Ozone Depletion.* Washington, D.C.: Investor Responsibility Research Center, 1988.

Cohen, Michael P. *The Pathless Way: John Muir and the American Wilderness.* Madison: University of Wisconsin Press, 1984.

———. *The History of the Sierra Club, 1892–1970.* San Francisco: Sierra Club Books, 1988.

Colby, Gerald. *Du Pont Dynasty.* Secaucus, N.J.: Lyle Stuart, 1984.

Conot, Robert. *A Streak of Luck: The Life and Legend of Thomas Alva Edison.* New York: Bantam Books, 1979.

Conover, Charlotte Reeve. *Dayton, Ohio: An Intimate History.* New York: Lewis Historical Publishing, 1932.

Corn, Joseph J. *The Winged Gospel: America's Romance with Aviation, 1900–1950.* New York: Oxford University Press, 1983.

Costello, John, and Terry Hughes. *Concorde: The International Race for a Supersonic Passenger Transport.* London: Angus & Robertson, 1976.

Council for Public Interest Law. *Balancing the Scales of Justice: Financing Public Interest Law in America.* Washington, D.C.: Council for Public Interest Law, 1976.

Craig, Richard A. *The Edge of Space: Exploring the Upper Atmosphere.* Garden City, N.Y.: Doubleday, 1968.

Crouch, Tom. *A Dream of Wings: Americans and the Airplane, 1875–1905.* New York: Norton, 1981.

———. *The Bishop's Boys: A Life of Wilbur and Orville Wright.* New York: Norton, 1989.

Crowther, Samuel. *John H. Patterson: Pioneer in Industrial Welfare.* New York: Doubleday, Page, 1924.

Culhane, Paul J. *Public Lands Politics: Interest Group Influence on the Forest Service and the Bureau of Land Management.* Baltimore and London: Resources for the Future/Johns Hopkins University Press, 1981.

Diebold, John, ed. *The World of the Computer.* New York: Random House, 1973.

Dobson, Gordon M. B. *Exploring the Atmosphere.* Oxford: Clarendon Press, 1963.

Dotto, Lydia, and Harold Schiff. *The Ozone War*. Garden City, N.Y.: Doubleday, 1978.

Drury, A. W. *A History of the City of Dayton and Montgomery County, Ohio*. Dayton: S. J. Clarke Co., 1909.

Dwiggins, Don. *The SST: Here It Comes, Ready or Not*. Garden City, N.Y.: Doubleday, 1969.

Ellis, Robert L., ed. *Taking Ideals Seriously: The Case for a Lawyers' Public Interest Movement*. Washington, D.C.: Equal Justice Foundation, 1984.

Environmental Protection Agency. *Can We Delay a Greenhouse Warming? The Effectiveness and Feasibility of Options to Slow a Build-up of Carbon Dioxide in the Atmosphere*.

———. *Effects of Changes in Stratospheric Ozone and Global Climate*. Vol. I, *Overview*. August 1986.

———. Vol. II: *Stratospheric Ozone*. October 1986.

———. *Assessing the Risks of Trace Gases That Can Modify the Stratosphere*. Vols. I, II, and III. December 1987.

———. *CFCs and Stratospheric Ozone*. December 1987.

———. *How Industry Is Reducing Dependence on Ozone-Depleting Chemicals*. A Status Report. June 1988.

———. *Regulatory Impact Analysis: Protection of Stratospheric Ozone*. Vol. I, *Regulatory Impact Analysis Document*. August 1, 1988.

Erickson, Jon. *Exploring Earth from Space*. Blue Ridge Summit, Pa.: Tab Books, 1989.

Farber, Eduard, ed. *The Great Chemists*. New York: Interscience, 1961.

Fisk, Dorothy. *Exploring the Upper Atmosphere*. New York: Oxford University Press, 1934.

Fox, Stephen. *The American Conservation Movement: John Muir and His Legacy*. Madison: University of Wisconsin Press, 1985.

Francis, John G., and Richard Ganzel. *Western Public Lands: The Management of Natural Resources in a Time of Declining Federalism*. Totowa, N.J.: Rowman & Allenheld, 1984.

Freedman, Warren. *Federal Statutes on Environmental Protection: Regulation in the Public Interest*. Westport, Conn.: Quorum Books, 1987.

Fuchs, Vivian. *Of Ice and Men: The Story of the British Antarctic Survey, 1943–73*. Shropshire, UK: A. Nelson, 1982.

Gibson, Arthur. *Concorde*. London: B.P.C. Publishing, 1976.

Gleick, James. *Chaos: Making a New Science*. New York: Viking, 1987.

Goldman, Eric F. *Rendezvous with Destiny: A History of Modern American Reform*. New York: Knopf, 1952.

Graham, Frank, Jr. *Since Silent Spring*. Boston: Houghton Mifflin, 1970.

———. *Man's Dominion: The Story of Conservation in America*. New York: M. Evans, 1971.

Gribbin, John. *The Hole in the Sky: Man's Threat to the Ozone Layer*. New York: Bantam, 1988.

———. *Hothouse Earth: The Greenhouse Effect and Gaia*. New York: Grove Weidenfeld, 1990.

Halaby, Najeeb. *Crosswinds: An Airman's Memoir*. Garden City, N.Y.: Doubleday, 1979.

Hamilton, Alice. *Exploring the Dangerous Trades: The Autobiography of Alice Hamilton, M.D.* Boston: Little, Brown, 1943.

Harris, Sherwood. *The First to Fly: Aviation's Pioneer Days*. New York: Simon & Schuster, 1970.

Harrison, Gordon. *Earthkeeping*. Boston: Houghton Mifflin, 1971.

———. *Mosquitoes, Malaria, and Man: A History of the Hostilities Since 1880*. New York: Dutton, 1978.

Hawke, David Freeman. *Nuts and Bolts of the Past: A History of American Technology, 1776–1860*. New York: Harper & Row, 1988.

Haynes, William. *American Chemical Industry*. New York: Van Nostrand, 1948.

Hays, Samuel P. *The Response to Industrialism: 1885–1914*. Chicago: University of Chicago Press, 1957.

———. *Beauty, Health, and Permanence: Environmental Politics in the United States, 1955–1985*. Cambridge: Cambridge University Press, 1987.

Hofstadter, Richard. *The Age of Reform*. New York: Random House, 1955.

Holdgate, Martin W., Mahammed Kassas, and Gilbert F. White, eds. *The World Environment 1972–1982*, A Report by the United Nations Environment Program. Dublin: Tycooly International Publishing, 1982.

Horwitch, Mel. *Clipped Wings*. Cambridge, Mass.: MIT Press, 1982.

Hounshell, David A. *From the American System to Mass Production, 1800–1932: The Development of Manufacturing Technology in the United States*. Baltimore and London: Johns Hopkins University Press, 1984.

Hounshell, David A., and John Kenly Smith, Jr. *Science and Corporate Strategy: Du Pont Research and Development, 1902–1980*. Cambridge: Cambridge University Press, 1988.

Howard, Fred. *Wilbur and Orville: A Biography of the Wright Brothers*. New York: Knopf, 1987.

Hughes, Thomas P. *American Genesis: A Century of Invention and Technological Enthusiasm, 1870–1970*. New York: Viking, 1989.

Ihde, Aaron. *The Development of Modern Chemistry*, New York: Harper & Row, 1963.

Ingells, Margaret. *Carrier: Father of Air Conditioning*. Garden City, N.Y.: Doubleday, 1952.

Jackson, Donald Dale, ed. *The Aeronauts*. Alexandria, Va.: Time-Life Books, 1980.

Jackson, Kenneth T. *Crabgrass Frontier: The Suburbanization of the United States*. New York: Oxford University Press, 1985.

Jacobs, David M. *The UFO Controversy in America*. Bloomington: Indiana University Press, 1975.

Jaffe, Sanford. *Public Interest Law: Five Years Later*. Ford Foundation, New York; American Bar Association Special Committee on Public Interest Practice, Chicago, 1976.

Jardim, Anne. *The First Henry Ford: A Study in Personality and Business Leadership*. Cambridge, Mass.: MIT Press, 1970.

Johnson, Mary Ann. *A Field Guide to Flight: On the Aviation Trail in Dayton, Ohio*. Dayton: Landfall Press, 1986.

Jones, Holway R. *John Muir and the Sierra Club: The Battle for Yosemite*. San Francisco: Sierra Club, 1965.

Kalman, Laura. *Legal Realism at Yale, 1927–60*. Chapel Hill and London: University of North Carolina Press, 1986.

Kasson, John F. *Civilizing the Machine: Technology and Republican Values in America, 1776–1900*. New York: Penguin Books, 1977.

Kay, David A., and Eugene B. Skolnikoff. *World Eco-crisis*. Madison: University of Wisconsin Press, 1972.

Kelly, Fred C. *The Wright Brothers: A Biography Authorized by Orville Wright*. New York: Ballantine, 1950.

Kloepfer, Deanne. *The Watt Record: James Watt and the National Park System*. The Wilderness Society, July 1983.

———. *The Watt Record: James Watt and the Bureau of Land Management Lands*. The Wilderness Society, October 1983.

———. *The Watt Record: The Environmental Policies of the Reagan Administration: Wilderness*. The Wilderness Society, December 1983.

———. *The Watt/Clark Record: The National Wildlife Refuge System*. The Wilderness Society, March 1984.

Knight, Geoffrey. *Concorde, The Inside Story*. London: Weidenfeld & Nicolson, 1976.

Lake, Laura M. *Environmental Regulation: The Political Effects of Implementation*. New York: Praeger, 1982.

Landau, Norman J., and Paul D. Rheingold. *The Environmental Law Handbook.* New York: Friends of the Earth/Ballantine, 1971.

Lash, Jonathan, with Katherine Gillman and David Sheridan. *A Season of Spoils: The Story of the Reagan Administration's Attack on the Environment.* New York: Pantheon, 1984.

Lassiter, Barbara Babcock. *American Wilderness: The Hudson River School of Painting.* Garden City, N.Y.: Doubleday, 1978.

Leland, Mrs. Wilfrid, and Minnie Dobbs Millbrook. *Master of Precision: Henry Leland.* Detroit: Wayne State University Press, 1966.

Leslie, Stuart W. *Boss Kettering: Wizard of General Motors.* New York: Columbia University Press, 1983.

Libby, Willard F. *Radiocarbon Dating.* 2nd ed. Chicago and London: University of Chicago Press, 1955.

Libecap, Gary D. *Locking Up the Range: Federal Land Controls and Grazing.* Cambridge, Mass.: Pacific Institute for Public Policy Research/Ballinger Publishing Company, 1981.

Lillard, Richard G. *The Great Forest.* New York: Knopf, 1948.

Loening, Grover. *Takeoff into Greatness: How American Aviation Grew So Big So Fast.* New York: Putnam, 1968.

Lovelock, J. E. *Gaia: A New Look at Life on Earth.* Oxford: Oxford University Press, 1979.

McAdie, Alexander. *The Principles of Aerography.* Chicago: Rand McNally, 1917.

McCormick, John. *Reclaiming Paradise: The Global Environmental Movement.* Bloomington and Indianapolis: Indiana University Press, 1989.

McHenry, Robert, with Charles Van Doren, eds. *A Documentary History of Conservation in America.* New York: Praeger, 1972.

Marcosson, Isaac F. *Wherever Men Trade: The Romance of the Cash Register.* New York: Dodd, Mead, 1945.

———. *Colonel Deeds: Industrial Builder.* New York: Dodd, Mead, 1947.

Marks, F. Raymond, with Kirk Leswing and Barbara A. Fortinsky. *The Lawyer, The Public, and Professional Responsibility.* Chicago: American Bar Foundation, 1972.

Marx, Leo. *The Machine in the Garden: Technology and the Pastoral Ideal in America.* New York: Oxford University Press, 1964.

Miller, Alan S., and Irving M. Mintzer. *The Sky Is the Limit: Strategies for Protecting the Ozone Layer.* World Resources Institute, Research Report #3. November 1986.

Morgan, Arthur E. *The Miami Conservancy District.* New York: McGraw–Hill, 1951.

Muir, John. *The Yosemite.* New York: Century, 1912.

Nader, Ralph. *Unsafe at Any Speed: The Designed-in Dangers of the American Automobile.* New York: Grossman, 1965.

Nash, Roderick. *Wilderness and the American Mind.* New Haven and London: Yale University Press, 1967.

National Academy of Sciences. *Halocarbons: Effects on Stratospheric Ozone.* Washington, D.C.: National Academy of Sciences, 1976.

———. *Halocarbons: Environmental Effects of Chlorofluoromethane Release.* Washington, D.C.: National Academy of Sciences, 1976.

National Aeronautics and Space Administration. *Present State of Knowledge of the Upper Atmosphere 1988: An Assessment Report.* Springfield, Va.: NASA, Scientific and Technical Information Branch, 1988.

National Oceanic and Atmospheric Administration. *Stratospheric Ozone: The State of the Science and NOAA's Current and Future Research.* Report to Congress and to the Environmental Protection Agency. Washington, D.C., January 1990.

National Research Council, Climatic Impact Committee. *Environmental Impact of Stratospheric Flight: Biological and Climatic Effects of Aircraft Emissions in the Stratosphere.* Washington, D.C., National Academy of Sciences, 1975.

Neider, Charles. *Edge of the World: Ross Island, Antarctica.* Garden City, N.Y.: Doubleday, 1974.

Nelkin, Dorothy. *Controversy: Politics of Technical Decisions.* 2nd ed. Beverly Hills, London, and New Delhi: Sage Publications, 1984.

Noble, David F. *America by Design: Science, Technology, and the Rise of Corporate Capitalism.* New York: Knopf, 1977.

Odishaw, Hugh, ed. *The Challenges of Space.* Chicago: University of Chicago Press, 1962.

Oppenheimer, Michael, and Robert H. Boyle. *Dead Heat: The Race Against the Greenhouse Effect.* New York: Basic Books, 1990.

O'Riordan, T. *Environmentalism.* 2nd ed. London: Pion, 1981.

Pepper, David. *The Roots of Modern Environmentalism.* London: Croom-Helm, 1984.

Peterson, Elaine. *Poof: The Aerosol Game.* New York: Carlton Press, 1989.

Petulla, Joseph M. *American Environmental History.* San Francisco: Boyd & Fraser, 1977.

———. *American Environmentalism: Values, Tactics, Priorities.* College Station and London: Texas A&M University Press, 1980.

Piccard, August. *Between Earth and Sky.* London, 1950.

Piccard, Jacques, and Robert Dietz. *Seven Miles Down: The Story of the Bathyscaphe Trieste.* New York: Putnam, 1961.

Pinchot, Gifford. *Breaking New Ground.* New York: Harcourt, Brace, 1947.

Pinkett, Harold T. *Gifford Pinchot: Private and Public Forester.* Urbana, Chicago, and London: University of Illinois Press, 1970.

Poe, Edgar Allan. *The Narrative of Arthur Gordon Pym of Nantucket.* New York: Penguin, 1975.

Pound, Arthur. *The Turning Wheel.* Garden City, N.Y.: Doubleday, 1954.

Public Land Law Review Commission. *One Third of the Nation's Land.* Washington, D.C.: Government Printing Office, 1970.

Pyne, Stephen J. *The Ice: A Journey to Antarctica.* Iowa City: University of Iowa Press, 1986.

Rae, John B. *The American Automobile.* Chicago: University of Chicago Press, 1965.

Ranney, Austin, ed. *The American Elections of 1980.* Washington and London: American Enterprise Institute for Public Policy Research, 1981.

Reich, Charles A. *The Greening of America.* New York: Random House, 1970.

Richardson, Robert D., Jr. *Henry Thoreau: A Life of the Mind.* Berkeley: University of California Press, 1986.

Rightor, Chester E. *City Manager in Dayton: Four Years of Commission-Manager Government, 1914–1917; and Comparisons with Four Preceding Years Under the Mayor-Council Plan, 1910–1913.* New York: Macmillan, 1919.

Roan, Sharon. *Ozone Crisis: The 15-Year Evolution of a Sudden Global Emergency.* New York: Wiley, 1989.

Robert, Joseph E. *Ethyl: A History of the Corporation and the People Who Made It.* Charlottesville: University Press of Virginia, 1983.

Ronald, Bruce, and Virginia Ronald. *Dayton: The Gem City.* Tulsa, Okla.: Continental Heritage Press, 1981.

Ronne, Finn. *Antarctica, My Destiny.* New York: Hastings House, 1979.

Rosenkrantz, Barbara Gutmann, and William A. Koelsch, eds. *American Habitat: An Historical Perspective.* New York: Free Press, 1973.

Rosner, David, and Gerald Markowitz. *Dying for Work: Workers' Safety and Health in Twentieth-Century America.* Bloomington: Indiana University Press, 1987.

Rotch, A. L. *Sounding the Ocean of Air.* London, 1900.

Sagan, Carl, and Thornton Page, eds. *UFOs: A Scientific Debate.* Ithaca, N.Y.: Cornell University Press, 1972.

Saloma, John S., III. *Ominous Politics: The New Conservative Labyrinth.* New York: Hill & Wang, 1984.

Sax, Joseph L. *Defending the Environment.* New York: Knopf, 1970.

Schieffer, Bob, and Gary Paul Gates. *The Acting President.* New York: Dutton, 1989.

Schneider, Richard J. *Henry David Thoreau.* Boston: Twayne, 1987.

Schneider, Stephen H., with Lynne E. Mesirow. *The Genesis Strategy: Climate and Global Survival*. New York and London: Plenum, 1976.

Sciarra, John J., and Leonard Stoller, eds. *The Science and Technology of Aerosol Packaging*. New York: Wiley, 1974.

Sealander, Judith. *Grand Plans: Business Progressivism and Social Change in Ohio's Miami Valley, 1890–1929*. Lexington, Ky.: University Press of Kentucky, 1988.

Shanks, Bernard. *This Land Is Your Land: The Struggle to Save America's Public Lands*. San Francisco: Sierra Club Books, 1984.

Sharts, Joseph W. *The Biography of Dayton: An Economic Interpretation of Local History*. Dayton: The Miami Valley Socialist, 1922.

Shea, Cynthia Pollack. *Protecting Life on Earth: Steps to Save the Ozone Layer*. Paper 87. Washington, D.C.: Worldwatch Institute, December 1988.

Shurcliff, William A. *SST and Sonic Boom Handbook*. New York: Ballantine, 1970.

Sicherman, Barbara. *Alice Hamilton: A Life in Letters*. Cambridge: Harvard University Press, 1984.

Simons, Geoff. *Eco-Computer: The Impact of Global Intelligence*. New York: Wiley, 1987.

Sive, Mary Robinson, ed. *Environmental Legislation: A Sourcebook*. New York: Praeger, 1976.

Skillern, Frank F. *Environmental Protection: The Legal Framework*. New York: McGraw-Hill, 1981.

Skolimowski, Henryk. *Eco-philosophy*. Boston and London: Marion Boyars, 1981.

Sloan, Alfred. *My Years with General Motors*. Garden City, N.Y.: Doubleday, 1963.

Smith, Henry Ladd. *Airways*. New York: Knopf, 1944.

Solberg, Carl. *Conquest of the Skies: A History of Commercial Aviation in America*. Boston: Little, Brown, 1979.

Stein, Leon. *The Triangle Fire*. Philadelphia: Lippincott. 1962.

Sugden, T. M., and T. F. West, eds. *Chlorofluorocarbons in the Environment: The Aerosol Controversy*. Published for the Society of Chemical Industry, London, by Ellis Horwood, Chichester, 1980.

Sullivan, Walter. *Assault on the Unknown: The International Geophysical Year*. New York: McGraw-Hill, 1961.

Talbot, Alan R. *Power Along the Hudson: The Storm King Case and the Birth of Environmentalism*. New York: Dutton, 1972.

Thoreau, Henry D. *The Selected Works of Thoreau*. Cambridge ed. Boston: Houghton Mifflin, 1975.

Turner, Frederick. *Rediscovering America: John Muir in His Time and Ours*. New York: Viking, 1985.

United Nations Environment Program. *Montreal Protocol on Substances That Deplete the Ozone Layer: Final Act*. 1987.

United States Congress. *Ozone Depletion, the Greenhouse Effect, and Climate Change*. Joint Hearing before the Subcommittees on Environmental Protection and Hazardous Wastes and Toxic Substances of the Committee on Environment and Public Works. Senate. 100th Cong., 1st sess. January 28, 1987. Washington, D.C.: Government Printing Office, 1987.

―――. *Ozone Layer Depletion*. Hearing before the Subcommittee on Health and the Environment of the Committee on Energy and Commerce. House of Representatives. 100th Cong., 1st sess. March 8, 1987. Washington, D.C.: Government Printing Office, 1977.

―――. *Stratospheric Ozone Depletion and Chlorofluorocarbons*. Joint Hearing before the Subcommittees on Environmental Protection and the Subcommittee on Hazardous Wastes and Toxic Substances of the Committee on Environment and Public Works. Senate. 100th Cong., 1st sess. May 12–14, 1987. Washington, D.C.: Government Printing Office, 1987.

―――. *Stratospheric Ozone Depletion*. Hearings before the Subcommittee on Natural Resources, Agriculture Research, and Environment of the Committee on Science, Space, and Technology. House of Representatives. 100th Cong., 1st sess. March 10 and 12, 1987. Washington, D.C.: Government Printing Office, 1988.

————. *Ozone Layer Depletion*. Hearing before the Subcommittee on Oversight and Investigations of the Committee on Energy and Commerce. House of Representatives. 101st Cong., 1st sess. May 15, 1989. Washington, D.C.: Government Printing Office, 1989.

————. *Stratospheric Ozone Depletion*. Hearing before the Subcommittee on Health and the Environment of the Committee on Energy and Commerce. House of Representatives. 101st Cong., 2nd sess. January 25, 1990. Washington, D.C.: Government Printing Office, 1990.

Viorst, Judith. *Projects: Space* (New York: Washington Square Press, 1962).

Wachhorst, Wyn. *Thomas Alva Edison: An American Myth*. Cambridge, Mass.: MIT Press, 1981.

Watt, James G. *The Courage of a Conservative*. New York: Simon & Schuster, 1985.

Watt, Leilani. *Caught in the Conflict*. Eugene, Oreg.: Harvest House Publishers, 1984.

Weiner, Jonathan. *The Next One Hundred Years: Shaping the Fate of Our Living Earth*. New York: Bantam Books, 1990.

Weinstock, Edward. *The Wilderness War: The Struggle to Preserve Our Wildlands*. New York: Julian Messner, 1982.

Weisberger, Bernard. *The Dream Maker: William C. Durant, Founder of General Motors*. Boston: Little, Brown, 1979.

Wenner, Lettie M. *The Environmental Decade in Court*. Bloomington: Indiana University Press, 1982.

Wessel, Milton R. *Science and Conscience*. New York: Columbia University Press, 1980.

Wilkes, Maurice V. *Memoirs of a Computer Pioneer*. Cambridge, Mass.: MIT Press, 1985.

Wilson, Andrew, and F. G. Clark. *The Concorde Fiasco*. Harmondsworth, Middlesex: Penguin, 1973.

Wilson, J. Tuzo. *IGY: The Year of the New Moons*. New York; Knopf, 1961.

Winkler, John K. *The Du Pont Dynasty*. Baltimore: Reynal & Hitchcock, 1935.

Woodbury, David O. *Battlefronts of Industry: Westinghouse in World War II*. New York: Wiley, 1948.

Worster, David. *Nature's Economy: The Roots of Ecology*. San Francisco: Sierra Club Books, 1977.

Wyant, William K. *Westward in Eden: The Public Lands and the Conservation Movement*. Berkeley, Los Angeles, and London: University of California Press, 1982.

INDEX

solar energy, 89
Solomon, Philip, 352, 360
  background of, 295–96
  on National Ozone Expedition,
    294, 314
Solomon, Susan, 292, 294
  background of, 285–86
  on National Ozone Expedition,
    294, 297, 302, 312, 313, 314,
    317
  ozone-depletion work of, 286–89,
    350
sonic booms, 149–50, 151–52, 153,
  160, 162
sound:
  abnormal propagation of, 129–30,
    132–33
  speed of, 146
Southern Ice Exchange, 57
Soviet Union:
  CFC-ozone policy of, 221, 318,
    336, 337
  space program of, 268
  SST program of, 155
space shuttle, 183–85, 197
spectroscopy, 134, 135, 158
Spencer, John, 208
Speth, Gus, 114, 115, 116, 118, 120
Spra-Tainer, 86
Sputnik, 268
SST and Sonic Boom Handbook
  (Shurcliff), 156, 160
Standard Oil Company of New
  Jersey, 35, 46–47, 49
Starr, Ellen Gates, 40
Starr, Walter, 349
State Department, U.S., 251, 253,
  259, 278, 305, 310, 312, 319,
  320, 321–22, 329
"steady state" conditions, 136
Steed, Joseph M., 225, 337
Stockholm Conference on the Human
  Environment (1972), 219–20,
  221, 263
Stockholm Declaration (1972), 252
Stockman, David, 241

Stoel, Tom, 125, 127, 220, 308
  in NRDC's aerosol-ozone project,
    192, 193–94, 195, 197, 199
Stohbehn, Ed, 125
Stolarski, Richard, 127, 183, 184,
  185, 187, 192, 285, 290, 296
Stone, W. S., 74, 75, 76
Størmer, Carl, 136
Storm King Highway, 104
Storm King Mountain, ix, 103–7,
  124
stratosphere, 129–48
  altitude of ozone layer in, 135
  discovery and naming of, 131–32
  manned balloon flights to, 137–44
  ozone depletion in lower vs. upper
    layers of, 247, 256
  sound refracted by, 132–33
Stratosphere-Troposphere Exchange
  Project (STEP), 340
stratospheric aerosols, 293
Stratospheric Ozone Protection Plan,
  281
Stratospheric Protection Task Force,
  259–60, 309
Straub, Bob, 206
Stroback, Donald, 278
Strong, Maurice F., 251
Styrofoam, 6, 169
submarines, 62
Suess, Hans E., 216
Suffolk County Mosquito Control
  Commission, 112
Sullivan, Walter, 9, 127, 268
Sullivan, William, 72–76
sulphur dioxide, 58, 61, 62
sulphuric gas, 360
Super-Constellations, 148
Superfund legislation (1980), 123
supersonic transports (SSTs), 145–67
  cost of, 155, 156
  international opposition to, 153
  opposition to U.S. program for,
    149–67
  ozone depletion from, x, 127, 157–
    66, 182, 197